RAF FIGHTER COMMAND

RAF FIGHTER COMMAND

'Defence of the Realm' 1936–1945

RON MACKAY AND MIKE BAILEY

FONTHILL

Cover: No. 66 Squadron Spitfires over the South Coast of England in summer of 1940. LZ: F is being flown by Plt Off. Colin 'Bogle' Bodie.

Fonthill Media Language Policy

Fonthill Media publishes in the international English language market. One language edition is published worldwide. As there are minor differences in spelling and presentation, especially with regard to American English and British English, a policy is necessary to define which form of English to use. The Fonthill Policy is to use the form of English native to the authors. Ron Mackay and Mike Bailey were born and educated in the United Kingdom; therefore, British English has been adopted in this publication.

Fonthill Media Limited
Fonthill Media LLC
www.fonthillmedia.com
office@fonthillmedia.com

First published in the United Kingdom and the United States of America 2019

British Library Cataloguing in Publication Data:
A catalogue record for this book is available from the British Library

ISBN 978-1-78155-727-3

Typeset in 10.5pt on 13pt Sabon
Printed and bound in England

Contents

List of Abbreviations

A&AEE: Aircraft and Armament Experimental Establishment
AG: air gunner
B: *Beobachter* (observer)
Bf: *Bordfunker* (radio operator)
Bm: *Bordmechaniker* (flight engineer)
Bs: *Bordschuetzer* (air gunner)
Epr.Gr.: *ErprobungsGruppe*
Epr.Kd: *ErprobungsKommando* (Experimental Detachment)
F: *Flugzeugfuehrer* (pilot)
N: navigator
RCAF: Royal Canadian Air Force
RNZAF: Royal New Zealand Air Force
RO: radar operator

RAF Ranks

ACM: air chief marshal
AM: air marshal
AVM: air vice-marshal
Cpl: corporal
Fg Off.: flying officer
Flt Lt: flight lieutenant
FS: flight sergeant
Grp Capt.: group captain
LAC: leading aircraftsman
MRAF: marshal of the Royal Air Force
Plt Off.: pilot officer

Sgt:	sergeant
Sqn Ldr:	squadron leader
Wg Cdr:	wing commander

Luftwaffe Ranks

Fw.:	*feldwebel*
Gefr:	*gefreiter*
GenMaj.:	*general-major*
Hptm.:	*hauptmann*
Ltn.:	*leutnant*
Maj.:	*major*
Ob.:	*oberst*
Obfhr.:	*oberfähnrich*
Obfw.:	*Oberfeldwebel*
Obltn.:	*oberleutnant*
Oltn.:	*oberstleutnant*
Stabsfw.:	*stabsfeldwebel*
Uffz.:	*unteroffizier*

Introduction

The creation of Fighter Command in 1936 and parallel appointment of ACM Dowding as C-in-C proved a providential act in view of the burgeoning military threat posed by Hitler's Nazi regime in particular. The intervening three years to the Second World War's start saw the mandatory replacement of the biplane by the monoplane as the more effective design, backed up by an efficient ground-support organisation that proved just sufficient to halt Germany's hitherto successful force the *Luftwaffe* in the summer of 1940.

The Command's perceived priority as a Home Defence entity gradually began to count against its involvement as the Allied Air Forces began to reach ever further into European airspace from 1942 onward. The range limitations imposed upon the Spitfire and Hurricane and even their Typhoon successor in terms of fuel capacity meant that their USAAF contemporaries largely carried the weight of the air battles extending across the continent. That notwithstanding, ground-assault and short-range escort operations ensured the RAF pilots still contributed to the task of wearing down the *Luftwaffe*.

Prior to D-Day, a further measure of punishment had been handed out by the twin-engined Beaufighter, and especially the Mosquito. The squadrons involved had ranged far and wide by day and night, adding to the destruction visited upon the enemy's industrial and military capacity by the Allied heavy bomber fleets. The advent of D-day allowed for the subsequent ground advance to be supported by operations primarily flown from continental airfields. However, home defence capability was still fully maintained despite the almost total absence of *Luftwaffe* intervention during the final months of the Second World War.

Fighter Command had been well tested in combat, and by VE-Day, the survivors could reflect upon a high degree of success in helping to subvert and ultimately lay low their often-skilful adversaries, even if they had fought in support of a sadly evil political concept. The price so many among their ranks had paid by the conflict's conclusion was arguably balanced-out by the resumption of Democratic principles across much of Europe and indeed throughout the world—that will remain their timeless legacy.

1

'The Greatest Flying Club in the World'

Preamble

Between 1066 and 1914, the British Isles was destined to remain inviolate from the physical depredations of an invading nation. The sense of both individual and corporate isolation from fear of occupation during this massive time span was almost palpable. Shakespeare's 'Sceptred Isle, free from the infection of War' as well as being regarded as 'The envy of less happy Lands' surely left its occupants with little or no apprehension regarding a momentous sea change in this outlook as the major European Nations headed towards the onset of what evolved into the First World War, with Britain's involvement commencing on 4 August 1914.

The Royal Navy's pre-eminence upon the Seven Seas had kept any nation with hostile intentions at bay as the Spanish Fleets in 1588 and French in 1805 had discovered to their immediate cost in their bids to clear a path for invasion of their island-based adversary. Kaiser Wilhelm II's fleet, as built up over the first decade of the twentieth century, could present a strong challenge but only provided it could break out from its North Sea ports—a difficult task in view of the Royal Navy's ability to basically mount an ultimately effective blockade. Therefore, how could the British population be compelled to directly suffer the scourge of conflict?

The hitherto unimaginable threat that came into being within months of the First World War's inception would be launched and brought to bear with frightening effect, not from the sea but rather the sky. Whereas the British and French currently had aerial forces on hand, these were comprised of standard aircraft designs with limited range and offensive load capacity that moreover were initially used for reconnaissance. By contrast, the Germans had entered the field of airship design; these huge machines possessed an endurance that soon saw them employed in attacks on Southern Britain while bearing generally sizeable bomb loads.

The grim portent for the British was encapsulated in the expression 'Britain is no longer an Island', certainly in terms of the man in the street avoiding

The Sopwith Camel would prove to be one of the major factors in turning the air war away from the German *Luft Dienst*'s hitherto superiority as 1917 evolved into 1918. The aircraft was not easy to control but proved to be a superb gun platform as many enemy aircrew found to their cost.

the impending aerial onslaught, albeit one that would prove to be staccato in nature over the ensuing four years. The total lack of a dedicated fighter and ground-support defence network became evident as soon as the first Zeppelin airships made their nocturnal presence felt. To the absence of anti-aircraft gun technology was added the basic inability of the fighter designs available to even attain the fairly high altitudes flown by the German machines, let alone be able to lock onto them visually without the aid of searchlight batteries, there being no electronic aids on hand to provide more precise guidance.

The subsequent involvement of the Gotha and Staaken bombers provided an even greater dilemma for the Royal Flying Corps pilots since these possessed a performance much closer to their RFC and RNAS opponents compared to the more pedestrian pace of the Zeppelin, several of whom were brought down after gunfire ignited the highly-inflammable hydrogen content that propelled these monsters aloft. It was as well that the infrequency of assault coupled with the relatively small numbers of attacking aircraft meant that the scale of punishment inflicted upon the British mainland was arguably more psychological than physical. Regardless of this, the general immunity of the enemy crews from effective counter-assault added to the man in the street's feeling of fear-fuelled vulnerability for him and his kin.

The blessed end of the First World War witnessed the victors treating the conflict as 'The War to end all Wars', with it being felt that the scale of both military and civilian slaughter could not conceivably be repeated if mankind

The Bristol Bulldog entered RAF service in 1929 as a replacement for the Siskin and Gamecock and equipped nine squadrons until 1936, when it began to be phased out of frontline service. Three sections of No. 17 Squadron are seen here; the section nearest the camera bear the markings of No. 3 Squadron, from whom they have been transferred.

was to advance—a naïve assumption in retrospect, but one genuinely felt in the period immediately following the 1918 Armistice and subsequent 1919 Treaty of Versailles. An almost inevitable follow-up from this understandable stance was the paring of military strength almost to the bone. In the case of the newly-formed RAF, what had been a force of some 3,500 aircraft with almost 250,000 personnel to fly and maintain the aerial machines was by 1920 reduced to a figure between 5 per cent and 10 per cent.

The established unit strength of the RAF was reduced to twenty-five currently-functioning squadrons with ten more being formed. Nor was the primary emphasis on Home Defence; the policing of Britain's global empire was regarded as meriting an aerial presence to add to that on the ground. Egypt and the Indian subcontinent—the latter's north-west frontier coming specifically in mind—saw the bulk of squadrons dispatched to these zones (that region's inhabitants' reaction to British rule still resonates in sadly current terms with religious-based antipathy directed at the entire Western World). The RAF's overseas deployment, in essence, provided an aerial version of the 'send a gun-boat' action with which to keep those offering a physical challenge to their colonial 'masters' firmly in place!

The sheer paucity of RAF strength in Britain was probably directly allied to the ultimately infamous 'Ten-year Rule' decreed by Westminster. This edict assumed that the nation would not be involved in a major conflict for that time period—a natural assumption in the aftermath of the First World War, especially when given

A pair of ground crew staff are holding on to the wing tips of a Bulldog as the pilot appears to apply full power to the Bristol Jupiter power plant. It was while flying a No. 23 Squadron example that Douglas Bader suffered an accident that cost him both legs, a drastic and seemingly intractable disability that did not inhibit him from again flying with the RAF from 1939 on.

'The Greatest Flying Club's' love affair with biplanes held sway well into the 1930s. The fighter version of the Hawker Hart bomber was the Demon that entered initial service during 1933. A total of 234 airframes were constructed with K2850 the ninth airframe in the first Hawker production run; Boulton-Paul were also involved. The open rear cockpit was a feature of all Hawker-built machines. The rear armament is mounted on a flexible Scarff ring.

the comprehensive defeat of the two nations most likely to take such an aggressive stance, namely Germany and Austria/Hungary. However, the continuation of the policy into the early 1930s would leave the country in an increasingly perilous position *vis-à-vis* the burgeoning but belatedly-recognised threat posed by a resurgent and revenge-seeking Hitler-led Germany backed to a lesser extent by Mussolini's Italy.

Between 1918 and the mid-1930s, the public image of flying in general was steeped in a romantic rather than military aura. To the exploits of civilian pioneers such as Lindbergh, Amy Johnson, Alan Cobham, and the like was added the appearance of the RAF's often beautifully painted biplanes flown by white-suited pilots and/or gunners. The image was further bolstered by the RAF's participation in the Schneider Trophy races, which culminated in Britain retaining the Trophy with the Supermarine S-6 floatplane during 1931. The annual Hendon Air Display saw bomber formations attacking and destroying artificial 'forts' and assaulting colonial 'natives' with nothing more lethal than flour bombs.

The fighter designs (Fury, Bulldog, Siskin, etc.), when not taking on the bombers, formed aerobatic teams that flew precise patterns. It was accordingly not surprising that the term 'The greatest Flying Club in the World' gained general currency during this extended period. The emphasis on technical development of airframes, engines, and other necessary advances lagged badly. So too did the accent on training for active combat, particularly among the fighter-based element; this was marginal to say the least, whether applied to tactics or to aerial gunnery—particularly the latter and vitally-necessary skill.

However, the response to any criticism directed at the Air Ministry could have been based on the following question: 'Where was the looming adversary that might induce prompt and full attention to these disciplines?' Germany with its Austro-Hungarian now-dismembered ally was seemingly prostrate in military terms thanks to the Treaty of Versailles's stringent conditions; France was a current British ally with little or no likelihood that this relationship would ever again slip into hostility as it had done intermittently over the preceding centuries; and Soviet Russia was geographically remote with its Communist Party hierarchy probably giving priority to maintaining a grip upon their far-flung national structure.

Staccato Expansion

In 1922, Sir Hugh Trenchard—who would forever be regarded as the primary founder of the RAF from its original RFC and RNAS status on 1 April 1918, and who moreover was a firm advocate of strategic bombing—was granted the right to form a Metropolitan air force assigned to Home Defence. This took the form of fourteen bomber and nine fighter squadrons, the imbalance towards the former category clearly reflecting his view that the best form of defence was offence.

The emphasis on striking at an adversary's heartland was based on the premise that dislocation of his industrial facilities would in turn deny his forces in the field the means with which to sustain an offensive effort. In the meantime, Britain's aerial defences would ensure that anything like the same scale of punishment would not be wreaked upon its industrial fabric. That was the reported theory behind the bomber/fighter-strength division.

Within two years, the intended expansion of the Metropolitan air force to thirty-five bomber and seventeen fighter squadrons respectively had reached the twenty-five mark. However, within this overall figure was a sub-total of thirteen squadrons that would be split between the Auxiliary Air Force created in 1925 (six) and the Special Reserve (seven). The initial four units for the former-named sub-force were formed that year, although none would switch from their original bomber status onto fighters until the mid- to late 1930s.

The expansion of the Special Reserve equivalent was similarly extended over the intervening six years or so. All these units were in effect part-time or 'non regular' in official terms, and the term that stuck was 'weekend fliers'; the personnel came from Territorial Associations, their normal civilian occupations restricting availability for service to the weekend. It would be a further five years before all would be brought into being.

By 1927, the number of frontline fighter squadrons assigned to Home Defence within what in 1925 bore the Air Defence of Great Britain (ADGB) title stood at just twelve, being equipped with the Gloster Grebe or Gamecock and the Armstrong-Whitworth Siskin. All were biplane in configuration with maximum speeds ranging between 134 and 156 mph—sufficient to overtake their RAF bomber contemporaries lumbering along at no more than 110 mph, if not those of other European nations. The number of squadrons contrasted sharply with the forty-unit figure on hand in France and Belgium on 11 November 1918. However, this doubtless left little sense of vulnerability in the minds of the politicians, whose priorities were perhaps more aligned towards economics as opposed to military necessity, especially with the 'Ten-year Rule' still holding sway in Parliamentary ranks.

As the 1920–1930 era was being transited, the Hawker Co. in particular produced a range of bomber/reconnaissance designs that followed the same construction pattern for the aforementioned fighters, being single-engined, fixed-undercarriage biplanes in configuration. The speed factor would reach towards the 200-mph level, but the first of two pure fighter types brought out around 1932 (Fury I) maintained a speed superiority of between 30 and 40 mph; the Fury II raised the margin slightly in 1936, but by then, the RAF was taking the initial step towards monoplane-configured fighters destined to (thankfully) displace their biplane predecessors in view of similar Nazi aviation developments.

In 1932, just one extra active fighter squadron had been added to the ADGB force while the overall intended total of fifty-two squadrons was still short by ten, the recently-elected Conservative Party having further delayed completion until 1936. As it was—and fortunately for the long-term survival of democracy throughout Europe—a sea change in political thinking now occurred. That the British had become aware of a still-democratically established Germany indulging

The turret version of the Demon was constructed under sub-contract by the Boulton-Paul Co. The aircraft bearing what looks like a turret is actually one from the Hawker production run. The concept of this armament arrangement may have played a part in the company's subsequent development of the Defiant, although the new machine would lack any forward firepower as on the Demon.

in secret military deals with Soviet Russia as one of several measures to subvert the 1919 Treaty of Versailles's severe terms seems to lend credence to the British Government's action in 1933.

The Nazi Party had only gained total autocratic rule in the course of that year but an official committee's conclusion focused its attention upon the Hitler-led 'government' and declared that Germany constituted a resurgent threat to European security that was likely to erupt within the current decade—a forecast backed by the military hierarchy and one that was tragically prescient. Being aware of the threat was one thing, but what measures to take to stem if not reverse the potential tide of aggression was another matter.

As a military power, Britain had hitherto pulled its forces back home upon the conclusion of previous European conflicts it was involved in. The critics of Neville Chamberlain's 'appeasement' of, or more diplomatically-couched discussions with, Hitler conveniently ignored the salient fact that there was no way in which physical pressure could be brought to bear upon the dictator by Britain at the time; only France and/or the Soviets among the major European powers was theoretically capable of doing so.

In the case of the French, its citizens had been psychologically and physically drained by the events of 1914–18 that had been added to by the Franco-German War's humiliating culmination in defeat during 1870. As for the Soviet government, it was ultra-suspicious of the motives of Britain and France or indeed of any nation not conceding the superior 'virtues' of Communism compared to Capitalism's iniquities as perceived and practised by Josef Stalin and his cohorts.

The Hawker Fury was to represent the pinnacle of biplane fighter design for the RAF during the early 1930s. This is the last of 117 built between 1930 and 1935, and an aircraft that broached the 200-mph maximum speed level for the first time. Although only three squadrons operated the Fury I, it would remain in frontline service until 1939. The red/white chequer board denotes No. 43 'Fighting Cocks' Squadron seen at the annual Hendon Pageant of 1935.

The need to consider expanding their military resources probably sat ill with Westminster. The effects of the Wall Street Crash and generally depressed state of the country dictated that all attention still be directed towards resurrecting the economy rather than diverting money away for whatever purpose, especially on the as-yet unconfirmed basis that conflict could envelope the nation in the near future. In the case of the RAF, the need to expand in both quantitative and qualitative terms was bolstered by the latest dire threat of aerial retribution from bomber assault.

Prime Minister Stanley Baldwin stated in 1934: 'There is no power on earth that can protect him [the man in the street] from being bombed ... regardless, the bomber will always get through'. His words echoed previous and equally dire projections for civilian casualty-rates emanating from several international sources over the preceding decade—this despite the fact that the experience of the First World War had seemingly proved otherwise. As it was, the anticipated scale of fatalities accruing from future assaults on Britain would prove to be far lower albeit still painful, but not so for its looming European adversary.

The question of how to mount an effective defensive system had to be addressed in one obvious and a second more-vague manner. The obvious solution was to create a force of fighters of quality that would out-perform their adversaries. Although by mid-1934, when the proposed Scheme 'A' Expansion Plan involving thirty-nine bomber and twenty-five fighter squadrons for Home Defence was laid before and approved by Parliament for initiation the following year, the emphasis on fighter design was still focused on the biplane, as the emergence of the Gloster Gauntlet and Gladiator would confirm.

However, the Hawker and Supermarine concerns were currently working on designs that would alter the basic fabric of fighter development in the form of the monoplane-configured Hurricane and Spitfire. The race was on to mount an effective challenge against any aggressor as Hitler-led Germany was to sadly present itself, and it would be a dangerously close-run one as the Nazis 'peacefully' extended their autocratic control within central Europe prior to the Second World War's late 1939 inception.

The more insidious and not-easily solved problem was to determine the in-coming attacker's presence in sufficient time to get the fighters airborne and up to the required altitude. Echo-sounding devices were short range and inefficient in function, while the use of ground observers to track the incoming formations would similarly be too belated in time-terms. The very fortunate 'break' for the nation came in the form of what was initially titled named 'radio-detection-finding', a term that evolved into 'radar'.

Scientist William Watson-Watt carried out experiments during 1935 that led to the system's development. However, it was really the successful efforts of Sir Hugh C. T. Dowding, currently the Air Member for Research and Supply and the imminent first C-in-C of Fighter Command, to secure the necessary funding from a naturally-sceptical Treasury faced with a currently unproven device that won the day.

Preparing for War? Hardly

The period in between 1918 and 1939 witnessed the RAF pilots—and their gunners in the case of twin-seat designs such as the Hawker Demon—indulging in flying skills that in the long-run did little or nothing to advance their state of readiness for aerial combat. They were usually attired in white overalls and leather helmets and flying boots. In the case of the fighters, very little gunnery practice was indulged in, which potentially was dangerously counter-productive for the future; this limitation was even more critical since ground-based targets rather than canvas 'drogues' towed behind an aircraft were usually involved, although the use of drogues became more prevalent towards the period-end.

The machine guns extended forward from the cockpit and their breech mechanisms were normally accessible should the weapons 'jam', so permitting the pilot a chance to clear any stoppage—no material advance from First World War operations there. The restriction to the pair of weapons on hand was none too critical when engaging the generally slender integrity of a canvas and wood aircraft, but it would be basically inadequate for handing out material damage to stronger-constructed airframes as was becoming ever more the norm during the 1930s with the inception of metal-clad designs.

As for learning how to manoeuvre their fighters in a superior manner to a potential opponent, the norm seems to have been for more indulgence in

The Fury I's performance *vis-à-vis* its RAF contemporaries was notable enough, but the Fury II pushed the margin even further. Maximum speed increased from 207 mph enjoyed by its stablemate to 223 mph and climb rate to 10,000 feet went up from 2,380 to 3,200 feet per minute. The enclosed main undercarriage is an obvious refinement. Strangely enough, the Fury II was gone from frontline service by 1938, although it had predated the Fury I as regards squadron assignment, doing so in 1931.

aerobatics or close-formation flying, neither of which could prepare one for the confusing and feral maelstrom that constituted the average 'dog-fight', rather than battle tactics. At least the largely fuselage-mounted weaponry virtually eliminated the need for deflection shooting—simply point the nose at the enemy and fire.

Navigation was primarily visual and indulged in at altitudes that enabled them to find their way by ground references; the restricted cockpit space did not allow for the presence of charts, etc. while the short-range nature of the single-engined machines basically dictated equally short-duration flights. Should a pilot end up lost, it was not unusual for him to land in a suitable flat area and 'ask the way' as it were from the local population. What was a primarily laid-back presentation of military activity created an aura of 'gentlemen aloft' in their silver-finished and often gaudily marked machines cruising through the skies, one that the media in particular latched on to.

Those among the population who attended premier occasions such as the annual Hendon Air Show would attest to much of the foregoing image of 'A Flying Club'—in this instance, 'The greatest in the World'. The 'blitzing' of wood-based strongholds and/or the harrying of their occupants—sometimes thinly disguised as colonial natives or other dissidents—involved the bombers; clearly, political correctness did not hold any sway within the society still possessing 'The Empire on which the Sun never sets!' The tight formation manoeuvres of fighter aerobatic teams probably added to this casually-confident image presented by Britain's aerial guardians.

The Gloster Gauntlet would represent the end of the line for RAF fighters with open cockpits, but its introduction into service in 1935 as a replacement for the Bulldog at a point when monoplane fighters were being designed or test flown—the Bf 109 being a prime example—did not bode well for Fighter Command. The Gauntlet did introduce a proper tail-wheel unit in contrast to the skid hitherto applied to RAF machines. Picture taken during King George V's Jubilee Review at Mildenhall in July 1935, including No. 19 Squadron as confirmed by K4095.

The RAF's dangerously extended involvement with the biplane saw the introduction of some beautiful unit markings that stood out particularly well against the airframe's silver finish. In this case, the colours on a No. 74 Squadron Gauntlet are yellow and black to signify the 'Tiger' motive, being the name applied to this particular RAF unit.

All in all, the fighting efficiency of the RAF with particular attention focused on its fighter strength was (perhaps thankfully) not tested *en masse* during the interwar decades. Having said that, the onset of the century's second cataclysmic global conflict was to bring the consequences of the foregoing lapses in combat training to bear down hard upon the service's aviators.

In stark contrast, the pioneer units of the *Luftwaffe*'s Fighter Arm (*Jagdwaffe*) were destined to participate in, and emerge from, the Spanish Civil War with well-worked combat disciplines, its pilots having been literally 'blooded' in the art of aerial combat against the Republican Air Force. They would accordingly hand out some nasty and often tragic punishment to Fighter Command that would consume far too many pilots before these lessons in overall battle tactics was taken on board during 1940–41.

The Eagles Gather

The clandestine events leading to the emergence of the *Luftwaffe* featured their public culmination on 20 April 1935. The date chosen was no coincidence since it marked the birthday of Adolf Hitler. As he gazed skyward at the impressive aerial parade put on for both his and the German nation's approval, he must have experienced a dark sense of satisfaction at having lulled his perceived Anglo–French opponents into a false sense of security. Moreover, here was a key element in his plans to overturn the unfairly-applied conditions of the Treaty of Versailles, against which he had long railed and ranted in countless speeches; the conditions were equally resented by many within German military and civil circles.

As it was, the available strength in qualitative terms at least was not much better than those of the RAF or the French Air Force. The Do 23 and Ju 52, although monoplane in their structures, were slow-flying machines with fixed undercarriages, while the He 51 biplane fighter (providing much of the *Jagdwaffe*'s initial establishment) possessed a performance barely on a par with the Fury I. However, about to emerge on the scene were two bomber and one fighter designs, all of monoplane configuration that between them would appear to alter the operational-efficiency equation sharply in the Führer's favour when compared to Fighter Command's current biplane establishment. These were the He 111 and Do 17 twin-engined bombers, and most daunting of all, the Bf 109. All three would enter service during 1937 and equally would be dispatched to Spain where their combat qualities would be tested to some degree during that unhappy Nation's Civil War, a degree that granted the *Luftwaffe* a clear head start over its Anglo–French future main opposition.

Although the top speed of the two bomber designs was not superior to the bulk of the Fighter Command fighters, their ability to absorb punishment from the latter's machine-gun-calibre weapons coupled with the relatively solid weight of return fire that could put out by a tight formation pattern would surely have proved to be to their basic advantage. As for the Bf 109, the overall performance along with its mix of bullet- and cannon-calibre weaponry would have cast

The Gauntlet II was externally similar to the Gauntlet I, but towards the end of the production run began to be fitted with a three-blade propeller as appears to be the case on K5332. A total of fourteen squadrons would take on the Gloster machine; unlike all its predecessors, it would see active service during the Second World War, in its case against the Italian Air Force in East Africa during 1941.

the RAF pilots on the back foot as regards even surviving in combat, let alone ending up as the victor.

On the other hand, the likelihood of a fighter *v.* fighter combat could have been discounted had the inability of the Bf 109 to reach British shores from Germany been maintained, the probability of a French collapse and the *Luftwaffe* operating from their vanquished adversary's airfields being an inconceivable issue at this time. What was a more logical alternative with which to match the *Luftwaffe* fighter establishment lay in dispatching a proportion of overall RAF Fighter Command strength to be based in France that would bolster the French defences, since that nation was in close geographic contact with Germany compared to Britain; the air space between these two long-term antagonists would certainly be fully taken up in the event of a future conflict.

So, as 1935 ended, the clouds of war were not yet clearly presenting a threatening presence, although the emergence the *Luftwaffe* did definitely create a further degree of apprehension within government circles with regards to the Führer's ultimate intentions towards his European neighbours. Hitler's illegal culling of the Rhineland back into the national fold within three months of the year-end would add to such apprehensions. Thankfully, in Britain, the Scheme A expansion plans announced the previous year coupled to the several single- and multi-engined aircraft designs intended for the RAF and/or already in prototype form would increase the prospects for the nation taking on an aerial adversary—German or otherwise—based on a sound footing.

The Gloster Gladiator was a refined version of the Gauntlet, the most obvious improvement being the sliding cockpit canopy along with a doubling of armament to four guns; the three-blade propeller introduced on the Gauntlet became a standard Gladiator fitting on later airframes. The aircraft would prove inadequate in respect of handling the challenge offered by the growing change to monoplane fighter designs. The colourful yellow/blue markings identify No. 73 Squadron.

A line of No. 72 Squadron Gladiators is caught on camera at Farnborough from where air exercises are being conducted. The wooden fixed-pitch propellers, non-retractable landing gear and mass of wire rigging between them created an overall speed-sapping performance, although the aircraft's manoeuvrability in the turn made it a difficult target—but air combat would always require a more positive action in order to achieve a victory.

2
Belated Rearmament

The anticipated mass expansion of the RAF as 1936 commenced was matched by a similar expansion in the command structure that replaced the ADGB and was five-fold in nature: Bomber Command, Coastal Command for seaborne operations, Training Command, Maintenance Command, and, of course, Fighter Command. Whereas the ADGB geographic spread was seemingly based largely in southern England, the new overall structure required access to the entire British and Northern Irish landscape; airfield-spread would soon span from the Shetland and Orkney Islands as well as on the mainland from Wick in Northern Scotland down to St Eval in Cornwall.

The burgeoning menace of Nazism was clearly demonstrated in March of this year when the *Wehrmacht* blatantly flouted the Treaty of Versailles by occupying the demilitarised Rhineland region. This action was the second of a series of similar bids by Hitler to purportedly bring about a reunified Germany that would be accommodated reluctantly or otherwise by the Anglo–French governments over the ensuing three years before they felt compelled to finally call the Führer's bluff.

Cometh the Hour, Cometh the Man

Air Marshal Dowding assumed charge of the newly-created command, one of five such structures that replaced the ADGB structure in 1936. Austere in personal manner and expression, a factor that landed him with the label 'Stuffy', he proved to be a first-class innovator in both technical and strategic terms that would prove of inestimable value both to his personnel and by extension to his nation. His strength lay in the ability to listen to and take on board positive information and moreover to face-up to those in either military but especially political authority who sought to autocratically alter or reject his measures—a stance extending up to Winston Churchill during the 1940 Crisis of the Battle of France (when one commentator described him as a 'genial Scot', he is supposed to have retorted: 'I am not genial and I am not a Scot', even though he was actually born at Moffat in south-west Scotland—presumably to parents with a non-Celtic background).

The entity that Dowding assumed charge of was still firmly wedded to the biplane design. However, by 1936, the existence of monoplane-format aircraft was clearly evident with all the perceived technical advantages—smoother aerofoil, retractable undercarriage in some cases, as well as enhanced engine output—that set its biplane predecessor on a dangerous overall back-step in terms of overall efficiency. It was as well that the Hurricane and Spitfire prototypes were on hand although the speed-performance of the latter was apparently still a matter for concern in the designer's mind.

By now the openly-declared existence of the *Luftwaffe* in 1935 was accompanied by the sight of a duo of bombers (He 111and Do 17) whose original civilian creation had conveniently been switched to a more hostile function. Due to be added to the ranks was the dangerously-efficient Bf 109, while the Ju 87 was to provide a close-support function for the *Wehrmacht*. The Führer clearly felt he had the aerial means to assist in enforcing his will, and it was Dowding's urgent duty to raise his command's efficiency to the same, if not superior level. The race was on.

Advance towards Modernity

The build-up of Fighter Command's strength was to gain steady pace following Dowding's arrival at Bentley Priory (Command HQ located north of London) in July 1936; this was with reference not just to aircraft and personnel but equally important to expansion in airfield numbers. The previous figure of nine that supported the seventeen assigned squadrons in 1932 was simply inadequate to cover an area larger than that spanning from Yorkshire in north-central England to the Channel coast region around Southampton. In retrospect, this geographic band permitted a theoretical defence of the major industrial zones throughout England and even probably the Scottish Lowlands. However, the actual number of fighters, even if all were operational in condition—a virtual impossibility in practical terms—could still have witnessed their being seriously outnumbered if not overwhelmed by an enemy bomber force.

Added to this was the current absence of an effective ground-based detection system that could alert the defenders in ample time to intercept and moreover to do so with some degree of accuracy. Aural warning was minimal and short-range in the form of echo-sounders whose efficiency even within such limitations was uncertain at best. Visual observation was often restricted by the weather conditions, but the existence of the dedicated members of the Observers Corps gave some benefit whenever possible (by 1939, a national web of 2,000 sites manned by some 30,000 personnel would be in place and answerable to the Air

K5083 made its inaugural test flight on 6 November 1935, four months ahead of its Supermarine rival. A full side view picks out the exposed engine exhaust ports and the single centrally-positioned vertical strut within the sliding canopy frame. Doped rear fuselage and wings and polished metal forward fuselage along with a brace strut for the horizontal stabiliser are points of note.

A front-angle view of the Hurricane prototype provides a good impression of the solid wing structure. The landing gear covers with a frontal gap between the extremities would be replaced by ones with a continuous front line. The flexible 'D' flaps at the cover-base would be discarded, while the retractable tail wheel would be fixed. Landing and navigation lights are not yet installed.

Ministry; in time, the prefix 'Royal' would be added to the organisation's title in well-earned acknowledgement of their vital service to the nation).

With France as a current ally, any future threat was regarded as emanating from across the North Sea, and it was on this premise that the now Air Marshal-ranked Dowding created the first two out of a final figure of four groups, Nos 11 and 12. These were split on an east–west line running just north of London, with No. 11 Group to the south and its 'twin' to the north but only as far as a line running through York. No. 13 Group was also on hand by the onset of the Second World War, but it took the Fall of France to create the fourth group (No. 10) in June 1940; it displaced the western segment of the original No. 11 Group's zone to cover a revised area running north from Southampton and west into South Wales. No. 11 Group had its revised line of demarcation running roughly east–north-east across the middle of East Anglia, while No. 12 Group's geographic tenure was extended to a line that was south of Newcastle on its eastern extremity. Finally, the remainder of England as well as Northern Ireland and Scotland was brought under No. 13 Group's charge.

Radar: A Key Defensive Godsend

The search for an effective early-warning system so critical to ACM Dowding's defensive network was ended primarily by a diminutive Scots scientist, Robert Watson-Watts. As is often the case, the evolution of Radio Detection Finding (RDF in its original title-format but now known as radar) came about in an indirect manner. Watson-Watt, as Superintendent of the National Physics Laboratory, was working on weather detection research. He noted that radio waves being 'bounced back' came not just from the atmospheric conditions but seemingly from passing aircraft. A report on the issue of radio detection as a tracking-method was completed and sent to Henry Tizard, serving as head of the Aeronautical Research Committee, a body formed in 1934 with a view to finding a functioning detection system.

Specific experiments by Watson-Watt and his team during 1935 utilising a bomber that reflected its 'signature' towards the BBC's Daventry station proved the potential efficacy of the scheme. Within a year or so, not only had further experiments greatly extended the original 8-mile detection range to 100 miles or more with the height factor raised to at least 10,000 feet, three of the initial cadre of five experimental stations were in operation and the way was clear for the wholesale expansion of a radar network the length of Britain's eastern, southern (and to a lesser degree, western) coastal fringes by 1939–40. The concurrent expansion of the Observer Corps would provide an absolutely necessary back-up support; this was due to the radar transmitter/receiver signals' inability to radiate inland that thereby rendered the system 'blind' in that direction.

The immediate priority in the absence of currently superior fighter designs was to establish a full and effective early-warning system based on this electronic-

K5083 in flight provides an enhanced view of its overall aerodynamic shape. The clean underside with the tail wheel in the retracted position is evident as is the lightly-framed cockpit canopy. The windshield frame is a single triangular piece that will change to separate sub-units linked at the top by a short horizontal metal strip. The 11-foot 6-inch Watts propeller bears a black/silver spinner.

A second view of K5083 shows the revised cockpit canopy with extra stiffening metal strips. Aerial mast is fitted but not the exhaust covers. Aircraft behind is the prototype Hawker Henley; intended as a light bomber, it never achieved this function and the few airframes ended up on target-towing duties. Note the wide-brimmed hat regularly worn by George Bullman during test flights!

The first production Hurricane reveals several features that required modification before the design could compete with its future Second World War adversaries. The twin-blade, fixed-pitched Watts propeller would be replaced by three-blade variable-pitch units, while armoured glass would be applied to the windscreen. A strake would be applied around the tailwheel and the twin-fork airspeed indicator would give way to a more streamlined 'L'-shaped unit.

operating equipment. This was destined to take the form of a twin layout of radar station chains. The obvious initial response was the formation of an initial twenty-strong number of radar sites largely distributed along Britain's east and south coastlines that was further extended by 1939–40 (during the 1950s, the author can recall the by-then redundant masts at Loth, south of his home in Northern Scotland). Each station possessed Multi-100-foot transmitter and receiver towers that formed what was titled the 'Chain Home' system and which could pick up aerial 'traces' upwards of 100 miles distant.

However, the transmission/receiver signals from the towers proved critically marginal in terms of range at minimum altitudes, and so a secondary set of sites was equipped with low-scanning radar sets in order to pick out attackers approaching close to the sea; these constituted what was titled 'Chain Home Low' in function. Whereas the Chain Home towers were consistently tall a two-fold structure system was brought into being for the Chain Home Low units. Those located on low ground or sea level featured standard tower frames in order to gain the necessary range-cover, but the transmitters placed at higher elevations could be mounted on smaller 20-foot gantries. In this manner, full warning could theoretically be given of aircraft encroaching upon British soil, although there were to be problems in guaranteeing the distance, approach-angle and numbers involved during the initial stages of the Second World War.

Radar's inability to scan to the rear was a key failure, but it was addressed, however incomplete through human resources. The formation of the Royal

The Supermarine F7/30 that preceded its illustrious successor was a world away in design efficiency. The fixed landing gear alone imposed a drag effect that reduced maximum speed to around 240 mph and the open cockpit promised a draughty ride for the pilot. Although accepted in principle by the Air Ministry, R. J. Mitchell decided on an alternative design—and the result was a quantum leap in fighter technology.

The prototype Spitfire demonstrates that leap in general, although the fighter would face similar necessary modifications. As with the Hurricane, the original propeller seen here would give way to variable-pitch units and the tail skid to a proper tailwheel. The lengthy pitot-mast located on the wing leading edge would be replaced by an underwing 'L'-pattern example and cowlings fitted over the engine exhaust stubs. The flat canopy would change to a 'blown' pattern giving the pilot enhanced headroom.

Observer Corps provided a body of men and women who manned their posts spread throughout the British hinterland. Their duty was to record and pass on the track of formations that had penetrated the radar 'screen'. History has recorded their vital and generally successful bid to inform Bentley Priory (Fighter Command HQ) of the *Luftwaffe*'s movements, whether by visual sightings or aural means when clouds intervened to cloak the formations.

Aircraft Efficiency

By 1936, the Air Ministry had surely become aware of the salient fact that the day of the biplane as a frontline concept was well out of date. Contracts for a range of designs had each been issued against the relative ministry specifications issued between 1932 and 1934, and the result was the imminent appearance within the next two years of the Fairey Battle single- and Bristol Blenheim, Vickers Wellington, Armstrong-Whitworth Whitley, and Handley-Page Hampden twin-engined bombers.

The latter-named trio would form the cadre of Bomber Command's strategic strike force up to the mid-point of the Second World War with the Battle and Blenheim serving in more of a tactical role. Fighter Command could similarly look forward to the introduction of the Hurricane and Spitfire within roughly the same time span; in the interim period and as in the case of the other RAF Commands, it would have to soldier on with the biplane as its primary equipment.

The current fighters on hand came from the Hawker and Gloster Company 'stables'. The former concern was providing the Demon (a twin-seat adaptation of the Hart bomber) as well as the Fury I and Fury II. The Fury 1 was greatly appreciated as an overall performer especially in aerobatics by the three squadrons operating the design; Nos 1 and 43 would retain the Fury I until conversion in late 1938 on to the Hurricane, but No. 25 Squadron would switch to the even-more superlative Fury II when it first entered service in late 1936.

This updated variant was to serve with five squadrons as well as seven Flying Training Schools (FTS). The maximum speed of 223 mph was regarded as the highest ever attained to date by an RAF biplane fighter while a climb rate of over 2,000 fpm to 20,000 feet, a range of 260 miles and a service ceiling of 29, 500 feet added to its overall top performance (the Fury I enjoyed a similar general performance output with a greater range of 305 miles but a maximum speed of 207 mph).

Gloster provided the Gauntlet and Gladiator, with the former displacing the Bristol Bulldog from mid-1935. The radial-engine machine featured a performance envelope that was similar in top speed and climb rate (230 mph maximum and 2,200 fpm up to 20,000 feet) but was well ahead of its Hawker competitors as regards range (460 miles) and service ceiling (33,500 feet). The introduction of a three-bladed metal propeller, albeit fixed-pitch on late production airframes, was

The first RAF unit to be equipped with the Mk I Hurricane was No. 111 Squadron based at Northolt in west London. Type A1 roundels are visible, but the aircraft are still to have squadron markings applied. The cruciform gun-bay cover and instrument venturi tube mounted below the cockpit windshield were features on early-production airframes.

of further operational benefit. The Hawker duo by contrast still operated on the standard two-blade wooden propeller.

The Gladiator, as with the Fury II, was an updated version of its predecessor that moreover signalled an end to one of the aspects of RAF design to date, namely the open cockpit, Gloster having fitted a sliding canopy on the aircraft. The Gladiator also introduced a necessary offensive measure in the form of its armament. Whereas the standard armament even on the present range of single-seat fighters consisted of twin Vickers machine guns, the Gladiator was outfitted with double the number.

The source of these weapons was the US-based Browning Co. from whom Britain had negotiated a licence for sub-construction that was duly fitted from the seventy-first airframe onwards. The day of the automatic gunsight still lay ahead, albeit none too distant, so the RAF fighters retained the 'ring-and-bead' design formed of a cockpit-mounted cross within a ring-frame and a vertical rod (the 'Bead') mounted above the engine cowling with which to aim at their targets.

The Gladiator in some ways provided a lead-in to the monoplane fighter age despite its biplane lineage. It was destined to be built in far greater number than its current contemporaries with nearly 500 airframes delivered by 1940 compared to an average of marginally more than 100 for the other three. Engine power-rating was raised by between 200 and 300 hp with maximum speed rated at 253 mph.

This picture caption could well read 'Out with the old and in with the New'. The Gauntlet biplanes neatly caught behind a trio of No. 56 Squadron Mk I Hurricanes have now been displaced in frontline service. However, they belong to another unit, since No. 56 converted from the Gloster Gladiator in April 1938. The Black lower-wing colour extends as far as the starboard landing gear.

A series of publicity pictures were taken of the modern Hawker design based at Northolt. In this view, seven Hurricanes hold a neat echelon to starboard. The side outline demonstrates the absence of a ventral strake around the tail wheel; the rudder was increased in area by being extended down to line up with the strake, an act that cured the problem hitherto encountered when attempting to correct a spinning action.

The most dramatic albeit somewhat enforced difference lay in its operational service. By the start of the Second World War, both Hawker designs were relegated to secondary duties as was the Gauntlet, although several briefly served against the Italians in East Africa during 1941, more out of necessity than choice since fighters of any vintage were in short supply in this theatre at the time.

The Gladiator served with Nos 607 and 615 Squadrons in France during the 'Phoney War' and a flight of 247 Squadron covered Plymouth Naval Base during the Battle of Britain; other units served during 1940–41 in Norway and the Western Desert, the latter area involving regular encounters with the CR.42 biplane in current *Regia Aeronautica* service. However, had Fighter Command not been so shorthanded at the time, it was likely the Gladiator would have suffered the same relegation from frontline service as its pre-war contemporaries, so its combat career was basically enforced rather than optional.

Relevant Shock—or Needless 'Wake-Up' Call?

The operational debut of the Bristol Blenheim Mk I at the start of 1937 have been cited in some post-war literary circles as providing a clear warning to Fighter Command that its fighters were dangerously outdated. The basis for this claim lies in the speed performance of the new bomber that was set at 260 mph maximum, a figure well above even the Fury II's equivalent figure of 223 mph from among the bulk of the command's older designs. However, by 1937, the Gloster Gladiator was on hand in sizeable numbers and its top speed was just 10 mph lower.

What is probably overlooked in making the assertion that the Blenheim's appearance had shaken up Air Ministry thinking on fighter design advancement was that well before then, the wheels were already fully set in motion for the introduction of the Hurricane and Spitfire; the previous June orders had been placed for 600 Hurricanes and 310 Spitfires respectively. The performance envelope of the Spitfire and its future Hawker contemporary had pushed the top-speed factor well beyond the 300-mile mark, while overall performance was similarly enhanced in comparison to their predecessors. Firepower in the form of eight machine guns was an even greater advance. Therefore, is it not reasonable to dispense with regarding the foregoing event as representing a 'wake-up' call?

'Pullll!' A No. 17 Squadron Mk I has bogged down at North Weald. While airmen push up against the wing undersides and two more stands by with supports to push under the wheels, the main group heave on the ropes; the strain is evident on the man's face nearest the camera. The venturi unit below the cockpit that powers the instrument panel was a feature on early production aircraft.

Ground Control System

A complex but flexible control system utilising information from both the radar stations and the Observer Corps with which to efficiently direct the fighters so that an incoming bomber force could be challenged was now being put in place. The core of the system lay in the Operations Room (OR) concept, a series of buildings (Blocks) that were constructed at HQs or on fighter airfields throughout the country. Each Group HQ possessed an Operations Room that supplemented the overall command's central location at Bentley Priory. A further subdivision of each group into several sectors was introduced, with each sector possessing between two and three airfields with one selected for the Operations Room function.

The principle of a 'Filter' Room initially set up within Bentley Priory but then extended to all Operations Rooms was only devised following the 1938 appointment to the post of Senior Air Staff Officer (SASO) of a man whose value in guaranteeing Britain's survival two years ahead would prove to be as inestimable in immediate terms then as Dowding's was over the several years since his stewardship of Fighter Command commenced. Air Vice-Marshal Sir Keith

Park, a First World War victor over twenty Germans, was the person responsible for introducing the Filter system.

Each Operations Room possessed a 'Filter' Room where the height, course, and numbers of 'hostile' formations were initially received and assessed. The information was passed to the Operations Room where markers showing these details were moved on a massive table bearing a grid-outlined map of the OR's geographic zone. The WAAF plotting staff so acting on the information via their telephone headsets moved the markers with long magnetic 'rakes' in like manner to gambling-casino croupiers.

A separate board was fitted with rows of lights with individual bulbs flashing the current status of each squadron, whether airborne or at the three 'Readiness' states on the ground—thirty minutes (airfield), five minutes (dispersal), or two minutes (cockpit). Sitting on a balcony above and behind the table was the controller with his staff. His primary function was to launch and direct his fighters towards the enemy, by anticipating the location where interception would occur—a difficult mental scenario made more so by the sometimes-misleading accuracy of the 'traces' thrown up on the radar set screens. Having the mindset of a gambler was clearly to a controller's advantage, only here he was not playing with money but held human lives at stake.

The flow of information from the radar stations and the Observer Corps proceeded in diametrically opposite directions under the system—downwards in the case of the former and upwards for the latter. In the former instance, Bentley

L1648 was assigned to No. 85 Squadron and arrived at Debden during September 1938. The fighter is seen in an embarrassing nosed-in attitude, with the Watts propeller seemingly minus the bulk of its blade surface. The Type A1 roundels would temporarily be displaced by the less prominent red/blue Type 'B' during the Munich crisis.

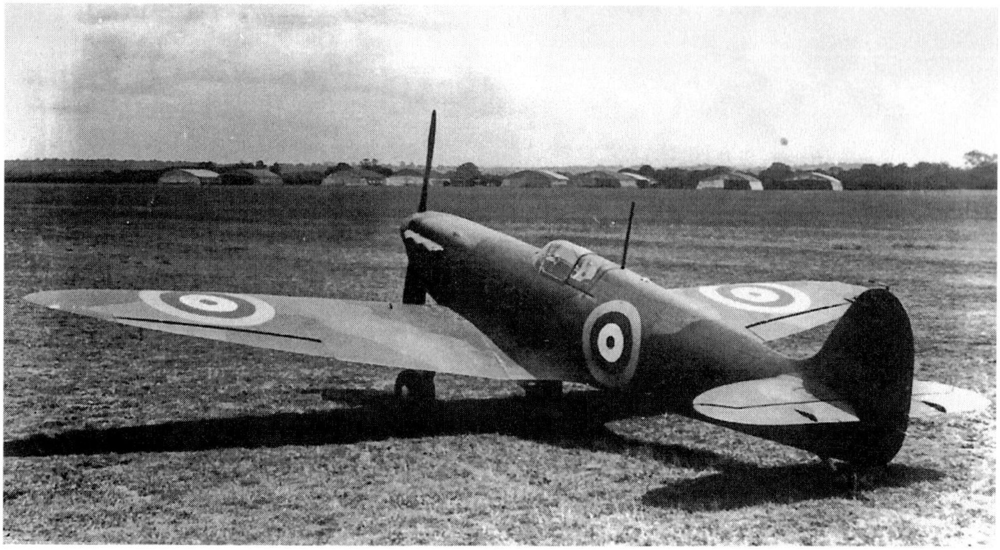

The first production airframe of the Mk I Spitfire was destined never to serve as an operational fighter. Instead, it was retained for maker's trials and other development work. It was subsequently modified to operational standard in terms of photographic reconnaissance duties during 1940, a function it performed until the following 1 June when it was reported MIA.

Priory's Filter Room would assess the overall effect upon the command's fighter disposition in relation to the height, direction, and size of each formation and which sector or sectors were best placed to intercept in time, passing down the facts accordingly to the relevant Group HQ. In practice, thanks to the pressures and confusion of battle as well as the often-marginal time in which to act, group and even sector controllers would themselves find it incumbent to assume the initiative in dispatching their squadrons.

Avoidable Vulnerability

The vital importance of the Sector Stations Operations Rooms to the overall ground-control system was destined to be placed in needless jeopardy during the Battle of Britain. For whatever reason, these structures instead of being buried underground were instead built out in the open. A certain measure of lateral protection was provided with a 'well' surrounding the block whose outer edges featured brick walls backing on to an earth mound in order to absorb blast damage from near misses.

No such protection other than the thickness of the block roof protected it from a direct bomb-strike, however. The same degree of vulnerability applied to many radar sites where their dislocation or worse still permanent destruction would literally blow 'holes' in this electronic and equally vital aspect of aerial defence. Only time and the *Luftwaffe* bombers would dictate the fate of both sets of structures.

Human Resources

The finest military equipment is basically redundant without properly-trained individuals to operate and, in this case, to fly and maintain the aircraft. From the very inception of the RAF, Sir Hugh Trenchard had insisted upon the establishment of an officer candidate's college (Cranwell) as well as a technical college (Halton) at which ground personnel could be trained in the art of aircraft maintenance with the emphasis on recruiting teenagers from the age of fifteen. Discipline standards at Halton were almost as strict for the apprentices as existed among their Cranwell-based elders.

The basic exclusion of the latter body of airmen from being granted access to aircrew status was marginally alleviated by just a select number of the best apprentices being offered the chance to learn to fly. Once qualified, however, there was a maximum of five years applied, after which they would resume their ground trade duties, their long-term value to the RAF being deemed more important in their primary sphere of expertise. The boys' guardianship was assumed by the RAF and strict conduct conditions included parental permission to smoke cigarettes and submission of a 'love-chit' should boys wish to meet with a girl.

The RAF's unconditional detachment from Army and Navy control was fiercely challenged during the initial existence of the Junior Service, but Trenchard's backing by the current Secretary of State for War and Air, the doughty if mercurial Winston Churchill, ensured that no reversal was deemed necessary

The simple beauty of the Supermarine design is fully evident in this shot of a Duxford-based Mk I, whose pilot is indulging in a roll. Note the repetition of the serial under both wings and heavy oil staining of the forward fuselage. The initial batch from which K9795 emerged bore an aluminium finish to the undersides.

or even desirable (Churchill was one among a number of leading figures in the government who purported to see the basic need to carry the fight to an adversary, with air power the quickest and hopefully decisive manner with which to strike at his heartland). There was a literal price to pay for independence, however, that came in the form of the annual budget estimates; these remained pitched at a figure that barely sustained the service's existence let alone allowed for any notable expansion up to the end of the 1920s.

AAF and RAFVR Development

The first addition to boosting officer numbers beyond that provided by Cranwell was introduced in 1924 in the form of what were short-service commissions with the selected candidates expected to join for a period of six years. Within a year of this scheme's inception, further sizeable additions to the short- or long-term (permanent) officer cadre of the RAF that were two-fold in nature commenced in 1925 with the creation of the Auxiliary Air Force (AAF).

The first five AAF units out of the ultimate total of seventeen came into existence over 1925–26, but all were assigned to light bomber operations. The remaining twelve were formed between 1930 and 1938, but the transition to fighters affected only eleven out of the overall figure of seventeen with the remaining six serving in bomber, army-cooperation, Coastal Command, or other roles. Furthermore, it would be roughly the period around the late 1938 Munich Crisis extending into 1939 before the transition would occur.

The third and probably most comprehensive boost to the RAF strength occurred in 1936 with the creation of the RAF Volunteer Reserve. In distinct comparison to the AAF personnel with its accent on commissioned officers, the intention was to attract air-minded individuals between eighteen and twenty-five years old from across the social spectrum, who would in common with their more class-based contemporaries learn to fly whenever their work allowed them to so indulge. An annual bounty of £25 was balanced by the requirement to attend an annual fifteen-day flying course.

A key difference between the two entities was that the AAF personnel were only accepted if they held a pilot's licence. This was a key factor that had hitherto put the average person out of the running on grounds of cost, whereas no such prerequisite was required for RAFVR applicants. An annual figure of 800 trainee pilots was the intention of the Air Ministry and this scale of output was maintained up to 1939.

The sheer scale of the numbers of pilots intended to be trained within the RAFVR Plan forced the Air Ministry to switch the emphasis from RAF instructors to civilian sources, and even by the year the reserve was created the number of flying schools on hand stood at thirteen. Those volunteers who avoided being rejected (or 'washed out' in service parlance) during the courses spanning between eight and twelve weeks in duration were dispatched to the RAF Depot, Uxbridge.

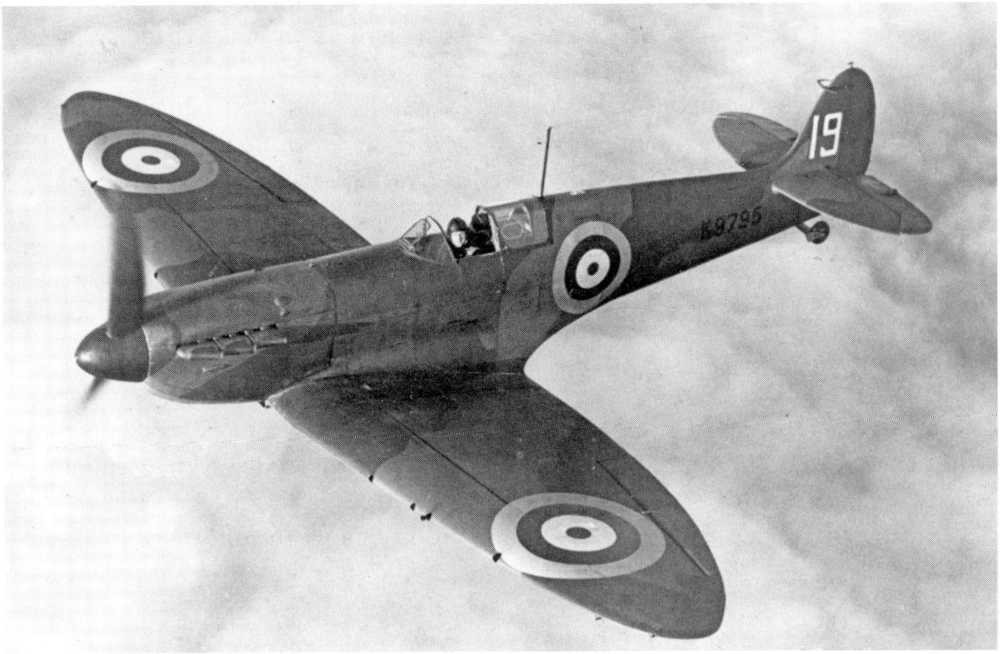

A Mk I Spitfire of No. 19 Squadron bears the unit number on the fin as the sole identifier. Fixed-pitch propeller, untapered radio mast, and flat-profile canopy are borne by what was the second airframe from the initial production batch during 1938. Type A1 wing roundels would give way to red/Blue Type B. An anti-spin parachute is fitted, and 'U' frame on fin prevents the canopy from snagging should the parachute be deployed.

A faulty axle stub that fractured after the fighter landed was the cause of Plt Off. Gordon Sinclair failing to prevent the No. 19 Squadron fighter from flipping onto its back. Sinclair was uninjured, but his subsequent transfer to No. 310 Squadron at nearby Fowlmere during the Battle of Britain could be treated as a form of rebuke—the squadron operated on Hurricanes.

Two weeks of drill and service indoctrination was followed by transfer to an Operational Training Unit (OTU) where introduction over six weeks to the aircraft-category each had been assigned to would take place. In this manner would a potential 'reserve' be available for call-up in the event of a national emergency—one that was being suspected was heading the way of the European democracies at an alarming pace.

RAF Snobbery? Perish the Thought!

The perceived 'junior' status of the RAF compared to its Naval and Army contemporaries has probably given the impression that its personnel were imbued with a greater sense of egalitarian perception. The traditions created and sustained over many centuries by the Royal Navy in particular has conversely laid it open to criticism of being too fixated and therefore too inflexible in its general outlook *vis-à-vis* the threat to its security from air power—a criticism that in retrospect could similarly be applied to the US Navy in the lead up to Pearl Harbor.

Security was meant to be watertight as regards awareness of both the public and even more so foreign governments' insight into the Spitfire's existence. The Mk I from No. 19 Squadron visiting nearby Cambridge airport has been surreptitiously snapped, otherwise had the two policemen been aware of the photographer's action they would have promptly taken legal action.

On a human level, the relationship within the RAF ranks has generally been regarded as being much more free and easy; examination of the situation prior to the Second World War and even in the conflict's opening months paints a markedly different picture. The British class system that was still markedly prevalent in civil life definitely extended its influence into the military world. Although the intention behind the Cranwell College's function was to recruit officer-candidates from across the broad spectrum of society there was a distinct tendency to focus upon individuals with a public-school background (the word public illogically refers to private fee-paying as opposed to state-funded pupils).

Officers and other ranks did no more mix than did those within the other two British services. There were separate catering facilities (known as messes) for officers, while NCOs and other ranks were further divided on this issue; the Officers' Mess amenities were also pitched on a higher level of quality. Officers wore superior-quality uniforms and also enjoyed the services of a servant known as a 'batman' who carried out menial duties such as bed making, shoe cleaning, and similar work on behalf of his commissioned 'master'.

While pilots and navigators largely enjoyed automatic commissioned status, many of the air gunners/wireless operators were not even raised to the basic rank of sergeant until the winter of 1939–40. Worse still was the treatment of other ranks aircrew following a sortie, whereas the officers could retire to the Officers' Mess, the hapless OR personnel could be selected for twenty-four-hour duties around the airfield if nobody else was available. At least one fighter squadron operated under RAF 'tropical hours' rules that saw all operational duties ceasing at 1 p.m., the rest of the day then being made available for social activities.

It is easily forgotten that Trenchard and the senior staff initially assuming charge of the 'junior service' were originally mid- or long-term serving members within the British Army or in some cases the Royal Navy and inevitably were imbued with their chosen service's sense of tradition; it is to their credit that the degree of formality applied within the RAF although noticeable in scale was gradually slackened. Having said that, it was the onset of the Second World War that arguably led to a sea change in attitudes between the ranks with the involvement of airmen from around the world eroding although not totally subverting the perceived need for such formal conduct.

'O, I have slipped the surly Bonds of Earth', the first line of John Gillespie McGee's poem 'High Flight' is exemplified by this superb shot of three steeply-banking Mk I Spitfires from No. 19 Squadron taken by the eminent photographer Charles Brown; an almost solid undercast and sun-shot background further adds to the stark beauty of the picture. Post-war inferences that the picture was 'doctored' do a discredit to one of the finest aerial cameramen to ever 'tread' the skies of Britain.

The Opposing Stance

The idea that it was the Nazis who initiated the clandestine birth of the *Luftwaffe* is a clear historical misnomer. The mix of subterfuge and legitimacy that preceded its inception was begun as early as 1923 when the democratically-elected government drew up plans for just such a resurgent entity. The aim was finally achieved from several angles. A key aspect was the granting by the victorious Allies of the right to operate civil airline facilities in the form of the *Deutsche Lufthansa* concern; here was the perfect platform for training a large cadre of aircrew with latent military service in view.

Leading German designers such as Ernst Heinkel and Claude Dornier ultimately produced prototypes (He 111 and Do 17 respectively) that were purportedly for commercial use but whose layout permitted their adaptation as bombers. Earlier in the 1920s, the Soviet government had connived at providing military training facilities for thousands of men. The provision of gliding clubs that was not prohibited under the Treaty of Versailles set the (therefore legal) conditions for even greater numbers of young volunteers who were subsequently to advance to powered-flight within the *Luftwaffe*'s ranks.

The Civilian Repair Organisation did a sterling job in returning often heavily-damaged aircraft to a fully-operational status. In this instance, L1942, belonging to No. 504 Squadron, was subsequently assigned first to No. 79 Squadron, followed by service with three secondary units prior to being struck off charge in 1944. TM codes for No. 504 Squadron displaced original AW letters after September 1939.

Even by 1936, the still-nascent *Luftwaffe* was reputed to possess a sizeable force of bombers, a proportion of which were He 111s and Do 17s, which possessed the range to strike at the perceived industrial arteries of the English element of Britain; the more-dated Do 23 and the shorter-range Ju 87 could be excluded from the strategic equation, but their absence would be balanced-out by the appearance of the Ju 88. What appears not to have been realised was the basic operational emphasis behind the deployment of the *Luftwaffe*—not as a strategic but rather a tactical air arm supporting the *Wehrmacht* in the field.

The rationale behind the German theory was in direct contrast to the strategic vision of Trenchard. In effect, the swift destruction of an opponent on the battlefield as envisioned by the 'Lightning War' (*Blitzkrieg*) method would render further material output from his industrial facilities redundant since there would be nobody 'in the military field' available with which to sustain the fight following defeat and surrender. However, it was fortunate for the Allies that Gen. Walter Wever (*Luftwaffe* Chief of Staff) who was a prominent proponent of strategic bombing and who had pushed through plans for the development of long-range bombers was killed just as Dowding took post and the Do 19 four-engined prototype then on hand was not advanced further (the subsequent and failure-inflicted development of the He 177 was to prove a further hindrance to any future for a *Luftwaffe* response to the Anglo–American strategic bomber equivalent).

When Göring was advised of the potential of the Do 19 design especially as regards its superior range and bomb-load capacity he is alleged to have said: 'The Führer will not ask how big our bombers are, only how many there are!' True or

The Mk I Spitfires of No. 19 Squadron seemed to have gained the attention of the publicity machine more than their No. 66 fellow unit at Duxford. The picture taken with war scant months distant shows all aircraft still fitted with the two-blade, fixed-pitch propeller, whose output was dangerously limited *vis-à-vis* its variable-pitch successor, even more so when a constant-speed unit was added to the latter during 1940.

not, the continued production-concentration went along the single/twin-engined route with tactical operations the continued and clear priority. This was a policy that would cost the Nazi regime dear in the years ahead, albeit reaping considerable initial success and conversely creating a morale-lowering experience for those attempting to stand up to the rampaging German forces.

Tactical Misapprehensions

There were two tactical factors—one already long-established and the other introduced during the late 1930s—whose retention within the command was to often prove tragically counter-productive. The first concerned the formation layout of a squadron whose pre-war average aircraft strength was twelve to fourteen. The basic sub-formation was a 'Vic' (V-pattern) of three aircraft labelled a section with two forming a flight and two flights constituting the full squadron complement. The arrangement was perfect in respect of keeping the unit in cohesive shape but was to prove very poor when attempting to avoid being taken unaware ('bounced' in RAF slang) by an adversary.

Other than the formation leader, all other pilots had to retain their attention upon station-keeping in order to avoid a collision, so the chances of picking-up an encroaching attacker before it gained firing-range were poor to minimal. The subsequent deployment of an extra fighter behind the formation whose solo weaving flight pattern permitted him a theoretically enhanced ability to spot an attacker was stopgap in nature; all too often, the measure led to what was christened the 'weaver' being taken down without warning to leave his colleagues still in mortal danger.

The mandatory adaptation of the *Luftwaffe*'s far superior *Schwarm* or 'finger-four' equivalent to the RAF's section would not be taken on board until around 1941 and then not comprehensively. The German lesson learned from the Spanish Civil War saw two two-aircraft sub-units each known as a *Rotte* (pair) flying in a well-spaced lateral pattern that was a duplicate of the fingertips on a human hand. Each fighter was also staggered in a marginally-vertical manner. The consequence was that each pilot had a clear sight of his segment of the sky while still maintaining contact with the other three.

Once battle was joined, each *Rotte* held together with the No. 2 guarding the leader's tail while the latter initiated a pass at an opponent; alternately, both could switch positions if necessary, for the No. 2 to assume the attack role. This contrasted sharply with the manoeuvring of a section in combat where it was unfeasible for the two wingmen to simultaneously function either in attack or acting as a cover. Acting as joint No. 2s reduced the overall striking power while it was basically difficult, if not impossible, for all three to cover one another in this 'odd man out' configuration anyway.

The other tactical misnomer concerned the manner in which enemy aircraft were to be intercepted. Nazi Germany's growing likelihood as the source for

No. 65 Squadron was based at Hornchurch and converted from Gladiators to the Mk I Spitfire in March 1939. The fighter being pushed back bears the more subdued Type 'B' roundel on the fuselage; this was introduced around April 1939 but was replaced by the Type 'A' towards the year's end. The de Havilland propeller is a standard fitting on all twelve fighters.

assault coupled to the distances the *Luftwaffe* would have to fly in order to bomb British targets would leave the aircraft bereft of fighter cover. The RAF fighters being accordingly free of counter-assault would launch their attacks that involved a set number (six) of what were titled Fighter Command Attacks (FCA). These involved specific approaches and/or various proportions of the overall squadron formation, with firing range dependent upon the approach angle. The harsh school of combat would dispel any notion of unimpeded success accruing from these manoeuvres, however.

Crisis Year

By 1938, the command's defensive structure at least in terms of its ground-control facilities was beginning to knit together but was still deficient from a point of view of overall national cover. The radar chain was incomplete, and it would be November 1939 before the coastline of England would be fully covered; the number of airfields assigned to Fighter Command was similarly short of the planned establishment figure. In the air, the numbers game was panning out in better fashion with a total of thirty-one squadrons; what was critically lacking, however, was the proportion of modern monoplanes from among the overall number on hand.

The first Hurricane squadron was to be No. 111 based at Northolt with the first examples beginning to displace the Gauntlet the previous December. Waiting to receive their first Spitfire Mk Is during the autumn were Nos 19 and 66 Squadrons based at Duxford, north of London. Therefore, it was that when the Munich Crisis occurred around September and Britain was plunged into a state of war situation, the outlook for Fighter Command as a viable defensive force appeared critical to say the least. Nos 85 and 87 Squadrons were converting onto the Hurricane around this period, while No. 600 Squadron was also converting but only on to the Blenheim Mk IF, whose performance was inevitably mediocre *vis-à-vis* the aforementioned duo. Only one more unit (No. 25 Squadron) would advance into the monoplane age with the Blenheim Mk 1F by the year's end.

Neville Chamberlain and the French Premier Daladier's negotiations with Hitler and Mussolini over the fate of the Sudetenland element of Czechoslovakia perhaps fortunately ended in an uneasy and sadly temporary lull along the path to the Second World War. Chamberlain's famous declaration of professed peace document signed by him and Hitler was touted as representing 'Peace in our Time' by the British Premier, a profound hope shared by many among the British population as well as the government that conflict had been thrust into the background in a long-term sense.

The starboard echelon formation caught on camera is being flown by pilots from No. 65 Squadron. All six Mk Is bear the 'bubble' canopy that replaced the original flat-line pattern on initial production fighters and provided the pilots with better headroom. A future change would be the replacement of the 'fork' pattern pitot mast seen here below FZ: L and FZ: O's port wings with a single tube at the base of the 'L'-shaped frame. Propeller on FZ: L seems to still be the original twin-blade, fixed-pitch unit of dubious performance.

On the RAF airfields, the personnel now gazed with regret at the sorry, drab condition of their aircraft, whose former silver finish with beautiful unit markings had been hastily covered up by brown/green camouflage patterns in anticipation of immediate hostilities commencing. The age of the peacetime airman and his distinctive-finished machine that was definitely obsolete in terms of combat efficiency had exuded a sense of gentle chivalry; that atmosphere was clearly gone for the foreseeable future and indeed would never be totally restored even following the conclusion of the now-looming conflict.

Combat Ready? Perhaps

As the war clouds started to loom ever-closer following Hitler's March 1939 annexation of the remainder of Czechoslovakia and his current threats towards Poland regarding the geographic 'Corridor' separating Prussia from Germany, Hugh Dowding would have been naturally concerned at the likely dilution of his overall strength thanks to the government's promises to dispatch elements to France.

By 3 September, when both nations declared war on Germany, there was still a shortfall of 25 per cent in the minimum need for fifty-two squadrons if the Home Defence force was to remain a viable fighting entity. Dowding's concern on this key issue was heightened by the decision earlier that year to allot four Hurricane squadrons for immediate deployment across the Channel; this figure would soon be increased by a further two Gladiator-equipped squadrons that in turn further reduced Home Defence resources to a two-thirds level.

In the interim months prior to the September declaration, there was a steady flow of Hurricanes and Spitfires into the command's hands. The question to be posed was how combat-ready was either fighter. The propellers in the case of both early production batches were still based on two-bladed units that did not possess any pitch control. The resultant climb rate, a factor that was of prime importance in gaining a height advantage over an approaching formation, was no more than adequate with these fighters as was the general performance in a combat scenario; power loss in contrast meant the broad-bladed Watts units provided a hazard by retarding forward motion that in turn threatened to 'stall-out' the aircraft.

The first three-blade replacements from de Havilland and later from Rotol were very fortunately coming 'on stream'. These featured a variable-pitch mechanism for the blades that combined with a constant-speed unit (CSU) in the latter case resulted in a far superior performance and therefore enabled the pilots to engage the enemy on equal, all-round terms. The blades could also be fully 'feathered'—that is, turned to a fine head-on angle following power loss, thereby reducing the potential 'stall' effect cast out by the rigidly-aligned Watts propeller.

Another negative aspect affecting the Hurricane in particular was the fitting of fabric-covered wings, a clear throwback to its Hawker biplane lineage, although their displacement by metal-clad equivalents was instituted early on in the production process. However, the control surfaces were not similarly adapted even as the Second World War commenced. So, it transpired that the air-pressure effect upon the ailerons in particular presented the pilot with an increased physical effort when indulging in more violent manoeuvres. However, when one considers how the arguably more direct approach and disengagement methods of the Fighter Command attacks were anticipated to be indulged in, then this physically-debilitating effect was probably never envisaged; the force needed to pull the control column back when pulling out of a dive was still noticeable. Fortunately, the ultimate fitting of metal-clad ailerons to both fighters would alleviate the overall situation to a sound degree.

Another important weakness for RAF fighters that had to be borne throughout a good proportion of the Second World War lay not with the airframe but rather the Merlin power source. The carburettor-based fuel flow system functioned normally at most angles of flight into which the aircraft was pitched other than when pushed into a dive; the negative 'G' forces encountered caused the chamber to be starved of fuel thereby leading to a power 'cut-out'. This problem would arise in full the following summer when encounters with the Bf 109 witnessed the benefit of the Daimler-Benz direct-injection system coming to the German pilot's assistance. Whereas the latter engine functioned perfectly in a dive, the failure of its Merlin contemporary often led to the pilot losing distance and/or visual contact.

Ammunition would prove to be another limiting factor in two respects: the striking power of the .303 bullet round was no more than sound in inflicting fatal damage to an airframe compared to the greater punch-power of even the heavier-calibre .5 (12.7-mm) bullet, let alone that of an explosive cannon-calibre shell; the other limitation applied to the round capacity for each weapon that formed a figure of 300 for both Hurricane and Spitfire. The total expenditure of even the 2,400 rounds on hand would take up no more than fifteen seconds, and therefore demanded a careful husbanding of resources—not the easiest thing to monitor in the feral atmosphere of combat and liable to leave a pilot very vulnerable should his guns run out when still engaging the enemy.

The windshields were initially formed of plain Plexiglas and were therefore incapable of withstanding what could for the pilot be a lethal penetration by any form of return gunfire from a bomber when indulging in Fighter Command attacks, or indeed in any air battle and even more so when encountering an escort fighter. The provision of toughened Plexiglas sheeting for the basic windshield would only occur during the winter of 1939–40 and right up into the spring. Nor was armour provision for the rear of the cockpit considered necessary as hostilities commenced; only then was shaped plates developed for location behind the pilot's head.

The Air Ministry's previous resistance to the idea was reportedly based on the assumption that the extra weight would have an adverse effect upon the fighter's centre of gravity (CG). It was only during November 1939 when Sqn Ldr 'Bull' Halahan, having realised how fortunate one of his No. 1 Squadron pilots had

A mix of service personnel and civilian onlookers aligning the boundary of RAF Biggin Hill east of London are watching two 'Vics' of Mk I Hurricanes from No. 32 Squadron as they roar overhead; the two pilots nearest to the camera already have full gear retraction. Picture was taken as the hostilities were just months or even weeks away from fruition on 3 September 1939.

been to survive his shot-up cockpit from behind, fitted out a Hurricane and demonstrated how the CG was not affected that the Air Ministry fell into line (however, Dowding had already raised the issue with the ministry at a meeting; when the committee members scoffed at the idea, he is alleged to have retorted: 'If Chicago gangsters can have it in their cars why cannot my pilots have the same!').

Fire penetrating into the cockpit was to cause severe burn injuries to numerous pilots surviving the incident, while this proved a fatal outcome for their fellow-airmen. The location of both wing-mounted fuel tanks for the Hurricane and a 'header' tank for both fighters positioned directly in front of the wind shield was the catalyst for each such incident. The problem was added to for the Hurricane pilots in that there was no panel separation between the fuselage and wing-roots around the cockpit area; consequently, the ignition of the wing tanks was a secondary source of exposure to the flames for the hapless occupant.

The foregoing limitations in performance and structural integrity were almost matched by what was to prove a priceless advantage over the Bf 109 or any *Luftwaffe* aircraft. This took the form of 100 octane fuel whose existence owed much to America, although the original tests had been carried out in Britain. That nation had the means to hold stocks of what was an expensive-to-produce commodity requiring equally expensive production plant facilities. The resulting 100-per cent increase in engine boost output from the original 6-pound in metric pressure turned out by the Merlin engine would be to Fighter Command's clear advantage in overall performance that included an enhanced climb rate so necessary to gain the same or greater height before engaging in combat.

All hinged upon whether the ever economy-minded British government could be persuaded to purchase large quantities as had been proposed by an RAF technical specialist during 1937. Consent was thankfully granted, and the first consignment arrived in Britain during mid-1939. For all Germany's undoubted technological expertise, the *Luftwaffe* was destined to soldier on with fuel achieving an increase in octane levels to a standard maximum figure of eighty-seven—still well short of its Allied equivalent, although marginal increases in quality did occur.

The RAF carried out a war exercise in August 1939, of which this trio of No. 85 Squadron Mk Is based at Debden, Essex, were a part. All are early production airframes with Watts propellers, non-armoured Plexiglas windshields and ring-and-bead gunsights. Unit codes are NO, but about to change to VY. The helmets and gasmasks are soon to become a permanent operational factor.

Armageddon Again on Hand

Across the North Sea, the ranks of the *Luftwaffe* were being stiffened by the recent return of the Condor Legion veterans from Spain. Their practised expertise in the art of combat was being passed on as the German military closed-up on the border with Poland in August, ready to launch combined ground and air assaults upon their Polish adversaries. The latter were similarly mobilised for battle; although exuding a mood of confidence as to their ability to withstand such an attack, the resources on hand were to prove utterly inadequate in qualitative terms notwithstanding the battle spirit and gallantry of their airmen and soldiers.

On 1 September 1939, the unprovoked Invasion of Poland unleashed the dogs of war, thereby initiating the series of malevolent actions over the ensuing six years that would consume tens of millions of military and civilian lives and alter the balance of power the length and breadth of the globe. Over the next forty-eight hours, Hitler was served with a Foreign Office directive from Sir Neville Henderson (Ambassador) stating that unless he was prepared to withdraw his troops from Poland, a state of war would be declared by Great Britain. At 11 a.m. on 3 September, Neville Chamberlain's sombre voice informed his nation by radio that the die was cast for hostilities to commence. All his efforts to achieve peace had been shattered, and he would be dead within sixteen months thanks to a cancer condition.

The scene is Biggin Hill and the Mk I Hurricanes of No. 79 Squadron still bearing fixed-pitch Watts propellers are revving-up; the ground crewmembers are standing by to act as visual 'guides' to the pilots as they taxi out. AL: T/L1718 in foreground will transfer to No. 111 Squadron and finally become a casualty of the Battle of France. The distinctive permanent hangar and its fellow structures will be *Blitzed* to destruction in August 1940.

3

Phoney War: A Vital Respite? September 1939–April 1940

The banshee yowl of the sirens cast their frightening notes over London among other cities and towns shortly following the Chamberlain broadcast's conclusion, and people stared fearfully upwards while they were directed into the shelters as they awaited the promised aerial assault envisaged by Stanley Baldwin. In the event, nothing happened, and so commenced a time period spanning many months before the full horror of the *Blitz* would descend upon Britain's mainland.

Out on the airfields, the personnel stood ready, if somewhat uncertain in expectation. Where were the *Luftwaffe* marauders, and when would they strike? The fact that the vast bulk of that force's strength had been dispatched eastward with the intention of hammering their Polish adversaries into the ground was probably not appreciated at this time—that besieged nation was surely another 'faraway country of which we knew nothing' to quote Chamberlain's words regarding Czechoslovakia during the Munich Crisis a mere twelve months previously.

'Friendly Fire' Tragedy

Fighter Command was naturally on full alert for the expected onslaught, but the very first 'action' on the 6th proved tragically counter-productive and would in retrospect be labelled the 'Battle of Barking Creek', this location being on the north bank of the River Thames but actually many miles distant from where the fatal encounter occurred. Separate formations from Nos 56 and 151 (North Weald) Squadrons and Nos 54, 65, and 74 (Hornchurch) Squadrons flying Hurricanes and Spitfires respectively were 'scrambled' in succession following a ground report from an Army unit further down the Thames Estuary (and presumably based in the Barking region) regarding what the soldiers thought was a 'hostile' aircraft. The multitude of successive 'plots' on the various radar screens were the likely catalyst for what ensued.

Air locks in the hydraulic system could easily lead to the embarrassing situation faced by the pilot of this No. 151 Squadron Hurricane. Fortunately, the partial collapse of the starboard main wheel left the propeller clear of the ground. The black underside of the port wing on L1768 is relieved by a plain aileron; the dark colour probably extends to the fuselage, with the remaining lower surfaces in white as originally introduced during late 1938.

Flt Lt Clouston's No. 19 Squadron Mk I Spitfire demonstrates the risks inherent in close formation flying. One of his section inflicted this potentially fatal degree of rudder and elevator damage to K8854; the pilot was fortunate to maintain control before force-landing on a racecourse. Incident predates the May 1940 introduction of fin flashes on RAF fighters.

The Hornchurch fighters then encountered what they presumably must have been informed was the prey. The resultant attack launched under FCA rules by one 'Vic' from No. 74 brought down two Hurricanes with one of the pilots killed, Plt Off. M. Hulton-Harrop becoming the command's first combat fatality—and all without hostile involvement. Fg Off. F. C. Rose escaped with his life, but this reprieve was only delayed until the following 18 May when he was the victim of a Bf 109 over France. Aircraft recognition skills must have been of an indifferent standard at this initial stage of hostilities, as indeed they were to prove during the entire course of the Second World War. However, the much more relevant question as to how a Bf 109, the sole single-engined fighter within the *Luftwaffe*'s current establishment, could have possibly ranged this far—unless dispatched on a one-way flight—is an issue that has seemingly never been raised in the aftermath of the incident.

Concentration across the Channel

The government's promise to France regarding air support was duly fulfilled. In the case of Fighter Command, this amounted to the immediate dispatch of four Hurricane squadrons (Nos 1, 73, 85, and 87) along with Nos 607 and 615 Squadrons with their Gladiator biplanes the following November. The first two units were assigned to the Advanced Air Striking Force (AASF), the other quartet becoming part of No. 60 Wing of the Air Component. The former sub-force was based well east of Paris and south of the city of Reims. The squadrons based at Vassincourt and Rouvres respectively were tasked along with several RAF bomber units with supporting the French along their borders with Germany at the juncture with Luxembourg.

Further north, the Air Component-assigned squadrons were part of the covering force for the British Expeditionary Force entrenched along the Franco–Belgian border; the city of Lille was the epicentre for their initial positioning with Lille–Seclin and Merville the main assigned airfields. Since direct access from their *Luftwaffe* airfields would entail traversing neutral Belgium, it was likely that not so much enemy activity over northern France would occur compared to the direct access across the Franco–German border further south. Nevertheless, the *Luftwaffe* could and did mount sorties that were routed over the North Sea. As it transpired, the initial months of the conflict would be largely passive in terms of *Luftwaffe* operations with reconnaissance much to the fore (the rather tardy conversion of Nos 607 and 615 Squadrons from Gladiators to Hurricanes commencing late April and early May 1940 would not have sat well with ACM Dowding since it spelled a further dilution in the overall availability of the Hawker fighter for Home Defence).

The operational conditions awaiting the personnel were far from satisfactory, while the number of aircraft involved provided no more than a token supplement to the French Air Force. Not that Dowding would have been too concerned given

King George's visit to France in December 1939 included inspecting RAF squadrons, in this instance No. 87 Squadron assembled at Lille–Seclin. Wg Cdr J. Dewar shaking hands wears Army-style boots and gaiters as does his companion officer. Dewar would become the highest-ranking casualty of the subsequent Battle of Britain, going MIA on 12 September during a routine flight from RAF Exeter where he was serving as station commander.

that his priority was the defence of Great Britain—that is, provided that further calls upon the Command's resources would not be made (in light of looming events, the situation would deteriorate to an extent that would cast in doubt the very ability of his pilots to confront the *Luftwaffe* with an adequate defensive response, but that crisis extended many months ahead).

There was a stark difference between the British and French aerial-defensive network particularly in electronic cover that would lead to fatal consequences for the Allied cause the following May and June. No equivalent to the Chain Home radar system was in existence; all was dependent upon visual telephonic and even aural means in the form of echo-sound equipment. Consequently, there was little ability to effectively handle the Anglo-French fighters so that an incoming formation could be promptly and properly intercepted, especially given the wide geographic spread from out of which the *Luftwaffe* attackers could emerge. The wasteful expedient of standing patrols that would appear to be the sole primary solution was further diluted if not rendered largely redundant by the very lack of aircraft numbers on hand with which to indulge this operational activity.

As regards the possibility of a land-based offensive, the Maginot Line of fortifications was confidently expected to repulse any *Wehrmacht* thrust; what was not probably anticipated was the involvement of the *Luftwaffe* in the forthcoming *Blitzkrieg* tactic that would thrust their opponents on a permanent back foot; in so doing, it would place an inordinate strain upon the air forces no

The early months of the Second World War raised the spectre of the Germans making use of gas as during the First World War; this was a fear that fortunately was not realised. However, practice gas alarms were initiated in France with this example using smoke canisters occurring in March 1940 at Lille–Seclin, Nos 85 and 87 Squadrons' base. The LK codes for the latter unit can be seen.

less than that borne by their equally hapless army colleagues. Regardless of the assault-pattern—*Blitzkrieg* or otherwise—that the Germans might adopt, the key weakness in this fortification system was its cessation at the northern end where the Franco–Belgian border commenced. The Belgian government had maintained its neutral stance and therefore could not countenance involvement in the scheme. As a result, there was no manmade impediment in the path of an invader along that country's western border.

The airfields assigned to the RAF were generally basic in format as regards the flying surfaces and technical support structures as well as living accommodation. The grass surfaces were often prone to failure in the face of wet conditions that led to landing accidents that over-stressed even the Hurricane's sturdy landing gear, while on occasions, no sorties could even be made. The lack of hangars and other technical sites made the task of the ground crew consistently bad and even miserable; the advent of one of the worst winters added to their travails.

Between September and the following early May, there occurred what the German dubbed '*Sitzkrieg*' and the French '*Drôle de Guerre*', appropriate euphemisms for the military stalemate that settled in wholesale fashion upon the Western Front. The French advance into German territory immediately following the declaration of war was short-lived and then reversed, after which both sides faced each other to indulge in a static confrontation reminiscent of the First World War. In the air, virtually a similar situation existed; reconnaissance flights were

A group of ground crew play handball beside a No. 85 Squadron Hurricane that reveals the fabric wing surfaces and cross-shaped gun panel applied to the first production aircraft. The Watts propeller and external venturi tube beneath the cockpit are other original fittings while the windshield lacks an armoured glass front. Engaging the *Luftwaffe* on even an equal footing would have been a daunting task with this dangerously unmodified machine.

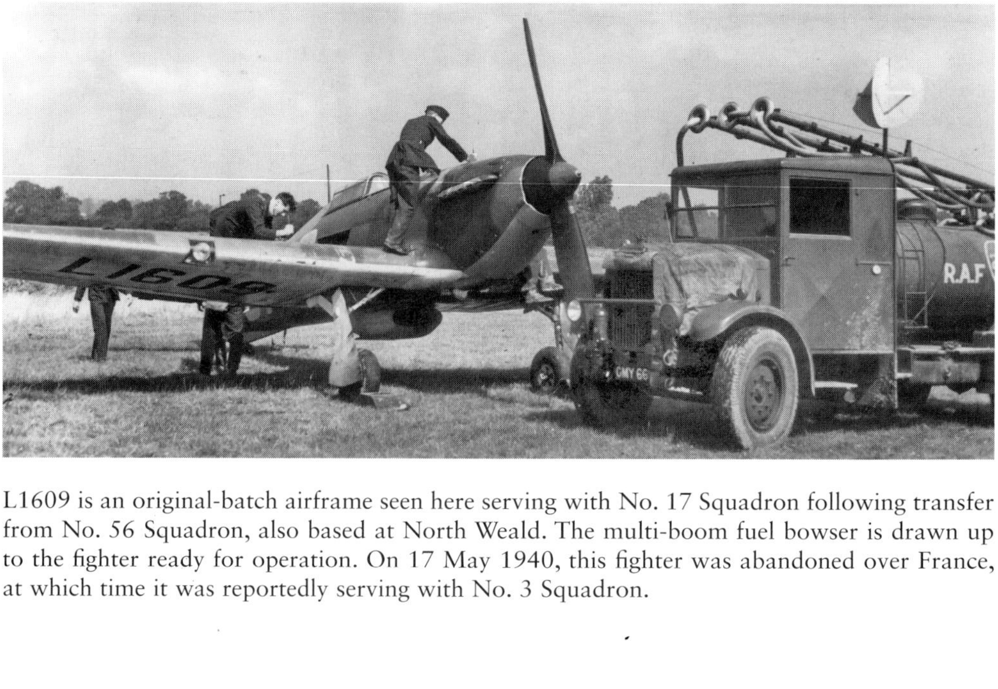

L1609 is an original-batch airframe seen here serving with No. 17 Squadron following transfer from No. 56 Squadron, also based at North Weald. The multi-boom fuel bowser is drawn up to the fighter ready for operation. On 17 May 1940, this fighter was abandoned over France, at which time it was reportedly serving with No. 3 Squadron.

sent out, but bomber assaults were not indulged in. There was little or nothing for the RAF fighter pilots to initially indulge their potential skills, but the occasional encounter would occur.

The high-flying reconnaissance invaders theoretically held all the cards in that establishing and tracking their approach and withdrawal was dependent upon visual means that in turn left the RAF pilots fighting an uphill battle to 'scramble' in time to gain the necessary interception altitude. Nevertheless, there were regular occasions when the situation worked out and even concluded favourably. One of the first involved No. 1 Squadron's Fg Off. 'Boy' Mould who intercepted a Do 17P from 2(F)123 on 30 October.

The bomber had previously been vainly pursued by two fellow-pilots, but the crew's luck was out the second time around. One prolonged burst of fire from astern was enough to ignite the fuel tanks and send machine and its hapless five-man team into a vertical and terminal spiral. Mould later inspected the crash site and expressed a sense of depression at having caused such human mayhem when he rejoined his colleagues who furthermore agreed with his view. The age of chivalry was not yet swallowed up by what was to evolve into an irreversible total war scenario.

The squadron's 'Killy' Kilmartin shared a Do 17 on the 23rd, but Sgt Clowes was fortunate to survive the loss of one elevator and the bulk of his rudder during the successful interception of a He 111. However, his assailant was 'friendly' in

A Mk I Spitfire serving with No. 19 Squadron at Duxford during the winter of 1939–40 displays the Type 'A' fuselage roundel introduced during November and retained until the Type A1 took its place the following May. The serial number is applied in very small form on the top of the fin, but later production batches would bear this on the rear fuselage.

the form of one from a group of Morane-Saulnier M.S.406 fighters that rushed in on the combat. Clowes held his nerve, landing at a higher speed than normal to avoid stalling-out, but still nosed-in at the airfield end; the Morane pilot reportedly baled out.

Fg Off. 'Pussy' Palmer was leading a section that took out a Do 17P of 4(F)122 from which the crew seemingly baled out after one engine was set on fire. On sidling up to the 'abandoned' bomber, he was met by return fire, the gun being fired by Ltn. Frankenberger (P). Having emerged intact from the situation intact—though lucky to avoid being struck by bullets that shattered the windshield—Palmer was nevertheless impelled to make a forced-landing in his somewhat shot-up fighter. Meanwhile, Kilmartin and Sgt Soper continued to harry the bomber, setting the second engine ablaze, whereupon Frankenberger also brought off a successful forced-landing. Such was the respect for his courage that he was subsequently released temporarily from French custody and entertained by the squadron personnel.

The spate of interceptions recorded and 'kills' submitted this day was to prove misleading in terms of regular recurrence over the succeeding winter months. As it transpired, similar albeit equally staccato successes by pilots from among the other three squadrons were recorded during November, including two Do 17Ps scored by Fg Off. 'Cobber' Kain from New Zealand. The No. 73 Squadron pilot was to go on to run up a total of sixteen 'kills' before losing his life in a seemingly needless aerobatic display. An even rarer if successful encounter on 21 November between Flt Lt 'Dickie' Lee (No. 85 Squadron) and a He 111 off Boulogne ended with the Stab./KG4 bomber being dispatched into the Channel to mark the unit's first 'kill'; this followed the downing of another He 111 from 2(F)122 on 2 November that marked No. 87 Squadron's 'debut', the victor being Flt Lt Robert Voase-Jeff (both pilots would be MIA within a week of each other during mid-August 1940).

It is to the credit of the pilots that they were able to reach relatively high altitudes, given that the bulk of the fighters were still operating with the twin-blade, fixed-pitch propeller. The onset of hypoxia via faulty oxygen equipment was another and potentially lethal problem, as was the danger from 'friendly fire' incidents involving their French counterparts. The application of a fin flash onto the full rudder outline was a visual measure for their Allies' benefit to denote the Hurricane's 'friendly fighter' status, but assaults still occurred, fortunately with little or no negative effect.

The appearance of first the Bf 110 and latterly the Bf 109 was destined to pose a stiffer challenge for the RAF pilots. The former machine, although twin-engined in layout and theoretically inferior to the Hurricane in overall performance, in practice proved to be a stolid opponent, especially in view of the mediocre Watts fixed-pitch propeller output that left the Hurricane as no more than an equal performer in an engagement; the heavier 'punch' of the enemy fighter's cannon/ machine-gun combination was also of especial concern.

Two No. 73 Squadron airmen strain on the winding-handles to operate the Mk I Hurricane's inertia-starter as the sergeant gives the signal to the pilot to press the starter button. The Watts propeller and 'kidney' exhaust cowl are features of an early-production airframe. Hopefully, the propeller would be replaced by a more modern de Havilland unit before the events of 10 May 1940 burst upon the Allied air forces.

Home Defence Activities

The *Luftwaffe*'s initial thrusts directed at British soil were launched not against the nation's southern fringe but rather further north in Scotland that was the location for two key maritime havens. The Naval Base at Rosyth in the Firth of Forth was targeted by Ju 88s of I/KG30 on 16 October. Nos 602 (City of Glasgow) and 603 (City of Edinburgh) were two auxiliary squadrons, both being equipped with the Spitfire.

On being alerted of the *Luftwaffe* raiders' approach, several sections were 'scrambled' from Grangemouth and Turnhouse and soon intercepted the nine-strong formation in the vicinity of their projected target. The result was in the RAF's favour, whose pilots brought down the bombers flown by Hptm. Pohle and Obltn. Storp into the sea. Pohle was the sole survivor from his aircraft after it had to be 'ditched' with Storp one of three out of the four-man crew surviving a prolonged immersion in the ever-chilly North Sea waters.

The next day, KG30 lunged at Scapa Flow (the other key Naval Base in the Orkney Islands) but achieved nothing at the cost of one bomber that exploded after being struck by the AA barrage. As it transpired, the anchorages were virtually empty since the warships had transferred to Loch Ewe on Scotland's north-west coast—an action initiated by the sinking just three days previous of the battleship *Royal Oak* by Gunther Prien's *U-47* as it lay in seeming security within the Flow. Further south, off Northeast England, a reconnaissance He 111 from Stab. I(F)122 was taken down by No. 41 Squadron and a Do 18 seaplane stood even less chance against a trio of No. 607 Squadron Gladiators. No. 46 Squadron administered a severe rebuff to *Küstenfliegergruppe* 406 four days later, downing three of its nine He 115 floatplanes attacking a convoy; a fourth damaged floatplane diverted into Denmark and internment while the convoy remained intact.

The first enemy aircraft to land on British soil in the Second World War was sought out by sections from Nos 602 and 603 Squadrons on 28 October, but initially evaded interception. Unfortunately for Ltn. Niehoff's crew in their Stab/KG26 He 111, it was anti-aircraft fire that finally caught the Spitfire pilots of No. 603's attention, whereupon they picked out their lumbering prey to deliver a series of assaults culminating in the bomber suffering a heavy crash-landing on undulating ground south of Edinburgh that shattered the nose section; Niehoff, who only subsequently had his suspected strained back confirmed as emanating from a fracture to his spinal column, was captured along with one of his three-man team, the others being killed during the air battle. So far, the *Luftwaffe* returns from these attacks had been abysmal, a pattern that would not materially alter over the ensuing winter months of 1939–40.

The probing attacks along the eastern seaboard continued to produce a drip-feed of *Luftwaffe* losses between November and the following April. KG26 bore the brunt of this, although *Aufklärungsgruppe Oberbefehlshaber der Luftwaffe* (Aufkl.Gr.Ob.d.L.) contributed three crews out of seven lost from other specialist units. Nor were all casualties caused by fighters since a number were simply MIA thanks to likely mechanical failure. The Royal Navy's bases at Rosyth and Scapa Flow continued to gain regular attention, with over half the confirmed 'kills' occurring off or on the Scottish coastline.

On 3 February, No. 43 Squadron dealt severely with a KG26 formation, downing three He 111s in the process. Six days after, a fourth *Geschwader* crew tasted the bitter seeds of failure at the hands of No. 602 Squadron, although half those on board survived the forced-landing east of Edinburgh; the minimal damage borne by the aircraft saw it restored to flying condition when it was assigned to the RAFWAFFE, a group of airworthy aircraft providing orientation and recognition instruction to Allied airmen.

Chivalry was still an item of faith among the ranks of the warring nations, including Germany. The He 111 of Aufkl.Gr.Ob.d.L. that was caught by Sqn Ldr Farquhar and Fg Off. Proudman forced-landed east of Edinburgh. The former-named RAF pilot decided to land near the bomber—an ill-advised action confirmed by the fighter overturning thanks to the unsuitable surface. Without hesitation, the *Luftwaffe* crew rushed over and helped their erstwhile 'foe' and undoubtedly embarrassed airman out of the cockpit. The facts were apparently later recorded in a parliamentary debate to confirm the still-ambivalent attitudes directed at the Germans and their military conduct.

No. 111 Squadron was detached to the author's home town Wick in Northern Scotland during February 1940. The unit's primary function was to protect the RN Base at Scapa Flow in the Orkney Islands. Two Hurricanes are being simultaneously refuelled; nearest machine L2001 appears to have no wing roundel. This aircraft reportedly 'stalled out' during a landing the following 19 June.

The relationship between RAF aircrew and their ground crew support teams was ever one of mutual respect with discipline more casually, if still firmly expressed from the top down. This is Flt Lt Peter Townsend with two airmen, all three then serving with No. 43 Squadron at Wick. Townsend became No. 85 Squadron CO in May 1940 when No. 43 also moved south to Tangmere on the Channel coast.

A further change in RAF markings occurred in April 1939 with the introduction of fuselage-mounted code letters, in this case US identifies the Hurricanes assigned to No. 56 Squadron. Type 'A' roundels indicate picture date was from around September. Tight 'Vee' formation was typical of RAF practice at this time but proved to be dangerously unwieldy in combat circumstances.

Two Mk I Spitfires serving with No. 609 (Yorkshire) Squadron are being readied for taxiing-out sometime during 1939–40. Aircraft in the background still bears an untapered radio mast but is adorned with the full code letter layout that surrounds the Type 'A' roundel. The auxiliary-formed unit converted onto the Supermarine fighter around the time hostilities began.

A full-strength formation of No. 19 Squadron Spitfires is seen against a heavy cloud background. All twelve carry the unit code letters of WZ in line with the general order of May 1939 for all fighter squadrons to adopt the code-letter scheme. A second change during February 1940 was the substitution of Type 'B' fuselage roundels by the brighter Type 'A' design.

The code of chivalry extended from the First World War to the present conflict had been further expressed by the British in that full military honours had been accorded the funeral of the two dead airmen from the 28 October crash-landing incident near Edinburgh; two weeks prior, the same service had been granted the two airmen whose bodies had drifted ashore from Hptm. Pohle's 'ditched' Ju 88. The looming all-out nature of warfare would cast such gestures firmly into the background as the true nature of Nazism demonstrated its autocratic tendencies in full measure.

One of the final casualties during this time involved a He 111 from among a six-plane 6/KG26 formation that having released over Scapa Flow on 8 April duly headed for home. Ltn. Weigel's 1H: DP was picked up by among others the No. 43 Squadron Hurricane flown by Flt Lt Peter Townsend not far distant from the unit's airfield at Wick; one engine was disabled, whereupon the bomber turned back and was safely deposited on the airfield. However, the natural light conditions must have been very poor because the two surviving crew members immediately threw their dinghy out having seemingly thought they had 'ditched', there being no other logical reason for the action (at least this is the anecdote that has been often quoted in post-war publications).

The encounters had clearly added little to the home-based RAF pilots' expectations of what fighter-to-fighter combat entailed. The sorties were conducted

On 8 April 1940, a KG26 He 111 bellied-in on Wick airfield in Northern Scotland; the crew were convinced they had ditched to the extent of deploying their life raft. Next day, it was occupied by three sergeant-pilots from No. 43 Squadron, based there to defend the naval base at Scapa Flow. 'Darky' Hallowes (left) rose to command No. 222 Squadron and amassed a total of seventeen personal and two shared kills by VE-Day.

at low to medium altitude and, with the exception of the Ju 88, against less mobile opponents who were almost exclusively on hand in single numbers when intercepted; in addition, they probably provided less of a defensive challenge even if being flown in formation as proved the case on 21 October with the He 115 force. The true test of individual if not also unit-strength engagements against the *Jagdwaffe* would provide a far steeper and lethal-leaning learning curve once the air war exploded into life with the invasion of Western Europe.

First Offensive Strike

Although the RAF was currently inhibited from bombing enemy land targets, there was no absolute inhibition placed on attacks directed at specific military targets where these were isolated from towns or cities. A case in point was the seaplane base at Borkum in the Frisian Island chain. Nos 25 and 601 Squadrons had each dispatched six of their Mk 1F Blenheims on 28 November. The protracted flight across the North Sea at low altitude and in murky conditions did not prevent the lead navigator from plotting a precise course that saw the fighters attain their target. The rather puny ventral 'gun packs' probably did not result in too much

The Blenheims Mk IF and personnel of No. 601 Squadron at Northolt are inspected by Sir Samuel Hoare (Secretary of State for Air) on 6 April 1940. The months of fruitless sorties will soon be a thing of the past, with daylight action over the continent giving way to an introduction to radar-backed night fighting while based at Middle Wallop. The Blenheims would be steadily phased out in favour of the greatly superior Beaufighter from September on.

damage being inflicted, but the shock to the enemy personnel's sense of well-being must have been sharp if not long-lasting. All twelve aircraft retuned safely, but no further offensive action of this nature was to be indulged in until the Nazi storm broke over Western Europe nearly six months on.

Turgid Times Ease

The severe winter conditions settling over Western Europe as 1940 was entered just added to the general mood of sterility among the RAF squadrons. The *Luftwaffe* still carried out reconnaissance sorties, weather permitting, but encounters with the enemy fighters proved to be few and far between at least until around March. The prohibition against mounting sorties over German territory was blatantly broken by No. 73 Squadron, albeit with initial bad results on one occasion when only one among a section of the unit's Hurricanes escaped being 'bounced' by Bf 109s.

No. 1 Squadron's pilots followed the official instructions to some extent with the pilots crossing the Franco–German border at maximum altitude but not penetrating very deep into hostile territory before circling back in a bid to entice their opponents over French airspace. Interceptions were made but frustratingly evolved into 'friendly' formations of French bombers or fighter escorts. The initial contact with the *Jagdwaffe* came on 29 March when Fg Off.s Palmer and Richey along with a newly-arrived colleague literally ran across a Bf 109 *Rotte* heading on a reciprocal course but were immediately 'bounced' by three others.

In the resulting mêlée, Richey closed upon one Bf 109 that initiated the evasive action of a steep dive to leave the Hurricane outpaced, but this advantage was dissipated when the 9/JG53 pilot entered into a prolonged straight climb. He paid for his laxity when Richey closed-up and delivered a series of bursts that saw the fighter exude black smoke before canting into a right-hand spiral that his adversary treated as terminal. In fact, Ltn. J. Volk carried off a crash-landing that left him intact in his badly-damaged machine.

Elsewhere, Richey's colleague 'Johnny' Walker's and his section downed one from a group of Bf 110s—an act that earned them a visit to Maxim's Restaurant in Paris following a promise by Air Marshal Barrett to grant this privilege to the first RAF pilot or pilots to destroy a '*Zerstoerer*'. Clearly the assumed threat posed by Willi Messerschmitt's 'twin' of the Bf 109 had gone before it, an operational factor that would be steadily countered and reversed in the summer skies over southern England.

On 9 April, Hitler's order to invade Denmark and Norway was initiated and the stage was set for a full-scale extension of the conflict across Western Europe. However, a full month was to elapse before the shadow of war loomed fully over France and the Low Countries. In this interim period, the air forces on both sides continued their largely probing sorties with reconnaissance flights still to the fore.

Interceptions by the Hurricane pilots were still sparse in numbers, but they yielded an occasional result, although not without cost albeit only in aircraft. 'Killy' Kilmartin (No. 1 Squadron) crippled a Ju 88 to the extent that it was forced to crash-land, but his fighter was set on fire by return fire and he was impelled to take the same drastic action as his victim. Eighteen days previous (2 April), he had shot down a Bf 109; to his Ju 88 today was added another Bf 109 from 7/JG53 at the hands of his colleague Flt Lt 'Johnny' Walker.

As April finally gave way to May, the RAF fighter pilots awaited the likely German offensive with quiet confidence. Their numbers were still small, but the encounters with the *Luftwaffe* had given an indication that the aerial aspect of their opponents' thrusts could be at least handled. Of course, there was no basic indication of the stunning '*Blitzkrieg*' offensive tactic that was about to burst upon Western Europe.

Despite the *Luftwaffe*'s dominance in northern climes, the Norwegian Campaign currently in full flow had not fully cast forth the weight of combined *Stuka* and *Panzer* assaults and their deleterious effect upon attempting to hold the line against the enemy's overall advance. The mountainous conditions tended to militate against the swift and widespread deployment of the *Panzer* columns, whereas the geography further south was much less inhibiting as events would all too soon demonstrate.

This No. 504 Squadron Hurricane has ended up on its belly following a combat with He 115 floatplanes on 2 April in which its pilot was wounded. The subsequent history of what is an original batch airframe is uncertain; one source states the machine was transferred to No. 46 Squadron and was lost on board HMS *Glorious* following the carrier's destruction on 8 June by two *Kriegsmarine* warships while sailing back to Scapa Flow.

Northern (Mis) Fortunes

The 'Phoney War' period was primarily ended on 9 April 1940 with the German invasion of Denmark and Norway. This was a move that caught the Allies squarely on the back foot even though initial preparations for securing the northern key port of Narvik, through which the enemy was trans-shipping vital iron-ore cargoes, were under way. On the other hand, the much greater distance between Britain and Norway compared to Germany placed an ultimately insuperable burden on adequately maintaining the Army units that were transported to the country's central region. An equally insuperable factor was the provision of proper air cover for the soldiers as they faced the onslaught from the sizeable *Luftwaffe* force swiftly entrenched upon major Norwegian airfields.

Fighter Command's initial effort involved a single Gladiator squadron (No. 263) whose aircraft had to be delivered by HMS *Glorious*; within a week of commencing operations from a frozen lake at Lesjaskog, the unit strength was almost totally dissipated either in combat or thanks to bombing raids, whereupon the personnel destroyed what was left and returned home. The almost parallel evacuation of the Army rendered any aerial replacement redundant at this stage. However, the second fighter deployment was to bear witness to a truly tragic and probably avoidable loss of life.

The assault upon Narvik was launched in late May with the twin hope of establishing a general hold upon northern Norway, this despite the fact that Germany's steady northward advance through the bulk of the country was presenting the Allied forces with little or no chance of reversing the overall situation by ejecting their more numerous and vastly better-supported adversaries. No. 46 Squadron's eighteen Hurricanes along with No. 263's Gladiators were similarly embarked on HMS *Glorious* thereby unknowingly setting in motion a holocaust destined to consume personnel from No. 46 and the warship's crew in joint martyrdom. The fighters were duly flown-off to Bardufoss and Skånland respectively.

During the period of 26 May to 7 June, the RAF pilots did their best to at least blunt the *Luftwaffe* bombing assaults, but once again, the Allied ground situation was already deemed untenable by the latter date. Orders were accordingly issued that day for withdrawal by sea and prior destruction of all equipment. In the case of No. 46, this entailed ten still-serviceable fighters, whereupon Sqn Ldr K 'Bing' Cross submitted a request that the aircraft be flown out to and landed on the *Glorious*—this despite the total lack of arresting equipment and the equal lack of carrier-landing training among the ten 'volunteer' pilots. The request was granted, and while the remaining personnel embarked at Narvik, Cross led his nine colleagues out over the northern waters to rendezvous with the *Glorious* in the early hours of the 8th. The Hurricane's rear fuselages had been weighted-down with sandbags in a bid, however marginal, to create a 'damping' effect on contacting the carrier's deck. In the event, all ten Hurricanes landed in sound order as did several Gladiators of No. 263 Squadron, and a course for Scapa Flow was taken up. Despite their superb action, a cruel fate still awaited most of the pilots among hundreds of their naval colleagues.

All proceeded in seeming sound order until late afternoon, when the enemy, in the form of the battlecruisers *Scharnhorst* and *Gneisenau*, appeared on the southern horizon. It seems almost incredible if not criminal that their presence was only picked up at this stage; had any of the carrier's Swordfish been launched on standard surveillance duties, then the chances of such an ambush occurring would have been greatly diminished if not totally cancelled-out, but all the aircraft had been 'struck-down' into the hangars. This lapse in basic operational discipline now saw the *Glorious* and her two destroyer escorts, *Acasta* and *Ardent*, engaged in a totally unequal contest that dispatched all three beneath the waves in brutally clinical fashion along with all but forty-three out of the 1,558 personnel on board; the frozen waters ensured that the vast bulk of those avoiding death during the action subsequently died of exposure. Only No. 46's Sqn Ldr Cross and Flt Lt P Jameson out of the entire party of RAF pilots lived through the incident, a stroke of extreme good fortune that saw both go on to survive the Second World War.

K9987 from the initial batch of Mk I Spitfires joined No. 66 Squadron in May 1939 and bears several changes from the original layout. The fixed-pitch, two-blade propeller has changed to a two-pitch, three-blade unit, and the 'Bubble' canopy replaces the flat-roofed unit. Small serial number on fin contrasts with the larger fuselage-applied example. Markings are confined to Type 'B' roundels.

A Lesson learned

The capture of a Bf 109 still in airworthy condition had enabled comparative tests to be conducted against a Spitfire. One of the future benefits accruing from the 'dogfight' aspect of the tests related to the physical restrictions that gravity (or 'G' stress as it was called) laid upon the RAF pilots. There had been occasions where the German pilot had somehow managed to hold a tight manoeuvre without apparently suffering the same sensory 'black-out' experienced by his opponent.

Examination of the Bf 109's seat provided the basic answer in that it was set at a distinct backward angle compared to the virtually upright stance within the Spitfire and Hurricane cockpits. There was no way in which to achieve a seat-frame adjustment but a solution to the 'G' problem lay with the rudder pedals. The single footrest currently fitted was replaced by a two-stage unit; when engaging in combat, the pilot shifted his feet from the lower to the upper foot-rest, an action that automatically tilted his body backwards in similar manner to the *Jagdwaffe* pilot's regular angle.

The pace of Fighter Command conversion onto the Spitfire was steadily mounting as 1940 began. In this case, a Mk I from No. 64 Squadron that lacks its individual letter is being manhandled into a hangar. Absence of fin flash and yellow surround to Type 'A' roundels indicates picture taken prior to these amendments that were introduced during May 1940.

Fighter Command Attacks

The basic premise behind the concept of the Fighter Command Attack (FCA) function seems to have been that RAF fighters encountering enemy bombers over Britain would do so without interference from escorting fighters. A further expectation was that the bombers would either hold formation or in individual cases still maintain a steady course even if isolated from its companions, thereby presenting a fairly easy target. Introduction of the system during the first half of the 1930s involved not just single-seat fighters but also the twin-seat Demon.

The conditions for operating the system were unforgivably rigid in that squadron COs were not to use any initiative to launch assaults other than in the prescribed FCA manner unless authorised by Command HQ. How the latter body could judge when to grant such a leeway while remaining stuck firmly on the ground really beggars belief. Firing range would be reached at 400 yards but gun harmonisation varied between 350 yards (Hurricane), 300 yards (Gauntlet), and 250 yards (Gladiator). The Demon gunners in contrast were first to deploy their guns and the pilot only had recourse to using his weapons when the gunner had expended all his ammunition or had been knocked out of action (during the ensuing Battle of Britain, the harmonisation applied to the Gladiator would become the standard).

No. 602 (City of Glasgow) Squadron operated from Drem, near Edinburgh, between October 1939 and August 1940, primarily in order to cover Royal Naval units based in the Firth of Forth. Here a 'Vic' of Spitfires swings in over what is a rather utilitarian airfield with a fourth fighter named *Chico* parked in the right foreground.

Single-Seat Fighter Attacks

The fighters would fly in three patterns depending on what was required of them. A wave attack on an intercepted formation would involve two 'Vics'; twice this number would form up when seeking out the enemy intruders. Attacks would be initiated and carried out from behind and slightly below. Attack initiation was preceded by the CO announcing either 'Stand by for No.' attack or just 'Stand by for attack' if unsure which variant to announce. In the former instance, the second CO's call would be 'No. … attack. Go!'

The Nos 1 and 2 attack variants were to be used against single aircraft within a formation as follows:

No. 1: 'Vics' in stepped-down line astern—leader fires at optimum range (400 yards) before breaking away and down; Nos 2 and 3 follow suit.

No. 2: Lead 'Vic' forms line astern, closes to 400 yards on a bomber on the formation's flank, then fans out and fires. Second 'Vic' takes on the other flank-positioned bomber.

No. 3: Both 'Vics' close in on separate bomber sub-formations (also expected to also be in 'Vic' layout) before each 'Vic' fans out with the individual fighters picking out and opening fire on its opposite number within the enemy formation.

Nos 4 to 6: Similar in function to Nos 1 to 3.

Twin-Seat Fighters

The approach-angle was variable with the gunner able to initiate firing both from ahead of and behind the target aircraft. A six-aircraft flight would take on a bomber 'Vic'; approaching into range from behind and below, ahead and below, or ahead out to one side before commencing fire.

Conclusion

All these manoeuvres and approach-patterns smacking of the aerial version of a parade-ground display took little or no cognisance of the fact that the likely reaction of the bomber formation would be to adopt some form of evasive action as well as having their gunners laying crossfire upon the obligingly-steady approach being conducted by their assailants. Indeed, the *Luftwaffe* did apparently operate such a system with a gunner in each *Kette* acting in a fire-control function for the flanking bombers.

During the Dunkirk evacuation, it appears that at least two senior COs who were of the vintage that had grown up with the FCA scheme fell victim to return fire, probably due to their indulging in one of the recommended attack-approaches. In effect, the 'Greatest Flying Club in the World' was currently prey to a dangerously anachronistic view of fighter tactics that was destined to cost it so highly in aircraft and pilot numbers as the Second World War entered its preliminary stage of consistently 'active' operations.

The beautifully lethal outline of the Spitfire is caught here by a factory-fresh Mk I from a production batch completed between January and August 1940. The two-pitch de Havilland propeller would give way to the vastly more efficient Rotol unit with its constant-speed mechanism. The fighter currently bears no armament while a tapered radio mast replaces the original untapered fixture. Black underside colour is restricted to the port wing.

Test pilot Geoffrey Quill flies P9450 that is modified in several ways. The two most critical are the three-blade, variable-pitch propeller and the addition of an armoured glass frame to the windscreen. The original flat-profile canopy is bulged to give the pilot better headroom. The first two refinements only came into service in time to take on the full offensive might of the *Luftwaffe* during 1940. Picture was taken during April.

4
Battle is Fully Joined

Daunting Deception Plan

The early hours of 10 May 1940 confirmed the RAF personnel's suspicions over the previous few days that they were now to be embroiled in a full-scale battle. The muffled sound of gunfire reportedly heard by the French companion of one pilot from No. 1 Squadron the previous evening had led him to suggest it was emanating from a French bombing range, but no overall reaction emerged from his colleagues at this point. It was the following morning before the first alerts and 'scrambles' occurred. Even then, the degree of contact with the *Luftwaffe* in the region covered by the Advanced Air Striking Force was subdued at least initially compared to the *Blitzkrieg* onslaught released upon Holland, Belgium, and north-eastern France that promptly drew the Air Component squadrons into heavy and sustained action.

The German plan was designed to lure the Anglo–French authorities into thinking their adversaries would repeat the Schlieffen Plan of 1914, whereby the German Army swept into Belgium and northern France with the intention of encircling Paris; on this occasion, Holland was included within the deception scheme. Having succeeded in drawing the Allies into advancing up into Belgium with the River Dijle as their intended central bulwark, the southern arm of the *Wehrmacht* offensive would thrust through the seemingly impenetrable Ardennes region. Located within south-western Belgium with its valleys and solid wooded clusters, it was there the *Wehrmacht* would attempt an encircling action in conjunction with the twin thrust to the north; what was known as the '*Sickelschnitt*' (Sickle-cut) would hopefully culminate with the Allied personnel being trapped and forced to surrender. The plan was certainly ambitious if not downright risky, especially if the bait was not swallowed and the southern-based units either did not achieve a break-out or encountered firm resistance even if they did.

Sqn Ldr 'Bull' Halahan (CO. No. 1 Squadron) stands by the rear fuselage of a Hurricane along with Flt Lt 'Johnny' Walker one of his flight commanders. The Type 'A' roundel and absence of a fin flash indicate picture taken no later than the German invasion on 10 May 1940. National colours on the rudder were a 1939–40 measure to ensure Allied fighters were aware of the Hurricane's 'friendly' status.

Sizing-Up

The *Luftwaffe* force comprised two *Luftflotten*—No. 2 under *Generalfeldmarschall* Albert Kesselring's command and No. 3 led by *Generalfeldmarschall* Hugo Sperrle. On hand were some 4,200 bombers, dive-bombers, fighters, and reconnaissance aircraft, of which nearly 66 per cent were operational. The penultimate category included around 600 Bf 109s and Bf 110s within *Luftflotte* 2 and 550 Bf 109s and Bf 110s within *Luftflotte* 3. Also on hand were nearly 500 Ju 52 transports used for paratroopers and equipment supply. Arrayed against this were over 1,200 French Air Force machines backed by the RAF's contingent of bombers and fighters, as well as the Belgian and Dutch Air Force. The clear quantitative inequality arrayed against Hitler's Air Force was furthermore nowhere near matching the quality of much of the *Luftwaffe*'s strength as was to become evident almost right away.

The aircraft of the neutral nations of Holland and Belgium through which the Germans launched their immediate assault were to be brutally swept aside as their mix of biplane and monoplane designs largely failed to approach the performance standards of their opponent's machines or in the case of the more modern designs were too few in number. Nor was the *Armée de l'Air*'s range of aircraft types generally capable of offering a serious, let alone sustained, degree of resistance to the mass of enemy bombers as they roamed across the battle zone under the protection of the Bf 109 and Bf 110 escorts. Those examples that were reasonably combat-efficient were just not on hand in enough numbers to make any difference.

The Dewoitine D.520's overall performance certainly matched that of the Hurricane, but the number on hand was restricted to one *Groupe de Combat* at this time. Its Morane-Saulnier M.S.406 and Bloch 151/2 'twins', although more numerous in service, were well outclassed in overall performance by friend and foe alike. Of the twin-engined designs—Breguet 693, Lioré et Olivier LeO 451, and Potez 63—the first two machines were fighter-bomber and bomber designs, while the Potez was already obsolete for its perceived multipurpose role as a bomber/reconnaissance/night-fighter. The LeO 451 possessed a top speed of around 300 mph as did the Breguet 693; the bomb load for the former machine was 1,200 kg. Defensive armament was at least adequate and, in both cases, involved partial cannon-calibre weaponry compared to the RAF's current dependency on bullet-fed guns.

No. 1 Squadron would be in the vanguard of the first serious challenge offered to the *Luftwaffe*, albeit piecemeal in nature. Among those going on to greater fame would be Fg Offs Billy Drake (left), Pete Prosser-Hanks (fourth from left), Paul Richey, and 'Killy' Kilmartin (fourth and third from right); all would survive the Second World War. By contrast, Fg Offs Lesley Clisby and Lawrie Lorimer (next to Drake) would be dead within ninety-six hours of the German invasion of France, Belgium, and Holland commencing.

Not that the RAF could guarantee making a more telling contribution to either the aerial battle or that on the ground, given the paucity of aircraft strength on hand that was furthermore coupled to a dangerously indifferent degree of operational quality. The single-engined Fairey Battle and twin-engined Blenheim bombers with their modest performance and bomb load, as well as their totally inadequate defensive armament, were unknowingly heading into a maelstrom comprised of both air- and ground-based firepower. Their Hurricane escorts were far too few in strength to do more than make marginal inroads into the swarms of fighters engaging the bombers, while the fearsome flak gun batteries on hand in quantity would reap a particularly frightening harvest within the ranks of the Allied bomber crews. Above all, there was the lack of an effective early-warning system as existed across the English Channel with which to allow deployment of squadrons in an orderly and timely fashion. A handful of mobile radar sets were on hand, but only one was operational on 10 May; even if all were functioning, the backup control rooms with which to filter the information down to the squadrons were absent. All of these sobering operational factors were looming up as the campaign commenced.

Battlefield Double-Bluff? (May 10–12)

The surge of the *Wehrmacht* and SS units assigned to invade Holland appeared to hold no immediate problems for the Anglo–French troops as they made their move into Belgium with a view to advancing up to and consolidating their defensive positions along the river Dijle; this ran on a north–south line just east of Brussels and up towards the port of Antwerp. What swiftly presented itself as a mortal threat to the scheme was a gap between the southern reach of the Dijle and the adjacent river Meuse to the south-east that was centred on the town of Gembloux. The German forces assembled along Belgium's border with Germany broke through the country's defensive network around Maastricht and forged the Maas river-crossings that had been previously seized by the *Fallschirmjäger* (paratroopers) in shockingly fast time; the *Panzer* units with supporting infantry that poured over the bridges were applying pressure upon the gap within twenty-four to forty-eight hours of the invasion's inception, thereby threatening to encircle the Allied line. The seeds for an Allied disaster had been sown.

If the ground assaults directed through Holland and southern Belgium could be regarded as the equivalent to a boxers 'right-hand jab', what was the real 'sucker-punch' that would scupper any realistic prospect for an effective Allied response was destined to be initiated on 13 May further south across the Franco–Belgian border with Sedan as its epicentre. Any natural doubt about being able to launch this new assault thanks to the difficult geographic conditions of the Ardennes Forest with its narrow, undulating roads traversing the tightly-packed forest of trees was soon dispelled. This was primarily due to the very effective *Stuka* bombing raids upon the admittedly scattered French defences backed up by the swift bridging of the Meuse; the resultant deployment of the *Panzer* units pouring across the pontoon bridges met little opposition from their French counterparts who were on hand albeit in nothing like the required concentration of force.

The Channel coast lay so far distant from the Meuse that there was no intention within the German High Command to have the *Panzer* forces proceed at other than a steady pace that would allow the supporting infantry to maintain contact. The decision of *Generals* Guderian and Rommel to make what was a head-long dash across France in a bid to cut the country in two faced the risk of a tank counter-offensive that could leave the German tanks cut off themselves. In addition, the infantry forces would be left far behind; the resultant vacuum in still unoccupied territory would only add to the chances of the *Panzers*' isolation. Fortune was to favour the enemy in that the expected resistance was only belatedly encountered and found to be ineffective when the columns had almost closed off the distance between their starting-point and the Channel coast.

Initial Fortunes (10–12 May)

10 May

Our average day is from dawn until dusk, which doesn't sound much I'll admit
But when dawn is at three and dusk is at ten—You'll agree, it's a bit of a s—t!!

The preceding bit of doggerel appeared in a book on the Battle of Britain, but the events now unfolding on 10 May would confirm its application to the air battle over the continent from today's date onward. The bulk of activity favoured the area covered by the RAF's Air Component, although the AASF bomber and fighter squadrons were also involved. In the latter instance, however, the dispatch of the Fairey Battle crews later in the day, whose attention was twice directed towards enemy incursions into Luxembourg, was made without their Hurricane escorts. Casualties were perhaps even higher than anticipated, with twenty-two aircraft lost out of the forty-eight attacking force—a grim portent of what lay immediately ahead for the survivors.

In No. 60 Wing, the first sorties flown by Nos 85 and 87 Squadrons went aloft around 4 a.m. as the skies resounded with the thunder of *Luftwaffe* bomber formations whose duty was to assault a sizeable number of airfields across northern France among other targets. It was not long before the first of a number of interceptions were made against what was to be largely reported as bomber formations up to *Staffel* strength that were bereft of fighter escort. The altitudes at which the bomber flew varied noticeably with several recorded at no more than 4,000 feet, well below the 10,000–15,000 feet of the remainder. The overall lack of numbers impelled the dispatch of the Hurricanes in no more than flights or more often sections, with the latter sub-formation sometimes reduced from three to two. Patrols over the unit-airfield or towards the Franco–Belgian border

The Phoney War (*Sitzkrieg* in German) ended abruptly on 10 May 1940. Support personnel at Lille–Seclin are working with ammunition containers close to a No. 85 Squadron aircraft. The fuselage roundel is a Type A1 variation with a thin yellow outer edge; this marking along with fin flashes was officially announced just nine days before the German assault was launched.

formed a proportion of the sorties, but there were occasions where the fighters were 'scrambled' upon receiving specific word of the approach of a bomber force.

The culture of Fighter Command Attack was clearly still in the minds of many pilots, with all the risk factors that the procedure inevitably cast up. An example involved a 607 Squadron section led by Flt Lt J Sample, who engaged He 111s of III/KG.1. The FCA No. 1 line-astern approach upon one bomber that appeared to be straggling culminated with the lead Hurricane encountering crossfire from the formation's gunners. The resultant damage was severe enough to enforce the pilot's bale out while the He 111 formation flew on still intact, although Sample's fellow-pilots reported smoke and 'feathered' propellers on at least one bomber. However, KG1's travails on the offensive's opening day were to add up to four He 111s MIA, one of which bore the *Gruppenkommandeur*, and two crash-landed on German soil.

No. 607 along with 615 had originally arrived in France equipped with the Gladiator biplane. Assigned to No. 61 Wing, both units were still in the initial stage of updating to the Hurricane when the Germans attacked. The squadron was absent from Merville when it was bombed, the pilots having been detached further west to Le Touquet on the Channel coast but was able to send up nine Hurricanes on one of the later sorties. As for No. 615, the mix of both designs within its ranks that rose up from Vitry on the 10th witnessed the pilots acquitting themselves in similar solid fashion.

There were occasions where single bombers were intercepted by more than one fighter that provided a better opportunity for making No. 1 attacks. Even so, the discipline of firing short bursts in view of the fifteen-second maximum content, beyond which all ammunition was exhausted, was sometimes overlooked in the heat of combat. However, even a prolonged burst of fire could not guarantee a 'kill'. An attack from astern or from the beam on the He 111 in particular could see the bomber absorb the punishment, given the bulky airframe coupled to the crude rubber wrapping around its fuel tanks.

The Do 17 and Ju 88 with their more slender and refined airframes were more susceptible to serious damage, but their air-cooled engines, in turn, were better suited to surviving the Hurricane's firepower than the oil-cooled Jumo motors on the He 111. The bald truth was that the bullet-calibre machine gun, as opposed to the cannon-calibre weapons in current use by both the Germans and the French, had its limitations in effectiveness even when well directed at a target. What was a vital changeover to more devastating striking power would evolve over the next twelve months but would come into wholesale force too late for the Battle of Britain period of operations.

Nos 3 and 79 Squadrons were similarly fed into the battle, and with sixteen Hurricanes, each were established within 63 Wing at Merville by mid-afternoon.

A Hurricane Section from one of the four squadrons assigned to the French-based air component fly a tight formation for the cameraman. Unit identification was often limited to aircraft letters, but red/white/blue flashes were applied to the rudders as is just visible on two of the fighters. These were used as friendly aircraft indicators for their French Air Force contemporaries who were inclined to fire first and confirm later.

The initial call for a sortie involved No. 3 who sent six fighters to patrol over Maastricht. The negative result in terms of interception was cancelled out during a second flight sortie towards Lille that ran into a He 111 formation from III/KG54 that was to simultaneously suffer the lethal intentions of two other squadrons. Bombs were observed being released as the fighters closed in with individual aircraft selected and homed-in upon, R/T problems likely intruding upon any form of mass assault or FCA indulgence.

Debriefing reports spoke of several bombers losing height as the formation headed homeward as well as displaying sagging landing gear, the latter a regular feature on the He 111. Plt Off. Frank Carey, who had already earned a DFM with 43 Squadron, observed one bomber he attacked losing all power and suffering the foregoing failure before falling down and impacting heavily with the ground. This and one more 'kill' along with a 'probable' brought his score to two full and four 'shared' victims, a figure that would rise to twenty-five and four respectively by August 1945.

No. 67 Wing

The scale of operations involving the wing was much reduced by comparison, but still bore results as well as casualties. The first patrol by No. 1 Squadron over the Maginot Line saw the successful downing of one Do 17Z from III/KG3. Conversely, No. 73 Squadron's interception of a 4/KG2 formation was negative in its outcome, Flt Lt R. Lovett being badly burned and impelled to force-land his Hurricane after incurring fatal damage from the gunners. The second squadron patrol had a more positive result with the fatal crippling of a 9/KG3 Do 17Z; shortly after, a reconnaissance sortie by a He 111 of 3(F)/121 ended in explosive fashion under Sqn Ldr J. More's gunfire.

Around the same time, 'A' Flight of No. 1 Squadron homed in upon a second III/KG3 Do 17Z that also stood little chance of surviving the five-strong force and its No. 1 FCA assault; Fg Off. Paul Richey was third in line and later reported how the final crash-landing left the crew alive compared to the reconnaissance crew's terminal fate. Subsequent sorties by both units were interspersed with the need to follow orders to transfer airfields—Vassincourt to Berry-au-Bac for No. 1 and Rouvres to Rhiems–Champagne for No. 73. Both new locations were bombed with minimal effect and while transferring to the former airfield, 'B' Flight ran across a He 111 formation from 3/KG53. In exchange for two of the four claimed 'kills' being confirmed, Fg Off. Lawrie Lorimer became the latest victim of return fire and jumped clear to land safely—a lease on life that had a mere ninety-six hours to run.

Another scene of activity during the Battle of France catches an anonymous squadron Hurricane under active servicing. The refuelling of the port wing tank is being accomplished via a small mobile container rather than a fuel bowser. The Watts propeller would leave the pilot with a dangerously limited climb rate and overall manoeuvrability even against the twin-engined Bf 110.

Daily Summary

The claims for 'kills' submitted during the course of the day bore all the hallmarks of the natural conflict between human logic and emotion. The fast-moving scenario of an aerial battle coupled to the mixture of enthusiasm and apprehension flowing through the mind of a pilot did not make for a guarantee of accurate accounting. As it was, the overall total of sixty confirmed and sixteen 'probable' 'kills' would be proven too generous, although the true total of thirty-five and fourteen respectively established after the Second World War was still a generous reflection of the cost to the *Luftwaffe* in facing up to the RAF alone. In fact, a total of 311 aircraft of all types had been destroyed or 'written-off' in respect of overall operations. The cost to the RAF fighter establishment was gratifying since most of the fifteen aircraft had completed forced-landings as opposed to their pilots baling out, while none of the latter were killed or became POWs. Steadily-deteriorating times lay ahead for both men and machines, however.

11 May

Across the Channel, the need to bolster the RAF ranks in France was continuing to be addressed with the dispatch of Nos 501 and 504 (Auxiliary) Squadrons within twenty-four and seventy-two hours respectively, with Bétheniville, Vitry-en-Artois, and Bapaume being the allocated airfields. No. 501's arrival that had bolstered

67 Wing's strength on the 10th was marred by the disastrous crash of the ensign transport bearing personnel that included pilots, three of whom were killed in the incident. On hand was a sergeant pilot still untried in combat, who would rise to the top of the list of 'aces' over the ensuing several months—'Ginger' Lacey.

Dutch Support

A measure of aerial support for the beleaguered Dutch forces was again provided this day from England-based No. 11 Group resources, but the results were again counter-productive in terms of their intended effect upon the *Luftwaffe*. No. 600 Squadron's Blenheim Mk 1Fs had been dispatched on the 10th to attack Waalhaven airfield that was the focus for the deployment of Ju 52 transports. Sure enough, they arrived as a formation of the *Tante Ju* aircraft (Auntie Ju in German slang) was arriving. Unfortunately, these were under escort by Bf 110s from I/ZG1 and the air battle that ensued was brief and bloody; only one Blenheim survived the encounter, while just two airmen on the MIA aircraft emerged alive. Clearly, the Blenheim's capability as a day fighter at least was tragically nil.

Three squadrons were dispatched during the day, with Nos 32 and 56 encountering no air opposition. Hurricanes of No. 17 Squadron, on what was the third sortie, swept across the North Sea and finally split up its flights between The Hague and Rotterdam. The Bf 109s of I/JG51 were similarly patrolling the region and lost no time in engaging their adversaries. The aerial jousting that filled the sky above the heads of the Dutch cast up the unwelcome sight of their 'Ally' being firmly placed on the back foot. Two Hurricanes from each flight were

The equipping of the Spitfire and Hurricane with variable-pitch propellers was still in the process of completion when the Battle of France commenced. P3428 is seen with this vital performance enhancement; although assigned to No. 245 Squadron as DX: N, it is unclear whether it served with the unit detachment that was involved in the Dunkirk evacuation. It was written-off on 26 June 1941 after a collision with electric cables.

shot down with two fatalities and two POWs incurred by the pilots. Sqn Ldr George Tomlinson (Squadron CO) staggered south to land his battered fighter on a Belgian airfield, where it appears to have been abandoned since he was flown back to Britain next day. Although one Bf 109 was lost along with its pilot and a second crash-landed, the fighter-to-fighter contest went to the *Jagdwaffe*. Two Hs 126 reconnaissance aircraft were also shot down to lessen the blow.

Belated Reaction

The onrush of German forces through south-eastern Belgium seemed to have only been belatedly reacted to since it was still unclear what the scale of assault was. At any rate, the attempts by several reconnaissance Blenheims to photograph activities round Maastricht and the Albert Canal came to naught since all were shot down—one by Belgian ground fire. The Belgian Air Force was the first to attempt a strike at the crossing-points, but of the nine Battles sent, only three returned and no material damage was inflicted; this was hardly surprising given the small bomb capacity and even smaller individual bombs capable of being borne within the bomb bays. The AASF parallel response was surprisingly limited with two Blenheim squadrons carrying out raids against what were described as 'concentrations' around Maastricht, presumably locations other than bridges. The full 'Crucifixion' of the AASF bomber ranks was accordingly on hold for another twenty-four hours.

The Air Component units were flying a mix of defensive and offensive patrols with the latter reaching as far as south-eastern Belgium. Pilots were flying at least two to three sorties on average as the waves of *Luftwaffe* attackers spread out over Belgium and northern France to attack a range of targets, airfields still being a specific source for assault. Sqn Ldr John Dewar's No. 87 Squadron was orbiting Brussels when a mass of Ju 87s from I/StG2 were encountered. The *Stuka*'s vulnerability to the Hurricane's eight-gun onslaughts was sharply demonstrated, a total of six either being shot down or crash-landing. Further 'kills' in other actions were recorded by Nos 79 (one), 85 (two), and 607 (four) from among a total RAF claim of fifty-five.

Although the raids on RAF airfields were not yielding too much in the way of destroyed aircraft or facilities, there were exceptions; for example, a Do 17 assault upon Condé–Vraux decimated No. 114 Squadron's Blenheims that incredibly were reportedly lined-up instead of being dispersed around the airfield perimeter and therefore proved easy prey for the enemy bomb aimers. Had they but known it, the crews of this and their fellow Blenheim and Battle squadrons not yet called upon were unlikely to survive long against the steadily-advancing enemy even when airborne thanks to solid fighter cover as well as massive flak battery support.

67 Wing

Early-morning sorties by Nos 73 and 501 Squadrons garnered at least two bombers, while Fg Off. Richey—part of 'A' Flight that had disengaged from interception of a He 111 formation that had itself turned back—came across a

Do 17P from 3(F)/10. A rather prolonged tail-chase that finally ended with the bomber apparently escaping intact although shot-up actually culminated in the crew abandoning their charge after it caught fire; their No. 1 Squadron tormentor diverted into a French airfield but damaged the Hurricane on landing, after which he was delivered back to Berry-au-Bac by his hosts. Escort duty for eight Battles from Nos 88 and 218 Squadrons was allotted to No. 73, but the German defences around Sedan decimated the bomber formation. A sole shot-up bomber from No. 88 Squadron got back while the death toll among the twenty-one MIA airmen was near 50 per cent (nine).

In the course of the day, all three wing units encountered a bomber formation that this time was escorted by the Bf 110. First to engage were Nos 73 and 501 Squadrons, followed minutes later by No. 1. In the increasingly frenetic combat sequence, a total of a double-figure of 'kill' claims were later reported. Post-war research established the loss of two crashed and one force-landed 4/KG53 He 111s, along with two Bf 110s from I/ZG2 whose surviving crew members baled out. In turn, Fg Off. Richey surrendered his second Hurricane for the day; he was 'bounced' by several Bf 110s and had to take to his parachute after the Hurricane caught fire (his abandoned Hurricane from the morning sortie was destroyed when the French airfield was bombed on 14 May).

'Lorrie and Leslie' was the expression among No. 1 Squadron for these two pilots. Fg Off. Clisby (right) was an Australian who was credited with a string of kills varying between nine and sixteen prior to his death on 14 May. Fg Off. Lorimer, by contrast, had little luck in this respect, but tragically sealed the friendship with his colleague, being shot down and killed while both were battling with Bf 110s of ZG26 on the aforementioned date.

Daily Summary

The Allied air forces' task was becoming ever-more onerous in the face of the mounting *Luftwaffe* attacks. The Hurricane pilots' claims for 'kills' were to prove out by a factor of two (fifty-five) to one (twenty-eight), against which a confirmed figure of fifteen Hurricanes, including five from No. 11 Group were either shot down or force-landed; at least eleven pilots were spared death or imprisonment. In truth, the numbers game was set to continue expanding in the *Luftwaffe*'s favour, given its massive superiority in aircraft. On the ground, the situation in Holland was rapidly approaching the point where sustained resistance was not possible. The situation in Belgium was scarcely less parlous for the Allies, while Luxembourg's tiny expanses were simply swallowed up.

12 May

Operational Diminuendo

A diminished degree of RAF support for the Dutch saw the mix of Hurricanes, Spitfires, Defiants, and Blenheim 1Fs covering the movements of Naval vessels off north-western Holland. Little *Luftwaffe* opposition was encountered apart from one sadly lethal occasion; three Blenheim 1Fs of No. 235 Squadron orbiting The Hague were hopelessly outnumbered and outgunned by eight Bf 109s; it was a wonder that the sole-surviving aircraft managed to escape its companions' fate.

The Crucifixion Commences

AASF bomber operations commenced at first light and were directed against *Wehrmacht* columns as well as the bridges around Maastricht over which they were advancing. A mix of three No. 103 Battles and nine No. 139 Blenheims lifted off and unknowingly headed into an aerial Armageddon provided by the lurking screen of Bf 109s. The fighters' task was made even easier by the absence of escorts for the hapless bomber crews, and seven were duly culled.

The next sortie involved just five Battles from No. 12 Squadron led by Fg Off. 'Judy' Garland that in contrast had cover from eight No. 1 Hurricanes led by Sqn Ldr Halahan. On approach to the targeted bridges, the Hurricanes took on an element of the estimated sixteen-strong defensive force. Unfortunately, the remainder joined in blocking the bombers' path along with the flak batteries that by now were firmly entrenched around the bridges. Two Battles fell to Bf 109 attacks, two to the flak guns, and one crash-landed on the way back.

The sheer, if hopeless gallantry of the crews was later recognised by Victoria Crosses awarded posthumously to Garland and Sgt T. Gray (observer) but unforgivably not to LAC L. Reynolds who was granted a meagre Mentioned in Despatches. Since both Gray's and Reynold's fate was in their pilot's hands, there should have been no award distinction—perhaps granting three VC decorations among one team was regarded as too 'generous'.

No. 1 Squadron also ended up to a lesser degree on the losing side with Plt Off. Lewis baling out of his burning fighter, Halahan force-landing and abandoning his charge, and Sgt F. Soper force-landing on return to Berry-au-Bac—at least all three were uninjured. Although several claims for Bf 109s and Hs 126s were submitted, most if not all were to subsequently remain unconfirmed. Worse still, by the morning's end, a further Blenheim sortie by UK-based Blenheims escorted by Nos 85 and 87 Squadrons had increased the overall bomber MIA cost to twenty-five, along with five Hurricanes, while the bridges remained intact.

A countermeasure of success attended No. 501 Squadron's activities, beginning with the 'scrambled' interception of the II. *Gruppe* element of a large KG53 formation and its I/ZG2 and I/ZG52 escorts; two He 111s were assessed as 'kills', although the second cost Fg Off. P. Raynor his life thanks to return fire. In the afternoon, a sortie to the Sedan area where the *Luftwaffe* forces were assaulting French ground positions saw the squadron pilots take on II/KG3's Do 17Zs along with two sub-units of French M.S.406s and Hawk 75s. The result was the downing or crash-landing of three bombers with damage to a further two.

In a separate incident, Plt Off. Ken Lee flying protective 'weaver' (known as 'Arse-end Charlie' in RAF parlance) spotted four Do 17s. Radio silence was currently in place, so he pulled up in front, waggled his wings, and dived towards the enemy. His assumption that the other three Hurricanes would follow him for an FCA No. 2 attack was not realised. By the time he realised he was alone, the Hurricane was closed-up to the formation and under intense crossfire, so he was fortunate to disengage safely. His debriefing 'kill' claim was reportedly backed by French observers on the ground, although how this was established is unclear (one of the other three pilots, Fg Off. M. Smith, was killed during a dogfight with Bf 110s). Another two He 111s out of a II/KG55 *Kette* (trio) were claimed by another squadron section, of which one was later confirmed.

Servicing facilities during the battle were often basic, as seen with a No. 85 Squadron party. Ammunition belts are being prepared for the Hurricane that is connected to a starter battery and with the harness straps hanging out ready for quick attachment should the scramble signal be given. Yellow diamond on the port-outer wing is a gas warning indicator.

Further north three 4/LG1 He 111s were shot down, all three being claimed by No. 607 Squadron although a cross-claim for one was submitted by No. 87 Squadron. Fg Off. Bill Gore leading the section baled out of his flaming Hurricane, but his luck was not matched later by Fg Off. Lewin Fredman; flying on a subsequent sortie as one of a mixed 607–615 formation, the 615 pilot was shot down during a battle with Bf 109s, though his loss was balanced up by one Bf 109 that was 'written off' in a crash-landing. No. 3 Squadron racked up a number of Ju 87 claims accruing from one action along with two Hs 126s later in the day, while No. 79 made several submissions for 'kills' although Plt Off. T. Parker's Hurricane was fatally struck by return fire from the Do 17Z he claimed as a 'kill' following his bale-out and safe return from behind enemy lines.

The latest unit that now arrived during the evening to bolster the Air Component ranks was No. 504 (Auxiliary) Squadron. The fifteen Hurricanes all landed at Lille–Seclin, but this was just a stopover prior to 'A' and 'B' Flights flying on to their assigned airfields at Bapaume and Vitry respectively. The feeding-in of flights and squadrons directly into the air battle was set to continue; ACM Dowding's nightmare scenario of a terminally-reduced force of fighters available for Home Defence was accordingly still extant as far as he was concerned.

Daily Summary

Despite the increasing presence of the Bf 110 and even more that of the Bf 109, the Hurricane pilots were still putting up a solid if geographically dissipated fight. A quarter of the sixteen fighters categorised as 'lost' witnessed their pilots' deaths, but fatigue was inevitably nibbling at the survivors' operational capability. The overall ground situation was on the point of evolving into sheer catastrophe with the Sedan 'breakout', with all that it portended for the encirclement and annihilation of the Anglo–French forces to the north.

The Dyke is Breached (13–16 May)

13 May

Dutch Finale

With its air force virtually destroyed and ground forces heading in a parallel direction, the omens for continued resistance were grim. No. 11 Group dispatched support with No. 264's Defiants covered by a 66 Squadron flight of Spitfires. Running into a Ju 87 formation placed the *Stukas* in an initial parlous position until a JG26 *Staffel* 'bounced' the RAF fighters to knock down five of the six Defiants and one Spitfire at a cost of one Bf 109. The sole other day's contribution was a section of No. 235 Blenheim Mk 1Fs. From this point onwards, the Dutch forces were on their own as regards RAF air, or indeed Allied support of any kind and capitulation loomed just forty-eight hours ahead.

Sgt Geoff 'Sammy' Allard has just returned from a successful sortie with No. 85 Squadron and is being congratulated on his latest claimed kill; he was credited with ten during the first week of the Battle of France period. Later promoted to flight lieutenant, he was killed in a flying accident the following March. N2319, a second production batch Mk I was believed abandoned in France.

Forging On

The *Wehrmacht* salient now established on the Meuse's west bank from Sedan northward towards Namur still did not galvanise the Allied military into action, nor was a similar reaction expressed as regards countering the separate *Wehrmacht* westward-orientated thrust into Belgium. In Britain, the dispatch of thirty-two fighter pilots over the ensuing twenty-four hours began with nine joining 73 Squadron. Activities involving the squadron included the downing of a solo 1(F)/122 Do 17P, followed by one flight's entanglement with an escorted II/KG55 force. Not long after, Flt Lt Pete Prosser-Hanks was leading 'B' Flight into what probably was the same formation. Fg Off. Leslie Clisby, an aggressive Australian, increased his claimed 'kill' total from four to seven but 'wrote-off' his Hurricane while landing beside one of his victims; three further 'kills' with one 'shared' were granted to 'B' Flight. In fact, KG55 surrendered six destroyed and four damaged bombers. This was a gratifying result, albeit not when weighed against the *Luftwaffe*'s huge logistical availability in aircraft compared to its opponent's steadily diminishing equivalent stock.

Further north, No. 85 Squadron handed out lethal punishment to II/KG54 but to the tune of three He 111s rather than the ten claimed, but Sqn Ldr J. Oliver baled out of his 'bounced' fighter on a later patrol. Another 'bounce' of No. 607 Squadron saw Sgt K. Townsend also taking to his parachute but unlike Oliver ending up a POW; then No. 615 lost Fg Off. Peter Murton-Neale to a II/ZG1 Bf 110. The ebb-and-flow of encounters involving Nos 3 and 79 Squadrons cost the *Luftwaffe* two Hs 126s, one Do 17, and one He 111, but sadly at a similar cost-figure in Hurricane pilots; all were from No. 3. Fg Off. D. Ball was shot down and later died from his injuries, but Flying Officers Wilfred Adams and Ray Lines-Roberts inexplicably collided over the airfield on return from an ironically combat-free sortie.

Daily Summary

The rather staccato and minimal scale of activity compared to the past three days provided no indication of the greatly-increased and sustained combat pressures ahead for what were already physically and mentally stressed personnel—ground crew as well as pilots. The burgeoning situation around Sedan was unknowingly signalling the ultimate end for Allied hopes of an effective stance against the invasion. From now on, the RAF was to be almost hounded both in the air and on the ground as their airfields were abandoned.

14 May

Crucifixion Crescendo

The Sedan breakout was recognised, however belatedly, as the principal mortal threat to an Allied victory. Consequently, the bomber squadrons were put on full standby with a series of raids spanning from soon after daybreak until the early evening. The aircraft were a largely dubious mix of RAF and *Armée de l'Air* designs. Alongside the Battles and Blenheims were a small contingent of Breguet 693s and LeO 451s. Further demonstrating the critical nature of the aerial counteroffensive were fifteen Amiot 143s, an angularly-ugly bomber normally assigned to nocturnal operations. Featuring a fixed-landing gear and lumbering along at less than 200 mph while bearing a bomb load of 1,320 kg, they were particularly ripe for wholesale slaughter. Supplementing the French fighter escorts of M.S.406s and Bloch 151s were Nos 3, 73, 87, and 607 Squadrons.

The plan of attack envisaged waves of bombers going out at three-hour intervals, a dispersal of effort that surely played into the *Luftwaffe* fighters' hands; the pilots would have ample time to ward off each wave, return to their airfields to replenish their armament and fuel reserves, and still be ready for subsequent Allied incursions. Equally surprising was the small number of aircraft involved in the initial three sorties. No. 103 Squadron was first up with six Battles under No. 73 Squadron escort, followed an hour later by four No. 150 Squadron Battles escorted by Bloch 151s; at around 9 a.m., No. 150 was also escorted by a Breguet 693 formation.

All three sub-forces were tasked with striking bridges, and while the Battle crews suffered no MIA casualties—probably due to the mist conditions affecting the flak gunners' sights—the French crews were marginally less fortunate; one bomber crash-landed following flak strikes and four others were damaged. This

L2020 from No. 253 Squadron has suffered damage to its de Havilland propeller blades as a result of a crash-landing. The tapes covering the gun apertures are absent to suggest the fighter was engaged in an action on this date, but details are lacking. Originally with 605 Squadron, it reportedly finished its days with No. 7 OTU.

easy-paced debut only provided a deceptive lead-in to what would evolve into an aerial rout that, in the RAF bombers case, culminated in one of the highest daily casualty-rates of the Second World War.

The German forces had the example of the Maastricht river and canal crossings as a benchmark for guarding the equivalent traffic channels over the Meuse; flak batteries were similarly entrenched around the pontoons and regular fighter cover was on hand, the joint air and ground effort having regular visibility as the mist dispersed, thereby granting extra time to respond to the bombers' approach. The sight of the Amiot 143 formation, by now reduced to nine, must have gladdened the hearts of the flak gunners and fighter pilots covering Bazeilles and Givonne.

The deadly *Flak-Vierling* 20-mm batteries took down one bomber, although the other eight did complete their bomb run; two further casualties were due to the Bf 110 fighters and the remaining six were very fortunate to escape with varying degrees of damage. Not surprisingly, this was the sole occasion that daylight operations for the Amiot 143 was conducted. Shortly after, one out of an eight-strong LeO 451 formation was flak-stricken as the bombers attacked.

The remainder of the day's operations with one exception fell to the AASF squadrons; the final raid was due to be mounted by No. 2 Group's home-based 21, 107, and 110 Squadrons. In the space of thirty-five minutes, no less than seventy-seven Battles and eight Blenheims from ten squadrons attempted to run the flak and fighter gauntlet for seven specified targets. The first wave of twenty-five Battles enjoyed the cover of four French M.S.406 and Bloch 152 units, but it availed the RAF crews naught. The streams of flak coupled with the depredations of 1/JG76's Bf 109s cut a swathe of destruction through the ranks of No. 12 (four), 142 (four), and 226 (three); six fighters were added to the MIA list, against which two *Luftwaffe* fighters were downed.

The next attack wave of eight Blenheims and twenty-three Battles swept in, with Nos 1 and 73 Squadron in attendance as the bombers approached the same spread of bridges. By coincidence, a Ju 87 formation from I/StG77 was preparing at attack Le Chesne nearby. The No. 1 Squadron escort element charged in and fell upon the *Stukas* before the waiting I/JG53 cover could intervene. For once, the debriefing claims for five 'kills' were out by one (six); better still was the further loss of four Bf 109s that almost matched the RAF pilots' separate claim figure. No. 73 Squadron also enjoyed a rather-less successful '*Stuka* party' after encountering a seven-strong group of I/StG76; this time round, two dive-bombers were lost and two badly damaged.

Sadly, these successes had to be put against the depredations incurred by the RAF bombers as flak along with the Bf 109s of I/JG53 took out eleven Battles and four Blenheims. Nor did No. 73 Squadron escape unscathed, since Sgts Basil Pyne and George Dibden fell victim to separate I/JG53 pilots and were killed. The final bombing sortie involved three No. 2 Group Blenheim units, but the planned escort cover failed to rendezvous, and the alternative presence of some M.S.406s and Bloch 152s was still not sufficient to prevent the Bf 109s and Bf 110s from downing five Blenheims with two more force-landing.

At least three other Hurricane squadrons bore multiple deaths among its personnel in the course of the day's operations, which spelt a grim portent for the RAF. The worst example involved No. 607 Squadron that was dispatched along with Nos 85 and 87. The intercepted formation with a large escort cover was attacked but the cost was high; no less than four pilots were downed. The

Two No. 85 Squadron pilots are rehashing a recent sortie to judge by Sgt Allard's hand action as he talks to Flt Lt Boothby. Allard was originally ground crew but had gained his wings in 1937. By 1 September, he would gain seventeen kills, all with No. 85. His meteoric success was sadly eclipsed by his death on 13 March 1941 when the Havoc he was flying crashed after take-off—a loose panel jammed the rudder causing a violent climb and stall action.

other two units took out two He 111s, but two of the No. 87 Sqdn pilots were killed. An evening patrol by just two Hurricanes witnessed the downing of both fighters, Plt Off. Chris Mackworth dying and Fg Off. Frank Joyce, later having a leg amputated following a heavy crash-landing. Two successive patrols near Louvain cost No. 504 three fatalities, including Sqn Ldr J. Parnall (Squadron CO).

Daily Summary

The burgeoning presence of both the Bf 110s and the Bf 109s was making the Hurricane pilots' task in challenging the bombers very difficult, and on numerous occasions, this turned lethal in human and material terms. In the former instance, fifteen pilots of the twenty-seven Hurricanes concerned were killed. The situation would not improve in the days ahead either aloft or on the ground as the *Panzers* began to blaze a virtually unhindered path across the French hinterland from their twin-salients flanking Sedan.

15 May

Ms Reynaud's remarks to Churchill's that the battle was lost was sadly prescient. The French in the north were withdrawing from south-western Holland and back into Belgium, while a British counterattack around Louvain was just a very temporary measure. Frantic requests for further fighter reinforcements were submitted upon which the Francophile Churchill reportedly demanded of the RAF that these be assigned to the campaign; this was a response that reportedly elicited ACM Dowding's historic written counter to the proposal.

Meanwhile, the air battle proceeded apace with defence of their airfields as much a priority for the RAF fighters as intercepting the enemy. The attempt to bomb Meuse bridges by Nos 15 and 40 Squadron Blenheims, with 'B' Flight of No. 607 Squadron as escort, led to the death of its CO, Sqn Ldr Lance Smith; No. 615 Squadron lost Fg Off. H. Fowler, although he did bale out. The *Luftwaffe* fighters were proving to be doughty adversaries, and although eleven were on the German loss list, two-thirds of the twenty-one Hurricane casualties were due mainly to the Bf 110s, with several Bf 109 'kills'. A measure of consolation was that eight of the RAF pilots escaped death or capture. The worst-affected unit was No. 3 Squadron whose morning patrol between Sedan and Dinant crossed the path of a small Do 17Z formation, with III/JG26 on hand. One of the bombers was damaged, but Sgt Jim Williams was downed and killed. Bf 110s from II/ZG76 then reportedly engaged the flight to cause the death of Flt Lt Carter and the bale out and subsequent capture of Plt Off. Noel Hallifax. Fg Off. C. Stone managed to force-land his damaged Hurricane at Vitry.

The sole action ending clearly in the RAF's favour involved a No. 607 section that engaged a 9/KG51 *Staffel* and claimed three; that number of He 111s were indeed shot down or crash-landed, although one may have been the victim of GCI/3 equipped with an element of the few Dewoitine 520s on hand. A morning raid on No. 1 Squadron's Berry-au-Bac airfield involved I and II/KG3's Do 17Zs, with III/ZG26's Bf 110s. A series of ever-frenetic dogfights ended with claims for four of the escorts that saw two destroyed, one in a failed crash-landing, and two moderately damaged in similar actions. In return, Fg Off. P. Richey was forced to take to his parachute and Flt Lt J. Walker ended up crash-landing.

A worrying aspect of the campaign that would plague all air forces during the Second World War was the issue of misidentification ('friendly fire' in modern parlance). Today's operations resulted in the latest Hurricane attack upon a reconnaissance Blenheim; Flt Lt John Owen (No. 504 Squadron) claimed a Ju 88 as 'severely damaged' when in fact he had unknowingly shot down a 53 Squadron aircraft, killing Plt Off. P. Bone and his two crew. Elsewhere, Fg Off. 'Cobber' Kain, the 73 Squadron 'ace', homed in on a second 53 Squadron Blenheim flown by Flt Lt B. Daly—the second time in twenty-four hours he had intercepted what he took to be an enemy bomber—but fortunately downed neither. Added to the often-indifferent aircraft-recognition skills of even experienced pilots, has to be considered in these circumstances the accumulation of fatigue over nearly one week and the swift-moving and confusing scenario of combat.

Daily Summary

Although the pilot fatality rate out of the number of Hurricanes lost—five out of twenty-one—was reduced as was the scale of activity from twenty-four hours previous, the stark fact was that the *Luftwaffe* fighters were handing out more punishment than absorbing it. More chaos was looming up as the *Wehrmacht*'s pace of advance forced several squadrons to abandon their airfields in the face of enemy occupation.

16 May

ACM Dowding's apprehensions regarding the dilution of Home Defence material and human resources continued to be justified from this day until around the 19th. The Cabinet decision requesting the feeding-in of further numbers of Hurricanes involved two forms of delivery. Six flights from UK-based squadrons were assigned on an intended permanent basis that would compulsorily end up 'temporary' within days, signifying the first stage. Five of these assignments were Nos 56/B, 229/B, and No. 253/B (Vitry), No. 245 Squadron (Moorsele), and No. 242/A (Lille–Seclin). The pilots bringing over the 253/B contingent could not regard the thought of engaging the enemy with much enthusiasm since their mounts were almost unbelievably still fitted with two-blade Watts propellers and fabric-covered wings, while the TR9 radio sets were extremely limited in range.

The onrush of the *Panzer* units towards the Channel coast was close enough to the AASF airfields to merit the transfer of its units out of their immediate or likely altered path, especially given that the enemy's intention could not be basically envisaged by the Anglo–French High Command. No. 1 Squadron's latest transfer that was originally from Berry-au-Bac to Condé–Vraux now involved an airfield at Anglure; No. 501 Squadron had similarly transferred out of Bétheniville to Anglure via Villeneuve and No. 73 out of Rouvres to Villeneuve. Adding further to the growing chaos was that the ground crew were finding it difficult if not impossible to achieve their own redeployment at the same pace. This limitation in turn was to hinder if not prevent the refurbishment to battle condition of numerous damaged Hurricanes, so resulting in a mounting tally of abandoned airframes. Already a total of eight unserviceable fighters were to be left behind at Bétheniville and Rouvres, the latter sub-group of five No. 73 machines being set on fire.

The pace of operations was regarded as moderate by the day's end if one judges the Hurricane casualty figure of thirteen compared to the previous three-day figure of fifty-two, but the five dead and one POW along with four wounded pilots bearing wounds would not have agreed with the assessment. Sgt L. Crozier from No. 85 Squadron had the misfortune to be shot down on take-off and was fortunate to survive his parachute descent with badly burnt hands. Earlier in the day, he had created the latest 'friendly fire' incident involving yet another No. 53 Squadron Blenheim; this was the second such incident in twenty-four hours for Flt Lt Daly's crew, but it was more critical since the three-man crew suffered serious burns in crash-landing their now-blazing aircraft at Glisy. It would appear to be the Blenheim's outline and radial engines casting up a resemblance to the Ju 888 that was leading to this unfortunately-recurring situation. Crozier along with Sgt

The fate of these three No. 73 Squadron pilots taken in France exemplifies the high cost in Fighter Command pilots' lives during the war. Sgt L. Pilkington (left) and Fg Off. N. 'Fanny' Orton flank Flt Lt R. Lovett; the latter-named airman was killed on 7 September during the first *Luftwaffe* attack on London. The same month a year later claimed his two colleagues in the course of operations over the continent.

H. Allgood subsequently survived being downed, but their squadron colleagues, Fg Off. A. Angus and Plt Off. M. Rawlinson, were killed in separate actions.

The sheer physical pressures being placed upon the pilots was now reaching the stage where the ability to remain alert was dangerously weakened with all that entailed for survival, especially when involved in close-quarters combat with the enemy fighters. A classic example of enforced relaxation involved Sgt Sam Allard (No. 85 Squadron). He landed off a sortie, but once power was switched off, he made no move out of the cockpit. Any concern among the ground crew that he had been badly injured was dispelled when they clambered up on the wings—the pilot was sound asleep and, even after a full night's rest, was still so comatose that he was allowed to remain in bed for most of the next day.

No. 615 Squadron lost Flt Lt Les Thornley, who was killed when the nine-plane formation was 'bounced' by Bf 109s. A second pilot, Plt Off. Tom Jackson, was fortunate to survive after strikes caused the Hurricane to burst into flames. The lack of fuselage side panels in the cockpit, allowing the flames instant access therein, undoubtedly left pilots extremely vulnerable to often ghastly burns; in this case, Jackson suffered serious face and leg burns before he exited his charge and parachuted down into enemy territory and capture. A third squadron pilot, Plt Off. Brian Young, ended up baling out but not before similarly being seriously burnt, his fighter also a 'bounce' casualty.

Daily Summary

The overall situation in the air continued to work in the *Luftwaffe*'s favour both in terms of striking out at multiple targets while whittling away at its adversary's ranks. The Hurricane reinforcements were to prove incapable of doing more than delaying the German onrush towards a complete encirclement of the Franco–Belgian and BEF forces.

Wholesale Withdrawal (17–20 May)

17 May

The first stage of reinforcement was completed today with the arrival of No. 601/A at Merville, the current home of No. 3 Squadron. Added to this now-thirty-six-strong sub-force were a further thirty-eight fighters shared between Nos 32 and 151 Squadrons and Nos 111/B, 213/A, and 601/B, who all landed at Abbeville, albeit with withdrawal to England in the evening in mind. So it was that the two days' support measures cast up the prospect of aircraft and pilot casualties, further exacerbating the situation as regards Home Defence sustainability.

Today's actions involved both positive and negative aspects. The Ju 87 was rightly earning a fearsome reputation as a pinpoint bomber that hitherto had handed out punishment at little cost from air opposition. Two separate interceptions by No. 11 Group squadrons seriously dented the reputation and were harbingers of future '*Stuka* parties', as they became labelled. First, No. 151 Squadron was near Lille when a III/StG51 formation was sighted. Sqn Ldr 'Teddy' Donaldson led his pilots in on a No. 1 attack that quickly evolved into a series of individual actions.

The slow-flying dive-bombers with single-gun rear armament were clearly no match for their eight-gun assailants, and subsequent claims for six definite and four likely 'kills' for once nearly matched the German record of seven aircraft lost. In the late afternoon, No. 17 Squadron waded into a larger Ju 87 force and culled four, of which three were total losses; Fg Off. Arthur Lines was initially posted MIA having been downed by a Bf 109 but he returned next day.

An arguably worse fate was that of No. 82 Squadron dispatched from RAF Watton to bomb German support units at Gembloux. Several hours later, the original twelve-strong formation was down to one badly-damaged aircraft staggering back to its airfield. The planned rendezvous with No. 87 Squadron around the target saw the bombers by then already decimated; to one flak victim was added ten summarily taken out by I/JG3 Bf 109s. Once again, the bombers' single dorsal turret guns proved tragically inadequate in countering the Messerschmitt fighters' machine-gun and cannon batteries.

The now-steady flow of pilots back to Britain for much-needed leave saw four 85 Squadron veterans included among the tally, with two replacements joining the squadron; as it was, none would return, and indeed the flow of such selected individuals was soon to be stopped permanently as matters on the ground in particular presented the Allies with a military *fait accompli*. It was not only the airmen who were feeling the strain, however.

A Hurricane from No. 501 Squadron has had its engine started via the trolley accumulator ('trolley-acc') stationed ahead of the starboard wing and one airman has just detached the power cable as his companion goes to haul the mobile unit clear of the fighter. Aircraft appears to have already been in action since the gun apertures are uncovered. The majority of Hurricane squadrons had left France when photo was taken in late May.

Aircraft serviceability levels were in some cases 'super-critical', although No. 504 Squadron's figure of two was probably an extreme case. Four replacements collected from the holding-point at Glisy were to be flown in by squadron pilots, but this still left the unit at half-normal establishment. Added to this was the general lack of spare parts for the fighters that were affecting their efficiency to a dangerous degree in some cases. Taking to the air with unserviceable flaps as an example was bad enough; to do so with the air-speed indicator at fault was even more potentially lethal, but 'needs must' in the critical circumstances facing the RAF.

How critical it was could be seen as Hurricanes were being pressed into the extra duty of tactical reconnaissance, this being ordered on the grounds that the assigned Blenheim and Lysander crews were palpably too vulnerable to be becoming regular casualties. Now, not only was there a risk of losing out to airborne gunfire, the risk factor was doubled thanks to the fighters coming well within range of the flak batteries. No. 607 Squadron launched two such sorties without incident. These duties sometimes resulted in contact with Hs126 as well as the newly-operational Fw 189 reconnaissance types.

The three AASF squadrons were currently installed at Condé-Vraux, Anglure, and Villeneuve west of Reims. No. 1 Squadron headed for Sedan to intercept reported Ju 87 formations, but instead tangled with V(Z)LG1's Bf 110s after carrying out a 'bounce' manoeuvre. The odds of up to 4:1 were formidable, but the results were very satisfactory—three of the five 'kill' claims were confirmed at the cost of Fg Off. 'Pussy' Palmer's Hurricane, from which he baled out. Sgt Frank Soper brought his shot-up fighter back, but it was a 'write-off' with numerous cannon and bullet holes and dents on the cockpit armour plate that had saved the pilot from becoming a fatal statistic. A sortie by No. 501 Squadron ended with one section strafing a tank column, although what good the bullets did to the vehicles or their crews was a clear case of 'peashooters against elephants'.

Daily Summary

The tightening net posed by the twin arms of the *Wehrmacht* forces coupled to the supporting aerial onslaught kept the RAF fighters under firm pressure, although the loss rate of fifteen Hurricanes was not matched by any pilot fatalities; in addition, the punishment handed out to the *Stuka* elements provided a small measure of comfort in the face of the failing overall defensive effort, whether expressed in ground or aerial terms.

18 May

The shrinking perimeters of the area occupied by the Allies while allowing their fighters marginally greater scope in intercepting the *Luftwaffe* saw any advantage cancelled out by the even greater concentration of the enemy bombers upon tactical support for the *Panzer* units in particular. Even when formations were picked up, the ensuing battle did not go in the RAF's favour. The mix of French-based units with those fed-in from across the Channel could lead to the latter's almost total lack of combat experience creating problems.

An early sortie by sections from Nos 85 and 87 Squadrons, along with 242/A Flight, which ran into a five-strong I/ZG26 formation, should have ended in the former's favour. Instead, the fixed, 'wooden' approach by the lead section probably contributed to the enemy fighters striking back to shoot down Flying Officers Derek Allen and Bill Lepine, with only the latter surviving as a POW. All three from the Canadian 242/A sub-unit were added to the casualty list, although Pilot Officers Russell Wiens, Marvin Brown, and Lorne Chambers all exited their aircraft, Chambers having suffered multiple burns when the Hurricane exploded just as he baled out. It would appear from Wien's account that the original enemy formation was further reinforced as the dogfight progressed, since he later talked of a double-figure number assailing his section. Whatever the circumstances, the counter-destruction of two Bf 110s was a marginal comfort for the RAF pilots.

The intention to send only flights whether on indefinite or day-long detachment was being clearly breached today with the full involvement of at least four squadrons (Nos 56, 111, 213, and 253). A further complication was the concentration by the afternoon of two squadrons and four flights on Vitry in particular; not only was this likely to place an even more inordinate strain upon maintenance work, there was the added risk of wholesale destruction should the *Luftwaffe* make a sudden strike before the Hurricanes could 'scramble'. The situation at Lille– Marcq-en-Barœul was scarcely better in terms of fighter concentration.

Armageddon finally came Vitry's way, a process that began earlier with the appearance of JG26 and ZG26 elements just as a 'scramble' was occurring. Plt Off. D. Bell-Salter and Sgt R. Brackley were culled shortly after take-off, both being fortunate to survive crash-landing their fighters. Not so fortunate was Fg Off. Tom Rose—already a survivor of the notorious 'Battle of Barking Creek' incident on 6 September 1939—who succumbed to a mass of Bf 110s, along with Plt Off. Tony Dillon. Also consumed in the air battle was Flt Lt Charles Darwood (111/B Flight). Flt Lt Fred Rosier the leader for 229/B Flight was very fortunate; his fire-stricken aircraft suffered a jammed cockpit canopy, but he emerged alive from the resultant disintegration of the Hurricane albeit with burns to his legs (this officer was destined to become the last C-in-C Fighter Command when it was dissolved in 1968).

The airfield's baptism was administered at thirty-minute intervals by three Do 17Z *Staffeln* from III/KG76. A bid by Sqn Ldr Donaldson to permit his pilots to 'scramble' upon sighting the first wave was denied and the trench-sheltering personnel experienced the frustration of watching the bomb-trains taking out nearly ten Hurricanes. There was no such hesitation in respect of the two following sightings and No. 151 along with other surviving aircraft lifted off. The raid saw the swansong for the airfield as an operational base, and by the day's end, its units had returned to England with the exception of 56/B Flight and No. 607 Flights, who transferred north-west to Norrent-Fontes. The die was being cast for the permanent withdrawal across the Channel of all AASF squadrons within the next forty-eight hours.

As ever, there were encounters working in the RAF's favour: II/ZG26 suffered the loss of Hptm. D'Elsa (*Staffelkapitän*) and three more crews, with three more Bf 110s bearing moderate to severe damage at the hands of 253/A and 111/B Flights; 56/B

Flight joined in and shared in the destruction of three II/KG1 He 111s under the Bf 110s escort; during the raid on Vitry, a trio of II/ZG76 *Zerstörers* fell, including that of the *Geschwaderkommodore* Maj. Grabmann (POW); and a KG1 and KG4 composite formation mourned the loss of three He 111s to the combined 145 and 601 Flights. The overall picture, however, was truly grim, with over thirty Hurricanes struck off establishment, along with seven pilots killed, five captured, and four wounded.

Daily Summary

The wholesale withdrawal of fighters across the Channel signalled the beginning of the end for continental-based squadrons. A further thirty-three Hurricane losses indicated the continuing severity of the battle, although a fair measure of punishment was handed out to the Bf 110 crews (twelve confirmed out of twenty-one claims).

19 May

The evacuation of Lille–Seclin and transfer to Merville of Nos 85 and 87 Squadrons (the latter unit doing so via Lille–Marcq from where it completed the foregoing move in the evening) saw both sharing with No. 3 Squadron. No. 504's move involved transfer to Norrent-Fontes. The now-truncated Air Component

The dearth of engagements with the *Luftwaffe* over France in the initial months of the Second World War left little scope for pilots to build up any score. A notable exception was Fg Off. James Edgar Kain, nicknamed 'Cobber'. The New Zealander was officially credited with no less than sixteen kills; tragically, on 6 June 1940, ordered back to England, he made several slow rolls before impacting with the airfield surface over which he had been aero-batting.

fighter strength was somewhat 'beefed-up' by the appearance at Merville of Nos 17 and 32 Squadrons from England, although the counter-withdrawal of 56/B from Norrent-Fontes seemed illogical. Strangely enough, No. 615 Squadron was still based at Moorsele, north-east of Lille, although their tenure of occupation was about to end next morning.

The day's events would witness a series of intense encounters that would yield a bloody harvest of death and destruction on both sides in what was a 'backs to the wall' scenario for the RAF. Although the northern zone of the ground assault was not neglected, the weight of *Luftwaffe* tactical support was probably directed towards the *Wehrmacht* columns striking for the Channel coast in the face of hastily-assembled French units whose resistance to the *Panzer* thrusts was basically ineffective in even slowing these down.

The Hs 126 units were busy in spotting duties, and it was the misfortune for a 2(H)11 crew to be consumed when their aircraft exploded under the fire of an 87 Squadron patrol, while two further Hs 126s suffered the same fate. This design was a fleeter contemporary of the RAF's Lysander that had suffered regular losses to date and today was no exception when a duo circling Lille–Marcq were given no quarter by Bf 109s from 2(J)LG2 or II/JG26.

By now, the dearth of AASF bombers was witnessing the truly desperate use of Lysanders in the role, while the Hurricanes were partially tasked with strafing sorties that posed the added risk of being downed by the flak gunners. In the former instance, three were detailed to join in with a force of Battles briefed to attack *Wehrmacht* concentrations around Saint-Quentin. The results were again tragic in that little or no damage was inflicted, all at the cost of six Battles and two Lysanders.

Although the *Luftwaffe* had the fighter resources with which to provide full bomber escort, the interception of formations that were bereft of at least immediate cover continued to be a feature of operations with a heightened chance for the Hurricanes to inflict damage almost at their leisure albeit sometimes with strong resistance from the enemy gunners. The latest *Geschwader* to suffer in what was arguably the worst case during the campaign to date was KG54; by the day's end, no less than fourteen He 111s had been struck off establishment with an equally high casualty rate in KIA crew.

There were at least four recorded actions that primarily involved Nos 85 and 87 Squadrons along with No. 3 Squadron and two composite units. Two He 111s were culled during a bombing raid on Lille–Seclin, and two afternoon actions saw five more 'kill' claims on each occasion. Lille was the epicentre for six crash sites and nearby Tournai for four, the remaining three spread further afield and the last a crash-landing back at its airfield. However, the formation escorted by II/ZG26 and I and III/JG3 resulted in the fighters killing three pilots, while Sqn Ldr John Thompson (111 Squadron CO) ended up force-landing his shot-up fighter.

The *Luftwaffe* fighter pilots ended the day the clear statistical winners since they shot down no less than twenty-two of the thirty-five Hurricanes; on the other hand, their *Staffeln* were short fourteen pilots thanks to the RAF pilots' endeavours. One of the more even contests involved the Lysander 'victors' who were taken on by fighters from Nos 85, 87, and 504 Squadrons. Four Bf 109s including the *Gruppenkommandeur* of II/JG26 (KIA) failed to return; the cost was three fighters with the new No. 504 CO Sqn Ldr John Hill and Plt Off. John Hardacre forced to bale out, as was Fg Off. James M. Strickland from No. 87 Squadron.

67 Wing

No. 1 Squadron's planned sortie to cover AASF bomber attacks around Saint-Quentin was diverted into an attack upon a III/KG27 formation near Rethel. Red Flight initiated the assault and Blue Flight, acting as top cover, joined in upon realising no escorts was present. The action ended with four He 111s falling within a triangle bounded by Reims–Soissons–Château-Thierry. Fg Off. Richey was very lucky to survive being injured by a missile that temporarily paralysed him before he regained control to put the Hurricane down for a force-landing; even then, he had to batter the jammed canopy off. No. 73 Squadron enjoyed a similar success against Ju 88s reportedly from KG51, downing three despite Bf 110 cover by V(Z) LG1; the pilots of two battle-damaged Hurricanes survived their crash-landings.

Daily Summary

What was the final day of sustained operations for RAF Fighter Command's units now penned within north-eastern France had been a brutal 'blow-for-blow' action: ACM Dowding's fighter ranks were cleaned out of thirty-five Hurricanes along with eleven pilots killed or POW and seven more suffering wounds. The final confirmed tally of forty-seven *Luftwaffe* aircraft, that was in itself no barrier to ultimate success, was the latest reminder to the German aircrew that the going was not going to get easier, especially as their ground advances brought them ever closer to the more concentrated and better-supported Home Defence resources across the Channel.

20 May

The eleventh day of the campaign would effectively end the Air Component's direct involvement in operations at least as regards defensive measures. Instead, there was an emphasis upon tactical reconnaissance sorties, although the Merville-based squadrons continued to dispatch patrols. Several Ju 88s along with reconnaissance Do 17 examples to the fore were downed, and strafing runs by the TR-assigned fighters brought a very small measure of destruction among the advancing columns.

Strafing was ever a dangerous act since the flak defences were difficult to perceive, whereas the gunners had a much better sight of the approaching attackers. One such sortie proved costly for 85 Squadron when Sqn Ldr Mike Peacock (CO) became the latest senior casualty while strafing a convoy near Arras; he along with Pilot Officers Dick Shrewsbury and Roger Burton were brought down and killed, although II/JG3 pilots in the area claimed two 'kills'; No. 213 also lost two pilots in similar ground assaults (one of the 85 Squadron 'victors' was Ltn. Franz von Werra, destined to be the sole recorded German aviator to escape from British captivity albeit into Mexico via Canada and the USA). The sole escort sortie involved Nos 17, 56, and 151 Squadrons shepherding Blenheims of Nos 21 and 107 Squadrons bombing Marquion.

The Belgian Air Force took delivery of a number of Hurricanes, but their involvement in combat was brutally swift. A German officer stands alongside one of two surviving fighters following Belgium's capitulation. The nearside airframe displays a mix of original and modified equipment in the respective form of the untapered radio mast and non-armoured windscreen and replacement three-blade propeller.

Daily Summary

From tomorrow on, the Air Component units would be operating 'from home' as it were. Before withdrawal, many unserviceable aircraft were destroyed, a figure that included a distressing number of Hurricanes adding up to nearly 400 lost on the continent to date.

Critical Attrition

The steady flow of Hurricanes away from Dowding's Home Defence requirements was naturally causing him concern; on the other hand, the outcome of what would be retrospectively termed the Battle of France was very much in the balance, at least during the opening phase. Although Prime Minister Churchill was a firm Francophile, he lost no time in promising maximum support for that nation's survival with aircraft the most visual and immediate sign of his goodwill. Even the breakout of the Ardennes-shrouded *Panzer* columns under *Generals* Guderian and Rommel's direction several days into the German invasion gave no immediate impression that an Allied collapse was inevitable, at least not in London.

So, the drain on Fighter Command's overall resources was set to proceed apace in the face of the C-in-C's mounting, but still unavailing opposition. He would finally 'bite on the bullet' on 15 May with a diplomatic, but skilled summary letter to the government that set out the consequences of running down Fighter

An early-production Mk I Spitfire judging by the untapered radio mast is rigged up for gun alignment; the ground is littered with spent cartridge cases. For some reason, the outer weapon has not been fired or is unloaded, while the action does not involve the starboard quartet of .303 machine guns. Type 'B' fuselage roundel dates this picture to between November 1939 and May 1940 when it was displaced by the higher-visibility Type A1.

Command's stock of fighters should the Germans conquer France and then logically set out to invade Britain, a measure that was acted upon positively by the politicians agreeing to halt the flow overseas.

Churchill's statement to his Cabinet on 13 May, in which he expressed his fears regarding the dilution of Fighter Command's strength in the Battle of France and the resultant negative effect upon Home Defence resources in aircraft and pilots, appears to render Dowding's subsequent letter-content redundant. However, although no more complete squadrons were intended to be dispatched to the continent, there was to be an intended flow of Home-based aircraft adding up to eight flights supporting those units based there that met with government approval following a Cabinet meeting on 16 May.

As it was, no further Hurricanes were sent following a further report by Dowding's representative who had visited France between 17 and 19 May, but the eight flights were already operating in France by then. Furthermore, at least four squadrons despatched their other flights to render the overall scheme redundant, however short-term this extra measure was to prove in practice. All these reinforcements were accordingly rendered equally liable to loss through combat or even to abandonment through battle damage and being incapable of return to airworthy condition due to the hasty evacuation of the airfield in question in the face of enemy advances—an aspect of the Battle that further added to the cost in fighters as well as pilots.

5

Dunkirk: The Fortuitous 'Miracle'

The Trap is Sprung

Any sense of a positive outcome for the Allied forces was by 21 May fully deflated since the campaign had now evolved into a raw battle for survival with the odds firmly stacked in Hitler's favour. The advance of the *Panzer* units towards the Channel that in turn would cut the northern-based defenders off from the French hinterland was about to be completed, after which the encircling arms of this western force coupled with the *Wehrmacht* elements pushing through Belgium would relentlessly constrict their adversary into unconditional submission.

As far as RAF Fighter Command was concerned, support operations with the exception of the three Air Component squadrons was now to be conducted from Southeast England with No. 11 Group the practical source for the airfield locations (reconnaissance operations were still partially being performed by Lysanders from two French airfields albeit at a continuing high cost). Hurricane squadrons were now sharing duties with the Spitfires, but the first sortie by the latter on the 21st resulted in the near-fatal downing of a Blenheim, whose pilot carried off a crash-landing south of Boulogne in his shot-up bomber. A He 111 and two Hs 126s were the unfortunate victims of the several patrols launched, but No. 253 Squadron lost its CO, Sqn Ldr E. D. Elliott (POW), and No. 229 Squadron lost Plt Off. Desmond Gower (KIA).

Merville was still operational, but only in terms of transport aircraft—these having brought in supplies for the BEF, who were then on hand to evacuate personnel and salvage any critically-important equipment. Also achieved was the restoration to flying condition of three out of sixteen abandoned Hurricanes. By the evening, the now almost deserted airfield was hastily finally abandoned in the face of approaching enemy units.

A close formation of twelve Hurricanes demonstrates how vulnerable the RAF fighters were. The need for each pilot other than the formation leader to concentrate on maintaining position for fear of collision wholly detracts from observing a 'bandit' in time to take the necessary corrective action and avoid being shot down, let alone take on an adversary on equal if not superior terms.

Tragically-Neglected Tactical Lessons

The *Luftwaffe* fighter tactics that had already spelled out serious problems for Fighter Command's pilots over France were seemingly not being taken on board by the bulk of its squadron personnel so engaged. The mandatory formation and FCA tactics adopted over the past decade were still being treated as good enough to ensure an evenly-fought if not successful outcome to any combat action. The main flaw in formation layout was the insistence in forming-up in ranks of three. Even when flown as a single 'Vic', the visual restriction in scanning the skies for an opponent was restricted to the leader, the other pair having to concentrate on formation integrity. The multiple flight (six) or squadron (twelve) formation proved to be even more dangerously limited in scanning terms. The apparent solution of stationing one or two pilots behind the squadron, whose function was to scan the skies as they flew a mobile 'weaving' pattern, sounded good in theory; in practice, all too many performing the duty would end up being the first to be 'picked off' by the opposition as they swept down to ambush the RAF fighters.

As for the Fighter Command Attack-variants, the Battle of France should have clearly cast up their potentially lethal limitations in the face of what were often fully-escorted bomber formations or even non-covered formations that did not oblige by flying in a non-deviating manner and moreover were capable of delivering a deadly weight of defensive firepower against the deliberate and steadily manoeuvring RAF fighters. In the event, where there was some understanding for persisting however briefly in the FCA tactics by those Home Defence squadrons as yet not blooded in combat; the same allowance was surely redundant in the case of the COs of already combat-exposed squadrons who still persisted with these tactics. The *Rotte/Schwarm* variants already proven as the vital elements for operational success were sadly to remain stillborn for many months as regards their wholesale adoption by Fighter Command.

Run-Up to Operation Dynamo

Patrols were now being mounted that ranged from around Dunkirk westward to the mouth of the Somme estuary. For the first time, the *Luftwaffe*'s Bf 109 and Bf 110 pilots were to regularly encounter the Spitfire and the punishment handed out to JG27 (five) today (23rd) was a clear, if not always consistent, portent that matters were not always going to run in their favour. Ironically, the *Zerstörer* crews came off relatively better compared to their single-engined contemporaries today, but this was a scenario that would be brutally reversed during the looming battle over southern England. The situation for the Hurricane pilots was not so comfortable with a kill–loss ratio favouring the enemy fighters; however, the

No. 610 Squadron was based at Biggin Hill during Operation Dynamo but operated from the forward Kent airfield of Hawkinge. The squadron is answering to the scramble order, with two Spitfires already full gear-up before clearing the airfield perimeter. Taxiing fighter on right has its individual letter almost obliterated and its path is dangerously close to any further oncoming companions.

summer and autumn months of 1940 would witness the Hawker design garnering a greater overall harvest in 'kills' compared to the Spitfire.

Today saw the start of an illustrious career for Flt Lt Robert Stanford-Tuck who scored his first three 'kills' out of a final Second World War figure of twenty-seven 'confirmed'. He had been appointed to No. 92 Squadron under Sqn Ldr Roger Bushell's command and was leading a flight. The squadron was 'bounced' by Bf 109s and Plt Off. Pat Learmont's fighter was set ablaze. Tuck latched onto a Bf 109 in what evolved into a protracted tail-chase culminating in a solid burst of fire that saw the machine swing drunkenly and descend steadily into a terminal impact according to Tuck. His insistence in maintaining visual contact during this time meant he broke, but survived, one of the cardinal rules of air fighting—never fly on a steady course for more than a minimum of time. A subsequent patrol involving the squadron was more expensive with Sqn Ldr Bushell and Pilot Officers John Gillies and P. Klipsch declared MIA following a dogfight with Bf 110s, the latter being the exception to surviving as a POW. Tuck's downing of two of the *Zerstörers* along with a second duo of fighters scored by Plt Off. Tony Bartley completed the day's tally.

The *Wehrmacht*'s advance up the Channel coast witnessed the seizure of Boulogne (24th) and a surge towards Calais that lay quite close to the port of Dunkirk, towards which the BEF and French forces were steadily withdrawing in reasonably sound order. Stanford-Tuck added to his tally with two Do 17s, but No. 92 Squadron lost Plt Off. Peter Cazenove (POW); No. 74 Squadron's four 'kills' spread over two patrols cost an equal number of Spitfires, with Pilot Officers Bert Aubert KIA and D. Hoare taken as a POW; Plt Off. Paddy Treacy and Sgt Tony Mould were the fortunate exceptions who regained friendly lines.

The day before, another future ace began his score in unusual circumstances following the force-landing of Sqn Ldr Frank White (No. 74 Squadron's CO) on Calais–Marck airfield with all this implied for his imminent capture by the rapidly-approaching *Panzer* units. A hasty rescue plan was formulated involving Flt Lt Al Deere, along with Plt Off. Johnny Allen covering a Miles Master trainer flown by Sqn Ldr Jim Leathart. All progressed in order up to the point where the Master had landed on the French airfield and its 'passenger' was on board. Allan now called-in the presence of a group of Bf 109s overhead before rushing in to engage. Deere descended to warn Leathart of the danger but was too late to prevent his take-off run—just as a 109 swooped down and fired. Deere's hasty burst of fire across the enemy pilot's path may well have put him off his stroke, but the yellow-sprayed undersides denoting its trainer status was a visual giveaway to this or any subsequent attacker and the prospects for its return to Britain seemed slim.

Leathart promptly 'aborted' the take-off, and having scrambled out of the cockpit, followed by a short time sheltering in a ditch, both officers cautiously emerged and took-off again, maintaining a northerly heading at minimum altitude to avoid interception that safely traversed the fortunately narrow 'neck' of the Channel. Meanwhile, Deere had caught up with the would-be 'executioner' to take him down before climbing to assist his now hard-pressed colleague. Visual contact was not made between the pair, but both pilots emerged unscathed from the combat and got back to friendly soil. The New Zealand pilot's successful involvement today was the first in a string of sometimes miraculously-pitched combat incidents—no wonder his post-war biography was titled *Nine Lives*, because this was a very pertinent title as future accounts in this book will relate.

The next day (25th), the recurring patrol pattern included two bomber-escort sorties involving Nos 17, 79, and 605 Squadrons, during one of which, a Ju 87 formation was encountered; its ranks were reportedly shorn of at least six bombers according to debriefing claims. Later in the day, while escorting Swordfish biplanes to bomb targets near Calais, No. 54 Squadron clashed with a combined Bf 109 and Bf 110 formation; the result was three 'kill' claims balanced up by the loss of two Spitfires. Plt Off. Johnny Allen baled out into the Channel safely and Plt Off. George Gribble belly-landed his near Dunkirk. Both pilots subsequently came back to Hornchurch, Allen having been picked up by an RN warship while Gribble would join the evacuee ranks out of Dunkirk. Sadly, such good fortune would not see Allan endure throughout the coming weeks as the aerial conflict headed towards a peak of feral intensity that would consume thousands of Allied and enemy personnel.

Fg Off. Colin Gray, a New Zealand and squadron contemporary of Al Deere scored his first of twenty-seven confirmed Second World War 'kills' today when he

The seemingly-fragile structure of the Spitfire is captured in this show of a Mk I serving with No. 54 Squadron. The auxiliary power unit is plugged in to conserve the internal battery system as well as guaranteeing a certain firing-up of the Merlin engine. Displacement of the fuselage Type 'A' by Type A1 roundels and addition of fin flashes is still to take place.

shot down a Bf109 over the French coast. Elsewhere a mid-air collision between No. 151 Squadron's Plt Off. Bushell and Flt Lt Fred Ives left the latter forced to crash-land his Hurricane at Nieuport; his fortune at surviving the incident tragically concluded with his subsequent demise as he was killed or drowned when the vessel evacuating him from Dunkirk was torpedoed and sunk with heavy loss of life three days later.

Also engaged in patrol duties were the Defiants of No. 264 Squadron whose pilots reported no interceptions. The day of this four-gun turret fighter as a viable fighting machine was still extant but not for much longer following the *Luftwaffe* fighter pilots' realisation of its total lack of forward fire-power; they swiftly took the necessary counter-measures that was to ensure its demise as regards daylight operations.

The first patrol that involved Nos 17 and 79 Squadrons (26th) resulted in one of the former unit's sections taking on six Bf 109s one being claimed as a 'probable'. 'B' Flight ran into a Do 17 and Ju 88 formation that ended up in the respective 'probable' and confirmed 'kill' categories but lost FS W. Jones who was killed. A subsequent late-morning patrol was about to commence its homeward leg when Bf 109s 'bounced' the squadron; during the resultant mêlée, Plt Off. Whittaker observed Flt Lt C. Adye's Hurricane bursting into flames, with the pilot baling out to float down into the Channel that was to become his anonymous grave.

Nine further formations were dispatched up to late afternoon, several of which encountered the enemy. In one instance, No. 19 Squadron's nine-strong force led by CO Sqn Ldr Geoff Stephenson latched onto some Ju 87s whose Bf 109 escort was too distant to interfere with the initial RAF assault. Stephenson was a disciple of the FCA system among other 'book' aspects of RAF thinking and led two sections in on a steady overtaking approach. Although several of the dive-bombers were hard-hit, with at least two descending sharply in flames out of five claimed downed, the last seen of the Squadron CO was his Spitfire gliding down while exuding a thin smoke trail, probably caused by engine overheat due to a punctured glycol tank. He did not return and ended up a POW, having crash-landed his fighter. The third section had engaged the escorts but lost Plt Off. Watson, although he did bale out.

Another heavily-imbalanced encounter with the *Luftwaffe* involved No. 54 Squadron. Sqn Ldr Leathart's three sections took on a mass of Bf 109s and Bf 110s covering Ju 88s bombing shipping between Calais and Dunkirk. The CO claimed one bomber and one Bf 110 followed by Al Deere taking out two more of the *Zerstörers* (German records showed two of the four MIA Bf 110s from I/ZG1 crashing in the region of these combats so granting some substance to the two RAF pilots' debriefing claims). All nine pilots survived the battle despite being outnumbered, but such positive fortune was not granted too often either to No. 54 or its fellow units.

By the day's end, twelve fighters were gone along with four pilots KIA and the others forced to bale out or crash-land their machines. Apparently, more than balancing up this negative statistic were the claims for twenty-nine 'kills' and eighteen 'probables'. This rosy outcome was far too good as records would later

The two RAF officers photographed here were evidence of the tremendous support accorded the service by the British Empire. New Zealanders Al Deere (right) and Colin Gray flew from Hornchurch with No. 54 Squadron during Dynamo and on into the Battle of Britain. They subsequently advanced to wing leader status as well as scoring seventeen and twenty-two confirmed individual kills respectively during the war.

confirm; all sides were to submit greatly inflated figures during the conflict—hardly surprising when given the frenetic pace of air combat that in turn allowed little latitude for accurate accounting at the time.

Critical Decision

The seeds for Allied disaster primarily sown on 12 May with the Sedan–Dinant breakout were now ominously maturing and back in London the government faced with the looming annihilation of its Army along with its equipment was pondering the unthinkable, but sole option—evacuation of the BEF. That conclusion was finally decided upon on the 26th, by which point the Germans were heavily investing Calais. In charge of the evacuation plan was Vice Admiral Bertram Ramsey, who less than four years ahead was destined to be Operation Neptune's chief planner, this being the naval aspect of Operation Overlord that culminated with the Anglo–American Invasion of Normandy. In stark contrast to these future events, British minds were currently directed towards an act of raw survival that, even if successful, would see the nation's military ejection from the European mainland and worse still the clear possibility of being successfully besieged if not also physically invaded for the first time in nearly 900 years.

Operation Dynamo

The seemingly terminal fate now awaiting the Anglo–French soldiers provided little scope for their salvation as the Germans closed inexorably in from all three sides. The shrinking perimeter was particularly shallow to the west with the selected—indeed the only—choice for evacuation being Dunkirk. The *Panzer* units were virtually within visual sight of the town and ready to administer the final blow to any hopes of escape when Hitler's military logic fortuitously struck. Known disparagingly throughout the Second World War by his General Staff as *der größte Feldherr aller Zeiten* ('Greatest Field Marshal ever'), he has since been credited with unilaterally halting the advance of his armoured units.

The reason for his decision—whether based on perceived critical supply deficiencies for the *Panzers*, a need for preservation of the force for future use against the French, or the perceived unsuitable geography of the region in terms of tank operations—unknowingly handed a lifeline, however temporary in practice to the Allied armies. The 'miracle', however unbelievable, was accordingly on hand, although its scale in terms of the human yield in both British and French personnel could never have been envisaged by even the most optimistic individual.

The casual stance of the pilot on his Spitfire's wing suggests he is at the second state of readiness. His Spitfire is certainly action ready, with patches over the gun apertures and parachute harness laid out in the cockpit. The Rotol propeller unit incorporated a constant-speed mechanism that proved vital in matching the aircraft's general performance with the Bf 109.

Command Priorities

If the planned evacuation was going to have any prospect of even partial success (the original estimate of some 45,000 troops being saved was mooted), then it was imperative that maximum air cover be accorded both the troops and their seaborne rescuers. The Battle of France had already claimed several hundreds of Hurricanes along with numerous pilots killed, captured, or rendered inactive through serious injury. Herein lay the primary problem for RAF Fighter Command in terms of human and material resources.

For a start, the available numbers of squadrons, and therefore of fighters on hand, was nowhere near the figure required to provide a comprehensive and regular defensive ring around the evacuation area. The unit figure of sixteen with an average strength of twelve operational fighters was materially inadequate for the overall task. Exacerbating the operational problem was the comparatively short-range nature of the Hurricane and Spitfire that normally allowed between one and a half and two hours' maximum flight-time. Furthermore, this endurance factor was achievable, assuming the fighters were not involved in combat when the extra engine-power required ate up the already meagre fuel reserves at a dangerously enhanced pace. Added to this was the inability for ground control to advise the pilots of likely *Luftwaffe* incursions as well as the strength of these potential strikes; this was due to the range at which the RAF fighters were to operate that put them well out of radio contact and by extension totally nullified the benefit of radar-based information.

The question of how to utilise the squadrons in practical terms was an added problem. Dispatching them in single squadron strength rendered them liable to being overwhelmed by the *Luftwaffe* fighters; the apparent solution of linking up two or three squadrons sounded a positive alternative. However, the varying manner in which some units operated was a hindrance to reaching a common operational function. The deployment of multi-unit formations raised yet another conundrum or 'Catch 22' scenario. If the entire force held ranks during a patrol, there was ever the risk of the *Luftwaffe* succeeding in penetrating to the port and surrounding beaches being used for embarkation and striking thanks to the patrolling RAF squadrons not making an interception. Even should interception be made an element of the force would have to remain as top cover to guard against the enemy escorts achieving a 'bounce'.

The relative lack of numbers of fighters placed a further restriction upon successful regular cover in that there would inevitably be periods when such cover was absent as indeed was to prove the case in the days ahead. With this unfortunate scenario was created the grounds for the BEF personnel's naturally-bitter, albeit misconceived, complaints especially regarding the perceived absence of the RAF fighters overhead during some of the *Luftwaffe* assaults. 'Where is the RAF' was a watchword that would extend well beyond the evacuation's conclusion and would see RAF personnel regularly abused and even physically threatened by the returning soldiers.

No. 56 Squadron operated out of North Weald from May 1940 but sent detachments to France during the German invasion. Press representatives are seen here watching a trio of Hurricanes taking off for what was probably escort for a Blenheim formation involved in attacks on German forces besieging Dunkirk.

'Action this Day'

The onus for the Operation Dynamo air-support measures fell squarely upon the shoulders of AVM Sir Keith Park since No. 11 Group in his charge was located within the several Southeast English counties closest to Dunkirk. The consequences of the sizeable losses in France now bore negative fruit by ensuring that the total number of fighters assigned to the operation was to be barely above 200 maximum, with that figure further reduced by the inevitable percentage of aircraft rendered unserviceable for various reasons (the need to cover the entire British Isles allied with the current greatly-depleted stocks of fighters on hand naturally contributed to this frustrating limiting-factor).

Nothing daunted, the airmen leant themselves to their very onerous duties that would see them tested to, and sometimes beyond, their physical and mental boundaries over the next nine days. A measure of comfort for the pilots in particular was the thought that the nation was freed of Allied involvement with the ever-likely subjugation and capitulation of France. The cooperation between the two air forces had been marginal both in terms of strategy and tactics, while now the RAF could act under its own operational terms. In addition, the squadrons were back on familiar territory and flying from their own relatively well-established bases compared to the largely basic and indifferent to poorly laid-out equivalents left behind across the Channel. In effect, they were 'playing at home' to borrow a sporting expression, although the 'sport' was deadly serious in nature, with the imminent threat of Nazi invasion backed by the well-drilled and skilled legions of the *Luftwaffe* clearly on hand.

Slow Beginning (27 May)

The odyssey of Operation Dynamo—officially spanning a week but extending to nine days in all—was duly commenced on 27 May. Activities were initially slow-paced thanks to the equally-slow build-up in suitable vessels with which to pick up the troops. The call to the British public for boats of any manageable and seaworthy scale, from pleasure craft upward, to be utilised for the evacuation was being responded to, but their assembly at designated ports under Naval supervision took time to establish; their regular presence off Dunkirk would only begin to make its effect felt on the second and third day of the operation. The port of Dunkirk's facilities was already under heavy air and even long-range artillery assault, and the atmosphere overhead was darkened by the thick and steadily persisting pall of smoke boiling up from ruptured oil tanks and extending many miles along the Channel coast.

The individual sorties flown today involved the already familiar mix of largely multiple-squadron formations whose brief was expected to cover not only the area around Dunkirk but also the sea-lanes extending back to Kent, where the intended disembarkation ports of Dover and Folkestone in particular were located—a heavy if not virtually impossible set of requirements for the hard-pressed pilots to fulfil as the evacuation was progressing

An interesting operational feature today was the engagement between No. 264 Squadron and some Bf 109s. Sqn Ldr Hunter (CO) ordered his pilots to form a circle, an action that emulated the Bf 110's similar tactical manoeuvre. The German pilots failed to either break their adversary's flight-pattern or gain any successes, while reportedly losing at least one fighter; it seems clear that they were as yet unaware of the Defiant's total vulnerability to frontal assault. A subsequent patrol-encounter with He 111s saw the *Luftwaffe* unit breaking ranks, and during the resultant pursuit by each squadron section, losing at least three bombers according to the submitted claim-reports.

This early-afternoon action heralded a period of intense enemy assault upon the port that drew in the RAF fighters. No. 74 Squadron under the command of Sqn Ldr 'Sailor' Malan had enjoyed several successes during a morning patrol and now, after abandoning their allotted height due to making no encounters, ran into a Do 17 formation. Two bombers were reported as crashing, but Flt Lt Paddy Treacy had to crash-land his Spitfire whose glycol-starved engine had seized up; the German-held site witnessed his temporary escape from capture.

Plt Off. Mike Maxwell (56 Squadron) was the victim of Belgian 'friendly ground-fire' who then faced the potential problem of 'friendly' identification when faced by soldiers as he landed by parachute—he simply had none. Fortunately, his 'captors' gave him the benefit of the doubt and transported him to Ostend from where he was repatriated. His No. 56 fellow-pilot Flt Lt 'Dicky' Lee, having already gone down behind and escaped from German lines during the Battle of France, suffered his second bale out, this time into the sea from where he was soon fished out (there would be no reprieve the third time round when he was posted MIA over the North Sea during the Battle of Britain).

Grounds for Hope? (28 May)

Although the *Luftwaffe* bomber force was more than sufficient to launch a sustained heavy assault, the actual scale during the day was limited with adverse weather conditions in the form of cloud and rain during the afternoon proving the main obstacle. Adding to this visual limitation was the continuing smoke-pall from the oil tanks smothering the town. The kill–loss ratio still appeared to favour Fighter Command at twenty-two to fourteen with the pilots of five fighters surviving.

The morning sorties with two exceptions comprised two- or three-unit involvement, and all witnessed engagement with the enemy. The single-operating squadrons absorbed nearly half the day's casualties beginning with No. 213; following successful cover for a Blenheim raid, the pilots assumed a patrol duty. Contact with Bf 109s cost two pilots: Fg Off. E. Winning (KIA) and Sgt Boyd, who baled out and was picked up out of the Channel. A later patrol with Nos 242 and 229 Squadrons added Plt Off. G. Stone to the fatality list, while Sergeants Samuel Butterfield and J. Lichman emulated Boyd's experience in baling out safely. The other two squadrons lost two and one aircraft respectively during the series of highly-pitched dogfights that in No. 242's case saw it being outnumbered by at least four to one.

The other 'solo' sortie was indulged in by the Defiants of No. 264 Squadron, whose hitherto almost miraculous good fortune was to desert them, albeit not for the last time. The ten-strong formation ran into a large Bf 109 group whereupon the pilots adopted their usual circular manoeuvre. Within a short time span, the formation began to disintegrate doubtless thanks to the superior handling and firepower of the enemy machines; three crews were taken down and worse still was the 100 per cent fatality scale.

The cramped Boulton Paul gun turret made swift exit almost impossible and was the probable reason for their occupant's fate; cockpit exit should have been easier, but perhaps the pilots were already dead. One of the surviving crews, Sgt Edward Thorn and LAC (Leading Aircraftsman) Fred Barker, not only survived their fighter's battering, but would advance to be one of the most successful Defiant teams during the nocturnal 1940–41 *Blitz* (the minimum rank of sergeant

Three Mk I Spitfires are seen at dispersal on Hornchurch from where they were involved in the Dunkirk evacuation. Picture is no later than May 1940 when the fuselage roundels changed to Type A1 and fin flashes were introduced. K9911 lasted until 8 August when Sgt Kirton was killed. K9907 in the middle was lost on 8 July along with the CO, Sqn Ldr Desmond Cooke.

not long introduced for RAF aircrew was still clearly pending for the gunners, although the issue would be addressed in time).

Al Deere's 'Nine Lives' Countdown (1)

The pressures of constant combat were reaching such a pitch for No. 54 Squadron that their removal for rest and recuperation purposes was scheduled for today—a move whose application would come too late as far as Al Deere was concerned. The squadron in the company of its Nos 19 and 65 contemporaries—the latter also listed for the same R&R treatment—lifted off on an early-morning sortie that involved just eight fighters in both these unit's case. Separation occurred thanks to the cloudy conditions and hardly had No. 54 reached the patrol start point when a lone Do 17 was sighted and pursued. Deere as leader closed on the bomber, but an accurate burst from the rear gunner punctured his glycol tank, so inducing a search for a suitable crash-landing site; the impact on a stretch of beach knocked the pilot out, but he recovered in time to vacate the steadily-burning Spitfire.

Deere's original intention to get back home via Ostend was soon quashed by the refugee-flow, so he turned his attention to Dunkirk. Having gained a truck lift to the town outskirts, he reached the harbour mole, but was halted by a major as he headed towards a berthed destroyer. His explanation of his status and need to get back and rejoin the aerial defensive screen was angrily refuted on the now-standard grounds of the RAF's defensive ineptitude. During the short altercation, the warship cast off, denying Deere his opportunity, but he joined the queue and eventually got on board the next warship that survived at least one bombing assault on its voyage to Dover. The stony silence emanating from his fellow evacuees during the crossing was further confirmation of their intense displeasure with the RAF that was hardly alleviated by Deere pointing out the operational strain to which he and his fellow fighter pilots were being subjected. As it was, four further and even more fraught incidents lay ahead of him over the ensuing months of 1940.

The day's activities had witnessed a further fourteen fighters being written-off RAF records, with a reverse claim of twenty-two 'kills' and several 'probables'; five out of the pilots had survived. The extremes of fortune were encountered by Plt Off. Ian Muirhead (No. 605 Squadron) and Flt Lt Fred Ives (No. 151 Squadron) who had baled out on the 27th and 25th respectively. They landed near Ostend and now embarked on a ship along with other RAF personnel, the vessel casting off in the late evening. Barely had the port been cleared when two torpedoes from an E-boat slammed into the hull and sent it within minutes to the bottom of the Channel. Muirhead managed to swim to a raft to become one of the roughly 11 per cent of the service and civilian passengers to come through alive, but Ives was listed among the casualty total. However, Muirhead's escape was sadly temporary because he was KIA the following 15 October.

Downturn in Fortunes (29 May)

To date, the evacuation process, although subject to steady enemy intervention, had not basically been materially affected. Although the limitations of the RAF fighter 'screen' had inevitably permitted access to the *Luftwaffe*, the bombers had not hammered the port facilities to a degree that prevented the troops being lifted off in sizeable numbers. What was the third full day of Dynamo was to force a switch from quayside evacuation to an enhanced use of the surrounding beaches; however, the issue was not deemed worthy of discussion during the morning and into the early afternoon. This was thanks to the indifferent weather conditions in the air that established an overcast low enough in particular to hinder dive-bombing.

Unfortunately, this welcome respite was then cancelled out as the cloud pattern dispersed and the first bomber formation of Do 17s appeared with a Bf 110 escort. The three Hurricane squadrons on hand made several claims against two losses, as did the Defiants of No. 264 Squadron. It was clear that these enemy fighter pilots had not yet discovered the armament 'Achilles' heel' of the Boulton Paul design, since neither the Bf 110 nor Bf 109 fighters engaging the unit scored any successes—unlike Sqn Ldr Hunter's team that claimed sixteen kills, with a Ju 87 the sole exception to its escort contemporaries.

Although the Hurricane was technically superior to the Bf 110 in overall performance, the odds in its favour when challenging Willi Messerschmitt's *Zerstörer* were cancelled out if not reversed in some circumstances as Sqn Ldr Edward Donaldson (No. 151 Squadron CO) ruefully discovered. He found

The Boulton-Paul Defiant enjoyed a rather brief and ultimately bloody combat spell during the summer of 1940, commencing with Operation Dynamo. On 29 May, L6957 PS: T staggered back to Manston with its starboard elevator shot-up, as seen here. Only the pilot was still on board the No. 264 Squadron fighter; his gunner baled out but did not survive the experience.

himself running into a Bf 110 *Schwarm* that latched onto his fighter and thwarted every attempt by him to outturn and out climb his opponents. Having firmly corralled him and appearing to be about to administer a *coup de grâce*; he initiated a vertical dive that saw the Merlin exude a heavy smoke-trail, a visual sign that probably convinced his tormentors their prey was doomed.

One of the No. 610 Squadron pilots lost on a late-afternoon patrol would likely have survived but for the notoriously-poor aircraft recognition skills existing among many Naval gunners. Sgt P. Jenkins' Spitfire was fatally crippled by misdirected gunfire and he promptly baled out to drift down into the sea, but still alive. When Flt Lt John Ellis swooped down towards a warship in Jenkin's vicinity to guide it towards his fellow pilot's watery location, he was also fired upon and forced to break away, thereby leaving Jenkins to drown or expire through hypothermia—a tragically needless loss.

Fg Off. Willy McKnight from No. 242 (Canadian) Squadron was subsequently granted official confirmation of first a Bf 109 and then a Do 17 as it retired towards the east. As it happened, he was fortunate to still be around given that he had been the perceived victim of a 'friendly fire' incident on the 28th. During the battle with Bf 109s, a fellow pilot reported that having downed one enemy aircraft, he opened up on a second that was McKnight's Hurricane; his aim was fortunately not so perfect, and although he was verbally lambasted after landing, McKnight kept the fact to himself on the joint basis that he had survived and that the 'assailant' was reportedly a particular friend. The incident amply demonstrated the basically nerve-driven confusion of aerial combat where seconds often meant the difference between survival and death.

It was around this point that the Ju 87s of StG2 led by Maj. Oscar Dinort appeared on the scene and began to deal out their accurate and often-summary treatment upon the port and its largely hapless occupants, as well as shipping laying or transiting offshore, all this despite the presence of up to four Hurricane and Spitfire squadrons. The joint presence of escort fighters from JG1 was a major and often fatal hindrance to taking on the enemy bombers as No. 229 Squadron in particular discovered; the conclusion of its feral battle with Bf 109s left it short five Hurricanes, with only two pilots surviving. Elsewhere, No. 64 Squadron lost CO Sqn Ldr E. Rogers along with Pilot Officers R. George and H. Hackney, none of whom survived. These combined casualties proved to be half of the day's negative tally in fighters, although the survival of five pilots somewhat balanced out this ever-dismal situation. A second CO killed was Sqn Ldr A. Franks leading No. 610 Squadron.

On the ground, the first signs of hope that the original estimate of a 45,000-maximum number of troops capable of being salvaged from the BEF entity was a pessimistic one was being proven. On this, the third full day of Dynamo, the figure stood at around 72,000. A further boost to this tally would be enjoyed the next day with Mother Nature providing a second bonus to add to the calm Channel waters.

Evacuation Upsurge (30 May)

The dawn light today revealed cloudy conditions over southern England that did not prevent the launch of the RAF squadrons. In contrast, a 'cloak' of sea mist and fog over the land approaches to Dunkirk, combined with the smoke pall drifting relentlessly from shattered oil tanks and other combustible stores, prevented any possibility of the lethal dive-bomber assaults launched the previous afternoon and evening being repeated; level bombing attacks were similarly inhibited while German artillery was at least diminished in accuracy. The switch to the beaches had seen the increased use of small boats that in turn transferred their human loads to properly-appointed warships and merchant vessels. The result was that, by the day's end, the evacuation-tally had been increased by a further 54,000 personnel. At this stage, nearly 40 per cent of the final figure of just under 340,000 individuals was either heading for or already back on British soil. However, a key alteration in the overall process was currently being actively mulled over and would be initiated on the 31st.

Douglas Bader's operational career commenced during the Dunkirk evacuation when he was serving as a flight commander with No. 222 Squadron. On 1 June, he was credited with a Bf 109 and shared in a He 111's destruction. This very assertive but courageously-spirited officer subsequently commanded No. 242 Squadron, as well as leading the controversial Duxford Wing during the Battle of Britain.

Although No. 11 Group was still dispatching multi-strength formations, these were expected to function as an integral wing. This was fine in theory, but it was largely incapable of being applied in practice. There was no time to establish how the wing could operate more efficiently compared to the previous policy of separating each squadron into lower-altitude operating sub-units with cover provided by at least one. It was even difficult to establish who the wing leader should be, while varying operational procedures further degraded the basic principle of formation-flying among other functions. Retaining a wing formation during a patrol also permitted a greater chance of gaps appearing in the overall fighter 'screen'. It would only be from the following winter onward that wing formations would operate in a regular and efficient manner.

In the event, the virtual absence of the *Luftwaffe* ensured that the manifold flaws in the acolyte wing system were not exposed. The 213 Squadron leader for one of the patrols dispersed his four-strong force on independent sorties, and it was his sub-formation that encountered one of the handful of enemy aircraft sighted; the Do 17 in question was last seen well shot-up with an engine on fire as it finally entered a cloudbank. A second Do 17 from a *Staffel* formation was similarly assailed by No. 245 Squadron, but it also faded into the clouds. This was the sum total of interceptions today.

Diplomacy Reigns (31 May)

Up to date, the act of evacuation had applied solely to members of the British Armed Forces, but now the process was directed to be applied equally between the 'Tommies' and their French counterparts. This alteration was likely an initiative demanded by the Francophile Churchill, but if so, it was nevertheless soundly reiterated by Admiral Ramsey on the grounds of diplomacy as much as military necessity. There was no doubt that the French authorities had hitherto been dismayed if not outraged by the British decision to pull their forces back across the Channel.

Perfidious Albion's reputation for joining in previous European conflicts but withdrawing to Britain at their conclusion was exacerbating such a reputation by presenting the nation's attitude in this instance as one where 'its soldiers would fight to the last Frenchman'. The decision to share the evacuation operation was perceived as going some way towards dispelling this unwholesome reputation—one that was militarily undeserved in respect of the BEF since the Germans were already well established to win the overall campaign in the west whatever the French—with the clear evidence of their comprehensive military collapse—might say.

One of the recurring puzzles surrounding Dynamo was why the *Luftwaffe*'s assaults were sometimes delayed in circumstances where operations were not hindered by adverse weather conditions, with today a clear example. The suggestion that the *Luftwaffe* was leaving the assault field free to *Wehrmacht* artillery units to strike home is flawed; the chances of accurately directing a shell onto a vessel for example were well short of the equivalent action by even a level-bomber, let alone the more pinpoint delivery of a bomb released from a Ju 87 or its Ju 88 dive-bomber 'twin'. Whatever the reasoning, this perceived lapse provided the latest bonus to advancing the evacuation-scale of personnel.

The new CO of No. 213 Squadron was destined to enjoy his tenure of office for less than one day, although he later resumed command. Sqn Ldr McGregor had been given a hasty conversion from his previous Spitfire experience onto a squadron Hurricane, but his operational inexperience with the Hawker fighter was the likely reason why he was forced to take to his parachute over Dunkirk after being shot-up to become one of five MIA casualties, two fatal. However, he managed to be picked up from the sea by a destroyer and landed in Dunkirk from where he was later brought back home.

No. 264 Squadron patrolling during the same time lost three fighters, two of whom collided, although the four airmen concerned were more fortunate in baling out or force-landing compared to a third squadron team who were killed.

A No. 264 Squadron Defiant air gunner stands in his flight suit ready to enter his turret; his somewhat wan expression probably relates to his thoughts on making a swift exit in an emergency. The cramped confines would make this difficult even without the flight suit's bulk. Note the extended footrest built into the frame in the wing root.

A subsequent evening sortie saw the squadron incur two further MIA casualties, from which only one crew survived their immersion in the sea while a third crash-landed in Southeast England (the martyrdom of the Defiant as a daytime fighter although on the fringe of catastrophe was still being held in abeyance for several weeks). On the beaches, the first half of the day had created serious problems for the boats inshore thanks to an unwelcome choppy sea-surface that thankfully subsided as the afternoon developed. Overhead, the RAF fighters were maintaining an unusually effective continuous barrier to *Luftwaffe* incursions; these were ironically proceeding in an equally continuous timeframe that, in turn, provided their opponents with regular interception opportunities. The opposing aerial forces each gave as good as they got, even if they did not win the day.

The sizeable numbers of RAF pilots who had baled out over the Channel and survived the experience were unaware of their good fortune. This was primarily due to the regular seaborne traffic whose crews could observe their descent and be on hand to pick them up. Had these vessels not been on hand, it was more than likely that the majority, if not all, would have perished due to drowning or hypothermia. The bald truth was that there was no current comprehensive British equivalent to the *Luftwaffe*'s Air-Sea Rescue Service (*Seenotdienst*) with its fleet of floatplanes, launches, and even moored platforms within which the aircrew could wait to be picked up. The provision of Air-Sea Rescue launches was being addressed; sadly, their regular availability supported by 'spotter' aircraft would only be on hand by the autumn, during which time many pilots would perish in the sea.

The number of troops so far evacuated was several times greater than the very modest forecast figure preceding the operation. To date, the five days had witnessed the activity conducted during the ever-extending hours of daylight, but it was now decided that the following day's operation would further extend throughout the night of 2 June; in addition, the vast bulk of the BEF troops still on hand would be granted priority of boarding, although their French contemporaries would not be ignored either—especially since the defence of the steadily-compressed, but still resisting Dunkirk perimeter was by now being primarily conducted by the Gallic nation's soldiers.

False Evacuation 'Dawn' (1–4 June)

The overall time scale for Dynamo that had now spanned five full days as June commenced was anticipated by Admiral Ramsey as coming to a close within the first two days of the new month; in practice, it would be almost two more days before the final human tally was completed, with some 28,000 French soldiers recovered during this final cross-Channel surge. The weather conditions of mixed cloud and clear visibility spells promised more enemy attention, which was duly delivered with punishing effect upon the shipping in spite of Fighter Command's defensive effort. Hornchurch's four Spitfire squadrons were first off and were soon embroiled in dogfights with Bf 109s and Bf 110s, with the former coming to the *Zerstörer*'s aid. Casualties were incurred by both sides, with No. 222 hard-hit to the tune of four aircraft and two pilots (Plt Off. Massey-Sharpe and Sgt L. J. White) killed.

One of the two squadron survivors, Plt Off. R. Morant, crash-landed his Spitfire in the surf at Bray Dunes well to the east of Dunkirk and later joined a group of soldiers trying to launch a boat with which to sail out to one of two destroyers; it was probably as well their effort failed because both warships were subsequently bombed, one fatally, the other badly damaged. Forced to make the protracted walk all the way to Dunkirk, the airman was fortunate to board a paddle-steamer that finally sailed, having survived at least one near miss from a bomb load that straddled its berth. Even then, the laying of mines by the Germans ensured that the sea-passage course taken up to Dover was one that regularly meandered away from the suspected sites.

There seems little doubt that the *Rotte/Schwarm* formation tactics as likely used against 222 Squadron were continuing to prove vastly superior in flexibility compared to the dangerously turgid 'Vic' and line-astern patterns currently utilised by their opponents. The greater degree of visual acuity accorded the *Jagdwaffe* pilots whether in formation or splitting off into *Rotten* (pairs) during a combat allowed them to engage or withdraw on favourable terms, whereas only

No. 65 Squadron was engaged both during the Dunkirk evacuation and in the Battle of Britain up to the end of August. A section is seen virtually at the point of becoming airborne from the airfield. R6714 and 6712 survived combat but were written-off on 16 October 1940 and 11 May 1941, with Sgt I. Patterson being killed during the former incident.

the leaders of the RAF sub-units were similarly blessed as were the 'weavers' to a certain extent. In spite of such tactics that accounted for the majority of the seventeen Hurricanes and Spitfires declared MIA by the evening, no less than twenty-nine *Luftwaffe* MIA casualties, including ten fighters, were recorded in its official records. In addition, five of the surviving pilots soon regained friendly shores. The German aircrew were under little lingering misapprehension regarding the challenge offered by Fighter Command, however fragmentary and dispersed such a challenge was currently amounting to.

The arrival of Ju 87s later in the morning saw their pilots adding yet another RN destroyer to their tally; HMS *Basilisk* had suffered an engine breakdown, a failure rendering her helpless to evade the torrent of bombs that fatally crippled her—she was probably the warship cited in Plt Off. Morant's aforementioned account. By the day's end, the destroyers *Keith* and *Havant* were also gone. The defensive firepower thrown up by such ships was basically inadequate to handle the weight of air assault; the corollary to this imbalanced situation was that the Naval gunners were constantly keyed-up and all too ready to operate on the principle of 'fire first and ask questions later'—hence the number of RAF aircrew commenting acidly upon the unprovoked fire directed their way should they approach anywhere nearby their nautical 'brothers in arms'.

For all the punishment being handed out by the enemy bombers, the steady stream of evacuees back safely to British shores was still being maintained, bringing the overall headcount to an amazing figure of 260,000 by this day's end. Hermann Göring's reputed boast to Hitler that he could prevent Dynamo ever being executed let alone attaining this level of success was being flung back in his face.

Clear visibility during the morning of the 2nd witnessed early engagements with the *Luftwaffe* bombers and their escorts, involving among the four squadrons then on hand the re-entry into the battle of No. 92 Squadron led by its new CO, Sqn Ldr 'Bob' Stanford Tuck, and initially flying the low position within the wing. Interception of a He 111 formation and its Bf 109 cover was made, but the future leading RAF ace was lucky to escape unscathed from the resultant dogfight, although credited with at least one fighter 'kill'; this was probably the one he saw breaking off and flying an undeviating course—an action that cost the pilot dearly since his aircraft was patiently closed-in upon and finally dispatched to bring Tuck's current 'confirmed' score up to seven. Nos 611 and 266 Squadrons, the latter making its first sortie, both lost two pilots killed, while No. 32 Squadron's sole loss, Sgt D. Flynn, survived albeit as a POW.

Air patrol activities were now curtailed until the evening, the morning flurry of activity presumably relating to coverage of those vessels still steaming back across the Channel since daylight operations were concluded. Evening patrols were launched with a view to providing reverse cover for those ships dispatched to pick up as much of the French forces either within the port or withdrawing from the defensive perimeter. By the day's conclusion, the Command was short eight pilots with only two surviving compared to *Jagdwaffe* claims for nineteen—one short of their opponent's total claim. Unbeknown to the thoroughly-exhausted RAF pilots was that the air battle of Dunkirk was effectively at an end, although

What appears to have been the final No. 222 patrol over Dunkirk on 1 June was an expensive one. One pilot was killed, one force-landed, and the third, Flt Lt Falkust, ended up making a forced-landing on Le Touquet in P9317. Unfortunately, the Germans were already in occupation and he ended up a POW. In the right background what appears to be a wrecked Hurricane is standing on its nose.

one morning patrol would be dispatched on the 3rd. As for the prospect of further French evacuation, virtually no personnel were found to be on hand to be picked up on the 2nd and 3rd, but a final shipping sortie during the next night succeeded in achieving a human haul of around 28,000.

Luck of the Draw?

During the course of Dynamo, a number of RAF aircrew with fighter pilots among this group had recourse to baling out of or crash-landing their aircraft, as well as avoiding capture. Their return to home soil should have witnessed them enjoying the same chance of evacuation as the BEF troops, but there was one sticking point based on emotion more than logic. This related to the growing frustration and anger among the Army ranks at the apparent failure of Fighter Command to prevent the steady pounding of Dunkirk, the beaches, and the myriad vessels.

On more than one occasion, the RAF individual concerned was ordered out of the waiting file with verbally obscene expressions. Plt Off. Cazenove (92 Squadron) was reminded on one of his three vain attempts that 'the ships were for the use of the BEF not the F-----g Air Force!'—the ultimate result was the start of five years captivity following the German capture of Dunkirk. Another pilot had recourse to physical force in knocking out the officer acting as the file marshal before boarding the vessel, but he could easily have been ejected by the troops witnessing the incident.

Al Deere's boxing expertise might have impelled him to this course of action on 28 May had he been similarly inclined, but he held back and managed to board a vessel later on. The relationship between the 'Brown Jobs' (Army) and the

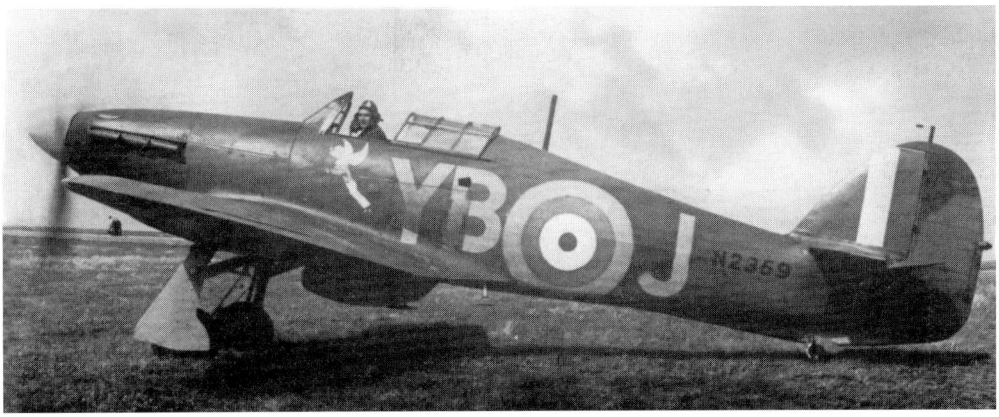

N2359 was produced and delivered to No. 17 Squadron during the winter of 1939–40. The squadron was involved in the Battle of France as well as Operation Dynamo. This Mk I Hurricane survived operations and OTU relegation until 11 June 1941, when it crashed. Note how the fuselage Type A1 roundel wraps around the base of the fuselage; the thick code letters and complete fin coverage for the flash are points of note.

'Brylcream Boys' (RAF), as each sardonically christened the other, was to remain under strain up to 1942 when planned and well-executed service interacting in North Africa began to improve matters from that stage of the Second World War onwards.

Conclusions

The 'miracle' aspect of the evacuation arguably owed as much to Mother Nature as to either Hitler's seeming vacillation in using his *Panzers* to administer the killer punch or the fighting qualities of the Anglo–French defenders holding the perimeter, within which the retreating personnel were converging upon Dunkirk. As it transpired, the almost consistently mild conditions applying to the usually variable and oft-turbulent Channel waters during the overall course of Dynamo undoubtedly played a key role in attaining the huge scale of operational success.

The natural bid primarily launched by the *Luftwaffe* but aided by a degree of *Wehrmacht* artillery support to deny the port facilities of Dunkirk to the British rescue effort was only partially successful. True, heavy damage was inflicted upon the overall area, but access to the extended length of the eastern mole as a vital embarkation point was never fully denied; although shipping was sunk in the approach channel, there was still sufficient room for transiting vessels to lay alongside the mole and load-up at least during the initial period of the operation. A move to the beaches as a regular evacuation location may well have been initiated thanks to the pounding the town was receiving, but although the pace of evacuation from the mole was probably lower and slower, its availability was still on hand right up to the last twenty-four hours of 3–4 June.

Nine RN and French Navy destroyers, along with nine merchant vessels and numerous other smaller boats, were lost to the combination of bombs, mines, and torpedoes. The ragtag of volunteer-manned vessels from civilian sources forever known as the 'Small Boats' gained the legendary status of being the key provider for the recovery process; in fact, the Royal Navy was entitled to claim such credit in practice, but the British media was responsible for creating what has become the on-going 'Small Boat' image the public still retain, if not also cherish, regarding Operation Dynamo. As it was, all the foregoing participants deserve everlasting national respect for what they had achieved regardless of the high human and material cost.

The major contradiction arising out of Operation Dynamo was experienced by the returning service personnel after they disembarked and were directed to the rail stations from where they would travel into the British hinterland. The welcome they received—with signs plastered everywhere in the seaports and along the rail routes, stating, for example, 'Well Done, men of the BEF'—elicited reactions ranging from bewilderment to acute embarrassment among their ranks. Far from feeling like conquering 'heroes' as the banners and verbal utterances were clearly proclaiming, they had thankfully emerged from a military disaster of the highest order.

The one vital factor that was destined to alleviate this current cataclysmic situation in time if not immediately was that the disaster was greatly more focused upon a material failure as opposed to a human one. The thousands of weapons and vehicles, along with an equal mass of ammunition and other support equipment, left behind in France had not been matched by the one source incapable of being replaced on the factory floor—the soldier. More than 210,000 British Army individuals, many having even retained their rifles, were safely back home and available for ultimate deployment on British soil or abroad. Huge as this figure was, it still only represented around 60 per cent of all BEF personnel; the bulk of the remainder were still actively involved further west and south within the steadily-shrinking interior of France as the Germans pushed for final victory—a goal destined to be achieved within a mere three weeks of Dynamo's conclusion.

The conclusion of the Norwegian campaign ended in tragedy for No. 46 Squadron, whose Hurricanes are previously seen being loaded for sea transport to that country. Having safely evacuated their fighters on to HMS *Glorious* on 8 June, the Hurricanes, along with all but two of the pilots, were lost with the bulk of the carrier's crew when the vessel was sunk by the battlecruisers *Scharnhorst* and *Gneisenau*.

6

Democracy at Bay: The Fight for Survival, June–August 1940

France's Fate is Sealed

Britain's military ejection from the continent had been basically completed during the first week of June 1940 with the conclusion to Operation Dynamo. Although there was still a sizeable contingent of the BEF on hand, its ranks were now engaged in a swiftly fruitless bid to assist in shoring up the remaining French defensive effort to stem the *Luftwaffe*-supported *Wehrmacht* and *SS* legions' burgeoning assaults into France's central hinterland.

Even at this point, the British Government doubtlessly chivvied by Churchill was assembling a supplementary force of men and equipment to be transported over the Channel in the hope their presence would further slow if not reverse the enemy advance. This act was to prove to be of no avail as the '*Blitzkrieg*' tactics swept all before it and gobbled up thousands of Anglo–French troops, a figure that included Gen. Victor Fortune's 51st Highland Division trapped by Gen. Rommel at Saint-Valery-en-Caux. In the air, the few remaining Hurricanes on hand could do virtually nothing to alleviate the plight of the ground forces.

Although the decision to send reinforcements was still being acted upon on 15 June—twenty-four hours after the Fall of Paris—counter-decision to curtail the activity and launch a second evacuation of the BEF via several seaports along the Normandy and Brittany coasts was initiated. Thousands of personnel were brought back safely, but there was a shockingly high death toll incurred at Saint-Nazaire on the 17th; the liner *Lancastria* anchored offshore had already embarked around 6,000 when a Ju 87 attack sent it to the bottom, along with an estimated two-thirds of its hapless human cargo.

A Mk I Hurricane belonging to No. 32 Squadron has been started-up and is ready to taxi out for take-off. The dormant pair of fighters in the background suggests that the active aircraft is taking off on a non-operational flight. Code letters and fuselage roundel are over scale in size, with the latter's yellow rim severed by the camouflage separation line.

The New Dark Age Looms

The logistical shortfall in military equipment resulting from the French Campaign was potentially lethal to all hopes of preventing a German invasion of Britain. Heavy artillery and tank numbers were frighteningly low, as were light weaponry and transport stocks. In the case of the RAF, the loss between 10 May and 4 June of several hundred fighters mainly Hurricanes along with pilot fatalities, injuries, and imprisonment had bit almost equally hard into Fighter Command's ability to withstand what was naturally regarded as an imminent aerial assault. That it did not commence in any concentrated form for up to five weeks must have come as a definite relief to ACM Dowding and his group commanders: Air Vice-Marshals Quinton Brand, in charge of the newly-formed No. 10 Group covering Southwest England; Trafford Leigh-Mallory, in charge of No. 12 Group; and, particularly, Keith Park, whose No. 11 Group pilots were arguably the most likely to regularly bear the main weight of assault.

The long-established figure of fifty-two fighter squadrons regarded as being the minimum required for even reasonably-effective defence of the national structure still fell well short of the target in mid-June. To the forty-three units on home soil of which forty-one were currently deemed operational could be added three full Hurricane squadrons back from France; however, the Defiant operated by Nos 141 and 264 Squadrons would finally prove to be lethally vulnerable and be withdrawn from daylight operations although not before suffering two devastating rebuffs. It was as well that the various factory sources for fighters were already increasing production rates by nearly half again on the May figure (229 Hurricanes and Spitfires) to an equivalent total of 304 by the end of June. On that date, the gross total of available fighters was just on the 1,000 mark; this statistic was misleading in terms of operational numbers that stood at just over 600 and included ninety-five Defiants and Blenheim Mk Is, both of which lacked the Hurricane and Spitfire's ability to even challenge, let alone exceed, the overall performance of the Bf 109.

Vital as it was, the recouping of this material shortfall was only one of the twin problems facing the command. Arguably worse was pilot availability in joint terms of numbers and battle experience. A proportion of those killed or captured in combat had garnered sound to good experience in aerial tactics; their absence accordingly denied the acolyte airmen the benefit of such knowledge being passed down as they prepared to enter the lists of combat. A further immediate loss to the command's fighting strength was the long-term absence from frontline squadrons of a further number of French Campaign survivors due to their being battle fatigued and accordingly assigned to secondary duties until regarded as fully recovered. An example involved several of No. 1 Squadron's 'veteran' complement, who fell into this category; at least their expertise could be passed on if so solicited, but their presence along with the other battle-weary veterans in a fighter cockpit would have been of arguably greater benefit to the nation's looming fight for survival.

As regards the pool of replacement pilots, the recently-formed Operational Training Units (OTU) programme anticipated a multi-month period of orientation for each trainee prior to posting to a squadron, but as the battle evolved and casualties began to mount, this was steadily reduced to a fraction of the original time span that, in some instances, involved between one and two weeks. As regards such a miniscule OTU time period, the opinion mooted by one government minister that the 'final polish' to the individual's performance could be achieved after assignment to a squadron was to prove cruelly negative.

In all too many cases, the pilot concerned was shot down and either killed or removed from operations through injury before learning enough of the necessary techniques that could help him to even survive the feral atmosphere of aerial combat, let alone flourish in combat experience. Dowding had opposed the OTU concept on the grounds that it diverted fighters and pilots from frontline service; however, the counter argument was that posting straight to a squadron especially in current circumstances was even more counterproductive since the pilots were too taken up with actual combat duties to grant time for bringing the newcomer up to operational scratch.

A Mk I Hurricane belonging to No. 85 Squadron has just attained minimum airspeed and is lifting away from the airfield, presumably the unit base at Debden. Of interest is the anti-glare shield, a horizontal metal flange just below and ahead of the cockpit. This is intended to cut out exhaust glare should the fighter be employed on nocturnal operations.

Setting the Trap

The transfer of *Luftwaffe* units to airfields closer to Britain was being fulfilled as swiftly as possible, with France and Belgium the prime locations along with Holland. In general, the personnel moved into established airfields; however, several airfields particularly around the Pas-de-Calais were being hastily carved out of the countryside. Such basically-provisioned strips that were no more than flat mown surfaces with minimal or even no solid support structures for accommodation or maintenance were assigned to the *Jagdwaffe* with an emphasis on Bf 109 operations.

The region was geographically the closest to Southeast England, upon which the main assault was due to descend, hence its selection for *Luftflotte* 2's single-engined fighters. This was not surprising since a lack of range was a major failing with the design and one of several operational factors that would work to the RAF's advantage. The range-degradation would prove even more restrictive for the Bf 109s serving with *Luftflotte* 3 positioned to the west where the English Channel is noticeably extended in width. However, the regrouping of all its Bf 109 units within *Luftflotte* 2 from mid-August on would at least alleviate the overall problem. The advent of external fuel tank stocks following the necessary attachments to later Bf 109E variants would occur too late to materially alter the situation for the *Luftwaffe* during the forthcoming battle.

The Bf 110 *Zerstörer*, unlike its single-engined contemporary, was not inhibited in terms of range thanks to its two DB 601 engines. In addition, it possessed a weight of firepower matching that sported by either of Fighter Command's premier fighters, while its top speed marginally exceeded that of the Hurricane. The high hopes for the design in terms of striking telling blows against Fighter Command had not been basically dented during the Battle of France; nearly fifty crews had been shot down or failed to return by the end of May, of which the Allied air forces and ground fire had accounted for a good number.

Three *Luftflotten* were assigned to the assault and positioned in a huge geographic arc spread between north-western France and Denmark–Norway. *Luftflotte* 3, with *Generalfeldmarschall* Hugo Sperrle's HQ in Paris, occupied the aforementioned zone, while from Brussels, the similar-ranked Albert Kesselring commanded his *Luftflotte* 2, whose airfields spanned north-eastern France, Belgium, and into Holland. The Scandinavian-based aircrews of *Luftflotte* 5 in *Generaloberst* Hans-Jürgen Stumpff's charge were already well aware of the multi-hundred mile North Sea crossing to be negotiated in attacking the northerly regions of Britain, since they had provided the great bulk of such operations to date (in the American Second World War film series *Why We Fight*, an excerpt in one episode depicts a drawing of Western Europe's Nazi-occupied coastline expanding into the shape of a whale's jaw that threatens to envelope the British Isles with the latter being clearly depicted as the biblical character Jonah. The depiction was a grimly apt presentation of the British nation's imminent annihilation by the Nazi hordes).

Initial Jousting

Although Göring and his commanders still held back from a full-scale assault thanks probably to Hitler's several bids to convince his primary enemy that it should negotiate with his regime, this did not mean that the *Luftwaffe* remained totally moribund in operational terms. Reconnaissance sorties were regularly flown, as were bomber intrusions, with the latter dispatched by night; both types of operations had in truth been occurring to some degree in April and May.

The moonlit conditions existing over England on 19–20 June promised a relatively smooth path to their various targets spread across the length of the country for upwards of seventy bomber crews. The possibility of being intercepted by RAF fighters was not on the airmen's minds, since the likelihood was minimal given their night-shrouded passage. Most of the units concerned duly made a safe return to their airfields, but a later headcount showed five He 111s absent from their dispersals. Worse still was that all five crews belonged to II/KG4.

No. 23 Squadron had recently been assigned to a night-fighting role, and at least two aircraft were aloft on this occasion. Elsewhere, Spitfires from Nos 19 and 74 Squadrons were also 'scrambled', although their inability to carry any form of electronic tracking devices meant that the 'Eyeball Mk One' was the sole means of seeking out a target. It was accordingly surprising that three of the He 111s were destined to fall to these fighters, even allowing for the moon-illuminated sky. Flt

Lt 'Sailor' Malan had probably not been long airborne from Hornchurch when he encountered the first of his two kills: 5J+GA was brought to earth some 20 miles north-east of the airfield. Malan's patrol then extended out towards the coast where he downed the He 111P2 that bore Hptm. Prochnow's (4/*Staffelkapitän*) four-man team to a watery North Sea grave.

Fg Off. Eric Ball (No. 19 Squadron) was victorious over 5J+FP that also fell in the sea while Fg Off. Petra (also 19 Squadron) shared 5J+AM during the first of two successful interceptions for No. 23 Squadron, albeit at a cost. Petra was forced to bale out, as was Sqn Ldr O'Brien, who was the sole survivor after his Blenheim went out of control. Finally, Flt Lt R. Duke-Woolley's gunfire was effective enough to compel Maj. Von Massenberg (*Gruppenkommandeur*) to force-land his bomber, so concluding a costly unit rebuff both in terms of aircraft and senior personnel within the crew complement. The harvest of nocturnal kills would not again attain this degree of success until nearly eleven months ahead, when the *Blitz* campaign would be nearing its conclusion, by which stage, the radar-equipped and heavily-armed Beaufighter was on hand in regular numbers.

Further north in the course of several small-strength probing sorties on 26 June, 3/KG26 surrendered two He 111s to No. 603 Squadron off the Scottish coast,

The ammunition-belt-draped airman on the left is feeding its bullet content into the magazine of one of the outer pair of guns; the weapons were staggered alternately to allow the magazines to be mounted in pairs and in tandem. His colleague holds the belt steady; the observer badge on his tunic indicates a former aircrew status, possibly as far back as the 1914–18 conflict.

and a 3/KG4 crew led by Hptm. Schroeder (*Staffelkapitän*) in 5J+BL was fatally downed by two 616 Squadron pilots off Hull; six days later, 5J+EL joined its companion bomber in death over the same zone, with No. 616 again the victor, but *Oberleutnant zur See* F. Koch's crew survived the 'ditching' even though the landing gear was extended. As June faded into July, the pinprick scale of assault extending from north-eastern Scotland to the Channel coast added twenty more aircraft to the loss tally by the month's first full week.

Extended Lead-Up to *'Adler Tag'*

The still slow-paced operational pattern of *Luftwaffe* activity as July was entered was brought to a more concentrated level commencing on the 10th, when what is still treated as the official beginning of the Battle of Britain was launched by Göring. However, the planned operations that had really commenced several days previous were largely confined to the sea lanes around the Thames Estuary and extending into the English Channel with various merchant convoys as the target.

Hitler's bid to negotiate a peaceful separation of Britain from the still European-based conflict was still under way, and it would only be on the 16th that his impatience with Churchill's total resistance to any such plan would erupt; on that day, the Führer issued Directive No. 16 in which he outlined the conditions under which an invasion might be carried out in order to permanently remove the threat to his future schemes for permanent European domination—however marginal that threat would currently appear to be.

Completion by mid-August of preparations for what was titled Operation *Seelöwe* (Sea Lion) was demanded, with the elimination of the RAF's ability to challenge the invasion forces an absolute prerequisite. Some post-war historians have asserted that Hitler's reputed attitude towards Britain's empire as being a stabilising factor in world affairs is reflected in the conditional nature of the directive's wording, especially the '(if necessary) to occupy it completely' phrase. He did hint, however obliquely, upon his willingness to leave the British Empire as a functioning entity provided the European hinterland was left to his and his Fascist Party's control; even if his suggestion had been accommodated, no real degree of trust in the continuation of such a policy when given his track record in deceit could have been indulged.

The primary aim of the German airmen was not so much to inflict destruction among the shipping as it was their hope of drawing Fighter Command into the air and seriously whittling down its ranks. The time lapse between incoming formations being detected on radar screens and the launching of fighters in time to attain an altitude at or above that of the enemy aircraft was particularly critical—even more so when given the location of AVM Park's airfields closest to such threats. Manston, Hawkinge, and Lymnpe were located right on the coast. This meant that the pilots either had to climb inland to gain height in order to avoid being 'bounced' by that element of the *Jagdwaffe* flying ahead of the bombers or trust to fortune in escaping attention should they take the direct outward route that also permitted a greater time span in protecting the convoy concerned.

Park was well aware of the 'Catch 22' situation facing him in fulfilling the duty of convoy protection. He clearly could not provide constant cover extending above the scale of a flight or even a section of fighters. This limitation in turn left the pilots involved facing heavy odds when an assault occurred; the strong fighter cover usually afforded by the Bf 109s—even if initially provided by the single JG51 *Geschwader* on hand until mid-month when JG2, JG26, and JG27 commenced operations—regularly left their RAF adversaries fighting for survival as opposed to warding off the bombers' malign intentions towards the vessels below. The alternative to patrol cover of 'scrambling' fighters in response to radar reports provided no guarantee of timely interception, while the forward 'sweeps' indulged in by a proportion of the overall German fighters cover and known as '*freie Jagd*' ('free hunt') was equally a constant threat to survival in the ensuing 'bounce' and/or dogfight scenarios visited upon the command's pilots.

It was somewhat of a wonder that the overall picture during the onset of the first 'official' stage of the battle tended to be even-spread, although theoretically advantageous to the *Luftwaffe* in terms both of unfettered bombing access and inflicting RAF casualties. Seven days previous (3 July), a large convoy heading for Canada had suffered heavy losses due to a combination of bomber and E-boat assaults. As a consequence, ocean-going convoys assembled in southern England would be redirected round the north of Scotland. Extending their route by several hundred miles was still preferable to the distinct possibility of incurring further losses as evidenced here.

Kanalkampf Fortunes

What the Germans described as the *Kanalkampf* or 'Channel battle' had been recently established by assigning two *Fliegerkorps* (II and VIII) to the duty. In overall command was Ob. Johnnes Fink, the *Kommodore* of KG2, who would quickly gain the sobriquet '*Kanalkampfführer*'. The mix of Do 17 level- and Ju 87 dive-bomber units was regarded as more than sufficient to close down this marine conduit, and the battering of Convoy OA 178 seemed to promise a swift and positive outcome to the action. Adding to the activity as the ships transited the eastern end of the Channel were long-range artillery guns positioned around Calais, but their effect, although spectacular, was at best marginal in terms of strikes.

The first full week of the battle's historically-defined first phase was focused not only on convoy interdiction but also attacks upon seaports albeit sometimes in an indirect fashion. Portland, for example, had already been focused upon thanks to the emergency diversion therein of Convoy OA 178 following its severe harassment on 6 July. Dover was another target probably due to the presence of the Royal Navy; Portsmouth's premier status for the Royal Navy was also targeted.

The turnout of fighters for Fighter Command as seen here at Hawker's Langley factory was never seriously affected by the *Luftwaffe* until the final stages of the Battle of Britain. Hurricane production was largely unaffected, while the bombing of the Spitfire's primary source at Woolston was more than balanced out by the alternative source Castle Bromwich that moreover was concealed within the Midlands' industrial zone.

Action over convoy 'Bread' on the 10th witnessed one RAF fighter downed against two Do 17s and three Bf 110s. The balance was much worse the next day, with six fighters and three pilots lost against no specific convoy-directed enemy aircraft, although four ZG76 machines were MIA during an attack on Portland out of fifteen aircraft declared MIA from all operations. Three pilots were lost the next day, while on the 13th, three fighters were downed, two from No. 56 Squadron with both pilots being declared MIA and two more Hurricanes damaged. The first full week of this phase of the campaign resulted in just two more aircraft casualties, with one fatality; of fifteen fighters listed as damaged, just three were 'Category E', the pilot of one being killed.

A Tragic 'Folly'

The second full week would prove to be sharply more expensive as regards both fighters and pilots; worse still was the greater percentage of deaths recorded (fifteen compared to nine), while a further five air gunners were added to the tally on the

19th. The latter group of airmen had been manning the turrets on the Defiants of 141 Squadron. What transpired here should have sounded the death-knell of the Boulton Paul design, but it would take an equal, albeit accumulative loss figure borne by 264 Squadron the following month to convince the Air Ministry that it had no place in daylight operations.

Although the *Jagdwaffe* had been involved in several encounters with the Defiants during Operation Dynamo and had inflicted casualties, the loss scale had been bearable in terms of continued operational ability. In addition, it seemed the salient fact that the fighter possessed no wing-mounted guns and was accordingly very vulnerable to attack from ahead or below was not taken on board. Today's experience would cruelly expose the deficiency. The squadron had been dispatched from Hawkinge around midday and was pitched into an uneven battle near Dover against the Bf 109s of III/JG51.

The formation of three line-astern sub-units theoretically permitted the leaders to scan the sky but proved no safeguard against the sudden 'bounce' initiated by the enemy. The German pilots delivered their swoop and follow-up passes in a manner that exposed the 'blind' spots on their frantically-manoeuvring adversaries and struck home with deadly effect. Within minutes, no less than six Defiants

A section of Mk I Defiants serving with No. 264 Squadron are holding a neat formation. The absence of any wing-mounted armament was to prove a fatal flaw in the use of the design during daylight operations. Once the *Jagdwaffe* pilots realised this limitation, they would engage from below, an approach angle that rendered the RAF fighter wide open to heavy and generally lethal punishment with little chance of defensive retaliation.

were summarily dispatched, with nine of the twelve crewmembers sharing their mounts' terminal fate; the gunner on a seventh that returned was later declared MIA, although he had baled out (the final moments of one Defiant slanting out of sight behind a tree-screen were captured on film with the commentator reportedly yelling 'There goes another Messerschmitt!!').

By the month's end, Fighter Command's casualties in direct combat continued to feature an overall 'drip-feed' figure. For instance, between 23 and 31 July, a total of fourteen pilots were killed and two survived bale outs, added to which, the material cost was six fighter 'write-offs' and eighteen suffering repairable damage. Normally, the death scale would have been more than acceptable, but not here when given the operational pilot strength and the continuing dearth of replacements coming from the OTUs. The *Luftwaffe* was also suffering on the same and sometimes greater scale, but still held the balance in terms of both numbers of personnel and operational experience—a factor that would weigh heavily upon ACM Dowding's and his immediate subordinates' minds.

A Necessary Expedient?

The convoys' presence in the narrow and accordingly bomber-infested Channel waters begged an important question: why were they being run? After all, the rail transportation system on the mainland could probably have almost as easily handled the movement of these ship-borne cargoes, of which coal formed a prominent percentage. It therefore would seem that the activity was sustained as much with a view to demonstrating that Britain was in charge of its maritime destiny as needing to do so due to an economic necessity. The Admiralty soon tacitly acknowledged the constant threat posed by the *Luftwaffe* bombers and *Kriegsmarine* E-boats by timing the west-bound convoys' passage into the Channel during the hours of darkness, but even this visual barrier did not hinder the latter from making their predatory presence felt, thanks to the *Freya* radar equipment tracking the vessels' progress. In addition, the short nocturnal phase at this time of the year did not grant the vessels much lateral movement before daylight again exposed their ever-vulnerable formations.

In the meantime, a distressing number of fighter pilots were risking and often losing their lives in the process, at a time when their numbers were barely sufficient to sustain let alone beat back the *Luftwaffe*'s manifold assaults. Moreover, the relative lack of a viable Air-Sea Rescue Service added to the problem in that some of the pilots died not while still seated in their cockpits, but as a result of exposure to the Channel waters into which they had safely parachuted. It seems tragically ironic that a sea-conscious nation such as Britain should have been placed well on the back foot in respect of comprehensive ASR facilities that was currently limited to a number of motor launches patrolling the Channel's length. This was a lapse verging on the disgraceful that compared starkly with that of Germany, a nation whose military inclinations were generally directed landwards within the

The quintet of fighter pilots seen at a DFC-awards ceremony attended by King George VI on 27 June are (right to left) Sqn Ldr Leathart (54 Squadron), Wg Cdr Malan (74 Squadron), Flt Lt Deere (54 Squadron) Flt Lt Stanford-Tuck (92 Squadron), and Fg Off. J. Allen (54 Squadron). Only Allen would not survive the conflict, being seen to crash during an attempted crash-landing on 24 July after his Spitfire was disabled in combat.

European continent and whose coastal fringe was much reduced compared to its current major adversary. Though the problem was being addressed, it was too late for those pilots lacking this vital support.

Al Deere's 'Nine-lives' Countdown (2)

Flt Lt Al Deere was by now a veteran fighter pilot with No. 54 Squadron who had already survived being forced-down near Dunkirk from where he was delivered back to Hornchurch. That occurrence was the first of several incidents that were mainly life-threatening and from which he was extremely fortunate to survive. On 9 July, the squadron flying its final sortie had engaged in a dogfight with Bf 109s, during the course of which, he downed a Bf 109 before squaring up to a second in a head-on approach—an action that almost proved fatal for the RAF pilot, since the two aircraft collided.

It was a miracle that neither fighter was destroyed, but in Deere's case, the engine with the propeller blade-tips distinctly curved backwards, immediately seized-up, and quickly began to exude a heavy smoke trail that obscured forward vision. The critically-affected fighter was directed back from the Channel waters as its occupant desperately looked for a crash-landing site near Deal. It was literally blind luck that enabled the aircraft with its Merlin now adding fire to the smoke banner to finally be put down in one piece since the area was liberally strewn with poles intended to lethally obstruct the path of the expected arrival of gliders.

The heavy crash-landing saw Deere escaping uninjured from the impact, but still at peril of dying thanks to a jammed cockpit cover. It was as well that the extra strength accorded him thanks to his skill at boxing enabled him to literally batter his way through the Plexiglas frame that threatened to become a fatal shroud and clamber clear of the fire-stricken airframe named *Kiwi* in recognition of his New Zealand origin. This was the true start of his 'nine-lives' legend, culled over the ensuing months of 1940, and was moreover an expression that he naturally utilised as the title for his post-war autobiography.

Pilot Training Deficiencies

The pre-war training of RAF fighter pilots was a world away from that due to be faced in the maelstrom of Second World War combat operations. For a start, the Air Ministry was not anticipating the presence of an enemy fighter force should Britain be aerially bombarded. Certainly, the circumstances that led to the Germans being located across the English Channel could never have been anticipated. The range-limitation on fighters in traversing the North Sea meant in turn that Fighter Command could expect to confront only bomber formations—hence the creation of the FCA tactical scheme arising from this understandable premise.

The cataclysmic events of May–June 1940 over France and the Low Countries that brought the *Luftwaffe* to Britain's 'front-door' should have woken the Air Ministry to the dangers of persisting with the FCA tactic, but post-war veterans' accounts of the subsequent battle over southern England still throw up consistent references to the various attack patterns being indulged in. However, the most critical operational problem arguably lay in the formations being flown, in particular, the reliance upon the 'Vee' sub-formation.

Not only was this arrangement inhibiting for the two wing men, in that they had to maintain visual contact with their leader as opposed to scanning the sky for enemy aircraft, when engaged in a dogfight, there was little if no chance for all three to provide mutual cover from counterattack compared to the enemy's twin-aircraft *Rotte* equivalent. In cases of the leader taking on a single fighter, there was less likelihood of the No. 3's guns being brought into action; bombers provided a better prospect of multiple engagement by the trio.

The emphasis on formation flying as opposed to learning the rudiments of how to survive the feral atmosphere of an air battle was basically being maintained even as the Second World War had been entered. Worse still, if not also inexcusable, was the relative lack of air gunnery practice that surely should have formed the kernel of each trainee's syllabus since this was the key to survival and success. Now, as the Battle of Britain steadily intensified, this basic lapse in instruction verged on the criminal.

'*Adler Tag*': The Die is Cast

As July wore on and the Channel actions dominated the *Luftwaffe*'s involvement, there was still little or no indication of when the offensive would switch into full gear. Hitler was still apparently vacillating on the issue, although patience with his democratic adversary's continued resistance to any form of negotiation was running thin and would finally dissipate on 1 August. On that day, he issued Directive No. 17, which demanded 'the overthrow of the RAF as soon as possible' after which accomplishment his airmen's attention would be focused upon 'seaports and land-based food storage facilities'. Among other provisions in what was a rather ambivalent set of conditions, Hitler required *Luftwaffe* resources to also be made available for 'support of naval operations against suitable targets' as well as being 'ready to apply full force to operation *Seelöwe*'. Finally, 'terror' attacks were to be initiated only at the Führer's discretion, although his volatile nature could change that situation in an instance regardless of the practical facts.

The full offensive's start date was left open to Göring and his commanders' discretion from 5 August onward and subject to the necessary preparations being completed—as well as Mother Nature in the shape of sound weather conditions. The summer of 1940 was to cast up spells of clear conditions that would normally have been welcomed by the RAF pilots but were heartily loathed whenever these arose since they provided no basic respite from having to face often multiple daily sorties that in turn drained the airmen physically and mentally. The breaks in such unwelcome conditions were naturally unpredictable but had already emerged on several occasions during July to totally preclude or limit *Luftwaffe* operations. As it was, the period between 2 and 7 August again cast up weather patterns that largely precluded any substantive effort in terms of bombing operations. The ensuing weeks of August and September would not be so obliging, however.

Priority for the *Kanalkampf* phase was still being granted as August commenced and was again encapsulated in the events of the 8th, when convoy Peewit (CW9) became the latest focus of attention. The vessels appear to have progressed with marginal disruption between entering the Channel and by-passing the Isle of Wight well to the west. It was at this juncture that the air battle began to take its toll on the RAF as well as the *Luftwaffe*, although three No. 11 Group pilots had earlier been killed as the ships entered the Channel. Ju 87s from *Luftflotte* 3 arrived under heavy escort but were nevertheless punished to the tune of nine downed with ten more bearing various degrees of damage; four Bf 109s and one Bf 110 shared this fate with a similar number of damaged machines. However, the cost to Fighter Command was proportionately more severe with twelve pilot fatalities added to those already lost further east. This attrition-rate if sustained or

Access to the ammunition boxes on the Spitfire were from the wing undersides; this proved an onerous duty when given the low ground clearance compared to the Hurricane, whose access hatch was also on the wing top surface. Despite this difficulty, the armorers would complete loading in between five and ten minutes on average as the battle progressed. Fighter seems to have seen action since the gun aperture covers are missing.

even approached in future would surely prove to be disastrous for any prospect of winning the battle. As for the convoy, barely one-quarter of the twenty ships escaped either destruction (six sunk) or damage by the evening.

On the other hand, the Ju 87's benefit to the overall success of the campaign was by now being thrown steadily into doubt. As a dive-bomber, its potential for pinpoint destruction was superb, but only if it was left undisturbed by aerial opposition. The relatively slow-paced descent in a dive created insuperable problems for any escort fighter since the latter could not sustain the same pace without risk of stalling out. Conversely, the slow pace of ascent following its bomb delivery left the Ju 87 totally vulnerable to counterattack that often was left free of any escort attention thanks to the foregoing problem for the Bf 109s and Bf 110s. The final operational demise for the *Stuka* (a misnomer since it generically means 'dive-bomber' and is therefore not solely applicable to the Ju 87) was only ten days distant from the action over 'Peewit'.

The launch of *Adler Tag* was further delayed due to the adverse weather conditions that only promised a distinct improvement on the 13th with the advent of a high-pressure front advancing from the Atlantic. In the interim period, the *Jagdwaffe* in particular attempted to lure Fighter Command into battle with sorties over Southeast England on the 11th. Although relatively unsuccessful,

The Spitfire's delicate undercarriage with its narrow track rendered itself to dipping sharply with the risk of snagging a wing-tip especially when moving over the uneven airfield grass surfaces that were still prevalent in 1940. This No. 19 Squadron fighter has ground personnel steadying the aircraft as it taxies over Fowlmere's surface. Raised elevators also prevent the aircraft from 'nosing-up' while manoeuvring in this manner.

a heavy raid further west drew the command into a contest that proved very expensive. Against *Luftwaffe* losses of thirty for the day was set twenty-seven, of which all but two involved the death of the pilot, a figure that encompassed a mix of combat-experienced and acolyte individuals; Nos 238 and 601 Squadrons each suffered four fatalities, Nos 74 and 111 Squadrons three, and several squadrons two. The next day was only marginally better, with fifteen MIA losses along with eleven pilots. Here was the recurring worry for ACM Dowding—not the loss of fighters that were currently being produced in more than enough numbers but the human cost. It was a central concern that would only intensify over the next four weeks before relief via enemy miscalculation would come to his and Britain's aid.

Deadly 'Furnace' Effect

One fear prevalent among both Spitfire and Hurricane pilot numbers was that of being burnt, with the Hurricane the more likely aircraft to create the scenario as exemplified by the experience of No. 56 Squadron's Plt Off. Geoff Page. The narrow cockpit confines coupled with the strong slipstream were the conditions for fire to create a 'furnace' effect that would swiftly raise the temperature and render the occupant helpless and unable to evacuate the fighter within mere seconds.

On the 12th, Page's unit encountered a He 111 formation that was surprisingly engaged from the rear, thus providing the gunners with a steadily-encroaching target. One burst of return fire ignited either the header-tank or a wing-tank because Page was suddenly engulfed by the burning fuel that invaded the cockpit. Within a matter of seconds, he had released his harness, slid back the canopy—a logical action that ironically increased the 'furnace' effect—and got clear, but already the searing heat had wrought a horrific degree of damage to his upper body that included his hands.

His descent into the sea saw him struggle free of the canopy but burn holes in his Mae West floatation gear left him with no buoyancy-support. It was more than fortunate that it was not too long before he was fished out by a vessel and delivered to hospital in Ramsgate, thereby saving him from death due either to exposure or loss of energy in remaining afloat and subsequent drowning. He now faced many months of specialist treatment for his burns under the supervision of Archibald McIndoe, a surgeon who would be responsible for resurrecting the physical and psychological fortunes of Page and dozens of his similarly-afflicted contemporaries.

Epr.Gr.210 leads the way

The initial application of *Adler Tag* was still twenty-four hours distant as dawn broke the next day, but the scale of assault launched on the 12th was an unconscious precursor. The relevance of the radar system to Britain's defensive screen was now perceived as important enough for interdiction by the *Luftwaffe*'s specialist unit *Erprobungsgruppe* 210. This specialist force of two Bf 110 and one Bf 109 *Staffeln* led by Hptm. Walter Rubensdörffer was tasked with precision-level attacks on targets. The various radar stations between Dover and as far west as Rye were homed-in upon by the bomb-bearing Bf 110s who disabled three of the four targets that strangely did not include Poling.

Further west, a force of Ju 88s utilised the cover provided by a larger KG51 formation heading for Portsmouth to totally knock out Ventnor's radar facility. This was the nightmare scenario for the RAF—the literal 'blinding' of the electronic support system that enabled interception of the incoming formations, however restricted in height and numbers calculation it might be. Fortunately, the swift provision of mobile set cover with which to largely plug the electronic 'gaps' convinced the Germans that the system was not materially affected—an interpretation that was to work in Britain's longer-term favour. Poling's similar dismemberment on the 18th was also covered-up, but by then, Göring's mindset regarding the value of the radar stations to the RAF pilots had decided him into suspending any further attacks.

Adler Tag Confusion

The offensive got off to a bad start, primarily due to weather forecasts that persuaded the High Command to hold back its forces. A basic technical failure throughout the *Luftwaffe* was now set to cost Ob. Johannes Fink's KG2 dearly; that failure was the lack of inter-unit communication. This critical limitation coupled with radio failure that prevented Fink learning about the weather-induced delay in launching *Adler Tag* meant that the attempt by the Bf 110 escorts from ZG26 to indicate cancellation through frantic manoeuvring around the Do 17 formation did not arouse the appropriate response. The now escort-deprived bombers, whose crews were unknowingly flying into an aerial storm, bore on through cloud-strewn skies towards their targets of Sheerness port and Eastchurch airfield, the latter not a fighter airfield and accordingly irrelevant. There they ran the gauntlet of Nos 74, 111, and 151 Squadrons, and by the time of the last fighter pass, the Fink-led formation was five crews short while the bombing results had little or no adverse effect upon Fighter Command's structure.

The variable weather conditions throughout the day caused several situations where bomber units turned back or where escorts were dispatched despite their charges not having been similarly dispatched. One raid that did produce results was an LG1 *Stuka* assault on Detling airfield that devastated the facilities and created a high death toll; the effect on No. 11 Group was again minimal since Detling was a Coastal Command base. These twin examples were to prove far from the last time non-essential locations in terms of Fighter Command's unfettered function would be targeted, thereby raising one more impediment to winning the battle. In fact, ten more non-fighter airfields would feel the weight of assault by the end of August.

Bomber operations the next day were largely very small in terms of individual formations apart from an abortive Ju 87 raid with Hawkinge the potential target; however, this force's Bf 109 cover dealt sharply with their adversaries to the tune of nine to one. Elsewhere, Epr.Gr.210 lost two Bf 110s during a snap raid on the ever-exposed Manston airfield and seven other aircraft were MIA from operations over Southwest England. KG55 mourned the loss of its *Kommodore* Ob. Stockl, whose He 111 also included Ob. Frank serving with *Fliegerkorps VIII*. As it transpired, any sense of looming relief from combat for the command was about to be dispelled as the 15th dawned.

The cloudless skies were never a welcome sight for the RAF pilots since the condition could almost certainly guarantee a *Luftwaffe* incursion. Here a Hurricane is on the point of flaring out for its landing; in the distance, two companion fighters are curving in towards the airfield. The grass surface on many RAF airfields were steadily giving way to paved runways and perimeter tracks.

Northern Misfortunes, 15 August

The current estimates of the RAF's available frontline fighter strength were such that the Germans regarded the figures as being basically inadequate to protect the major segment of Britain stretching from the south-west Channel and up the east coast as far as southern Scotland. The presence of *Luftflotte* 5 in Scandinavia now saw the He 111s of KG26 along with the Ju 88s from KG30 and ZG76's Bf 110s called into action. The natural expectation was that their targets in Northeast England would be bereft of effective fighter cover, but the crews were unknowingly heading for an individual and corporate Armageddon.

Matters went critically astray well before the first 'traces' appeared on the radar screens. The plan was for a force of He 115 floatplanes to fly a course pointing them towards the Firth of Forth well to the north of the main force's track. Unbelievably, the latter's navigators ending up flying a course almost parallel to their predecessors, thus destroying any chance of the He 115 'feint' being focused upon by the defenders—such as these were expected to be, given the supposed paucity of fighters covering the region.

The lead attack element involved seventy-two KG26 He 111s with twenty-two Bf 110s from I/ZG76 with which No. 72 Squadron made the sole initial contact.

Hptm. Werner Restemeyer's Bf 110D was blown apart when the massive detachable 'belly' tank erupted thanks to an accurate bullet strike. Further RAF squadrons were vectored onto the formations as they flew in some confusion down along the coast, all the time under ever-heavier fighter assault that ultimately culled eight of the Heinkels and seven Bf 110s, with a further number regaining the continent in varying states of distress and bearing dead or injured crew members.

Meanwhile, the fifty-strong Ju 88 force was heading for Driffield further south but ran into Spitfires of No. 616 Squadron and 73 Squadron's Hurricanes. Although the unescorted bombers pressed on to attack the airfield, they were seven crews short as they headed back across the North Sea with three further teams having to crash-land on return. Behind them, they left a trail of devastation that included ten aircraft—all Whitley bombers of No. 102 Squadron, since Driffield was a Bomber Command station.

Operations further south had been fully in swing by this point, with Ju 87 assaults directed at Hawkinge and Lympne, level-bomber attacks on Eastchurch and Rochester, and a low-level strike by Epr.Gr.210 on Martlesham. Further west, *Luftflotte* 3 headed for several targets to put No. 10 Group under similar pressure to its eastern 'neighbour'. However, by the day's end, over 2,000 individual *Luftwaffe* sorties had been flown, but the overall results failed to match the loss of seventy-five aircraft.

Among the personal casualties was Hptm. Rubensdörffer. He had led Epr. Gr.210 on the day's final attack, but probably due to the hazy atmosphere, he mistook Croydon airfield for the Kenley-intended strike; the formations now encountered Nos 32 and 111 Squadrons and the *Gruppenkommandeur*'s fighter was one of six Bf 110s and a single Bf 109 to succumb to their attackers during a furious and sustained dogfight and pursuit at minimum altitude. This specialist unit would witness a multi-fold change in leadership as Rubensdörffer's successors were similarly lost in action.

The casualty-rate among the Bf 110 ranks in turn formed one-third of the day's loss tally, with II/ZG76 the second heavily-depleted element from that *Geschwader*. The planned rendezvous with a Ju 88 formation was to prove stillborn, the cancellation of the bomber's participation not having been received. Instead, the eighteen-strong formation found itself running into a mass of RAF fighters from five squadrons. The heavier armament of the *Zerstörers* availed them little in the ensuing air battle that saw four shot down over or forced to crash-land on British soil, while a further seven found their final resting place in the sea; worse still was the survival figure of just three out of the twenty-two airmen.

Since the official start of the battle, no less than twenty-eight Bf 110s had been declared MIA, with a further number suffering various degrees of damage extending up to total 'write-off' in three cases. This latest savage rebuff to the much-vaunted long-range fighter's combat reputation would soon see its theoretical relegation from a hitherto independent role to one requiring cover-support from its Messerschmitt 'twin' as demanded by Göring; in fact, the Bf 110 would still fly escort sorties bereft of such cover in the future.

The precise harmonisation of a fighter's guns was a basic and vital requirement. In this shot, a Mk I Hurricane belonging to No. 87 Squadron has been raised into a horizontal alignment and retained in that position by twin jack units. This aircraft was later converted to a Mk IIA (with revised serial DR355) and shipped-out to the Soviet Union.

The overall *Luftwaffe* loss tally reflected a mix of bomber and fighter subtotals, with the Bf 110 figure nearly two-thirds of those borne by the bombers (twenty-four to thirty-seven) while 'write-offs' of returning aircraft were two and five respectively. Five more aircraft with two *Aufklärungs* (reconnaissance) examples among the total were also destroyed. The RAF could not rest on its laurels, since thirty-one fighters were destroyed, including four 'write-offs', while the human cost was twelve killed and three captured; a senior death involved Sqn Ldr Terence Lovell-Gregg (CO, No. 87 Squadron).

Al Deere's 'Nine Lives' Countdown (3)

That a fighter pilot had to experience a degree of luck in surviving combat was a truism exemplified by the varied experiences of Flt Lt Al Deere from 54 Squadron. On 15 August, he nearly lost the third of his Second World War 'nine-lives' experience, which on this occasion was arguably due to over exuberance. The final day's sortie during what had been one of the hardest day's actions to date was launched from Manston's coastal location and saw No. 54 Squadron climbing without interception to a height that for once placed them well above the incoming enemy force, whereupon the nine pilots followed instructions to take on the escorts.

Deere had already downed a Bf 109 and latched onto the tail of a second. However, he only closed to firing range when above Calais-Marck airfield, whose circuit was occupied by several fighters—two of which made for him in a bid to cut off his now-belated retreat. Deere was quickly fighting for his very existence as his assailants remorselessly followed his every evasive manoeuvre and finally landed heavy strikes on the Spitfire that by now was down to less than 2,000 feet.

It was fortunate by then that friendly soil was looming up, forcing the Bf 109s to disengage, but any sense of relief was soon dispelled when the engine started to falter before bursting into flames. Inverting the aircraft, Deere attempted to bale out, but got snagged-up on the fuselage via his parachute pack. The ground was looming terminally up when he somehow was cast clear, but he suffered a bad wrist injury due to striking the tail plane and barely managed to then pull his ripcord before floating down to land close to the now-disintegrated fighter.

16 August

Tangmere was one of seven sector stations in No. 11 Group, but its immunity from attack was now at an end as battle was renewed on the 16th. The Ju 87 force involved destroyed or badly damaged all the hangars, as well as numerous support structures, but the Operations Block remained intact. Ventnor was again bombed despite Göring's previous injunction to the contrary; severe restriction in function for several days was the result thanks to the scale of renewed destruction.

West Malling was again bombed, but planned strikes on Hornchurch and Biggin Hill never materialised—a treble stroke of fortune for the command despite the

A Mk I Hurricane assigned to No. 607 Squadron is photographed at its current base of Tangmere. An auxiliary squadron formed in 1930, it transferred to this No. 11 Group airfield during the height of the Battle of Britain, September. Its status as an 'original' production airframe is confirmed by the untapered radio mast, but it is likely updated by the Rotol propeller with its vital constant-speed unit (CSU).

feelings of the personnel at the former airfield. The geographically-isolated nature of Manston that left it exceptionally prone to 'sneak' raids at low level saw it receive the latest baptism of fire with the airfield well hammered and two aircraft destroyed. It was hardly surprising that the men's morale was reaching an almost mutinous level.

'Singular' Award

The Victoria Cross is Britain's highest military award, and it still seems unbelievable that only one was granted to a Fighter Command individual during the entire course of the Second World War. Flt Lt James Nicholson (249 Squadron) was leading a section that was 'bounced' by what he later described as Bf 110s. His Hurricane was set on fire and the flames enveloped the pilot who had suffered injuries from 20-mm splinters. His immediate desire to bale out was momentarily halted when he caught sight of his assailant; he accordingly closed-up on the *Zerstörer* and shot it down before clearing the cockpit. He floated down to earth with severe burns to his hands and lower torso, his trousers having been largely burnt-off. Even this aspect of his venture was far from passive because he was shot at and injured by a Home Guard member as he neared the ground.

German losses totalled ten Bf 109s MIA (one lost to mid-air collision) and two fatal crashes on return; six Bf 110s MIA plus three 'write-offs' on return was added, along with seventeen bombers, one of the fighters being flown by Maj. Karl (II/ZG2 *Kommandeur*) who lost his life. Nearly half of the latter (eight) involved Ju 87s downed during the Tangmere action. The cost to Fighter Command was twenty-two fighters shot down or otherwise 'written-off', with nine pilots killed, one (Fg Off. Henry Ferriss) to a collision with a Do 17 during a head-on approach by No. 111 Squadron.

Included in this figure was Plt Off. 'Billy' Fiske, an American 'volunteer' with No. 601 Squadron; he crash-landed his fire-afflicted Hurricane back at Tangmere but subsequently died from his burns. No. 266 Squadron was particularly punished during what was its baptism of fire in combat, with three, including Sqn Ldr Rodney Wilkinson (CO), killed and five Spitfires lost—an initial experience that was to be paralleled by more than one unit during the battle. The score was marginally levelled up by the fatal downing of Hptm. Karl Ebbighausen (II/JG26 *Kommandeur*), an equally senior loss.

The RAF defenders' undoubted surprise at the lack of *Luftwaffe* offensive inroads into British airspace the next day was heightened by the almost perfect weather conditions overhead. The exact reason for the enemy's failure to utilise these very favourable conditions remains unclear, although the scale of losses over the past forty-eight hours may have resulted in the *Luftwaffe*'s inertia. The morrow would harshly dispel any lingering illusions as to an extension of relief for Fighter Command, however.

The propeller on VY: Q is revved-up by the mechanic in the cockpit as its pilot begins to board his charge—right foot in the extended 'stirrup' frame and left leg about to be raised onto the wing surface. Rolled-up sleeves suggest the flight is non-operational since combat altitude usually demanded heavier clothing due to the frigid atmosphere. Overlapping propeller spinner indicates unit is a Rotol-produced item.

The Human 'Crisis'

The immediate technical crisis for the command was already being further heightened by a human crisis in the form of both pilot numbers and their individual combat effectiveness. No less than seventy-eight pilots were KIA and twenty-seven were wounded between 10 and 17 August, which was negatively matched by just seventy replacements being fed into the squadron ranks since the beginning of the month. Further 'combing' of the various other commands—Bomber, Coastal, and Training—as well as the FAA, who had already fifty-nine volunteers, some before the battle even commenced, was bringing in pilots to supplement those received from the OTUs. However, effecting an instant switch from flying usually more sedate aircraft types to handling a high-speed fighter was far from easy, especially when faced with the extreme pressures of combat operations.

Two squadrons were about to be declared operational. The Czech pilots manning No. 310 Squadron would be granted operational clearance on the 17th as would No. 1 (Canadian) Squadron, just in time to participate in one of the stiffest tests for Fighter Command to date. There was a further source from which pilots could be placed on frontline service, but the individuals concerned were currently being held back for linguistic as much as technical reasons. Nos

302 and 303 Squadrons were staffed by airmen from Poland. The natural desire to get at their truly-hated adversary was tempered in their host's minds by their general lack of English knowledge. Until this could be brought up to a level where RAF terminology was clearly understood, they were being retained in a training-up function that in turn left them extremely frustrated (a number of their individual contemporaries were already operational within several squadrons thanks probably to a superior knowledge of English).

The Hardest Day? 18 August

At this stage of the battle, the operational aircraft statistics were continuing to reflect at least a 3:1 factor in the *Luftwaffe*'s favour. On hand across the Channel were 1,040 bombers, of which one-quarter were Ju 87s; the *Jagdwaffe*'s equivalent figure of 940 included just short of 200 Bf 110s, which left a marginally-superior number of Bf 109s to challenge their single-engined RAF contemporaries. However, the figure of around 920 Blenheims, Defiants, Gladiators, Hurricanes, and Spitfires on operational status out of marginally more than 1,000 in squadron service with which to directly challenge the enemy's principal assaults along Britain's southern stretches was diluted by around 22 per cent thanks to the need to staff No. 13 Group covering Northern England, Scotland, and Northern Ireland.

The non-operational 302 and 303 (Polish) Squadrons' complement of Hurricanes had also to be excluded. The net figure was further reduced by unserviceable aircraft, while the Blenheim, Gladiator, and even the Defiant elements were questionable assets to pit against the *Jagdwaffe*. Furthermore, the need to concentrate on fighter destruction alone was a luxury handed to the *Jadgwaffe*; in contrast, the RAF fighters had to avoid direct contact as much as possible in order to bring maximum pressure to bear upon the German bomber strength that was the key to perceived German success.

Although the overall pressure upon Fighter Command's personnel was now to be a constant for much of the ensuing August period and well into September, there were to be several days when the operational tempo reached an almost unbearable level; such was the case on 18 August, a day that witnessed one of the highest number of RAF sorties and whose results proved to be a catalyst for tactical changes within both Fighter Command's and the *Luftwaffe*'s structure to be applied henceforward.

To date, the key importance of the sector stations in the carrying out of timely, if not always height-advantaged or numerically-superior, interceptions of the incoming formations had not seemingly dawned upon the German High Command. Nor were the Germans aware of the extreme vulnerability of the surface-built operations blocks. However, the benefit to Fighter Command arising from their efficient function was now to be placed under almost unremitting strain and dislocation over the next twenty days following Göring's injunction to Kesselring and Sperrle to direct their full attention towards Fighter Command's airfields.

There are few Hurricane survivors from the Battle of Britain; this is an original from the first production batch that was completed with fabric wings. On 18 August 1940, the wounded Plt Off. Looker brought his No. 615 Squadron charge back with heavy damage. Aircraft now hangs up in London's Science Museum. The stencilled serial is incorrect and should read as L1592.

Kenley was one of the seven No. 11 Group Sector stations and was scheduled for multiple KG76 assault with the final element involving a target approach at minimum altitude by nine III/KG76 Do 17s. This formation took off from Cormeilles-en-Vexin and skimmed across the Channel and then the English countryside; in doing so, the bombers provided little warning via the radar screens, although ground-observer reports did filter in to Kenley. As it was, their final approach was met by a barrage of light-calibre guns as well as parachute-assisted cables (PAC) fired into their path as the aircraft traversed the target.

The resultant strike proved expensive for both parties. The airfield was heavily damaged with three of the four hangars set ablaze and other buildings totally or partially destroyed, although the operations block was spared. On the other hand, of the nine-strong formation, only five regained French soil. Fw. Petersen's bomber leading the port-side *Kette* was hauled out of the sky by a PAC, over whose site this sub-unit had tracked, and *Unteroffiziers* Gunther Unger and Schumacher were subsequently forced to 'ditch' their shot-up aircraft.

Hptm. Roth's (9/KG76 *Staffelkapitän*) Do 17 with Obltn. Rudolf Lamberty as pilot was set on fire and finally made a heavy crash-landing just north of Biggin Hill. One of the three crewmembers, Fw. Eberhard, parachuted, and he did so with the blazing aircraft now so low that his canopy opened and swung its charge just once before depositing him unharmed on the ground. The crash site's location induced the crew and their captors to hastily seek shelter when the airfield then became the subject of attack.

What should have been the initial assault on Kenley involving dive-bombing by II/KG76's Ju 88s and a level bombing by Do 17s of I and III/KG76 was as much foiled by the disruptive effect of a head-on assault launched by No. 32 Squadron during final run-up to the target as by the vast, smothering plume of smoke arising from the smashed facilities that would have thwarted the former type of bombing approach. In the event, the Ju 88s diverted to West Malling's already well-punished facilities. Kenley's sister-sector station nestling scant miles away at Biggin Hill was later attacked by KG1 but with surprisingly minimal effect on this occasion—a stay of execution that would extend to the month's end when the aerial axe would harshly descend.

The latest attack on Manston could have reaped a rich reward in fighters and/or pilots. I/JG51 were orbiting the area as a protective force for returning bombers when its leader sighted No. 266 Squadron alighting there to refuel. The resultant descent and firing pass ended with two Spitfires destroyed and six others receiving degrees of reparable damage; the pilots were thankfully absent from their already-stationery charges before the sudden assault's onset. Six days previous, No. 65 Squadron had been even more fortunate to escape a 'snap' attack by Epr.Gr.210 that caught the Spitfires as they frantically 'scrambled'; only one fighter failed to get off due to bomb-blast stopping its propeller, but no aircraft or pilot casualties were otherwise incurred.

Another *Zerstörer* martyrdom was unknowingly looming that involved all three ZG26 *Gruppen* during the course of two sorties. The first involved twenty crews supporting the planned KG76 follow-up raid on Kenley. A strong force of Spitfires and Hurricanes engaged the in-coming formations, and as the Bf 110 pilots tangled with No. 32 Squadron, they were in turn 'bounced' by No. 64 Squadron. The German crews attempted with some success in deflecting attention away from their Do 17 charges, but soon began to absorb casualties. The result was the absence from Saint-Omer of five crews from I *Gruppe* and four from II *Gruppe*. Hptm. Herbert Kaminski from the former sub-unit succeeding in 'ditching' and along with Uffz. Strauch was fortunate to survive a prolonged period in their dinghy until rescued by a *Kriegsmarine* vessel. The second sortie raised the MIA figure to thirteen, with three 4/ZG26 and one 8/ZG26 aircraft involved. The horrendous aircraft loss-tally was equalled by the human cost of eighteen dead and six *Kriegsgefangenen* (POWs).

The punishment inflicted upon the Bf 110 contingent was destined to be shared by their Ju 87 companions as the day wore on. Over 100 *Stukas* from StG.3 and 77 lifted off from their Caen airfields and took up a course for the region around the Isle of Wight, their targets being Poling radar station and Gosport, Thorney Island, and Ford airfields. Some 150 Bf 109s provided the cover force. Once again, the former target was the sole one directly affecting Fighter Command's viability, the airfields accommodating Research, Coastal Command, and Fleet Air Arm in function.

Serious damage was certainly inflicted at all four locations, but the RAF pilots were still able to penetrate the fighter screen that should have seriously intruded

Plt Off. A. Lewis grabs his parachute harness from the stabiliser surface as a mechanic springs from his No. 85 Squadron Mk I Hurricane ready to operate the auxiliary power trolley beneath the starboard wing. Picture taken at Castle Camps, a satellite airfield for Debden. Lewis scored a string of victories before being shot down and injured flying with No. 249 Squadron during September; however, he did survive through to 1945.

upon their adversaries who were outnumbered by more than two to one. The range limitation of the Bf 109, coupled with the inability to accompany the Ju 87s during their attacks without laying themselves open to exploitation, probably played a part in what was a recurring problem for the *Jagdwaffe* pilots. Only two No. 601 Squadron Hurricanes were shot down, with four more fighters damaged.

As for their charges, three Ju 87s were taken out during the attack on Ford along with one of the Poling attackers, but this figure was well exceeded during the attack on Thorney Island by I/StG.77. No. 43 Squadron interceded during the actual assault to reduce the thirty-one-strong formation by five and then Nos 152, 601, and 602 Squadron joined in. The single 7.92-mm rear-firing gun was no match for an eight-gun barrage delivered at minimum range against a slow-moving if manoeuvrable airframe as evidenced once again today.

By the time the enemy force was free of the lethal storm of gunfire, seven more crews had been shorn from its ranks and two more were 'written-off' following fatal crashes in Normandy. The hitherto fearsome reputation earned by the Junkers dive-bomber had now been so sharply eroded that the stage was accordingly set for a significant reduction in the *Luftwaffe*'s bomber strength. This was the case even if the *Stuka*'s use for other than shipping or coastal-fringe targets was not valid in terms of the overall bombing offensive—at least not until air superiority was a proven fact.

The raids launched further east by *Luftflotte* 2 during the late afternoon witnessed KG53's He 111s and KG2's Do 17s dispatched to attack North Weald and Hornchurch respectively. Both being within No. 11 Group, AVM Park called upon No. 12 Group to 'scramble' squadrons that would remain as cover for these airfields while his group strength was utilised in making direct interception of the incoming bombers. In the event, neither assault materialised since increasing cloud cover forced a complete withdrawal well short of the targets; the four He 111s and a single Do 17 culled from the formations suggested sound escort cover in the face of a significantly higher *Jagdwaffe* loss-tally. No. 12 Group's prompt reaction naturally provided no hint of the looming dispute on tactics that would pit AVM Leigh-Mallory against his C-in-C and AVM Park's views on how to dispose the command's squadrons against the *Luftwaffe* incursions.

The 'Butcher's Bill' for both sides was high as regards aircraft and airmen. A figure of sixty-nine *Luftwaffe* aircraft was deleted from its overall establishment either through loss in combat or through bearing irreparable damage on return while a further twenty-six aircraft suffered degrees of reparable damage with several airmen dead or injured; this was out of a total number of just under 1,000 individual sorties. The greatest MIA casualty was the Ju 87 at sixteen; Bf 110 strength was reduced by thirteen, with twelve Bf 109s added in; and standard bomber ranks were reduced by twelve.

Ltn. Hans-Otto Lessing was a II/JG51 pilot who greatly admired his *Staffelkapitän* and leading *Experte* Hptm. Horst Tietzen. Just twenty-four hours prior to the 18th, he had written home expressing the opinion that he 'would not change places with a king', so great was his enjoyment as a fighter pilot and further that 'peacetime would seem boring after this'. Today, he and his superior, whom he so respected,

Time was of the essence in replenishing the fuel, ammunition, and supporting facilities on the command's fighters and getting them back up in time to effectively challenge the *Luftwaffe* formations. The blown covers on the gun apertures indicate the Fowlmere-based Spitfire has seen action and needs to have a new set of ammunition boxes that are being inserted.

were united in death when both became victims of No. 501 Squadron pilots. Other notable losses were Maj. Reinhold Tamm (II/KG53 *Kommandeur*) and Hptm. Herbert Meisel in command of I/StG.77. Such losses were slowly but inexorably eating into the future efficiency and spirit of the *Luftwaffe* crews just as much as the reverse casualty-tally was doing so to their opponents.

Fighter Command's aircraft losses totalled thirty-one, but more serious was that eleven pilots were killed or died later and only one of the other nineteen escaped injuries that also rendered eleven of this number out of action for the remainder of the battle. The severity of these casualties was heightened by the fact that they arose from just over two-thirds of the overall 600 sorties flown this day, the remainder involving convoy cover and potential enemy reconnaissance incursions. Fighter numbers might well be away beyond the German Intelligence Service's current estimates, but the burgeoning crisis regarding pilot numbers was a major barrier to Fighter Command remaining a viable threat to the *Luftwaffe*'s hopes of gaining air supremacy.

Slaughter of the Innocents (1)

The fate of one casualty encapsulated the inevitable risk inherent in pitching acolyte pilots with minimal experience into the battle. Plt Off. Neville Solomon had arrived at Debden on 15 August and now was part of a squadron sortie dispatched along with several other units to intercept the retreating *Luftwaffe* force. Solomon was stationed as 'weaver' at the rear, no place for even an experienced pilot let alone one totally bereft of combat experience. The squadron duly entered the fray but when the air battle was over Solomon was nowhere to be seen nor had his disappearance been observed by anyone. His life had almost certainly been brutally expunged by a Bf 109 and his Hurricane despatched into the Channel since he remains MIA to this day.

The Claim Game

Several adverse factors tended to come into play when claiming an adversary as even a probable, let alone a confirmed kill. The obvious one was the inadvisability of following the stricken aircraft to final impact with the ground, especially when flying thousands of feet up. Added to the real chance of being 'picked off' while maintaining prolonged visual contact with the victim was the responsibility towards one's fellow pilots in keeping the pressure on the enemy aircraft still milling around as well as keeping them free from being 'bounced'.

Another misleading factor *vis-à-vis Luftwaffe* aircraft was that of smoke trails issuing from the engines. Whether this was due to the German fuel's lower octane-quality compared to that in RAF use or some other technical reason, distinctive trails would tend to exude; this was the case with the Bf 109 (and later the Fw 190) when indulging in the 'split-S' or half-roll manoeuvre, resulting in

'We few, we happy few, we band of brothers.' Shakespeare's immortal words particularly apply to the pilots of Fighter Command during the Second World War and are no more appropriate than during the Battle of Britain when the odds against survival, let alone success, were initially stacked in favour of the *Luftwaffe*. The group of No. 601 Squadron personnel grouped around a Hurricane's tail sums up this general attitude.

regular claims that the Hurricane or Spitfire's strikes had induced fatal damage. The He 111 was also prone to exuding smoke trails, as was the Ju 88; in their case, the strikes appeared to induce this condition but may have been at least partially due to the bomber pilots' pushing open their throttles to gain extra power.

Even the emergence of flames from the engines or airframe was not always absolute confirmation of the aircraft's imminent destruction. Regular instances of fires being started and subsequently extinguished either by crew actions or through slipstream effect, etc., would occur among the ranks of the Anglo–American Bomber Commands as an example. Only where an aircraft blew-up or disintegrated in mid-air or a pilot abandoned his single-engined machine could a kill be truly registered—and then strictly-speaking only if backed up by eyewitnesses.

One of the principle reasons for excessive claim figures especially arose when formations engaged one another. An aircraft would be set upon and seen by its initial attacker to fall away spinning and/or trailing smoke, fire, or both. The same aircraft could then be latched on to by one or more adversary as it wallowed towards the ground or in some cases was brought under control. The true *Luftwaffe* casualty figures would only be confirmed after the Second World War, following examination of salvaged records that were generally meticulously maintained.

7

From Crisis to Salvation

The events of what was to become known in post-war Britain as the 'Hardest Day' of the battle naturally did not sit well with *Reichsmarschall* Göring when he held his conference twenty-four hours later. Several decisions were accordingly made that affected overall *Luftwaffe* operations, only one of which materially advanced the offensive's effectiveness in its application:

1. The withdrawal of all Ju 87 units from direct involvement in the battle was immediately put into effect although the units were held in readiness; their future use was anticipated once Operation *Seelöwe* was initiated.
2. Göring acknowledged, however reluctantly, that there were serious limitations in the deployment of his beloved Bf 110 *Zerstörer* as a pure fighter *vis-à-vis* its overall performance against the RAF fighters. Instead provision was to be made for Bf 109 support when flying future sorties. This was a case of 'robbing Peter to pay Paul' because the action would thereby place one more limitation upon the single-engined machine's unfettered deployment as a superiority fighter.
3. A more positive and ominous decree for Fighter Command's immediate fortunes related to the concentration of all Bf 109 units within *Luftflotte* 2's sphere of influence, this to be supposedly balanced out by the redeployment of *Luftflotte* 5's Bf 110 force within *Luftflotte* 3—an action that clearly contradicts Göring's injunction contained within (2) regarding Bf 109 support.

As it was, the greater number of Bf 109s amassed particularly at close range to No. 11 Group's airfields was likely to make the task of breaking through to the bombers even harder than was the case to date. Over the last eight days of August and the first week of September, Fighter Command's pilots and support teams would be hard pressed to a point where the enemy appeared to be winning through to victory and thereby clearing the way for Operation *Seelöwe*'s initiation.

The second Polish fighter squadron to be formed, but the first to see direct action in the Battle of Britain flying within No. 11 Group was No. 303. These three Mk I Hurricanes are lifting off from what is certainly Northolt, the sensor having totally blanked out the background. The unit was credited with a high kill rate between its introduction in late August and the battle's official conclusion on 31 October.

20–23 August

To date, the *Luftwaffe*'s attention had not been regularly concentrated upon the RAF's airfields assigned to Fighter Command. Certainly, a number of airfields had been attacked, but on at least several occasions, the locations were assigned to other commands—Driffield (Bomber Command) and Detling (Coastal Command) were cases in point. For the bulk of the next eighteen days, the enemy's concentration would be far better focused upon those airfields serving Nos 10 and 11 Groups, with a consequent dislocation in proper function.

Between the 20th and the 23rd, the weather came to the defenders' relief. Operations were restricted to warding off attacks on convoys with occasional inland attacks also mounted. During this time, being conscious of an inordinate number of pilots not surviving their descent in to the Channel, ACM Park issued an order that his pilots should not venture out beyond land to any extent except in extreme circumstances. Bombers should be the priority for attack wherever possible—an increasingly difficult act to carry out in the face of the increased scale of fighter support. On a higher level, he requested that No. 12 Group provide cover for his airfields on the northern fringes of No. 11 Group, an act that further increased Leigh-Mallory's ire at not being more deeply involved in the main battle.

24–31 August

The 'Battle of the Airfields' commenced in earnest on the 24th, with North Weald, Hornchurch, and Manston receiving punishment. In the latter case, the airfield's proximity to the Kent coastline and minimal distance from the French coast had already rendered, and would continue to render, it particularly vulnerable to 'sneak' assault. This latest assault had reduced its facilities to a state of virtual ruin, while the morale of the airmen permanently stationed there was arguably at rock bottom.

In truth, its use as a forward base was almost criminal in nature since any aircraft 'scrambled' either had to fly inland to gain any measure of height or were vulnerable to a 'bounce' if heading directly towards the incoming formations. The final decision to abandon the airfield towards the month's end came none too soon as far as the fighter pilots, and even more so the ground support personnel, were concerned and may have been delayed in similar manner to persisting with the routing of convoys through the Channel on the grounds of not giving the Germans a psychological advantage.

The next day, Hornchurch, Debden, and Warmwell (No. 10 Group) were targeted, but the defenders largely saved the No. 11 Group duo from serious assault; twenty-four hours later, the overall picture was more fraught. On this occasion, no less than six airfields—all but one in No. 11 Group—were bombed in the course of three separate raids. Already, a worrying pattern of deteriorating kill–loss ratios was emerging to add to the material damage suffered on the ground.

Although the *Luftwaffe* had reportedly lost around 100 aircraft, Fighter Command's establishment in aircraft had gone down by over seventy, while a good proportion of their pilots had been killed or injured. Park was none too happy with No. 12 Group's inability to reach Debden in time to avert its assault, despite the airfield being mere miles distant from Duxford. This was not the first time in recent days that these circumstances had arisen, and Park now issued an order to his controllers to route any call for No. 12 Group support via Fighter Command's HQ.

A brief respite in operational activity on the 27th was displaced the next day by two more airfields being bombed, although one suffering its second ordeal (Eastchurch) was not a fighter base. At this point, *Luftflotte* 3 was ordered to transfer its attention to nocturnal bombing operations, but any prospect of relief for Fighter Command due to diminished *Luftwaffe* numbers was not yet in the offing as *Luftflotte* 2 more than kept up the pressure, particularly on the 31st. No less than six of No. 11 Group's airfields along with Duxford were assailed, but Eastchurch again appeared on the target list.

Equally punishing was the mounting material and human cost, with no less than ninety-four RAF fighters 'struck off charge' along with a fair number of their occupants. The worst statistical day was the 31st, when the *Luftwaffe*'s thirty-nine aircraft casualty list was equal to that of Fighter Command. On this basis of machines written-off and pilots killed or injured, the odds against sustaining the battle, let alone winning it, were lengthening with no sign of improvement. Nor was Mother Nature intervening. The largely brazen skies existing during this phase of the battle would continue to mock the defenders in their desire for the weather conditions to deteriorate and so bring a measure of relief from the present scale of assault.

The loss of 145 pilots, sixty-four of whom were killed, in the week of 24–31 August constituted a huge diminution in pilot numbers, not only quantitatively, but also in operational experience, since a proportion were combat veterans reaching back as far as Dunkirk. The replacement personnel were more and more proving to be acolytes regarding their experience—or rather non-experience—of aerial fighting. This unfortunate circumstance not only affected new pilots posted in direct from an OTU, but also individuals already in regular service. Al Deere recollected greeting a fellow New Zealander joining No. 54 Squadron who had been trained as a light bomber pilot followed by minimal flight time in a Spitfire; he further professed complete ignorance of how to operate its gunsight since he had no experience of firing the fighter's weapons.

Between June and September, No. 92 Squadron was assigned to No. 10 Group guarding the western stretch of the Channel coast. In this view, what looks like one section in the far centre is starting its take-off run while two of what will form the other section is taxiing out with the third Spitfire of the sub-unit partially visible on the right.

The End for a Folly

The bloody repulse suffered by No. 141 Squadron on 19 July that witnessed its withdrawal from daylight operations was still not convincing enough proof of the deadly fallacy behind the Defiant's use as a day fighter since No. 264 Squadron were still functioning in the role—a role that could be summed up as 'chase me and I will shoot you down' and therefore lethally naïve in the current operational circumstances. Of course, the increasingly desperate state of Fighter Command's overall strength probably, if barely, justified its frontline presence. Today's event would bring about a sea change for the design that henceforth would revert to nocturnal duties.

On the 28th, Maj. Galland was leading JG26's III/*Gruppe* providing close escort to a KG53 formation as the bombers were crossing-in near Dover. He later claimed that his sight focused upon an initially unidentified and smaller formation that was below the He 111s and paralleling their course. Then the realisation that the 'bogies' possessed gun turrets with their barrels angled-up towards his charges struck home. Immediately he called for a 'bounce', whose swift effect was to cause what was No. 264 Squadron's fighters to be diverted from their intention to lethally enfilade their prey with concentrated gunfire and to now scatter in what was vain evasion efforts.

Sqn Ldr Garvin who had replaced Sqn Ldr Hunter following the latter's loss on the 24th managed to jump from his fire-stricken aircraft but not his gunner, Flt Lt C Ash. The CO was the sole survivor from the total of four Defiants downed while two further crews staggered back to Hornchurch in their shot-up fighters. This second drubbing in four days (three MIA crews including Hunter's and a fourth aircraft written-off along with Sgt W. Machin killed) appears to have been the evidence if any was really needed that the Defiant's relegation from daylight operations was mandatory.

Al Deere's 'Nine lives' Countdown (4)

The confusing imbroglio emanating from a dogfight was ever likely to cast up the chance of what is now termed a 'friendly fire' incident. The split-second confusion of what was a swirling mass of aircraft did lead to misidentification as Deere asserted on this occasion. The squadron had tangled with the Bf 109 escorts for a Do 17 formation but whether his assailant was a fellow-unit pilot or from another squadron is unclear. Regardless of this, he was able to safely abandon the Spitfire and make a protracted descent—right into a farmer's prize plum tree, an act that was not to its owner's pleasure as expressed forcibly to Deere.

Biggin Hill's Final Martyrdom (30 August)

Biggin Hill was one of seven sector airfields whose geographically-central location in terms of approach to London had rendered it a prime target along with nearby Kenley and it had already received heavy, if not lethal, attention to date. Today's assault was destined to administer the worst blow, however. It was late in the day when Epr.Gr.210 headed inwards at an oblique angle before swooping upon its airfield prey. The force of just nine Bf 110s (still quoted as Ju 88s in some contemporary accounts of the battle) struck home with deadly force. To the toll of over forty dead, many in one of the designated shelters, was added the destruction of numerous structures and the severing of the operations block's power cables.

Three further raids during the next forty-eight hours witnessed the operations block being directly struck and its communication links again severed. A transfer of its staff and facilities to a local building ensured some form of sector control was regained, but the immediate reduction in quality of the ground-to-air guidance system was now wide open to exploitation by the Germans. A similar dislocation of the sector station facilities at Hornchurch, Kenley, and Tangmere that formed the eastern and southern ring of airfields around London was only adding to the overall disruption in the command's control efficiency at this crucial juncture in the battle and presaged even worse times ahead for Dowding's defensive network.

'Big Wing': Fact or Fiction?

A major bone of contention that grew into a feud during and after the battle was concluded cantered round the concept of a 'Big Wing' formation as put forward by AVM Leigh-Mallory, and that resulted in such an entity being created and operating from Duxford and Fowlmere. The basic brief for No. 12 Group was the protection of the Midlands' industrial resources, but a secondary requirement related to No. 11 Group; this was the protection of AVM Park's northerly airfields (Debden, North Weald, in particular) while their squadrons were up. The implied 'side-lining' of No. 12 Group from joining-in the main action to the south did not sit well with Leigh-Mallory nor with some of the pilots for which thirty-year old Sqn Ldr Douglas Bader was a prominent spokesman and arguably the catalyst for what would evolve into the 'Duxford Wing'.

Bader was a Cranwell College graduate officer who shortly after graduation had lost both legs in an air accident involving a Bristol Bulldog of No. 23 Squadron (an incident that he attributed to 'my own bloody fault!') and following his invalidating-out of the RAF, he had only rejoined in 1939. He asserted that the current policy of dispatching single squadrons should be superseded by multi-unit formations; in effect, force should be met by force. An admirable theory, it blatantly ignored the current operational circumstances:

1. The overall number of fighters on hand between No. 11 Group and the supporting squadrons from No. 12 Group was still too small to handle the scheme efficiently;

this central factor in turn challenged the accusation of operational 'timidity' being displayed by AVM Park that was the basis for the 'Big Wing' alternative.

2. The extra time-factor in assembling Wings would eat dangerously into their ability to match if not exceed the altitude levels of the incoming formations—one of Bader's stated dictums being 'he who controls the height, controls the battle'.
3. The still-uncertain state of the radar system in guaranteeing the height and direction of the enemy formations as well as numbers involved when coupled to the enemy's ability to launch several either simultaneous or successive sub-forces could result in the attackers slipping through thanks to the defenders either being dispatched too late or alternately being in the wrong position.

The seeds for the wing's creation were only sown on 30 August when Bader led his No. 242 Squadron up from Duxford to cover North Weald as requested by No. 11 Group. His biography recorded that he disregarded the controller's instructions by swinging well to the west in order to gain a favourable up-sun angle—despite the radar plots on the incoming formation indicating the more south-east angle of approach to North Weald (official squadron records by contrast indicate otherwise in that the controller's course vectors were adhered to).

The subsequent action witnessed a plethora of kill claims and the thwarting of the airfield's intended attacking formation. In fact, the enemy formation had been briefed to attack other targets further west; moreover, at least one other squadron was involved in this engagement. When congratulated by Leigh-Mallory on his return, Bader asserted that the tally would have been multiplied in proportion to more than one squadron's presence. This was a concept that the AVM took on board, arguably as much as a swipe at his C-in-C and No. 11 Group contemporary as it being a viable option that would advance his group's involvement in the battle.

Worse still, as well as extremely discourteous to Dowding and Park, was the reported selling of the scheme to the Prime Minister by Peter McDonald, Bader's adjutant and a serving MP; unaware of the involvement of several other squadrons in the 30 August sortie, the often romantically-inclined Churchill probably accepted the concept as a superior method of striking at the *Luftwaffe* (although he must have also had some knowledge of the ever-tenuous state of Fighter Command's resources that in turn should have tempered his enthusiasm).

The upshot of all this manoeuvring, political and otherwise, was the assembling of Nos 242 and 310 (Czech) Squadrons along with No. 19 Squadron at Duxford's adjacent Satellite Fowlmere into the original wing that would later be expanded due to the inclusion of Nos 312 (Polish) and 611 Squadrons by mid-September; however, the latter unit was only declared fully operational several weeks later and operated on detachment from Digby further north.

The first sortie was made on the 6th; overall, results accruing from its operation during the rest of September and into the October period of the official battle would be at best spotty both in terms of successful interceptions and numbers of kills. However, the concept still had a future role to play in Fighter Command

No. 310 (Czechoslovakian) Squadron was formed in July 1940 and was based between then and June 1941 at Duxford. As such, its function was as an element of the controversial Duxford Wing during the latter stages of the Battle of Britain. The largely bare tree line around what was still a grass airfield forms a backcloth to one of the squadron's Mk I Hurricanes.

operational planning when the fight was taken over the Channel and into the *Luftwaffe*'s backyard from 1941 onward.

A noted author's assertion that Leigh-Mallory's purported enthusiasm for mass formations was not matched on 15 August given his minimal response to *Luftflotte* 5's attack on Driffield should be put in proper context. The 'Big Wing' theory so often ascribed primarily to him was of course not his but rather Bader's and only retrospectively taken on board by the No. 12 Group C-in-C on 30 August as recorded in this account.

Al Deere's 'Nine Lives' Countdown (5)

No. 54 Squadron's Al Deere had already been four times through the combat 'mill' in terms of survival, but what was to transpire on 31 August would surely top the list of his manifold escapes from serious injury or death. The squadron was on the point of being belatedly 'scrambled' from Hornchurch at the very point where a He 111 formation having broken through in still-intact form was now zeroing-in upon the airfield. Deere had reached the runway's end with his section, and all three Spitfires accelerated desperately down the runway after the other fast-receding sections in what now became a vain race to get airborne before the first bombs struck home.

An eyewitness, Richard Hillary of No. 603 Squadron, who was himself within seventy-two hours of suffering horrendous burn injuries later described what occurred:

> The slug-like shapes of the bombers slide out of the sun's glare and the high-pitched scream of their bombs intermingled with the sound of the Spitfires taking off. I

> watched as all three aircraft were thrown apart by the explosions, the leader [Deere] going over onto his back and sliding along the runway while the other two aircraft were blasted aside.

These normally terminal circumstances for one or more of the pilots were amazingly held at bay, although Deere in particular was very fortunate. First of all, his viciously inverted contact with either the runway surface or the cockpit canopy resulted in a deep score to his scalp before the fighter ground to a halt. Worse still was his inability to exit the aircraft that was now exuding the distinct odour from ruptured fuel tanks with all that implied for a truly horrible conclusion to the sortie.

Plt Off. Edsall had luckily landed right side up, and having got out, albeit with a bad leg injury, he crawled over to his leader's battered aircraft that lacked one wing and the engine. After several minutes' desperate effort, the cockpit door was released, allowing Deere to scrabble clear, whereupon the duo limped away across the bomb-scared surface and ultimately into the hands of the medical staff. As for Sgt Davies, his Spitfire was bodily transported clear of the airfield but also settled down in an upright position, leaving its occupant to spend up to an hour regaining access to the airfield. This triple dose of individual good fortune was very much the exception to what befell so many of this section's contemporaries within Fighter Command.

1–6 September

Diminishing Returns: A Death Blow?

The effective commitment of squadrons and their pilots once the battle had been fully entered into had been put under increasingly inordinate strain. To the steady whittling down of the more experienced pilots was added the decimation of those relatively combat-raw squadrons fed into the conflict. A typical example involved No. 616 Squadron who arrived in naïvely confident mood at Kenley on 20 August; two weeks later, no less than thirteen Spitfires were MIA or written-off while to the five pilot fatalities was added four injured and one POW. The scale of material and human casualties merited the squadron's withdrawal from direct combat.

The policy of squadron rotation to and from the main battle zone was by now facing diminishing returns in terms of pilot experience in combat. Whereas the squadrons sent for rest and recuperation in the initial stage were doing so with an element of their personnel now up to scratch in overall combat techniques, the serious loss of ever-more experienced pilots as the fight intensified meant that there was nothing like the same prospect of 'rested' squadrons re-entering combat with many seasoned veterans. The case of No. 85 Squadron provides a good example of this 'Law of diminishing returns' scenario.

Having participated in the Battle of France, the unit retained a number of the survivors and were commanded by a fellow veteran, Sqn Ldr Peter Townsend, who had previous service with No. 43 Squadron. The squadron had operated from Debden and Martlesham on the fringes of No. 11 Group during July and up to 19 August. Although the pace of battle was not so intense, the constant strain was undoubtedly leaving its mark on the airmen, although fighter and pilot loss was minimal despite steady encounters with the *Luftwaffe*. A transfer to Croydon occurred on the 19th and the ensuing period up to the 26th witnessed no casualties, although two Hurricanes were damaged. Matters turned steadily sourer from the 26th onward, however.

On that day, Plt Off. John Hemingway was forced to bale out, becoming the first combat victim. A two-day spell passed, during which two fighters were damaged, but the casualty rate shot up over the next four days as follows. On the 29th, Flt Lt Harry Hamilton was killed and Sgt John M. Ellis and Sgt Frank Walker-Smith baled out of their Bf 109-stricken aircraft, as did Plt Off. James Marshall the next day. A tussle with Bf 110s on the 31st now cost the squadron its CO, although Townsend did survive his bale out, albeit with a toe injury that led to its amputation, while Plt Off. Pyers Worrall joined his CO in mid-air after his Hurricane was fatally crippled; three more fighters were damaged.

The bloody climax that led two days later to No. 85's withdrawal into No. 12 Group occurred on 1 September. The swirling air battle that involved the squadron on the day's second sortie resulted in four Hurricanes shot down. Fg Off. Gowers and Sgt J. Booth baled out, but the burns suffered by Booth coupled to a heavy landing subsequently led to his death in early 1941. Fg Off. Patrick Woods-Scawen also jumped, but as in too many other Second World War instances, his parachute failed him. Finally, Sgt Ellis's body was never found, and it is likely he tragically lived up to his middle name, Mortimer, which translates from its French origin to 'Dead in the sea' (*Mort-en-Mer*).

Every one of these pilots had served either during the Battle of France and/or in the course of its equally intense and feral successor. Although one or two of the veterans from the former campaign had survived, the possibility of the squadron's prompt return from its rest-spell into the fray was at best unlikely; this was especially given the relative dearth of combat-experienced personnel in reserve as opposed to the bulk of pilots falling into this category who were already serving 'up front' within the main battle zone.

The ABC System: A Necessary Operational Palliative

This scenario that was being generally visited upon other squadrons similarly hard-pressed and hard-hit was surely the catalyst for Dowding and Park's agreement to create the ABC squadron system that in turn sought to patch up the gaps in Fighter Command's fighting structure, however piecemeal and uncertain that system might be.

Dowding had anticipated the problems inherent in maintaining a numerically effective pool of units and pilots exemplified by No. 85 Squadron's aforementioned situation. With this in mind, he had resorted to creating a three-tier squadron system as follows:

A. Squadrons bearing the prefix were those based within No. 11 Group and added to by the Duxford and Middle Wallop (No. 10 Group) squadrons.
B. Squadrons with a leavening of experienced pilots who were on hand at airfields within the two support Groups and who could be called upon to relieve units within No. 11 Group.
C. Squadrons such as Nos 54 and 85 retired from the battle and utilised to train-up acolyte pilots prior to their posting within No. 11 Group.

There was inevitably a fine balance to be struck between retaining enough veteran pilots on hand in the 'B' and 'C'-categorised squadrons with which to instruct the newcomers without further reducing the numbers of their fellow-veterans fighting the main battle 'down south'. The dispatch of 'B'-category squadrons into the main battle zone was a clear gamble since a good proportion of their pilot establishment not being combat experienced meant they were open to harsh, if not fatal treatment by the enemy prior to attaining the basic knowledge that would first guarantee their survival and ultimately lead to an ability to mount an effective challenge.

Slaughter of the Innocents (2)

The peremptory switch from flying multi-engined aircraft to a fighter was not the best way in which to enter any air battle, given the feral circumstances existing in southern British skies in the mid-1940s. After joining No. 38 Squadron in January 1938, Fg Off. Arthur T. Rose-Price had served as a flight commander, but since

No. 602 (City of Glasgow) Squadron spent the period between September 1939 and August 1940 in defence of its Scottish homeland before transferring to Tangmere. By then, the fin flash along with the Type A1 fuselage roundel were becoming standard markings. Serial number is faintly discernible between the unit code letters.

January 1940, he had been instructing on an OTU before being posted to No. 501 Squadron on 2 September, where his Fighter Command career was measured in mere hours. Arriving during the morning, he had been immediately 'scrambled' on a sortie. His second sortie during the afternoon saw his unobserved disappearance over Dungeness, his epitaph a sad 'MIA' since his body was never recovered.

Intelligence Lapse

The fear that the *Luftwaffe* would target the main sources for fighter production was never to be tested until well into the battle, when the situation was already in hand. On 4 September, the bombers were briefed to take out the Hawker factory, a prime production centre for the Hurricane and based at Brooklands. The attackers duly got through but picked out a second plant and delivered a devastating blow. Tragic though the human casualty and material scale of loss subsequently proved to be, what had been struck was the Vickers factory that was manufacturing the Wellington bomber—Bomber Command's loss was Fighter Command's undoubted gain.

The failure at Brooklands was one more example of faulty intelligence, although a good degree of fortune went the RAF's way on this occasion. The vulnerability to assault of the relatively few major fighter-production plants had thankfully not been exposed to date, and, indeed, these would remain inviolate

Sgts Joan Mortimer (left) and Helen Turner flank Flt Off. Elspeth Henderson. All were serving personnel at Biggin Hill during the height of the battle and were involved in incidents arising from the regular severe punishment the key airfield sustained that earned each a Military Medal. Picture was taken in October 1940.

until the course of the battle was swinging ever-more in Britain's favour. The Supermarine factory at Woolston in Southampton was particularly vulnerable since it stood out, positioned as it was alongside the waters of the Solent. Plans were currently well in hand for the massive 'shadow factory' at Castle Bromwich, Birmingham, to supplement and ultimately dominate overall Spitfire production strength, however.

September's Crucial Manoeuvres

Fighter Command was still very much on the back foot as September commenced, but already its greatest, albeit unknown, ally—Adolf Hitler—was in the process of setting in motion a tactical alteration that would ironically evolve into a counterstroke to his hopes for victory. The accidental discharge of bombs over London on 24 August was destined to set in motion a naturally unperceived 'reprieve' for Dowding and his sorely-tried 'in the field' group subordinates. Churchill had seized upon the incident to dispatch Bomber Command against Berlin.

The several operations did little damage to the city's infrastructure but induced in Hitler an inordinate desire to strike back, not in a logical manner, but rather an emotional one. He revoked his sanction on 'terror' attacks during a speech on 4 September to a packed audience in his capital's *Sportpalast*. Among his peroration was the phrase 'If the British launch heavy attacks on our cities—then we will eradicate theirs!' The die was cast for the switch from attacking Fighter Command to one directed against the British population. The man and woman in the street would shoulder the burden that had hitherto been bearing the Service entity to the ground and thereby ensure the survival of the nation, however cruel the immediate human cost would be.

7–14 September

Operation Loge

The absence of any substantial 'traces' on the RAF's radar screens as Saturday the 7th dawned and developed into yet another unwelcome fine-weather day was puzzling to say the least. The reason for the lack of action unknowingly lay in the events accruing from the accidental bombing of London on 24–25 August; Operation Loge was the result, for now the *Luftwaffe*'s attention would be primarily, though not wholly, concentrated on Britain's capital. Hitler's latest, but by far the last example of his phobia regarding *Vergeltungsangriffe* (revenge attacks) had been set in motion, and Göring was on hand at Kesselring's HQ at Cap Gris-Nez near Calais to 'take command'.

The diversion of the bomber formations away from attacking the airfields was to provide the crews with the opportunity to penetrate to their target with minimal challenge from Fighter Command. The initial radar responses were recorded as the afternoon approached its juncture with the evening. The build-up over the Pas-de-Calais of what finally constituted a massive 'air bridge' of some 300 bombers escorted by around 600 fighters was not reacted to at first. It was clear AVM Park was anticipating that the overall force would split into separate elements, each tasked with a specific target. The onward movement across the Channel and over the Kent countryside witnessed no such separation, and it appears that the lead elements were still free from lethal attention as they approached the River Thames.

From this point onward, a desperate race evolved between attacker and defender that ended in the former's favour. Park not only unleased his squadrons but called for back-up from Nos 10 and 12 Groups. Even so, the first wave of bombers appeared to have made their bomb runs upon the capital's commercial docklands in unhindered manner before meeting opposition from the Hurricanes and Spitfires. Further to the east, the pilots of those squadrons making contact were astounded, if not daunted by the sight of the forces arrayed against them, as well as their aerial 'spread' both vertically and laterally.

The height advantage enjoyed by the *Jagdwaffe* escorts placed the RAF attackers at a disadvantage, but the resultant mass of engagements, although causing casualties among thirteen of the participating squadrons—four Hurricanes, with one pilot killed and three wounded, for No. 249 Squadron and three No. 43 Squadron Hurricanes, with two fatalities being among the most affected—witnessed a final toll of forty *Luftwaffe* aircraft either downed or written-off on return against the RAF's twenty-four 'total loss' figure.

The 'high tide' of *Luftwaffe* daylight domination over Southern Britain was now set to ultimately diminish to the point of extinction within 1940. What was much more rapidly decided within less than two weeks was the fate of Operation *Seelöwe*. It is supremely ironic that today's mass raid was, in the eyes of the British military hierarchy, one indication that *Seelöwe* was in fact on the point of being initiated; the other indications lay in the concentration of barges along the Channel coast from Dunkirk to Ostend coupled with the transfer of the Ju 87 units to airfields close to the French coast and the favourable moon and tide conditions. The code word 'Cromwell' indicating an imminent invasion was accordingly flashed to all military units, ordering them to their battle stations along the Channel coast.

The *Luftwaffe*'s return later that evening of the 7th heralded the start of the nocturnal *Blitz* campaign that would, over the intervening months of 1940 and on until early May 1941, land painful, albeit non-terminable blows upon British cities along with their hapless populations. As London absorbed the first of fifty-seven nightly beatings, the RAF fighter pilots had no way of knowing that their adversaries had committed a major blunder in their campaign to destroy Fighter Command. All that could be anticipated by the young men congregating in local hostelries and enjoying the beer and spirits available was that another hard day of combat lay ahead with no relief from the dreadful pressures of combat on the horizon.

Flt Lts Peter Townsend (left) and Ceasar Hull are seen at Wick while serving with No. 43 Squadron. Both were posted to other squadrons in May, Townsend assuming command of No. 85 Squadron that he led until mid-1940. Hull went to Norway with No. 263 Squadron where he was wounded and upon recovery, returned to No. 43 Squadron this time as CO on 31 August. His tenure of office proved tragically brief; during the first mass daylight raid on London (7 September), he was downed and killed.

Little of operational consequence happened on the 8th to the undoubted relief of the RAF; No. 43 Squadron that had lost its CO, Sqn Ldr Ceasar Hull, the previous day was pulled out of the line to be replaced by 607 Squadron. The next day, heavy cloud delayed *Luftwaffe* intervention until late afternoon when the acolyte No. 607 pilots received a brutal baptism of fire, losing six Hurricanes and three pilots killed. Elsewhere, the Duxford Wing for once caught an escorted formation approaching North Weald. A number of kills were registered, but two Hurricanes and two Spitfires were lost. The latter casualties were self-inflicted in the form of a collision as No. 310 Squadron attacked a Do 17 formation. Flt Lt Gordon Sinclair managed to clear his fighter safely, but Fg Off. John Boulton was less fortunate and was killed.

Adverse weather totally hindered any enemy activity on the 10th, while a similar weather pattern to the 9th delayed any *Luftwaffe* incursions the next day. A combined KG1 and KG26 force lunged towards and penetrated as far as London; any sense of success among the crews was sharply reversed thanks to the loss of ten bombers, with seven in the MIA category. The punishment in turn was due to a combination of fuel-limitation suffered by the Bf 109 escorts and wayward rendezvousing by the Bf 110 contingent that left their charges open to unfettered assault. Elsewhere, a second escorted force attacked Portsmouth and Southampton with surprisingly little result.

The KG1/KG26 formation had been met by a wing of Spitfires that unusually emanated from both Nos 11 and 12 Groups with the former command represented by Sqn Ldr Malan's No. 74 Squadron based at Hornchurch along with No. 266 Squadron. Although five fighters received various degrees of damage, only one was actually lost; this was a No. 611 fighter set ablaze and flown by Sgt Fred Shepherd who suffered the cruel fate of a burning parachute that duly cost him his life.

Mother Nature provided yet another adverse weather pattern on the 12th, followed by a similar one the next day. Improved weather conditions on the 14th surprisingly still did not elicit serious *Luftwaffe* involvement other than some probing sorties. The relative respite from sustained operations on all but two of the past seven days was physically beneficial to the RAF personnel, but it naturally left them with a nagging doubt that the situation could possibly remain so quiescent. In Berlin, a decision with immediate tactical and longer-term strategic implications was being announced by Hitler on this day.

Luftwaffe Operational Limitations

The operational strain upon the *Luftwaffe* personnel was as great as that faced by their adversaries, regardless of Germany's superior numbers in both human and material terms. In the case of the *Jagdwaffe* pilots, although the numbers of Bf 109s in particular was materially the same as Fighter Command, the latter force could not present its total strength in direct combat since a good proportion had to be retained throughout the British mainland. A further diminishing factor up to mid-September was both the shortage in pilot numbers coupled with the lack of combat awareness among many of the replacements and consequent extreme vulnerability to being downed in combat.

Where the *Luftwaffe* undermined itself in the long run was the absence of any equivalent to the rotation from constant combat status of either the pilots or their units as operated by Fighter Command. Once on combat status, there the units remained along with their airmen. Even worse was the lack of relief from operations; again, this contrasted sharply with RAF practice of granting some time off-duty, extending up to twenty-four hours within seven days. The fact that the RAF were serving within their own national surroundings compared to the Germans who were immersed within an alien countryside and population did not provide the same grounds for relaxation in the latter case of course.

The regular presence in combat enabled those *Jagdwaffe* pilots imbued with a higher skill in gunnery to run up impressive numbers of kills, but there was a downside even to this seemingly positive outcome: whenever any among this number was killed or captured, the effect was often morale-lowering within the unit's ranks, on the basis that if the *Experten* were being culled, what hope was there for the less well-endowed in combat experience? But even these top-grade pilots were prone to the growing pressures of aerial strife that could surreptitiously gnaw at the most outwardly confident individual's mindset as Maj. Galland for one would later attest.

Sqn Ldr Don Kingaby, seen here at Hornchurch in early 1943 as CO of No. 122 Squadron, fought as a sergeant in the Battle of Britain with Nos 266 and 92 Squadrons. By June 1941, he had scored sixteen of his twenty-one confirmed kills, all but two being Bf 109s. He won the DFM three times, an amazing tally, since what was an NCO's equivalent award to the officer's DFC was very sparingly granted during the Second World War.

Kanalkrankheit

Although the German aircrew were numerically superior to their opponents, the same close-knit bond applied within their ranks along with the same sentiments regarding those among their ranks who were lost. Whereas the RAF aircrew ultimately sensed that the battle was swinging in their favour, the reverse feeling of frustration gradually expanding into a mood of despair at the inability to succeed in achieving air supremacy certainly afflicted the rank and file of the *Luftwaffe*. During the course of the battle, there arose an additional hazard that steadily bore down upon the psyche of the *Jagdwaffe* pilots in particular. The expression for this was *Kanalkrankheit* or Channel sickness.

The mandatory traversing of the English Channel whether at its narrowest point around the Pas-de-Calais or further west was regarded with a distaste amounting to phobia. The prospect of having to 'ditch' within the watery surface that was unpredictable in terms of motion as well as temperature cast a pall upon the mind of many individuals from the Bf 109 units. Baling out was even more risk-laden unless the *Seenotdienst* was on immediate hand. It was little wonder that as soon as the cockpit fuel-warning bulb lit up, its occupant was under extra pressure to disengage and hope—especially on extended sorties or when incurring material battle damage—that the engine would not quit, or the airframe fail to hold together before the continental coastline was safely attained.

Seelöwe's Limitations

The stunning success of the Germans in conquering all but one of the major nations bordering the North Sea within a matter of two months was to bring its own ultimately insuperable problems in bringing the exception, Great Britain, within their unconditional control by similar physical subjugation. The English Channel constituted a formidable geographic barrier that would require a sizeable invasion fleet of landing craft to be on hand, but the resources in terms of such specialist vessels were non-existent. Moreover, the timescale within which a crossing would have to be made in 1940 was no more than three months at the most; the sea and weather conditions even by September could easily render an assault difficult if not impossible.

Grand Admiral Erich Raeder was ever-doubtful regarding the ability of his badly-truncated *Kriegsmarine* strength to hold off Royal Naval intervention unless the RAF could first be rendered powerless. His *Wehrmacht* contemporaries were more sanguine as regards this aspect of *Seelöwe*'s evolvement, however. The *Luftwaffe*'s debilitating effect upon the Allied armies during the recent land campaigns was expected to exert the same deterrent effect upon any attempted naval intervention regardless of the Royal Navy's strength and commitment.

There was an on-going ambivalence regarding the scale of the operation as well as in terms of where its focus should lie. The original plan to invade on a front extending between Ramsgate and Lyme Regis using three armies had been subsequently amended to a more concentrated lateral spread from Brighton to Folkestone with the *Fallschirmjäger* troops being added-in. Why these specialist forces had hitherto been excluded confirms the degree of planning uncertainty; their prior presence within the extremely poorly-provisioned defensive network then existing after Dunkirk would probably have hastened a British collapse 'in the field' even before the seaborne forces had landed in any force.

The *ad hoc* provision of landing craft numbers—adapting commercial barges and other vessels, many of which had no power source and would have to be towed across the Channel—was likely to adversely affect Germany's economy thanks to their absence. When suitably amended for the carriage of personnel and equipment, these vessels were assembled in seaports extending west from Antwerp as far as Dunkirk where their vulnerability to assault by RAF Bomber Command was highlighted. Prior to the invasion's launch, the laying of minefields along the fringes of the invasion force's primary channels would be indulged in.

Hitler's mood swings regarding both the feasibility of *Seelöwe* and arguably even the need for Britain to be invaded in the light of his peace offerings had dragged on up to the end of August. It was then that he announced he would make a final decision on 10 September; in fact, he extended this further to the

The Mk II status of MN: A/P7297 is confirmed by the bulge on the forward lower engine cowling that covers the Coffman Starter. Its service with the Belgian squadron was the fifth in sequence since its service debut in the summer of 1940, during which time it was converted to a Mk VA. The aircraft ended its days at No. 53 OTU.

14th despite all basic preparations including minefield completion being in hand. His latest decision was probably due to the still unfinished business with Fighter Command.

'*Der Tag*', RAF Style

History has noted that the climactic battles fought by Britain in 1815 and 1940 occurred on a Sunday. In the former case, with the undoubted assistance of the Prussians under Gen. Blücher, Napoleon Bonaparte's twenty-two-year rampage around Europe was brought to an end. Fully 125 years on, Britain and its Commonwealth stood out against the seemingly irresistible advance of another former corporal, Hitler, and his Nazi hordes. This time round, not only the European continent, but great swathes of the globe were at risk of 'sinking into the abyss of a new Dark Age' to quote Churchill from one of his emotively-pitched speeches during June 1940. So it was that Fighter Command stood by on 15 September as another pleasant, if somewhat cloud-spilled atmosphere pervaded the dawn light.

The day before, Hitler had expressed a view that within a mere handful of days, the RAF's will to resist would be irretrievably broken by his *Luftwaffe*; added to this was his further optimism that the onset of the *Blitz* signalled by the first London raid would force the British Cabinet to bow to the people's call for an armistice and peace negotiations in the light of the capital's hammering (why the bulk of the over 40 million citizens who were still basically free from similar physically and mentally enervating treatment should follow suit was not considered).

The focus of assault being away from the airfields over the past week meant that their facilities could be brought back to at least a bearable level of operational function; the Spitfires and Hurricanes could be 'scrambled' and directed towards the enemy in a less frenetic manner that also was basically free of *en route* interception and dispersal by the Bf 109s in particular. So it was that AVM Park's reaction to the initial build-up of aircraft numbers over the Pas-de-Calais was to send his squadrons aloft in successive pairs that supplemented the single-squadron standing patrols already patrolling the Channel coastal fringes. The full five-squadron 'Duxford Wing' was also called upon and headed towards London as the *Luftwaffe* closed in on the capital.

Initial Play

Historians have generally alluded to the weight of bomber assault on the 15th as approaching or equalling that of 15 and 18 August for example when the sortie figure rose into the hundreds. This was certainly not the case during what would be the first of two attempted thrusts on London. The forty Do 17s of KG76 and KG3 were led by Maj. Lindenmeyer who held his relatively small force in good formation; this was despite the attentions of the RAF fighters engaging in relay form from the coast onwards that culminated over London with the appearance of the Duxford Wing. Even this fifty-strong sub-force's attentions did not prove to be overwhelming in destructive effect, although six crews were MIA before the Channel coastline faded away behind the retiring bombers. A combination of dogged defensive response by the gunners added to by reasonable support from the escort had secured the return of the other bomber crews.

AVM Park's response in launching his entire fighter strength had run the risk of a second wave assault occurring before sufficient pilots could return, rearm, and refuel before getting airborne again. This was the possible dilemma he now faced—and with the Prime Minister, who had made a snap visit to Park's HQ on hand. To the question posed by Churchill as to the command's available reserves, Park could only respond in a totally negative manner. It appears that he was referring to the situation as it affected No. 11 Group. Even so, what was available from either Nos 10 or 12 Groups would not have been so large in strength nor found it easy to respond in time to fly the extra distance from their further-flung airfields in order to engage the *Luftwaffe* crews before they attained their selected targets.

P7420 was one of the 1,000 Spitfire airframes built as Mk IIAs between June 1940 and July 1941. It was assigned to No. 19 Squadron at Fowlmere where this photograph of its still uncoded fuselage was reportedly taken during a refuelling process. Unlike P7297, it failed to survive beyond 15 November 1940 when it was written-off following a crash-landing in Suffolk.

The Follow-Up

It was early afternoon before the *Luftwaffe* made its second assault bid, by which time No. 11 Group was fully recharged in terms of operationally-ready fighters. Once again, the scale of bomber participation was no more than moderate at 114, although the provision of well over 300 escorts promised an intense series of engagements for the RAF pilots. Five sub-forces were involved that flew a rectangular pattern spread across 6 miles, and the forward three preceded the rear two by some 3 miles. The left-hand column involved III/KG2 and II/KG2's Do 17s, while the right side was headed by II/KG3's Do 17s with a composite I and II/KG26 formation of He 111s behind. Finally, a second composite formation made up from I and II/KG53 was placed up front between III/KG2 and II/KG3.

London was the main focus of attention and, once again, the bomber crews faced an almost constant degree of attack passes from their assailants as they adopted a more protracted inward course. Whereas the morning attack force had flown straight from Cap Gris-Nez to Gravesend on the Thames before turning left towards their targets, this force headed almost due west from the Cap to Dungeness on the Kent coast from where a north–north-west course was held for Gravesend. Whether the extra distance flown made any difference to the scale of damage or loss suffered by the Germans cannot be confirmed. What was obvious was that the air battle was just as intense as the preceding one, while the casualty rate was noticeably greater.

AA gunfire on the Thames Estuary joined in to speckle the sky with multiple bursts, one of which initiated the ultimate demise of the II/KG53 He 111 concerned. With one engine knocked out, the bomber could not hold formation altitude especially with the bombs aboard. Even when jettisoned, the power loss saw the bomber lose its position, so Obfw. Schmidhorn turned back, seeking cloud cover to avoid the fighters. The sparse layers on hand soon disappeared and the crew came under an attack that killed a gunner and set the failed engine on fire; the final result was a successful forced-landing in mid-Kent while harried all the way down by the trio of fighters. This was reportedly the final one of the six *Geschwader* losses, all but one of which was culled on the inward leg.

One of the RAF Squadrons (No. 257) was aloft for the first time under Sqn Ldr Stanford-Tuck's command. He had recently been sent to take charge of what was regarded as a demoralised group of pilots. He wasted no time in sorting most of them out and now led them back into the fray where a dogfight developed with a Bf 110 formation. Tuck's expertise saw him take down one *Zerstörer* and inflict enough damage on a second to be granted a probable. Pete Brothers, a newly-appointed flight CO and former ace with No. 32 Squadron, added a Do 17 and a second listed as a 'Ju 88' to the success tally. The pilots' morale was evidently boosted by the operational success, and No. 257 subsequently progressed in an upward manner that was undoubtedly due to Tuck's firm but fair stewardship.

The Duxford Wing was again called into action, but this time around, it was caught at an altitude well below that of the oncoming formations, a situation that the enemy escorts were quick to take advantage of. In combats that ranged from the Channel coast to London, a total of five fighters were shot down, although only one pilot (from No. 302 Squadron) was killed; one of the surviving four ended up as a POW after chasing (probably ill-advisedly) an opponent well across the Channel, an act that reportedly ended with the ditching of his severely-damaged Spitfire.

By the day's end, several *Luftwaffe* units found their ranks had been shorn of near-*Staffel* strength numbers. To the six each declared MIA by KG76 and KG53 was added eight from KG2; a further nine MIA crews were shared between several other of the participating *Geschwadern*. MIA fighter casualties totalled twenty-four out of the remaining *Luftwaffe* losses, while at least three further aircraft staggered home to crash-landings with damage assessed at 50–60 per cent—figures that indicated a write-off status.

The overall *Luftwaffe* loss figure of fifty-six was clearly below that of either 15 August (seventy-five) or 18 August (sixty-nine), but the sense of failure accruing from today's operations ran much deeper compared to what were seen as heavy but temporary setbacks to the campaign on the other two days. The heady sense of imminent victory had seemed to be sustained especially in the two weeks preceding Operation Loge. This was probably heightened by the Intelligence reports that indicated ever-fading RAF strength in respect of both fighters and combat-experienced pilots.

Gen. Kesselring had reportedly stated that the former figure was probably no more than between fifty and 100, and that the turn on London would raise the attrition rate in the *Luftwaffe*'s favour. Imagine the chagrin of his crews when the opposition showed little signs of permanently buckling but instead continued to rise-up in almost undiminished force; this was especially the case today, so it was no wonder that individual crewmembers were making cynical statements when intercepted, such as 'Here come those last fighters!' The way ahead to a successful outcome was not only uncertain but also seeming to be fading inexorably away—a view shared by Hitler that was within forty-eight hours of being confirmed by him.

Five pilots belonging to No. 85 Squadron are depicted behind one of their Mk I Hurricanes following the Battle of Britain's conclusion. The CO, Sqn Ldr Peter Townsend, holding the Alsatian, commanded the unit between May 1940 and June 1941. The propeller blade displays the tally of squadron kills. Horizontal hexagon was one of the two flight symbols; the other flight bore a vertically-aligned example.

Birth of the '*Jabo*'

To date, the *Luftwaffe*'s bombing campaign over Southern Britain had exclusively involved conventional means of delivery by aircraft types specially designed for the function. Fighters had hitherto functioned in their primary role as escorts tasked with warding off all RAF fighter countermeasures. The rationale behind the latest form of bombing could be viewed as no more than a desperate and small-scale measure, especially since it involved a single *Staffel* within each *Jagdgeschwader*. Göring in his wisdom now decreed that the sub-units would have their fighters converted to carry bombs that in the case of the Bf 109 amounted to weapons of no more than 250-kg capacity. The first two so adapted belonged to the attack-specialist Epr.Gr.210 along with LG2. By 20 September, the *Jagdbomber* ('*Jabo*') Bf 109s were on hand in the Pas-de-Calais and duly prepared to launch their initial sortie.

In fact, the intention behind the measure was the latest attempt to draw Fighter Command into a battle of attrition with the *Jagdwaffe*. The likely presence of the '*Jabos*' within the overall formations would compel the RAF to make a challenge in a manner that had hitherto been generally resisted when the controllers had been confident that they were dealing with a pure fighter sweep. The semi-stratospheric approach altitudes by the Bf 109s added pressure to the attempts to make the necessary height before encountering their adversaries; this was not always possible, especially in the case of the Hurricane, whose performance also fell off noticeably in these circumstances.

The operational pace varied during the four-day period leading up to this switch. The 16th remained devoid of serious action and AVM Park resisted the *freie Jagd* thrusts each of two-*Gruppe* strength launched next day. On the 18th, a major raid against Tilbury Docks, east of London, was initiated by the recently-arrived Ju 88s of III/KG77. The bid ended in a serious setback for the bomber crews thanks to a massive response by Fighter Command involving nearly twenty squadrons, including the Duxford Wing. The resultant battle over the Thames that lasted some fifty minutes culled eight crews from the surprisingly unescorted formation before the British coastline was left behind. The lead bomber bearing Maj. Kless (*Gruppenkommandeur*) was probably the final casualty with the Maj. one of the fatalities (Bader's pilots alone claimed three times this figure in kills). Unbeknown to the surviving personnel as they landed back at Asch in Belgium was a second even-greater cull awaiting the *Geschwader* before the month's end.

Yet another day's inactivity due to the poor weather that was a regular feature of British autumns changed tantalisingly on the 20th when the *freie Jagd* formation surrounding the LG2 *Jabos* swept towards and over London where the bomb loads were duly scattered with unknown, but doubtless minimal effect. Fighter Command's reaction was initially the usual negative one, but several squadrons were then 'scrambled' only to face 'bounce' actions that took down seven Spitfires and Hurricanes along with four of their pilots; only one Bf 109 pilot was MIA in return.

The likelihood of continued bombing attacks of this nature forced Dowding into an immediate countermeasure. This consisted of two flights of fighters operating out of Gravesend; their pilots' duty was to fly patrols above the Channel coastline in a bid to monitor any incoming formation in order to determine whether it contained a *Jabo* element. This was a duty fraught with danger for the isolated airmen flying in solo or duo form, apart from which there was no guarantee of picking out bomb-laden fighters from the mass formation even when left unhindered from attack. The still fairly-desperate times merited the measure, however, although the benefits accruing to Dowding and Park's control of the overall battle remained uncertain.

Belated Success

To date, Britain's aircraft production capacity, particularly in relation to fighters, had hardly been affected by direct assault. Several of these locations had been targeted, but they had either been missed or in the case of the Short plant at Rochester or de Havilland's at Hatfield was involved with bomber, not fighter, development, respectively involving the four-engined Stirling and twin-engined Mosquito. Parallel attempts to disrupt aero-engine production with the Rolls-Royce factories at Derby and Crewe in mind had been equally unsuccessful.

It was only as September was entering its final phase that the situation altered in the Germans' favour, although even then there was a degree of failure involved as on the 24th. The latest briefing for Epr.Gr.210 once again directed its Bf 110s at the Woolston factory on the Solent that had been the prime production source for the Spitfire. The formation managed to penetrate the defences and the pilots duly laid their bomb loads. Nearly 100 factory staff were killed, but this was due to the shelters in which they were incarcerated being struck; whatever damage was inflicted upon the factory structure did not materially hinder the flow of airframes.

Woolston's immunity from severe punishment was to continue for a mere forty-eight hours. *Luftflotte* 3's KG55 He 111s rose up from their airfields in and around Paris on the 26th and headed across the Channel. Despite being intercepted during target approach, the formation remained intact and completed the bomb run at a cost of one bomber. The result was that the plant was basically wrecked, a situation that promised a gross disruption to new airframe production. This positive result for the Germans would have been much more critical to Fighter Command's chances of survival had it occurred earlier.

By this point in the battle, alternative and much larger-scale production means were on hand at Castle Bromwich in Birmingham, a location that moreover was far harder to strike at since it lay beyond escort cover *vis-à-vis* daylight strikes and was shielded by the dark regarding nocturnal sorties. Although the Woolston structure was badly damaged, the heavy machinery was not so affected. A proportion was transferred to other locations and the remaining element provided a basis for the painfully-gradual resumption of production.

KG55 had been very active elsewhere in between the twin and vastly-different Woolston attacks. The Bristol Co. possessed a major factory at Filton in the city bearing the company name; among the designs under construction was the Beaufighter, whose importance to effectively challenging the *Blitz* campaign was to prove vital, albeit tardy in application due to production delays. The *Geschwader's* 58 crews had anticipated some form of interception but they received a fortunate tactical break. AVM Brand on studying the radar plots decided the attack would be made against the Westland Co. factory at Yeovil well south of Bristol and directed his No. 10 group fighters to the area.

The result was that KG55's target approach was totally unopposed and the near-100-ton bomb pattern laid upon the factory created havoc, although not as much as was due to be borne by the Woolston strike. Turning for home, the He 111s immediately found themselves under belated but sustained attack by two squadrons. One bomber was swiftly dispatched by an AA Battery's fire and crashed violently, killing four airmen out of the five on board. Two more bombers were fatally damaged and abandoned before the Channel coast appeared, with a fourth crew successfully force-landing around this time. The quartet of losses was added to by two Bf 110s from the III/ZG26 escort MIA with a third written-off after its return.

As a sergeant pilot with No. 1 Squadron, Fg Off. A. Clowes had survived a mid-air collision with a French fighter that had excised most of the rudder and one elevator; he was fortunate to be able to force-land his Hurricane. Still with No. 1 at Wittering in October, he is climbing into JX: B's cockpit. The black stripes on the body of the bee motive applied to the engine cowling are not only decorative but signify his kill record to date—nine—that was also his final total during the Second World War.

Two days on, KG55 was again dispatched to the region to resume the assault on Filton and a separate facility at nearby Yate. In the interim period, No. 504 Squadron had been transferred to Filton and their presence was reinforced by three further squadrons when the He 111 force supported by Epr.Gp.210 and with ZG26 escorts appeared in sight. The subsequent encounter witnessed only the Epr.Gp.210 aircraft gaining access to Filton, although the punishment inflicted was much reduced compared to the 25th. Why the He 111s did not also succeed is a mystery since their ranks remained intact.

That this was a fortunate outcome for the crews was due to the efforts of their Bf 110 colleagues in staving off the Spitfire and Hurricane thrusts, albeit at some cost. Five of the *Zerstörers* were shot down, and only two of the ten airmen concerned survived; a sixth fighter was involved in a mid-air collision that consumed the three *Luftwaffe* and RAF individuals concerned. Epr.Gr.210 also suffered as it returned four crews short. The latest senior fatality within the *Gruppe*'s ranks was Obltn. W. Roessiger, who was a veteran from the initial battles in July; also downed was Hptm. Lutz (*Kommandeur*).

Eastern Travails (1)

The Ju 88 was the newest and arguably the best-performing of the three bombers prosecuting the conflict to date, but its ability to withstand fighter assault without the benefit of fighter escort was problematic at best. The defensive armament consisting of several single-mounted machine guns was not guaranteed to ensure survival against the gun batteries mounted by the Spitfires and Hurricanes; the close-packed crew sitting inside a heavily glazed cockpit was wide open to injury or death, especially from frontal assault.

KG77's punishment on the 18th was the latest evidence of the design's short-comings, but nine days later, I and II *Gruppe* prepared to emulate III *Gruppe* in penetrating beyond Tilbury and into London. The escort provision was flying well ahead in a bid to draw the RAF fighters into combat that would end with their being on the ground due to fuel shortage before the Ju 88 formation arrived—at least this was the scenario quoted by a leading Battle of Britain author. Whether correct or not, the rendezvous point at which the escort would evolve was reached with none around; instead, a hostile 'escort' turned up consisting of at least 100 fighters that proceeded to make steady inroads into the outnumbered formation.

The culling of fully twelve bombers extended along both the inward and return route with the bulk of those machines lost coming down in Kent and Surrey. Five were already gone at the point of bomb release, with a sixth downed over London to be followed by two between bomb release and the coast. A further four crews went down in the Channel, including one that 'ditched', but only three of the sixteen airmen survived. The casualty rate on the other eight Ju 88s was almost as grim at twenty dead out of thirty-two. This was a truly bloody 'butcher's bill' for what was not even a successful operation in terms of bombing, as well as being the second disaster to overtake the *Geschwader* in September.

Eastern Travails (2)

The value of the Bf 110 as a pure fighter had already been well cast into doubt. Balancing out its formidable firepower was its rather ponderous performance against single-engined opposition that saw even the more pedestrian Hurricane gaining a regular advantage. This was the reason why Göring had ordained that a Bf 109 escort was mandatory from 19 August onward. That was only feasible when making penetrations within Bf 109 range, something that was impossible for *Luftflotte* 3 when advancing at any distance into Southwest England as for example on the Bristol raids.

V/LG1 had been part of a mid-morning fighter 'sweep' with Hptm. Liensberger (*Gruppenkommandeur*) in charge. The formation had swept in south of London and ran into No. 249 Squadron among other units. Liensberger was engaged by Plt Off. Percy Burton and pursued southward until both aircraft came together in deadly embrace, all three airmen forfeiting their lives as both machines slammed into the ground. Whether Burton had run out of ammunition and resorted to ramming his prey or had closed-in too tightly to avoid the mutually-fatal impact could never be confirmed.

The fate of Lienberger's fighter was mirrored by six more, two each from the unit's three *Staffeln*; only one pilot and two gunners came through alive from their aircraft's descent on land. The very high fatality rate was not uncommon on the Bf 110 and was likely due to the protracted bale out procedure for the pilot in particular. In place of a simple one-piece canopy, the *Zerstörer* featured a top panel and two side panels. The former had to be released before the other two could be pushed downwards—a similar situation as on the P-38. The gunner's single-piece canopy on all variants up to the 'E' was unlatched and jettisoned by a lever. Both airmen then faced the possibility of making contact either with the horizontal stabiliser or less likely the vertical fin after vacating their positions. Attempting an exit, especially if the fighter was going out of control, would be an uphill task at best.

Slaughter of the Innocents (3)

Fg Off. Michael G. Homer was originally a Bomber Command pilot who had been awarded the DFC during his operational tour. A posting to No. 1 Squadron at the beginning of September was followed by a transfer to the Duxford Wing's No. 242 Squadron on the 21st. The relatively sparse time span in which to adapt to the greatly-differing flight characteristics of a fighter compared to a bomber, as well as gaining even a basic knowledge of how to survive an air battle, probably contributed to his loss a mere seven days after taking up his latest post.

September Finale

The aircraft and personnel-casualty statistics from the 15th onward had revealed a grimly favourable balance in the RAF's favour. On only two days (the 24th and the 28th) had the daily losses risen above the *Luftwaffe* figures (eleven and ten, and seventeen and twelve) and indeed the margin was anything up to 100 per cent on twelve of the remaining thirteen days. On the 30th, there occurred what was the last sizeable pitched battle. During the morning, two closely-spaced bomber sorties under direct escort and with further indirect support hovering between Dover and Dungeness were both directed at Biggin Hill and Kenley. A third raid launched further west before midday involved some 100 aircraft split between Bf 110s and Bf 109s indulging in a *freie Jagd*. Finally, the last concerted effort was initiated by KG55 with the Westland factory at Yeovil, the briefed target.

There were rebuffs suffered by several RAF units, beginning with No. 229 losing three Hurricanes and one pilot killed during the first enemy incursion. No. 56 Squadron lost two Hurricanes while challenging the *freie Jagd* attackers and three more were shot down or written-off during the KG55 incursion, happily with no pilot fatalities. Several other squadrons suffered single or in one case double loss; the latter was self-inflicted when Plt Off. Vernon Simmonds collided with Plt Off. Robert Kings, both No. 238 Squadron airmen managing to bale out during a routine patrol.

The *Luftwaffe* was not having matters its own way, either for the bomber or fighter elements. KG55 had witnessed success in several of its recent operations but had paid a steady price in crews. Today's planned raid upon the Westland factory at Yeovil by forty-three He 111s was backed up by fifty-two Bf 109s and forty Bf 110s. The course was to Portland Bill from where the final bomb run was commenced, but the first fighter opposition was encountered off the coast. A good degree of cloud cover was present over the land and this was a factor that likely featured in the resultant tragedy.

The lead *Beobachter* zeroed-in on what was taken to be the factory complex but was actually the small town of Sherborne several miles west of Yeovil. The bomb patterns ploughed through the town, killing a number of civilians and destroying property with no benefit to the campaign. Adding to the failure was the cost to the formation; four bombers were dispatched to a watery grave in the Channel. There was a total crew loss on three, but the fourth machine, a He 111P-2 from 3 *Staffel*, was 'ditched', an act survived by four of the five airmen who were later picked up by the *Seenotdienst*. The aircraft also bore Maj. E. Kuehl, the *Gruppe*'s operations officer who had prepared today's operational order and who was among those saved.

The day's operations for the *Jagdwaffe* was a disaster in terms of losses, with thirty-two aircraft struck-off *Luftwaffe* records. Bomber losses were almost half at fifteen, both figures reflecting the mix of MIA and written-off airframes. JG26 had been one of the leading *Geschwadern* in garnering success during the battle, but today it surrendered four pilots, of which two were killed with a fifth Bf 109 written-off. Equally punished were JG2, with three MIA losses along with their pilots and Uffz. Zeller and Fw. Neumann killed in a take-off collision. Worst affected in terms of aircraft attrition (eight) was JG27; five pilots went down with two survivors among their number, while three further Bf 109s were written-off. One of the *Geschwader*'s POWs was extremely fortunate to end up so. Obltn. Fischer attempted a crash-landing in a public park, but the battle-damaged Bf 109 overturned; the cockpit frame was crushed flat, but the pilot amazingly escaped intact. JG52 contributed one-third of the thirteen other fighters struck off official records.

The Bond's Inevitable Strains

The close-knit relationships established on a fighter squadron could and did produce an increasingly inordinate strain upon the pilots in particular. This was a negative aspect that displayed itself as the air battle erupted into full life since at this stage of the Second World War, the bulk of pilots had previously served and therefore interacted for many months. The corollary to this was that every individual loss was keenly felt, given that the total unit complement was not far above double figures and was further subdivided into flight strength (the officially laid-down unit figure of twenty-nine pilots barely reached above twenty even by the battle's climatic period).

No. 603 (City of Edinburgh) Squadron had spent almost the first year of the Second World War in Scotland. The pilots had gained a modicum of combat knowledge in engaging the *Luftwaffe* raids on naval units around the Firth of Forth and the occasional attacker off the East Scottish coast but were not called upon to bolster No. 11 Group's hard-pressed strength until late August. Fg Off. Richard Hillary related how 'all sixteen of us headed south to Hornchurch in a mood of quiet elation', the inference being that they would match up to anything their adversaries could hand out; as it transpired for them and other acolyte squadrons, the grim reality of the battle would soon sharply intrude upon any such expectations.

Before the month was out, the fairly-well-bonded squadron had suffered three fatalities. First to demonstrate the often-brutal brevity of operational flying was Plt Off. 'Broody' Benson, so nicknamed due to his solemn demeanour. His death on the 28th was mirrored by the first of two brothers to fall. F/L Harold K. McDonald had joined the squadron well prior to the Second World War and was reunited with his kin, Plt Off. Donald K. McDonald, during July in what was to evolve into a tragically-brief event with the latter's loss over the Channel. An exact calendar month on their union in death was confirmed when 'H. K.' was shot down over Kent.

Next to go was Fg Off. R. 'Bubbles' Waterston, a fellow Edinburgh citizen to the McDonalds, who was downed by Bf 109s over London on 31 August. Although Richard Hillary survived his bale out and descent into the Channel on

3 September, the hideous facial and body burns arising from being momentarily trapped in his Spitfire's flame-stricken cockpit left him facing many months of remedial skin surgery granted to him and others by the skills of Archibald McIndoe at his specialist hospital in Kent. His close friend Fg Off. Peter Pease's five-month spell with the squadron was closed out twelve days later when he engaged a bomber formation whose escort cover shot him down; his CO, Sqn Ldr George L. Denham, was more fortunate in managing to jump from his crippled fighter during the same afternoon combat.

The 'grim reapers' tally was somewhat reduced, albeit still painful during the ensuing three weeks. On the 27th, Plt Off. 'Pip' Cardell jumped clear from his fighter but suffered the particularly horrible fate of a parachute that failed to deploy and was fatally propelled into the Channel waters. Most of the foregoing pilots had served some length of time with No. 603, but the latest casualty, although a veteran of the July period, only lasted eight days; his arrival on 30 September from No. 54 Squadron, a unit that had been through the combat 'wringer' since Dunkirk, ended with Fg Off. Henry Matthews crashing to his death on 7 October.

The ability of the Hurricane to withstand such severe damage as inflicted on this No. 87 Squadron fighter was a hallmark of its survival in combat. However, the punishment was self-inflicted on 24 October 1940, when another Hurricane collided with LK: T, Plt Off. J. R. Cock making a superb effort in landing the crippled machine. The other pilot baled out from P3404 but tragically suffered parachute failure.

October Diminuendo

The Battle of (or more accurately for) Britain was already over as far as the possibility of the nation's immediate physical subjugation was concerned. Hitler had issued his proclamation on 19 September in which he had stated that the 'Invasion was postponed indefinitely'. This would be followed during October by *Generalfeldmarschall* Keitel in command of the German High Command (*Oberkommando der Wehrmacht* or OKW) announcing that all plans for an invasion were now in abeyance until the spring or even summer of 1941—by which latter stage the Führer would have committed the fatal blunder of invading Soviet Russia, thereby initiating the very situation any warring nation rightly feared, namely a two-front conflict.

The fight for survival was still on as far as Fighter Command's personnel were concerned, but the onset of the autumnal weather patterns gave increased hope that the worst was over for 1940 at least. The high-level fighter incursions still had to be dealt with, however enervating the process of gaining the necessary altitude before engaging their opponents was proving to be for the RAF pilots. The Hurricane pilots were really pushed to do so in comparison to their Spitfire colleagues.

The indulging of *Störangriffe* (Intruder raids) on specialist targets with those devoted to aircraft production a top priority had not reaped too much success but one strike on 3 October by a Ju 88 from I/KG77 could have had serious consequences for the development of the de Havilland Mosquito. Obltn. Fiebig delivered his bomb load squarely on the plant and the result was an 80 per cent loss of material along with twenty-one staff deaths. Fortunately, the prototype airframe was located elsewhere. The Ju 88's four crew had little time for congratulations because ground fire fatally crippled the bomber and it crash-landed mere miles distant from Hatfield (ironically, Fiebig had not found his briefed primary and had chanced across this target instead).

A break in the regular indulgence of *Jabo* operations occurred on the 7th when Westland's factory at Yeovil was again focused upon; this time round, the duty was assigned to II/KG51's Ju 88s with a substantial escort consisting of Bf 109s and Bf 110s. Elements of four squadrons rose to challenge the incoming formation, and the resultant battle concluded with almost even loss figures of eight (*Luftwaffe*) and six (RAF). The single Ju 88 failing to return was flown by Obltn. Hey (I/KG51) and initially lost one engine to assault from Plt Off. Robert Doe (No. 234 Squadron). The bombs were jettisoned, and a turn southward made; the now-isolated bomber was wide open to further attack, which duly arrived. Three more Spitfires descended upon their lone, lumbering prey and their gunfire set the fuselage ablaze; this left the pilot with no option but to order a bale out that all four airmen survived.

Once again, it was the Bf 110 elements from ZG26 that absorbed the punishment with fully seven crews lost out of an overall total of nineteen from all today's operations. There was an exact split between those airmen killed and

The pilot of V7608, whose serial number can be partially discerned beneath the fuselage colour band, is preparing to start up his Mk I Hurricane. The black port wing underside merits the application of a yellow rim to the Type 'A' roundel to make it stand out. Fighter also bears an anti-glare strip aligned ahead of the windshield. Squadron was based at Kirton-in-Lindsey at this time.

those surviving with four of the pilots included in the former category. Here was further proof if really needed that the *Zerstörer* was basically unable to survive a one-on-one encounter with its RAF opponents or indeed in future against the Soviet and USAAF fighters (sadly for RAF Bomber Command, its looming utilisation as a night fighter would witness its crews reaping a bloody harvest during the nocturnal bombing offensive).

No Security Anywhere

North Weald lies upwards of 80–100 miles distant from the sea and so would seem to be safe from surprise assault; on 29 October, this assumption was found to be false. No. 257 Squadron, led by CO Sqn Ldr Tuck, was taking off when a *Jabo* formation from II/JG2 swooped upon the airfield; the blast wave from one bomb threw Sgt Alex Girdwood's Hurricane on its back, whereupon it fell back to earth and expunged the pilot's life in its violent explosion. Plt Off. Franek Surma avoided a similar fate, but having gained several thousand feet altitude, his Hurricane was fatally struck by gunfire and the Pole baled out of the doomed fighter.

The Polish pilot's problems were destined to mount to a likely terminal conclusion as he floated down, only for his parachute canopy to tangle with a tree and leave him dangling. The location was outside an inn whose clientele included several French servicemen. They gazed upon Surma and thought he was '*un sale Boche*' (a dirty German). This was hardly surprising because Surma was wearing a *Luftwaffe* airman's flight jacket that he had 'liberated' during the German onrush into Poland the previous year.

This, coupled with Surma's agitated accent suggesting a Teutonic origin as he struggled to free himself, persuaded the Frenchmen that they should solve the problem by climbing up and wrapping the parachute cords around the neck of the 'German'! Good sense prevailed and Surma was assisted down out of the tree by other people in the vicinity where his true status was confirmed, and profound apologies expressed by his potential executioners. By the time Tuck reached the scene, Surma was well alight with alcohol; afterwards, his CO persuaded the Pole to dispense with the offending garment.

The twelve-strong enemy formation was reduced by a quarter by the time it left British airspace. No. 249 Squadron based at North Weald pursued the retreating formation led by Flt Lt 'Butch' Barton; he latched onto and downed Fw. Rank's 4 *Staffe*l Bf 109, and a second *Staffel* machine flown by Obfw. Harmeling (POW) was credited to Plt Off. Michel Maciejowski; finally, Plt Off. Bill Millington was granted Obltn. von Schenk's 5 *Staffel* aircraft from which he baled out, but his and Fw. Rank's injuries led to their subsequent deaths.

Post-Mortem

The reason for the official dates of the battle spanning 10 July to 31 October are obscure to say the least. Although muted in relation to what had transpired up to its 'conclusion', the *Luftwaffe* was still carrying out operations over Southern Britain and airmen on both sides continued to face death and injury. The post-war Battle of Britain Clasp award was granted on the foregoing time span only, which was manifestly unfair especially for those participating prior to or after the stated dates.

As the days and weeks slipped into winter, the RAF took stock of the overall situation. For a start, the falsely romantic, if not naïve, atmosphere that had spawned the 'Greatest Flying Club in the World' had been ruthlessly cast aside. The hard crucible of combat had ensured that not only were the tactics hitherto considered suitable for air battles—the FCA system in particular, but also the formation patterns flown—basically flawed, the pre-war relationship between officers and other ranks was undergoing a radical change.

In the former instance, the *Luftwaffe*'s superior tactics in the air had wrought mandatory changes. As regards the latter situation, the steady influx of wartime volunteers added to those pre-war members of the Volunteer Reserve was breaking down any class barriers between themselves and the regular-service officers.

Furthermore, a number in these two categories were either already assuming or were destined to establish themselves in the post of Squadron CO and even higher; in addition, many such graded personnel surviving the Second World War would gain permanent commissions to further degrade the class-distinction aspects of service life in which the RAF had hitherto dabbled, albeit to a lesser degree than the other two services.

The figure of 544 Fighter Command aircrew lost in the battle ran the gamut of service experience and combat prowess. The 'Grim Reaper's scythe' had demonstrated no distinction in terms of age, rank, or background. The deaths encompassed eighteen-year olds up to several individuals well above thirty years; combat-raw sergeants shared a fatal communion with wing commanders; and individual backgrounds ranged from labourers and craftsmen to public school graduates. As for combat experience in such feral circumstances, there was never any guarantee of survival, with seasoned aces taken down alongside acolytes on their first sortie.

Evidence of the geographic spread of the command's airmen was clear. Not only did a sizeable contingent of men and women from Canada, Australia, New Zealand, and other British Empire countries answer the call to assist the 'Mother Country', Poland, Czechoslovakia, France, Norway, and other lands now under

In late 1940, No. 71 Squadron was the first of three fighter units to be established for staffing by American volunteer pilots, all three bearing the title of Eagle. XR: Z's codes are prominently applied around the Type A1 roundel: the 'Sky S' tail band, which obscures the aircraft serial finishes at the camouflage separation line.

the unhappy yoke of Nazism had added their national weight as did those individuals from the USA who turned a blind eye to their country's neutral stance. Democracy's eternal battle with autocracy had been encouragingly, if rather tragically, demonstrated over British skies in mid- and late 1940.

Now the longer-term challenge to beat back and ultimately demolish the forces of Fascist intolerance would be taken up. The sole element of subjugated Europe holding out militarily had survived, but totally lacked the material and human means with which to gain a substantial foothold on any key element of the Third Reich's ill-gotten empire. A hard, unpredictable road lay ahead in order to achieve that laudable end.

8

Groping in the Dark

The original intention of the two central European adversaries in the execution of air assaults was that this would be conducted by daylight; only in this manner could targets be specifically located and accurately bombed. A by-product arising from the decision was the hoped-for avoidance of non-combatant casualties by focusing exclusively on the enemy's identified industrial and military resources. As it transpired, the experience of first the RAF followed by the *Luftwaffe* in being badly rebuffed by the respective defensive networks led to or probably enforced the decision that operations would have to be switched to night-time hours, however restrictive this might be in overall operational terms.

The subsequent accusation and counter accusation regarding a deliberate descent into indiscriminate bombing could be perceived to be in the *Luftwaffe*'s disfavour. Its bomber crews had hammered a number of cities and towns in between attacking Poland and the onset of the Western European Campaigns between April and June 1940. The result was a mix of legitimate target assault and sometimes blatant attacks on locations with little or no war-production capacity. The RAF policy up to May was to refrain from any bombing operations over Germany, with propaganda leaflet sorties the norm.

Both Britain and Germany were basically unprepared in terms of effective countermeasures to combat the nocturnal over-flying of their hinterlands as the Second World War commenced. In the former case, the potential situation was measurably worse in that no electronic support equipment with which to home-in upon the night-shrouded attacker was on immediate hand as the *Luftwaffe* massed for large-scale attack at much shorter range to their targets compared to RAF Bomber Command. Added to this, by 1939–40, was the German advance in remote navigation and bombing equipment that at one point would threaten to render even minimal-size targets liable to pinpoint attack by bombers so outfitted. An alternate use of the equipment was for the specialist bombers to illuminate major cities with flares to act as beacons for the main bomber force.

No. 604 Squadron converted onto the Blenheim Mk 1F in 1939 but flew daylight operations until June 1940. It then transferred to Middle Wallop to conduct tests with the initial flow of Air Interception (AI) radar equipment. Picture was taken in April at RAF Northolt. Outline of the belly-'gun-pack' can be discerned on the nearest aircraft; individual aircraft letters are not yet applied.

Why such research was deemed necessary for the benefit of what was a daylight tactical as opposed to a strategic-operating entity seems to be contradictory, but at least the *Knickebein*, *X-Gerät* and *Y-Gerät* equipment variations were on hand; in contrast, RAF navigator/bomb aimers were bereft of any electronic support at this time. Instead, they had to rely upon Mother Nature in the form of clear weather that permitted visual scanning for suitable landmarks. Conversely, Astra-navigation could be carried out when cloud cover intervened to prevent a sight of the ground.

Knickebein (Crooked Leg)

The first of the range of electronic devices with which to deliver attacks on British targets was not only the simplest but moreover was available to all bomber aircrews; this was due to its adaptation from the standard Lorenz beam-approach equipment that was basically very precise in azimuth terms. An aural support was provided to the pilot in the form of continuous Morse code signals—if veering off course, the letter 'E' (dots) on the left and letter 'T' (dashes) on the right would be heard. The steady 'on course' tone would accordingly be produced by the merging of the twin Morse signals.

Five VHF stations were set up along Western Europe between Denmark and France from which beams were directed against the selected target and which when the bomber crossed their path would initiate the requisite signal for bomb release. Range was restricted in practical terms to around 200 miles, with the bombers also having to attain an altitude around 20,000 feet in order to continue receiving the ground-transmitter signals. In addition, the aircraft's beam signal steadily widened as the distance increased, but even then, its approximately 1-mile spread at maximum range was sufficient for an 'area' assault if weather conditions intervened to block a visual sighting.

The existence of *Knickebein* had been confirmed by Dr R. V. Jones, a brilliant scientist. Examination of the Lorenz equipment had revealed a refinement quality too high for its original function and the subsequent aerial searches for beam signals by aircraft of Beam Approach Training Development Unit (BATDU) ultimately succeeded in pinning down the station locations. The initial antidote was provided by hospital X-ray sets (coded 'Aspirin' in response to the 'Headache' term applied to the German equipment) that were used to 'jam' the signals. A more subtle method was the introduction of special transmitters that focused upon and distorted the beam signals. It was not too long before the *Luftwaffe* aircrew began to lose their unconditional faith in the efficacy of *Knickebein*, resorting to standard navigation techniques that inevitably degraded the locating of a target, let alone its precise punishment.

The Burgeoning Onslaught

The *Luftwaffe* bombers being encamped on the near continent left the southern part of the British Isles within their operational range while southern Scotland and Northern Ireland was capable of being struck from both this southerly axis or from the Scandinavian-based units. The relatively few sorties flown at night over southern England and its eastern seaboard brought little destruction in its wake on land, but the continued minelaying in the nation's sea lanes was more productive in terms of sunken and damaged shipping.

The technical means with which to stem if not reverse the onset of regular attacks by night was minimal both in respect of electronically-outfitted aircraft and anti-aircraft weapons. The recent disaster on the continent had robbed the British Army of a high proportion of its overall 3.7-inch artillery content. What was left in Britain along with the less mobile 4.5-inch guns and lighter-calibre weapons such as the Bofors 40 mm amounted, for example, to less than 60 per cent of the total heavy gun establishment regarded as the minimum for overall national cover—a calculation that in itself could be treated as woefully inadequate. It would require months of productive effort to bring the figures up to the theoretical figure, and in the meantime, the attackers would remain free from serious interference among their ranks. Nor was the gun-laying radar equipment on hand in any quantity with which to bring more accurate fire to bear upon the individual bombers. The same technical disability applied to the searchlight batteries intended to work in partnership with the guns.

A passive form of defence lay in the use of barrage balloons; these were massive fabric-manufactured and inflatable units fitted with a 'Y'-pattern stabiliser resembling elephant ears. They were raised and retained aloft by a winch-driven cable that could extend thousands of feet. Their deployment was useful for deterring the dive-bombing of targets, but their presence could and sometimes did prove a lethal barrier to any aircraft unfortunate enough to become entangled in either the balloon surface or the cable. Contact between a major component such as a wing and the cable could result in its excision with an even greater chance of the aircraft's destruction being realised.

If the ground defensive network proved to be virtually moribund in mid-1940, the same almost shocking deficiency applied to Fighter Command's nocturnal resources. The absolute need for airborne radar equipment with which to pick out, close in upon, and dispatch a *Luftwaffe* bomber was being addressed, but once again, although the first sets were becoming available, these were both far too few in number by the *Blitz*'s inauguration on 7–8 September; in addition, their efficiency level was simply woeful. Another key deficiency was the immediate lack of Ground-Control Interception (GCI) stations, whose controlling staff using their sets could direct the night fighters towards a 'hostile' plot at a distance close enough for the airborne set to register a 'contact' signal; the rest of the interception was then up to the aircrew in question.

The range of aircraft designs forming Fighter Command's night defensive force demonstrated the *ad hoc* nature of this function. The sole type that could be regarded as even generally suitable for the duty was the Bristol Blenheim Mk 1F. A derivative of the original bomber variant, the main difference lay in the provision of a 'gun-pack' mounted below the forward fuselage and bearing four .303 machine guns. The first AI sets had been installed and tested in this variant as early as the previous August, with Nos 23 and 604 Squadrons involved to date. Already, the first kill had been attained on 2–3 July—admittedly not by a standard squadron, but by the specialist Fighter Interception Unit (FIU) whose work on such equipment would steadily advance its ultimate efficiency levels. A key disadvantage of the Blenheim lay in its speed performance—or rather, its marked inferiority *vis-à-vis* any of the three *Luftwaffe* bombers prosecuting the 1940–41 offensive.

Three other aircraft-types were 'volunteered' for the role, of which only one could be treated as anything approaching a viable candidate. The Hurricane and Spitfire were proven machines in combat, but only by day. To send pilots aloft within a darkened environment with either machine basically unsuited for nocturnal operations demonstrated the desperate straits the RAF was facing. The following limitations applied: neither possessed the necessary fuel endurance; the confined cockpits did not provide very good scanning platforms; and the inability to carry any electronic search equipment meant the 'eyeball Mk I' was the sole source for detection of the enemy aircraft (successfully spotting an aircraft at night was likened to trying to track down a fly within the darkened confines of a massive structure such as a cathedral).

Above: The crew of a Blenheim squadron tasked with night-fighting duties are clambering aboard. The Bristol design was barely adequate to the task with a performance just matching that of the He 111s and inferior to that of the Ju 88s, the main adversaries during the 1940–41 *Blitz*. Nor was its firepower good, consisting of four machine guns in a belly pack and a single gun in the turret. Letter 'R' is part of the RO code for No. 29 Squadron that switched onto the Beaufighter beginning September 1940.

Below: The previous picture's identity with No. 29 Squadron is confirmed by the pilot who is now clambering into the cockpit. He is Plt Off. P. Kells and the squadron is currently based at Coleby Grange in Lincolnshire. Airborne radar was not only primitive during the onset of the *Blitz* but was also not available in enough numbers, leaving crews not so outfitted to make visual and largely failed attempts at interception.

But needs must and the fighters were deemed of some use especially in moonlit conditions.

The third single-engined type called upon was one that conversely had failed by day, namely the Boulton Paul Defiant. There is no doubt that the greatest advantage over its single-engined contemporaries lay in the four-gun turret; coupled with this was a rather better flight endurance on its 105-gallon capacity compared to the eighty-plus gall capacity of the aforementioned pair. The provision of a two-man crew further improved the chance of visually engaging a target, however marginal the prospect would generally prove in practice. As with its single-engined contemporaries, the 'eyeball Mk I' would have to suffice for achieving contact since a radar set was not initially deemed a practical proposition thanks to cockpit limitations.

Although some Mk I Defiants would reportedly be equipped with AI Mk IV during the late winter and spring of 1941, regular on-board radar provision would arrive with the introduction of the Mk II Defiant. In either case, the dual task of flying the fighter while interpreting the set-screen's readings would surely have proved to be a very demanding activity. However, the *Blitz* had run its course by the time of the new variant's introduction into service; moreover, the growing availability of the custom-built Beaufighter clearly rendered its single-engined contemporary redundant in its perceived nocturnal role and a percentage would be switched to secondary, albeit still important, duties such as target-towing or ASR.

The flexibility of the rotating gun turret bestowed a key advantage on the Defiant compared to a wing-mounted gun platform. Whereas the latter layout forced its possessor to make either a level approach or stand on its tail to fire a 'shotgun' burst ahead of the target; the Defiant could approach undetected from below, fly below and/or parallel with its prey, and fire into the fuselage or better still the wings that bore the fuel tanks. The few successes attained with this aircraft utilised the technique—a technique that tragically would be adopted wholesale by the *Nachtjagd* against RAF Bomber Command from mid-1943 and reap a huge harvest in bombers and crews in its wake. As it was, the Defiant crews serving in the ultimate figure of seven squadrons and assigned the duty largely suffered under the same visual limitations.

There was one bright if still nascent star on the horizon in the form of the Blenheim Mk 1F's successor, the Beaufighter. Not only was its performance envelope streets ahead of the Mk 1F: the aircraft had been designed from the outset as a fighter although its deployment as a night fighter had arguably not been perceived. The superb and rugged aerodynamic outline was supplemented by two powerful Bristol Hercules radial engines. Better still was the armament consisting of six outer wing-mounted machine guns that were backed by four 20-mm cannon in the lower nose compartment. The first production airframes were on the point of assignment to No. 604 Squadron just days before the *Blitz*'s onset; among the unit's pilot complement was one destined to be a premier exponent of night-fighter operations.

The 'Happy Times', *Luftwaffe* Style

The foregoing title refers to the two periods of 1940 and early 1942 when the U-boat crews played havoc with the Allied merchant fleets respectively traversing the North Atlantic and US East Coast convoy routes. The initial period of the *Blitz* could likewise be placed in the same category and granted the same sobriquet since it would play out firmly in Germany's favour, for all the promises of better things to come for the RAF night-fighter resources. London suffered its tormentors' attention virtually exclusively for almost two months. The proximity of the capital to the bomber airfields and the geographic 'giveaway' of the River Thames in clearer conditions rendered the capital an easy victim. Added to these purely military factors was the propaganda value of striking at the heart of Hitler's stubbornly-resistant enemy and hopefully weakening the city population's and even the nation's will to resist in the process.

The clinically-effective bombing of the London Docks infrastructure on 7 September was a clear exception to the subsequent battering of not only the capital, but all of Britain's cities. The concept of nocturnal 'area bombing' as opposed to achieving surgical strikes on purely commercial or military targets within a metropolitan area arguably bore first fruit in September 1940. The physical invisibility of specific valid targets meant that there was no guarantee of success even when deploying electronic means for their detection and exclusive assault—thus the deployment of ever-expanding bomber forces with which to saturate the general target area with the prospect of achieving some measure of success. Total War was accordingly on hand in an inevitable manner that encompassed civilians as well as military personnel in its remorseless passage.

That this harsh expansion was evident lay in the manner of the weaponry now being utilised by the *Luftwaffe*. The standard range of aerodynamic bombs was directed via the bombsight method and these had some prospect of landing near or on an identified target. Not so the so-called 'land-mine', which was an adaptation of the naval magnetically-detonated weapon. The *Luftmine* (LM) came in two sizes of LMA (500 kg) and LMB (1,000 kg) whose explosive content was around two-thirds of gross weight. This fearful degree of blast effect was truly indiscriminate in that these weapons were not aimed but released attached to a parachute, thereby rendering any pretence at accuracy null and void—a pure 'terror' device whose military value was as secondary as it was haphazard in application.

Gunnery Woes

The immunity from any appreciable degree of loss that marked the *Blitz*'s progress between September and the year's end was demonstrated on the first night. Out of the approximately 250 crews who reached London, just two—a 6/KG4 He 111 and a 4/KG54 Ju 88—failed to return. In the fire and smoke-shrouded city, over 400 civilians lay dead, a figure that would be multiplied over 100-fold across Britain's length and breadth before the campaign's conclusion the following May. The weather-affected night of the 10th that limited bomber numbers was to prove an exception in terms of freedom from major assault. The following night witnessed an event aimed at boosting the citizens' morale if nothing else.

The numbers of 3.7-inch guns assigned to London's defence were low in total as well as still lacking a comprehensive GL radar back-up with which to more accurately engage the incoming bombers. With this in mind, the authorities decided the next night to indulge the gunners in the discharge of a steady mass barrage. The resultant counter-noise to the nine-hour procession of bombers and the scream and detonation of their loads was intended to demonstrate that the defenders were not supinely absorbing the punishment but were striking back; the citizens would have had no real knowledge of the lack of success attending the expenditure of thousands of shells, however.

The duty of the gunnery personnel that encompassed both male and female ranks—the latter initially assigned only after the *Blitz* was concluded—was physically demanding. The gun sites were basically exposed to the elements no matter where they were stationed. The heavier 4.5-inch weapons were fitted with a metal framework that did little to expel the weather conditions while their 3.7 contemporaries lacked any cover. Nor were the operators manning the predictor equipment adjacent to the guns any better provisioned. Added to this physically debilitating situation, especially in poor or winter weather conditions, was the risk of injury or even death, thanks to stray bombs or fragments from their own expended shells.

No. 25 Squadron was in the forefront of aerial radar development, although in this picture, the Mk IF Blenheims are carrying out a convoy patrol in early 1940. The gun pack outline on L1437 can be discerned along with a cradle frame directly behind. The first sets were delivered and tested as early as September 1939, but their performance boded ill for the prospects of even picking up another aircraft let alone providing an accurate approach to within firing range.

Night-Fighter Travails

The manifold operational limitations imposed upon the Army anti-aircraft (AA) gunners at this stage of the *Blitz* was largely paralleled by their fellow defenders aloft. The switching of selected Hurricane and Spitfire squadrons to night operations demonstrated the desperate state of the command's countermeasures. The lack of a heater meant that the extremely low temperatures encountered at the bombers' altitude ate into a pilot's physical energy that in turn adversely affected his reactions; this was the case regardless of the fighters' short flight endurance. As regards electronic assistance, not only could AI equipment not be fitted in the cockpit, but VHF radio equipment was not on hand.

The gunsight's presence meant its bulk ironically hindered the ability to scan the instrument panel. The striking power or rather the limitation in striking power posed by the largely machine-gun-equipped machines would provide no more guarantee of success in taking down a bomber than in daylight— that is, assuming any could be picked out within the depressingly vast expanses of the night skies. The 20-mm cannon was due to be installed as standard both to the Mk V Spitfire onwards as well as the Mk IIC Hurricane, but the presence of both current designs within the night-fighter ranks would be gone before the advent on operations of these heavier-armed variants—by which stage, custom-built night fighters would assume the role anyway.

The experience of No. 85 Squadron was probably typical after Sqn Ldr Townsend (CO) was informed the unit had been selected for the revised role in October. He couched a letter to No. 12 Group requesting several amendments to the Hurricanes that included the following: VHF radio; the smaller Prismatic gunsight to allow better instrument scanning; and improved cockpit lighting. An anti-glare shield fitted above the engine exhaust manifold was also suggested, although the blinding glare from the normally-exposed item should have been a matter of mandatory amendment. The application of black paint to the airframe was certainly applied to the squadron aircraft, but the original RDM2 issue had poor adhesive qualities.

Even when these corrections were made the average sortie imposed an enervating weight upon the pilot. Flying even in good weather conditions still left him reliant upon his skills alone as he carried out his patrol over a specific area while remaining above the maximum altitude assigned the AA batteries when over-flying London in particular. Adverse weather increased the chances of going astray and unable to find one's assigned or even any airfield. Regardless of this complication, the completion of any sortie was fraught with difficulty; the bare minimum of airfield and runway lighting was permitted in order to avoid possible assault by enemy bombers, a factor that made for a serious and sometimes fatal outcome when attempting a landing.

The autumn and winter months would drag on with little or no success in even tracking down the enemy intruders, let alone shooting one down. Sqn Ldr Townsend made an interception on 25 February involving a Do 17 from 4/KG2.

The distinctive outline of a Boulton-Paul Defiant is emphasised by the sunlight as the fighter flies low over the airfield. The inability to carry on-board radar equipment in the Mk I left the crew with no option but to hunt down the bombers visually—a daunting and largely frustrating measure. On the other hand, the four-gun turret was potentially effective especially when intercepting a target from underneath.

The bomber was fatally crippled and fell from the skies to explode on impact; one of the four crewmembers died thanks to a failed parachute with his three companions captured. Any sense of achievement by the victorious pilot must have been tempered by one huge bonus—the aircraft's lit navigation lights that attracted his attention.

Diminishing Returns?

The relaxed manner in which the *Luftwaffe* crews approached the initial series of raids on London would not be sustained forever. Granted the overall lack of ground and airborne resistance to their presence over Britain's capital and several other cities made for what was a straight-forward duty of completing each sortie. What could not be guaranteed to remain equally pacific was the weather; unpredictable shifts in wind, cloud patterns along with rain showers (or later as winter set in, snow, sleet, and frost) was destined to impose an increasing load of pressure upon pilots and navigators (*Beobachter*). That pressure was further extended as the bombers reached ever-further afield across the national hinterland to seek out and deposit their loads on other cities.

A confirmed but very meagre total of six bombers were brought down over Britain or in the sea during September. Of this figure, two were due to AA fire's immediate or subsequent effect, one to collision with a barrage balloon cable, and one to the pilot losing control according to the sole survivor among the four-man crew. The remaining pair of crews could count themselves very unfortunate to be intercepted by a Blenheim from No. 25 Squadron (on the 14th) and a Defiant of No. 141 Squadron (on the 17th); the latter team from KG54's ranks was the first of three to be MIA within five nights so the unit's morale must have been low to say the least.

No. 25 Squadron's involvement in the defensive screen was important in that it had been testing the principle of AI interception with the first sets on hand. Moreover, the victor, Plt Off. Mike Herrick, had already racked up his first night kill on 4–5 September, a He 111 of *Stab* I/KG1 before his follow-up victory on the 14th. The overall efficiency level of the equipment that was barely operational was to prove very unpredictable for several months ahead, so it says much for this pilot's skill if not also tenacity that these successes had been achieved (the squadron's imminent conversion to the Bristol Beaufighter would ensure an enhanced aircraft-performance as well as introducing much-needed striking power compared to the Blenheim's paltry 'gun-pack').

October 1940

Although the daylight battle was largely given over to the *Jagdwaffe*, the nocturnal presence of what was a formidable number of bombers from the two *Luftflotten* over Britain was still somewhat staccato in numerical terms. Although London was targeted with three-figure numbers on four occasions in the first half of October, there were other nights when little or no sorties were flown to the capital; a number of other cities were also attacked. The disheartening aspect for the RAF and the AA gunners was the continuing marginal scale of bomber losses credited to the defences. There was a degree of 'operational' casualties occurring on the continent—take-off and landing crashes, etc.—but even when these were added into the loss percentage the effect upon the *Blitz* campaign was still marginal.

Civilian casualties began to rise steadily as the assaults gathered pace and furthermore took on an 'area' dimension to their activities. The massive layout of London in particular that involved intermingled industrial plant and housing inevitably resulted in the latter absorbing punishment. Air-raid shelter facilities were inadequate and tragically vulnerable in many cases, while use of the capital's underground rail system could only accommodate a small proportion of the total population. It was little wonder that many military personnel, especially those in the RAF coming into contact with the citizens, felt a sense of inadequacy bordering on shame at their Service's current failure to stem the enemy's aerial tide.

'Black Beauty'

The Bristol Beaufighter was to prove one of the premier RAF designs in the Second World War that was destined to serve in a multi-combat role almost akin to that of the Mosquito. Its inception as a night-fighter proved to be very timely, if also rather tardy; whether its use in this duty was previously envisaged by the Air Ministry is unclear, but its overall aerodynamic qualities coupled both to its ability to mount heavy armament and accommodate AI radar equipment was to prove an urgently-required boon for Fighter Command. The *Luftwaffe* crews were in for a shock, whose effect was only gradually going to be realised as sufficient numbers of the twin-engined machine arrived on the squadrons selected for night-fighter duties.

The Beaufighter was basically an adaptation of its Beaufort torpedo-bomber contemporary. To the rugged nature of the latter's airframe was added the increased power of the Bristol Hercules radial with a 1,130-hp output that far outpaced the 770-hp equivalent for the Beaufort's Taurus power plants. The range factor was nearly half again *vis-à-vis* the Beaufort, although service ceiling was marginally less. The destructive punch provided by four 20-mm nose-mounted cannon and six wing-mounted machine guns was a huge bonus in the bid to bite into the enemy's ranks.

The pilot sat behind a very short nose cone that, along with generous cockpit glazing, provided him with enhanced all-round visibility. The space in the rear fuselage for the AI equipment was of generous proportions and moreover was heated; this was a distinct bonus for any radar operator formerly serving as a gunner on the Blenheim whose turrets granted the icy slipstream unfettered access. All in all, the two-man crew were provided with a superb aerial platform with which to go into action.

Slow Beginnings

Three squadrons—Nos 29, 600, and 604 Squadrons—had already been testing out the very new and often malfunctioning AI radar sets in their Blenheim Mk 1F aircraft since the year commenced. Not only were these prone to failure on being activated, the screens were affected by 'ground-returns' that created a visual blocking on their surfaces known as 'grass'. Another problem was that the echo from another aircraft could be picked up regardless of whether it was heading towards or away from the night fighter—no use for the chances of an interception if the set picked out a 'bogey' falling into the first category. During September, conversion to the Beaufighter was begun and the AI sets were installed regardless of their still frustratingly- wayward level of function. No. 604 Squadron based at Middle Wallop led the way; the airfield's location north of Southampton placed it directly in the path of *Luftflotte* 3's access to targets in central and north-western England, but the slow pace of the new design's delivery up to the year's end was to leave the German airmen in relative security from attack.

There were twin and interconnected problems to be overcome before an effective defensive response to the bombers could be mounted. The first was the

'The Shining Sword' that would cut a steadily-expanding swathe among the ranks of the He 111s and Ju 88s made its appearance during the autumn of 1940. The Beaufighter's four 20-mm cannon and six .303 machine guns provided a fearsome degree of firepower and any bomber crew homed-in upon by the Mk IV radar set fitted would be fortunate to escape being summarily dispatched. Overall, RDM2 black paint was the original camouflage applied to RAF night fighters.

performance of the AI sets that to date had hardly raised confidence among the aircrew as to their overall level of efficiency. To the problem of gaining clear visual readings on the two screens was added an initial inability to guarantee holding the 'blip' representing the potential target in a steady manner during the approach. The natural tendency to point the aircraft's nose directly at the 'trace' had to be dropped; instead, the operator had to anticipate the target's movements in advance in a similar manner to a fighter pilot utilising his skill at deflection shooting. Both actions involved an artful technique that was more easily managed by some airmen than others.

November 1940

Bomber operations during the penultimate month of 1940 reflected a steady dispersal of their numbers across the British landscape as London's companion cities felt the weight of the mainly He 111 and Ju 88-borne bomb loads. Although the capital was raided twelve times between 1 and 15 November and bore four heavy assaults towards the month's end, there were a further thirteen major and two heavy-scale attacks delivered elsewhere.

Any pretence at restricting the bomb loads to military or industrial sources alone were by now long gone, if this was ever feasible in the first instance. The *Luftwaffe*'s range of electronic devices with which to launch attacks on specific targets could only be indulged in by a limited number of bombers. However, the British equivalent countermeasures to confuse the transmissions of signals providing the precise route to and concentration upon a target were already coming into force; their effect, although not consistently effective, were still providing a measure of hindrance to the *Luftwaffe*'s hope of laying waste key sources of production such as the Rolls-Royce factories at Derby and Crewe. The era of 'area' assault in the nocturnal skies over Europe had accordingly been established in a manner that would bring the concept and even more brutally the meaning of Total War to all the major participants on the continent. In the case of Britain, one specific raid during the month was to create an autocratic expression courtesy of Dr Joseph Goebbels that epitomised this inevitable stance—*Coventrieren*—originating with the attack on Coventry on the 14th.

Coventry possessed a sizeable industrial base that included six major factory complexes and rendered the city a priority for a devastating attack. The weather conditions were in the *Luftwaffe*'s favour; visibility was sound and further improved by the presence of a full moonlit sky that rendered the target exposed without the need to deploy any guidance from KGr100 'Pathfinders' for the 550 crews assigned the operation; the specialist unit's crews did operate their *X-Gerät* equipment, but only against a region of the city rather than a specific industrial target. Its *Luftflotte* 3 companion unit II/KG55 joined in with a mix of parachute flares and SC1400 and SC1800 bombs. All too soon, Coventry's centre, along with other districts, was submerged amid flame and smoke as the raid progressed along its ten-hour length. Despite the absence of over 15 per cent of the total force, the remainder had succeeded in tearing the heart out of the city. Dr Goebbels subsequently crowed about the Luftwaffe's ability to *Coventrieren* (Coventrate) British cities in similar fashion.

The single Do 17 crew actually culled by AA fire could count themselves particularly unfortunate because not only were they the exception failing to regain their airfield, none of Obltn. Preiss's five-man team survived the bomber's loss. This solitary statistic was doubled twenty-four hours later during the latest major London raid. Even then, the 5/KG53 He 111 failed due to the weather rather than the defences; the airframe iced-up, causing the bomber to fall away and break-up in mid-air. The general immunity from any material RAF night-fighter threat was currently holding good, although a portent of things to come was about to select Uffz. Sondermeyer's 3/KG54 crew flying B3+YL for its debut.

On 19–20 November, No. 604 Squadron dispatched several Beaufighters, each being allocated a patrol area with one aircraft flown by Flt Lt John Cunningham along with Sgt John Phillipson (radar operator). Several 'contacts' were made that ended indecisively until the latest example was successfully held and closed upon to evolve into Sondermeyer's Ju 88. The resultant cannon shell and bullet fusillade did not immediately bring the bomber down but was sufficiently crippling to force the pilot to reverse course from his Birmingham-briefed target and head south after jettisoning the bombs. One crewmember was already dead, and by the time the Channel coast was looming, the now fire-stricken bomber's condition impelled Sondermeyer to order a bale out; he and only one of the other two airmen

The Mk IF Blenheim seen here was serving with No. 154 OTU when photographed, but it demonstrates its likely night-fighter service thanks to the angled-out aerial protruding from the port wing leading edge. The signals on the early set screens were often badly compromised by ground return echoes that were known as 'grass' for the pattern these cast up.

survived the incident. Thus was the stage set for the air battle to be carried to the enemy in a more certain, if sometimes staccato manner.

Only two more crews were lost over Britain before the month's end, with neither due to RAF intervention. The AA gunners disposed of a 5/KG55 He 111 during the raid on Bristol on 24–25 November, but the second crew in their 1/KuFlGr 606 Do 17 were primarily victims of electronic countermeasures in the form of 'Meacon'. This involved feeding misleading signals into the *Knickebein* navigation/bombing system's ground transmitters to throw the crews using it off course. The subsequent meandering flight pattern finally led to *Leutnant zur See* Sauersacker blundering into Plymouth's barrage balloon complex. Contact with a steel cable subsequently caused the crew to abandon their mortally-crippled mount further to the west.

X-Gerät

The introduction of the *X-Gerät* system provided the first of two electronic quantum leaps in precision focus upon a target as developed by the Germans. The equipment was allocated to a single unit, KGr100, whose He 111s were fitted with twin receiver masts. The equipment operated on a frequency range more than double that of *Knickebein*. On the ground, the Wotan I monitoring stations broadcast a steady stream of directional pulses to the *X-Gerät* sets; these were absorbed and analysed to provide the pilots and observers with the information that maintained the aircraft on a precise aural track.

The aircraft's track was intersected by three radio beams upon final target approach. The first intersection prompted the crew to be prepared to activate an *X-Uhr* clock on reaching the second intersection. When attained, the observer pushed a button on the *X-Uhr* that activated a single arm. When the third intersection was reached, a second button was pushed that stopped the first arm but activated a second arm. This rotated until it linked up with its partner. At this point, the union of the arms activated two electrical contacts that duly released the bomb-bay content.

The existence of *X-Gerät* was already known to the British authorities by the late autumn, following the discovery via 'Y'-service intercepts of transmission traffic to the Wotan I stations. However, the requisite means with which to disrupt the system were to prove more difficult to develop compared to *Knickebein*, nor was their effect upon its function as comprehensive or as effective.

German measures to limit the negative effect of the British transmitters included operating on a wide range of frequencies that would swamp the 'rogue' equipment's signals. Another measure was to delay switching on the X-beam transmitters until shortly before the bombers reached the targeted source. Further measures involved one or more frequency switches during all operations, alteration of the crossbeams, and, finally, the use of additional frequencies as the aircraft were on final run-up to the target. Although all the measures were recognised and challenged, the overall efficacy of *X-Gerät* was seemingly not badly disrupted.

December 1940

The initial onset of winter with its often-variable weather conditions was still the primary hope for at least inhibiting the full force of the *Luftwaffe* attacks. Conversely, the lengthy periods of darkness permitted the enemy bombers the opportunity to spread their efforts over many hours with a parallel extra degree of pressure not only bearing down upon the RAF pilots and Army gunners but also on the population and the civil defences with the Auxiliary Fire Service, Air Raid Wardens, police, and medical staff literally in the firing line.

As for the bomber crews, their task in bringing the necessary scale of effective punishment to the British industrial output was still a daunting one and beset by several problems. A key issue was the availability of aircraft numbers along with their bomb-carrying capacity. The He 111, Do 17, and Ju 88 had been devised with tactical operations in mind, and the result was a modest to poor return in this category; this varied between 1,000 and 2,000 kg, with only the He 111 enjoying the maximum internal capacity figure. In addition, the ability to carry individual bombs of more than 250-kg weight internally was denied due to the bomb-bay dimensions and layout; the external mounting of larger-capacity bombs created a

What looks like a blanked-out background done for security reasons provides a sharp platform with which to study a No. 256 Squadron Defiant's upper profile in relation to the gun turret's movement. The section between the cockpit rear and turret has retracted as has the fuselage length behind the turret; the resultant clearance provides the gunner with an enhanced degree of gun depression as well as greater forward azimuth cover.

drag factor that ate into fuel reserves as well as maximum speed unless internal capacity was reduced as compensation.

The fuel capacity on all three designs was adequate in attempting to reach any selected target in the British Isles. On the other hand, the carriage of even a full internal bomb load, let alone externally-mounted weapons, degraded the range factor when carrying out longer-distance raids well into the British hinterland. The countermeasure was to reduce the loads that in turn lessened the potential damage inflicted. Navigation to targets at any material distance was likely to prove a challenge to the *Beobachters*' (navigators) mental skills. By now, the regular corrupting of the *Knickebein* electronic guidance system was almost certainly having a negative effect upon the airmen's trust in the system's efficacy. The moon period was a continuing major factor in deciding when raids should be mounted. The resort to visual navigation methods was accordingly only sound when the crews were presented with reasonable to fully clear weather conditions such as during these periods, but cloud cover could and did intrude during any night to inhibit this basic target-seeking alternative.

Regardless of these limiting factors, the destruction being handed out was of a painful albeit not terminal scale. The classic example was Coventry, where industrial output was brought back to sustainable levels within week of 14 November's seemingly cataclysmic event. On a more strategic level was the target selection that switched between inland locations and seaports. The regular concentration upon key ports such as Liverpool, Bristol, and Southampton would clearly boost the U-boat offensive that was currently placing a serious brake upon the vital import of commodities with which to sustain Britain's war effort, as well as providing foodstuffs for its population's survival.

The cities of Manchester and Sheffield were placed on the target list for the month, both enduring two sizeable attacks from among the figure of sixteen launched in total. Liverpool, Bristol, and Birmingham also suffered two successive *Blitz* assaults within twenty-four hours, while Southampton and Portsmouth were struck. The emphasis on seaports that appears to have been addressed in December would be maintained; however, the early months of 1941 would place a weather-dictated break upon overall operations that would accordingly inhibit this element of the offensive.

The total of 2,854 tons of explosives and 11,000 incendiary containers estimated as being released during the month was hardly more than RAF Bomber Command would be destined to deliver against one German target in the years ahead. It highlighted what was a recurrent problem for the *Luftwaffe* in terms of effecting long-term dislocation to Britain's industrial base. A partial solution was to lie in the split between the proportion of explosive and incendiary weaponry.

The bomb was useful in destroying structures but could not guarantee similarly affecting the often-vulnerable internal content of heavy machinery for example. In contrast, the incendiary weapon could ignite the operating fluid of any such equipment, resulting in its partial or total disposal as a functioning entity (the Americans would learn this from their successive August and October 1943 raids on Schweinfurt's ball-bearing plants when the explosive/incendiary split was reversed in favour of the incendiary on the latter mission with greatly-enhanced destructive effect compared to the first mission). The incendiary would dominate the *Blitz* scene as 1941 commenced.

Passive Response

The provision of 'decoy' sites positioned near to likely target cities was yet another passive countermeasure intended to divert bomb loads away from their primary source. The initial quota was positioned close to RAF airfields and displayed the same lighting system in a bid to attract the attackers' bombs. The need to construct similar sites in the vicinity of large towns and cities took on a more complex aspect, however.

The main difference between the original and follow-up sites was that the latter had to be more 'active' compared to the 'passive' presentation enjoyed by the former. It was no use producing an instant-glowing inferno to the incoming bombers in a bid to distract them from the nearby target. What were code-named 'Starfish' sites were positioned in trios around six major cities in central and the West of England. Rows of drums filled with highly-inflammable material and grouped in pairs within metal-framed structures over which was slung hessian covers formed the basis of each site. The drums contained enough material to accommodate any multi-night assault indulged in by the attackers.

The Havoc I was a Plexiglas-nosed version of the Havoc II that was officially designated DB-7, of which 100 were supplied to the RAF. Mounting eight machine guns 'up front', service as a pure night fighter was restricted to No. 85 Squadron from March 1941. As with all current RAF night fighters, the aircraft were painted in RDM2 black as seen on BL228 taxiing out at Debden.

Firing-up required both fine judgement and luck since the intention was to do so before bombing had commenced but to do so in a manner that duplicated the build-up of bomb and incendiary-induced fires along with smoke patterns. During the period between December and May, an estimated 10 per cent of the firing-up activity gave returns regarded as 'excellent' by attracting three-figure numbers of bombs and incendiary loads; on a handful of other occasions 'good' results were recorded, the criterion being the attraction of double figures of explosive or incendiary-cluster weapons up to fifty. Meagre as these figures appeared, any dilution in the weight of actual target assault was to be welcomed.

DB-7: A Mixed Response

If the entry into combat of the Beaufighter promised a positive outcome to the night conflict for the RAF, the almost parallel introduction of a second night-fighter system would prove to be beset with inevitable problems that rendered it largely and dangerously ineffective. The RAF had assumed ownership of over 200 Douglas DB-7 Boston twin-engined aircraft, originally intended for the French *Armée de L'Air*, but they diverted to Britain before that nation's military collapse; these also became a part of the 300 constituting Britain's original order from Douglas.

The intention was to supplement the current number of squadrons assigned to the night-fighter role—six Blenheims/Beaufighters, three Hurricanes, and two Defiants—with nine further squadrons. No less than twelve among this expanded figure would fall into the AI-bearing category, within which the DB-7 would feature. However, the initial planned deployment of the American design was hardly positive; assignment to No. 93 Squadron for twelve aircraft was to see them used for releasing long aerial mines on a trailing cable into the path of the enemy bomber stream—a measure highlighting the still-desperate state of Britain's aerial response and one that would harvest little success before the design's withdrawal the following October ('Mutton' was the code-name for similar operations using obsolescent Handley-Page Harrow transports).

A more positive utilisation of the DB-7 was destined to be commenced in the New Year. The overall batch was split between the standard bomber version with its glazed nose section for the navigator and what was titled the Havoc. This was a conversion of the Boston, with four machine guns initially positioned in the lower nose. Then other airframes had the original nose section replaced with a 'solid' nose cone that contained eight machine guns in addition to carrying the 'arrow' tracking aerial for an AI Mk IV set. No. 85 Squadron would take on its first examples during February.

The depressing lack of fighter or AA kills continued virtually apace during the month. On at least three occasions, the *Luftwaffe* dispatched sub-forces to between two and four targets, with Liverpool, Sheffield, and Birmingham the recipients of major assaults. London was less attended to on these nights but received the first example of the heaviest-calibre bomb to be dropped during the *Blitz*. This was the 2,500-kg weapon named 'Max', whose carriage was specifically allotted to III/KG26—doubtless with a view to striking at specific locations in connection with the application of *Y-Gerät*. Whether Victoria railroad station was the target on 22–23 December was undetermined, but the blast effect on the terminus was minimal, although a signal box and numerous buildings alongside were devastated

The side profile view of an unmarked Havoc II provides a good view of the overall outline. The AI Mk IV transmitter aerial is just visible on the nose-cone along with the port-side receiver aerial; light patches are covers for several of the twelve machine guns. Also shown below and ahead of the windshield are the vertical aerials for the Rebecca blind-landing equipment. No. 85 Squadron supplemented its Havoc I complement with the Mk II from July 1941 until July 1942.

with traffic halted for twenty-four hours. The AA gunners' expenditure of nearly 29,000 shells overall this night brought no confirmed victims; the ninety-two fighters sent aloft were equally thwarted.

The single partial-success for the RAF occurred next evening as the light was fading and Flt Lt Cunningham was orbiting his No. 604 Squadron aircraft south of Lyme Bay. It was Fw. G. Deininger and his crew's misfortune to be visually spotted and homed-in upon as their 3/KGr100 He 111 6N+DL approached the coast. The sun's afterglow was fast diminishing as the Beaufighter closed in from behind and below before delivering a solid burst of fire that initiated a huge flash around the fuselage, upon which the bomber heeled downward and disappeared into the cloud base. Cunningham's later report that his victim had been dispatched proved inaccurate; Deininger managed to retain control of the burning and controls-damaged machine, jettisoned the flare load, and staggered south to a heavy crash-landing near Caen following total power loss that ended with his incurring injuries requiring hospitalisation.

January 1941

The growing emphasis on Britain's seaports was evident in January's target selection, although the weather conditions during the month were poor enough to restrict operations for thirteen nights. In spite of this, no less than seven major and seven heavy raids were launched, with port facilities the focus on eight occasions. The results continued to be painful but were far from terminal in their effect upon Britain's ability to import the vital food stocks and equipment, with which to respectively sustain life and advance the war effort. The real threat to the nation's survival was still in the hands of the *Kriegsmarine*'s U-boat service, whose crews had wrought severe depredation among the convoy ranks to date.

Y-Gerät

The latest refinement to the *Luftwaffe*'s electronic equipment was the single-beam, range-measuring *Y-Gerät* that had been introduced soon after the onset of the *Blitz* and was assigned to the He 111 crews serving with III/KG26. Whereas the crews of KGr100 were primarily tasked with releasing incendiaries, the dispatch of explosive weaponry was the duty laid upon their *Y-Gerät* colleagues. Although ground transmitters and their operating staff were involved in similar manner to the *X-Gerät* system, a greater degree of actual directional control was placed upon these personnel than upon the aircrew.

The He 111s bore transponders with which the ground controller measured the precise distance along the beam that the bomber was flying via a second transmitter/receiver that 'triggered' the airborne sets. There was an operational bonus granted the *Löwengeschwader* teams that was denied their *X-Gerät* contemporaries. Unlike the latter, it was now not necessary for the pilots to continually track along the beam; instead, they could adopt a separate off-beam course until such time as reconnection was necessary, and bearings could be taken on the aircraft signals with which each bomber could be duly vectored back onto the beam. As soon as the calculated range of the target coincided with the on-board equipment, the bombs were released.

Countermeasures were about to be put into operation by utilising the *Y-Gerät* range-measuring signals. These were picked up and retransmitted to the enemy ground station transmitters via the BBC. The receipt on board the bombers of two simultaneous, interlocking signals emanating from varying distances was expected to throw the range-information calculations out of kilter, with the result of the bomb loads being deposited well astray of the intended target.

GCI: A Quantum Leap

Up to now, the relatively few AI-equipped night fighters had been forced to seek out their prey. This was a task that required a degree of fortune in either gaining a visual sight of a bomber or picking-up a 'contact' on the set screens; the latter action was limited to the scanning distance of the set that was measured in no more than several thousand yards depending on the altitude being flown. What was required was a ground-based guidance system with controllers directing the pilot who would orbit within the GCI-allocated airspace; then he would await the details of a bogey's height and direction towards which he would be directed, until AI radar range was attained.

Seen here is one of the clearest and most detailed depictions of the Havoc Mk I's Turbinlite mounting. The massive facility is faired into the aircraft's nose and the transmitter aerial for the radar set is neatly slotted into the starboard side of the frame. The four individuals in civilian clothing may well be technicians involved with supervising the equipment's proper function.

Five GCI sites were now functioning between Southampton and Lincolnshire, these being the initial crop of forty-seven planned sites by mid-1941. Their circular zones overlapped one another and extended out into the Channel and North Sea, thereby providing advance warning of bombers; the overlaps also permitted the handing-over of a night-fighter team from one controller to another should the pursuit not produce a result within the original control zone. Now what was needed was a sizeable increase in Beaufighter delivery to the squadrons, but this highly desirable situation was not to be fully addressed until the latter weeks of the overall *Blitz* offensive.

Lone Wolf Legend

The use of single-engined fighters in the nocturnal battle was currently producing little results in interception, let alone lethal contact, but one individual was about to buck this trend in no uncertain manner. Flt Lt R. P. Stevens was attached to No. 151 Squadron based at Wittering with detachments at Coltishall for the Hurricanes and Defiants under current unit charge; Stevens flew within the Hurricane element.

On 15–16 January, he was among the forty-three pilots assigned to challenging the relatively small numbers mainly heading for Derby in the face of cloudy and snow-flecked weather patterns. Two separate waves came in, the second in the early hours of the 16th, and it was likely the unlucky duo of crews were culled from the separate sub-forces to judge by the times of the encounters. First was a 4/KG3 Do 17 (5K+DM) that was downed near Brentwood along with all four on Uffz. Schindler's crew.

Stevens must have then landed and taken-off on a second sortie because the second encounter around 5.32 a.m. was fully four hours after the first. This time, Ltn. Moehring's team suffered the seeds of defeat in their He 111 A1+JK, although only the 2/KG53 bomber and one crewmember became fatal casualties after the bomber descended into the sea off Canvey Island; the other three parachuted into captivity. Thus was recorded both the squadron's first kills at night along with Steven's ultimate tally of fourteen victories, the majority collected before the *Blitz* was completed (exactly eleven months later, he would be MIA from an 'Intruder' operation over Gilze-Rijen in Holland).

February 1941

The adverse weather conditions regularly encountered during January were intensified during February, and the *Luftwaffe*'s ability to mount major raids was totally rendered null and void. The scale of assault was accordingly low overall with one exception, the Welsh port of Swansea. The city bore the brunt of three attacks involving a total of 169 bombers in all that reached their goal. Clear conditions on the second and third nightly sequence aided the attackers in landing punishing blows to the city centre and to a lesser degree the dock facilities that were the primary source for assault.

The dearth in bombers culled to date by Fighter Command took a step up during February, although the figure of six was still very marginal. A single Do 17 downed on 4–5 February was added to on 15–16 February by Flt Lt Cunningham; Sgt Philipson was by now replaced by Sgt 'Jimmy' Rawnsley, who would become the regular radar operator. The GCI system was playing a material part in directing the crew within AI range onto a III/KG27 He 111P-2 (G1+FR) that, as with Fw. Deininger two months previous, was orbiting just off the coastline to await the onset of darkness before proceeding towards Birmingham.

Fortune was not to prove anything like so kind on this occasion as the Beaufighter once again adopted a low approach upon the unsuspecting bomber flown by Ltn. E. Beckmann. The cannon and bullet combination struck home to initiate a fierce fuselage fire. Again, the bomber descended steadily as visual contact was initially lost; the next sighting related to the bomb load as it was jettisoned presumably at low altitude since the sky was quickly lit-up as the He 111 impacted, killing all four crewmembers.

The immediate result was the Air Ministry's christening of Cunningham with the nickname 'Cat's-eyes'. This alluded to his reputed above-average visual acuity being the prime reason for his success. AI radar was still very much on the secret list as was the Beaufighter and the title was officialdom's way of disguising these facts (the pilot was apparently presented with a cat during the Second World War, which was ironic, given that he had an intense dislike of the feline breed).

Two more bombers were MIA on this night, although one landed at Steeple Morden while a He 111 was crippled by AA fire before finally brought down by a balloon cable. The *Luftwaffe* offensive was dishearteningly progressing with little counter effect upon its ranks and indeed the remaining three months of the *Blitz* would see its strength only marginally whittled away. For the defenders, the prospect of the assault extending into the remainder of 1941 if not further was extremely unsettling.

There was naturally no knowledge of Hitler's plans for Operation Barbarossa among the ranks of the RAF in particular, although 'Ultra' intercepts were already indicating his intention to invade Soviet Russia—a battle casting two dictatorships against each other and one that would create the first indication of the way forward in first countering and ultimately crushing the Führer's mortal threat to democratic standards.

The final February week following the Swansea battering was free of other than minor-category raids on several nights with no real activity otherwise. The relative freedom from national assault was not to be sustained as more regularly favourable weather conditions began to return over both the continent and Britain. The *Blitz* was about to enter its final and horribly concentrated form, this despite the steadily-improving defensive network.

March 1941: The *Blitz*'s Ghastly Culmination

To date, the *Luftwaffe* pattern of attack had largely tended to focus upon single attacks on any selected target with the alternative of striking at more than one source during the same night. Now the pattern would tend to accentuate a concentration over several nights against one location; this was an act that seemed to suggest the intention was as much to strike at the citizens' morale as it was to inflict material destruction. The final week apart when continental weather intervened, March would realise a sizeable degree of dislocation to the British industrial structure, although one that remained well distant from terminal in effect (the total of over 4,000 individual bomber sorties launched sounds impressive but the bomb/incendiary tonnage they could deliver was no more than that dropped by RAF Bomber Command on far fewer operations from 1943 onward).

The first city to suffer this was Cardiff in Wales; its port facilities were tailor-made for attack and three raids were launched during the first week with a surprisingly low average of fifty-three bombers. Only the second raid resulted in material damage, but there was naturally no guarantee of future assaults not garnering increased scales of destruction. The AA defences were at their current and barely adequate establishment around all the major ports but moves were already afoot to transfer upwards of eighty guns either from non-coastal industrial cities or from the production lines that would bolster the port defences; emphasis was placed upon the extra coverage going to locations handling the Atlantic convoy traffic. The paucity in numbers demonstrated how the weapons industry was still striving to make up for the losses incurred in France the previous May and June.

March was to witness the first notable 'bite' into *Luftwaffe* ranks by the defences, although the casualty percentage in no way inhibited the Germans either in terms of aircraft strength or the effect upon the crews' morale. Four He 111s were MIA during the first week, two falling to fighter- or AA-inflicted strikes. The figure was extended to no less than ten over the seven following days. One fell to AA fire, but an interesting feature of the nine RAF credited kills was the almost even split between twin- and single-engined squadrons, five to four respectively.

All but one in the latter category involved Defiant crews. The four-gun turret on the Boulton Paul design could be regarded as no more than adequate to inflict fatal damage to the solidly-protected He 111s and Ju 88s; on the other hand, a well-directed and sustained burst of fire could and obviously did sometimes achieve the desired result as witnessed here. The advantage the Defiant enjoyed over its single-engined contemporaries was the ability to make an approach from other than a horizontal angle. This not only provided a better chance of remaining unobserved unlike the Hurricane or Spitfire, whose final attack-angle placed it more within a gunner's vision-scan; with their more steadily-paced approach, the Defiant pilots were also granted a greater time span in confirming the bogey as hostile before engaging.

No. 96 Squadron was a relative latecomer in terms of service during the *Blitz* since it was only formed in December. Subsequent service up to the following October was at the satellite airfield of Cranage near Manchester from where the crews operated to provide cover to this city and the key port of Liverpool; however, it was March before the Defiant began to displace the Hurricanes forming the original squadron complement of fighters.

The existence of GCI guidance probably helped the non-AI-equipped fighters to at least be placed in the general path of the bomber stream, however loosely flown this was in practice. On 12–13 March, the record number of fighters sent up (over 250) proved a mixed blessing for the ground controllers in trying to handle so many at any one point, but a degree of success did attend the night's operations. Fg Off. F. Hughes, after taking off from Tangmere on the Channel coast, was twice directed towards a bogey, and on the second occasion, he picked out Stabsfw. K. Bruening's G1+GN. The 5/KG55 He 111 absorbed several short bursts that ignited one engine, after which the bomber described a fiery trail to finally impact south-west of London, only the pilot surviving. This was Hughes' fourth kill out of eighteen in a distinguished night-fighting career that culminated with assignment to No. 604 Squadron; his first two victims were gained during the finally-disastrous appearance by No. 264 Squadron in the Battle of Britain.

However, it was the steady inflow of the AI-equipped Beaufighters with its fearsome degree of firepower that promised real and regular problems for the enemy. No. 604 Squadron's hitherto main presence in the nocturnal battle was now being bolstered by the appearance of Nos 29 and 219 Squadrons, with all three units joining in the harrying of their adversaries. Fg Off. K. Geddes commenced his path to swift 'acedom' alongside Flt Lt Cunningham this same night. The No. 604 Squadron pilot caught a Ju 88 from 6/KG76 (F1+OP) assigned to Portsmouth, whose pilot, Fw. K. Berger, was the sole survivor among the four crew, his bomber crashing well west of the target.

On the 15th, Flt Lt Guy Gibson was on readiness with No. 29 Squadron based at Digby, Lincolnshire. This airman had already completed a tour with No. 83 Squadron's Hampden bombers and had eschewed the normal 'rest' from active operations in favour of flying night fighter sorties. Along with Sgt R. James, he took off, and during the patrol, he latched onto Ltn. G. Stugg's 2/KG1 He 111 (V4+HK). The hapless four-strong crew stood little chance of survival when their stricken aircraft was dispatched to plunge into the North Sea. Gibson in contrast would go on to resume operations with Bomber Command, rising to wing commander rank and leading first No. 106 and then No. 617 Squadron; the latter unit consisted of handpicked veteran crews who would breach the Möhne and Edersee Dams on 16–17 May 1943. Tragically, he would join tonight's victims in death during September 1944.

Twenty-four hours previous, another squadron pilot who unlike Gibson was a regular member scored his second in an ultimately major list of twenty-nine kills; these were destined to be achieved both in the night fighter and Intruder operational roles. Fg Off. 'Bob' Braham's radar operator Sgt Ross directed him onto Obltn. H. von Keiser's Do 17 U5+DA off the Lincolnshire coast and the Stab/KG2 bomber stood little chance of surviving the blast of gunfire that sent it into the cold waters along with all four occupants. His success was one of two squadron kills; Wg Cdr S. Widdows (CO) downed a 4/NJG2 Intruder R4+GM that took the three-man crew to their deaths, this time on land. An overall figure of six confirmed victories was achieved on this occasion.

The remainder of March saw a notable regression in the number of nocturnal kills. Compared to events up to the 15th, just one crew was confirmed as falling on 16–17 March. Even this was probably self-inflicted since Ltn. E. Arz called-up to say he was baling out his 2/KG51 crew without the precise reason being reported. In the meantime, the bombers rained down destruction on London, Plymouth, and Clydebank in particularly severe measure, as had been the case earlier to Portsmouth. By the month's end, the cumulative total of civilian deaths incurred since the *Blitz*'s onset was just under 29, 000 and 40,000 injured, with the months immediately ahead likely to increase these figures noticeably, given there was no sign of the offensive even slackening, let alone being turned back.

April 1941

The continued attention to seaports on Britain's western fringes impelled ACM Sholto-Douglas to transfer several night-fighter squadrons from Scotland to Southern England with a view to intercepting the bomber stream. Events confirmed this act was timely since, of the 21 April assaults listed as 'major' or 'heavy', a sizeable proportion involved the maritime target category spread between Portsmouth and Clydeside. Plymouth and Belfast were to be severely punished as was London, when the largest bomber force ever dispatched (712) struck home on 16–17 April.

The emphasis on radar-equipped night-fighter squadrons guided by GCI stations to counter the *Luftwaffe* raiders was not yet capable of being put into full operation due to lack of aircraft numbers, so recourse still had to be had to sending up single-engined fighters as well. April saw the respective sortie totals of 342 and 842 recorded; in the same period, over 5,400 sorties spread between the two *Luftflotten* were sent out. However, the withdrawal of a sizeable number of *Gruppen* with which to support imminently-pending land operations in the Mediterranean was to place an added strain on the crews still on hand. This entailed crews flying more than one sortie on any one night; naturally, the distance to be flown was restricted to southern targets with London the obvious source, but the extra pressure placed upon the personnel was not welcomed.

The number of functioning GCI stations was now up to ten, eight of these covering Southern and the East of England with two in Scotland. Two recent technical advances had improved the link-up with the fighters. The first was an accurate height-reading system and the second was an equally effective IFF set that assisted the controllers in fully identifying their aerial charges from other screen 'traces' as the former were brought into AI-contact range.

The month commenced badly for I/KG27, which lost four crews along with four others from several *Gruppen*. However, all but one was downed during daylight while conducting individual raids, the exception being Ltn. E. Menge's V4+AR from 7/KG1. The He 111 was unfortunate enough to encounter Flt Lt

The group of aircrew congregated in front of a trio of Mk I Havocs equate in overall numbers to the three-man teams for the aircraft. The extended entry hatch frame for the pilot is demonstrated here. Aircraft letters placed on the nose were a feature on the Havoc–Boston airframes.

Cunningham's Beaufighter during the Bristol raid of 3–4 April; the fusillade of gunfire tore the machine apart, leaving the remnants to fall into the Channel off the Isle of Wight along with its crew.

The Cunningham–Wransley team were now one short of ace-dom, but that target was attained four nights later during major raids to Greenock–Clydeside and Liverpool. Six III/KG26 He 111s were assigned to Greenock, among which was 1H+GT flown by Ltn. E. Hartmann. The 9 *Staffel* bomber was crossing the English coast when its Beaufighter 'nemesis' struck home. The Channel waters swallowed up the bomber whose fuselage probably acted as a tomb for all but one crewmember, whose body was later washed ashore (a claim for this aircraft by Flt Lt J. D. Ward, an 87 Squadron Hurricane pilot, was also granted according to a leading author on fighter aces).

The cull of victims by single-engined fighters was further boosted the next night by Plt Off. R. P. Stevens, who would claim his second duo of kills in an illustrious, but ultimately fatal operational career. His first kill was Obfw. H. Muller's 1G+FR, the 2/KG27 machine that was culled some thirty minutes before he closed upon the 3/KG55 He 111 bearing the *Gruppenkommandeur* Hptm. O. Bodemeyer. G1+DL fell many miles to the east of its companion in fate, but this time, all four of the crew baled out.

The lack of radar equipment in the Mk I Defiant did not hinder several crews from gaining a series of kills during the *Blitz*. N1801/PS: Y, a No. 264 Squadron night fighter, displays five swastikas that represent the figure credited to Fg Off. F. Hughes and Sgt F. Gash; this was far from being the final figure for the pilot, which reached a further eight while flying Beaufighters with Nos 125 and 600 Squadrons.

All four of the night's casualties were incurred by the single-engined 'brigade', with the efficacy of the Defiant's four-gun turret again proving its value. The ability to make the same low approach as the Beaufighter, but without the need to rise to a level position before delivering its lethal gunfire, was proven once again. The fighter flown by Sqn Ldr A. Sanders (No. 264 Squadron) was steadily directed by GCI control towards what evolved as an III/KG26 bomber bound for Coventry.

Plt Off. Sutton opened fire initially upon approach and then at minimum range, after which 1H+ET turned over and plunged to be abandoned by three of the four-man team before final impact. The other loss was a second KG55 bomber (G1+LS) that uniquely bore a twin-gun dorsal weapon; the added firepower availed Obltn. J. Bartens' crew nothing when Plt Off. J. Davidson's quartet of .303s tore into the airframe, killing the pilot and one among his three colleagues. This was Flt Lt D. Darling's third No. 151 Squadron kill alongside Steven's contribution on the night.

The next night's cull was six, four of which definitely fell to fighter assault and with three of this sub-total being credited to Defiant crews. Tonight was also the final kill in twelve confirmed victories for Sgt E. Thorn and his gunner, Sgt J. Barker,

A Mk I Defiant assigned to No. 125 Squadron is receiving attention from an inordinate number of ground crew, indicating this is a PR picture. Squadron was formed as the *Blitz* ended in May 1941 and commenced a lengthy seven-month conversion onto the Mk II Beaufighter that was only completed in September 1942. The forward alignment of the machine guns, and the two-piece landing gear cover are points of note.

the others having been granted during the May–August daylight operational spell for No. 264 Squadron. The latest KG55 loss was G1+DM, a 4 *Staffel* bomber heading for Birmingham; the He 111 was caught and downed south of London to leave one survivor among Uffz. A. Mueller's (killed) crew. The next night again saw the majority of victories (four out of six) going to single-engined fighters with Flt Lt Stevens adding two more to his tally.

The intermingled presence of single- and twin-engined aircraft was casting up the problem of double-claimed victories. The Cunningham–Wransley team's experience on 7–8 April was repeated four nights later. The single He 111 downed over land was 1G+HT of 9/KG27 that was claimed by a No. 307 Squadron Defiant flown by Sgt F. Jankowiak and J. Lipinski after it was struck and dived away with pieces shredding off. Then the No. 604 Squadron crew intercepted a bomber that matched Lipinski's report of it being northbound. This time round, the bomber was reported as definitely crashing, all on Uffz. L. Roeth's crew being killed. Unlike the previous occasion, there is no confirmation of the Defiant crew being granted a kill alongside the Beaufighter team's confirmation.

Although the *Blitz*'s overall effect was continuing to be far from terminal, the effect upon the citizens was continuing to be serious as the bombers hammered their targets. Plymouth was almost devastated by a series of four attacks within nine days, and Belfast's martyrdom was arguably almost as severe during April; London also suffered with a mid-month raid that lasted over eight hours and resulted in the sole example of in excess of 1,000 tons of bombs and incendiaries dropped upon a single target. The April cull of bombers, although gratifying to date, was not materially halting the offensive, nor was the figure of around thirty more taken out by the defences before the month's end—a figure added to marginally by unconfirmed aircraft losses over the sea or the continent—leading to this highly desirable situation.

The introduction of Beaufighters in sizeable numbers was the main aerial hope of impinging materially upon the *Luftwaffe*'s strength. Production of airframes was beginning to increase albeit in a frustratingly staccato manner. The Bristol design clearly held more than an overall performance edge upon the currently available German bombers; even the more higher-performance Ju 88 was hard-pressed to evade or outmanoeuvre its assailant, while the heavy firepower was capable of bringing down any opponent.

As in March, April's second half witnessed a downturn in confirmed kill figures, although nothing like as minimal. A trio of kills were recorded by No. 604 Squadron on 15–16 April, but a fourth bomber from which three crewmembers jumped out after being engaged by Flt Lt Cunningham was brought back to a crash-landing near Caen. The precipitate action by these airmen was probably due to their mishearing of the pilot's words—'*Bomben raus*!' ('Drop the bombs!')—thanks to only picking up the latter word, the English translation being 'Out!'

The same scale of success was recorded next night by No. 219 Squadron with two going to Wg Cdr T. Pike (CO). First a Ju 88 from 4/KG1 was dispatched along with all of Obltn. E. Schlecht's (*Staffelkapitän*) crew; one hour later, 2/

KG28 lost 1T+EK that broke up in mid-air, half of Uffz. T. Hammer's (POW) team failing to survive the experience. Pike would gain a final total of six kills and moreover would rise to the premier RAF post of Chief of the Air Staff after the Second World War.

The sadly-meteoric operational career of Flt Lt Stevens continued three nights later with a single kill. Apart from following the general directions from the ground, he also focused upon any notable AA concentration in the confident hope that a bomber would be in the gunfire's vicinity. On this occasion, the unfortunate victim came from the ranks of 7/KG54. Obltn. J. Baierl was steering 5J+JR over Kent when the No. 151 Squadron Hurricane discharged its eight-gun battery. The German pilot attempted to crash-land his fatally damaged bomber, but it broke-up on impact; Baierl and one crew member survived from among the four on board. The sole other loss tonight was ascribed to the AA gunners as was another on 27–28 April, when again just two kills were recorded over British soil, the second going to No. 219 Squadron.

Y-Gerät: Success or Failure?

The ability of the British to apply a really deleterious countermeasure to the *Y-Gerät* equipment was ever open to question. To date, no III/KG26 bomber downed over land had remained intact in sufficient form to provide an examination of a set in the same manner as its *X-Gerät* companion from the bomber pulled ashore at Bridport. Interrogation of *Gruppe* POWs had yielded no admission that the final 'release' signals had been tampered with to any degree. The fact that near misses had been recorded in respect of specialist locations on some raids seemed to back up such assertions, but thankfully the scale of actual impact upon sites such as the Rolls-Royce factories was none too great—and accordingly provided a degree of hope that the signal-interruption action was having some negative effect (one apparent worry for the enemy crews was the possibility of the night fighters being able to 'track' along the beams—a situation that never evolved but one which probably planted the seeds of doubt in the system's infallibility among its operators).

May 1941

Ugly Martyrdom

Liverpool was a priority target since its port facilities were a prime source for the mass import of goods. The city had absorbed numerous raids since the *Blitz* commenced, but the experience as May commenced was to test its citizens to the utmost and probably bring many to the point of thinking about the need to even negotiate with the enemy, such was the physical and psychological pressure placed upon their shoulders. Clydeside and London would share the punishment, but it was Liverpool that bore the brunt commencing on the 1st, when the sirens sounded their heart-searing notes.

R2274 was the fifth airframe from a production run of 150 commenced in March 1941. It went to the A&AEE to be fitted with the Boulton-Paul turret. Although operationally evaluated by No. 406 Squadron, what was designated the Mk V never progressed beyond this stage. The total of ten machine guns and the Beau's reduced cannon armament of two would have been a fearsome force to run up against.

The northern city was vastly greater in spread than other badly-blitzed contemporaries such as Plymouth, but the pounding it received over eight nights ran the death toll up to 1,900, as well as badly dislocating the port facilities. The explosion of an ammunition ship in one dock area put the facility out of total commission for months ahead to add extra pressure upon the ability of the other docks to handle the overall import load. The generally clear conditions with the expanding moon period assisted the bombers in delivering their loads, although the destruction of thousands of houses was an indication that the raids involved a mix of precision and 'area' assault.

The defences did gain a small measure of success on 2–3 May, with two aerial and one AA success, a fourth bomber being MIA to unknown causes. Over double this figure (nine) was realised the next night, of which seven were culled by the duo sub-forces of Beaufighters and Defiants; engine failure was the cause for one of the remaining losses. The steady haemorrhage within the bomber ranks was being sustained twenty-four hours later with three night-fighter kills and two more casualties on technical grounds that induced Obltn. M. Baumann to 'ditch' 3Z+FP (6/KG77) thanks to engine failure—an act that killed him and two of the other three airmen—while a second KG77 Ju 88 (3Z+EC) crash-landed following fuel failure. Seven further crews tasted the bitter seeds of defeat during the next two nights, all but one succumbing to fighter attacks.

By far the best record of success to date occurred on 7–8 May, when a round dozen of crews failed to return. Ten fell to fighters with the single-engined machines responsible for six, to which were added one lost to ground collision and one listed as MIA. I and II/KG55 were particularly affected since five crews in all were gone. The culling of this number of bombers within one week, gratifying as it was for the RAF and AA gunners, was still proving little hindrance to the continued prosecution of the *Blitz* and the overall weight of assault. Only the onset of the midsummer months that presented the minimum in terms of a nocturnal cloak could hopefully retard the worst effects of the offensive.

Nos 255 and 256 Squadron Defiants were enjoying a good run of success with four and three kills scored in forty-eight hours; the former unit claimed no less than three on 8–9 May, and ironically, all three He 111s concerned came from II/KG55 so adding to the *Gruppe*'s misery. Fg Off. Bob Braham was up from No. 29 Squadron's new airfield at West Malling as I/KG27 was heading for Derby with seven He 111s. The unlucky exception to completing the raid was 1G+MK, which was picked up after crossing the Channel. The bomber's clinical dispatch over the London suburb of Wimbledon was matched by Ltn. D. Staehle's four-man crew; this was Braham's third Beaufighter victory.

Unknown 'Climax'

London's status as a major industrial city and national capital had rendered it open to regular assault, with several instances when it was heavily attacked. Several raids were launched to coincide with the full moon as well as low-tidal conditions, when the latter limitation directly affected the Auxiliary Fire Service's ability to draw sufficient water reserves from the Thames. A prime reason for the launching of the raid on 10–11 May was reported to be its value in cloaking the imminent wholesale withdrawal of both *Luftflotten*'s strength for participation in Operation Barbarossa, the Invasion of Soviet Russia. True or not, the citizens were in for what transpired as one of, if not the worst night's experience during the *Blitz*'s entire eight-month course.

The laying of *X-Gerät* beams on the city was an indication of *Luftwaffe* intentions, and the full moon and the Thames's ebbing water state boded ill for the Civil Defence personnel. The first attack wave of nearly 600 individual sorties appeared towards midnight, and over the ensuing six hours, many major conflagrations were created with the possibility of 'firestorms' arising—a nightmare scenario that never materialised in Britain, but ironically would be visited in dreadful format upon several German cities in the future (AVM 'Butch' Harris, upon viewing the late December raid that devastated the City of London from the roof of the Air Ministry, had said: 'They are sowing the Wind—and they will reap the Whirlwind'. As future C-in-C Bomber Command, his prescient observation would be fulfilled in the course of what was sadly a Total War).

Up aloft RAF Fighter Command had launched the first counter wave of over 300 fighter sorties, and although immediate results indicated that as many as thirty-three bombers had been culled, the true figure (eleven) was one-third in

The 'Arrow' aerial on the nose cone of a Merlin-powered Mk II transmits the radar signals and the starboard wing's receiver aerial is also depicted. External aerials on RAF aircraft were immeasurably less cumbersome and accordingly speed-sapping compared to the bulk of their *Nachtjagd* contemporaries. Note how the RDM2 paint has partially worn off the nearside propeller cover.

comparison; even then, only six were confirmed as coming down on British soil. Tonight was another severe rebuff for KG55, with five among the overall total being lost. One among this number confirmed was G1+BT with Stabsfw. Adolf Schied as pilot and Lt. Martin Reiser as *Beobachter*. The crew had completed their run and landed back at Lille-Nord, only to be ordered to make a second sortie—an issue for which they were unprepared according to Reiser. The second run was completed and the He 111 was heading back when a fighter landed fatal strikes upon the aircraft. Both Schied and Reiser managed to bale out, but only the latter came through alive.

An early loss was A1+JN flown by Fw. R. Fuerthmann with Hptm. A. Hufenreuther in practical charge. The deliberate zigzag course to London and bomb run had barely been completed when the 5/KG53 He 111 was badly damaged by a No. 74 Squadron Spitfire. The steadily descending aircraft was finally eased into a crash-landing near Ashford that fortunately stopped short of a solid line of trees. All four crew survived the immediate crash, but the pilot subsequently died.

Finis

The horrendous smoke pall over London, under which around 2,000 individuals lay dead among large tracts of devastated and communications-choked districts, left the authorities with frightening visions of immediate follow-up strikes that could easily overwhelm any attempt to save London from larger-scale punishment. Only time would confirm that the raid spelled the practical end to the *Blitz* in its current punishing form for the remainder of the Second World War.

The growing, albeit staccato, pace of Beaufighter production coupled with good GCI support as well as equally expanding AA gun and searchlight numbers would probably have begun to really bite into the enemy bombers' strength, although whether sufficient to even blunt the offensive's effect over the remainder of 1941 will ever be a matter of conjecture. The advent of the even more high-performance Mosquito to the nocturnal battle during 1942 would have surely accelerated the prospect of landing punishing blows, but this matter was equally placed in almost total abeyance.

There would be spasmodic attempts at its resurrection especially in early 1944 when Hitler ordered its renewal with London as the epicentre. By then, the pendulum would swing squarely in the favour of Fighter Command and AA Command. This factor coupled with the totally inadequate resources placed on hand—both quantitative and qualitative—ensured that the 'Baby *Blitz*' would achieve nothing other than the loss of numerous aircraft and crews against even less material damage to Britain's industrial infrastructure.

But all of this lay well ahead of the British population on what was a shatteringly bleak Sunday morning in 1941. However, from this point on, Fighter Command would be able to regroup, especially as regards the permanent daytime deployment of its Hurricane and Spitfire squadrons and look towards carrying the aerial battle to Hitler's Third Reich. As regards nocturnal provision, the advent of the Beaufighter and still-nascent Mosquito into the night-fighter role was destined to ensure a solid barrier against further *Luftwaffe* bomber assaults, minimal though these were to prove.

9

Taking the Fight to the Enemy

Conflict's Recurring Conundrum

The conclusion of every military conflict along with the various stages or campaigns contained therein casts up a central conundrum: does the victor attain this end thanks to a positive stance—that is, the superior application of its personnel and support material—or is it the converse failings of the vanquished that leads to a negative result as regards its aspirations?

The conduct of the Second World War for the Allies as exemplified by the Battle of Britain was a typical example of this. Nazi Germany had prepared for war and duly pursued its warped dreams for European conquest in a frighteningly efficient and all-conquering manner between September 1939 and the summer of 1940 before coming up against its first important stumbling-block in Britain and its Empire. That the isolated and equipment-shorn adversary across the Channel could resist either the temptation of negotiating a political settlement or alternatively of putting up an effective military resistance should the former scenario be rejected was clearly inconceivable to Hitler or indeed to many neutral sources, Winston Churchill's brilliantly-inspired rhetoric notwithstanding.

The *Luftwaffe*'s ultimate failure was already being accelerated in that direction thanks to faulty intelligence as demonstrated by Ob. 'Beppo' Schmid's *Studie Blau*. His mid-July report both understated British fighter-production levels as well as being ignorant of the Civilian Repair Organisation's (CRO) supplementary part in returning battle-damaged fighters to combat status; he also paid no heed to pilot resources as being the more critical factor. In early August, he informed Göring that over 350 RAF fighters had been destroyed between 1 July and now, while his estimate of Fighter Command's frontline strength was barely 500. Such naïve understating of the command's operational strength would be repeated by Gen. Kesselring and influence his support for a switch to attacks on London beginning on 7 September.

This No. 615 (County of Surrey) Squadron Hurricane is one of 1,000 Mk IIAs produced during 1940–41. It bears a presentation reference to the London Borough of Croydon that is a Surrey town. The fighter served with two further RAF units prior to transfer to Russia on 15 October 1941, but whether it operated with No. 141 Wing is unclear.

Schmid clearly had no knowledge of Fighter Command's structure, neither regarding the specific location of fighter airfields nor had he similar knowledge both of sector airfields and the joint-vulnerability of these and their operations blocks. Another overestimation was the quality of the German fighters *vis-à-vis* their RAF single-engined adversaries. Although not so misleading regarding the Bf 109's performance in this respect, he badly overstated the same comparison as regards the Bf 110, as the *Zerstörer* crews soon discovered.

In the course of the Battle of Britain, the *Luftwaffe*'s superiority in numbers of aircraft was not as striking in terms of actual operationally-available aircraft, but the nett figure was still well ahead of that enjoyed by RAF Fighter Command. Even more striking was the quality of its aircrews, particularly those within the *Jagdwaffe* element. Not only did many enjoy a longer-term and superior combat experience, the advantage in formation and battle tactics lay firmly in their hands and led to a serious draining of their opponent's ranks during the initial and central stages of the battle, especially when indulging in the forward-scanning *freie Jagd* manoeuvre.

However, the battle had witnessed their ranks being steadily thinned out in terms of both middle- and senior-serving aircrew while an added twist to combat pressure was the relative lack of off-duty periods or leave compared to the RAF's regular indulgence in these tension-easing actions. Even more enervating for the *Jagdwaffe* pilots, in particular, was the absence of any scheme to rest those perceived to be suffering combat fatigue—in effect, 'The last man shall go on' seems to have been the inflexible policy adopted by the *Luftwaffe* High Command.

One picture in a sequence taken at Digby shows a corporal-rank mechanic from No. 401 (Canadian) Squadron. The Hurricane prototype originally had fixed panels around both cockpit sides, but the starboard example was amended to one that acted as an emergency 'knock-out' unit, which is detached in this case. The anti-glare strip on Canadian Hurricanes was normally angled upwards.

That the *freie Jagd* tactic, although originally sanctioned by him, was ultimately reined-in by Göring after the bomber commanders complained they were being left bereft of cover and exposed to steady losses was of vital importance to Fighter Command's pilots; the reduction in premature interception meant they were now granted better prospects of gaining access to the bombers, which, after all, formed the principal means of turning the battle in the *Luftwaffe*'s favour. But even before this sea change occurred, Göring and his senior staff had made the first of two crucial miscalculations.

The initial error related to the CH/CHL radar network whose regular function was of key importance to Fighter Command's continued efficiency. The assaults of 13 August specifically aimed at a number of sites had punched at least one major 'hole' in the system. The prompt repair in the network via sister-stations and/or mobile sets should still not have deceived the enemy into thinking that repeat attacks would not attain the desired aim of 'blinding' the electronic guidance system for the RAF fighters, but thankfully this was the attitude adopted by the *Reichsmarschall* during his 15 August meeting with his *Luftwaffe* commanders (a second and more long-term 'puncture' achieved at Poling on the 18th equally held no sway with Göring in dissuading him from his decision).

The second and arguably the battle's key miscalculation occurred in September. Although a proportion of the sorties directed at RAF airfields had not always been on actual Fighter Command airfields, sufficient dislocation to No. 11 Group's locations and in particular those possessing sector control facilities along with a steady whittling down of pilot strength had placed Fighter Command on the back foot to the extent that it faced an imminent collapse in overall effectiveness between mid-August when the assaults commenced and 6 September.

The almost peremptory switch from this increasingly advantageous situation to the onset of the nocturnal *Blitz* that was immediately preceded by the 7 September daylight raid on London provided a critical envelope of relief in terms of revived airfield operational ability thanks to the cessation of direct *Luftwaffe* assault. Added to this relief factor was the now-enhanced opportunity for squadrons to be safely dispatched in ever-greater numbers with the renewed prospect of engaging the enemy on their own operational terms of timely launch twinned to height advantage on interception. These were measures that saw their immediate successful culmination eight days later during what is now recorded as the official 'Battle of Britain' commemoration date, before being extended further on into the autumn as the campaign petered out.

No. 257 (Burma) Squadron moved to Coltishall in Norfolk in late 1940 where a series of official photographs were shot. Heading this pilot line-up (right) is the CO, Sqn Ldr Bob Stanford-Tuck. He was a leading ace with twenty-seven confirmed personal and two shared kills but ended up a POW after crash-landing his Spitfire in France during January 1942.

Bullet *v*. Cannon shell

The weaponry introduced into aerial warfare during the First World War utilised what is now treated as bullet in character. The individual round was intended to strike its target with maximum velocity still in intact form while relying on the force of impact to wreak maximum damage. The general calibre of the machine guns from which they were fired was .303 inches (7.92 mm) and the effect of even a short burst of fire was usually enough to either fatally weaken the airframe or set the aircraft on fire; the wood and canvas airframes then on hand were very susceptible to any degree of damage or were natural fire hazards respectively.

For the greater part of the period between 1918 and 1939, the notion that an enhanced form of striking power was not deemed necessary certainly held sway within Air Ministry circles; the mindset was maybe driven as much by economics as operational necessity. The sheer mass of surplus ammunition stocks after hostilities ceased coupled to no obvious source against which they could be used probably were the prime reason; it should also be considered that until the 1930s, aircraft construction was still firmly wedded to non-metal-clad designs. What had proved adequate to bring down an aircraft between 1914 and 1918 was still regarded as matching the requirements for RAF fighters in particular.

The alternative to the striking power of the .303 was either a heavier-calibre successor or what became known as a 'cannon' projectile that possessed an explosive capability as opposed to the 'solid-shot' nature of a bullet. The former alternative that was favoured by the Americans was the .5-inch bullet. The roughly 60 per cent increase in calibre as well as an increased length was to witness *Luftwaffe* aircraft being severely damaged by the USAAF bomber gunners or often torn apart by the four- to eight-gun array mounted on the P-38, P-47, and P-51 fighters as they bid to protect the B-17s and B-24s engaged in the daylight offensive.

The destructive effect of an explosive shell would appear to be superior to any bullet-calibre contemporary, and indeed, the .303 was truly outclassed on several aspects. The obvious one was its relative ineffectiveness against more sturdily-constructed airframes as was the general case with metal-based airframes. The fact was brought home during the Battle of Britain when a large number of German bombers, particularly the He 111, sustained heavy, but not fatal damage to limp back for a normal or crash-landing. Not only did their airframes hold out, the crude rubber wrappings around the fuel tanks simply denied any penetrative leeway that would set the fuel content alight.

The wholesale introduction of cannon-calibre weapons was spearheaded by the *Luftwaffe*'s Bf 109s and Bf 110s, although a handful of Spitfires were equipped and briefly used during the Battle of Britain. The combination of 20-mm cannon and 12.7-mm (.5-inch) machine guns proved a fierce striking combination for the Bf 109, but low muzzle-velocity effect provided by the former weapon type during 1940 was a basic problem that unfortunately would be corrected as the conflict expanded. Once corrected, a properly directed burst of fire often brought

The snow-strewn surfaces of Coltishall form the backcloth to one of No. 257 Squadron's Hurricanes as its pilot watches a section fly overhead. The auxiliary battery unit is plugged-in ready for the fighter to be fired-up. Note how the aircraft's code letters partially seen between two of the airmen are painted around the serial number.

about the desired result with less expenditure of shells in relation to total carrying-capacity compared to the .303.

There again, the extended value of the cannon shell—as with the .5-calibre bullet that the USAAF fighters were to demonstrate with great effect from 1943–1944 onward—was its twin use for assaulting ground-based targets. There was little or no manner in which the .303 could guarantee for example blowing up a railroad locomotive and its load of trucks or similar solidly-constructed forms of transport or structures.

The one drawback for the cannon-calibre weapon lay in the limited wing-stowage capacity for what were very large shells compared to the bullet. This was where the .5 arguably came into its own as the best compromise between the two other 'challengers'. The number of rounds capable of being carried was roughly equal to its less-effective predecessor, but the striking power directed at a target with reference to aircraft was virtually the same as its cannon-calibre contemporary.

Defence to Offence Hiatus (Winter 1940–41)

The final two months of 1940 included the still-controversial 'retirement' of Sir Hugh Dowding and Keith Park, their replacements being AVM Sholto-Douglas and AVM Leigh-Mallory respectively. Dowding was at the age when retirement normally beckoned, but the circumstances of both changes was tinged with perceived but basically ill-founded accusations (with both new incumbents

Four pilots from No. 71 (Eagle) Squadron are obliging the press visitors to Kirton-in-Lindsey by indulging in a practice scramble; in the lead is Fg Off. Eugene 'Red' Tobin' with Plt Off. Kolendorski on his right. Picture was taken in March 1941; the latter was killed in action on 17 May while Tobin suffered the same fate the following 7 September.

leading the charge) regarding the handling of the battle. The 17 October conference at which these matters were discussed included just one operational pilot—none other than Douglas Bader whose 'Big Wing' theory was expounded to those present.

There was no contemporary of Bader's present to even attempt to put the case for the Fighter Command's and No. 11 Group C-in-C's conduct of the battle, but the imbalance perfectly suited their critics' largely theoretical stance on the subject. The case for more offensive action during the battle would certainly prove relevant to forthcoming operations as the fight was taken across the Channel but was never to prove valid in terms of the summer skies of 1940. Apart from Bader's biography, none of the several participants and leading aces of the Battle of Britain's books support his contentions but rather contain references of unconditional support for Dowding and Park.

Italian Fortunes

The *Regia Aeronautica*'s participation in the battle was short-lived and counterproductive, as well as belatedly delivered. Mussolini had dispatched a force of BR.20 twin-engined bombers, along with CR.42 biplane escorts that were assembled and stationed in Belgium during September. It was not until 29 October that the first sortie was made, with Ramsgate in Kent the target. Little or no damage was made upon what was a small town of virtually no military or war-production significance. The formation returned without loss, and for the ensuing twelve days, the aircraft rested upon their dispersals.

On 11 November, ten bomber crews and twenty-two CR.42 pilots were briefed and took off to head in the direction of the Thames Estuary. At nearby Martlesham Heath, No. 257 Squadron's CO was taking the medical officer's advice to refrain from flying due to an ear infection. The subsequent act of taking his gun to go bird shooting was to end in frustration. At one point, he observed his pilots lifting off and heading towards the coast, and by the time he regained the airfield, it was too late for him to participate in whatever action transpired. On the formation's return, Flt Lt 'Cowboy' Blatchford filled his CO in on what happened.

The oncoming Italians were sighted off the coast and almost simultaneously Blatchford picked out what was No. 46 Squadron's Hurricanes closing in on the enemy's left flank. It took a short visual scan for the unfamiliar Italian aircraft outlines—especially the CR.42—to confirm their 'hostile' status and both squadrons swooped in for the kill. Blatchford homed-in on one BR.20 and saw his burst of fire result in the bomber going into a loop manoeuvre that culminated with the aircraft flopping on its back at the apex and descending in an ever-accelerating manner to finally tear apart under the aerodynamic pressures. Blatchford later opined that the pilot was killed, and fell backwards while still holding the control column, an act that in turn automatically induced the loop action.

Although three fighters were downed along with three bombers the RAF pilots acknowledged both the desperate skill of the Italian crews in staving off the initial assaults until these succeeded in breaking up the bomber formation as well as the great difficulty in trying to out-do the CR.42s, whose lower speed was balanced by a better turning circle *vis-à-vis* the Hurricane. Blatchford had a protracted fight with one of the biplanes that finally saw the Hurricane closing in just as his guns fell silent.

In like manner to Ken Mackenzie's Battle of Britain experience, he made physical contact in this case with his propeller against one wing that chewed up the trailing edge. The result was not conclusive as regards dispatching his opponent, but the several inches excised from two blade-tips made for an eventful return flight and landing, Tuck's reaction was incredulity that his normally easy-going Canadian colleague could even think of undertaking such a potentially lethal step, a step that he regarded his Polish pilot element being more capable of indulging, given a naturally more feral attitude towards their adversaries. Unbeknown to the RAF was that today's action was the final bid by the Italians to launch a sortie over British soil.

The scale of enemy air operations on the 11th was one of the largest to develop during November. The Italian formation had been part of a three-pronged force directed against convoys. Earlier in the day, several further attacking forces had penetrated as far as the London area but with virtually no material effect in

A sergeant is closely supervising one of the squadron Mechanics as he attends to the port main undercarriage strut's brake system. Fighter is a Hurricane belonging to what was originally No. 1 (Canadian) Squadron on arrival in Britain but was changed to No. 401 (RAF) Squadron in early 1941. Head-on view shows how the brake drum is angled slightly inward in relation to the vertical strut.

causing damage or casualties. Arising from these sorties, a total of eight *Luftwaffe* bombers and fighters shared the fate of their Italian contemporaries.

Although the nocturnal 'Blitzing' of London was being expanded to steadily encompass Britain's industrial cities *Luftwaffe* daylight operations were still being carried out on a reduced scale that still merited a sizeable Fighter Command presence right up to the year's end and even beyond. Reconnaissance sorties were regularly indulged in, as were occasional fighter 'sweeps'. Single or several-strong sorties were conducted against key targets such as military production factories, while the Ju 87 reappeared to assist in delivering several attacks upon convoys.

One of the top-ranking German casualties as 1940 neared its end involved the *Kommodore* of JG2, Maj. Helmut Wick; his combat skills matched that of his First World War predecessor, Manfred von Richthofen, which the *Geschwader* bore as its title. By 29 November, this *Experte* had run up more than fifty *Abschuss* (kills) but was clearly showing the strain of prolonged combat both as a commander and pilot. The day's second sortie saw him hoping to increase his tally, but after his *Schwarm* engaged a Spitfire squadron that lost one to Wick, his fellow pilots lost

In early 1941, a series of publicity pictures were shot at Coltishall then home for No. 257 Squadron; however, the revelation of the unit's codes was also published, forcing a code-change to FM. The Hurricane seen here is parked upon metal frames secured into the soil by lugs. The tendency for aircraft to puncture their wheel covers on this surface type was often realised.

visual contact. Obltn. Rudi Pflanz then observed a fighter pursuing another Bf 109 and administering the fatal blow prior to his confirming the victor was a Spitfire.

The RAF pilot had bare seconds to savour his success before Pflanz closed in and dispatched him and his mount into the chilled, remorseless Channel waters along with the Bf 109 that had been flown by Wick. During the dogfight that had involved the intervention of No. 609 Squadron, a survivor had heard one pilot say: 'Whoopee, I've got one!' The airman in question was Flt Lt John Dundas, a veteran of the battle who was declared MIA after the squadron landed. The 'grim reaper' had again bitten into the ranks of the combat-seasoned personnel on both sides of the conflict (Dundas's brother and fellow fighter pilot, Hugh, would advance to a stellar RAF career in both the Second World War and post-war, finally retiring as a group captain).

Sqn Ldr Stanford Tuck was by now a leading double-figure ace and in charge of No. 257 Squadron. Faced with a demoralised group of pilots on arrival in early September, he had promptly assessed this operationally debilitating situation; with a mix of bluntness and encouragement, he had instilled in them a measure of confidence and pride that resurrected the squadron to 'top-line' status. On 9 December, he was either vectored on to or visually encountered a Do 17; the resultant pursuit must have been rather protracted since the aircraft's final demise was north of Ostend in Belgium. Three days later, his squadron was involved in a battle with Bf 109s off the Suffolk coast, during which he shot one down into the sea.

Technical Advances, RAF

By this point in 1940, the Mk IIA Spitfire was entering into service. The variant still retained the standard eight .303 battery, but the main change concerned the Merlin XII that was attuned to accommodate 100 Octane fuel and featured a Coffman cartridge starter in place of the former electrically-activated unit. Of the 940 airframes built at the Castle Bromwich factory, the final 170 would be adapted as Mk IIBs to carry the twin cannon and four machine-gun combinations that would feature on the majority of subsequent Spitfire airframes; a number of IIA airframes were also retrospectively converted to this format.

Its Hurricane partner's Merlin has been similarly uprated in power terms; the Mk XX's extra horsepower capacity raised the variant's top speed to around 350 mph, an increase that still left the fighter outpaced by its contemporary and even more so by its principal current opponent the Bf 109E. On the other hand, the standard firepower retained by the Mk IIA had been increased to twelve machine guns on the Mk IIB, although the increased firepower was likely to only prove less ineffective in achieving the downing of the *Luftwaffe* bombers. Cannon-calibre weaponry was the answer, and this was finally being addressed, however belatedly, not only for the Spitfire and Hurricane, but also for future designs.

Technical Advances, *Luftwaffe*

Across the Channel, aerodynamic developments were similarly gathering pace. The Bf 109E that had formed the core of the *Jagdwaffe* strength was soon to see it first being supplemented and ultimately replaced by the 'F' model. This airframe had been 'cleaned up' with a more streamlined propeller cover and engine cowling, slimmer radiator covers, retractable tailwheel, and removal of the stabiliser support struts. Firepower was marginally reduced and completely fuselage-mounted, consisting of twin 7.92-mm machine guns and a 20-mm MG-FF cannon firing through the propeller hub; the latter would be displaced initially by a 15-mm MG151 on the F-2 followed by a 20-mm MG151 on the F-4.

With a top speed of 390 mph at 22,000 feet, a maximum climb rate of 3,300 fpm at 5,000 feet and a service ceiling of 37,000 feet the latest Messerschmitt variant would prove a marginally more formidable adversary than its 'Emil' predecessor. The overall performance would prove to be inferior only in terms of turning circle when matched even against the Mk V Spitfire but diving at maximum speed induced such wayward effects upon the ailerons that full

Flt Lt Eric 'Sawn-off' Lock gives a thumbs-up sign from his Mk V Spitfire cockpit. This officer had a meteoric rise to combat fame, scoring twenty-three kills between August and November 1940 before being wounded and hospitalised for over six months before resuming operations. All but three of his final total of twenty-six victories was with No. 41 Squadron; the remaining three were with No. 611 Squadron that he commanded for a few weeks before his death over France on 3 August 1941.

hand-grasp sometimes backed by knee-pressure upon the control column had to be applied. The centralisation of the armament was welcomed by the top *Experten* but not by the rank and file for whom the art of deflection shooting was a difficult one to master. The 'F' model's absence of a cone of fire compared to the 'E' model's fuselage/wing-mounted weapon's ammunition 'spread' now made it even harder to land strikes on an adversary.

Into the Unknown

The 'bullish' stance adopted by the new C-in-C of Fighter Command and the head of No. 11 Group was now to be put into action as soon as possible, but the question to be begged was in what manner and how effectively. The short-range nature of the two current fighter designs did not allow for more than a shallow penetration of the northern French, Belgian, and, to a lesser extent, Dutch national territories. Nor were the potential replacements in the form of the Typhoon and Whirlwind likely to add materially to the range factor, at least as regards the Hawker design.

In the USA, the North American Co. was designing a fighter whose future impact upon the enemy's ability to defend even its own airspace would be called into question and found wanting. What evolved into the Mustang and entered RAF service around 1942 still required drastic modification in terms of engine power before such an impact could be realised, however; in addition, it would be the USAAF far more than the RAF who would wield this weapon in the stated manner. So it was that Fighter Command entered 1941 with the aforementioned operational limitations.

Stirring-up the Hornets' Nest

Both Sholto-Douglas and Leigh-Mallory's concept of meeting force with force was to focus upon fighter squadrons being formed and dispatched in wings as per the Bader experience. However, other means of disturbing the German infrastructure 'in the field' as opposed to the central intention of bringing the *Jagdwaffe* into action were to be indulged in. Sub-forces varying between two and four fighters were to be sent out at low level; their pilots would seek out targets of opportunity that would supplement the anticipated disruption to the enemy personnel's psychological state. Code-named Rhubarbs, these were initiated at the start of 1941. A normal pre-condition was the onset of low cloud patterns.

Crossing into occupied Europe at minimum altitude even under the foregoing circumstance was still fraught with risk thanks to the substantial flak presence at the coast and extending into the near continental hinterland, while the *Jagdwaffe*'s manifold locations added to the defensive network in similar manner to the RAF's 1940 experience. The sole advantage compared to the *Luftwaffe* experience was in evading capture should a pilot be downed; there was a chance of gaining access to the ever-expanding resistance network and evading capture denied to the German crews coming down over Britain. However, one logically had to survive the loss of their fighter and that was a bonus denied to all too many of the airmen entering the MIA category in the months ahead.

The pinprick nature of the Rhubarb activity was no way in which to bring up the enemy fighter strength in numbers. Instead, squadron and sometimes wing-strength formations were dispatched in similar manner to the enemy's *freie Jagd* sorties, bearing the respective code-names of Rodeo and Ranger in the hope of eliciting such large-scale responses. However, the German radar staff was as competent at distinguishing between these sorties and likely bomber formations as their British counterparts, and they accordingly withheld their pilots from engaging.

Drawing the *Jagdwaffe* into battle could only be expedited by the threat of a bomber assault accompanied by a strong escort presence in the same manner as for the recently expired daylight battle over Britain. There was a prime difference in circumstances, however; whereas the target availability in Britain was crucial to the nation's survival in being kept intact, the same rule was largely absent in the reverse circumstances. The available targets within escort range were relatively small in terms of Germany's industrial capacity, while Bomber Command's strength was no

An early 1941 picture depicts a pair of Mk IIA Spitfires serving with No. 602 (City of Glasgow) Squadron as they squat in their well-established dispersals consisting of walled-in earth banks; unit is currently stationed in Scotland. P8047 in foreground served with four squadrons and an OTU before being struck-off charge (SOC) in 1944.

more than adequate in terms of numbers as well as bomb-carrying capacity. So it was that the available JG2 and JG26 *Gruppe*n stationed across northern France and Belgium would constitute the major opposition to the RAF invaders.

An Embarrassing Revelation

The championing of the 'Big Wing' concept had played a notable part in the elevation of both current Fighter Command incumbents into their posts. For whatever reason, on 29 January, Leigh-Mallory decided to carry out an exercise purporting to show the efficacy of the scheme as based on an actual Battle of Britain case when two key airfields were attacked. The attacking force not only got through to the selected airfield targets but did so before the wing fighters even lifted off. Whatever the reasons for this situation, the result was a tactical 'black eye' for the No. 11 Group AOC, which his ego and doubtless backing from his immediate superior still managed to cover up since he would subsequently advance to assume Sholto-Douglas's post in late 1942.

Test Run

The first ever escorted bomber formation launched under the Circus code was sent out on 10 January. The single Blenheim flight was shielded by the three Hurricane units forming the North Weald Wing led by Wg Cdr Victor Beamish as well as Wg Cdr Harry Broadhurst's Spitfire wing from Hornchurch; Biggin Hill's complement of three Spitfire squadrons patrolled the Channel to act as withdrawal cover. The airfield target in the Pas-de-Calais was duly bombed, although the total of around 6,000 lb released did not achieve much in the way of damage. The meagre enemy fighter presence was easily brushed aside while casualties on either side were minimal. The very easy-paced experience encountered on Circus. No. 1 was not to prove the norm on subsequent raids, once the late winter and early spring weather arrived to promise improved conditions along with extending daylight hours.

Although the wing concept was in existence at North Weald and Hornchurch, it was only during March that the airfields of Kenley, Biggin Hill, and Tangmere became the epicentres for the same three-squadron structure. The wing commanders appointed were respectively Sqn Ldrs. John Peel, 'Sailor' Malan, and the effervescent Douglas Bader; in addition, Sqn Ldr Reginald Kellett had taken over at North Weald. The launching of further Circus operations following January's inaugural run had been left in abeyance as a result, but once all the wings had worked up to an accepted level of operational efficiency, the way was clear for Leigh-Mallory to initiate regular thrusts of this nature into Nazi-occupied airspace.

The desire to bring the *Jagdwaffe* into a hopefully deleterious battle similar to that applying during the middle stage of the Battle of Britain was given an added twist following the launch of Operation Barbarossa on 22 June. Hitler's politically

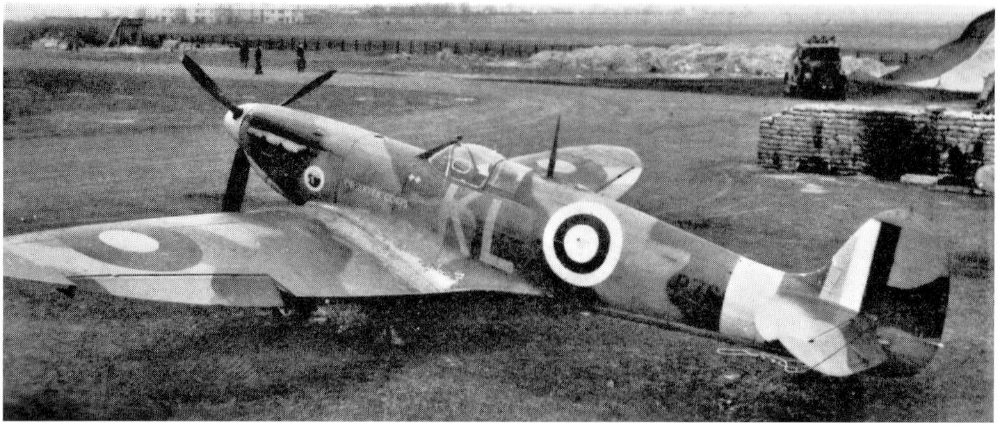

Hornchurch was home for No. 54 Squadron on five occasions during 1940, including periods involving the Battles of France and Britain. The latest return was in February 1941 when some Mk IIA Spitfires were transferred-in from No. 41 Squadron. KL: Z/P7618 bears the name 'Observer Corps' that would be prefixed by 'Royal' when that fine body of men and women was honoured by King George VI. This fighter was MIA on the 24th of the month.

convenient Non-Aggression Treaty with Stalin's USSR in August 1939 had now run its course and the Führer's long-term obsession with the need to crucify Communism and its adherents had come to fruition with the invasion of Soviet Russia. Churchill's support for his unexpected and politically-incompatible 'ally' demanded any and every measure to reduce the military pressure now bearing down with frightening efficiency upon a dangerously unprepared adversary. Britain could do nothing practical to draw the *Wehrmacht/SS* legions away from their immediate and seemingly unstoppable task of destroying Russia as a military entity.

The sole obvious source of intervention lay with the *Luftwaffe* support for the operation. Could a sustained air offensive as envisaged by the RAF draw a sufficient proportion of the German's aerial strength away from its Eastern Front involvement? This was the duty handed down from the command's political masters that was eagerly accepted by Sholto-Douglas and Leigh-Mallory in particular. What they announced was a 'non-stop offensive' that would evolve with the Circus and parallel operational variations.

From a German point of view, the need to balance the large-scale dispersal of units away from the assault on Britain with the need to defend against RAF incursions was arguably simpler. There was little threat to the German war effort as regards daylight attacks on its infrastructure from fighter-backed bomber formations. Consequently, the availability of the resident elements of JG2 and JG26 from April onwards with which to defend the obvious regions open to fighter-supported attack was regarded as more than sufficient to act as an effective defensive shield (in retrospect, the German's response to the 'non-stop offensive' expression was to dub it the 'nonsense offensive' as events would appear to confirm).

Stepped-Up Performance

The RAF's dependence upon the bullet-calibre weaponry, whether for bomber defence or fighter attack, was rather belatedly being corrected in wholesale manner as 1941 was commencing, and was an action taken none too soon. Both the Spitfire and Hurricane were adapted in this manner, although the application of the full four-cannon battery to the latter in the form of the Mk IIC was not largely duplicated on its Supermarine stable mate. In the Spitfire's case, only two of the four available cannon mountings were almost wholly destined to be utilised from the Mk VC onward during the Second World War; final post-war variants would be configured with the full complement, however.

The Spitfire Mk V was the practical replacement for the Mk III. The latter variant had been envisaged as accommodating the Merlin XX as its power source, but in addition was to be equipped with a strengthened fuselage and engine

This steeply banking Spitfire Mk VB R6923/QJ:S is the mount for Sqn Ldr Jamie Rankin, who was currently the CO of No. 92 Squadron. The simple beauty of the Vickers-Supermarine airframe is admirably caught here in plan form. The bulged fairings for the cannon ammunition drums are offset to the outside of the weapons. This aircraft is an original Mk IA converted to Mk V standards.

mounting, additional armour plating, retractable tail wheel, and a forward rake of the main undercarriage by 2 inches—this adjustment being intended to counter the Spitfire's tendency to nose-up in rough ground conditions. Further refinements were complete landing gear covers in flight and wing tips 'cropped' by several feet with a view to increasing the fighter's roll rate.

Although chosen in place of the Mk III, the Mk V's choice for production was nevertheless apparently envisaged as a temporary expedient ahead of the latter's entry into service—an ironic perception since it became by far the most produced Spitfire variant. The fact that the Mk V incorporated little or nothing of the Mk III's refinements other than the clipped-wing configuration on the low-flying (LF) variant reinforces the 'expediency' assumption (a similar situation would arise between the Mk VIII and Mk IX; the major difference was that these marks' introduction into service would merely be reversed compared to the Mk III's non-appearance).

The Merlin XX had a notably enhanced power output compared to its predecessors, but the decision was taken to mount the Merlin 45 on the Mk V on the grounds that the power output could permit the fighter to gain access to the same height as the Bf 109F. This operational factor would be crucial if a second Battle of Britain scenario appeared likely to arise in mid-1941, but the same consideration was relevant in reverse as Fighter Command anticipated going over to the offensive.

The performance envelope of the Mk V's Merlin 45 witnessed a maximum speed of 369 mph at 20, 000 feet, reducing to 346 mph around 25, 000 feet, and a climb rate of around 2,600 fpm up to 20,000 feet, reducing to 1,600 fpm up to 30,000 feet. Service ceiling was assessed at 36,000 feet, with a further 1,000 feet regarded as an 'absolute' maximum. One serious and recurring problem was oil freezing in the propeller constant-speed units (CSU). Over-revving was one undesirable outcome but equally unwelcome was a converse loss of rpm in the climb. This was a flaw that would take time to counter but would clearly place pilots on a potentially lethal back foot in combat.

The initial production batch of Mk Vs appeared in service during the spring, but the first 100 airframes still bore machines guns and were designed Mk VA. The first cannon-armed variant was the Mk VB, but the airframes so designated only mounted single cannon bays. Finally, the Mk VC emerged with the requisite double cannon bay layout (the clipped-wing VB and VC variants would appear from 1942 onwards). Nos 91 and 92 Squadrons took on the Mk VB as early as February–March and No. 74 followed suit in May, when the first Mk VA deliveries involving No. 41 Squadron also occurred, although these were supplanted by the Mk VB around July. The need to swiftly press the Mk V into wholesale service in order to properly challenge the Bf 109F was of paramount concern.

Operational Limitations

The bid to draw the *Jagdwaffe* into combat on RAF terms was destined to run into arguably more difficulties than that borne by the German's 1940 offensive. For a start, the region under potential threat from the bombers was no larger and, moreover, held a far lesser degree of suitable targets either of an industrial nature or relating directly to the *Luftwaffe* that could in the latter instance inflict serious, let alone terminal, limitations on its operations. An even greater limitation factor lay in the resources devoted to the actual assault; the small number of bombers sent out on individual sorties saw to this. In summation, the assaults held no material threat to Nazi Germany's national survival in the same manner as had confronted Britain in 1940.

The greater time factor enabling the Germans to react to the raids further ate into the opportunity to engage the *Jagdwaffe* pilots when they were at an inferior altitude; added to this was the deployment in similar manner to Fighter Command of small sub-units tasked with patrolling at altitude and monitoring any incoming force's composition and strength, and these would radio back the presence or absence of bombers within the *Pulk* (formation) for the controllers to dispatch or withhold their fighters accordingly.

Should the situation merit 'scrambling' the Bf 109s, the *Staffeln* concerned would climb as quickly as possible, but on making an interception, they would skirt round the opposing mass of aircraft instead of rushing straight into combat, awaiting the opportunity to make a quick 'pass' wherever gaps appeared. The mass of RAF fighters accumulated around the bombers were now destined to suffer the same limits on combat flexibility and consequent frustrations accruing from this basically rigid stance whenever the *Jagdwaffe*'s pilots chose to intervene in what was a logical 'strike and run' manner.

A classic example of the tactic arose during one Circus operation when Wg Cdr Stanford-Tuck's Duxford Wing was the focal point. A number of Bf 109s were stalking the formation, an act that culminated with the leader being warned of a potential 'pass' directed at his section. This day, his No. 2 was a relatively 'new boy' whom he had selected by way of encouragement. The approach of one *Rotte* was signalled-in evermore urgently to Tuck by other wing pilots as the pair inexorably headed his way.

At the last moment, he swerved and avoided the fire of the *Rotte* leader but recovered promptly to latch on to and dispatch the enemy No. 2; sadly, by then, Tuck's No. 2 had been summarily disposed of by the German No. 1 to demonstrate the summary nature of air combat. After the Second World War, Tuck discovered the *Rotte* leader was reportedly none other than Adolf Galland, the JG26 *Kommodore*; this is according to the Germans, but records indicate he scored no kills during Tuck's tenure as the Duxford Wing CO when the incident occurred—according to Tuck.

New Zealand Prime Minister Mr Fraser is about to exit the cockpit of a No. 92 Squadron Mk VB at Warmwell on 26 July 1941 during his visit to Britain. The IFF wire stretching back from the Type A1 roundel to the stabiliser could be a lethal impediment to any pilot baling out who was unfortunate enough to make contact with its guillotine-sharp edge.

Combat Fatigue?

Tuck was very fortunate to still be in circulation following the events of 21 June. On that day, he had flown a non-operational 'sortie' from Coltishall that took him down over the Thames Estuary. At this point, he illogically banked east and commenced a prolonged course out over the North Sea. His year-long spell on active operations probably played a part in what transpired by inducing a mix of combat fatigue mingled with casual confidence since he was completely 'bounced' by three Bf 109s.

He managed to survive the initial onslaught of gunfire that struck his aircraft, and having fought off the momentary sense of panic, he now banked in a bid to take on his assailants, hopeless odds or not. One Bf 109, likely the one making the firing pass, flashed in front of him and paid the price when Tuck's superb deflection-shooting skills dispatched him into the sea—one down, two to go. One of the other two was taken on in a continuous, twisting dogfight that finally ended with Tuck the victor, at which point his instrument panel was riddled and cockpit hood blown off by the third Bf 109, whose pilot described a wide circle before heading straight for his apparently doomed opponent.

The resultant exchange of fire left the Hurricane surprisingly free of further damage, while sufficient punishment had been dealt out for the glycol-spewing

Although this Hawker Fury fighter is seen in modern surroundings of the former RAF airfield of Duxford, it is an original airframe. The colourful markings of No. 43 (Fighting Cocks) Squadron include the bird motif on the fin surfaces along with the black/white chequerboard design. This aircraft is fully airworthy and performs at displays during the summer months.

No. 3 Squadron's initial conversion from Gladiators to Mk I Hurricanes only lasted from March to July 1938, when the action was reversed; the original conversion was repeated on a permanent basis in May 1939. This picture was taken during the 1939 operational period since L1940 in the foreground's construction was after July 1938. The Type 'B' fuselage roundel and absence of a fin flash were features applied between September 1938 and 1939.

Flt Lt John Kent from Canada is second from left as he walks along with a group of pilots from No. 303 (Polish) Squadron. The unit was assigned Hurricanes during the Battle of Britain and Kent served as a flight commander between July and October before transferring to No. 92 Squadron as its CO.

The ground crew are assisting the pilot of a No. 222 Squadron Mk V Spitfire as he readies himself for a sortie. The Type A1 roundel indicates picture taken prior to mid-1942 when the fuselage and fin design changed to the Type C1.

The pilot of the No. 222 Squadron Mk V Spitfire has just fired-up the Merlin as indicated by the flames issuing from the exhaust stubs that bear 'fish-tail' apertures. The knock-out emergency panel on the cockpit canopy is clearly shown.

This low-angled view of the Spitfire confirms that it is the Mk VB version. The cannon armament is limited to a pair of 20-mm weapons compared to the later Mk VC, which had provision for four, although few mounted the extra pair. The Mk V formed the base for the superlative Mk IX. Note the aircraft letter repeated under the nose panel.

No. 87 Squadron was one of several squadrons tasked initially with night fighter duties but subsequently carried out Intruder operations over the continent. The overall black camouflage borne here with the sole colour variation a red propeller cover changed to ocean grey/dark green above and black beneath for the latter-stated function. Fighter is a Mk IIC variant armed with four 20-mm cannon that proved useful for assaulting ground as well as aerial targets.

The beautifully pristine condition of an LF Mk VB assigned to No. 316 (Polish) Squadron is captured here. The clipped-wing structure permitted a faster roll rate, although overall performance was still well below that of its Fw 190 adversary. Ocean or mixed grey displaced dark earth on RAF fighters in August 1941, but dark green was retained, as seen here. Serial number is applied in small scale on the rear fuselage band.

The Bell Aerocobra's RAF service was brief and involved only No. 601 Squadron before withdrawal from combat duties. The mechanics are draped with belts of bullets or cannon shells in the case of the two airmen alongside the engine. The cannon barrel protrudes prominently from the propeller spinner cover. The unit's winged-sword emblem can be discerned below the windshield.

The distinct, if angular, outline of the Westland Whirlwind is demonstrated in this picture of P7048. The fighter was assigned to No. 137 Squadron following its creation in late 1941; ironically, after surviving on operations, it was sold back to Westland. Note the feathering effect on the wing surface camouflage pattern. Pilot's view from the cockpit was superb.

No. 175 Squadron went operational on the Mk IB Typhoon in June 1943. What is probably a publicity picture shows HH: N being readied for a ground-attack sortie to judge by the pair of bombs ahead of the starboard wing that appear ready to be lifted and attached to the underwing pylons. The fighter's first-class camouflage condition suggests a fairly short time on frontline service.

A view of the port wing surface on a Mk IB Typhoon picks out detail on the armament compartment. The hatch covers are separate units for each weapon up front with a single overall cover at the rear. The outer ammunition drum is being fed with the 20-mm shells. Note the recoil springs on the gun barrels; later production airframes were equipped with sheaths for these currently exposed sections.

Right: The rocket rail on a Mk IB Typhoon is the subject for discussion. The pilot stands between two members of the British Army that includes what looks like a Highland Regiment officer. Note the rolled-up trouser bottoms and very casual footwear worn by the pilot. Picture taken during the summer of 1944 to judge by the cut-down D-Day bands on the inner wing.

Below: This is an FB Mk VI Mosquito, but it did not serve with an operational squadron. Instead, it was used as a test bed for Monica IIIe—the tail-warning device fitted to heavy bomber rear fuselages—and other technical refinements relating to fighter operations.

An aerial view of Flt Lt Jan Zumbach's Spitfire Mk VB provides a clearer sight of the Duck artwork. The head clearance for taller pilots was rather marginal, even with the bulged canopy fitted to the Spitfire. Yellow-striped outer-wing leading edges became standard on RAF fighters from August 1941 on.

HJ728 was an F Mk II Mosquito from a batch constructed between March and May 1943. The pristine condition, lack of squadron markings and several civilian staff attending to the aircraft indicate it is yet to be delivered from the factory to the RAF.

The Mk V Hurricane bore a universal wing that could accommodate the carriage of bombs up to 500-lb weight, eight rockets, or two 40-mm cannon as seen here. KZ193 also bears a tropical filter under the nose, although it only served with No. 164 Squadron in Britain. By 1943, when this final variant entered service, it was seriously outperformed by the *Luftwaffe* fighters, and its use over Northwest Europe was steadily curtailed over the intervening months.

A rear-angle view of what is believed to be EK183 assigned to No. 56 Squadron picks out the thin yellow stripe applied on the upper wings. This was an early indicator to other Allied pilots of the Hawker design's friendly status that predated the underwing black and white stripes serving as a more visible indicator. The huge bulk of the airframe and the even-greater size of the propeller is evident. Pilot's retractable footrest is a point of note.

Three veteran fighters fly a tight echelon-right formation for the photographer. The combat days for the Mk I Spitfires are far behind them as they are now serving with the Empire Central Flying School. The Supermarine duo both served with four operational squadrons prior to reassignment to the ECFS. The de Havilland propeller on the nearside aircraft was a standard fitting on early-production Hurricane airframes, but in fact, Z4791 never reached an operational unit.

This is the business end of a Mosquito FB Mk VI that picks out the four machine guns mounted in the nose compartment. The elliptical panel, whose outline is visible below, contains the apertures for the quartet of 20-mm cannon in the forward bomb bay—a fearsome overall array of firepower. Flat-fronted windshield was standard on all fighter variants.

Right: 'Johnny' Johnson is posed with his black Labrador, Sally, with a Mk IXE Spitfire as background. Although his rank insignia is invisible, he has attained wing commander rank and is leader of No. 127 Wing, 2TAF, an all-Canadian force of three squadrons. Picture was taken at Bazenville in France during late July 1944.

Below: No. 616 Squadron, an auxiliary unit originally formed in Yorkshire, was selected to be the first to convert onto the Gloster Meteor, the Allies' sole operational jet-propelled aircraft in the Second World War. By the time this picture was taken, the squadron was stationed on the continent but no contact with their *Luftwaffe* contemporary, the Me 262, ever occurred—probably a good thing, with the RAF design's notable inferiority in top speed being a key limitation.

Hurricane Mk I, serving with No. 1 Squadron in France during early 1940.

Blenheim IF, ZK: P, No. 25 Squadron stationed at North Weald in early 1940.

Spitfire Mk I, PR: L of No. 609 (White Rose) Squadron serving at Middle Wallop, summer 1940.

Defiant Mk I, PS: V of No. 264 Squadron based at Hornchurch in summer of 1940.

Whirlwind I, HE: H flying out of Warmwell during 1941.

Above: Havoc Mk I, YP: F of No. 23 Squadron operating from Middle Wallop in spring of 1941.

Below: Beaufighter IF, NG: O, No. 604 Squadron stationed at Middle Wallop in 1941.

Mosquito FB Mk VI, UP: J of No. 605 Squadron flying out of Bradwell Bay in early 1943.

Above: Typhoon Mk IB, PR: D serving with No. 609 (White Rose) Squadron in early 1943.

Below: Mustang III, PK: F of No. 316 (Polish) Squadron based at Ford in early 1944.

Meteor Mk I, YQ: U of No.616 Squadron based at Manston in the summer of 1944.

Tempest Mk V, SA: A assigned to No.486 (New Zealand) Squadron, Hopsten (Germany) 1945.

Bf 109 to head for home. Tuck's receding prospects of regaining British soil soon culminated in a compulsory bale out and descent into the mercifully-calm North Sea. Inflation of his dinghy and plugging of several small holes still left him adrift with no immediate sign of rescue; his luck was in, however, when a coal barge whose crew witnessed the combat arrived on the scene and picked him up. What was known as 'Tuck's luck', a reference to his several fortunate escapes from death or injury both pre-war and in combat, had once more favoured him greatly.

A Vain Hope

The launch of Operation Barbarossa into the hinterland of Stalin's corrupt empire was naturally regarded as a military Godsend to the previously hard-pressed British. As with Poland, there was nothing material that the nation could do to assist their now equally, if not more mortally, pressed Ally 'in the Field' as it were. All that could be considered was how to draw a measure of the German forces off the Eastern Front with the emphasis logically directed against the *Luftwaffe* contingent. There was no possibility of forcing the redirection of the *Luftwaffe*'s bomber strength towards the west. However, as regards the *Jagdwaffe*, the situation appeared more promising. If enough aerial pressure could be applied over France and Belgium thanks to the constant presence of the RAF bomber/fighter formations, it was expected that the current defensive force represented by JG26 and JG2 would require bolstering in strength in order to hold back these assaults. That was the theory to which both Dowding and Park's successors were upholding.

As the summer progressed the RAF sallied forth on regular Circus operations, but their efforts to attract a greater reaction from the *Jagdwaffe* were retrospectively proven to be in vain. Not only were the current numbers of fighters on hand when Barbarossa erupted capable of handling their adversaries, the casualty rate inflicted upon the RAF was to prove far greater than that suffered by the *Jagdwaffe*. The only consolation arising from this depressing situation lay with those pilots fortunate enough not only to survive being shot down, but also to evade being captured. Their descent into occupied Europe provided them with the chance of gaining access to the local resistance movement, who could in turn provide them with the means to eventually regain British soil—an advantage totally denied their German contemporaries coming down over Britain the previous summer.

Although JG26 in particular was to enjoy a notably superior kill–loss ratio in the course of this type of operation, there were instances when the scores were almost evened-up, as on 21 June—ironically, just twenty-four hours prior to the momentous events far to the east that erupted and would give hope to pressurising the western-based *Jagdwaffe* units in the near future. Two separate Circus operations were met by elements of JG2 and JG26, and in the course of the sometimes-frenetic engagements, a figure of eight out of the twelve JG26 *Abschuess* submissions were granted against RAF records of six fighters MIA. In turn, the *Geschwader* suffered the loss of nine Bf 109s shot down or written-off in crash-landings, with three pilot deaths.

There could have been a further pilot casualty, a key one at that, in the shape of the *Kommodore* Maj. Adolph Galland. He had already downed a Blenheim during the first Circus and now, on the second, engaged a Spitfire from No. 611 Squadron that caught fire and fell away. It was then that Galland committed the cardinal combat error of watching his victim going down. Suddenly, the starboard fuselage and wing was riddled by return fire from another Spitfire and one fuel tank exploded while he was gliding back to base; although struck by fragments, he was extremely lucky to avoid serious injury as he hastily evacuated his charge and parachuted safely to be later dispatched for treatment to a local hospital. His survival spelt misfortune for the Allied pilots he would shoot down over the ensuing five months, thereby raising his tally to 104. However, he was then detached from combat duties to serve as *General der Jagdflieger* in place of Ob. Werner Moelders following his death in November 1941.

The Master Departs

Douglas Bader was a remarkable individual as a fighter pilot, all the more so since, by 1941, he had been bereft of both legs for nearly ten years; the cause was a flying accident in a Bulldog fighter of No. 23 Squadron that he was to acknowledge after the Second World War was his 'own bloody fault'. Invalided out of the RAF in 1933, he returned in 1939 and persuaded the authorities of his ability to fly an aircraft in a full operational capacity. During the Battle of Britain, he commanded No. 242 Squadron that became the core of the 'Big Wing' based at Duxford and Fowlmere.

By 9 August, Bader, as leader of the Tangmere Wing, was probably reaching the point where his reactions in the air were, like other aces, such as Stanford-Tuck, becoming dangerously extended. His naturally stubborn nature was at last beginning to reconcile itself with this situation, and he had reportedly agreed with his wife that it was time to come off operations. On his latest operation, he had already downed a Bf 109F and, according to his biographer, had become isolated from his squadron when he subsequently intercepted a small enemy formation.

His immediate reaction was contrary to all operational principals that he had instilled in his pilots and seemed to confirm his operationally-exhausted state of mind. A pilot on his own either had to quickly seek a link-up with others or, failing that, should head homewards. Anybody admitting to doing what Bader was doing would have been severely reprimanded by the man himself. As it was, Bader closed in on the formation, shot one down, but then collided with a second that was lagging as he banked away. The Spitfire's tail was knocked off and the decapitated machine hurtled towards the ground. Initial attempts to bale out were lethally hindered by one artificial foot jamming under the rudder pedal, but somehow, the leg-restraining strap tore; he was cast out into mid-air, whereupon

No. 616 Squadron operated on Mk IIs during its initial spell with the Tangmere Wing led by Wg Cdr Douglas Bader, whose name adorns the cowling. The chipped-tooth grin belongs to Fg Off. J. E. 'Johnny' Johnson then a squadron member who is destined to run up a score of thirty-four personal and seven shared kills by VE-Day—a tally that will be the highest figure for an RAF and Commonwealth air force ace.

he deployed his parachute and floated down to be immediately captured by some soldiers.

After the Second World War, an examination of the circumstances surrounding Bader's loss settled on a more logical explanation. Apparently, an *Abschuess* claim that related to his fighter was granted to one or other of the JG26 pilots concerned. However, further research made within the past year or so has added to the confusion. It is now alleged that a collision did not take place with a Bf 109, but that his aircraft's demise was at the hands of another squadron member. No matter the circumstances, Fighter Command had been deprived of its latest ace and senior-serving officer. Nevertheless, the inspiration he had provided to those within his command would resonate throughout the years and air battles ahead, none more so than with one individual who would feature as one of the premier pilots in Fighter Command.

Bader's Apprentice Blossoms

No. 616 Squadron was part of the Tangmere Wing and one of its number was still a relative unknown, Fg Off. 'Johnnie' Johnson. He had joined the squadron in September 1940 and after the unit transferred into the wing had incurred Bader's justified wrath on one operation. Sighting a mere handful of Bf 109s, he yelled out

'Look out!!' instead of making a calm, precise report. The formation immediately lost its cohesion and descended into a shambolic state as the other pilots broke away. Back on the ground, Bader asked for an explanation before lambasting the hapless Johnson in front of the entire assembly.

Having done so, the wing commander soon recognised the latent qualities of a good fighter pilot in Johnson's persona. On a subsequent operation, Johnson became separated from the formation and was assailed by a number of Bf 109s. Just when the situation was verging on the terminal, he was spotted by one of Bader's section from which he had become detached; Bader reacted by orbiting in a manner that permitted Johnson to link up and all four returned home. This timely salvation of Johnson's career would have fatal consequences for numerous *Luftwaffe* airmen in the years ahead.

By 9 August, he had amassed three confirmed kills along with several probables. This figure was destined to be repeated over ten-fold before the war in Europe was concluded, during which time Johnson rose to the rank of group captain as well as commanding three separate wings at various periods. His final personal figure of thirty-four kills and a further number of shared victories was to place him at the head of the Royal and Commonwealth Air Forces' list of aces.

The battles between the RAF formations that had gained the nickname of 'beehives' and the *Jagdwaffe* defenders proceeded apace as summer began to ease into autumn. Although the German pilots continued to enjoy a kill–loss ratio in their favour, this appears to have been as much due to the restrictive nature of the RAF formation pattern as to the technical superiority of the Bf 109F over the Spitfire Mk II, although nothing like as wide a margin *vis-à-vis* the Mk V. As it was, a much darker prospect for the Allied pilots' survival chances in combat was unknowingly looming on the horizon, one that would persist well into 1942 before the latest Spitfire variant arrived on the scene to again level up the odds.

Hurricane Offensive Operations (1940–1941)

The use of the Hurricane as a superiority fighter from 1940 onwards was perhaps wisely run down in terms of operations over Western Europe, although final exclusion from this primary duty was not realised until the autumn of 1941. The Hawker design's ability to handle even the Bf 109F, let alone the Fw 190, was to prove increasingly in doubt—the maximum speed differential favoured the Fw 190 by around 80 mph, a margin that would later be paralleled by the Me 262 *vis-à-vis* the P-51. The Hurricane was accordingly switched to other combat duties that were important in keeping pressure upon the enemy but provided a better chance of evading the aerial defences, although this was never unconditionally guaranteed.

The advent of the 'non-stop offensive' provided the means for the Hurricane squadrons' deployment in the full range of specialist operations: 'Rhubarb', 'Rodeo', 'Ramrod', 'Ranger', 'Circus', and, finally, 'Roadstead'. The Rhubarb and Rodeo sorties were suitable in that the individual or small formations indulging in this form of 'hit and run' activity usually flew in weather conditions that left the pilots with a chance to both strike at targets of opportunity while also remaining exempt from air interception.

Nos 607 and 615 Squadrons were in the fore in what were effectively Intruder raids; however, the machine-gun batteries with which their Mk I and IIA variants were equipped could not inflict effective damage on more solid structures. In addition, the ever-alert flak batteries were a cause of regular attrition among the ranks of these units and their fellow-Hurricane contemporaries. It was not until the winter of 1942–43 that this activity was halted on the grounds that the return in terms of disruption to the German military strength was not worth the cost.

As regards a direct fighter function, the Hurricanes participated in Ranger operations. These involved formations of wing proportions carrying out 'sweeps' along the enemy coastline with a view to drawing the *Jagdwaffe* into an air battle. With Spitfire squadrons usually part of the formation structure, this provided a form of security for the Hurricane pilots should an engagement occur. Circus duties were also indulged in up to late 1941. An interesting feature of the Hurricane's presence came during the latter stages of these operations. By late autumn, several squadrons were flying aircraft modified to carry up to 500 lb in bombs. On occasion, these replaced standard bombers as the 'core' of the Circus sortie.

A section of No. 79 Squadron Hurricanes is 'shadowed' by the photographer's aircraft. All three came from a batch of 1,000 built between August 1940 and July 41. NV: M is a Mk IIA, the other two being Mk IIB variants. All three later served with No. 141 Wing in Northern Russia during late 1941. Operations over France and the Low Countries rendered the Hawker design very vulnerable to fatal punishment when encountering the Bf 109F and Fw 190.

No. 402 (Canadian) Squadron was the second of the 'Hurribomber' units, as the Mk IIB was known. They were tasked with attacking targets in France from November 1941 and AE: K is seen at Warmwell being loaded up with 250-lb bombs. As good a fighter as the Hawker machine was, the conversion to Mk V Spitfires the following March was probably met with relief.

No. 402 (Canadian) Squadron was the first to train-up on the Mk IIB Hurricane with a view to making bombing raids across the Channel. Known as 'Hurribombers' the Hawker fighters usually mounted 250-lb-calibre bombs on the wing racks. No. 402 commenced this type of operation in Nov. 1941 but only did so until conversion on to Mk VB Spitfires the following March. Note the aircraft letter repeated on the lower engine cowling.

Hurricane Mk II

The momentous events of 1940 arguably witnessed the Hurricane at what was the near-peak of its performance scale. Further development comparison with the Spitfire in this respect was to see the Hawker design steadily, but inexorably lagging behind in its perceived primary function as a superiority fighter. The airframe was incapable of being further aerodynamically refined both in terms of the fuselage and particularly the solid wing structure, and it would be relegated to secondary, but nevertheless important duties, such as ground-attack and Intruder operations over north-western Europe; however, continued function as a fighter would apply overseas for some length of time.

Whereas the Mk I had operated as a pure fighter to date, the intention with its successor was for use in a multi-role combat function as mentioned in the foregoing paragraph. The uprated Merlin XX (1,260 hp) now fitted with a two-stage supercharger and impelled by a Rotol constant-speed unit was mounted in Mk I P3269 that served as the Mk II prototype. Maximum true air speed (TAS) was 348 mph at 17,500 feet, where the supercharger kicked-in; this figure would be somewhat degraded by up to 20 mph as extra weaponry and external racks along with tropical filters were added to the AUW figure for subsequent Mk II variants.

No. 151 Wing, comprising Nos 81 and 134 Squadrons, was sent to northern Russia in autumn 1941. During the six-week detachment flown from Vayenga (now Severomorsk) near the key seaport of Murmansk, a total of twenty kills were registered. The four Hurricane Mk IIBs from the former-named unit that bear tropical air filters fly a tight formation over the airfield.

A group of personnel from No. 134 Squadron are scattering in a vain attempt to avoid being showered by the snow nestling on the dispersal camouflage netting. Unit identity is confirmed by the letter mix of 'G' for the squadron and 'O' for the individual aircraft letter. One of the two Cyrillic numbers for Soviet identification purposes applied behind the roundel is partially seen behind the airman on the right.

A close-up view of a Mk IIB Hurricane demonstrates the overall weapon layout. The extra pair of .303 machine guns is staggered vertically and has the muzzles slightly protruding compared to the main bank of four further inward. The enhanced firepower was still barely adequate for guaranteeing destruction; hence the parallel introduction of cannon-calibre guns in their place.

There was to be four sub-variants of the Mk II, beginning with the still standard-armed Mk IIA. However, this variant was further divided into Series I and II batches. The Series I airframes initially included 100 Mk Is modified to Mk II standard as a stop-gap measure; 60 per cent were allocated to training units following the full-flow of Mk II airframes from Hawker's and Gloster's factories by the time the converted aircraft were available for operational reissue, the remainder having been dispatched to Russia.

The Series II allocation built specifically by the Austin Co. were all intended to have enlarged coolant header tanks with a view to its service in 'tropical' theatres, a feature that marginally extended the nose contour. During flight testing, negative handling characteristics displayed by the first few aircraft so outfitted, soon resulted in the cancellation of the tank modification programme for the remaining airframes.

In the light of the urgent need for heavier-calibre guns than the .303, it seems illogical that the Mk IIA's retention of its Mk I predecessor's eight-gun battery did not prevent production proceeding well into 1941 before conversion of subsequent airframes to the other three variant's standard of firepower occurred. Even then, there was only an increase in the number of machine guns to twelve installed in the Mk IIB; this arrangement in one anonymous pilot's caustic opinion 'only provided 50% more chance of more peas bouncing off *Luftwaffe* armour!'

It took the introduction of the Mk IIC in concert with the Mk VB Spitfire to bring RAF fighter striking power into the modern world via the 20-mm cannon, although greater use of the .5 machine gun in place of the .303 would arguably have been of almost equal benefit to the pilots. The Hispano design was drum-fed as was one of the two Oerlikon variations, the other being a belt-fed system by Châtellerault. The first two in turn merited the fitting of 'blister' covers on the upper-wing surfaces so as to accommodate the drums' outline. Access panels behind the wing spar were also deemed necessary to permit weapon detachment. Hispano won the day and the Mk I and II variants were installed, each gun having a drum capacity of 100 rounds.

A single test aircraft, V7360, adapted to MK II standard had already flown with No. 151 Squadron during the Battle of Britain and gained at least one kill. More comprehensive investigation involved thirty airframes that were created at the end of 1940. These shared the three aforementioned systems between them, with ten forming an experimental 'pool' for final experimental work. With this completed satisfactorily, the initial issue of cannon-armed Mk IICs to operational squadrons commenced in March 1941, the first of around 4,700 destined to come off the production lines up to September 1944.

Whirlwind Fortunes

The Westland Co. had produced a novel all-metal, stressed-skin design with a distinct structural outline. The Whirlwind was of twin-engined layout; powered by the Rolls-Royce Peregrine in under-slung nacelles and featuring a cruciform tail layout as well as a cockpit canopy mounted on top of the fuselage, the first prototype was airborne during 1938. The production machines, 112 in all, were equipped with four 20-mm cannon and a bomb load of 1,000 lb was standard. Maximum speed was on a par with the Mk 1 Spitfire (360 mph) at 15,000 feet, climb rate to 15,000 feet was around 2,500 fpm, and the service ceiling was 30,000 feet.

The perceived primary intention behind the Whirlwind's development in an anti-bomber function would logically have witnessed its introduction within the Battle of Britain. Whether it could have served as an effective companion to the Hurricane and Spitfire by the time of entry into RAF service in July 1940 was never put to the test. Maintenance problems, especially in respect of the engines and a high landing-speed that restricted the use to larger airfields may have been relevant factors in holding back its use. Full operational status was not confirmed until November when the Battle of Britain was effectively concluded.

How it would have performed on its own when running up against the Bf 109 in particular was to remain a moot point; any Second World War twin-engined aerofoil was generally hard-pressed to survive against single-engined opposition, as evidenced by what could be regarded as the Whirlwind's contemporary the Bf 110. The altitudes flown during the battle were of a nature that would have seen

A close-up view of a Westland Whirlwind in flight confirms the massive overall shape compared to standard fighter layout. The appearance was deceptive in terms of performance since the aircraft possessed sound manoeuvrability and equally sound top speed. However, the uncertain behaviour of the Peregrine engines was probably the reason for the restriction in numbers of squadrons being assigned the fighter (two).

the maximum speed factor noticeably reduced; on the other hand, the Whirlwind possessed a good degree of manoeuvrability that could have provided a challenge to the *Jagdwaffe* in a dogfight.

The Whirlwind's perceived function was basically altered at its point of full operational availability thanks to Germany's repulse in its bid for invasion and subjugation of its bitter adversary. With Fighter Command refreshed and potentially poised to take the offensive to the Germans, the Whirlwind's heavy armament and bomb-carrying capacity made it an ideal candidate for the fighter/bomber function; in addition, a greater range capacity meant the pilots could range further into occupied Europe and even western Germany as far as the Rhine.

An unforgiveable lapse in internal layout was the absence of a fuel tank cross-feed system. This raised the possibility of disaster should an engine be disabled on longer-range sorties since the other fuel tank would have to sustain the aircraft in flight—provided all the content was not exhausted before attaining friendly shores. Another problem related to the use of oil under pressure instead of the normal linkage controls for the engine throttles and airspeed controls. Flying at higher altitudes adversely affected the system with the engines tending to desynchronise. The solution was to push the throttles forward and pull the airspeed control levers back—a sound solution in normal flight, but not guaranteed to increase survival if engaged in a combat at the time.

The concept of a fighter that could serve in a long-range offensive as opposed to short-range defensive function as currently in force up to 1940 was given credence with the creation of the Westland Whirlwind. Added to this was the presence of a battery of cannon-calibre weapons as seen on P7055; these would provide a punishing strike force against ground and shipping targets as well as aircraft.

No. 137 Squadron bore the title ‘Fellowship of the Bellows’ as its particular ‘sponsorship’. Access to the Whirlwind’s cockpit required a physical effort given the height of the wing surface. The photo angle picks out the generously ‘blown’ pilot’s canopy as well as the port wing’s split flap outboard of the fuselage.

Operations

No. 263 Squadron was the first of only two units to convert onto the Whirlwind. The first period of operations involved the somewhat prosaic one of convoy patrol commencing December 1940. The ultimately eight airfields on which the squadron was based were all ranged along the central and western fringes of the Channel. From June, the pilots were engaged in more offensive-minded ‘sweeps’ over enemy territory that included interdiction strikes on airfields in the Normandy region. On one famous operation, the aircraft acted as escort to a Blenheim force that penetrated as far as Cologne on the Rhine where specific targets were attacked. However, the cover provided only extended to Antwerp. The heavy armament was also useful for shooting-up shipping in the Channel and out into the North Sea as the RAF attempted to deny these waters to the Germans; the sparse ammunition capacity of sixty per 20-mm gun dictated careful use by the pilots, however.

On occasions such as the interdiction sorties, No. 263 ran into Bf 109s and the resultant dogfights witnessed the RAF fighters standing up quite well to what was a higher-performance machine. It was somewhat ironic that non-operational losses proved to be higher compared to those incurred on operations. In September 1941, the second and sole other Whirlwind Squadron (No. 137) was formed with No. 263 transferring some pilots and support staff. The operational debut was marred by the death of the CO Sqn Ldr J. Sample during the first week, but after a short non-operational respite, the succession of ‘sweeps’ and coastal patrols from airfields in Norfolk was maintained during the winter.

Two mechanics have detached the nose compartment panels on their Whirlwind in order to gain full maintenance access to the quartet of 20-mm cannon; the huge overall size of the weapons is clearly demonstrated. There were useful not only against aircraft but also against ground or sea-borne targets.

No Chivalry at All!

Aerial combat has been regularly presented as a more 'clean and equal' method of engaging an enemy with little or no thoughts of straying from the Geneva Convention or the rules of war in the process. The bald truth was that each fighter pilot went aloft with a view to surviving the 'kill or be killed' fate awaiting him. Air battles were hardly conducted in any other manner, and the idea of a 'Knights jousting in the Sky' contest was quite bluntly a million miles distant from that sanitised image.

An anonymous pilot who participated in the Battle of Britain placed the art of successful fighter combat in its true context. He was quoted as follows: 'Being involved in a dogfight is akin to a bar-room brawl with the lights way down or even out. Each participant has a knife in his hand and he goes seeking an adversary with his back to him'. The experienced pilot employed the final one of 'Sailor' Malan's 'Ten Rules of Air Fighting' dictum, namely 'Go in quickly!—punch hard!—get out quick!' The virtual plethora of combat-film clips on hand tend to confirm the fact, in that the vast majority reveal a victim being blasted at close range—no head-on charges or granting an adversary an equal chance to focus his gunsights upon the assaulting fighter there.

Shooting of a more relaxed nature is the clear intention of two pilots from No. 122 Squadron. Right-hand officer is Flt Lt H. 'Darkie' Hallowes, a flight commander and Battle of Britain ace with nineteen kills on No. 43 Squadron. Aircraft are probably Mk VBs with which the unit was equipped by the early 1942 date of Hallowes' arrival at Scorton.

A more controversial issue was the question of when to desist from actually killing an opponent as opposed to downing his aircraft, which was when the Geneva Convention came into force. Should an airman bale out, and regardless of whether that happened over hostile or friendly soil, the Convention forbade any further attempt to end his life. In practice, his safe descent into friendly territory where he could be available to again take to the air was regarded as almost a traitorous act by some pilots—the question in their minds was 'What if he kills you (or worse still a colleague) on his likely return to combat duties?'

Better to end his life in order to avoid that possible outcome, whether or not he was helplessly dangling under a parachute, fleeing his crash-landed aircraft, or any other scenario where he would be regarded as meriting exclusion from a combatant status under Convention rules. The Second World War was a Total War in many respects, of which this issue was one and aircrew on both sides of the conflict did indulge in taking out their opposite numbers in the foregoing manner. However, the mindset of most fighter pilots was firmly opposed to such a concept, brutally practical as it would be regarded by its proponents.

10

Advantage *Jagdwaffe*: The Fw 190 Menace

Kurt Tank's Genius

The constant debate regarding the qualities and limitations of radial engine design against the in-line alternative had seen the development of aircraft types that utilised both systems. Among the major military nations, the tendency to favour the radial engine had been more prevalent up to the mid-1930s. The air-cooled nature of the design allowed for a fair degree of security from lethal punishment by bullets, while the relatively slow speeds then being flown meant that the engine's sizeable mass was of little significance in terms of improving air-speed performance.

In contrast, the in-line's slimmer profile meant it enjoyed a noticeably lower drag factor in advancing an aircraft's speed performance as witnessed by the Hurricane, Spitfire, and Bf 109, for example. The one weakness lay in the need to provide oil-coolant reserves for the engine; should this be compromised through the coolant tank being punctured, the result was swift seizure of the engine. Nor as aviation technology advanced was the radial engine demoted from first-line consideration as witnessed by the USA, whose premier Second World War fighters were largely dependent upon this power design.

The Second World War was still two years distant from its inception when the Nazi Air Ministry (*Reichsluftfahrtministerium*—RLM) presented a demand to the Focke-Wulf *Flugzeugbau* to submit the specification for a single-seat fighter. In turn, the company's technical director, Kurt Tank, presented twin projects that would be built around the radial twin-row BMW 139 or the liquid-cooled Daimler-Benz DB 601. In time, the latter power plant would be used for the Fw 190-D9 and Ta 152, but in the meantime, engine stocks were already being allocated to the Bf 109 and Bf 110 in particular, hence the likely reason for the BMW's selection.

The beautifully sculptured airframe was fronted by an equally beautifully-streamlined cowling and generous propeller spinner cover. On the second prototype, this took the form of a ducted unit that was subsequently replaced by an engine-cooling fan as a standard feature. Another even more key alteration on later prototypes was the replacement of the BMW 139 by the 801D that raised power output to 1,700 hp on take-off—well ahead of the Spitfire Mk V's 1,415-hp figure—and would moreover be the power source for the 'A', 'F', and 'G' variants up to the introduction of the Fw 190D-9 in late 1944.

Planned firepower on the Fw 190A-1 was initially set at the surprisingly puny level of four 7.9-mm MG17 machine guns, two ahead of the cockpit and wing roots respectively. Future variants would mount a more daunting scale of firepower; the fuselage-mounted 7.9-mm guns were supplemented by two 20-mm MG-FF cannon in the wing roots on the A-2. The A-3 variant then saw the displacement of the MG-FF cannon to the outer wing sections and the wing-root positions equipped with the MG151. This latest armament variant represented a weight of firepower that would make short thrift of any aircraft, especially a relatively slender airframe borne by most fighters.

The assessed performance figures were just as impressive. Maximum speed was around 400 mph at 20,000 feet, falling to 355 mph at sea-level; climb rate averaged 2,350 fpm and the service ceiling of just over 37,000 feet was an ominous portent of continuing problems for the RAF. Even more ominous was the superb manoeuvrability of the fighter. It proved stable in a dive and the ailerons acted in a manner that provided a very tight turning circle. The climb rate was another fine feature compared to both current and future RAF or *Luftwaffe* contemporaries. Tank's creation in the form of the A-1 and A-2 variants was ready to enter the combat lists as 1941 was beginning to descend towards its conclusion (a fall-off of power above 23,000 feet on the Fw 190A-I was corrected by the fitting of a GM-1 power boost system). So it was that the extended 'Winter of Discontent' for Fighter Command was duly commenced.

Circus Planning Limitations

The concept of the Circus type of operation that involved a mere handful of bombers backed up by double figures of fighter squadrons might suggest that an adversary would find it almost impossible to make any inroads upon the former sub-force. The practical situation cast up a much more open and difficult task for the escorting force, however. The cover afforded the bombers at any stage of the operation was not universally continuous even within the comparatively short distances to be flown to the targets; this limitation owed everything to the very short endurance of the Hurricane and Spitfire, both having been conceived with Defence of the Realm operations as opposed to striking deep into the enemy hinterland. The alternative was to utilise a 'relay' system of cover whereby squadrons—comprising two-thirds of the overall escort force, other than the seven assigned to continuous escort—would cover the main force prior to and during its withdrawal from the target area.

No. 71 (Eagle) Squadron exchanged its Hurricanes for the Mk IIA Spitfire in August 1941, but the almost parallel advent of the Fw 190 on operations would prove a very stern test for the American pilots. In this case, on the 27th, Hawkinge airfield took in this fighter that was well shot-up around the rear fuselage; it was later updated to a Mk V standard but the Fw 190 would still have been as superior an opponent.

The original pristine camouflage on these two Mk VB Spitfires from No. 72 Squadron has inevitably deteriorated thanks to a combination of weathering and the scuffing effect of ground crew footwear particularly upon the wings. M/W3316 and L/W3437 from 'B' Flight are ready to start-up and follow RN: F out onto the perimeter track at Biggin Hill. Picture was shot during August 1941.

Just as the USAAF fighters would experience in 1943–44, so the art of accurately feeding-in the units assigned to rendezvous duties depended upon precise guidance by the RAF ground controllers and interpretation by the wing commanders involved. The difference was that the Americans would be operating over far greater distances, but regardless of this, any lapse in proper rendezvous *vis-à-vis* both time and assigned location could leave the bombers liable to assault, more perhaps so in America's case—a direct attack against the German hinterland spelled immeasurably more trouble for that nation's industrial and military infrastructure than what were admittedly pinprick forays over France.

First Encounter

The briefing for one of the two latest Circus operations was held on 27 September, with Sqn Ldr J. Rankin leading the Biggin Hill Wing as high cover for twelve Blenheims raiding Mazingarbe in the Pas-de-Calais (Circus 103B). By now, the much larger Short Stirling four-engined bomber was also forming the bombing kernel for these sorties, but the Blenheim was still the more-regularly used machine (the previous day, six Hampdens had participated, but this was a relatively rare event for the Handley-Page 'twins'). On the way home from the operation that had involved tangling with Bf 109s from all three JG26 *Gruppen*, one CO sighted several bogeys behind and below and ordered four No. 609 Squadron Spitfires to investigate. The resultant contact was inconclusive in terms of either sub-formation landing strikes, but what impressed the RAF pilots was the speed and general movement of the still-unidentified fighters; what was clear was that they were not Bf 109Fs since they bore radial engines.

Subsequent to debriefing, the information was channelled upwards. The response from those within the RAF's senior echelons was that the aircraft were Hawk 75s, a US design originally exported to the French Air Force but expropriated by the Germans following France's collapse. As sturdy a design as the Hawk might have been, there was no way in which it could have been flown in the manner demonstrated on this day since its overall performance barely matched up to the Hurricane, let alone more advanced-performance designs as this example had apparently demonstrated. II/JG26 had begun conversion to the Fw 190 during late August and all too soon was in a position to supplement the original Bf 109E and Bf 109F elements of JG2 and JG26 in taking on the RAF incursions. This all-round superb aerial fighting machine was to evolve into one of the premier fighter designs of the Second World War and would prove a redoubtable foe to the RAF in the immediate future as well as the Allied air forces for the reminder of the conflict, as its nickname *die Würger* (Butcherbird) would grimly highlight.

The initial operational sorties of the II/JG26 Fw 190s occurred as August merged with September, but it was the 17th before the *Staffel*'s first *Abschuess* was recorded during the largess Circus operation to date, with Obltn. K. Ebersberger (4/JG26 *Staffelkapitän*) shooting down one of two Spitfires claimed by the *Gruppe*.

The latest Circus on 28 September 1941 cost the RAF nine aircraft, a figure that included Mk VB W3824 serving with No. 129 Squadron. A *Luftwaffe* NCO is seen examining the fuselage that sits on what seems to be a railway wagon with its hinged side hanging down; one wing is stacked against the 'inverted-V' wooden frame. Transportation to a smelting-down plant may well be the aircraft's final destination.

The next day, one of the RAF kill claims was stated to be a Curtiss Hawk—a clear if natural misunderstanding of what the radial-engine fighter actually represented.

The feral nature of aerial combat ensured that no pilot, however experienced, was able to unconditionally guarantee his survival. Hptm. Walter Adolph was a veteran of the Spanish Civil War who had amassed a total of twenty-five *Abschuss* up to 18 September. The II *Gruppe Kommandeur* was leading a force of nine Fw 190s providing cover for a tanker that was attacked by escorted Blenheims, one of which was shot down. For whatever reason, Adolph circled the crash site, and before his attention was brought back aloft, he was plucked out of the sky by a fighter—at least that was the impression gained by his colleagues on return, who did not witness the circumstances of his demise; the subsequent washing-up of his body in Belgium confirmed the fact with the victor being a No. 41 Squadron Spitfire.

Senior and combat-experienced pilot losses such as Adolph always impinged upon the overall morale, if not efficiency, of any unit's personnel. The RAF probably knew this to a similar if not greater degree. During 1941, several Battle of Britain aces were culled. Sqn Ldr J. Mungo-Park, with eleven kills and now CO of the Biggin Hill Wing, lost out to fighters on 27 June and Flt Lt Eric Lock, with twenty-six kills, was downed on 2 August. This duo represented just the tip of the iceberg as regards what was being lost to the RAF in terms of either current or potential combat expertise.

There was some consolation in the battles being fought over Nazi-occupied territory in that the chances of an Allied pilot regaining British soil were immeasurably superior to that of a German downed over Britain. Whereas the latter could expect no succour of any kind from their adversaries, an Allied evader was granted the chance of gaining not only shelter but the likelihood of access to a local resistance movement body that in turn could facilitate his successful escape into neutral Spain or Switzerland, and in the former case, a subsequent repatriation.

A typical example involved Flt Lt D. Crowley-Milling, a former member of the (then Sqn Ldr Bader's) No. 242 Squadron during the Battle of Britain. On 21 August, while serving as a flight commander on No. 610 Squadron, his Spitfire was cut out of the formation and shot down. He parachuted safely and quickly was picked up by the local population. His subsequent transfer southward towards the Franco–Spanish border zone proceeded in order, and he gained entry to that neutral country. Most evaders were processed in proper order; however, in his case, he was unfortunately incarcerated in the notorious Miranda Concentration

The Bell Aerocobra made a brief and unsuccessful entry into Fighter Command's infrastructure. The design that one anonymous USAAF source described as 'Good for doing low, slow and wide circles' was assigned to No. 601 Squadron who paraded their new charges at Duxford in October 1941. Only a handful of sorties were subsequently flown over the ensuing months before the squadron converted onto the Spitfire.

Camp for three months, during which time he contracted paratyphoid from which he thankfully emerged in full health before his dispatch to Gibraltar and homeward passage during December.

By late autumn, the Bf 109E contingent among the French-based units were showing their fading operational vintage against the Spitfire Mk V and their numbers would rapidly diminish by the year's end. A similar situation for example applied to JG26's overall aircraft establishment in terms of the Bf 109F's frontline service, although operationally, around 25 per cent of the serviceable figure as the year closed still involved the Messerschmitt fighter (the *Ergänzungs* (Operational Training) *Gruppe* was equipped almost wholly with the combat-retired Bf 109E by then).

Winter Hiatus

The restricted hours of daylight during the winter period naturally limited air operations, particularly in relation to large-scale sorties as exemplified by the Circus variation. Instead, RAF Fighter Command indulged in small-scale variations such as Rhubarbs. The dispatch of pairs of fighters that would seek out targets of opportunity presented the *Luftwaffe* with a problem in countering these incursions. On the other hand, the low-level nature of these intrusions brought the ground defences into play; in the process, the flak gunners added to their tally that included several notable casualties.

On 28 January, Wg Cdr Stanford Tuck bade farewell to his former flight commander from No. 257 Squadron: Flt Lt 'Cowboy' Blatchford, who had visited him at Biggin Hill—unknowingly for the last time ever. Tuck and Plt Off. Harley (RCAF) flew off on a sortie against alcohol vats south of Boulogne. The low cloud base provided a fine cover, but the fighter's entry into France was picked up. Even so, the duo of Spitfires remained undetected as they reached and successfully shot-up the target before turning for home. Unfortunately, the minimal weather conditions led to the Spitfires flying directly over the heavily-defended seaport.

The flak batteries latched onto Tuck's fighter and strikes landed fatal blows on the airframe. The chances of safely crash-landing his aircraft appeared nil as it descended inexorably over the built-up surroundings. When hope was almost expended, a clear area appeared into which Tuck directed his doomed machine. However, as he approached for a crash-landing, a flak battery opened up despite the fighter being clearly disabled. In his frustration, Tuck fired a short burst on his assailants before putting the fighter down for a heavy landing.

After exiting the Spitfire, he was roughly apprehended and dragged over to the battery's pit where he gazed upon the shattered weapon and the several inert bodies of the gun crew—his bullets had literally blown the gun barrel apart. Where he had expected to be lynched for his action, instead he was congratulated by his captors for his perceived gunnery skills. Tuck had survived to face over three years of captivity and safe return home; in contrast, Blatchford, as CO of

A. O. Weekes (standing) and FS C. A. Joseph, both from the Caribbean West Indies, are snapped along with a Mk VB. Both wear the revised-pattern flying boot that was more comfortable than the fur-lined, sponge-soled predecessor. Solid wheel disc with the tire-pressure valve outlet was seen on many Mk V Spitfire airframes.

the Digby Wing, would doom-spin into the North Sea in late May 1943 after his fighter was damaged by a II/JG1 pilot and the resultant attempted ditching proved fatal.

Operation *Donnerkeil*

The *Kriegsmarine* duo of capital battleships, the *Scharnhorst* and the *Gneisenau*, along with the battle cruiser *Prinz Eugen*, had been contained for several months within the French port of Brest and had been accordingly well supervised by the RAF and Royal Navy. The situation was clearly not to Hitler's advantage and plans for a breakout of the warships was laid on. But the obvious direction for their return to German waters was not to be taken up. Instead, the potentially suicidal course through the English Channel as opposed to the extended but apparently more secure route via the Atlantic was to be indulged in.

Fortune favoured the initial action due to the failure of the normal air and submarine surveillance on the night of 11–12 February when the operation commenced. The vessels escorted by a sizeable destroyer and E-boat contingent proceeded under air cover provided by JG2 and JG26 as supervised by Ob. Galland. The daring nature of the operation continued to work in Germany's favour as no British reaction to the warships progress under admittedly poor weather conditions occurred before the Channel stretch was nearing its end. Only the chance observation of a pair of Spitfires, one piloted by Grp Capt. Beamish, alerted the authorities to the fact.

By now, the aerial cover was primarily in the hands of JG26 and its pilots were ready for the first belated reaction from their adversaries as their naval charges sailed past Cap Gris-Nez. Both the RAF and Royal Navy possessed dedicated torpedo squadrons, but the sole unit on hand was the Fleet Air Arm's No. 825 Squadron operating on the Swordfish biplane. The six crews led by L/Comm. Esmonde set off from Manston but only one of the five Spitfire squadrons assigned as cover rendezvoused.

The consequent massacre of all six aircraft along with the bulk of the crews to flak and fighters was due to their No. 72 Squadron cover being totally engaged with the *Jagdwaffe* and unable to come to their assistance as they commenced their torturously slow attack run (the slow progress of the Swordfish led to some Fw 190 pilots reportedly having to lower their undercarriage in order to make a suitably-paced attack approach upon their lumbering prey, the observation being made by one of the five FAA survivors). Half of the losses were credited to the eight-strong formation from III/JG26 with Ltn. Paul Galland, Adolph's brother, one of the victors; the other half was divided between JG2 and the ships' flak batteries.

The subsequent movements of the three warships remained free of damage from following groups of standard and torpedo-bombers as well as Royal Navy warships, but a more subtle explosive barrier finally struck home on the

No. 303 (Polish) Squadron took on the Mk V Spitfire in August 1941 but only operated across the Channel in October. In this shot, a Spitfire is raised up for a gun-alignment test. Aircraft bears the 'Kosciuszko' badge under the windshield in honour of the Polish patriot bearing the name. Picture taken at Northolt in early 1942.

Sgt Robertson (right) does not seem to take his colleague Sgt Handley's advice on combat tactics too seriously to suggest this is a publicity picture. Both pilots from No. 402 (Canadian) Squadron wear standard flying boots, but uniforms suggest non-operational flying. The 'Sky' fuselage band is applied on the ventral strake and the light colour highlights the starboard entry-point for the lifting bar.

Scharnhorst in the form of the first of two sea mines whose effect was not fatal but did retard her progress somewhat. The *Gneisenau* also suffered a sea mine strike after previously suffering mechanical failure, but it similarly regained control to reach the Elbe along with her companions around midnight.

The British had been tactically 'bearded' in their own backyard, but the perceived humiliation was misleading, albeit almost palpable at the time. The transfer of the warships to German waters was undoubtedly a tactical success but more significantly a strategic defeat in the long term. This was because now the Royal Navy could interdict the warships' future movements much more easily compared to their greater ability to break out into the Atlantic from Brest with enhanced prospects of evading interception.

Circus operations were resumed in early March when weather conditions permitted and now utilised the far more efficient Douglas Boston as the bomber element. The *Jagdwaffe* units continued to enjoy a superior kill–loss ratio thanks to the Fw 190's superior flight qualities against the Mk V Spitfire. However, a contributory factor was the insistence on some RAF squadrons flying line-astern sections.

As with the former practice of 'weavers' positioned behind the formation, so the last pilot in each line was wide open to being brought down thanks to being

No. 1 Squadron was the second unit to convert onto the Mk IIC Hurricane during July 1941; it was further tasked with carrying out Intruder operations in which the heavy-calibre weapon would be particularly effective. The CO, Sqn Ldr McLachlan, and Flt Lt Kuttelwascher, from Czechoslovakia, would run up an impressive list of kills along with destruction of rail traffic and other ground facilities during 1941–42.

'bounced' from above or behind. The 'finger four' pattern long adapted by their adversaries was still not being appreciated as the surest way in which to gain both formation security through mutual observation coupled with the ability to engage in greater and more efficient attack mode. The tragic result was a steadily mounting scale of casualties thanks to such inflexible formation tactics.

Ambush!

New Zealander Al Deere had emerged from the Battle of Britain as an ace and progressed to the rank of squadron leader by April 1942. His appointment in as CO of No. 403 (RCAF) Squadron based at North Weald followed a liaison visit to the United States where he lectured on fighter tactics. The further prospect of his assuming a wing-command position in the near future seemed sound following an interview with AVM Leigh-Mallory, but the events of 2 June were destined to cast a pall upon this. Deere had been well briefed on the operational qualities of the Fw 190 as he led his pilots in a twelve-strong formation to link up with the other North Weald units in a planned twin-wing Rodeo over the Pas-de-Calais; as it was, he had flown operations from August to December 1941, when the fighter was already serving on the Western Front, but whether his squadron had ever encountered Tank's design in this time was unclear.

Already aloft as the RAF formation crossed into France were elements of I and II/JG26 led respectively by Hptm. Johannes Seifert and Maj. Joachim Müncheberg. The former sub-force was picked out closing from behind on No. 403 Squadron flying high cover, whereupon Deere gave the order to 'break' in a manner that had one section on the right sweeping upwards while the other two sections banked round into the attackers. It was as Deere's element was turning that Müncheberg's formation pounced from the right. The fight was on but had begun in the worst possible manner for the dispersed RAF formation.

Deere observed one Spitfire breaking in two thanks to the concentrated fire from a Fw 190. He was moreover taken aback by the contrast between the former tactics of Bf 109 pilots in making swift passes and away, whereas his present assailants were staying around to 'mix it' with their adversaries. Of course, his experience during late 1941 was probably earned during the Circus operations when the 'strike and run' tactic suited the *Jagdwaffe* pilots; in contrast, the clearly superior performance of the Fw 190 permitted a continued form of engagement.

Having expended his ammunition with no discernible result he turned for home with his No. 2 Sgt Murphy holding position. As the Channel was being crossed, two Spitfires were seen from which the pilots baled out into the waters. Following landing at Lympne on the coast, the fighters were refuelled before heading for Rochford where the full scale of the disaster was revealed. Seven pilots were MIA and one of the five surviving Spitfires written-off.

The immediate upshot of the operation was the relegation of the squadron to Northern England. When Deere gained another interview with Leigh-Mallory to

No. 243 Squadron had a chequered career in the war. The unit's presence in Malaya during the Japanese assault saw its outmoded Buffalo fighters shot out of the sky. The trio of Mk VB Spitfires was photographed following the squadron's reformation in the UK during June; its stay was short since after converting to Mk VC Spitfires the squadron departed for north-western Africa in December 1942.

discover the reason why, he was amazed to receive a verbal reproach from the C-in-C in terms of being too aggressive in his actions—this despite his superior's regular *ukase* to the command to 'seek out and destroy the enemy!' Throughout the Second World War, Leigh-Mallory's attitude to combat operations was ever ambivalent and sometimes in direct contrast to his stated dictum mentioned here. Deere would take his squadron north, but it would be nearly twelve months before he realised his ambition to lead a wing.

Stirrings in the Wind

The almost critical need to redress the imbalance between the RAF and *Luftwaffe* fighter forces was being addressed in terms of Spitfire development even before events conspired to literally deliver an intact Fw 190 into British hands—a good example of how luck almost as much as technical superiority plays its part in a conflict. As matters transpired, the improvement to the Supermarine design owed more to its power source than any alteration in the airframe.

The Mk V's Merlin 40 Series engine was equipped with a single-stage supercharger that conferred serious limitations upon its combat performance, especially at the altitudes at which the Fw 190 was being encountered. Rolls-Royce had been working on the development of a vital replacement, featuring a two-stage supercharger. The required compression ratio (boost

A No. 64 Squadron Mk V with the lower engine cowling panels detached is undergoing a test at full power. The airmen sitting on the stabilisers are preventing the tail from rising under the fierce airflow. The fighter's serial number is obliterated by the 'Sky S' fuselage band. This unit was the first to convert to the greatly superior Mk IX during June 1942.

pressure at altitude) was easily achieved. Not so easily achieved was the higher efficiency level required from the supercharger in order for it to function in the face of a parallel increase in temperature. Exhaust turbos as fitted for example to the P-47 proved inadequate in terms of weight, and also provided no equivalent to the Merlin's ejector exhaust boost effect.

Instead, a mechanically-driven system was tested and found to be the basic solution. The static-rig tests utilising a modified blower from a Rolls-Royce Vulture was coupled up to a Merlin's inlet. The result was an increase in power output by 300 hp at a 30,000-foot level compared to the Merlin 46. The problem of temperature increase (205 degrees at maximum revs in FS gear) that posed a knock-on risk effect of 'detonation' was solved with a coolant. The resultant air drag caused by the slim oil cooler under the port wing being replaced by an expanded radiator cover, similar to that under the starboard wing, fortunately did little to retard the performance benefits in spite of this structural amendment. What was to be the Merlin 60 Series was destined to basically alter the current imbalance between the Spitfire and Fw 190.

The air tests with the Merlin 60 engine produced a maximum speed of 408 mph and a climb-rate of 3,950 fpm along with a service ceiling of 43,000 feet. These were prime performance factors that promised a definite switch in Fighter Command's favour once sufficient numbers of both the Mk IX and its Mk VIII contemporary were on hand. The *Jagdwaffe* pilots would furthermore have no initial way of visually identifying the reason for the change in combat fortunes;

Stanisław Skalski and Tadeusz Czerwiński hold the Polish eagle emblem against a Spitfire cowling. The former airman ran up a string of victories first in Poland (six) followed by a further sixteen with three RAF squadrons and the Polish Fighting Team, a detachment sent to North Africa in 1943. He ended up as leader of No. 133 Wing. Czerwiński later became CO of No. 306 (Polish) Squadron but was KIA several months after this early 1942 picture was taken, when both were serving with No. 306 at Church Stanton.

this was due to the Mk IX that would introduce the power plant on European theatre operations still being based upon the Mk V airframe (the Mk VIII would serve exclusively in the Mediterranean and Far East theatres).

The Threat Fully Revealed

On 23 June 1942, Obltn. Arnim Faber, the III/JG2 adjutant, was part of a 7 *Staffel* formation that tangled with Spitfires returning from an operation against Morlaix airfield. The weather conditions must have been heavily affected by visibility or Faber's compass must have failed—how else to explain his subsequent appearance over and landing on the Welsh airfield at Pembrey that was nearly 100 miles north of the Normandy coastline. The pilot was apprehended before he could destroy his fighter. This was an A-3 variant with its BMW801D engine producing 1,700 hp; firepower was composed of pairs of MG151s, MG-FFs, and MG17s, more than sufficient when properly directed to bring down any opponent.

The *Luftwaffe* fighter was duly taken up and fully tested in all performance aspects. The results provided a sobering lesson to the RAF in just how advanced Tank's design compared to its current adversaries in Fighter Command. The performance comparisons against the Mk VB were as follows:

1. At all speeds up to a 25,000-foot altitude, the Fw 190 enjoyed a minimum advantage of 20 mph and 35 mph depending on the specific height being flown.
2. The maximum climb factor up to the same altitude was around 450 fpm better with the Fw 190 while pulling into a climb from high cruising speed as well as doing so after pulling out of a dive left its RAF adversary hopelessly adrift.
3. The initial impetus in a dive created a similar scenario while overall manoeuvrability was superior in all aspects other than turning circle. Only by maintaining maximum cruising speed could a Mk V pilot hope to evade being 'bounced', and that by entering into a shallow dive—not a very comfortable situation in any circumstance.

Conversely, the assignment of the first Mk IX Spitfires with the Merlin 60 Series to No. 64 Squadron earlier in the month constituted an as-yet unfulfilled hope that the air battles between these two fighter types would advance in the RAF's favour once-sufficient numbers of both this variant and its Mk VIII contemporary were on operational hand. Even if this was to be the case, the switch in favour of the RAF would probably depend almost as much on pilot efficiency as on aircraft performance.

No. 174 Squadron's experience with the Mk IIB Hurricane from March 1942 was to prove expensive. The fighter-bomber operations against targets across the Channel in an aircraft increasingly outperformed by the *Jagdwaffe*, as well as facing often formidable flak defences proved costly, climaxing with Operation Jubilee when no less than five pilots were lost. Picture was taken at Manston around June.

Operation Jubilee, 19 August 1942

Although RAF Fighter Command operations over France in 1941 and up to mid-1942 had sometimes witnessed contests pitched on a squadron or more rarely at wing-level, the opportunity for a full-scale air battle was basically absent until 19 August 1942. The Allies planning for the invasion of Western Europe faced serious obstacles, with the ability to establish and retain a viable beachhead being an obvious priority. With this in mind, an operation named Jubilee was set in motion to test the viability of gaining access to a seaport, through which equipment and personnel could be properly channelled. The choice for what was recorded as a 'reconnaissance in force' was to be directed against the French port of Dieppe, whose defences would be attacked by a large Canadian Army force supported by British commandos; a sizeable number of Churchill tanks would also be on hand and the fleet of landing craft would have a strong naval and air force backup.

Leigh-Mallory amassed a total of forty-nine pure fighter squadrons that included the recently introduced Mk IX Spitfire and Hawker Typhoon within the figure; also on hand were eight Hurricane squadrons flying fighter-bomber operations and four Mustang squadrons making their operational debut. The JG2 and JG26 opposition possessed an operational strength that was well outnumbered by their direct contemporaries. On the face of it, the *Jagdwaffe* appeared in for a difficult, if not uphill struggle to contain the RAF effort. However, this quantitative disability had to be set against Germany's clear qualitative advantage in equipment and personnel. A further RAF limitation was that the four Mk IX Spitfire squadrons were not long on operational status and the Typhoons, although sound in performance, were no more than adequate when operating at other than low altitude. Numbers alone were not necessarily guaranteed to turn the battle in the RAF's favour, given that the Mk V pilots were still on the performance back foot *vis-à-vis* the Fw 190.

The omens for a successful landing were already poor in terms of absolute security since the operation had been cancelled and then restated despite the advice of Gen. Montgomery among other senior Army staff. Matters were further soured on the day when the landing force was picked up in mid-Channel by one or more *Kriegsmarine* vessels who alerted the port authorities. The Canadians were heading straight into a holocaust that would consume hundreds in death and witness a majority of the remainder ending up in a *Stalag*. The bulk of the tanks never cleared the harbour beach area and ended up battered hulks along with a number of their landing-craft bearers.

Pilot sitting on the right has a comfortable upholstered 'perch' compared to his four colleagues occupying more uncomfortable chairs as they watch two others indulging in a game of quoits. Hurricane code letters do not relate to any frontline squadron so picture may be taken at an OTU or similar secondary support unit.

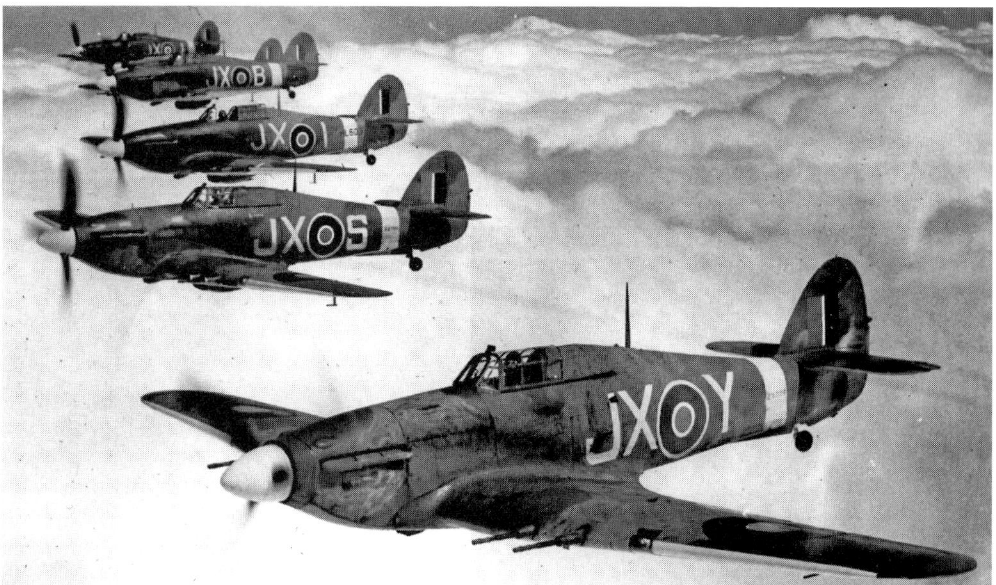

A starboard-echelon formation of Mk IIC Hurricanes from No. 1 Squadron depicts the final camouflage pattern applied on its fighters; the undersides appear to have lost their black colour that was a feature during the previous few months after the original overall black was dispensed with. Picture was taken not long before the switch to the Typhoon that began in July 1942, the revised Type C1 markings having only been introduced the month before.

USAAF Fortunes

One of the first USAAF groups to arrive in Britain prior to Jubilee was the 31FG, whose pilots must have rejoiced when the planned use of the P-39 Airacobra was switched to the Mk V Spitfire. The three squadrons were dispersed between Biggin Hill, Kenley, and Tangmere and were being tutored on combat techniques by experienced RAF pilots. Little actual combat had taken place since commencing action at the start of August, but this changed sharply when the squadrons were 'alerted' on the 18th.

Today's operations would witness each squadron flying at least three sorties with the 308FS (Kenley) setting the pace. An encounter with an Fw 190 formation resulted in Lt. F. Hill claiming one kill; the cost was Lt. Inghram who baled out—a likely victim of Ltn. Prym (4/JG26)—to be picked up from the Channel waters by a German vessel. The squadron's second sortie was more expensive in that one pilot Lt. Dabney was MIA to be later confirmed as killed. Lt. Sam Junkin (309FS) also submitted a kill claim but would not return in his Spitfire. Instead, scarcely had he called out over the radio when his fighter was terminally damaged, forcing him to bale out, a shoulder having been badly injured in the process.

The 307FS was the unluckiest since it lost three fighters whose pilots were respectively listed as POW (Lt. Tovrea), KIA (Lt. E. Wells), and MIA (Lt. R. Wight); the ever-tragic casualty figure was added to by the 309FS's Lt. L. Collins. The group's combat learning curve had been pitched very high thanks to the experience of Jubilee, but its pilots would steadily redress this imbalance following the unit's transfer to the Mediterranean for Operation Torch in November, after which it advanced through North Africa, Sicily, and Italy.

The American pilot's rather harsh experience in facing the *Jagdwaffe*'s combat veterans was being paralleled by their RAF 'cousins' as they joined in the prolonged air battle over Dieppe. The sighting of the invasion fleet by two JG26 pilots dispatched on a reconnaissance sortie elicited a prompt response from both the *Geschwader* and its JG2 companion unit within *Luftflotte* 3. The *Jagdwaffe*'s initial RAF targets were probably the fighter-bomber squadrons as they launched their low-level assaults; the first pure fighter *v.* fighter combat involved the North Weald Wing against a mixed I and II/JG26 force. In the whirling imbroglio into which the dogfights descended, the RAF pilots claimed five kills against a confirmed absence of six Spitfires on return to their airfields. The seeming equality in kills to losses was not to be borne out either in this case or indeed accruing from the overall battle—if *Luftwaffe* records are to be accepted on face value.

A series of publicity pictures was shot while the 31FG was in England. Mechanics with their distinctive 'jockey' caps, are working on a 308FS Mk VB. The RAF fuel bowser was typical of British 'back-up' services to the USAAF during its build-up period in Europe before its own ground-support facilities were shipped wholesale across the Atlantic in late 1942.

Merston on the south coast was home for No. 412 (Canadian) Squadron in June 1942 when it hosted members of the 31FG who were to gain a degree of operational experience flying with the RCAF pilots. Third from right is Maj. Harrison Thyng who was the first CO of the 309FS and a ten-kill ace during the war: he retired as a brigadier-general in 1966.

The 'Biter' nearly 'Bit'

'Johnnie' Johnson who had originally cut his combat 'teeth' within Bader's Tangmere Wing was by now a squadron leader with a DFC and Bar and in charge of No. 610 Squadron equipped with the Mk VB. He was also an ace, with six confirmed and four probable victories and therefore an aggressively competent pilot. During the West Malling Wing's sortie following on after the North Weald Wing's action and having shot down an Fw 190 and shared the destruction of a Bf 109F, he then sighted another Fw 190.

Johnson initiated an attack curve, only to have his adversary take him on in a series of manoeuvres that steadily ate away at Johnson's confidence; from anticipating a kill, he was now under imminent threat of becoming a victim himself as he threaded a path low down over Dieppe with the Fw 190 in relentless pursuit. He finally decided upon a desperate move to shake off the *Luftwaffe* pilot. Seeing a Royal Navy destroyer ahead, he headed directly towards the warship in a deliberate bid to have the ships AA gunners open up.

The move did not end with the Fw 190 being taken down, but on emerging from the hail of fire, Johnson found himself free of his opponent, whereupon he headed back to West Malling, doubtless relieved with the encounter's outcome. Sometime later, intelligence reportedly picked up an alleged statement from a German pilot named 'Matoni' inviting his opponent from Operation Jubilee to a return contest. Regardless of the facts, the surname of what was assumed to be an Italian proved to be well wide of the mark; the 'Italian' was in fact Obltn. Walter Matoni, a II/ JG26 combat-tested pilot who would amass a sizeable score and also advance to survive the conflict.

The decision to withdraw the attacking forces from Dieppe was reportedly issued well before midday, but the extraction of the pitifully few numbers still able to do so lasted into the early afternoon, given the consistently-severe scale of defensive firepower poured upon them from the heights surrounding the seaport. At least the naval support was granted relative immunity from air assault, although the destroyer HMS *Berkeley* was so crippled by bombs delivered by two Fw 190s of 10 (*Jabo*) JG2 that she had to be subsequently sunk. The steady withdrawal of the Allied vessels during the afternoon continued under the RAF umbrella, but the air battle continued well into the early evening.

A total of ninety-six kill claims were accepted by No. 11 Group's senior hierarchy, of which fifty were related to fighters, all but three that were identified as Bf 109s being Fw 190s. The remainder was spread between the bomber units operating the Do 217, Ju 88, and He 111. In sharp contrast, the listed losses for the two fighter *Geschwadern* were pitched at around twenty-five with a similar figure for the bombers, this being quoted by a leading JG26 historian. Total RAF losses were confirmed at 106, signifying a conclusion in clear favour of the *Luftwaffe vis-à-vis* the foregoing figures. The Fw 190 had again demonstrated its basic pre-eminence in combat over Dieppe, but twin operational factors were scheduled to occur that would see this early autumn and large-scale contest as

The third of the three Eagle squadrons was No. 133, formed in July 1941. It progressed from Hurricanes and Mk IIA and VA Spitfires to the Mk VB, an example of which is seen taxiing out from what was probably Great Sampford, the satellite airfield to Debden. Conversion to the Mk IX would occur during the early autumn 1942.

The shallow ground angle and relatively compact outline of the Spitfire is highlighted by the airman standing on the wing root of this Mk VB belonging to No. 310 (Czech) Squadron. It was assigned in mid-1942 as shown by the Type C1 markings introduced around June and lasted until 29 January 1943; that day with W/O Petr in charge, it was downed by Fw 190s over Morlaix, France.

signalling the beginning of more challenging times for the pilots of Tank's *Würger*. The steady build-up of Spitfire Mk IX strength would impinge upon the Fw 190's ability to unconditionally control the skies at medium to high altitudes.

Nor was the situation going to provide greater security from lethal interception at minimal altitude. The latter situation would arise during the 'tip and run' bombing raids along the southern British coastline originally launched in early 1942. The challenge would not bc primarily mounted by the Merlin-engined Spitfire, but by Hawker's latest design, the bulky but solid-performing Typhoon, which would have the 'legs' on its adversary, though with a variable degree of success in the months up to mid-1943 (the early 1943 operational debut of the Griffon-powered Mk XII Spitfire with good low-level performance would further add to the Fw 190 pilot's problems).

The shape of momentous things to come was unknowingly embodied in a proposal submitted by British test pilot Ron Harker serving with the Air Fighting Development Unit (AFDU), Duxford. This was the substitution of the Mustang's original Allison power source with a Merlin. This is the airframe into which the Rolls-Royce engine was mounted and flown by Harker during April 1942. The seeds sown by the experiment would reap an increasingly savage harvest among the *Luftwaffe*'s ranks from the beginning of 1944 onwards.

11

Regaining the Initiative (June 1942 into 1943)

'The Dawn Beckons'—Tantalisingly

The advent of the Mk IX Spitfire within the ranks of Fighter Command held a naturally latent promise of more productive times for those pilots serving with the squadrons so equipped. No. 64 led the way during June 1942 and a further four squadrons—Nos 133 (Eagle), 401, 402 (RCAF), and 611 Squadrons—had converted to the type by August. The quiet confidence that a marked improvement in combating the *Jagdwaffe*'s fighters was on hand had been demonstrated during tests between Armin Faber's Fw 190 and a Mk IX. The results were as follows:

Maximum Speed (Altitude)

2,000 feet	7/8 mph advantage to the Mk IX
5,000 feet	no advantage
8,000 feet	8 mph advantage to the Mk IX
15,000 feet	5 mph advantage to the Mk IX
18,000 feet	5 mph advantage to the Mk IX
21,000 feet	no discernible advantage
25,000 feet	5/7 mph advantage to the Mk IX

Climb Rate

Up to 22,000 feet	little difference
22,000 feet and over	Fw 190's rate declines rapidly, whereas the Mk IX's rate increases

Dive

The Fw 190 is faster, especially at an initial stage, but the margin is not as great compared to the Mk V.

Manoeuvring

1. The Mk IX can outturn the Fw 190.
2. The Fw 190 can outmanoeuvre the Mk IX thanks to its superior roll rate.
3. The Fw 190 had a marginal advantage when either pulled into a climb from a cruising-speed situation or conversely when coming out of a dive.
4. The Mk IX could not be caught in an attempted 'bounce' if cruising at high speed and also sighting its opponent when it was still out of range. At lower speeds, the Mk IX was vulnerable thanks to a slower acceleration rate. However, the same circumstance applied to the Fw 190; otherwise, it enjoyed a higher acceleration rate under all flight conditions.

The general impression was that the Mk IX was well up to scratch in providing a sound attack and evasive platform for its pilot in future combats. On the other hand, the variant would not 'reign supreme' against the Fw 190 as one leading RAF ace and commander asserted in a post-war TV documentary—but then Douglas Bader was never one to hold back with his opinions. In truth, pilot skill would determine the outcome as much as the fighter's technical performance.

The Mk IX Spitfire was basically responsible for tilting the combat balance lost by the Mk V against the Fw 190 back in the RAF's favour. No group was more ferocious in hammering home the advantage than the Polish pilots such as this individual in his No. 302 Squadron machine. The similarity of the Mk IX to its predecessor lulled many enemy pilots into a false and often lethal sense of security.

Autumn Fortunes

As the autumn of 1942 wore on, the fighter pilots on both sides of the Channel continued to engage in actions that were on nothing like the scale of the Dieppe operation. The launch of Fighter Command squadrons on the various types of actions such as Rhubarbs, Roadsteads, and Rodeos introduced since 1941 was sustained. On the other hand, an escort duty similar in some respects to the Circus operations was now deployed, albeit in a more open manner. The advent of the 8th Bomber Command's daylight offensive on 17 August saw the relatively few B-17s of the 92nd, 97th, and 301st BGs and soon-to-appear B-24s of the 44th and 93rd BGs testing their mettle against targets located almost wholly in France.

At this initial stage of America's aviation presence over Western Europe, its provision for fighter cover was equally minimal; only the 1st and 14th FGs (P-38s), and 31st and 52nd FGs (Mk V Spitfires) were available in Britain and would soon be dispatched to North Africa for permanent inclusion within the 12th and 15th USAAFs. Apart from the 4th FG that was created out of the former RAF 'Eagle' squadrons, the onus for escort cover was placed upon Fighter Command when called for. This duty was capable of being fulfilled in the current circumstances of what were generally short-range penetrations into the enemy's occupied hinterland.

As it was, the confidence of the American military that their heavy bombers would be more than capable of handling the *Jagdwaffe* on their own, given the degree of defensive firepower on hand, coupled with tight formation flying, was not to become blunted for months ahead. The limited-range capability of the Spitfire meant that when the bomb groups operating up to the end of 1942

The ever-graceful profile of the Spitfire is captured in this view of a Mk VB assigned to No. 121 (Eagle) Squadron and named *Olga* as shown directly beneath the windshield. By September 1942, when the photo was taken, the squadron was based at Debden; at the month's end, along with its Nos 71 and 133 fellow units, it would form part of the USAF's 4th Fighter Group as its 335th Squadron.

had their attention directed at the U-boat pens along the French Atlantic coast, with Saint-Nazaire a particular focus, the RAF and 4 FG escort provision was accordingly restricted to delivering their 'Big Friends' across and back over the English Channel stretch of the overall routes.

An Avoidable Disaster?

No. 133 Squadron was the last of three units created between September 1940 and September 1941 that was staffed by US personnel serving with the RAF. The entry of the United States in the Second World War and the arrival of the USAAF's 8th Bomber and Fighter Commands were now to lead to the three squadrons being reformed as the 4th Fighter Group within the 8th Fighter Command, with Debden their permanent base. The ceremony attended by ACM Sholto-Douglas and B/Gen. 'Monk' Hunter (CG, 8th Fighter Command) occurred on 29 September, but the ranks of No. 133's pilots on parade were starkly minimal in comparison to its 121 and 133 contemporaries. The reason for this disparity was barely seventy-two hours past and constituted a simple tragedy.

The squadron, having only converted onto the Mk IX during August, had been assigned to provide an escort facility along with Nos 66 and 401 (RCAF) Squadrons for the B-17s of the 301 BG scheduled to bomb two airfields on the Cherbourg Peninsula. The wind forecast that would be a salient element within the incident was presented as around 100 mph from the south, but in fact was to develop from the north-east; the projected cloud cover of 8/10 over the primary was similarly wayward in that a solid undercast across the entire English Channel and northern France became the norm for the entire mission.

Taking off from a staging airfield in Southwest England (Bolt Head), No. 133 Squadron's twelve pilots had been assigned the 'target cover' aspect of the mission, but a third factor in the disaster was that the formation was unknowingly being blown off course to starboard and out over the Bay of Biscay. By the time this error had been confirmed and the ETA rendezvous with the bombers came and went, Flt Lt Brettell turned for England. Descending below the cloud base, the pilots sighted land they assumed was part of Southwest England and began searching for an airfield. The Spitfires were at low altitude when they flew over a town that was expected to provide a bearing—only to discover the 'town' was the large and heavily-defended naval port of Brest.

The flak batteries were ready and poured up a merciless hail of fire that claimed several of the fighters; of the rest, all but Lt. R. Beaty were compelled to force-land through lack of fuel. Beaty miraculously managed to get within several miles of the English coast from where he was able to direct his now-powerless charge into a safe crash-landing (Brettell ended up in *Stalag Luft* 3 and was one of the fifty officers executed in the wake of the 24–25 March 1944 'Great Escape').

A pair of Mk VBs squat in their dispersal, probably at Hornchurch during the first half of 1942. The pilot's overall feeling of facing the Fw 190 with what is a generally inferior variant will start to alter come June; it is then that the squadron will be first to convert onto the Mk IX and with this have an opportunity to challenge, if not also best, their formidable adversary.

Operational Priorities

The several qualities of the Fw 190 were seen to lend themselves not only to the superiority fighter role, but also that of reconnaissance and ground attack; the air-cooled BMW801 promised more security from critical damage than the oil-cooled DB600 Series mounted on the Fw's contemporary, the Bf 109, when indulging in the latter duty. The current problem in utilising the design in such operational roles was logistical due to the still-tardy production rate. The A-4 version coming on stream with JG26, for example, featured a water-methanol boost system that improved power output up to 16,000 feet. The current availability of *FuG* 25Z IFF sets now allowed the *Jafue* controllers to monitor several formations at the same time. The improvement in turn witnessed the various *Gruppe* control locations handing over the duty to the central *Geschwader* controller.

The A-4's availability made its comprehensive appearance in Northern France all the more ironic in view of plans being mooted by the *Luftwaffe* authorities. This was for the Channel-based *Geschwadern* to transfer onto the Bf 109G in order to permit the aforementioned switch to multirole duties. The Messerschmitt fighter in its current G-4 format was a superb machine, especially when indulging in high-level dogfights but suffered a serious limitation in firepower that consisted of a mere two fuselage-mounted MG17s and one MG-151/20 cannon. This was barely adequate to take out a fighter, let alone a heavy bomber as was increasingly likely to occur with the advent of the USAAF's daylight offensive.

The cameraman taking this picture of a No. 243 Squadron Mk VB Spitfire must have palpitations on studying the result considering how close his subject came to his aircraft. The angle shows how the aircraft letter is applied below the squadron letters' level and the yellow stripes along the wing leading edges.

JG26 already possessed Bf 109G-1s assigned to the *Höhen Staffel*, but the conversion of II *Gruppe* onto the fighter was originally intended to be fully implemented as 1943 commenced; this was evidenced by the presence of several Bf 109G-4s within the sub-unit establishment by December. In the event, the conversion was duly carried out—not by II *Gruppe* whose successive *Kommandeur* somehow managed to resist the requirement until it was rescinded—but rather by their III *Gruppe* contemporaries. This was as far as a wholesale switch was to occur for the foreseeable future.

Year-End Experiences

The fitful pace of operations experienced by the 8th Bomber Command during the first eight or nine months of its existence owed much to the dearth of both material and human resources. The American military was still stretched almost to the limits over this time, and aviation's 'New Kid on the Block' was placed in the priority shadows, particularly following Operation Torch, the invasion of North Africa; the 97th and 301st BGs were dispatched to the Mediterranean and not immediately replaced in Britain, leaving just four B-17 and two B-24 groups to take the strain.

The scale of individual mission numbers even before the transfer took effect was hardly enough to reach a triple-figure level on more than a handful of occasions.

The first was 9 October when Lille was targeted by seventy-nine out of 108 dispatched. The large RAF fighter support added to by the 4th and 14th FGs did not prevent III/JG26 gaining access to and landing a degree of punishment upon the formations; three B-17s and one B-24 went down, although the crew from one of the Boeing machines was saved after it was successfully 'ditched'.

The packing of fighter squadrons closely around a bomber formation had cast up the problem of handling the 'hit and run' tactics rightly employed by the *Jagdwaffe* units during Circus operations. On the other hand, the deployment of fighters on this occasion—involving sub-forces allotted to the main and diversionary bomber formations—had appeared to be too loose in application when considering the reportedly unfettered access gained by JG26 to their primary prey. The need for pre-emptive measures to tackle one's adversaries before they were ever able to approach, let alone engage, the bombers would not be mulled over and activated for a long time ahead—neither by the RAF nor USAAF hierarchies.

There was also a key difference between escorting the RAF medium bombers generally forming the core of Circus operations and the immeasurably heavier-armed USAAF heavies. The RAF bombers' defensive armament was generally no more than adequate—and absolutely abysmal in the Blenheim's case—in order to withstand any fighter assault while continued dependence upon the .303 bullet was a further barrier to providing a sufficient degree of effective firepower.

The pilot of a Polish squadron is leaping from his Mk V Spitfire cockpit, the enthusiastic expression suggesting a successful sortie. The clue to this fighter belonging to No. 302 Squadron, the first all-Polish unit in Fighter Command, is the 'inverted L' letter ahead of the roundel, the squadron codes being WX. Thick white socks and heavy flying boots would ward off the worst effects of the often-extreme temperatures encountered at operational altitudes.

In the latter instance, there was the (sadly naïve and ultimately discredited) theory that a fighter escort was an optional extra as opposed to a necessity, given the bombers' perceived ability to basically survive the anticipated *Jagdwaffe* assaults with minimal casualty rates, this being due to the sheer weight of defensive firepower cast up by the formations' gunners. The relatively short ranges largely being flown at this stage of the daylight offensive provided more false evidence of this 'unescorted bomber' policy—even if the 'unescorted' part was equally false.

As it was, 1942 concluded with a stalemate in terms of direct fighter combat and with the *Jagdwaffe* units in France, Belgium, and Holland firmly entrenched and demonstrating little sign of buckling under the strain; this was hardly the case elsewhere, whether their contemporaries were facing the Russian onslaught particularly around Stalingrad or the Anglo–American on-surge in North Africa. The new year promised no discernible advance in Allied aerial fortunes over Western Europe and indeed would see a degree of retrenchment in operational effectiveness as the Allied Bomber Commands thrust ever deeper into the Third Reich.

High-Level Incursions

The likelihood that the *Luftwaffe* would enter into ultra-high-level flights in order to achieve reconnaissance information was ever on the minds of the RAF hierarchy. Efforts were accordingly made by Supermarine to develop a Spitfire that would be capable of challenging these incursions. The aircraft the Germans had on hand for this was the Ju 86, but the initial planned use was not reconnaissance but rather bombing raids in retaliation for the increasing blows being handed out to Germany by RAF Bomber Command as 1942 progressed towards its conclusion.

The planned variant was the Mk VI, and its features included a pressurised cockpit, a 'C' wing with tapered tips that extended the overall span to 40 feet, 2 inches, and a Merlin 47 rated at 1,415 hp. The bulk of the ninety-seven airframes ultimately constructed were intended for home-based operations, but five were also sent to the Middle East to replace the current Mk Vs of the Special Performance Flight (SPF). Eight squadrons were to utilise the mark with No. 124 the first to be assigned a number in July 942. In the event, the altitude performance in particular was inadequate in attaining anything like the altitude required to get at the Ju 86s; it was as well that only a handful of flights were made by the *Luftwaffe*.

A follow-up to the Mk VI was the Mk VII that not only achieved the required performance, but also introduced amended power and structural features becoming standard from the Mk VIII onwards. The circular oil cooler under the port wing gave way to a rectangular structure the same as that under the other wing. The change was brought about due to a redesigned cooling system for the Merlin 61, 64, and 70, which also had multi-ejector exhaust stubs. The overall length was increased thanks to the longer engine-mount frame and a retractable tailwheel was added. The need to lock down the Mk VI's canopy was avoided and the Mk

The Mk VI Spitfire was the first of two successive marks developed to intercept ultra-high-flying *Luftwaffe* aircraft. The variant was the first to utilise the Rotol four-blade propeller but used the single-stage Merlin 47 for power, with firepower the same as on the Mk VB. The tapered wingspan was increased to 40 feet 2 inches. Only ninety-seven airframes were completed but performance was inadequate as regards the key issue of maximum altitude.

Although designated as the NF Mk XV Mosquito, the main emphasis behind its swift creation was to combat anticipated daylight incursions by ultra-high-flying Ju 86s. The extended wings, Merlin 70s, pressurised cockpit, and substitution of cannon by a ventral machine-gun pack and other equipment lightening enabled the five aircraft ultimately adapted to reach away over 40,000 feet. However, with no *Luftwaffe* activity, the aircraft finally went from the command's high-altitude flight to No. 85 Squadron.

VII's sliding version undoubtedly increased the pilot's sense of comfort should an emergency arise. A maximum speed of over 400 mph and maximum altitude of 44,000 feet was confirmed; as with its predecessor, no operational activity against the enemy high fliers was achieved by the four home-based squadrons to whom the variant was assigned during 1943–44.

Low-Level Incursions

The creation within the two Channel-based *Geschwadern* of specialist fighter-bomber sub-forces—10 (*Jabo*) JG2 and 10 (*Jabo*) JG26—had been effected back in March 1942. Their operational function contrasted with the original use of the Bf 109E in the duty during the battle of Britain. Whereas the latter had made their approaches at high altitude and scattered their single bomb loads accordingly, the two aforementioned units were generally indulging in strikes delivered at low level. This was a tactic that placed the RAF and ground radar and gunnery defences on the back foot in being able to muster a timely response.

The selection of targets containing some element of benefit to Britain's war effort appeared to have been granted priority up to the last months of 1942. It was then that a *Führerbefehl* (Hitler ordinance) was issued, whereby the pilots would seek to deliver their loads against locations that were to be purely 'civilian' in nature. The Nazi leader had fallen into one of his rages following RAF Bomber Command's raids in recent weeks and now wanted the *Luftwaffe* to launch *Vergeltungsangriff* (revenge attacks) against his adversary. What constituted such targets was not made absolutely clear. For example, on 27 November, a *Rotte* from 5/JG26 shot-up a train whose locomotive exploded; the resultant tidal wave of debris enveloped one Fw 190 that carried its pilot to his death (a locomotive would appear to be a legitimate source for attack as it could be utilised for hauling military loads; on the other hand, if pulling a passenger train, it was being equally interpreted as legitimate fare under the *Führerbefehl* despite its current 'civilian' function—yet another example of the expansion of the global conflict into a 'Total War' scenario).

A joint JG2/JG26 mass assault had already occurred on 31 October; the *Jabo* units were supplemented by Fw 190s specially converted for the operation that was directed at Canterbury in Kent. The attack duly went in against the city centre and the low approach coupled with equally low cloud visibility ensured that the defences were caught out; just a single JG2 fighter was actually intercepted and shot down over British soil. A second more notable casualty was incurred by 8/JG26, namely Adolph Galland's younger brother, Paul. He attempted to engage a Spitfire harassing a fellow pilot but stalled-out, so allowing his opponent to close upon his Fw 190 and dispatch it in flames into the remorseless Channel waters (Adolph Galland's other brother, Wilhelm-Ferdinand ('Wutz'), would also not survive the Second World War after being shot down by 56 FG P-47s the following 17 August while serving as III/JG26's *Kommandeur*).

The pilot of BM271/SK: E serving with No. 65 Squadron appears to be following directions, although the beckoning individual doing so may only be just making some form of gesture to the airman in the cockpit. Two ground crew are holding onto the wingtips with the nearside individual lifted-up off the ground. Picture taken at Gravesend in late 1942.

No. 453 (Australian) Squadron had been mauled during the Malayan campaign but was disbanded and reformed at Drem in Scotland during June 1942. The FN codes are a current misnomer as they had been applied to the-former No. 331 Squadron Mk VB Spitfires now assigned to No. 453; they would be displaced by the letters FU and the squadron would move south to Hornchurch during September.

1943

The ranks of Fighter Command that had hitherto demonstrated its main reliance on the Spitfire and Hurricane now also involved a steady build-up of both the Hawker Typhoon and the de Havilland Mosquito in numbers; the Bristol Beaufighter's introduction as a night fighter during 1940–41 was similarly having its presence expanded within the command. A fourth and largely sidelined design was the Westland Whirlwind twin-engined fighter/bomber that had entered service in 1940–1941 and would serve as a frontline aircraft until mid-1943.

Fighter Command's Spitfire establishment was destined to reflect the upsurge in numbers of Mk IXs entering service as the year progressed, although the demands of the Mediterranean theatre witnessed the parallel deployment of the variant to support the drive of the 1st and 8th Armies across North Africa. On the other hand, the Mk V was continuing to serve with a sizeable number of squadrons, despite its perceived serious performance limitations when encountering the Bf 109 and even more so the Fw 190.

A Notable Rebuff

The Fw 190 to date had held the ascendancy over Fighter Command as the records of both JG2 and JG26 reportedly confirm. That happy situation for the *Geschwader* personnel was to suffer a heavy reverse on 20 January, with the latter entity the principal victim; as it transpired, the punishment was to be shared between the Spitfires, Typhoons, and ground defences, but this factor was of no consolation to the pilots involved in the action. London was chosen as the target for the latest *Vergeltungsangriff* (revenge attack) with the actual bombing to be carried out by the specialist 10 (*Jabo*) *Staffeln* in current JG2 and JG26 service; the force was to be supplemented by fighters detached from JG2 and a Paris-based *Jagdschule* (fighter school). Escort cover was provided by JG2 and JG26. The attack plan was to be three-fold in application and involved just short of 100 fighters; the majority of these were Fw 190s, but 6/JG26's Bf 109s made up the remainder.

The actual bombing force was to approach in two waves, ten minutes apart, while III/JG26 would follow, but climb to altitude and loiter off the English coast, the intention being to intercept any pursuing RAF fighters as the attackers withdrew. This arrangement was sound theoretically, but it would only work out in terms of a strike free from defensive interdiction as far as the initial wave was concerned. However, matters turned sour even before the main event was launched. A projected reconnaissance run by two Fw 190s was caught by No. 609 Squadron Typhoons over the Channel, with Ltn. Hans Kuemmerling dispatched to his death and his companion forced to run for home.

In spite of this, the two *Jabo* sub-forces not only encountered no opposition after they emerged from solid cloud into clear skies over the English landscape,

In the summer of 1943, a series of publicity pictures were shot with No. 181 Squadron the centrepiece. A row of its Mk IB Tiffies—the Hawker fighter's nickname—forms an appropriate backcloth to the squadron pilots sitting at the front and backed up by an equally sizeable party of ground crew personnel. The unit was carrying out a mix of Roadstead, Rhubarb, and bombing sorties around this period of the war.

they managed to reach the capital—where a further bonus was the total absence of barrage balloons with their lethal cable-supports. The overall bombing results were another matter, in that along with claimed strikes on the London docks was included a fair number of civilian casualties in several housing areas; this included the bombing of a school that killed thirty-eight children and six teachers—a surprising lapse in view of the clear conditions and probably caused by a faulty release mechanism rather than a failed bomb run on a perceived legitimate target.

The 'so far, so good' situation for the initial thirty-four-strong sub-force that lost just two at the coast—one fighter crash-landed by Ltn. Hermann Hoch (POW) and one flown by Obfw. Paul Kierstein (KIA), the latter pilot being downed by Wg Cdr R. Milne (Kenley Wing Leader)—was not to hold good for the second wave. The defences were clearly alerted by now, so the prospect of having to fight their way through without the risk of heavy loss was probably the catalyst for the decision to turn back. As it was, the formation was still harried during what appears to have been a shallow penetration over enemy territory.

A total of five more JG26 pilots would not regain their airfields as the frenetic action spanning around fifteen to twenty minutes now ensued. However, the

Dennis Crowley-Milling, a former member of Bader's No. 242 Squadron during the Battle of Britain, had subsequently been shot down but evaded capture in mid-1941. He was given command of No. 181 Squadron in September 1942 and is seen in the cockpit of his Mk IB Typhoon. The CO's pennant accompanies artwork depicting Hitler awaiting a blow from a bomb; the squadron served in the 'Bombphoon' role from March 1943.

major punishment was handed out to the Bf 109s of the covering III *Gruppe* force. Ltn. Kurt-Erich Wenzel (KIA), Uffzs. Heinz Marquardt, and Hermann Buddes (both POW) all tasted defeat at the hands of No. 609 Squadron whose Typhoons were based at Manston and accordingly in perfect geographic position to engage the enemy as they retired over Kent. The fourth *Gruppe* casualty to a Spitfire of No. 122 Squadron was Uffz. Helmut Peters who joined Manzel in death, albeit during a failed crash-landing at Ardres in France.

The sole Fw 190 loss during the action was that flown by Fw. Alfred Barthel. The pilot baled out of his 5 *Staffel* machine that was fatally crippled by a No. 340 (French) Squadron Spitfire, but he failed to survive descending into the Channel. Two more pilots managed to stagger back to heavy or crash-landings. The third-wave formation's claim for three Spitfires, of which two would be recorded in RAF records, was a counterstrike hardly measuring up to the loss figure that was further increased by at least one fighter from JG2. The involvement of the Typhoon in handing out this punishment was both a harbinger of more to come for the *Jagdwaffe* as well as an affirmation to the RAF authorities that the Hawker machine was worth proceeding with in combating low-level incursions.

A familiar face in unfamiliar surroundings. 'Gabby' Gabreski was destined to become a senior figure and high-scoring ace with the 8th Fighter Command's 56th FG. Prior to joining the Group in mid-1943, he requested attachment to an RAF fighter squadron to gain combat experience. His Polish family roots saw him joining the No. 315 Squadron; he is vacating his Mk IX Spitfire on completing his first operational flight during January 1943.

Thirsting for Revenge (1)

By March 1943, Al Deere had been off operations for round ten months and was naturally keen to regain that status, with command of a wing his priority. He still possessed grim memories of the previous June's debacle between his No. 403 Squadron and JG26, and part of his desire in returning to the aerial frontline was to exact revenge for this beating. The chances of doing so were regarded by him as being enhanced if the Mk IX Spitfire came into his hands compared to the trusty but largely inferior-performing Mk V that had borne him into the unequal battle in 1942.

His wish bore fruit in both respects during mid-month when his appointment as CO of the Kenley Wing was switched to Biggin Hill; Kenley Wing Leader 'Dickie' Milne was shot down at this time and his place now taken up by one of Bader's protégé's, 'Johnny' Johnson. Both of his squadrons, Nos 341 (Alsace) (a French-staffed unit) and 611 Squadrons, now operated on the Mk IX to fulfil the second part of his expectations. Deere planned for a basic operational freedom of action not only at squadron but down to section level.

The latter-mentioned sub-units now not only flew in four-aircraft form, but on Deere's instruction did so in the 'finger-four' pattern compared to the line-astern equivalent that was still generally in vogue within Fighter Command. Deere's command in the air was absolute in terms of routes and timings, etc.; sightings

An awards ceremony on 16 October 1943 was the occasion for Wg Cdr Deere to receive one of his several decorations. The presence on left of Maj. Eugene Roberts (78FG) who wears an American DFC and Col. Hub Zemke (56FG CO) suggests this is the DFC granted him by the US authorities. All three distinguished airmen survived the war.

of enemy formations by any element was acted upon by them once Deere was informed of these 'contacts'. In effect, the initiative for overall action as well as mutual support during any aerial contest was not wholly laid upon Deere but was shared with the squadron and section leaders.

The initial contact with the *Jagdwaffe* proved frustrating when a sortie to catch out the JG2 *Gruppe* based at Triqueville and led by Obstlt. Walter Oseau failed; this was due to the Fw 190s spotted taxiing out by Commandant René Mouchotte (341 Squadron CO) as the wing swept in at low level ready to strafe the airfield, managing to get airborne and disperse in time. A second formation closing from the south was then engaged, but fuel restriction caused the wing to disengage with honours clinically even—two Fw 190s to two 341 Squadron Spitfires downed, but with Raoul Duval evading capture and regaining British soil.

Deere's tally against the Fw 190 had already begun on 16 February when flying as a supernumerary with No. 611 Squadron. On that occasion, he shot one down into the Channel near Calais. His first confirmed kill as a wing commander came on 4 May over Belgium, and before he relinquished command during September, he added one more kill and one probable to bring his tally to seventeen confirmed kills. This was his final figure in the Second World War as the bulk of his duties now assumed support posts such as CO of the Central Flying School's Fighter Wing; the sole operational experience was with the 145 French Wing around D-Day.

'Johnny' Johnson

One of Douglas Bader's protégés was 'Johnny' Johnson, who by early 1943 was Al Deere's contemporary as the CO of the nearby Kenley Wing. His two-squadron force was Canadian, whose pilots were regarded as particularly strong-willed to the point of rebelliousness—a stance that Johnson discovered was overstated at least aloft when they displayed sound individual and corporate discipline. One aspect of current squadron procedure that surprised him was the continued reliance upon line-astern sections.

Johnson was all for the 'finger-four' pattern that largely emulated the *Jagdwaffe*'s *Schwarm* in overall function. One of his wing commanders (Syd Ford, leading No. 403 Squadron) expressed the view that the line-astern arrangement was basically as sound in operation, while the other (Foss Bolton, in charge of No. 416 Squadron) was vaguer in his preferred choice. Johnson suggested the latter squadron fly 'finger-four' with Ford's unit retaining his option of continuing with the present formation or taking up Johnson's suggested alternative. After a few sorties, a definite choice was made that came down on the side of Johnson.

'Johnny' Johnson presents a more studied expression to the camera just over two years on from his carefree grin captured in Chapter 8's photo content. He is now a wing commander with medal ribbons for a DSO mounting what appears to be a badge for a second such award (left), alongside a DFC with a rosette also indicating a second such award. The tunic's open-top button was an unofficial indicator that the individual concerned was an RAF fighter pilot. Picture was taken no earlier than late 1943.

Although he had respected Bader as a leader, he declined from unconditionally following his air-fighting rules. When intercepting the enemy, Bader would automatically take the lead when initiating the attack; in contrast, Johnson would deploy that part of the wing that was in the best position to take it on, while retaining the overall cohesion of the wing in the subsequent action. Another change involved reassembly after a battle. Before taking off, Johnson would designate a rendezvous location that the pilots would head towards after action was broken off. This was a sharp contrast with what had previously happened when the pilots would make their own way home—thereby increasing the chances of being intercepted in unfavourable circumstances and without proper support.

Thirsting for Revenge (2)

'Johnny' Johnson's operational career had taken a previous step-up in June 1942, when, as a squadron leader, he was appointed to his first unit command, No. 610 (County of Cheshire) Squadron, which was currently equipped with the Mk VB Spitfire and was an element of the Tangmere Wing. At this stage of the war, he would have been under little or no allusion of the Fw 190's ascendancy in combat and would have to strike a balance between forcefulness and caution when encountering the enemy—not an easy thing to achieve in such imbalanced circumstances.

The hard facts of operational life struck home for the squadron during an early 1943 sortie to provide close escort cover for a Ventura squadron attacking a target at Caen in Normandy, a region protected by JG2. The bombers were positioning themselves marginally below the cloud base, an action that inhibited No. 610's ability to manoeuvre vertically so Johnson held back with a view to orbiting the target following the assault and so provide a bulwark against *Jagdwaffe* counter assault. This was proceeding in order when what appears to have been a *Gruppe*-strong force from the numbers involved (thirty) shot through a gap in the clouds and descended upon the squadron.

At odds of over 2:1, the omens for survival were poor and almost immediately lengthened when one Spitfire's tail was shot off with the pilot managing to bale out, albeit just off the Channel coast. Johnson observed another Spitfire trailing heavy smoke and advised its occupant to jump as he appeared to have little chance of getting back; the Polish pilot displayed his nation's talent for stubbornness and held course for home. Meanwhile, the remaining ten pilots were at least succeeding in diverting the Fw 190s from pursuing the bombers to the extent that Johnson could finally call for his colleagues to disengage and dive northwards.

The original formation was split into three segments, but the third one consisting of just two fighters was not only out at a distance but flying higher and taking no evasive action. The inevitable result was that both were fatally crippled and set on fire to become total losses. The seven Spitfires on hand held course for Westhampnett (the satellite to Tangmere) where they encountered their Polish colleague who had beat the odds in recrossing the Channel in his stricken

BS456/UZ: Z from No. 306 (Polish) Squadron reveals several features on the Mk IX compared to the Mk V. The carburettor air intake extends forward of the wing leading edge, although early Mk V airframes modified to Mk IX standard retained the shorter-length fitting. The six exhaust stubs replace the three larger cowlings and the four-blade propeller is substituted for its three-blade predecessor.

Spitfire and one other who had also made a solo return after his fighter was badly damaged and knocked out of the battle.

To lose only three pilots in these 'backs to the wall' circumstances was somewhat of a mercy, but several days later, another pilot was lost in the latest air battle. As with Al Deere's even more traumatic experience with No. 403 Squadron in mid-1942, so Johnson must have harboured a strong desire to gain his revenge on the earliest possible occasion—an urge that would initially be settled by early April.

Thirst Slaked

On 3 April, the Kenley Wing was briefed for a sortie that was loosely linked with a Typhoon attack on Abbeville airfield. The wing would arrive at altitude in the immediate area following the bombing of the airfield in the hope of intercepting any enemy aircraft that had 'scrambled' as a result of the assault upon their base. The Kent-based controller informed Johnson of a twenty-plus indication on his radar screens flying well below the wing's 20,000-foot altitude. Matters then took a potentially nasty turn as the wing was closing-in from up-sun but still with no visual sighting; the controller announced a second formation approaching from behind, whose presence held the attendant risk of the Johnson-led force being 'sandwiched'.

The overall situation was made clear almost at once as the first enemy formation in the form of two sub-units totalling twenty-two Fw 190s hove into view. The two wing squadrons duly initiated the classic 'bounce' action that in Johnson's case placed him behind a Fw 190 on the extreme left side of what was a II/JG26 *Staffel*. His first burst of fire missed, but the second delivered after he corrected his aim smashed into the starboard wing root and set the fighter on fire. A final burst and then the Mk IX was pulled-up into a climb followed by the others.

It was now that the controller advised an immediate withdrawal, which was obeyed by all twenty-three surviving pilots. Although the debriefing kill claims later granted totalled six, this figure was reduced by half; according to the *Geschwader* records, three pilots were KIA over France this day, and a fourth from 10 (*Jabo*) was lost during an attack on Eastbourne, the victim of a Northolt Wing Spitfire. This was an unusually expensive twenty-four hours for what was a premier *Jagdwaffe* body.

The adaptability for manifold duties was a hallmark of the de Havilland aircraft. In this picture, a plan view of an FB Mk VI from below picks out the port wing pylon with its concave interior that accommodated the cylindrical shape of bombs. The cartridge slots for expended cannon shell cases are another point of note as is the split set of bomb doors with the forward section accessing the 20-mm weapons, the rear the available bomb bay.

Growing Strike Power

The creation of No. 2 Group back in 1936 had witnessed the original establishment of Fairey Battles and Bristol Blenheims suffering heavy and often unsustainable casualties over the period between 1939 and 1942. Their displacement by more modern and efficient types with the Boston, Mitchell, and Mosquito featuring prominently had in turn seen an unrelenting pressure placed upon the *Jagdwaffe* in its bid to stem the regular assaults upon a range of targets spread across northern France and the Low Countries; this duty was to grow ever more burdensome as the VIII BC heavies began to add to the pressure by expanding operations into Germany.

Although more fast-paced, manoeuvrable, and better provisioned in defensive armament than their hapless predecessors, there was still a need to provide escort cover for the first two named aircraft, the Mosquito being regarded as capable of handling matters on its own; this was a duty that Fighter Command was more than willing to accommodate. Ironically, set against this function was the true, if unpalatable, fact that the Spitfire's original concept in which it had proved its value during the initial period of the Second World War was to prove an insuperable barrier to supporting Allied aerial thrusts into the heart of the Third Reich.

Biggin Hill: Fighter Command's PR Station?

Since the Second World War, whenever memories of Fighter Command are evoked, the name of Biggin Hill tends to come to the forefront. It is likely its prominence stems from its central location within No. 11 Group during the Battle of Britain. As with Bassingbourn and Debden's similar post-war prominence within 8USAAF bomber and fighter circles, so Biggin's similar easy access to London may have played a part in attracting the media's interest in the airfield and its personnel since a large element of this literary body was based in the British capital. Whatever the reason, the fact is that Biggin Hill's name and reputation remains synonymous with all that the British aviation-minded public feel for how Fighter Command conducted itself throughout the conflict.

The airfield's perceived premier status stretching from the Battle of Britain to the steadily-effective advance into Western European skies by the RAF in conjunction with its Commonwealth, continental, and USAAF contemporaries in 1944 was probably based in part on its media exposure. Linked to this was the international co-mingling of squadrons and personnel. By mid-1943, the command structure had several prominent airmen within its ranks. 'Sailor' Malan was now a group captain and the station commander; Wg Cdr Al Deere of immortal 'nine-lives' fame was leading the Biggin Hill Wing; and Canada's Sqn Ldr Jack Charles was present, as was Commandant René Mouchotte (CO of No. 341 Squadron).

Over the previous three years, the squadrons based at 'Biggin on the Bump' (a term referring to its perch on lower-lying surrounding countryside) had amassed a total of kills almost on the 1,000 mark and this target was reached on 15 May 1943.

RAF Biggin Hill was one of the most famous airfields within Fighter Command. This photo exemplifies the international nature of the command's ranks. The four officers in the centre are (left to right) Jack Charles (Canada), René Mouchotte (France), 'Sailor' Malan (South Africa), and Al Deere (New Zealand). The three RAF pilots amassed a total of fifty-nine confirmed kills during the Second World War. Mouchotte was the sole fatality, being shot down on 27 August 1943.

On 15 May 1943, Biggin Hill was two short of the 1,000 confirmed kills registered by its manifold squadrons to date. Sqn Ldr Jack Charles is chalking up the desired figure following a 'sweep' that netted two victories for him and one to Commandant René Mouchotte. An inability to identity to whom the second kill could be granted ended with both officers sharing the sweep-stake sum—a whopping (by 1940s standards) figure of £300 (equal to $1,200).

Mouchotte and Charles each scored a kill that between them brought the figure to 1,001; no clear conclusion emerging as to whom had been first to succeed resulted in the £150 sweep-stake sum being divided between the duo. The subsequent banquet in London to celebrate the event had 1,000 guests present, but the fact that the sizeable cost entailed in putting on the event was reportedly recovered from among the No. 11 Group squadrons if not further afield was not greeted with enthusiasm.

'A Busted Flush?'

The creation of the Spitfire and Hurricane was based upon their primary function being as defensive fighters. Both designs proved their worth in this role during 1940, but with the switch from defence to offence, a growing and basically insoluble problem arose as the battle was taken into the western fringes of the Nazi Empire; the issue concerned was that of operational range——or rather, and particularly in the superior-performance Spitfire's case, the serious lack of range.

The need for RAF Bomber Command to be provided with adequate escort cover in its bid to strike at the enemy's industrial heart was placed in abeyance from the winter of 1939–40 until mid-1944. During this time span, the bombers exchanged the desirable option of focusing on targets in daylight to the enforced and much more-vague policy of assaulting an entire town or city in the hope—not always fulfilled—of gaining access to their production sources. This was area bombing with all it implied in terms of inaccuracy and non-combatant casualties.

More efficient medium bombers in the establishment of No. 2 Group such as the Boston and Mitchell along with the USAAF's Marauder were on hand in steadily-growing numbers by 1942–43. However, it was the advent of VIII Bomber Command operations using the B-17 and B-24 that promised no respite for the German military and economic structure during daylight; the four-engined duo's intervention along with their RAF strategic colleagues signalled the still largely-nascent policy of 'Round the Clock Bombing'.

The initially confident hopes of the Americans that their heavies could dispense with escorts did not prevent calls for the Spitfire to provide cover during the Mighty Eighth's first autumn and winter on operations. Until late January, all their targets were within the occupied countries on Germany's western boundaries; consequently, the Spitfire squadrons assigned to the duty could maintain regular contact with the 'Big Friends' other than when the missions were directed against the U-boat bases along the Biscay Bay coastline.

The overall situation converted into an increasingly negative mode when the USAAF heavies began to carry out strikes into Western Germany as the offensive was expanded in the light of equally-increasing bomber, personnel, and support equipment resources. It was then that the 85-gallon internal fuel capacity of the Spitfire truly played its part in inhibiting any continued escort provision; once beyond the restricted range provided by this minimal figure, the bombers were left to their own defensive means for salvation. Consequently, the RAF pilots were only able to take their charges so far into the continent's landmass before an enforced withdrawal took place; a similar cover-range applied during the bomber's return leg.

'Johnny' Johnson recalled Wally Macleod one of his Canadian pilots imbued with a particularly aggressive streak bemoaning the fact that the wing was restricted to medium bomber escort duties. On one occasion, he said to his CO words to the effect of 'Why can't we stick two drop-tanks under our wings and head for Berlin where we could get stuck-in and give the enemy a licking?' However, the increased range factor, when so accoutred with the maximum extra capacity of 90 gallon, still provided a flight endurance barely half that of the P-51. In practice, this would take the fighter no further than the German border and this maximum range factor would be further eroded if combat ensued during the outward stage.

Johnson was fully cognizant of the Spitfire's qualities as a superiority fighter, but in his post-war conversations, he would sadly acknowledge that the duty was inexorably being taken in hand by the P-47, P-38, and, most effectively of all, P-51, with their greatly-enhanced range capability. His use of the expression that heads this section was a bitter comment on Fighter Command's pride and joy's exclusion from sharing in the overall duty that would have undoubtedly added to the *Jagdwaffe*'s woes.

Whirlwind Fortunes 1942–43

No. 263 Squadron commenced 1942 flying regular convoy patrol sorties but suffered a short period 'grounded' due to problems with the fighters' Peregrine engines before resuming a mix of operations. Added to convoy patrols was Rhubarb-type activity that included attacks on airfields and shipping. From early autumn to the Whirlwind's formidable gun power was added the striking power of bombs up to individual weights of 500 lb; the latter was utilised with some effect against shipping from this point until the end of 1943, although aircraft numbers on hand were inhibited through lack of regular replacements.

No. 137 Squadron's entry into service with the Whirlwind during late 1941 had seen its CO lost in an accident, while four further pilots were lost during the February 1942 'Channel Dash' of three *Kriegsmarine* capital ships. The squadron's location in Southeast England during 1942 and into 1943, coupled with its fellow unit's operations further west, meant that the whole of the Channel and northern France was open to assault, with the aforementioned target category regularly homed in upon.

The Hispano quartet of 20-mm cannon was to prove the bane of many locomotives and the crews of vessels. In the latter case, the gunfire provided solid cover whenever bombs were borne. However, the combination of low-level approach and a propensity for the fighter to adopt a tilt to port created a potentially lethal problem. The official advice was for pilots to either drop both bombs simultaneously or to release the port-mounted example if intending to make more than one pass—the latter action hardly being recommended in

A Whirlwind serving with No. 263 Squadron is photographed 'all down and dirty' (in modern aviation parlance); undercarriage along with full flaps is lowered as a final landing approach is in its final stage. The squadron operated on the Westland design for three and a half years until Typhoon conversion occurred in December 1943.

the case of anti-shipping sorties where the flak defences were difficult enough to survive during a single pass.

The design's frontline presence was sustained throughout 1943 despite the relative lack of numbers, as well as the growing availability of contemporaries such as the Typhoon and Mosquito that were available in far greater quantity. No. 137 was perhaps illogically switched onto the Mk IV Hurricane in mid-year; the perceived equal, if not superior performance of the Westland fighter was probably balanced out by the rocket-carrying ability of the Hawker machine; this category of armament was used against the same range of targets, in particular shipping. The Whirlwind's operational value was still evident to the extent that No. 263 continued operating it until the year's end when the squadron converted onto the Typhoon.

'Instep' Operations

The emphasis on Fighter Command operations during the Second World War has tended to be centred on combating the *Luftwaffe* bomber and fighter assaults upon the British Isles along with the reverse actions in challenging that force over the landscape of Europe. What has tended to be overlooked is the period between early and mid-1943; this was when support was provided to RAF Coastal Command in its key strategic battle against the U-boat service with reference to the movements of its vessels across the length and breadth of the Bay of Biscay. The 'Battle of the Bay' would swing operationally to and fro in each side's favour during this central phase of the overall North Atlantic campaign.

The harassment by Coastal Command's aircraft of the *Kriegsmarine* crews, whether in transit to strike at or return from the Atlantic convoy routes or more directly attempting to interdict the specific convoy route to and from Gibraltar and further around the west African coastline, went initially unchallenged by the *Luftwaffe*. This was due in part to priority being granted to air attacks on the British convoys plying the Gibraltar route that thereby supplemented their U-boat colleagues' efforts. This was a satisfactory arrangement up to 1942, given both the lack of sufficient naval escorts as well as carrier-borne or land-based RAF fighter resources with which to challenge the often-costly strikes against the plodding merchant vessels.

As the overall conflict began to turn however slowly in the Allies favour, the maritime fliers began to apply more effective pressure upon their underwater adversaries. Improved-quality depth charges and later the Mk 24 'homing' torpedo, along with the 'Leigh-light' that pierced the cloak of darkness around a surfaced U-boat, presented a growing threat to the submariner's safety. The bulky Sunderland flying boat, soundly-efficient Wellington and the now pedestrian-paced Whitley bombers were the platforms from which the attacks were being delivered.

An FB Mk VI Mosquito whose starboard tanks are being refuelled ready for the next sortie bears the red/white-quartered square on the nose confirming the squadron's Polish status. Aircraft is believed to belong to No. 307 Squadron that flew this variant during late 1943 when the crews were involved in the Instep campaign over the Bay of Biscay.

However, until mid-1942, there was an absence of multi-engined fighters in *Luftwaffe* service assigned to any of the airfields along the Biscay coast.

A *Staffel* of Ju 88Cs moved to Bordeaux–Merignac in south-western France, although it is uncertain which unit these belonged to at the time; what was confirmed was that by August, the unit became the nucleus for V/KG40 with its full *Gruppe* strength on hand by September. Here was a serious counter threat to the Coastal Command fliers, a threat that soon materialised when Ltn. Stoeffller shot down one out of two Wellingtons (ironically, the duo was not command-assigned machines but were in transit to the Middle East) but was forced to 'ditch' his fighter thanks to return fire.

During the remainder of 1942, as the air battles became evermore intense, the chief RAF fighters on hand were Beaufighters with Nos 235 and 248 Squadrons in the forefront of the action. The 'Beau' was a formidable adversary for even the Ju 88C, but during December, an arguably more formidable opponent made its initial appearance over the Bay—the Mosquito, whose greater range capability among several operational attributes was of prime importance to impeding V/KG40's freedom of movement as far as the northern Spanish coast.

No. 264 Squadron currently operating on night fighter duties sent a detachment to Predannack in Southwest England; from there, the crews would fly 'Instep' or 'Day Ranger' sorties. The latter involved 'freelance' activities designed in this case to draw out enemy aircraft; the 'Instep' sorties were a direct counter to aircraft already airborne on maritime operations and therefore more likely to result in a combat. After the entire squadron had transferred to Predannack around March, regular 'Instep' operations were conducted with crews flying in sections of four aircraft.

Between this time and the first Mosquito victory on 11 June, it was the Beaufighters of Nos 235 and 248 Squadrons, added to by No. 404, that featured on the kill list. Then, on 11 June, Fw. F. Hiebach's 15/KG40 fighter was credited to Flt Lt J. Singleton and Fg Off. W. Haslem. Ironically, this crew was one of several on detachment from No. 25 Squadron and due to return to their squadron following the sortie. Five of the six Mosquito F Mk IIs were at minimum altitude when they encountered the same number of Ju 88Cs. They swiftly reversed their dangerously inferior tactical situation by climbing up behind the enemy formation that was around 7,000 feet and orbiting in an upward manner.

Singleton as leader ordered his colleagues to 'break' and seek individual targets. In his case, the return fire from several of the Ju 88 gunners as he closed-in seemed to indicate the enemy formation was holding together rather than actively seeking to similarly 'break' in attacking mode. Hiebach was flying in the rear position and Singleton's wide-deflection burst of fire before he levelled-off induced a large smoke plume from the port engine after which the Ju 88 peeled off and down to starboard. The descent angle was halted low down over the sea, but the relentless barrage from several subsequent bursts of fire finally saw two of the three airmen bale out with one impacting against the tail. Seconds later, the fighter flicked onto its back and fell into the dark maw of the Atlantic along with its pilot (the RAF

The daylight RAF interdictions over Western Europe were greatly intensified by the winter of 1943–44, with the FB Mk VI Mosquito a prominent element. Two armourers are attaching bomb-hoist frames prior to loading the weapons in the rear bomb bay. Cannon apertures and gun muzzles create the very appropriate impression of shark's teeth.

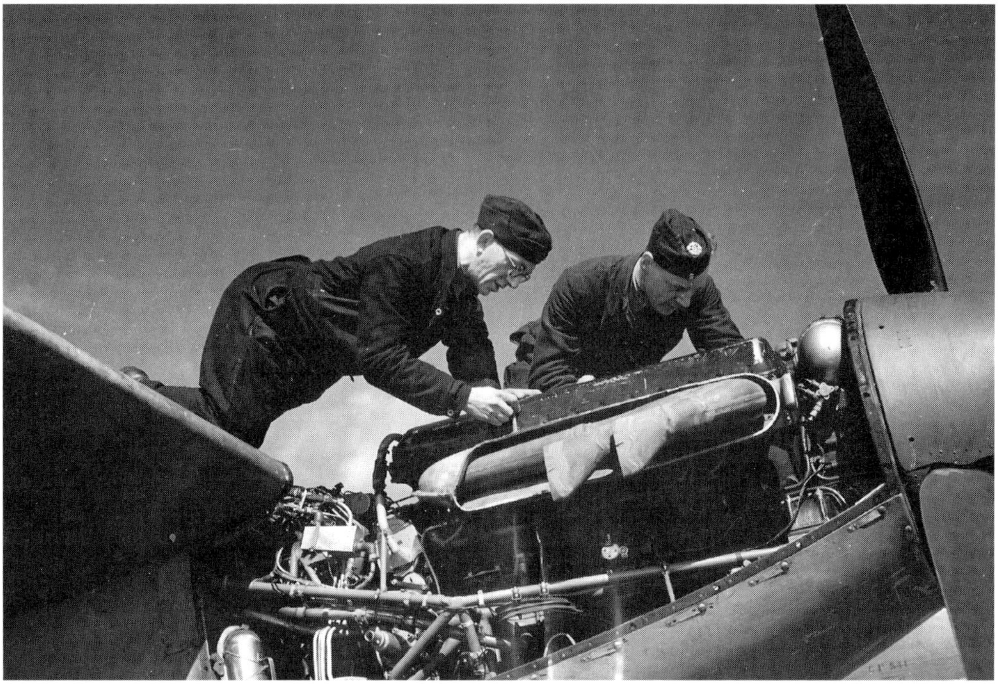

The innards of a Mosquito's Series 20 Merlin engine are being worked upon by two mechanics. Detachment of the exhaust fairing reveals the distinctive pattern for the exhaust stubs nicknamed 'Saxophone' for obvious reasons. The glycol tank is mounted between the propeller and top of the engine block and a fire extinguisher is positioned against the base of the engine nacelle as seen at the bottom left of the picture.

crew were also destined to down three bombers on 18–19 March 1944 during Operation Steinbock and end the Second World War with seven kills).

The success was undoubtedly marred by events just forty-eight hours later when three of a section, which included a pilot from No. 410 Squadron, were intercepted and downed by Fw 190s of 8/KG2. The fighters had been based at Brest with a specific brief to tackle the Mosquito threat among other RAF incursions over the Bay that might come within their range. However, the suggestion holds sway that the Mosquitos were unfortunate in that the original reason for the Fw 190's dispatch was to intercept a raid on a Brittany target by Venturas of No. 464 Squadron that then culminated with the Fw 190s running into the section on their homeward leg.

Unknown to either side was that the Battle of the Atlantic that had seemed destined to provide Germany with a possible long-term advantage in strangling vital human and material supplies to Britain during March–April had been permanently reversed thanks to the events in May. The consequent decision by Adm. Dönitz to withdraw his U-boats due to the hammering they had received during that month had created a situation where the Allied naval and air forces would from now on hold an increasing advantage in ensuring their seaborne adversaries would never again regain the initiative and indeed would be pushed onto a permanent and finally failed back foot.

No. 264 Squadron was withdrawn from Predannack in July, having lost another Mosquito in non-direct combat circumstances. The day after the trio of losses, W/O Hendra was on the port side of the 'Instep' section. Fg Off. W. Kent scanned across the formation to see his companion's Mosquito suddenly describe a sharp upward climb angle that ended with a stall and spin action; following the impact with the sea, the tail section from behind the wing bobbed up along with the crew dinghy but no further sight of either crewmember was gained.

Fighter Command's direct involvement in 'Instep' operations was far from concluded at this point. Nos 25, 151, 157, 307, 410, and 456 Squadrons had all assigned three fighters to the duty, although the former-named unit's cadre had returned to their airfield at Church Fenton during mid-June. A number of V/KG40's and I and III/ZG1's Ju 88Cs were credited to these crews during the remaining months of 1943. The first was on 19 June when Ltn. W. Gutermann's crew in F8+LY were forced to 'ditch' their Ju 88C following interception by No. 151's patrol. Uffz. W. Derr's crew were less fortunate, going MIA with the kill also credited to No. 151. Then, on 11 September, three fighters from No. 307 (Polish) Squadron latched onto Uffz. F. Huber's fighter and clinically dispatched it along with the crew.

September's cull of V/KG40 crews reached four in all. On the 21st, it was No. 456 that was reportedly the victor over Uffz. J. Heicke whose crew joined so many others in gaining an anonymous maritime grave. Four days later, No. 307 Squadron ran across eight Ju 88s, double the patrol's strength; in spite of this numerical imbalance, the three Polish and one RAF pilots engaged the formation, and when the air battle was over, only six Ju 88s were on hand. Stabsfw. K. Linden (14 *Staffel*) and Ltn. E. Kromer (15 *Staffel*) had fallen during the action with a 100 per cent fatality figure. In turn, FSs. L. Lowndes and I. Cotton had joined the duo in death after Obfw. K. Gaebner had latched onto their Mosquito.

The final credits granted to Fighter as opposed to Coastal Command fighter crews as 1943 faded away all went to No. 157 Squadron. On 20 November, Flt Lt G. Dyke put in a claim for a probable accruing from a joint Beaufighter–Mosquito patrol, along with three 'damaged' claims by two other pilots. The sole Ju 88 loss involved Obltn. H. Schuster, *Staffelkapitän* of 3/ZG1. Finally, a trio of kills were registered on 1 December with ZG1 the sufferer. Uffz. A. Meierl (3 *Staffel*), Ogfr. M. Vetter, and Ltn. G. Neumann (both 2 *Staffel*) were part of a formation bounced by the Mosquitos. Flt Lt Dyke added two to his tally with Fg Off. B. Whitlock the other victor; all nine airmen were listed as MIA, even though the first-named pilot's crew were seen to be in their dinghy.

The steady cull of the *Luftwaffe* aircraft over the Bay was balanced out by the sizeable number of Coastal Command crews losing out due to their less-manoeuvrable aircraft and average to poor armament provision; even the heavily-armed B-24s flown by the RAF and the US Navy's 479 anti-submarine group were not exempt from fatal assault. In spite of this casualty rate, the battle over the Bay was steadily turning to the Allies' advantage, with the U-boats being harried evermore as they attempted passage to and from the main Atlantic combat zone.

Above: The Rolls-Royce Merlin being an oil-cooled engine naturally resulted in a regular degree of seepage out of as well as on to the cowling panels. Two airmen are cleaning the port-side lower panel with some form of detergent mixture. The machine guns in *Daisy Mae*'s nose compartment have been removed and the wheel tarpaulin cover provides a necessary protection from seepage.

Left: Grp Capt. John Grandy (left), Duxford Station CO; Wg Cdr D. E. Gillam (middle), CO of the first Typhoon Wing; and a senior member of the AFDU operating from Duxford are in discussion. Grandy and Gillam were Battle of Britain veterans with the former rising to Chief of the Air Staff (CAS) after the war.

12

'The More Violent Storm'

The Typhoon

The Hawker fighter design that would earn the title heading for this chapter was under consideration, even as its predecessor was taking to the air in prototype form. The development and initial operational experience of the aircraft would be fraught with problems that would all but lead to cancellation, while the original concept of service as a superiority fighter was not destined to materialise; on the other hand, the low-level performance and deployment in ground attack would place it among the premier designs serving the RAF in the Second World War.

Specification F18/37 entailed the prototype construction of not one, but two distinct airframes powered by the 1,800-hp Rolls-Royce Vulture (R) and the 2,000-hp Napier Sabre (N). The all-up weight (AUW) estimates were 8,900 lb and 9,250 lb respectively, figures that reflected in part the much-increased engine weights compared to the Hurricane. The sturdier overall airframe and the wing section in particular was a second noticeable difference that, in time, would add to the aircraft's use in its revised role.

The all-metal construction utilising a steel and duraluminium tube method was added to by flush-riveted light alloy skinning; the inclusion of split flaps was another feature, while the generous-sized gun bays outboard of the landing gear promised a heavy firepower base. Perhaps not so sound was the cockpit access that consisted of a 'car-door' frame on both sides—not so easy to exit in an emergency and a layout that would change in time to a bubble canopy on later batches of the Mk IB.

The 'R' prototype named Tornado was first to fly on 6 October 1939 and was regarded as generally satisfactory, a status that included the engine—an ironic factor for the future when the Vulture's choice for the twin-engined Avro Manchester bomber turned out to be a retrograde step since the power plant did not live up to expectation. The 'N' prototype named Typhoon followed suit in the

The first Tornado prototype's outline is similar to its Hurricane predecessor as regards the nose contour, exhaust stubs, and radiator scoop. Aerodynamic problems caused the radiator scoop to be moved forward under the nose. Centrally-mounted doors for the landing gear were not fitted. This prototype has a Rolls-Royce Vulture engine.

following February, but the onset of the Battle of France resulted in the head of the Ministry of Aircraft Production (MAP) Max Beaverbrook calling a halt on the project and switching the continued priority to Spitfire and Hurricane production; a wise move in the light of impending events over Southern Britain.

By early 1941, development of the single Typhoon and now the pair of Tornado prototypes on hand had been resurrected, but the Air Ministry then took the decision to proceed only with the former. This action provided a second ironic situation in that the Typhoon example had cast up recurring problems both in terms of airframe and certainly engine function. The power output was not deemed sufficient for the fighter to function fully as a new-generation machine especially when above 20,000 feet, while the actual maximum speed fell well below the assessed figure of 460 mph. More serious was a central fuselage failure during one test flight that fortunately ended with test pilot Philip Lucas making an uneventful landing. The future seemed at best uncertain for the aircraft in the light of these several problems.

Faith in the Hawker Co. staff's ability to surmount the current range of difficulties was evident with the placing of an order for 250 airframes, although at this point, the remainder of the complete 1,000 total airframe contract was to have originally been mainly allocated to the Tornado. There was a degree of dissent within some RAF circles as to the need to progress with the Typhoon. The feeling was that the Spitfire was fully capable of taking on the *Luftwaffe* on equal, if not superior, terms, so why devote resources to a supposed replacement when the intended successor was still not fully up to the task? This stance was probably

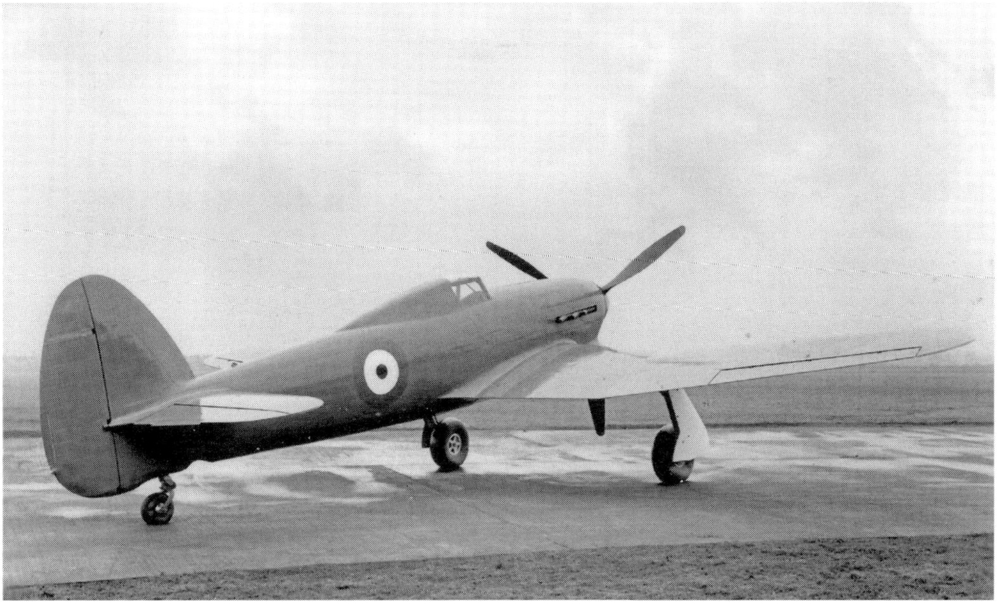

P5212 was the first Typhoon prototype. The airframe's overall outline is akin to that of P5219, but the radiator has been removed to directly under the nose. Power was provided by a Napier Sabre 1 with a 2,020-hp output. First flight was on 24 February 1940.

further bolstered when serious problems continued to arise during the Typhoon's early stage in operational service.

Into (Conditional) Service

The first batch of production Mk IA and IB airframes began to roll off the assembly lines at Hucclecote in September 1941 with No. 56 Squadron then at Duxford, the first recipient. Nos 266 and 609 Squadrons were second and third in line, but not until February–March 1942 did both receive their first Mk IAs. The Mk IA variant was no better equipped in firepower terms than the Mk IIB Hurricane, but plans had been in progress to outfit the design with four 20-mm cannon that would become a standard item and was duly initiated within this batch.

The fact that the RAF was still persisting with .303-calibre bullet ammunition when the *Jagdwaffe* and other air forces, including the USAAF, were regularly applying either cannon-calibre weaponry or, in the latter case, the much heavier .5 bullet was symptomatic of an overcautious view towards necessary change; this was despite the evidence already accrued from the air battles of 1940 that the punishment inflicted by the .303 held no guarantee of successfully bringing down an adversary.

By now, the Fw 190 had been making its superior presence felt in the skies over France and Belgium for several months, but any likelihood of the Typhoon joining in with the hard-pressed Mk V Spitfire was never destined to materialise. On the

The Mk IA Typhoon was equipped with twelve .303 machine guns, and R7579's starboard wing displays the bullet case ejection chutes. Some Mk IAs were subsequently retro-fitted with 20-mm cannon while the small windows on the cockpit fairing were deleted. The engine is a Napier Sabre rated at 2,100 hp compared to the 2,020 hp of the first prototype P5212's power plant.

other hand, the Typhoon's better performance at medium to low-level altitudes was an unconscious portent of problems for the *Jagdwaffe* in another sphere of operations—namely 'tip and run' raids along the Channel coast. In the interim period, the pilots manning the first batch of Typhoons faced a series of mandatory checks that could cost their pilots dear if not applied.

The first concerned the absolute need to wear an oxygen mask prior to start-up. Tests at the Air Fighting Development Unit (AFDU), Duxford, confirmed a dangerous level of carbon-monoxide seeping into the cockpit as soon as the engine started up. Bob Stanford-Tuck had experienced one of his 'lucky' incidents when serving with the unit. He had been about to take off on a test flight when he was called to the telephone. The Typhoon was already running-up and had to take-off soon to prevent the engine overheating, so Tuck almost ignored the call before being persuaded to do so. His place was taken by an Argentinian named Dack, who duly took off, only to be observed in a steep terminal dive not long after take-off. The autopsy of the shockingly limited body parts of the unfortunate pilot revealed a large carbon-monoxide content in the liver segment on hand.

The ever-uncertain weather patterns existing over the British Isles created regular wet and associated damp atmospheric conditions. This was normally no great impediment to start-up on other engine types such as the Merlin, but not so the twenty-four-cylinder Napier Sabre. The Coffman starter unit was apparently not powerful enough to guarantee automatic start-up. Consequently, the fuel–oil priming mix was changed to a 70–30 per cent level that was intended to prevent the fuel from washing the oil out of the cylinders during the priming action.

A mechanic attends to the massive Sabre engine fitted on Typhoons. The circular-shaped coolant header tank is positioned directly behind the propeller spinner. Tank had a capacity of 7¼ imperial gallons. (33 litres). The Sabre engine would prove to have a prolonged history of problems that were only generally solved by the latter stages of the war.

The Typhoon's oil tank was positioned directly ahead of the cockpit windshield and this aircraft's tank is being topped up by the mechanic on the left. Unfaired cannon barrels indicate an early-production Mk IB. Engine cowling panels are propped up against the wing leading edge. Note the black/white stripes that were a 'friendly fighter' indicator to Allied pilots unfamiliar with the design's appearance on operations.

Uneven running was another regular problem; the result of this was that the wear-effect upon the sleeve valves could cause them to jam, with the knock-on effect being an explosion within the relative cylinder. If this occurred at any stage in a flight, the almost certain result was total engine failure and the attendant need to bale out or attempt a crash-landing if the circumstances permitted. The latter option was not recommended over water, however. This was due to the large circular radiator scoop under the nose, whose presence could act as a 'drag' that would pull the fighter under the surface with little chance of its occupant evacuating safely in time.

A truly lethal problem that was beyond the control of the pilot concerned was the tendency for the tail section to become detached when the airframe was put under pressure in a dive. A distressing number of Typhoons were destined to be so affected, with an attendant extreme mortality rate among their hapless pilots. The ultimate cure would be the fitting of 'fish-plate' strips over the seam where the fuselage and tail sections were linked-up. However, elimination of elevator 'flutter' due to the mass-balance's location being altered would primarily cure this lethal situation.

'To See was to Live'

One of the absolute priorities for any fighter pilot was the ability to spot an adversary before he could move into a lethal strike position. In the case of the initial batches of Typhoons to come into service, there was a critical lack of a rearward clear view. The solid pylon fairing directly behind the pilot forming the rest of the cockpit structure imposed a dangerous limitation in this respect. In time, Hawkers would introduce Plexiglas panels within a frame outline that would go some way to solving the problem. However, the unconditional solution would only arrive during the production of subsequent Mk IB airframes during mid-1943 when a full-blown sliding canopy would replace both the pylon structure and the 'car door' outline around the pilot's seat.

The theory behind the construction of a solid pylon was asserted in some circles to be down to the perceived nature of future aerial combat when the design was first proposed. The high maximum speed up to the mid-400-mph level anticipated to be flown by the Typhoons were expected to render close-in encounters such as dogfights totally redundant since the fighter would never be able to be bounced—a scenario that would be rendered invalid by events from the very onset of the Second World War.

The designer team should have been aware of the true nature of fighter *v.* fighter combat that was still holding true to First World War experience, albeit at a faster pace even in 1939–40, when the prototypes were just making their initial flights. It would equally seem that they enjoyed ample time between then and the start of production in late 1941, within which to carry out the structural alteration. But the pressures of conflict and the need to establish an efficiently-functioning design as quickly as possible at the time of Britain's very survival likely overrode this seemingly marginal, but vital adjustment.

No. 56 Squadron was the first RAF Fighter Command unit to be equipped with the Typhoon. Two sections are taking up close formation and are probably heading out on an operational sortie. The narrow yellow identification stripes on the upper wings are seen on the two nearest aircraft, in addition to the black and white underwing stripes.

A Hesitant Union

The previous experience of the personnel manning the first three squadrons to convert onto the Typhoon had been with the Hurricane and Spitfire. Both these types were well-proven designs with a sound to good track record in aerodynamic and mechanical efficiency. When the airmen were made aware of the impending change, there was likely an initial curiosity regarding the still-unknown performance envelope of the Typhoon; doubtless the No. 56 Squadron contingent would have expected that Hawkers would have developed a fighter that was similar in overall manner to the Hurricane albeit in an enhanced form.

Their first sight of what was a 7-ton machine compared to the lighter-weight 'Hurri' must have caused them to hold back on judgement. As for the 'White Rose' and No. 266 Squadron pilots, the same experience must have arguably evinced more startling if not daunting reactions; compared to the almost dainty Supermarine machine, the new fighter presented a hulking if not brooding appearance with its bulky fuselage headed by an equally prominent radiator scoop and linked to massive thick-chord wings. The thought that the 'new kid on the block' could deliver even the same combat performance capability as its joint predecessors when weighing-in at almost twice the weight must have seemed rather doubtful to put it mildly (a similar reaction was voiced by pilots of the former trio of 'Eagle' squadrons transposed during late 1942 into the USAAF's

This picture depicts the original cockpit pattern for the Typhoon. The rear section is fixed in position with the radio mast in the centre. Exit from the cockpit in an emergency was not easy since all three panels enclosing the pilot had to be released; the pilot had to cross his arms to grasp the jettison handles in order to effectively carry out the procedure.

Compare the original cockpit pattern on the Typhoon with the revised canopy applied to later production batches of the Mk IB. Not only does the pilot have a better all-round vision, but the ability to jettison the sliding portion would provide a far better chance for a swifter as well as a safer bale out to be made.

4th Fighter Group when first sighting their intended and extremely bulky P-47 Thunderbolt replacements for their Mk V Spitfires).

The serviceability levels among the initial cadre of aircraft delivered to these squadrons was to prove frustratingly staccato to the point where serviceable numbers on any one day were minimal. The Sabre engines continued to cast up a plethora of problems. Failure to start-up after two of three attempts could lead to the mandatory replacing of the 'safety disc', cooling and reloading of the starter, and manual turning of the propeller with the fuel cock 'off' in order to expel excess fuel from the manifold and plugs—a time-consuming duty and one that left the offending Typhoon taking off late and thereby compromising prompt formation assembly.

The tremendous surge of power released when take-off was commenced was an issue causing concern among the pilots. Winding the rudder trim fully to the left did not automatically ensure the torque-effect, creating an incipient swing to starboard would be cancelled out; the result was that the fighter could easily assume a wayward angle of run that would witness a dangerous proximity to the runway edge before the control column eased the aircraft into the air. Engine vibration in flight was experienced regularly until the problem was traced to the propellers not being properly balanced; the pilot's seat was also adapted to a sprung-laden format in a bid to further reduce the vibration factor.

Two armourers are loading their Tiffie's port-side cannon by feeding the 20-mm belts into their boxes. Surface of the outer gun-bay cover shows the oval interior of the bulge that fitted over the visible ammunition-feed drum when the cover was closed.

A major problem encountered in the Sabre's function even after the Typhoon had entered operational service was cylinder sleeve distortion. The Napier products were often failing when still well short of the time span between mandatory major overhaul of the engine. The initial solution was found in the involvement of the Bristol Co., whose sleeve units used on the Bristol Taurus that enjoyed a lifespan several times more between major overhauls could be machine-adapted to Sabre requirements; a 'marriage' between Napier and English Electric as well as the import of specialist machine tools from the USA with which to bring the former-named Co.'s own products up to the proper efficiency level was also instrumental in stabilising the situation.

Points For

Flt Lt (later Wg Cdr) Roland 'Bee' Beamont was destined to become a leading proponent for the Typhoon's continued service on operations, especially after taking command of No. 609 Squadron in October 1942. He made his first flight on 8 March 1942 and recalled the difficulty in getting airborne without his aircraft adopting the aforementioned propensity for swinging to starboard. Once aloft, however, he felt at home in the air, with stability and control judged 'excellent' in his view, although a high noise-level accompanied by vibration was experienced in a sustained dive; the resultant zoom-climb to 15,000 feet was equally stable in execution.

On the other hand, gun-aiming stability appeared to be good even at higher speeds; the air pressure upon the control surfaces was also not likely to prove too inhibiting if pitch and roll manoeuvres were to be initiated in combat when flying at full throttle. The wide-track undercarriage made for a more relaxed landing run than the narrow-track equivalent on the Spitfire—something that the Battles of France and Britain veteran would never realise operationally since his Second World War experience would be exclusively centred on the Hurricane, Typhoon, and Tempest.

Although Beamont's reactions to the Typhoon's general performance were basically positive, they must be regarded as emanating from an operationally-experienced airman. A proportion of the pilots on the first squadrons were not anything like as versed in the art of airmanship as 'Bee', so their approach to the '7-ton monster' was generally cautious to the point of near-apprehension. Complaints about the heavy nature of the controls, the restricted view from the cockpit, and, most pertinent, the adverse performance at altitudes above 20,000 feet was common.

Nothing could be done in respect of the first complaint, while the question of adequate sighting from the cockpit would be corrected in time. As for the limitations on likely combat performance at higher altitudes, the pilots could not anticipate the fighter's redeployment from this perceived function to the lower-altitude functions of defensive and conversely daylight Intruder operations. Only time would establish the Typhoon's positive use in these joint

A view of the early Typhoon's 'car-door' fitting picks out the top canopy panel with its 'tear-drop' pattern that houses the rear-view mirror. Pilot's handgrip panel is open. W/T stencil at bottom left indicates bonding of the airframe and control surfaces that prevents static electrical build-up and ensures enhanced radio transmission and reception.

activities to which would be added a third and arguably most effective duty as a rocket-bearing ground attacker.

The lessons to be learned regarding the mediocre high-altitude performance of the Hawker fighter were taken on board following a series of 'sweeps' into which it was pitched. There was little need to confirm its limitations against the *Jagdwaffe* because it quickly became evident that it was being outpaced by the Spitfire element within the force dispatched, a fact that did not make for overall formation integrity as well as raising the risk of the enemy pilots exploiting any noticeable 'gap' within the overall ranks.

During this stage of its deployment, there were calls from some quarters for the entire project to be scrapped; it took the efforts of Beamont among others to champion the design's cause, but the first few months in operational service did not bode well for the continued presence of the Typhoon as a pure fighter. The resurrection to unhindered service could be said to originate from an outside source—the *Jagdwaffe* itself or more precisely those JG2 and JG26 *Staffeln* assigned to 'tip and run' attacks.

Many British towns 'sponsored' RAF aircraft during the war. The Borough of Sutton and Cheam's coat of arms is positioned on R8199, which went to No. 56 Squadron. This aircraft was sadly shot down on 1 June 1942—by Spitfires. 'Trestle Here' stencil is applied to the bottom of the fuselage band.

A Necessary Precaution

The standards of aircraft recognition whether expressed by ground observers or, even more important, by aircrew were never consistent, and in many cases, they verged on the dangerously abysmal. A case in point was the Blenheim and Ju 88, with the RAF bomber being shot at and sometimes downed in mistake for the *Luftwaffe* machine. A similar visual comparison between the Typhoon and Fw 190 might appear to cast up little problem in separate identity; the Sabre in-line against the BMW radial engine and the greater bulk of the Hawker fighter would appear to settle the issue.

However, there was enough quiet concern, not so much about misrecognition with the Fw 190, but rather the chances of 'friendly fire' being directed upon the still-unfamiliar machine by other RAF fighters or ground gunners, for distinct markings to be applied. The first introduced in November 1942 consisted of nothing more than white paint applied to the propeller spinner and forward engine cowling back to the wing-leading edges. Within a month, this order was cancelled, and the white removed in favour of four slender black stripes applied on each wing underside between the fuselage and aileron inner-line.

A further amendment requiring white alternate stripes between the black was quickly issued; this was probably deemed necessary, since the black stripes alone might not show up so distinctly. There was to be a number of occasions extending into 1943–44 when this visual 'signal' still did not prove sufficient for Allied pilots and AA

Although much larger, the Typhoon still bore a dangerous resemblance to the Fw 190. The initial attempt to mark the fighter as a friendly aircraft to Allied pilots is seen here. Narrow yellow bands are applied to the top and bottom wings in line with the inner cannon fairings. The non-slip surface on the wing root is almost worn away.

units to desist from opening fire, with some of the pilots so engaged being injured or killed in the process—reinforcing the accusation of poor aircraft recognition standards throughout the Anglo–American military ranks during the Second World War.

Compressibility: A Pointer to the Future

Air pressure, unlike water, is an invisible barrier militating against forward motion, although both enjoy the same restrictive force. As aircraft speeds built up to and beyond the 400–500-mph level in the course of the Second World War, so the still-unknown phenomenon of what would be acknowledged as compressibility began to make itself felt, though sadly at an initial cost in airframes and sometimes pilots. The Typhoon's powerful engine combined with its great weight was to bring the issue to the fore when the fighter was pushed into prolonged dives when flying around 30,000 feet and upwards.

The effect on the airframe varied from mild vibration to violent buffeting and change of trim as well as sharp pitching both up and down. The overall result was the loss of all ability to maintain control of the plummeting fighter until altitude was well below 20,000 feet and, in some extreme incident, even much lower. Having established with a test Typhoon that something was badly awry—the monitoring Hurricane pilot having noticed the wool tufts applied to the test fighter's airframe were flowing forward instead of backwards—further tests were initiated. 'Bee' Beamont experienced a truly vicious one when detached to Hawkers—ironically when testing for the cause of another failure, namely the current spate of tail structures becoming detached.

The steady equipping of squadrons assigned to the Typhoon during 1942 did not automatically exclude further use of the Mk IA. In No. 182 Squadron's case, the switch to the Tiffie included a few of the machine-gun bearing variant as seen here; the photo angle prevents identification of a specific airframe via the serial or aircraft letter.

In this instance, the tail remained intact, but as he headed down from around 30,000 feet, what was initially a steady, controllable descent developed into an apparent fight for survival. The controls stiffened as the fighter began an incipient urge to swing to port and the buffeting built up throughout the airframe. Two-handed pulling on the control column gained no positive response from the elevators while the port-inclined roll became more intense despite his attempt to similarly manipulate the ailerons. The engine was throttled fully back, but Beamont's sense of apprehension was only eased when, at around 15,000 feet, first the buffeting, then aileron response was eased and gained respectively.

When fully stabilised, he headed back and landed without incident, the airframe showing no sign of the pummelling it had endured. One post-flight comment related to his body temperature as 'no longer cold' compared to its chilled state when the dive was commenced. There appears to have been little or nothing that could have been done to promptly stabilise the fighter in such circumstances, so perhaps it was as well that the bulk of future Second World War operations would be conducted at altitudes away below the level where 'compressibility' was likely to be encountered.

Structural Crisis

The Typhoon's litany of technical problems extending from its very inception to an operational spread of many months attained a really frightening level between late 1941 and most of 1942. A rash of structural failures affecting the tail section occurred that involved around thirty aircraft and resulted in the deaths of virtually all the pilots concerned; the drastic aerodynamic imbalance resulting from these failures would cast the fighters into a gyrating manoeuvre that gave little chance for each occupant to evacuate safely from what was already a difficult cockpit frame to open quickly even in level flight.

The problem that was raised regardless of whether the aircraft was being sharply manoeuvred or flying in more sedate circumstances was thought to be the result of 'flutter', although the contention was challenged. However, the series of strengthening modifications to the fuselage and tailplane did not seem to halt the continuing run of failures whose cause was frustratingly unclear. Thankfully for all concerned on operational squadron service, the fault was latterly traced to the elevator mass balance or rather its position and the adverse manner of the airflow over its surface that contributed lethally to the 'flutter' build-up; once this was altered from an external to an internal location, the incidence of further failures fell away.

Mk IA/R7700 was used by A&AEE to test the 'fish-plate' tail strengtheners, seen as a dark shadow on the fuselage colour band. Plates were added to counteract the tendency for tail units to fracture at this point, reportedly due to extreme vibration induced by elevator flutter. Solid rear cockpit fairings on early Typhoons were replaced by the Plexiglas shape seen here.

Initial Operations

Nos 56, 266, and 609 Squadrons would form the kernel for Typhoon operations in the aircraft's original perceived role as a pure fighter during 1942. The three squadrons were dispersed between Duxford (Nos 266 and 609 Squadrons) and Snailwell (No. 56 Squadron), some 25 miles east. The delivery of Typhoons was very staccato, with No. 609, for example, experiencing a two-month delay until 1 May, when it possessed sixteen fighters, all but four Mk IA variants. Along with its sister unit, it formed the Duxford Wing, but nearly two months elapsed before it was regarded as worked-up sufficiently to anticipate active operations. Although only acquiring their initial cadre of fighters by the early spring, the first sorties by No. 56 were flown during June. The operational debut was unfortunate in that a 'friendly fire' incident involving No. 401 Squadron Spitfires resulted in two Typhoons and one pilot being lost. A further attack occurred the following month.

No. 266 had actually commenced operations in late May but continuing low levels of serviceability plagued its ranks and very few sorties were achieved until well into July when it linked up with No. 609 to commence wing-strength 'sweeps'. These operations were in turn largely plagued by failure to engage the *Jagdwaffe* until 19 August over Dieppe during Operation Jubilee. Even then, only one No. 609 Squadron pilot managed to claim shooting at a Fw 190. As for No. 266, its pilots were engaged by fighters—not Fw 190s but Spitfires, with the incident fortunately concluding without casualties. Clearly the outline comparison with the Fw 190 was confusing other RAF pilots and indeed would do so intermittently for the ensuing months of 1942 and right through 1943, when the 8th Fighter Command would initiate friendly-fire incidents.

There had been a small measure of success for No. 266 in August. One pilot had brought down a Me 210—probably the Epr.Kd. aircraft MIA over the sea on the 12th—while operating from Matlaske in Norfolk. The next day witnessed a radar-directed interception against another EprKd.210 Me 210 engaged in maritime reconnaissance that similarly ended with the aircraft crashing into the North Sea. A fellow squadron recently converted from Hurricanes to Typhoons (No. 1) had been posted to Acklington in Northeast England during July, from where the conversion from Hurricane Mk IIC to the Typhoon took place. The location promised little action with several hundreds of North Sea miles to be traversed, but on 6 September, the *Luftwaffe* obliged when what were identified as two 16/KG6 Me 210s, Willi Messerschmitt's latest creation and a basically flawed predecessor to the Me 410, was intercepted by Plt Off. T. Bridges and Sgt D. Perrin.

The latter pilot closed quickly in a dive upon Fw. H. Mosques's aircraft that sustained multiple strikes and whipped over on its back to descend into the ground minus the crew; unfortunately, parachute failure cost both men their lives. Meanwhile, the climbing turn to starboard adopted by Obltn. W. Maurer (*Staffelkapitän*) initially held his assailant at an out-of-range distance, but he forfeited the advantage by then reversing this manoeuvre into a dive. Bridges was

No. 609 (White Rose) Squadron's move to Manston in late 1942 coincided with Wg Cdr 'Bee' Beamont's assumption of command. Under him, the unit indulged in nocturnal operations with railroad targets a priority. The name MAVIS is applied in script ahead of the cockpit. Parallel rows of nine locomotive markings above the walkway attest to its pilot's penchant for shooting up this form of transport! Picture was shot in May 1943.

R8224 was a Mk IB that served with No. 56 Squadron before transfer to No. 609 Squadron. Aircraft is being refuelled from a tractor-towed fuel bowser. The wing bears a variation in its friendly aircraft stripes, since there are normally four black and three white stripes. Dark colour on spinner is seemingly applied in a wavy pattern.

able to use his fighter's faster acceleration rate to close the gap, and the result was the firing-up of one engine and a trail of structural debris. The stricken aircraft also crashed, but by then, both crewmembers had safely parachuted, although Maurer was fortunate to survive his immersion in the sea thanks to pick-up by a lifeboat.

Leading the Way

No. 609 Squadron witnessed the slowest entry into combat with the Hawker fighter, but it was arguably destined to receive the most attention during the Second World War, as well as in terms of post-war publicity; this was no reflection upon any other Typhoon-based unit but rather followed the dictates of media exposure. Although launching the first sorties in July and August, the pace of operations then stagnated, apart from which standby patrols became the squadron's 'bread and butter' until October. It was around this point that an officer famously associated with the Typhoon's development and who would also be fighting vigorously and finally successfully for its continued deployment arrived to take over command—'Bee' Beamont (his predecessor was Sqn Ldr Paul Richey who had fought gallantly with No. 1 Squadron during the Battle of France).

The mix of operations other than in the high-altitude fighter role originally considered for the Typhoon really began to take shape during late 1942. The concept of Rhubarb sorties was deemed to suit the design; not only could it strike with speed and accuracy compared to the Hurricane while delivering a weight of assault with its cannon, but the activity was equally capable of being launched by night as opposed to the current daylight method of approach. Beamont's pilots largely expressed concern regarding operating by night over enemy territory—probably due to the uncertainty of regaining home soil if any of the design's current technical problems manifested themselves during a sortie—but events saw a gradual change of mind among their ranks.

Reasonably clear or moonlit skies was a usual prerequisite for nocturnal operations if suitable targets were to be picked out and approached at a distance where the pilot would have time to properly focus his gunsight and line up for attack. Whereas daytime operations merited a low-level crossover into enemy territory to avoid the defences, the night-time equivalent was made at around 10,000 feet before descending to the recommended search altitude of between 1,000 and 2,000 feet that provided the best compromise between picking out details at a long enough range to deliver the assault.

A favoured target type was locomotive-hauled traffic in both passenger and freight terms; the former category was included since the civilian populations in the occupied countries were excluded from travel due to curfew restrictions. The locomotive drivers and firemen in charge of the locomotives were generally civilian staff, but their lives were unfortunately secondary to interdicting the German transport system as well as a sad reflection on the priorities of fighting and winning a conflict.

In a further move to avoid misidentification by Allied fighter pilots, the propeller spinner and forward engine cowling on early production Typhoons was sprayed white. This gave way in November–December 1942 to black and white stripes under the wings. In this instance, the anonymous Mk IB bears both variations.

One advantage compared to the Spitfire was the solid-wing structure that provided a steady platform for the cannon shells' discharge. The slender and therefore more flexible Spitfire equivalent was deficient in this respect, apart from which only two cannon-calibre weapons were generally mounted despite the aircraft having provision for four gun bays. A further advantage was in respect of range. Whereas the Spitfire's internal fuel capacity was 85 gallons, the equivalent figure for the Typhoon was 140 gallons, a total that allowed an appreciably greater penetration of the enemy hinterland with the attendant increase in vulnerability to assault in geographic terms.

Beamont had led the way in this operational sphere. The attack run was normally concentrated upon the locomotive, whose boiler was extremely vulnerable to puncture and likely explosion from the solid punch delivered by four 20-mm cannon, after which the entire train-length was rendered stationery and ripe for follow-up assault. The Germans being aware of the situation regularly attached flatbed wagons bearing 20-mm flak guns. Their firepower was a constant threat that had to be accommodated but could be largely thwarted by fast, low approaches. Attacking in pairs further divided the defensive effort.

No. 486 Squadron

The entry of No. 486 Squadron, a New Zealand-established unit, into the combat lists with the Typhoon tends to be overshadowed by the emphasis on No. 609 Squadron's parallel activities. Conversion from the Hurricane to the Typhoon occurred around June; the previous two months had seen the pilots co-operating with the Turbinlite Havocs in what was to be an overall failure in the attempt to combat nocturnal *Luftwaffe* bombers. The promise of a switch to regular daylight operations must have pleased the personnel, although their enthusiasm would surely have been tempered in similar manner to the other squadrons regarding their mounts' current problems.

By the beginning of October, the squadron was stationed at Tangmere on the Channel coast, a primary location for making interceptions of the 'tip and run' assaults. On the 17th, 10 (*Jabo*) JG26 dispatched a *Schwarm* from Saint-Omer, with the town of Hastings as the target. The strike was completed, and the pilots turned for home, only to be suddenly confronted by the Tangmere Typhoons. Three managed to escape, but Fw. Carl Niesel's Fw 190A-4 was hauled from the sky to descend fatally into the sea. His loss was the first of several fighters claimed before the year's end by No. 486 as well as No. 609; the A-4 variant's state-of-the-art performance with water-methanol power boost enhancing low- to medium-altitude engine output was seemingly availing it little against its RAF adversary, although the margins between successful and failed interception was to prove ever small during the remaining several months of this attack pattern before the activity was permanently dropped by the *Luftwaffe* High Command.

An interesting variation in the victim types being successfully downed by the Typhoon squadrons related to the *Luftwaffe*'s long-range reconnaissance (*Fernaufklärung*) Bf 109F. On 17 December, No. 486 Squadron pilots reportedly engaged two during what were separate sorties by 4(F)123 fighters and shot both down. The fact that both were engaged in this function would suggest they might have been flying at medium to high altitude where their adversaries' performance advantage would arguably not have been so sound. On the other hand, such operations could also be indulged in at low level; this being the case, the Typhoon would have had the edge in these engagements. This was not the only occasion in which the specialist Bf 109Fs would be successfully intercepted.

Critical Meeting

The series of meetings at Fighter Command in 1942–43 culminated with one in January at which the die was finally cast on the Typhoon's future. 'Bee' Beamont, who had flown the fighter while on detachment to Hawkers, appeared to be the main if not sole supporter for the design. Arrayed against him were a number of colleagues and superiors at group and command level who were pushing for its exclusion in favour of continued Spitfire production. On the face of it, the Supermarine fighter held the cards in terms of proven success compared to the Typhoon's technical- and operationally-chequered history to date.

Beamont pointed out the virtues of the Typhoon in matching or outpacing the Spitfire—a performance that outflew the Bf 109 and Fw 190 in terms of speed and that also provided a greater range capability; easy to fly and docile in

This Mk IB is heavily damaged on its starboard stabiliser and vertical fin. It is an early-production aircraft as confirmed by the V-pattern rudder mass balance below the fin flash. Note the tail wheel's plain surface compared to the anti-shimmy pattern carried by most Typhoons.

Yet another Mk IB that never entered RAF operational service, R7881 was used for experimental purposes as a night-fighter prototype by the RAE. The propeller diameter of 14 feet did not allow for much ground clearance, especially on take-off.

landing approach; rugged in withstanding damage; and a better weapons platform internally and externally. Even so, the technical problems that still persisted and seemed to provide no guarantee of being corrected would appear to have thwarted all his attempts to sustain the fighter in service in the eyes of its detractors—that is, with the important exception of AM Leigh-Mallory, now C-in-C Fighter Command, who gave the 'green light' for its continued service.

Leigh-Mallory's decision seems to have been somewhat ambivalent when given his tendency for cautious advancement. After all, the need for continued build-up in Spitfire strength had been pushed by him in the past—so why persist with an aircraft that was already deemed redundant as a superiority fighter? Whether he had been influenced by Beamont's enthusiastic pitch in similar manner to Bader's regarding the 'Big Wing' concept being clearly superior to AVM Park's more scaled-down disposal of his fighters in 1940 remains a moot point. Whatever the facts, the way ahead for a positive operational future beckoned tantalisingly at this stage (in contrast to the limitations inherent in the 'Big Wing' concept, the Typhoon's revised role would be steadily and finally fully proven over the remainder of the Second World War).

'Tip and Run' Countermeasure

The initiation of *Jabo* strikes against targets along the Channel during 1942 had witnessed the overall advantage going to the attackers. Their low and fast approach provided little warning to the defences; their attacks were accordingly delivered with little or no hindrance from Fighter Command whose fighters comprised mainly of the Spitfire Mk V were hard-pressed to close with their opponents even when managing to make interceptions that proved to be relatively few in number.

The physical destruction wrought by these raids known as 'tip and run' were not too serious, but the morale effect upon the civilian population was arguably of a depressing nature given that they inevitably suffered injured and fatal casualties with basically non-industrial coastal towns such as Folkestone and Eastbourne being among the locations targeted. The attacks commencing in early 1942 also added to what was a very gloomy period for Britain in military terms with reverses in North Africa and the Far East as well as the ultra-critical Battle of the Atlantic, whose loss would certainly impinge upon the very survival of the Allied bid for victory.

Nos 486 and 609 Squadrons' arrival on the south coast during October signalled a renewed determination to at least blunt the effect of the assaults if nothing else. On 31 October, the mass raid on Canterbury led to minimal casualties among the JG26 ranks thanks to low cloud conditions that in turn thwarted the RAF's defensive effort. The London strike the following 20 January was much more severely punished although the Typhoon's contribution was more directed against the Bf 109 'cover' force than the second-wave of attackers. No. 266 Squadron had arrived on the Channel coast further west around the same time with the

R8884/HF: L, seen at Gatwick on 20 April 1943, provides a fine study of an early Typhoon. Aircraft bears a solid radio mast and unfaired forward cannon-barrel sections. Full friendly fighter stripes are applied under the wings along with yellow upper-wing stripes level with the inner cannon barrels. This No. 183 Squadron fighter was SOC on 16 August 1943.

intention of supplementing Fighter Command's general cover against attacks by either JG2 or JG26.

The continuing pattern of low-level approach and departure from the selected target location was to prove difficult to counter and almost as much reliance was placed upon the AA defences to at least blunt if not repulse the *Jagdwaffe* raiders. The gunners scored two kills against JG26 within six days, beginning on 15 January. A raid against the town of Rye was intended to be conducted by the *Jabo Schwarm*, but operational and technical problems on the first two occasions forced a return and reloading. The third attempt was successful for all but one of the 3/JG26 escort; Uffz. H. Bremer's Fw 190 was fatally struck as the force approached and descended into the sea. The other loss appears to have been Ltn. H. Hoch, recorded in *Geschwader* records as a victim of 'light flak' that day.

The records at this time confirm the risks other than fighters or AA fire that were attendant upon low-flying 'strikes'. On the 4th, during a raid on Winchelsea, Fw. H. Muller's fighter had one wing impact with what was described as an overhead cable—probably a power line; the scant altitude and violent manoeuvre described by the aircraft provided no opportunity for him to bale out before the inevitable crash and disintegration of the airframe.

The incidence of successful RAF interceptions was never to rise above a small, if steady level, but this was of little consolation for the *Jagdwaffe* pilots concerned.

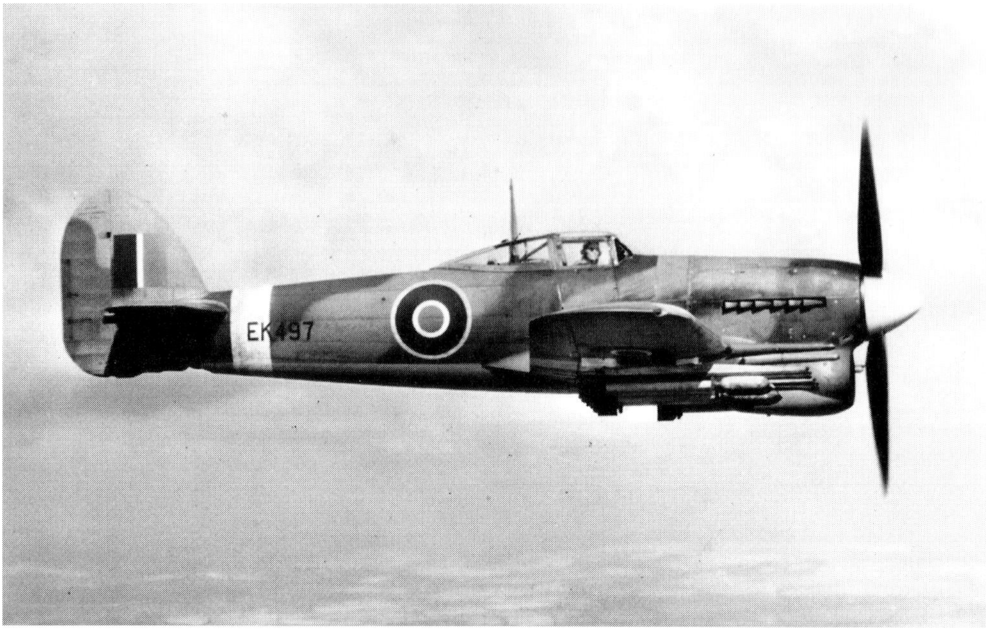

EK497's operational debut was delayed until October 1944 as it was first utilised by Boscombe Down for external stores trials as seen in this picture. It was released for service with No. 183 Squadron that by the aforementioned month was located at Ursel (B.67) in Belgium. Its ultimate fate was cruel; during the *Jagdwaffe* mass attack on 1 January 45 (Operation *Bodenplatte)*, Fg Off. D. Webber was engaged and shot down—by a USAAF P-51.

In mid-February (the 14th), III/JG2 dispatched a small force to shoot up a reported flotilla of Royal Navy MTBs operating off Cap Gris-Nez. Their progress had been picked up by radio-intercept and No. 609 'scrambled' accordingly. The resultant combat over the warships ended narrowly in the RAF's favour, with a trio of Fw 190s joining two Typhoons in their watery graves.

Twenty-four hours later, with the RAF Circus bombers attempting to bomb what was officially described as a merchant blockade runner named *Tōjō* berthed in Dunkirk but was confirmed post-war as the night-fighter control vessel *Tōgō*—an action supplemented by the B-24s of the 44 BG—Uffzs K. Bruhn and J. Kemper from 7/JG26 were fatally involved in the air battle surrounding the USAAF raid with Spitfires from Nos 331 or 332 (Norwegian) Squadrons adjudged the victor.

The following week saw Ltn. H. Thiessen (8/JG26) and Uffz. E. Wilkemeier (III/JG54) failing to withstand the challenge posed by No. 609 Squadron Typhoons. The next day (the 27th), the Kenley Wing ran into III *Gruppe* away out over the North Sea; a No. 402 or 403 Squadron flight swooped on the 5 *Staffel* element who flew on woodenly and paid the price. Ltn. K. Mueller-Goebs, an acolyte pilot, never survived what was his inaugural combat sortie, and Uffz. H. Gomann was very fortunate to bale out at minimal altitude and survive the potentially terminal descent.

Although the loss scale among the marauding *Jagdwaffe* pilots during March hardly attained a double-figure level, there was one major casualty among the *Jabo* element of JG26. Obltn. Paul Keller, the 10/JG54 *Staffelkapitän*, led fifteen fighters to an attack on Ashford. His action in shooting-up a fuel truck rebounded fatally when the concussion wave or metal fragments touched off his bomb. The senior loss towards the month's end was preceded by a concentrated loss pattern over four days in mid-month. On the 11th, a mid-air collision with an unidentified companion sent III/JG54's Fw. A. Stern to his death. Fw. E. Bosch, a 10 (*Jabo*) pilot, was caught by two No. 609 Squadron Typhoons and downed off Dunkirk during return from a raid the next day. The daily tally continued with Obfw. H. Meyer falling to a Kenley Wing Spitfire and the grim sequence concluded on the 14th when Ltn. E. Haehne collided fatally with a No. 340 (French) Squadron Spitfire.

No. 1 Squadron had transferred from Acklington to Biggin Hill in March but moved again to Lymnpe on the Channel coast soon after to participate in the 'tip and run' counter action. While at Biggin, two kill claims were submitted for an interception on 13 March, neither of which appear to have been confirmed against JG26 records, although JG2 was probably the suffering unit. A more positive note was struck on 9 April when a single section linked up with No. 611 Squadron. The patrol's eastward path along the French coast encountered several Fw 190s hovering over one of their motorboats seeking Uffz. K. Heck, previously downed by a No. 609 Squadron pilot. The resultant short, but sharp combat ended three to nil in the RAF's favour. Two Fw 190s were taken out by the No. 611 contingent. The third flown by Ltn. O. Backhaus was the victim of Sgt R. Hornall; the wheels were seen to descend before the fighter snapped on to one side, with the pilot vacating the cockpit, but he did not survive the loss to join his two fellow pilots in death.

Tip and Run's Culmination

The final months in which the coastal towns of Southern Britain in particular were subjected to regular low-level assault was May–June, and the results were somewhat mixed for the *Luftwaffe* marauders. The damage and casualties inflicted were sometimes heavy, but the defenders enjoyed a degree of success with the AA gunners thinning the enemy ranks on occasion. On the 30th, the twenty-one-strong SKG10 formation swept in towards Torquay, but it was met by a hail of gunfire that fatally crippled three Fw 190s while two more pilots failed to return, with one recorded as involved in a mid-air collision.

One of the AA victims sadly became the catalyst for an unforced tragedy. Gefr K. Laue's 5 *Staffel* aircraft that was mortally-damaged and inexorably sagging out of the sky impacted with the roof of a church within which children were engaged in a Sunday school gathering. Laue's bomb became detached and dropped squarely onto the building, killing twenty-one of the hapless youngsters while the equally hapless pilot died in the shattered wreckage of his fighter that had ploughed into a group of houses, leaving one woman with severe burns, but not adding to the death toll.

This Mk IB from No. 1 Squadron at Tangmere suffered engine failure on take-off. The intact propeller indicates the landing gear collapsed only when it became entangled with the barbed-wire around the airfield perimeter. The damage was extensive enough for salvage action to be declared. Incident occurred during June 1943.

The coastline of Suffolk and Norfolk witnessed regular assaults upon several seaside towns, with Yarmouth and Lowestoft the main targets either for aircraft jettisoning their loads or, in this instance, selected for the latest low-level assault. Yarmouth had suffered heavily from III/SKG10's depredations on the 7th and 11th. The next day, the unit dispatched twenty-five Fw 190s from the *Gruppe* to attack the latter location. The force was sighted as it approached, but cable damage prevented the sirens being sounded. Within minutes, fifty-five people were either dead or seriously injured and many commercial buildings or houses were destroyed or damaged to add to the already sorely-tried town's structures.

Three days later, the latest dose of intended punishment was thankfully diverted by the interim delivery of a sizeable number of barrage balloons that thwarted the enemy pilots, but did not prevent a good proportion from turning away and venting their spleen against an alternate location along the coast. The East Anglian population would have had no insight into the imminent and permanent cessation of the low-level threat by day; SKG10's services were required to bolster its fellow units based in the Mediterranean, now that victory in North Africa had been confirmed during May with all that implied for a planned invasion of the Island of Sicily.

Further south at Bournemouth (23 May), a devastating SKG10 raid in human and material terms still cost the unit two fighters along with a further

A Mk IB displays a 44-gallon tank sprayed medium sea grey on the wing pylon. The cannon barrels appear to be in different colours and their apertures are blanked off. The exhaust stubs have a shallow plinth surround but these were often removed in combat.

two involved in attacking adjacent Hastings. As late as 1–2 June, II *Gruppe* recorded successive daily losses over British soil. One was to unknown causes at Ipswich, the other to Fg Off. Davies piloting a No. 609 Squadron Typhoon—a fitting tribute to the Hawker design's efforts at helping to at least stem, if not reverse the tide of these attacks. From this point on, the *Geschwader*'s presence in northern skies would be encountered by night, there to meet the challenge of the more immediate and effective cover provided by the command's night fighters.

The 'Bombphoon'

The potential of the Typhoon other than as a fighter was recognised fairly early in its operational career. The sturdy Hurricane airframe had lent itself to the carriage of bombs up to 500 lb in weight for the Mk IIB variant and armed with these weapons attacks were made on various land and seaborne targets during 1941–42. However, the inability to extend the design's performance envelope coupled with fairly limited range proved to be inhibiting factors in the fighter's use in this capacity, although sorties were to prove a regular feature as late as the winter of 1943–44.

The Typhoon by comparison promised not only a better performance with which to survive on operations; the solid-wing structure also permitted the carriage of much heavier bombs up to 1,000 lb, hence the creation of the 'Bombphoon', as the aircraft became known by the media if not also subsequently by the squadrons assigned the duty. The first squadron formed in September 1942 was No. 181, quickly followed by Nos 182 and 183. By the year's end, no less than seven squadrons were either operational or working up to this level. The intention to bear bombs up to 500 lb in calibre was currently thwarted by a production shortage as all stocks were understandably being allocated to Bomber Command, but the supply situation would attain a level where both command requirements could be accommodated. A future extension to the carriage of the 1,000-lb weapon would also be achieved. This ability to carry externally-mounted weaponry was also the first stage in the Tiffie's ground-assault operational function that would culminate with its use as a rocket-firing platform.

Airfields were a regularly briefed target type with locations in France and the Low Countries favoured for assault. The intention behind these attacks was twofold: to maintain pressure upon the *Jagdwaffe* units with a view to depleting their strength and/or destroying their ground support facilities; and in doing so, restrict the enemy pilots' ability to direct their forces not only against the medium bomber squadrons but, from mid-1943 onwards, against the B-17s and B-24s of the 8th Bomber Command as they faced ever-longer missions into central Europe. The extended periods flown without Allied escort at this stage of the Second World War left the bomber gunners with ever-diminished firepower on the return route so any measure to cut down on *Jagdwaffe* activity was to the USAAF crews' benefit.

The carriage of a maximum bomb load that was reaching up in weight towards any of the medium bomber types in Anglo–American service meant that attacks against those of a purely industrial nature could also be indulged. After all, the 1,000-lb bomb was the second largest in the USAAF bomber's current arsenal with which they were carrying out their strategic brief; the delivery of this type of bomb would accordingly provide an equally effective form of striking power upon factories, shipbuilding yards, or similar sources of a strategic or tactical nature.

Anti-shipping sorties provided another target variation. The swift approach of the fighters against what were generally slow-moving vessels would appear to hand the advantage to the attackers. However, this advantage was eroded by the presence of flak guns either on the merchant ships or their escorts, the latter custom-built for the defensive duty that could lay down an often-lethal weight of counter fire. With this in mind, attacks were usually initiated in pairs with each approaching in train; the first bearing no bombs would use its cannon to distract or disable the target ship's gunners in order to allow its companion the chance to strike with minimal or no interference. The bombs were released in a manner that would 'skip' them off the water surface and into the hull when the three-second fuse delay would (hopefully) expend itself at the point of impact.

A close view of a No. 183 Squadron Mk IB Typhoon clearly depicts the revised 'bubble' cockpit canopy that was the main external difference from the original fixed-frame unit. The fixed radio mast has given way to the flexible 'whip' aerial behind the cockpit, but what is the penultimate Typhoon in outward appearance still requires the change from a three-blade to four-blade propeller.

Cut and Thrust

No. 3 Squadron, having now converted onto the Typhoon, had re-entered the combat scene on 16 May, a quiet debut that was brutally dispelled on its third sortie forty-eight hours on. A raid on Poix airfield succeeded in its intention, but the formation headed home at low level instead of climbing to meet its No. 486 Squadron escort. This was to prove very costly after a group of Bf 109Gs from I/JG27 descended upon their adversaries and took down no less than four Typhoons, a fifth falling to flak, leaving only three to get clear. Seven weeks later, a second mauling was suffered during a Roadstead off the Dutch coast; this time round, Fw 190 elements of JG2 that included two *Experten* (aces) shot down a further three.

By mid-year, no less than fifteen Tiffie squadrons were operational from coastal airfields in Southern Britain. The constant and variable types of assaults ranging from Ramrod to Roadstead added to the overall pressure placed upon the enemy defenders, albeit at a steady cost that added up to sixty-six fighters and a proportion of their pilots in the four months ending 30 September. The low- to medium-level nature of many sorties naturally invited lethal attention from flak, but the still-formidable *Jagdwaffe* made its joint presence felt as evidenced by No.

A group of seven pilots along with fellow aviators and the occasional ground crewmembers are gathered in front of an anonymous squadron Typhoon. The collar-and-tie attire of the majority suggest a non-operational flight is involved. The restrictive nature of the clothing item would dangerously inhibit head movement in combat; another danger was collar shrinkage, leading to strangulation if the individual should end up in the sea.

3 Squadron's torrid experience among others. The human cost left the command structure short of two wing leaders and nine squadron COs among those declared killed or MIA.

Surviving the 'Beast'

The Typhoon's airframe conferred a mix of good and bad fortune for those pilots involved in accidents whether over land or sea. In the former case, there would be a sizeable number of crashes where partial or almost total disintegration of the aircraft would seem to have left the pilot with marginal chances of escaping serious injury or death. What was arguably an extreme example concerned a fighter that was making its landing approach to a Kent airfield during August 1943.

Regarding himself as too close to the preceding fighter, the pilot inadvertently stalled due to pulling up the nose. The resultant cartwheel action tore one wing and the entire engine away, while the fuselage immediately behind the seat also separated. The truncated fuselage section came to rest up in the air with the seat against the airfield surface—as for the pilot, he was assisted from the remnant with no more than shock and a few bruises. On 26 January 1944, a power loss just after take-off from Lymnpe and subsequent contact with a concrete defence post inflicted almost the same damage scale on FS H. Bletcher's Tiffie, but he also emerged intact.

There were similar cases of disintegrated airframes so drastically affected where the occupant survived, although not always so physically intact as shown above. Even when cases arose where the fighter had become inverted in the course of the incident, the occupant was as likely to emerge alive as to end up on a morgue slab. The Tiffie may well have been regarded as somewhat of an unpredictable machine, but the robustness of its airframe was the basis for likely survival in circumstances that would not be guaranteed for those operating on many of its fighter contemporaries.

In contrast, the chances of safely ditching a Typhoon generally ranged from minimal to nil. The primary reason for this normally terminal action could be traced to the large air intake located directly behind and below the propeller. The initial contact of the intake with the sea automatically drew the nose downwards to induce a diving action that totally submerged the entire airframe within seconds, thereby granting the pilot little chance to get out before being dragged

The engine, fuselage directly behind the pilot seat, and starboard wing have been torn away after the Typhoon stalled-out and cartwheeled to its destruction at New Romney in August 1943. A fitting testimony to the inherent strength of what remained lies in the fact that the pilot survived the incident—physically, if not also psychologically.

The Mk I Tempest prototype HM599 utilised the engine destined to become the Sabre IV. The clean nose underside is due to the radiators being accommodated in both wing roots; it also bears a sliding canopy that would become a standard Tempest feature, unlike the radiator design that would revert to the 'chin' position as seen on HM595.

under and smothered. However, there were—sadly not so many, but occasional—instances where the occupant did survive the experience.

In late September 1943, Flt Lt Charles Brayshaw had taken off on a sortie and had barely cleared the Channel coast when all power was lost; the Typhoon sagged sharply downward to strike the sea and promptly sink, taking the now-unconscious pilot with it. Brayshaw fortunately came-to quick enough to release his harness, detach the cockpit flexible panels, and swim upwards to the surface where he was plucked out by a fishing boat. It is likely the sea depth was not too deep for him to avoid being drowned, but fortune still played a major part in his survival.

The Typhoon's Successor

What was intended as an aerodynamically-refined version of the Typhoon to be titled the Mk II was first mooted as early as 1940. The primary alteration related to the wing structure that was intended to be thinner-sectioned and laminar-flow in design; it would also possess a semi-elliptical plan form in contrast to the tapered rectangular pattern borne by the Typhoon. The shallower depth forced a change in fuel tank disposition from total containment within the wings to an extra 76-gallon header tank unit. The need to lengthen the overall nose section to accommodate the tank in turn forced aerodynamic stability adjustments; these took the form of expanded stabiliser/elevator surfaces and a curved fairing for the fin/fuselage junction.

Another initial refinement was the replacing of the chin-mounted radiator unit with twin units extending along the inner-wing leading edges, similar to those on the Mosquito. However, these did not record any measurable increase in efficient function and so a return to the standard nose location was introduced on the first Mk V prototype; this was HM595 that still displayed its original Typhoon lineage with its 'car-door' cockpit and fin retained at least initially. The main external Tempest V features, such as the 'bubble' canopy, fin-fairing, and 'chin' radiator cover, would later be adopted. The Mk V version of what was finally retitled the Tempest was preceded by the following five variants: Mk I powered by a Sabre IV (HM599); Mk II powered by a Bristol Centaurus (LA602 and LA607); Mk III powered by a Griffon IIB (LA610); and Mk IV powered by a Griffon 61 (LA614).

However, development problems with the Sabre IV caused delays in its final availability, and although the Centaurus was to prove an efficient power source for what emerged as the Tempest Mk II, its availability was far too late to meet the required current deadline. As for the two Griffon-powered variants, the respective allocation of the IIB to the Mk XII Spitfire and Griffon 61 to its Mk XIV successor was the likely reason why Hawker axed both projects.

So it was that the Sabre II-powered Mk V came to the fore more by default than by logical choice. HM595 first took to the air in September 1942, but it was the following June before the first production airframe (JN729) followed it into flight. By then, the chosen armament of four Hispano Mk V 20-mm cannon was fitted. These featured a much shorter external barrel length of 8 inches compared to the Typhoon; however, even this aerodynamic excrescence was completely eliminated with the introduction of the Series 2, whose reduced length could be completely accommodated within the wings.

The shape of even better things to come. The prototype Tempest Mk V HM595 is seen at Hawker's airfield at Langley during September 1942. The transition to its ultimate distinctive outline compared to its predecessor is still to evolve since it bears the Typhoon's fixed canopy structure and fin and rudder.

Performance comparison tests against the Mustang III, Mk XIV Spitfire, Bf 109G, and Fw 190A revealed a speed gain below 20, 000 feet of between 15 and 20 mph that was reversed by the first two designs at higher altitudes but only equalled or not matched by the respective *Jagdwaffe* examples. Turning circle by comparison was inferior to the two Allied fighters but was similarly equalled or exceeded in the case of the German duo. The roll rate was the least satisfactory aspect, especially regarding the Fw 190 that was already known for its superlative function in this respect. Only the Bf 109G was equalled in the action, while 350 mph was a minimum-required figure beyond which the Spitfire could be effectively challenged. Finally, zoom climb and dive performance was also superior, and since the Tempest would not be fighting its own kind, the ability to take on and best the Bf 109G and Fw 190 in general boded well for the Tempest's operational future.

A full plan view of HN599 from below demonstrates the manner in which the radiator frames extend forward from the main wing pattern. Also obvious is the distinct change in the wing shape from the Typhoon's tapered rectangular outline to one more in common with the Spitfire.

13
From Nocturnal Defence

Home Defence

The conclusion to the 1940–41 *Blitz* on British cities coincided with the now steady upsurge in Beaufighter numbers. What was proving to be a superb state-of-the-art night fighter had already made its presence felt among the ranks of the *Luftwaffe*'s nocturnal raiders; on the other hand, the numbers of victims falling to the Beau's fearsome array of machine-gun and cannon-calibre weapons had resulted in little more than putting the smallest dent in the offensive's effectiveness. By May, when Hitler switched his attention away from Britain in anticipation of striking at Soviet Russia, the number of squadrons operating on the Bristol twin had only grown to six, although five other units would carry out conversion by the following January; one of the latter, No. 406, was formed on 10 May, hours ahead of what was to signal the *Blitz*'s ghastly official climax over London.

The onrush into Soviet Russia had naturally involved the wholesale transfer of many *Luftwaffe* units away from Western Europe to a figure that left nine *Gruppen* compared to the original figure of fifty. A further dilution in aircraft numbers for continuing any direct assault on British cities involved five *Gruppen* being reassigned to maritime duties, although these could be switched back to the campaign if deemed necessary. Of course, maritime operations did include attacks on merchant shipping and minelaying in British sealanes, activities that added to the 'blockade' aspect of the overall assault upon Britain as exemplified by the U-boat campaign.

The odds against penetrating the enemy hinterland with impunity were accordingly stacking up against the *Luftwaffe* crews tasked with maintaining the bombing campaign. Not only were the night fighter and even AA gun numbers increasing, but the GCI and gun-laying equipment on respective hand for the RAF and Army were presenting a more formidable barrier to even attaining, let alone returning safely from, their targets. The period of an aerial 'happy times' was fading away and would become just a permanent memory.

NF Mk II DZ750 came off the Hatfield production line in the winter of 1942–43 after the revised night-fighter colour scheme was mooted; however, she still retains the RDM 2A special night colour that highlights the national markings. Service with four operational units followed by two spells at OTUs culminated in the aircraft crashing at Cranfield on 25 April 1945—the author's seventh birthday.

The Mk IV Hurricane was basically identical to the Mk IID but featured the 'universal' wing structure that enabled a range of external equipment to be borne with no adjustments required to either the armament circuits or fuel system. The slim lines of the 40-mm cannon are clearly displayed. No. 164 Squadron was one of six to take on the variant in June 1943, but by February 1944, the Hurricanes were gone from service over north-western Europe, with the Typhoon taking over.

A further limitation in safe transit was the searchlight provision that was linked with night-fighter operations. The individual sets were arranged in huge 'boxes' extending many miles in breadth and depth. Night-fighter crews would position themselves above a searchlight within each 'box'; when a bomber was caught in the 'box', it would be homed-in upon visually, but the radar operator would still maintain his electronic 'contact' in order to ensure making final interception should the prey escape the beams.

This procedure unknowingly mirrored the original German technique known as '*Helle Nachtjagd*' ('illuminated night-fighting') that also involved searchlight-assisted interception. On the other hand, the German lack until 1941–42 of both GCI systems, as well as the *Freya* and *Würzberg* ground radar equipment, placed absolute reliance on interception guidance by visual means alone.

Turbinlite Operations—A Redundant Fiasco?

Mingled among the more logical methods of airborne interception was at least two schemes, the first of which, launched during the *Blitz*, verged upon the edge of desperation if not madness. Code-named 'Mutton', the plan was to use aircraft in the 'sowing' of aerial mines with the intended aim of presenting a lethal barrier to the *Luftwaffe* bombers' progress. No. 93 Squadron was the major source for carrying out the sorties, using obsolescent Harrow twin-engined transports and later Havocs. The vast area to be covered even by a full squadron of aircraft clearly provided little chance of success; operations extended from late 1940 until April 1941, when all operations ceased.

The second scheme might have held some merit had it been launched at the beginning of or even during the *Blitz*, but instead it was brought into being when the campaign was already concluded; in addition, it was persisted with far too long, but even more illogical was its reliance on a mix of electronic and visual cooperation between two aircraft—this at a point when electronic means of hunting down an aircraft were becoming more and more established in terms of quality and quantity.

Between July and December 1941, ten flights (numbered 530 to 539) were created using Douglas Havocs. The aircraft were equipped with a powerful searchlight as well as their AI sets. Each flight was initially assigned to a squadron, all of whom flew Hurricanes. The plan was for a Havoc to take-off along with a Hurricane for what would nowadays be termed 'Hunter and Killer' sorties. The Havoc would track down an enemy aircraft until within a 900-foot range. At that point, the searchlight would be switched on to illuminate the target for the Hurricane pilot.

The practical results between the first operational sorties in October 1941 and the end of 1942 were virtually nil. The initial problem lay with the Hurricane squadrons not always having aircraft or pilots to spare, since the priority was for their aircraft to be used in Fighter Command's daylight operations, especially with Sholto-Douglas's 'non-stop offensive' in current mind. As a consequence, the flights

A Mosquito night fighter has been raised into the horizontal position prior to a gun-firing test. The eight bright and pencil-thin tracks of the discharged weapons are highlighted by the enveloping gloom of an evening sky. Any form of strike from such a massive weight of firepower would be certain to end in a critical or fatal result for the selected victim whether aerial or ground-based.

were soon expanded to squadron strength, with each consisting of joint Hurricane and Havoc flights. Even then, the practical difficulties of getting the fighter into the firing position proved difficult enough with the target maintaining a steady course and proved almost impossible in the event of the pilot taking evasive action. Over the entire lifetime of Turbinlite, just four engagements justified claims for either a kill (one), a probable (one), or even damaged (two). There was at least one serious friendly-fire incident accruing from these operations before a halt was finally called and total disbandment effected in January 1943.

Luftwaffe Operations, May–December 1941

The 10–11 May raid on London, regarded as the *Blitz*'s climax, was an almost accurate assessment of the situation, but it was marginally incorrect. During late May and June, separate raids on Manchester and Birmingham flown by near- or exceeding three-figure numbers of crews from the four *Gruppen* assigned the duty was added to by a sixty-strong strike at London.

The bomber types involved were as follows: I/KG2, Do 217E; III/KG30, Ju 88A-4; Epro/KG30, Ju 88A-5; and II/KG40, Do 217E and Do 17. All four of these units appear to have been dispatched to their airfields following the *Blitz* campaign since none are recorded as serving within either *Luftflotte* prosecuting the offensive, nor was the Do 217 on hand until mid-1941. As regards the bomber establishment, the Do 217E was a theoretically more efficient successor to the Do 17, whose current involvement seemed retrogressive since it had been excluded from regular *Blitz* operations fairly early on. However, the advance in overall performance was not strikingly better, while single-engined flight was unpleasantly difficult to sustain. The Ju 88 variants on hand were reasonably efficient machines in basic performance and bomb-load capacity, although the latter was nowhere near the 3,000-kg equivalent total enjoyed by the Do 217, even if it had to carry two-fifths of its maximum figure externally.

The June trio of major city raids, along with a fourth in mid-month against the south-east naval port of Chatham, produced a surprising variation in bomber casualty rates. The relatively deeper-penetration runs to Manchester and Birmingham were achieved with a gratifying (to the *Luftwaffe* crews) figure of around 2 per cent, albeit not for the five teams failing to get back. In contrast, the marginal penetration by the sixty crews assigned to Chatham (13–14 June) resulted in a 5 per cent loss rate for what was a far more marginal time spent over hostile territory—perhaps the target's proximity to London had attracted more concentrated attention in particular from the night fighters.

The foregoing casualties were spread across several *Gruppen*, including the specialist KGr100 who lost two over Chatham and a further one within the ensuing seventy-two hours, all victims of the Beaufighter. The overall loss figure accrued on 13–14 June was actually six, the other three involving I/NJG2's Ju 88s, whose function was Intruder in nature. By the month's end, this *Gruppe* would be short five crews as well, although one would be self-inflicted. On the night of 13–14 June, Uffz. V. Alt was circling low over a ditched He 111's crew in their dinghy—too low, he dipped a wing into the sea, a contact that propelled aircraft and crew to a needless fate compared to the bomber crew who all reportedly survived. His colleagues both fell to Beaufighter attack.

Operations over and around Britain during the mid-summer period of 1941would appear to reinforce the 'backwater' nature of this activity. Hitler's initially-confirmed hopes for a rapid Russian military collapse and surrender seemed to justify concentration on this geographic sphere to all other campaign's virtual exclusion from similar prosecution. After all, once Stalin's empire had been conquered, full attention could be brought to bear upon Britain; bereft of all external support, Churchill's island fortress could be duly hammered into like submission as its current ally. The dreadful scenario was encapsulated in a Nazi song, whose final lines—'*Heute gehört uns Europa, und morgen die ganzen Welt*', translated as 'Today Europe belongs to us, and tomorrow the World'—loomed large.

During the winter of 1942–43, No. 29 Squadron flew a mix of defensive night-fighter sorties and latterly offensive Ranger patrols over the continent. The predatory outline of a Mk IF Beaufighter is caught here as V3824 heads out, its black overall colour only broken by the code letters and national insignia. The Bristol-built machine gave way to the Mk XII Mosquito during May.

A 'Beneficial' *Führerbefehl*

By October, one serious threat to the RAF was being permanently cancelled by Hitler, not on operational, but rather on psychological grounds. The action affected the attempts by I/NJG2 to carry out Intruder attacks over Eastern Britain, a duty that had been commenced almost twelve months previous. Although the small number of crews available to the *Gruppe*-strength unit was barely adequate for the task, the presence of their marauding Ju 88s could have had a debilitating effect both upon Bomber Command operations and OTU instructors and pupils had more effort been put into the activity.

The Führer's warped logic could not countenance whatever degree of punishment was being handed out, not because of the likely scale of loss being borne by his adversaries, but because it was not being evidenced by his nation's population since it was not occurring over the Third Reich. The withdrawal to *Reichsverteidigung* (Defence of the Reich) of the aircraft and crews would ensure that any successes would be directly witnessed. It so happened that, to date, the crews had not achieved very much in hindering RAF operations while a steady loss rate among their ranks had been rung up. However, as Bomber Command built up in strength, the potential chaos among its formations especially during assembly and even more so on return would undoubtedly have been progressively more severe.

A very belated operation, code-named Gisela, in March 1945 proved the point. The Ju 88s involved caught the command crews as they returned and entered the circuits, shooting down around twenty Halifaxes and Lancasters; it was as well that VE-Day was looming up within a matter of two months. So it was that the 1941 decision to withdraw I/NJG2 was the latest example of how Hitler's decisions unconsciously benefitted the Allied cause during the Second World War; in this instance, by saving the lives of hundreds, if not thousands of British and Allied aircrew personnel who would otherwise have fallen victim to the '*Fern-Nachtjäger*' assaults. Given the scale of punishment handed out during Gisela, it is clear that constant 'intruding' would have reaped a bloody harvest in bombers and crews with all that was inferred for overall morale.

The 'Meacon' Strikes

Among the several passive systems introduced to distract and 'way-lay' the *Luftwaffe* crews during and subsequent to the *Blitz* was the electronic countermeasure code-named 'Meacon'. Enemy radio beacons operating on a medium frequency band sent out a two-letter Morse code identifier followed by a prolonged time-lapse that enabled the crews so tuned-in to determine the signal's direction. No. 80 Wing built-up a series of receiver/transmitter sets intended to prevent the fliers from correctly identifying their own transmitter station as opposed to the fake 'Meacon' signal.

It was all too easy to overshoot a target in the dark, and in 1942, one device intended to provide the necessary braking force was the Youngman 'frill cake' that encircled the centre-rear fuselage and spread out in the pattern seen here on W4052. It recessed into the airframe when retracted, but although tried out in this 'finger' format or as a solid shield, neither proved of practical value.

The system involved separate locations for the receivers and their directional aerials and the transmitters. The German-based signal's receipt by the receiver set was then passed over to the transmitter set who would repeat it. This action alone was only liable to create and sustain confusion among the crew concerned should the aircraft be further away from the genuine source than that of the 'Meacon', otherwise the stronger signal from the genuine source would override the 'Meacon' in intensity. It followed that, once the aircraft had penetrated to any depth over hostile territory, the growing likelihood was that the false signals would become ever-more effective in their wayward effect.

An early and crucial success was the KG100 He 111 lured to a final force-landing in November 1940. In more recent times, no less than three Ju 88A-5s from I/KueFlGr 106 were reportedly so deceived that all three pilots flew into the higher ground over the Yorkshire coast; the cloud and mist conditions then existing may have been a greater contributing factor to these losses, however. A more likely candidate for 'Meacon' treatment was a companion *Gruppe* bomber pilot Uffz. E. Herms; he was engaged in a shipping sortie over the Irish Sea, but the subsequent wandering pattern adopted culminated with a landing at Chivenor in Southwest England. Whereas the crew's flying career was over their charge was destined to operate with the RAFWAFFE, the specialist unit operating *Luftwaffe* aircraft for recognition and orientation studies among Allied aircrew.

The previous 23–24 July, two Ju 88s from I/KG30 were regarded as falling victim to 'Meacon' treatment. The first flown by Ltn. W. Dieterich ended its return flight from Liverpool on the wrong side of the Channel, having force-landed on the Isle of Wight. The crew of its *Gruppe* companion in fate was so confused that, as they clambered from their bomber on what they took to be a *Luftwaffe* airfield, they were surely shocked to be confronted by armed RAF personnel stationed at Lulsgate in Somerset. Uffz. W. Hosie's crew joined their colleagues in captivity, but their mount was also later dispatched to No. 1426 (Enemy Aircraft) Flight, alias RAFWAFFE.

Winter Doldrums and Spring Resurgence

The increasingly-marginal scale of *Luftwaffe* operations over Britain between June 1941 and April 1942 was naturally welcome. Not only was the nation's industrial and maritime base able to function with minimal dislocation, the constant need to alert the population to the likelihood of attack through sounding sirens was equally diminished, a factor that in turn allowed the people to sleep or work on undisturbed. A good proportion of the operations involved the anti-shipping element of *Luftflotte* 3 along with its reconnaissance *Staffeln*.

As 1941 evolved into 1942, the bomber strength of the *Luftflotte* fell away until only II/KG2 was on hand by mid-February; III/KG40's He 111s were serving as one of the five anti-shipping units. In addition, the transfer-in of all of NJG1 indicated a growing emphasis on defensive as opposed to offensive operations;

A group of No. 604 Squadron aircrew was taken at their Officers' Mess, Middle Wallop, in 1942. Wg Cdr John Cunningham (Squadron CO) is third from right with his navigator Plt Off. 'Jimmy' Wransley the diminutive figure on the end. There were several Norwegians serving on the squadron, two of whom are fourth and fifth from left, with the latter showing his wings on the opposite side of his tunic to that of his RAF colleagues.

the latter duty now involved the *Jabos* of 10/JG2, later supplemented by 10/JG26 following the inception at the beginning of 1942 of what were attacks primarily delivered against locations scattered along the Channel and East Anglian coastlines.

The steady expansion of Beaufighter-equipped squadrons was ironically paralleled by the extremely sparse availability of raiders on hand to be intercepted or downed. During this time, two among several future aces were cutting their teeth. No. 29 Squadron's 'Bob' Braham earned the sixth out of twenty-three confirmed kills on 23–24 October, when Uffz. F. Hall's Epro/KG30 Ju 88 was downed into the sea off Lowestoft along with its four-man crew. Fg Off. Mike Herrick (RNZAF) was victorious over Obfw. Otto Wiese's crew in their I/NJG2 Intruder on 23–24 June. By a grim irony, both RAF pilots would be shot down within days of each other during June 1944 with their victor the same Ltn. Robert Spreckels of JG1, and with only Braham surviving as a POW.

Upsurge in Activity

The arrival in February 1942 of ACM Arthur 'Butch' Harris to lead Bomber Command had recently witnessed an official shift from the attempt to strike Germany's industrial resources in isolation to one that included a parallel strike at enemy morale. The limitations inherent in surgical attacks by night with the equipment on hand had forced the policy change to one that was 'area bombing' in nature—the explosive and incendiary saturation of a city with a view to gaining some measure of success.

The initial raids on the Hanseatic Baltic seaport of Lübeck had literally burnt out the centre of the town. The fact that it possessed a wealth of ancient wooden structures aided the grim process as would be again proven when its commercial and structural 'twin' further along the Baltic coast (Rostock) would be subjected to three successive nightly assaults several weeks later. The concept of Total War as rendered during the *Blitz* was now due to rebound with stunning force against the Nazi perpetrators.

The raid and its effect had struck at Hitler's ever-unpredictable state of mind. In this instance, he decided upon a countermeasure that directed his bombers not towards Britain's industry, but rather its citizen's morale. The focus for the attacks would be upon locations with a cathedral. The rationale behind the decision was centred upon the German *Baedeker* tourist guide to British cities possessing such a structure. To do so with the current bomber establishment within *Luftflotte 3* was not a viable choice; consequently, several *Geschwader*'s fourth sub-unit normally assigned to training and secondary duties were transferred-in. On the other hand, the availability of KG2 with all of its Do 217Es would provide a central focus point for all planned operations.

Hitler's decision was announced during a speech on 26 April, by which time the first sortie had been launched against the West Country town of Exeter. The results were minimal on this occasion, but subsequent raids would intensify the assault and attendant material and human destruction. Next on the list was Bath, which was totally devoid of ground defensive measures and suffered accordingly, with some bombers descending to minimum altitude and directing their bomb loads in dreadfully effective manner during successive nightly attacks.

Although the command's night-fighter resources were more than adequate, the loss scale borne by the *Luftwaffe* was small at only four bombers downed, all but one by Beaufighters. An initially surprising inclusion in this total was the Do 17Z that was part of 12/KG2, but the training status of the *Gruppe* clearly reflected the utilization of this now operationally-dated variant. Uffz. Kuglat's crew were on the performance back foot and paid the price when Flt Lt Strange from No. 219 Squadron sent their bomber down into the Channel.

A switch away from the west saw the bombers directed towards Norwich starting on 27–28 April and repeated two nights later. In this instance, the efforts of the night fighters to make effective interception at least on the first occasion were reportedly thwarted by the low-level approach adopted by the attacking force. Over 230 citizens were killed, including the best friend of co-author Mike Bailey. The young schoolboy had been with his grandparents when a bomb that badly damaged Mike's house impacted right by the Anderson shelter in which the trio were, none of whom survived the detonation. In between the Norwich raids, the *Luftwaffe* turned its attention on York to badly damage the centre and destroy the centuries-old Guildhall among other buildings. The death toll within the city brought the fatality figure to around 800, accruing from all the attacks to date;

By the time No. 96 Squadron converted on to the Mk VIF Beaufighter in late 1942, there was little trade in *Luftwaffe* attacks on Britain, so the massive 'snake' of 20-mm shells being fed into V7848's ammunition boxes would see scant use. However, a move to West Malling in late 1943 witnessed its involvement in the baby *Blitz* raids on London when the crews scored several kills. Pilot's access hatch and extending ladder stands out.

a heavy toll, but one that was destined to be clinically miniscule in what awaited the Germans as 1942 extended into 1943—truly a case of 'He who lives by the Sword shall die by the Sword'.

Exeter and Cowes on the Isle of Wight bore the brunt of the punishment during May's first week. The centre of the first location was devastated, while Cowes received a serious battering. Only four bombers failed to join their colleagues back on the continent following the Exeter raid, with three more deleted from the Cowes force—a seemingly marginal total, but not when aligned against the small overall numbers of bombers involved, being no more than eighty in all. More important than the statistical factor was the total lack of negative effect upon the national war effort. Painful as the material and human loss arising from the *Baedeker* offensive might be, the ultimate benefit to Nazi Germany's bid for overall success was frankly nil. Little or nothing was going to stem the tide of military force against the Third Reich as its cohorts sought to hold out against the burgeoning Allied aerial might.

Mosquito: The Shining Sword's Twin

The advent of the ubiquitous Mosquito on active operations that would expand into a first-class multirole combat function had commenced with the passive, but equally vital role of high-level reconnaissance. The design's development as a fighter among other options had not been ignored, and by early 1942, the first examples of the Mk II were supplementing the PR Mk I reconnaissance and bomber 'B' Mk IV in service. Nos 151 and 157 Squadrons were among the initial recipients of the fighter version that in this instance was subordinated to a night-fighting role.

With four machine guns mounted in the nose and four 20-mm cannon located in the forward bomb bay, the Mk II was custom-built to present a truly lethal barrier to any *Luftwaffe* aircraft venturing over British soil. Here was a real partner for the Beaufighter in terms of comprehensively-effective home defence. It was as well for many of the German airmen prosecuting the *Blitz* that the offensive was over, although no consolation to their successors tasked with penetrating hostile airspace in smaller numbers against this increased threat.

Technical Advance: Radar

By this stage, the double-screen layout of the original AI Mk IV radar sets was being displaced by the uprated Mk VIII, which moreover possessed a single screen displaying the height and azimuth dispositions as well as the range of the enemy aircraft in enhanced detail. In addition, the pilot was provided with an indicator so he could work in conjunction with the navigator from the point of initial contact by the latter until closing within visual distance of the targeted aircraft when confirmation or otherwise of its hostile status would be determined.

Countermeasures (RAF)

No. 85 Squadron's transfer from Hunsden north of London to West Malling in Kent had placed its crews in a better position to engage the nocturnal raiders; the new airfield's location was in a direct line between London and any enemy aircraft heading towards the capital. The current CO, Wg Cdr John Cunningham, was by now a leading night-fighter ace, and his leadership over the intervening eight months would further bolster the unit's reputation as a top performer in nocturnal activity. The need to present a firm challenge to *Luftwaffe* assault by night would be raised a notch around this time, with the operational debut over South East England of two higher-performance aircraft types, the Fw 190 and the Me 410, from April onwards.

No. 85 Squadron was based at either at Hunsdon or West Malling in mid-1943 when this picture was taken of its senior staff. *From left to right*: Wg Cdr John Cunningham (CO), Flt Lt Tim Moloney (Adjutant), Sqn Ldr Peter Green ('A' Flight CO), and Sqn Ldr Edward Crew ('B' Flight CO). Cunningham was the top RAF night-fighter ace: Crew went on to command No. 96 Squadron shortly after depicted here.

Enter the Nocturnal Fw 190

The somewhat 'penny-packet' nature of *Luftwaffe* incursions over Britain in mid-1943 would witness the inclusion of a single-engined variation in the form of the Fw 190s from I/10 *Schnellkampfgruppe* (SKG) as a prominent participant. With a bomb-carrying capacity of a single weapon, the fighter's involvement over Southern Britain resurrected memories of the original 1940 *Jabo* operations and the more recent 'tip and run' attacks. These daylight incursions at least had some prospect of aiming at a specific target, whereas the latest venture smacked of nothing more than scattering bombs over a general area.

The drag effect of the externally-mounted bomb did not materially hinder the Fw 190's performance that accordingly presented a tough interception challenge even to the fleet-footed Mosquito. A further limiting factor was the relatively short time span in which to close upon the fighter before it had traversed the roughly 70–80-mile distance from the coast to London. Prompt GCI guidance played a part in interceptions as evidenced on 13–14 June when Sandwich radar advised Wg Cdr Cunningham (No. 85 Squadron CO) of a 'contact' as he and his navigator 'Jimmy' Rawnsley were orbiting off the Kent coast at 23,000 feet in their NF Mk XII.

The first confirmation of a bogey was gained around 2,500 yards and well below, whereupon altitude was reduced, and visual sight established around 1,000 yards with the bogey now around 20 degrees higher. Closure and positive identification were followed by a burst of fire that did not have the anticipated effect, so Cunningham further shortened the firing distance. The second fusillade of cannon shells and bullets struck home and the Fw 190 was cast violently out of control; Ltn. H. Ullich was ejected into mid-air with serious injuries that did not prevent him from deploying his parachute. His charge slammed into the ground with its bomb still attached, the resultant explosion echoing around for miles. The crash site, around 30 miles from the capital, demonstrated the foregoing point regarding the time limitation available in which to ensure interception and dispatch of the *Luftwaffe* attackers before they achieved their goal.

A subsequent encounter with a bomb-laden Fw 190 on 6 September was to create a potentially serious outcome for Cunningham and Rawnsley. The German pilot was first intercepted off the mouth of the Thames, but his course took him northwards as opposed to the capital. The initial burst of fire had no effect and Cunningham held back momentarily before closing-in again, much to Rawnsley's dismay since he had observed with his binoculars that the bomb was still firmly in place. A second burst of fire still had no terminal effect and it was only on the third delivery that the cockpit canopy flew off accompanied by fragments of metal; some of the latter probably caused the damage to one engine's radiator and glycol tank that induced an immediate switch-off and propeller 'feathering' action. Not long after, Cunningham told Rawnsley to hook up his parachute pack and be prepared to 'step out' since an unaccountably high degree of altitude loss had been suffered; fortunately, the descent was held at 5,000 feet, and after skirting the Thames Gunnery Zone, a safe return and landing was made at West Malling.

SKG210's Mini-Disaster

SKG210's nocturnal debut had proved to be somewhat of a disaster that moreover was self-inflicted. The projected raid on London by thirty Fw 190s did not materialise after the pilots closed in north of the Thames Estuary and released nearly all their loads short of the capital. What was an operational failure then developed into a navigational farce for no less than four of the force as they wandered over the southern fringes of the Estuary. At West Malling, the airfield lights and beacon were switched on following the duty controller's order, after he picked out the sound of an approaching aircraft; this duly fired a recognition flare and switched on its lights to make a perfect landing and taxi-run up to the control tower. When two airmen approached the pilot, they were unable to understand him—until one realized Fw. O. Bechtold's hostile status, ran to get his rifle, and duly apprehended the bemused pilot.

What was an event of some uniqueness initiated a sequence of almost equally-bizarre scenarios. Shortly after Bechtold was seized, the harsh note of another approaching aircraft was heard that evolved into a second Fw 190. Having landed, it too taxied across the airfield; when identified as hostile, a vehicle converted to a mobile gun battery with Vickers machine guns made to cut the pilot off from any attempt at regaining flight. Ltn. F. Setzer must have belatedly realized his error because he swung around in a bid to take-off. The RAF gunner's first burst of fire did not halt the fighter's frantic progress, but the second put an end to the bid for flight by setting a fuel tank ablaze, whereupon Setzer jumped out of his now-stationary charge. His attempt at evading capture was brief and

The assumption that black camouflage was the effective way with which to conceal an aircraft from sight was found to be suspect by 1943. Instead, a disruptive pattern of dark green and sea grey medium was adopted by Fighter Command; it is demonstrated by V8442 that still bears an AI Mk IV or V radar set judging by the external receiver aerials on the starboard wing.

probably would have failed anyway, considering he was both wounded and been badly burnt when the Fw 190 caught fire.

Almost immediately, the sound of yet another aircraft orbiting the airfield was picked out, but this time, Obfw. O. Schulz would not even achieve a safe landing. The RAF Regiment and Army personnel tasked with the airfield's defence had received instructions that the enemy pilots were mistaking the airfield for a German location and were to treat any aircraft as hostile—a blanket instruction that could have been fatal had the invisible machine been Allied. In the event, the gunfire latched onto the Fw 190, but whether this had the desired effect in Schulz's force-landing short of the airfield seems a matter of conjecture; he had amazingly escaped injury and was being 'entertained' by civilians when later arrested.

So far, the worst affected among the trio of captives was the injured Ltn. Setzer, but good fortune was about to totally desert one of their colleagues who had become similarly disorientated. Obltn. K. Klahn's increasingly desperate attempts to pick out a suitable landing site of any kind finally prompted him into baling out—a fatal decision in his case, since his parachute had not had time to fully deploy before he struck the Kentish soil. Whether he had not realized his parlous situation regarding altitude or was unable to regain a safe altitude before jumping could never be determined.

A footnote to this night's dramatic events related to the intact nature of Fw. Bechtold's Fw 190A-4. It was first flown to the Royal Aircraft Establishment (RAE), Farnborough, for evaluation, but days later and suitably embellished with RAF camouflage and markings, it became the latest member of the RAFWAFFE with whom it flew until the following October; tragically, it was involved in a fatal crash on the 13th that consumed Flt Lt E. Lewenden, the 1426 Flight CO.

SKG10's navigational misfortunes were given a further negative 'boost' a mere five weeks later. On this occasion (20 May), the airfield in question was Manston and the Fw 190 was piloted by Uffz. H. Ehrhardt; his base at Saint-Omer was also on the fringes of the Channel, but the error appeared less excusable unless his compass was out of order. As with its West Malling contemporary, the fighter ended up with No. 1426 (Enemy Aircraft) Flight following tests conducted at the Aircraft and Armament Experimental Establishment (A&AEE), Boscombe Down.

Battle of the Insects

Aircraft recognition was a subject that was often a vital factor affecting survival in aerial combat. There was, however, an art to perfecting one's knowledge, apart from which the level of enthusiasm in studying the matter varied from person to person. An added difficulty, not to say mortal danger, lay in the existence of respective Allied and German aircraft designs that were similar in overall outline. For instance, the rear view of a C-47 and a He 111 presented the same low-wing, close-packed engine mounts and sharp outer-wing dihedral. Other dangerously similar twins were the Bf 109 and the P-51B, the P-47 and Fw 190, the Blenheim and the Ju 88, and the Hampden and Do 17.

What has the appearance of a clown's nose conceals a lethal surprise for enemy aircraft attempting to penetrate Britain's aerial defences. The Mk XII Mosquito was the first to bear centimetric-wave radar equipment in the form of the home-built AI Mk VIII that almost did away with external aerials. The four machine guns had to be deleted, but the four cannon-calibre weapons in the bomb bay could bring down aircraft without further assistance.

In June 1943, the first examples of the Me 410 *Hornisse* (Hornet) appeared in the west, having been assigned to V/KG2 and based in northern France. The latest of Willi Messerschmitt's designs to enter combat, the Me 410 mounted two DB 601 or DB603 inline engines on a low wing frame; along with an overall plan form similar in proportions to the RAF's own 'insect', the Mosquito, as well as a general performance at least approaching that of its de Havilland opponent, there was clearly every chance of confusing one with the other, especially at night.

The first opportunity to test out the RAF crews occurred on 13–14 July. No. 85 Squadron's Fl/Lt Bunting and his navigator/AI operator Plt Off. French were up on patrol near Dover when they were warned of a north-bound bandit. Scarcely had this been closed-in upon when a second aircraft was picked out, upon which Bunting diverted his attention. Although initially overhauling the bogey that had now adopted a slight climbing attitude, problems with the Merlin engines overheating and the resultant drag caused by the need to open the engine radiators saw the gap again widen.

All too slowly, the Mossie was brought into visual contact, with the lighter northern horizon providing an enhanced degree of sighting. The low wing position compared to the RAF design's mid-wing setting, as well as its underslung Merlin engine mounts contrasting with the centrally positioned DB603s, was enough to satisfy the 'stalkers' that the bogey was definitely in the hostile category. Turbulence caused by the Me 410's motion threw Bunting's aim off on his first pass, but the second attack upon the still-unwary two-man crew sealed their fate along with their charge. U5+KG burst into flames, was propelled onto its back, and descended inexorably into the North Sea. One technical insect's sting had proved lethal to the other.

Countermeasure (*Luftwaffe*)

The need for some form of defence against attack from the rear was a key issue for the Allied and Axis crews operating by night. In the former instance, Bomber Command featured an electronic device code-named 'Monica' that indicated the approach of an aircraft but could not differentiate between friend and foe; only the rate of closure could perhaps suggest a night fighter rather than another RAF bomber. The *Luftwaffe* equivalent was *FuG* 217.

The Me 410 was proving to be somewhat of a problem for Fighter Command, even without the initial benefit of *FuG* 217. It was a full month before Bunting's confirmed success was matched by the squadron's Sqn Ldr G. Howitt on 22–23 August, although records indicate a further three machines lost over the sea around the month's end. Interceptions of what were assumed to be Me 410s were being intermittently made, but the aircraft in question proved very hard and generally impossible to be held onto or closed-in upon. The suspicion that electronic means were on hand for the enemy pilots as regards indications of aircraft encroaching from behind was suspected by 'Jimmy' Rawnsley in particular.

The *FuG* 217 sets were relatively limited in both lateral and vertical coverage. In the former instance, the scanning arc extended only 20 degrees on either side of the fuselage; vertical coverage was better, although the arc was only 30 degrees above and 50–60 degrees below the aerial's horizontal line. The maximum

The pilot of an FB Mk VI Mossie has almost cleared-up the landing gear even though he has barely gained marginal height off the airfield surface. This variant was powered by the single-stage supercharged Merlin 20 Series ranging from 21 through 22 and 23 to 25. A companion aircraft in left background appears to be canted over to starboard with what seems like a bent propeller blade supporting this impression of undercarriage collapse.

range was 5,000 metres. The chances of a night fighter latching onto a *FuG* 217-equipped bomber in undetected manner was being seriously compromised.

The air battle over Southern Britain had seemingly become an uncomfortable scenario for Fighter Command's crews, but this was fortunately a misnomer. Apart from the Me 410 and Fw 190, the remaining bomber types prosecuting the offensive—if the relatively small numbers involved could perform in a sustained and punishing manner that merited the foregoing title—were not of a similar calibre in performance. Granted the Ju 88 and its Ju 188 successor could provide a fairly tough challenge, but the Beaufighter and the Mosquito, in particular, held the edge in speed and firepower. As for the other bomber variants, neither the Do 217 nor the He 177 *Greif*, now appearing on the scene as Operation Steinbock beckoned, possessed anything like the means to outrun, outmanoeuvre, or outfight the RAF night fighters.

Odds Against...

The higher-performance Me 410 and Fw 190 notwithstanding, the remaining variants in current service were truly fighting a vain contest in terms of sheer survivability. The raids on Lincoln and Grimsby on 17–18 August was the latest, but far from the last, occasion when the defences would reap a bloody harvest. Two Do 217s of 3/KG2 and single losses from 5/KG2, I/KG6, and a Stab I/KG6 were all swallowed up by the North Sea. KG2's suffering was added to by one further casualty.

Fw. R. Holz, who was presumably one of the formation heading for Grimsby, found his Do 217M firmly held within the blinding lights of a group of searchlights. Before he could free U5+DR from this potentially lethal visual stranglehold, the directed fire of the AA batteries linked to the batteries struck home with deadly effect. It was as well for the four crew members that they were able to abandon their bomber and parachute down into captivity unlike most, if not all, of their fellow airmen descending terminally into the sea.

One of this unfortunate number was on board U5+AK, which was struck and temporarily went out of control following a fighter attack. Assuming the bomber was doomed, two crewmembers jumped out with only Uffz. D. Arlt surviving—Uffz. W. Schneider having probably fallen into the sea since he is MIA to this day. Given his action, it was ironic if not also tragic that Ltn. Roesner was able to regain control of his battered but still intact bomber and bring his charge back safely.

Not only was nearly 10 per cent of the overall attacking force lost, but the twin targets remained basically inviolate from assault. Far to the north-east, Bomber Command was raining down nearly 600 bomb loads upon the research establishment at Peenemunde. History records that, although immeasurably more punishing, the immediate overall effect upon Germany's development of V-1 and the ballistic V-2 weaponry was disappointingly marginal; however, fear of further raids prompted a dispersal of facilities that in turn delayed the subsequent V-1 assault upon Southern Britain by up to two months, thereby providing a measure of long-term success.

… and Ever Increasing

The overall assault effort handed out by the *Luftwaffe* bombers during 1943 had never reached other than a marginal level of disruption to Britain's war production resources. A combination of minimal aircraft numbers and an ever-more efficient nocturnal defence network had seen to this parlous situation for the airmen prosecuting the offensive. During the same month as *FuG* 217 made its regular appearance, the increasing odds against survival continued to be demonstrated.

The fitting of GM-1 nitrous-oxide that boosted engine power to the Ju 88S-1s of KG6 availed neither of the two *Geschwader* crews heading inwards on the late evening of the 8th. The first, flown by Fw. W. Kaltwasser, was caught on approach to Dover and taken out by No. 85 Squadron's Flt Lt Bunting (the pilot's name translation of 'Coldwater' was a grim reference to his watery Channel grave). Further north over the Thames, Fg Off. S. Holloway was guided towards Ltn. H. Kalff's 3E+US that was given short thrift from the Mosquito Mk XII's gun battery; the doomed machine took its three-man crew to a similar maritime tomb as its unfortunate companion.

The forward section of an anonymous Mk VIF Beaufighter is caught in the glare of a floodlight as the crew stand by on the left while last-minute preparations are made for the night's operation. The main wheels are covered to guard against oil residue dripping from the engine nacelle. The dark streaks from the slots for spent machine-gun cartridges stand out against the light. These guns were split between four in the starboard and two in the port wings.

The Ju 188 was an improved version of the Ju 88, with heavier armament including a power turret, expanded interior crew space, and bomb load among other improvements; there was also an equal advance in speed and range. The E1 version was on operational hand by August, with I /KG6 a recipient, but on the 15th, the *Gruppe* was given a shock lesson in tactics and once again the teacher was No. 85 Squadron.

Sqn Ldr W. McGuire was aloft and orbiting off the Suffolk coast when the first indication of a westward-heading bogey was transmitted to him by his radar station controller. Momentary confusion between this and another aircraft 'blip' was resolved into the former aircraft definitely as a hostile, and McGuire duly closed from above upon what was evolving into Ju 188 3E+FL in Hptm. H. Waldecker's charge. Hunter and prey gained sight of each other and the grim contest commenced.

As it descended in a shallow dive, the clear, full moonlit conditions provided no visual relief for the enemy crew, even if their bomber had escaped still intact from McGuire's initial aim that nevertheless set the port engine on fire. Waldecker's desperate alternate sharp turns to port and then starboard availed him nothing as McGuire closed to minimum range and this time administered a terminal burst of fire. The burning bomber adopted a vertical attitude that saw the airframe breaking up prior to impact, and only the pilot and one of his three companions escaped their aircraft's fiery fate.

Within fifteen minutes, a second I/KG6 Ju 188 was destined to suffer the same fate at McGuire's hands. This time around, 3E+RH was encountered before it had crossed further west over British soil in the vicinity of Clacton-on-Sea. The Thames Estuary waters became its grave as did Ltn. W. Hayn and crew. Thus it was that 3E+ FL, being the joint-first example of the recently-operational Ju 188 to crash on British soil, was later examined in as much detail as its shattered carcass could provide. The *Gruppe*'s misery was compounded by a third loss credited to Fg Off. H. Thomas, from which none of Ltn. K. Geyer's crew emerged alive.

'The Last Blitz'

The period between January and May 1944 would witness the final attempt by the *Luftwaffe* to mount the nearest to a concerted bombing offensive over Britain since the *Blitz*. In the event, the raid pattern would be primarily directed against London with steadily-diminishing effect from the equally-diminishing bomber strength available to former-*Oberst* and now-GenMaj. Dietrich Peltz. He had been previously grandly appointed *Angriffsführer* ('attack leader') England by Göring but was already facing an uphill struggle to gain enough numbers of, and quality in, aircraft with which to even hope for a conclusive result either in material destruction or in lowering the nation's morale.

The *Luftwaffe* Order of Battle on 20 January amounted to 491 aircraft, of which 431 were serviceable. Included in the total was forty-six He 177s, all but

Full flaps have been deployed by the pilot as his Mosquito crosses the runway threshold and 'flares out' prior to making what should be a sound landing run. The photo angle does not permit a clear view of the squadron code letters, but the more vertical cockpit framing suggests a fighter as opposed to a bomber/PR variant.

four action ready. The range of the other aircraft types ranged from the somewhat outdated Ju 88A-4 to the more combat-efficient Ju 88S, Do 217, and Ju 188. Also on hand were the Fw 190s of I/SKG10. Only the He 177 was capable of delivering a bomb load akin to that regularly borne by the Lancaster and Halifax, while the Fw 190's contribution was marginal to say the least.

Aligned against the German airmen was sixteen Beaufighter Mk VIF or Mosquito XII–XIII squadrons. Their radar equipment extended from four units still operating the Mk V dual-screen system to ten utilising the Mk VIII and two who possessed the best equipment in the Mk X. The latter was an adaptation of the American SCR720B, whose 3-cm wavelength signal placed it above even the 10-cm Mk VIII equivalent regarding overall efficiency. Comprehensive GCI coverage was on hand to direct the fighter crews, while AA and searchlight back-up was equally massive in scale.

Changed Tactics

Although the *Luftwaffe* never adopted the 'bomber stream' concept of RAF Bomber Command, there was a basic, if enforced, change compared to 1940–41. Then the bombers had come over in the course of a large time spread of anything up to ten hours. The current presence of a solid night-fighter screen allied to equally solid AA and searchlight provision compared to the very limited equivalent defensive structure during most of the *Blitz* rendered the foregoing option redundant. Instead, the overall force would occupy the minimum amount of time over its target although still arriving in no more than individual *Gruppe* strength. Moreover, target approach would be made at higher altitudes and in a steady descent; the return leg would be made at full throttle and as low as possible.

Another seemingly illogical alteration lay with target-marking methods. These would follow the RAF pattern of flare release as opposed to utilising the electronic *Knickebein* and *Y-Gerät* equipment on regular hand. The deployment of the two systems in question was dependent on target weather conditions, as follows:

1. The *Ablauflinie* ('Line of Departure') marking method was applied in clear conditions. A group of incendiary bombs was released in a line at right angles to the briefed target approach and at 6 kilometres from that area. When level with the flare line or *Ablauflinie*, each crew would make a timed bomb run. Selected crews in the initial attack wave would supplement the mixed colour and white incendiary pattern laid by the Pathfinder crews by releasing incendiary bombs on the lateral fringes of the target area.
2. *The Leuchtpfad* ('Path of Light') marking method operated in up to 6/10 cloud cover. A line of seven alternate white and coloured flares was laid 6 kilometres distant. Each bomber selected a flare while using a gliding approach from either upwind or downwind; bomb release was carried out within the time span stated at briefing.
3. A *Leuchtpfad* variation anticipated the crews on reaching the last flare sighting a second laterally-applied *Leuchtpfad* with its central coloured flare in direct line with the first target-maker flare up ahead. The short life of each flare dictated the regular renewal of the complete system in time with the briefed arrival of each bomber wave. Delays in scheduled wave arrivals merited the laying of red flares to windward of the target area and at right-angles to the wind direction, following which target re-illumination would resume with the same pattern and colours. Incorrectly-laid patterns would require releasing a flare beside each wrong marker—none too easy to achieve and moreover laying the crews open to extended orbiting of the target and possible interception by night fighters.

All depended upon the target-marking specialists of I/KG66 achieving their goal in the same manner as their RAF contemporaries. However, whereas the latter force sometimes ended up illuminating the wrong area of a city or releasing on its fringes, the Steinbock experience would on more than one occasion end with the designated target not even being remotely homed-in upon with a resultant dispersal of bomb loads over entire regions of Southern Britain.

The structural cross-pollination in Mosquito production sometimes led to visual confusion. The 'Thimble' nose cover first appeared on this variant's Mk XII predecessor. However, the Mk XIII seen here is part of an HK-prefixed airframe batch that featured both 'Thimble' and the bulkier 'Bull' nose outline. Only the serial number confirms its production status. The cartridge ejection slots for the 20-mm cannon are clearly depicted.

First Strikes

I/KG66 had been specially trained in the Pathfinder role for the main force operating from airfields widely spread between western France and Germany. The initial strike on 21–22 January was impressive as regards bombers dispatched during the two-stage raid—447 in all—but the results were extremely disappointing in their effect; barely 200 aircraft, of which 20 per cent were recorded by the British monitoring service as bombing London, even crossed over hostile territory. The cost was not negligible either at sixteen.

The operational debut of the He 177 over Britain proved particularly fraught, with no less than four bombers lost. One was abandoned on the way over, a second crashed during the return flight, and two fell to the defences. One of the remaining duo that came from KG40's ranks was in Obltn. Waterbeck's hands. His bomber was vectored on to by a Mk XII Mosquito of No. 151 Squadron, flown by W/O Kemp. South of London, gunfire lanced into the bomber's port wing, igniting the fuel tank and sending it into a descending spiral that the pilot seemed incapable of correcting; a measure of control was seemingly regained, but the shallow angle of impact shattered the airframe, killing him and one member among the two still on board.

A full eight nights elapsed before the second thrust at London was launched. Once again, there was a marked difference between German claims for launched sorties (nearly 300) and aircraft recorded over Southern Britain (100). A similar casualty total of seventeen was suffered, split between losses to the RAF and AA and 'operational' crashes on the continent. The campaign's debut was proving a failure both as regards its overall effect upon the capital and the relatively high cost. Matters were destined to slide into a steady decline over the ensuing several months of the offensive, although strikes on London in the second half of February were to give a false promise of better things to come.

London was still the epicentre for the bombers, but the first February raid was very restricted in scale, with Me 410 and Fw 190 involvement alone. The next three assaults were similar in both scale and unit involvement, a strange situation given the still-adequate strength of aircraft on hand, but matters advanced on 13–14 February, when ten *Gruppen* were alerted and provided an average of eleven bombers. The raid produced the latest disappointment for Gen. Peltz since just five of the bomb loads were recorded within the city's boundaries. Worse still was the technical situation facing I/KG100's He 177s, which saw eight 'abortions' primarily due to engine problems out of the thirteen dispatched. In addition, ten crews were lost, with all but one being declared MIA.

The short-lived upsurge in Steinbock fortunes came five nights on when nearly 200 crews, of which 60 per cent were plotted over British soil, took off. Bombing was widespread throughout London, with 480 fires being recorded along with 180 deaths. The crew casualty list totalled nine, but two among the figure were victims of Intruder attack by Flt Lt Kipp in his No. 418 Squadron Mosquito; both were from 3/KG54 and were approaching their Juvincourt airfield when downed—yet another reminder of how there was by now no guarantee of security from assault for the *Luftwaffe* at any stage of an operation.

Over the next six nights, the capital absorbed four raids. An even greater number of fires were recorded thanks to a heavy incendiary content, with over 200 deaths on 21–22 February, although German claims of 171 crews bombing conflicted with the less-than-half figure tracked in over the country. A gap of twenty-four hours was followed by the next raid that delivered 81 tons of bombs and incendiaries, which created 230 fires including a severe one in Victoria Docks; casualties were fortunately much less (twenty-nine). The cost was thirteen crews, five of which descended on British soil.

The penultimate assault in the tight-knit sequence was rendered the next night, and although the 161 crews rostered fell to around 33 per cent reaching London, the effect of their loads was disproportionate, causing the deaths of around 300 people mainly in residential districts, although causing minimal industrial or commercial damage. Twenty-four hours on, and an estimated 100 tons of weaponry was dropped mainly in the very centre upon what were briefed as 'the Westminster area of government buildings'. So the Baby *Blitz*'s focus on London had reached its climax with no material benefit to the enemy. Regardless of this, the population must have been shaken by this upsurge in activity, with no guarantee of its reduction, let alone cessation in the immediate future.

No. 409 Squadron was the second Canadian unit to convert onto the Mosquito NF Mk XIII in March 1944 following operations with the Beaufighter since January 1942. The starboard Merlin is receiving the full attention of two mechanics with a third airman working on the landing gear. Cut-down D-Day stripes confirm picture taken well after Operation Overlord.

The Growing Price

Not only was the bombing effort losing its impetus, the cost to the personnel was steadily rising as the superior performance of the night fighters was being brought to bear. The latest London foray proved to be a 'red-letter night' for No. 29 Squadron, whose crews were credited with five confirmed kills and three damaged. Flt Lt Pargeter headed for a searchlight concentration that had ensnared Fw. Wudzig's 8/KG6 Ju 88A-4; separate bursts of fire as the Mosquito closed in to 200 yards witnessed the bomber falling away and its crash site later tied in with Pargeter's combat report.

His second victim was a Ju 188 that was also picked out by searchlights. This time round, a protracted tail chase ensued, with Fw. Von Pawelsz executing a series of twisting manoeuvres that thwarted his attacker until near West Malling. Then, with the range closed completely down, the final burst of fire set the bomber ablaze and it flopped into a spiral action that saw just two of the five-man crew bale out prior to the fatal impact. Sqn Ldr Kirkland's and Flt Lt Barry's separate culls of Do 217Ms from I/KG2 and Fg Off. Provan with his 2/KG66 '*Pfadfinder*' were the other squadron victors.

Gun 'Strike'

The pre-eminence granted the RAF defenders during the Second World War has tended to totally diminish the part their ground-based Army colleagues manning the AA guns played in thwarting the *Luftwaffe*. By the inception of Steinbock, the numbers of 3.7 and 4.5 weapons extended to several thousands and were supported by efficient gun-laying equipment and radar-directed searchlight batteries. A duo of crews felt their malign effect during the 20–21 February raid on the Capital.

Ogfr. J. Kretlek's 2/KG54 Ju 88A-4 was heading in over south London when a battery opened up, with one shell disabling the port engine. The signal to bale out was responded to by his three fellow airmen, but what prevented the pilots from following suit could never be determined as he went in with his bomber near Brookwood. A second *Gruppe* bomber encountered gunfire over the Thames Estuary that persuaded Uffz. G. Klunker flying his first sortie to abandon it and

Another NF Mk XIII forms the background for a discussion between a flight sergeant (left) and what is a member of the aircraft's ground crew and who is working on the starboard engine, whose lower cowling lies on the right. Aircraft in background seems to bear Type A1 fuselage roundels, although this was replaced by Type C1 long before the squadron took on the Mosquito.

jettison the bomb load. Almost immediately, a strike on the tail threw the aircraft into an attitude that forced the pilot to order a bale out; only Gefr G. Grosspietsch (*Beobachter*) managed to do so, the other three ending up MIA after the bomber crashed into the estuarial waters.

An approach from the east of London the next night was being made by a Ju 188 from 6/KG2 in the hands of Uffz. R. Elster when a Stebbing-based AA battery locked on to the bomber and opened fire. A single shell from among the barrage impacted directly with the port engine, the effect being to cast the bomber into a steep and ultimately terminal dive. The centrifugal forces impinging upon the crew was the likely reason why only one among the five on board finally escaped the deadly pressure to bale out scant seconds prior to the final impact.

'In Transit' Peril

Yet another operational variation was being indulged in, which related to where the attacks were launched and completed. RAF Bomber Command crews served at one airfield during their tour of operations. In 'Steinbock's' case, it was not unusual for a crew to take-off from their airfield in Germany and land elsewhere in France or Belgium, or to reverse the process. Another regular indulgence was for crews to fly 'in transit' from their main base and take-off from the assigned forward operating location; these extended from Châteaudun, south-west of Paris, to Soesterberg, central Holland.

To the extra expenditure in fuel and time was now added the distinct risk of being intercepted *en route* by RAF or USAAF fighters, especially during daylight hours; the growing presence of the B-17 and B-24 fighter escorts was particularly inhibiting to the *Luftwaffe* crews' security, as was Fighter Command's presence. On 29 February, Maj. Helmut Fuhrhop (*Kommandeur* of I/KG6) lifted off from Chièvres, Belgium, along with another crew, with Dreux, west of Paris, their destination. The Spanish Civil War veteran and his fellow Ju 188 pilot were close to Saint-Quentin when the nemesis in the form of eight No. 609 Squadron Typhoons crossed their path.

The weather conditions of snow squalls and a pattern of patchy low cloud might have saved the German duo had Fg Off. De Moulin and two others not caught the bombers' shadow reflecting from the cloud banks and flitting from left to right just above the formation's minimal altitude. In a frantic banking manoeuvre that barely avoided initiating a collision, the trio with the other five trailing behind rapidly caught up with their prey in a now-clear stretch of airspace.

De Moulin later recalled that the resultant and unequal air battle was akin to a pack of dogs savaging two hares; it was a case of 'fire at will' when close enough, with no order of assault among the formation—so much so that there was a danger of accidental strikes from the mêlée. The return gunfire availed either crew nil as the streams of cannon shells tore into the bomber structures to set both ablaze, with them hurtling to an inevitable explosive disintegration that expunged the lives of the ten crewmembers and three ground personnel on board.

A Steady Deterioration

As March opened, the latest thrust against London (1–2 March) did not live up to the February experience; of the 120 crews involved, only ten got through to the primary, with bomb loads otherwise widely scattered between Hampshire and Kent. Almost a full two weeks elapsed before the next raid of any size, when just over half the 140-strong main bomber force again struck London; the planned diversionary raid by Fw 190s further west was a failure as it was late in application while the radar 'traces' moved at a rate too fast for these to be other than fighter-orientated. The ample use of *Düppel*, Germany's equivalent of the RAF's radar-blinding Window, actually confirmed the main formation's approach route. Worse still was the loss of seventeen aircraft, eleven of which were lost or crashed other than on British territory. A particularly hard-hit unit was KG30 '*Adler*', which ended up minus six crews.

Fortunes of War

A seventh KG30 crew led by Ltn. E. Wolf in 4D+DM returned without Uffz. J. Wiesmaier (BS). The gunner was manning the lower-rear position when a night-fighter pass caused the gondola to break up. Wiesmaier was doubly fortunate after being cast out into mid-air in that not only was he not injured, his parachute pack was attached, and he was able to float down to become a *Kriegsgefangener*. What was initially an abrupt termination to his continued freedom would become a blessing seven nights later when two of his three companions' fortune would run out in a far starker manner. Their Ju 88A-4's downing by Fg Off. Hippert of No. 410 Squadron killed Wolf and Uffz. R. Ober (BF), although Ogfr. H. Moller (B) joined Wiesmaier in captivity.

Wolf's crew had been one of 144 crews sent out on the latest run to London. Although over 200 fires were started, the bombing effort was again well scattered and afforded little material damage to other than private properties. Nine out of the near-100 bombers crossing-in failed to regain their airfields. One of those was a KG6 Ju 188E-1 flown by Lt. G. Lahl, who became the second of Sqn Ldr E. Bunting's latest clutch of kills. The No. 488 Squadron pilot had previously gained his first victory with No. 85 Squadron (a Me 410 on 13–14 July), and tonight's second victim brought his confirmed tally to seven. The Ju 88A-4 in question belonged to 9/KG30, but the Mk XIII's powerful armament dispatched Obfw. N. Mayer's charge in flames, with him and one other crewmember perishing in the process.

London was on the target list on two more March nights, the first being 21–22 March, when 140 crews from eleven units were briefed to attack the Isle of Dogs in the East End—presumably with its dock complex as a focal point. Yet again, a sizeable percentage were unsuccessful in their primary task since only 110 crossed-in, of which exactly half released over their capital target.

On 24–24 March 1944, a Ju 188 participating in Operation Steinbock exploded under the gunfire of the Mk XVII Mosquito flown by Fg Offs E. Hedgecoe and N. Bamford (RO). The fireball that both aircraft and crew were enveloped within stripped most of the camouflage away, as well as the rudder fabric, and the crew were very fortunate to safely attain their airfield. The Mosquito was declared Category 'E', while its pilot was subsequently killed in a bad-weather accident.

Eight crews were downed over Britain or listed as MIA and two more crashed on the continent.

The month's final capital run went out three nights later, and of 130 crew rostered, exactly the same figure (110) was recorded as overflying Southern Britain, with sixty bombing London. This time around, the cost was noticeably higher. Eleven crews were listed MIA, a further seven crashing either on take-off or return, abandoned, or, in one case, shot down by its own flak batteries.

Three Ju 88s from KG6 were part of the 24–25 March 'blood debt', with two of them providing the AA gunners with a relatively successful 'bag'. First, Ltn. H. Besser's A-14 variant was assailed shortly after bombing. The initial effect from the strikes was nil, but shortly after, the airframe broke up with the sections descending near Hornchurch; only Ogfr. H. Wissel (BS) got out alive. Thirty minutes before, the gunners scored against 3E+HT to send it into an irrecoverable dive; tragically, the bomber descended directly upon a house, killing not only all four on Uffz. K. Luetcke's crew, but three women and two children.

Northern and Western Fiascos

The first of four raids meriting a 'major' title to targets other than London was mounted against Hull on 19–20 March. The east coast seaport's location enforced a several-hundred-mile traversing of the North Sea that, in turn, tested the inexperienced *Beobachter*'s navigational skill. A line of *Lux* buoys was dropped into the sea as an additional visual aid to the twin *Knickebein* electronic beams cantered on Hull. What should have been a reasonable concentration of aircraft and their bombs over the city turned out as a complete fiasco.

None of the small minority from the 131-strong force who claimed to have either released their flares or dropped their bombs on target did so. Nor was the figure of 103 crews claiming to have even crossed-in anywhere near the 50 per cent equivalent total picked up by the British monitoring staff. What was confirmed was the excision of nine more crews from *Luftwaffe* records. KG30's combat travails during the month continued with II *Gruppe*'s ranks shorn of four more crews.

The inward route brought the bombers south-west towards the northern fringes of Norfolk. No. 25 Squadron based at Coltishall, near Norwich, dispatched Flt Lt Singleton in his Mk XVII Mosquito; the unit was one of the only two operating the Mk X radar set. The ensuing several hours witnessed both a climax and near-nadir in both the fighter and its crew's fortunes. Neatishead GCI station directed the pilot to climb rapidly on an 80-degree course that took the aircraft

A particularly onerous but necessary ground crew duty was to sweep their assigned aircraft clear of snow, especially when it coated them with a heavy blanket as in this instance. The icing-up of wing surfaces that sapped their ability to support the aircraft in the air was a constant threat to both aircraft and crew survival prospects with landing and take-off arguably the twin worst scenarios.

out over the night-shrouded sea. A large clutch of bogies flying from starboard to port was advised and a 'trace' at 8 miles' range was soon established on Fg Off. Haslem's screen.

What was identified as 'a Ju 188' was opened up upon at close range. The resultant disintegration of the airframe showered debris in the pursuer's path and probably initiated the subsequent near-lethal problem affecting both Merlin engines. Almost at once, a second 'trace' similarly flying in a north-west direction was homed-in upon and, once again, a single burst of fire consigned another 'Ju 188', according to Singleton, to a marine grave along with all five occupants.

A third 'trace' was developing even as the second bomber plunged towards the sea scant distance from its companion in fate. Once again, the 'Ju 188' came into sight, but this time the bomber was describing a sharply-weaving flight manoeuvre. The first burst of fire ignited the starboard engine, and all too soon, a familiar pattern of airframe failure emerged as the riddled fuselage gave way. The doomed machine's downward path culminated in its disintegration on the sea surface (in fact, only one of the Junkers was lost this night and was believed to be the victim of AA guns stationed near Hull; the likelihood is that the trio of crews were part of the KG30 contingent recorded as bogies by the GCI station).

Less than fifteen minutes had elapsed between the three victories, but Singleton and Haslem had little time to savour their success before they faced a serious problem. Both engine temperature levels were steadily rising, and the 'feathering' of the port engine only placed extra pressure upon its twin. Opening-up the port engine and reducing revs maintained what was a slowly descending flight attitude and matters remained relatively stable until the aircraft was in Coltishall's landing pattern. It was then that the starboard engine failed and burst into flames, and before the pilot's intention to belly-in the Mosquito was completed, the port engine seized up after power had been applied.

Fortunately, the aircraft was in a level attitude, and although the impact was sharp, the airframe stayed intact, allowing the crew to scramble clear as it ground to a halt. The fire was extinguished by no more technical means than ground personnel throwing soil upon the cowlings. A post-mortem confirmed the glycol tanks had been punctured, so it was fortunate that the distance to land was not too far, otherwise the result would have been a descent into the sea with little likelihood of surviving either the impact or an extended exposure to the wintery North Sea.

Eight nights later, an equally abortive effort was launched against the West Country port of Avonmouth, part of Bristol. The failure was less explicable when given the relatively short Channel crossing and several *en route* landmarks. The fact of one I/KG66 *Pfadfinder* crew finally being shot down miles south of the target when approach was to have been made from due north is a small indicator of how dispersed the general performance of the 114 crews was that were sent out. Like Hull, Avonmouth remained inviolate from assault, and it was not until the Germans announced a 'successful' outcome that the British authorities became aware of the raid's intention.

The FB Mk VI airframe formed the basis for several subsequent Mosquito variants, including the NF Mk XIX and now the NF 30; this was, in fact, a development of the NF Mk XIX, but featuring Merlin 70 Series engines with two-stage superchargers compared to the single-stage facility on the Merlin 20 Series power plant borne by its predecessor. A total of ten squadrons, including seven for home-defence, were so equipped during 1944–45.

A similar experience of corporate failure was destined to accompany the follow-up raids to either of these cities during April. The order of projected attack was the same, with Hull appearing on the briefing maps on the 20th. A marginally greater-strength force (130) was involved, of which sixty were logged as crossing-in, but none of which landed their loads anywhere near the city boundaries. Three nights later came the follow-up bid to bomb Avonmouth, with 117 crews alerted. The same pattern of assembly over Guernsey, a direct northerly course to the Bristol Channel before making two flare-marked turns to starboard and finally a due south bombing run from the latter, was set out.

This time around, the percentage of attackers recorded over British soil was barely 30 per cent of the foregoing figure, while their bomb loads were scattered along the Channel coast. Whereas twelve crews were declared MIA or in one case crashed on return from the March raid, this sorry statistic was increased by one here. Two were downed over Southern Britain, eight declared MIA, and three crashed on return or, in one case, was shot down by a night fighter over Carentan.

Steinbock's Effective Demise

The second Hull attack had been immediately preceded by the latest and destined to be the final run to a target regarded as falling into the 'major' category. To date, the thirteen previous attacks had involved nearly 2,000 crews being briefed, of which just 1,500 had been 'logged-in' over Southern Britain; worse still was that the proportion of those crossing-in and reaching the Capital dropped to 527, with only four occasions when their numbers exceeded sixty and none attaining triple figures. Total tonnage released was 1,780 with what was a particularly derisory figure of 690 landing inside London's boundaries, albeit painful in terms of destruction and casualties inflicted.

London's Dockland formed the target for the attackers who would approach from Holland, swing in towards the city from the north-east, and depart in a south-easterly direction to finally disperse to their airfields over Boulogne. A major error in wind forecast—briefing stated this as coming from north–north-east, whereas British forecasters confirmed its diametrically opposite south–south-west course—should not have proved too critical since its strength was none too high. Nevertheless, although fifty-three crews did cross-in with a good proportion attaining their basic goal, the figure only represented around 40 per cent of the total force. The resultant effect upon either the city or its designated commercial quarter was at best marginal.

This was certainly not the case for the *Luftwaffe* personnel since, several hours following the 1 a.m. time for the raid's inception, no less than sixteen were either not accounted for or had crashed on return; a seventeenth had suffered the fate of falling victim to a No. 25 Squadron Mosquito near Schiphol in Holland. The bomber, a 7/KG2 Do 217M-1 was one of five *Geschwader* machines included within the loss total. KG6's trio of MIA losses was added to by a fourth that crashed on return. The same figure applied to the KG54 contingent, of which one was self-inflicted.

Uffz. H. Brandt's Ju 88A-4 had taken-off from Wittmundhafen and released his bomb load before being engaged by AA batteries over south-east London. The apparent escape from serious damage was temporary because at some stage the port engine caught fire. The final outcome was that Brandt, having presumably caught sight of an airfield, executed a safe belly-landing—on what he later stated under interrogation was assumed to be located in Holland. The four crewmembers must have been chagrined to discover the hostile identity of the airmen greeting their exit from the still-alight aircraft; the flames were quickly extinguished by the airfield personnel serving at Bradwall on the Thames Estuary, a forward base for Intruder twin-engined fighters heading out to the continent.

Steinbock's Final Convulsions

Before April was out, the *Luftwaffe* made its third bid out of a final figure of four to attack Bristol, but once again, the gods of war or, more bluntly, the indifferent to woeful performance of the participating crews contributed to another complete failure. What few bomb loads were released came down on locations anything up to 70 miles south of the target city. Of the thirteen crews MIA, crashing, or shot down by an intruder over friendly soil, just one was claimed by AA batteries and one by a night fighter.

The AA victim was a Ju 188A-2 belonging to 1/KG2 in the hands of Obltn. W. Christoff. After being engaged and struck, it was observed entering into a steady dive from 17,000 feet that culminated in a total disintegration within a wood and consumed all five crewmembers. Of interest to the authorities was the Jumo 213 engines from what was the first of this Junkers bomber variant to crash on British soil; the power plants were dispatched to RAE at Farnborough for detailed examination.

Uffz. R. Detering's Ju 88A-14 belonging to 4/KG30 had crossed the coast and when picked up by Sqn Ldr E. Barwell's Mk XVII was engaged in a weaving flight motion. A single burst of fire smashing into the starboard wing root and engine was followed by the bomber going into a vertical dive that evolved into a spinning action with sections falling off. Amazingly, only one among the four airmen failed to get clear, although the pilot received injuries.

With London finally removed from the target maps, the focus for assault during May witnessed the key naval base at Portsmouth continuing to be the main source, along with a final lunge at Bristol, while Plymouth, further west, was struck during the final night in April. III/KG100 transferred further north in France from where its crew would be part of a supposed mass assault numbering 400 aircraft—a figure quoted at briefing that was patently false; the figure of actual attacking bombers would be set at around seventy.

The battleship *King George V* said to be the reason for the sortie was the catalyst for the *Gruppe*'s presence since it was tasked with dropping the *Fritz X* guided missile. It was a state-of-the-art weapon and typical of the quantum leap in such technology that placed the German military science dispiritingly way ahead of their Allied contemporaries; the specialist bomb had already claimed several warships sunk or heavily damaged in the Mediterranean. Whether or not the Royal Navy's capital ship was in Plymouth was a moot point since adverse weather and a smokescreen, allied to late flare marking, largely thwarted the *Luftwaffe* crews' bid.

Ltn. Palme, flying in 6N+IT, did manage to commence his bomb run, but following what he regarded as AA gunfire crippling the Do 217K-3, as well as seemingly damaging his *Fritz X*'s flight controls, he jettisoned the bomb. All attempts to regain control of his charge proved fruitless, so he gave the order to bale out. In fact, his bomber had been fatally damaged by a Mk XII Mosquito flown by Sqn Ldr D. Williams from No. 416 (Canadian) Squadron. No sooner was the bomber dispatched than a second 'trace' appeared on the fighter's Mk VIII screen.

This was Hptm. Pfeffer (III/KG100 *Gruppenkommandeur*) who had circled the target area several times before deciding to 'abort' the sortie. His persistence at trying to sight the base and deliver his weapon proved his and the crew's undoing as Williams latched onto 6N+AD as it retreated. The starboard wing was set ablaze and the huge machine slammed into the Channel; two crewmembers had already baled out and miraculously survived their immersion to reach the land in their dinghy later in the day.

Bristol–Portsmouth 'Follies'

Forty-eight hours following the Bristol raid came the first of four runs to the Royal Navy's principal base of Portsmouth. As was the case over Hull and Bristol, nothing of any consequence was suffered either by the port facilities or the city's inhabitants. This was despite its prominent geographic location that the *Pfadfinder* crews of I/KG66 again failed to illuminate for the crews of the several assigned *Gruppen*. Of the six crews declared MIA, two were from 1(F)/121 tasked with photo reconnaissance of the port.

The first of these special-duty Me 410s had been involved during the scheduled time for the raid but had suffered engine damage that compelled a return ending in a fatal crash at Le Havre. Several hours later, Obltn. H. Kroll (*Staffelkapitän*) was on what was listed as his second flight to the area and was still 50 miles south of the objective when his presence was advised by Wartling GCI station to Flt Lt Branse Burbidge flying a No. 85 Squadron Mosquito. Flt Lt Bill Skelton picked up the Me 410's 'trace' at 3½-mile range and the fighter closed in from directly behind.

The range was down to 500 feet before the pilot was able to confirm the bogey's hostile status, after which he fired a seven-second burst that set the starboard engine on fire. A second attempt to fire was foiled by the guns jamming due to overheating. With his target in a gentle weaving and downward path, Burbidge pulled alongside to observe the cockpit hatch open before easing back and commencing a second attack; before this could be initiated, the Me 410 canted into a steep dive that culminated in an explosive contact with the sea. Kroll was killed but *Oberfähnrich* Meyer having vacated his position was later picked up in his dinghy. The Mosquito team would go on to become a leading exponent in the art of Intruder operations.

The second monthly thrust at Portsmouth was laid on the next evening, but total failure attended every effort of the fifty hostile pilots overflying the region around the city. The steady haemorrhage of lost crews continued with a total of six MIA and one lost on return. However, one among the former figure was not directly involved in the bombing effort. Lt. W. Wenning in his Me 410 from Stab/KG51 was carrying out an Intruder sortie when his path crossed that of an Airspeed Oxford; tragically, the *Luftwaffe* pilot's attack curve ended in a collision that took the two-man crew along with the RAF pilot Plt Off. Moore to their mutual deaths (this unit had caused mayhem among the returning B-24s of the 2nd Bomb Division on 22 April, when a mere handful of crews interdicted the formations as night was falling).

The first two weeks in May involved virtually no concentrated bombing effort other than on the 14th, when the fourth and final thrust against Bristol was launched by 150 crews, a figure that fell by two-thirds according to numbers of bombers picked up by the monitoring staff. Once again, the plotted bombing incidents were between Southampton and Portsmouth and a long way south-east of the city. Added to the complete lack of success in even attaining the target was the absence of eleven crews MIA and a further two involved in non-combat incidents.

Portsmouth was targeted on two occasions during May, the first commencing the night following the Bristol fiasco. Nothing tangible was achieved by the participants in terms of effective bombing, and four crews were lost in the process. One of the two downed over enemy soil was picked up by its aerial executioner flying a weaving course away north of the base. The Ju 88A-4 had been damaged by AA gunfire, whose effect had probably caused irremediable damage to the controls, hence the illogical flight direction. Uffz. H. Meyer's crew were given no quarter by Fg Off. D. Arnold's No. 456 Squadron Mk XVII Mosquito, whose bullet and cannon fusillade from close up sent their machine into a vertical and terminal dive.

What was the ultimate large-scale raid launched under the Steinbock umbrella was again directed towards Portsmouth on 22–23 May, but 'the hoodoo' hanging over all previous attempts to strike at the base held full sway. Although 80 per cent of the seventy-five participating crews were tracked-in over land, not one landed their bomb loads on the target area. Eight crews in all were MIA, two of whose intention had been to lay mines within the port's navigable channels.

Summary

Steinbock's inception had been based far more on an emotive reaction to the Allied bombing of Germany rather than on any realistic prospect of landing even a painful, let alone serious measure of punishment upon Britain's economic structure. For a start, both the quantitative and qualitative reserves of *Luftwaffe* bombers, as well as a good proportion of their crews, was not up to the task. In the former case, only the He 177 and to a certain extent the Ju 188 could approach the performance and load-carrying capacity of RAF Bomber Command or indeed the 8USAAF's B-17s and B-24s. The deployment of aged-service variants such as the Ju 88A-4 emphasised the paucity of the available bomber resources.

The quality of the aircrew graduating from 1943 onwards was being steadily eroded in comparison with the very high standards enjoyed up to then, standards that were superior in time span and instruction *vis-à-vis* the Allied air forces. The reason for the deterioration was both strategic and tactical. As Nazi Germany's resources were placed under increasing pressure on the Mediterranean and Russian Fronts, as well as at sea and in the air, the consequence was that the availability of equipment and particularly fuel with which to complete a continued high quality of training was conversely placed on the back foot in terms of priority.

Aircrew personnel were accordingly being turned out in ever-shortened time spans, with all that implied for their chances of functioning properly when engaged in combat. The tactical problem arose when the marauding USAAF escorts along with RAF intruders made their presence felt across the expanse of the Third Reich; training flights were under constant threat when conducted anywhere within the range of the Allied fighters. The effect upon the German training system must have been deleterious to say the least.

Even if an enhancement in aircraft and crew quality had been on hand by 1944, the bald fact remains that the defensive situation facing the attackers would have been as formidable as the one faced by RAF Bomber Command during the winter of 1943–44. Both the Beaufighter Mk VI and the several Mosquito night-fighter variants, backed by comprehensive GCI facilities, were well placed to hand out punishment on an unacceptable scale. In the event, the duo managed to achieve this during the four-month duration of Steinbock, while the equally sizeable AA gun and searchlight facilities added to the punishment.

Another failure factor during the campaign lay in the tactics adopted. Despite Göring's injunction to the contrary, the raids were launched during non-moonlit periods. This in turn created a staccato pattern of operations, although the ability of the night fighters to seek out their prey regardless of the visibility on hand would have rendered operations during moon periods as particularly lethal. True or not, the switch from the 1940–41 use of electronic target-identification methods to the 1944 use of flares placed an inordinate degree of responsibility upon the *Pfadfinders* of I/KG66, a duty that fell lamentably short of fulfilment on numerous occasions.

London's lure as the epicentre of the offensive confirmed the emotive basis for its launch. What Bomber Command was not to achieve in hammering at Berlin was even more a parallel cause for *Luftwaffe* failure. In any case, the city was but a part of the overall national productive output, the vast bulk of which remained inviolate from assault. In truth, the Führer appeared to be relying upon the morale effect on London's citizens to lead, in turn, for a plea to consider negotiations with the enemy. Admittedly, the civilian level of morale was to some degree stagnant after almost five years of conflict, but the possibility of such a compromise being raised among the British population in general was verging on the laughable. The die was cast for the conflict to progress in a manner that would give no quarter to Hitler and his gang of physical and intellectual thugs—unconditional surrender was the loud Allied call.

14

To Nocturnal Offence

Turning the Tide

Fighter Command's recovery from the Battle of Britain witnessed a degree of its strength focused upon carrying the fight to the Germans. The obvious basis for this was by day, but the hours of darkness were to provide a parallel pattern of assault. The non-availability of custom-built qualitative designs with which to launch such assaults deep into the enemy's hinterland was evident during 1940–41. The twin-engined Bristol Beaufighter was coming onto stream at this time, but the current priority for its operational function was to stem if not reverse the *Luftwaffe* assault upon Britain's cities; any offensive use of the design was understandably not under immediate consideration as the *Blitz* commenced.

No similar constraint was applied to other fighter types, however, with the Mk IF Blenheim and the Defiant being placed in the forefront, their targets the *Luftwaffe* bombers as they took off or landed back. The proximity of many of their airfields in terms of range made this possible; No. 23 Squadron's 'twins' were provided with wing racks, with which to supplement their meagre internal bomb load and duly dispatched from late December onwards. Although confirmed successes were few and far between during the ensuing winter months, the shadowy presence of the RAF aircraft surely exerted a psychological influence upon the German crews out of all proportion to the actual numbers involved.

The duty of carrying out what were in effect Intruder operations but on a larger scale with more effective aircraft was initially presented to squadrons operating on the Hurricane Mk IIC. The cannon-armed fighter provided a solid base for such operations. On the other hand, its relative lack of range meant that such forays were conducted at rather short range, with the northern fringes of France along with Belgium and sometimes western Holland falling within the Hawker fighter's province.

A view of Sqn Ldr Smallwood's No. 87 Squadron Mk IIC highlights the sharp outline of the Hurricane. The striking power of the four cannon-calibre weapons would bring devastation to any target the gunfire was focused upon. The sole restricting factor was the smaller ammunition content compared to the .303, a factor basically cancelled out by the enhanced weight of firepower.

Two sections from No. 87 Squadron are caught on camera as they hold a good formation pattern. However, the nature of Intruder operations usually merited the dispatch of the Hurricanes in single or at most double numbers. The Type A1 roundels and light 'Sky' code letters would appear to compromise the shadowy colour scheme.

The relatively small force of fighters on hand with which to carry out these operations resulted in little hindrance to the overall function of the *Luftwaffe* at this stage of the conflict. On the other hand, it was an indication, however minimal, that the German crews could not anticipate an unhindered progress in successfully carrying out their sorties. The RAF pilots were further tasked with attacking any suitable target, ranging from rail traffic to shipping or any other source that might be perceived to assist the Nazi war effort.

The interdiction of the airfield network in France, Belgium, and up into Holland from which the *Luftwaffe* bombers operated was of importance to at least causing some degree of dislocation to the crews' operations as well as to their morale. The RAF pilots would hover in the vicinity of selected bases and await the first sign of a bomber. The best time to engineer an assault was arguably at the conclusion of a raid. Not only was the aircraft in question running short of fuel, their occupants were physically tired and probably in a relaxed psychological mindset—the dangers all behind them with a safe landing looming ahead.

The ability to react promptly when ambushed in such circumstances was not easily achieved, and the outcome was often fatal for both bomber and crew. A knock-on effect when this situation arose was the disruption to any other crews making their final approach or already in the airfield circuit. The airfield lights would be extinguished with no immediate guarantee for the crews still aloft in their critically fuel-short machines when re-illumination would occur; were they to hold off until, as it were, 'normal service was resumed' or should they seek out an alternative airfield, assuming one was within reasonable distance as well as free from hostile attention?

The Risk Factors

The act of flying Intruder operations especially during the hours of darkness meant that any such foray held a range of potentially lethal situations for the attackers. Those operating on single-engined designs were wide open to failure should their power source be adversely affected either due to enemy action or to technical problems. Making attacking approaches at minimum height against, for example, rail, road, or canal-bound traffic held the risk of what was known as 'target fixation'; it was all too easy to be so focused on firing that pull-up from the strafing run left too little margin for clearing the target with a fatal collision the result.

The interdiction of airfields meant that closure towards this target category, particularly when making a pass at aircraft within the circuit, would certainly attract the full attention of the flak guns that could lay down an often-solid barrage of return fire. This was the reason for a number of RAF casualties, one of the more prominent being Flt Lt R. P. Stevens. During the latter stages of the *Blitz* and the course of 1941, the No. 151 Squadron pilot became the doyen of the single-engined night fighters operating on the Defiant and, in his

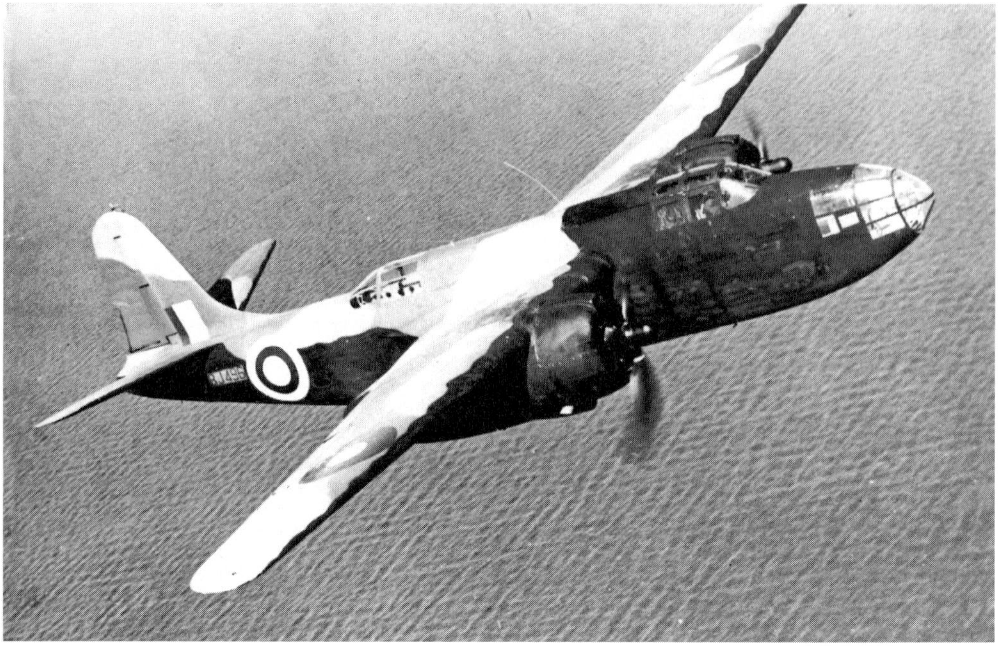

The DB-7 Havoc in its original form was envisaged as a bomber bearing a three-man crew whose navigator occupied the nose compartment. The lengthy endurance and internal bomb bay, as well as a four-gun layout in the nose side panels, made it suitable for nocturnal operations with Fighter Command, and with Intruder activity specifically in mind. Note how the black underside paint is carried onto the upper edges of the wings and stabilisers.

case, the Hurricane. Bereft of on-board radar equipment, they had to rely upon visual contact alone. In Stevens' case, he amassed the incredible total of fourteen confirmed kills by late October.

In mid-1941, the squadron's Mk I Hurricanes gave way to the better-armed Mk IIC, the four 20-mm cannon advancing the RAF fighters' striking power not only against aircraft, but also against ground targets. It was likely that this was the reason for Stevens taking off on 15–16 December and heading out over the North Sea towards southern Holland. During the course of his aerial hunt, he must have overflown the major airfield of Gilze-Rijen. Whether he was initiating an attack or not, the tragic result was the crash of his fighter in the vicinity of the airfield accompanied by his death.

Nocturnal 'Leader': No. 1 Squadron

Having transferred to the south coast in June 1941, No. 1 Squadron's companion unit at Tangmere was No. 1445 Flight, currently training-up on Douglas Havocs fitted with the Turbinlite searchlight, this to be used to pick out enemy bombers that were intended to be shot down by the accompanying single-engined fighter.

The Hurricane pilots were assigned the duty of assisting the flight in its activity when not indulging in normal operations that saw its Mk IIC variants attacking shipping in particular; strangely, operations were minimal in scale up to the year's end, and when flown, the accent was as much on night as daytime activities.

The same degree of operational lassitude extended into 1942, with adverse weather the prime cause. On the other hand, liaison flights with No. 1445 Flight continued when the conditions allowed. A notable operation was the squadron's involvement in *Donnerkeil*, the escape of the three *Kriegsmarine* warships through the Channel, when attacks were made against the escorting vessels that ended with two pilots MIA; otherwise, the absence of *Luftwaffe* bomber formations over Britain in any numbers, whether by night or day, left Fighter Command in general able to continue expanding its offensive capability. The Circus daylight regime commenced in 1941 would proceed apace when conditions permitted.

No. 87 Squadron had helped to initiate night Intruder operations during the latter four mouths of the *Blitz*. Its targets had been primarily the French airfields from which the bombers were operating, and a measure of success had been achieved. However, the departure of the bomber *Geschwadern* to Russia had seen these sorties steadily diminish as autumn gave way to winter. The circumstances that impelled Hitler to call for the Baedeker mini assault on selected British cathedral cities did not directly prove to be the catalyst for Nos 87 and No. 1 Squadrons renewing the previous year's Intruder assault on the enemy bomber formations. Instead, the greatly intensified bomber traffic commencing in late April, did likely induce a similar increase in the command's countermeasures.

As the situation turned out, it was the latter unit that was first into action and two among its complement of pilots were destined to make a name for themselves in this specific function. Flt Lt Karel Kuttelwascher from Czechoslovakia had flown with the French air force in 1940 before joining the RAF. By early 1941, he was flying on operations and had been credited with one Bf 109 kill that would rise to four by June. Kuttelwascher's companion and Intruder exponent should not have been continuing on operations. Sqn Ldr Jim MacLachlan had flown in Malta during 1941 but following several kills had lost his left forearm in a combat. Repatriated to Britain, his indomitable spirit had brought him back into operational service with No. 1 Squadron as its CO the previous October.

The combination of the four-cannon armament coupled to fuel capacity increased to 185 gallons with the addition of twin 44-gallon drop tanks meant that the fighter's ability to hand out severe punishment while loitering over the continent up to nearly four hours meant the pilots could either cover a large geographic area or wander to and from selected airfields at will. The squadron records indicate that certain airfields between Paris and Rennes (Brétigny, Saint-André, Dreux, Évreux, and Rennes itself) were regularly scheduled for supervision, a fact that suggests the squadron had been assigned this zone of operations. Trouble was unknowingly brewing for the bomber crews.

Two ground crew armourers are replenishing the port wing compartment on a No. 1 Squadron Mk IIC Hurricane; the belt-feed drums are laid out on the wing along with the compartment covers that possess a 'bulge' to accommodate the drums' extended height above the wing surface. Unsheathed cannon barrels reveal their recoil spring sections. Symbols under the cockpit indicate three railroad engines and one aircraft credited as kills to this fighter.

A leading exponent of night-Intruder operations was 'Mac' MacLachlan who, along with Flt Lt Kuttelwascher, formed a deadly duo flying with No. 87 Squadron. Loss of his left forearm in Malta in no way inhibited his return to combat during late 1941, and he ran up a score of five kills to add to eight Mediterranean victories. Three more were earned flying daylight Intruder operations with the ADFU in 1943 before he was tragically lost on 18 July.

The Grim 'Fruits of Victory'

April Fool's Night was to prove a savage experience bereft of humour for a Ju 88 crew at the hands of Kuttelwascher. He had taken-off just ahead of his CO, and after reaching Évreux, where nothing was discovered, he moved on to Melun with its lit flare path over which a Ju 88 was orbiting, its navigation lights clearly and fatally visible. The two short bursts of fire from close behind induced a fierce blaze in one engine followed by a steep irrecoverable dive that consumed the bomber and its crew. A second Ju 88 was picked out, but only slightly damaged during the course of the three-hour sortie.

MacLachlan had no success this night nor was he any more fortunate on the 16th, when both set out. In contrast, Kuttelwascher increased his margin over his CO. This time round, he successively orbited near three of the previously-mentioned airfields but drew a blank before retracing his flightpath to the second, Saint-André. Here he found two aircraft with navigation lights on; one extinguished his promptly, but whether this was on being warned from ground control or through belated discovery was uncertain. His companion was still lit up when the Czech's cannon shells doomed the machine as well as its occupants to an explosive end.

The Baedeker raids commencing on 23–24 April extended over successive moon periods whose light conditions were an aid to the Hurricane pilots, in this case initially benefitting the No. 1 Squadron CO followed later by Kuttelwascher. Attempts to infiltrate the circuits at two airfields failed, but Évreux yielded a better result in the form of a Do 217 taking off. Its progress was clinically terminated within a minute or two; a second bomber, although damaged, escaped thanks to MacLachlan running out of ammunition. Kuttelwascher's single victim was based at Rouen-Boos and was taken down after the Czech had completed a circle over the airfield.

Over the ensuing month or so, almost all the aircraft kills would fall to these two pilots. Six would be claimed by Kuttelwascher during May as opposed to two by his CO. A double victory was realised on 30 April–1 May, but the pinnacle of his combat career arose four nights later over Saint-André. A group of He 111s returning from a truly devastating raid upon Cowes (Isle of Wight) were picked out in the landing circuit. The RAF assassin slotted in behind one bomber that slumped fatally to the ground following multiple strikes that set an engine ablaze; the next bomber in the aerial procession fared no better and plunged into a wood; the third potential victim in line was hit but not actually seen to crash although Kuttelwascher's claim that he witnessed three separate fires appeared enough for the authorities to grant him all three as kills.

MacLachlan had been similarly blessed the night before over Dinard. He recollected the first bomber was caught during its landing approach and the effect of his short burst of fire was the severing of one engine from its mounting and the bomber's violent plunge to earth. 'Mac' immediately sighted another aircraft above, and having closed in from below, he discharged his cannon; fire

Flt Lt Karel Kuttelwascher from Czechoslovakia was 'Mac' MacLachlan's fellow exponent in the art of night Intruder operations. His eighteen confirmed kills were registered between January 1941 and July 1942; all but three scored during daylight operations were gained during the first six months of 1942 when No. 1 Squadron was pursuing its nocturnal path. Kuttelwascher remained in Britain after the Second World War and flew with British European Airways but sadly died of a heart attack in 1959.

immediately took hold, but this time his victim's demise extended over several miles in a shallow dive prior to the final impact. A double confirmed score on 3–4 June would close off his score while with No. 1 Squadron.

Kuttelwascher's record of victories would extend further into the summer as well as being greater to the tune of seven kills, with several damaged claims added. Nor were these attained as solely single victims on each occasion. The first double came on 3–4 June, with Saint-André again the focal point. This time, he latched on to one of a pair of He 111s and gave it and its crew no-quarter as the flame-wreathed aircraft descended to its fate. After engaging a Do 217 that evaded his lethal attention, he picked out one of a quartet that was closest to his course and sent this to an equal fiery fate.

The second doubles sortie on 1–2 July was unknowingly the squadron's swansong in its current Intruder role. Dinard airfield's light pattern caught his attention, above which he encountered and dispatched a Do 217. The second Do 217 victim may have escaped had the searchlights that latched onto the Hurricane destroyed its pilot's night vision; as it was, his eyes were sufficiently unaffected for him to continue his firing pass and send the aircraft into a steep irrecoverable dive north of the airfield (unbeknown to him was that all further combat success would be denied him, even when he later resumed operations with No. 23 Squadron and its Mosquito F Mk IIs).

The 3–4 June successes for Kuttelwascher were paralleled that night by MacLachlan, and it was the airmen based at Saint-André who were initially punished by him since he had preceded Kuttelwascher by one hour. The sight of well over ten Do 217s circling the airfield must have been stunning, but he controlled any urge to rush in upon the formation. Instead, he infiltrated its ranks

An underside view of Z3778 demonstrates how regular operational service soon led to heavy staining of the lower airframe, with oil secretion and radiator exhaust prominent factors in the deterioration. The squadron's transfer to Acklington in June and conversion onto the Typhoon was in progress when, on 14 August, JX: Y was written-off following a crash during a landing overshoot of the airfield.

steadily to catch one bomber barely short of the runway's end; it never reached that desirable goal because the cannon shell fusillade took it out of its now minimal height level, leaving it to smash into the ground.

He was instantly 'coned' by searchlights but evaded their beams and climbed away. To his undoubted surprise, the airfield lights remained illuminated, so he again closed in upon the remaining group of Do 217s continuing to circle, their crews seemingly unaware of the carnage below. His first intended victim also on landing approach was struck, but not fatally damaged; the second one flying appreciably higher was not so fortunate since MacLachlan's gunfire plucked it out of the sky to impact close to the airfield perimeter.

Target Variation

The downing of *Luftwaffe* aircraft, with bombers a priority, was of palpable benefit, however marginal, to the Allied cause. Another target category casting up a bonus for the Intruder pilots or crews was the destruction of all forms of transport with railway locomotives a particular prize. The vulnerability of this form of transport to assault by heavily-armed fighters such as the Typhoon was evident. A solid strike upon the boiler would either puncture the metal skin, allowing the highly-pressurised content to dissipate, bringing the machine to a halt, or better still would induce an explosive effect that would tear the locomotive asunder (in the longer term, the dislocation of the rail network would work in the Allies favour both in tactical and strategic terms).

The almost total lack of success in engaging the *Luftwaffe* crews by the other No. 1 Squadron pilots at least saw their frustrations partially alleviated by their looking out for the rail-bound alternative as laid down by the RAF hierarchy. Having said this, there was a regular number of pilots specifically dispatched to take out locomotive-hauled traffic. For example, on the last night in April, six pilots were sent out in full moonlit conditions, and between them, they immobilised or damaged upwards of twenty locomotives. Although some of the driving teams were probably French, the fact that only German personnel were permitted nocturnal travel meant that passenger trains could be attacked with little or no likelihood of death or injury for the oppressed population in this or any other Nazi-occupied land.

The ever-fickle hand of fate would witness only Kuttelwascher surviving the conflict. Following a spell off operations at an OTU after relinquishing command of No. 1 in August, 'Mac' joined the Air Fighting Development Unit (AFDU) from where he began to fly Ranger sorties on Mk IA Mustangs in June 1943. He added three to his tally on his first sortie on the 29th, but tragedy intervened during the second daylight sortie on 18 July. Along with Flt Lt Geoff Page, the duo undertook

No. 87 Squadron spent most of 1942 at Charny Down before deployment to North Africa in November. It continued night-intruder operations from May, but with the all-black scheme displaced other than beneath by dark green and medium sea grey. *Night Duty* was one of two Mk IICs bearing presentation names relating to the nursing profession. Photo taken in September when Type C1 markings were now the norm.

an operation to France, but during its inward course, his Mk I Mustang was seen to exude a strong smoke trail. The resultant attempted crash-landing culminated with the airframe shattering, and although McLachlan was extricated still alive from the wreckage, he subsequently died in a German field hospital on 31 July.

Strategic Build-up

The need to harry the enemy in every way possible was a natural priority for the RAF not only by day but by night. The latter situation had become ever more evident as RAF Bomber Command expanded its presence over the Third Reich's territory at an initially painful and largely result-less pace. As early as the winter of 1941–42, the growing presence of the *Nachtjagd* had presented serious problems for Bomber Command. The tendency for the crews to filter towards their targets in a loose manner had presented the *Nachtjagd* pilots with the opportunity to home-in upon single targets when guided by their radar stations, and the casualty rate grew at an alarming pace.

The counter challenge to this aerial version of 'spider and fly' tactic was initiated in early 1942 with the advent of the 'bomber stream' concept. Now, instead of operating in a loose pattern akin to the *Luftwaffe* experience over Britain in 1940–41, the RAF bombers were to form up in a more compact, albeit general, formation that would concentrate the overall force. Instead of arriving over enemy territory during a multi-hour period, the revised procedure concentrated the assault effort in a far more limited time span often lasting less than thirty or forty minutes over the selected target. The knock-on effect of this operational revision was that the *Nachtjagd* concept of having their fighters orbiting specific radar-directed locations to await the arrival of a single target was made redundant.

The bomber stream concept had reaped its initial reward at the end of May when over 1,000 bombers attacked the city of Cologne; a swatch of devastation was accomplished at the (then) minimal cost of forty-one bombers, an action that concentrated the minds of the Nazi hierarchy as to how effectively challenge this looming and probably mortal threat to their national structure. As it transpired, Bomber Command's logistics could not sustain the assault on this level of activity for more than the immediate future and the campaign resumed a normal intensity that did not materially punish Germany's industrial structure unduly up to the year's end.

The Havoc's entry into service as an Intruder saw the aircraft issued to No. 23 Squadron. The temperate camouflage seen on the preceding example was replaced with an overall application of RDM2 black, whose adhesive quality was indifferent to poor, hence the lighter patches around the forward wing surfaces between the fuselage and engines. Note the reduced area of the yellow rim on the A1 roundel.

No. 418 (Canadian) Squadron was formed at Debden in November 1941, equipped with the Boston III and commenced Intruder operations in March along with No. 23 Squadron, and in August, with No. 605 Squadron. The normal nose-mounted machine guns were supplemented by a ventral gun pack containing cannon-calibre armament. An airman is directing the pilot of TH: C on what is an unusually clear day, given Britain's wayward weather patterns.

'Battle of the Ruhr'

ACM 'Butch' Harris's central aim to bring the conflict home to the Nazi hierarchy would never be relaxed during his tenure as C-in-C Bomber Command. Post-war critics of the manner in which he prosecuted the campaign have asserted that he thought his crews could reduce Germany's resistance to a point where they would see the folly of their actions and sue for peace; his statement during the subsequent onset of the Battle of Berlin during late 1943 would appear to support these criticisms. Harris was a man who stood by his assertions as well as the actions of his 'Old Lags' as he would allude to his airmen then and up to his death in 1983. He sensed that the battering of Germany's industrial and military infrastructure was adding one more penalty upon that nation's ability to resist the steadily crushing weight of the Allied onslaught.

A full year after Harris had taken charge, the command's strength in aircraft numbers, as well as the greater performance qualities of the Halifax and Lancaster that had come on stream during 1942, gave him the chance to indulge in a several months-long assault upon Germany's industrial core, the Ruhr. The persistent smoke blanket hanging over the key region had greatly inhibited visual sight of the various targets, but now the RAF had access to a precision marker system code-named Oboe and the cloak of industrial fog no longer guaranteed immunity from attack.

This took the form of two tracking stations, the first of which transmitted a beam signal that guided the flare-marker aircraft—in this and future instances, the fleet-footed Mosquito—along a north–south curve. The second station's beam signal intersected with the other at the designated target site at which point the flares were released. The Krupp's complex at Essen was selected on 5–6 March, and the outcome was material destruction among the plant facilities and surrounding factories compared to the sizeable town's virtual immunity from attack up to this stage of the conflict. Here was a mortal threat to any similar location, although the curvature of the earth currently restricted the maximum signal range of Oboe to no further than the Ruhr region.

The 'Stinger' Arrives

The first real boost to the concept of Intruder operations was destined to arrive during 1942. Although home defence needs still gained a degree of priority, given that there was no absolute guarantee of a second *Blitz* campaign not recurring during 1941–1942, the operational debut of the de Havilland Mosquito in its fighter format was on hand as the third full year of the now-universal conflict evolved. The NF Mk II was simply an AI Mk IV radar-equipped variant of the first F Mk II batch, totalling 278 airframes in all. By April, Nos 151 and 157 Squadrons were operational with the company's 'Wooden Wonder'.

A Havoc from No. 23 Squadron is being prepared for take-off from Ford sometime during late 1941. The pilot is already in position with the navigator negotiating the angled access hatch to the nose compartment; this is his position for the entire flight as the cockpit bulkhead denies movement back into the main fuselage—not the best location in a crash-landing.

A second view of *Evelyn* from the port side shows the nose hatch closed, Pratt & Whitney Twin Wasps having been started using the APU on the left and now straining under full power against the wheel chocks. The placing of the aircraft letter on the forward fuselage was a regular feature with the Douglas aircraft. The twin 'troughs' for the nose-mounted guns stand out in both photos.

A third squadron (No. 23) converted from the Boston Mk III to the Mosquito in June, but its activities with the Douglas design during 1941 had placed it as the premier twin-engined Fighter Command unit to indulge in Intruder operations. The original machines were the DB-7 variant originally intended for delivery to France but switched to Britain after that nation's collapse. The nose armament of four and later eight .303 machine guns of what was designated the Havoc were mounted alongside the Plexiglas nose compartment.

Operations commenced in March, and with the *Blitz* still in full progress, much of the crews' attention was directed towards airfield interdiction. Although able to fly further and over a longer time span than their single-engined contemporaries, the fact of what was a further handful of aircraft that also possessed no more than average striking power could do little more than add somewhat to the *Luftwaffe* crews' discomfiture, though the ability to carry a reasonable bomb load was a benefit.

The *Luftwaffe* had largely decamped east for Operation Barbarossa, and the pace of night-fighter activity had in consequence dropped noticeably away; the *Baedeker* raid sequence in April–May was but a blip in terms of regular raids by large formations, so Air Ministry thoughts were turned towards utilising the NF Mk II Mosquito on nocturnal duties over the continent. The fearsome firepower of its cannon and machine-gun quartets allied to its greater overall performance *vis-à-vis* the Havoc–Boston made it a prime candidate for the task. The Mosquito stock on hand was assigned to home defence, but a simple solution was found. This entailed removing the radar equipment from twenty-five airframes as well

A fine upward-angle camera shot has focused upon DZ715/UP: L as she flies in close formation with a fellow squadron aircraft. Both belong to No. 605 (County of Warwick) Squadron, whose crews operated the Mk II in an effective Intruder role between February and July 1943 while based at Castle Camps.

as adding extra fuel tanks and dispatching these fighters to No. 23 Squadron. Between mid-1941 and December 1941, the squadron carried out its Intruder assignment, after which it was posted to Malta from where it performed the same function over several months.

Wg Cdr S. Hoare (CO) had led the way on the very second night sortie when he downed a Do 217 while claims for two kills were submitted by a second pilot forty-eight hours later—a good start for the squadron, especially since it possessed but two operational Mosquitos at this point. A proper aircraft establishment was soon on hand and with these the sortie numbers steadily built up. Losses were borne—three on one night—to somewhat balance the not inconsiderable number of registered victories. Another pilot and navigator team were very fortunate when, with one engine 'out' due to failure they crash-landed at Manston—running into a steam roller whose bulk fortunately left the main airframe intact, although shattering the port engine nacelle.

The Stinger's Companion

The Bristol Beaufighter had justly won its spurs as an all-round performance night fighter during the course of the *Blitz*. Although more pugnacious in overall outline compared to the more-slender Mosquito, the sturdy nature of its construction allied to an even greater firepower—four 20-mm cannon nose and six wing-mounted machine guns—made it a worthy combat contemporary. Another likely advantage lay in the twin Bristol Hercules radial engine that could withstand as great a (if not greater) degree of punishment from battle damage than the Merlin mount on the Mosquito; this was thanks to the latter's dependence on coolant-control that would be lost if the tank was punctured and the fluid drained away, leaving the engine to seize up.

A subtler albeit beneficial advantage of the Hercules related to the crew's aural comfort. 'Jimmy' Rawnsley who would operate on both types during the Second World War asserted that, whereas the Hercules engine gave off a bearable 'snoring' note, this applied far less pressure to one's hearing compared to the Merlin's snarling, crackling noise pitch that could and did induce a headache on occasions. Of course, his observer's location being further back in the Beaufighter's fuselage compared to his forward position in the Mosquito cockpit that placed him level with the Merlin's bulk may well have made the difference in the level of noise toleration.

As with the Mosquito's adaptation to more offensive operations, so the same thoughts among the RAF hierarchy would be directed towards the Beau as it was generally dubbed being similarly utilised. The generous basic fuel capacity within the thick-wing platform permitted it to accommodate a total of 510 gallons in four tanks that, in turn, made the aircraft capable of ranging well into Western Europe. An extra 74 gallons could be added if the machine guns gave way to the two tanks containing this additional fuel load. The reduction in firepower still left the design with a strong striking ability via its quartet of 20-mm cannon. The lack

Mk VIF Beaufighter V8613 bears no squadron markings but was reportedly assigned to No. 68 Squadron. That unit took on the variant in early 1943 and conducted Ranger sorties by night out of Coltishall. The external aerials barely impeded the aircraft's performance; this was in comparison to its *Nachtjagd* opponents who flew with massive nose-mounted aerials almost until the end of the Second World War when centimetric-wave radar was belatedly introduced.

of a bomb bay was the sole deficiency *vis-à-vis* the de Havilland design, but the scale of on-board armament still provided a sound basis for conducting Intruder operations at least against ground targets. However, there was to be a period where the Beau's attention would be directed against their *Nachtjagd* opponents.

Fighter/Bomber Command Link-Up

During the Second World War, the experience of all the major combatants in the European theatre of operations when setting out to carry the aerial battle to their opponents provided a salutary lesson in overconfidence in all three instances. The *Luftwaffe*'s bid to hammer Fighter Command out of existence as a proposed prelude to invasion manifestly failed and recourse had to be had to assaulting Britain's industrial capacity by night. The USAAF's 'unescorted bomber' theory was brought to a very bloody and virtual permanent conclusion by the events of October 1943 when the bomber force was torn apart, losing 148 MIA crews in just four missions.

In the latter case, the mandatory continuation of the daylight offensive was first restored to stability and then transformed into the Allies favour by the presence of—and more pertinently, the proper operational deployment of—the trio of American escort fighter designs, with the P-51 arguably the one that was destined to reign supreme over its adversaries, no matter where they were encountered above the Third Reich's ill-gotten empire. But what of the third aerial combatant in the form of RAF Bomber Command?

As with the *Luftwaffe*, the early months of the Second World War witnessed the RAF crews operating by day. However, the lesson of attempting to challenge its adversary's defensive screen while relying solely on its own bomber resources to attain targets with acceptable loss ratios was more swiftly, and bloodily, brought home during the winter of 1939–40. Several very costly encounters forced the command to consider operating over Europe during the hours of darkness, with all that this implied for loss of accuracy. As matters transpired over the ensuing months of 1940 and 1941, the nett result was, as one senior figure asserted, 'the exporting of X number of bombs to the Continent'; not only were the briefed targets being missed, they were not even being located in the majority of cases.

From 1942 onward, the command's operational function became somewhat more focused in terms of target accuracy, although involving what was an 'area' bombing policy. A basic inability to guarantee picking out specific industrial or

The Beaufighter's long-range ability coupled with its heavy mix of cannon and machine-gun weaponry made it an ideal candidate for Intruder operations as Wg Cdr Braham was to prove with No. 141 Squadron. This former No. 604 Squadron example has the unit's code painted out, although the NG letters can just be discerned. Picture was taken no earlier than the summer of 1942 when the Type C1 markings were introduced.

military complexes within a city mass had the knock-on effect of encompassing the population regardless of whether any individual was contributing to the war effort. The latter consideration was covered by the 1943 Casablanca Conference *ukase* on the Allied bombing policy that listed the final element of its overall intention to be 'the undermining of the German Nation's morale to a point where its capacity for continued resistance is fatally weakened'. The meaning of Total War in its inevitable ruthless format would to be brought to bear upon the Nazi regime.

The tendency in numerous post-war documentaries dealing with the strategic bombing offensive to assert that flying by night was a safer option to the daylight alternative is a grossly-misleading statement. The cloak of darkness was only of benefit if the defenders, in this case the *Nachtjagd*, had been deficient both in numbers and expertise, but sadly that was never the case for the bulk of the Second World War. Just as the *Jagdflieger* pilots successfully blunted all attempts by the USAAF 'heavies' to attain their goal while operating without heavy and regular escort cover, so the same degree of pressure was being brought to bear upon RAF Bomber Command, whose defensive armament was even more incapable of handling the Ju 88 and Bf 110 nocturnal marauders than the plethora of .5-calibre weaponry borne by the B-17s and B-24s.

It was not until the advent of Operation Overlord and beyond that invasion that the RAF could feasibly launch its heavies on daylight operations. Prior to that, the crews were forced to soldier on, with no prospect of any large-scale fighter cover in the night-shrouded European skies being a viable option. The best that could be done to at least alleviate the situation was to dispatch fighters in a bid to either interdict the *Nachtjagd* airfields or to intercept aircraft while they were airborne. In the latter instance, it was the Mk VIF Beaufighters from No. 141 Squadron that came into their own during mid-1943.

'Catch as Catch Can!'

A device code-named 'Serrate' had been developed that had the intention of acting as a lure to entice enemy aircraft onto the RAF aircraft equipped with a set. The initial 'contact' was established on the twin screens of Serrate that homed-in upon the Bf 110 and Ju 88s' *Liechtenstein* on-board radar transmissions, after which the standard AI set's screen took over the hunt once the latter was guided close enough to make contact. The Beaufighter would steadily manoeuvre onto the attacker, thereby transforming him from the potential hunter to the quarry (the 'traces' on the set's twin screens, one for azimuth and one for elevation assessment of the bogey's distance and vector angle, resembled the outline of a fish's skeleton frame, hence the code-name's explanation). No. 141 was based at Wittering with Sqn Ldr Bob Braham already an ace and destined to be a leading expert in Intruder operations during the Second World War. This was the squadron that would be equipped with Serrate and tasked with seeking out the German crews.

Wg Cdr 'Bob' Braham studies a map along with his most-regular navigator Flt Lt 'Sticks' Gregory, with whom he paired-up following their transfer to No. 141 Squadron in late 1942. Braham had already scored twelve kills with No. 29 Squadron and would add to his final score of twenty-nine confirmed by May 1944. However, nine would be shot down after he left No. 141 Squadron and while he served in a senior post at No. 2 Group HQ. On 25 June, he undertook his latest solo sortie by day but was shot down and captured along with Fg Off. Don Walsh (N).

The equipment was fitted and flight-tested by mid-June, and on 14–15 June, it was adjudged clear for active operations to commence. Braham led five other crews aloft in the full knowledge that the 197 Lancasters and Halifaxes heading for Oberhausen in the Ruhr would still face the full force of triple figures of night fighters. Trailing the stream from behind and below—the suspected attack angle currently favoured by the *Nachtjagd* crews—Flt Lt 'Sticks' Gregory (so named due to his pre-war profession as a jazz band drummer) was operating the AI set in the hope of picking up a trace; any such contact made that was finally established as hostile would see him switch to the Serrate equipment with which to guide Braham onto the target.

As the bombers were heading home and crossing over Holland, Braham suddenly sensed excitement in his navigator's voice as he announced: 'Bob, I've got a signal, turn gently port'. A short pause, then: 'Bob. I think this one is behind us; the signal is strong'. Braham said: 'Have you anything on the AI yet?' Gregory replied: 'No but keep on turning'. For the pilot, it was an eerie feeling knowing that the sortie was probably developing into a deadly hide-and-seek match with an as-yet unseen foe, especially when Gregory announced: 'I've got an AI contact,

2,000 yards behind; bank hard as possible to port'. Braham's next question was 'Are you sure it isn't one of our bombers?' The response was (rather illogically) 'Yes, it isn't. The Serrate and AI signals line up. Keep turning, he's only 1,000 yards and twenty degrees to your port as well as slightly above. Now ease the turn and watch it; you're closing fast and should see him very soon. He's still well over to port and about 600 yards distant'. Then Braham said, 'I've got him, I've got him!' with a yell.

The moonlight had assisted the pilot's vision in picking up what was identified as a Bf 110 heading south, and he crept up to 400 yards before unleashing a torrent of fire that smothered the airframe and doubtless caused physical mayhem among the hapless crew. The brightly burning machine fell away and was observed by Gregory to finally impact on the north-east fringe of Holland's massive marine bay, the Zuiderzee (post-war research confirmed the crash site as north of Steveren). This was Braham's fourteenth confirmed kill and the first in a run of five Bf 110G-4 victims over the ensuing two months; it was also the sole success scored from among the six crews this night, some of whom suffered set failure. Nineteen bombers had been culled from the stream, making a loss rate whose 10 per cent figure was unsupportable in the long run if the campaign was to remain viable, but one less aerial 'sting' had been deleted from the defenders' ranks.

Ten nights on and the bomber assault on Wuppertal in the Ruhr witnessed nine crews lifting off from the forward base at Bradwell on the Thames Estuary to trail the stream out over the Belgium–Holland border. Gregory picked up an AI contact, but whether Serrate also entered into the interception is unclear. At any rate, the Bf 110 appeared in sight at a minimum distance that still permitted Braham to land a devastating weight of firepower in two swift bursts; the flame-shrouded aircraft took its crew to their mutual deaths close to Gilze-Rijen where Flt Lt R. P. Stevens had met the same fate eighteen months before. The third Bf 110 victim was downed during the 8–9 August raid on Mannheim, but even better fortune lay ahead of Braham nine nights distant.

The pace of Serrate operations never materially slackened as the offensive was conducted on every available night when the conditions permitted its launch; the shorter summer nights dictated the distances the command could penetrate into the Third Reich. There was one looming limitation for No. 141 Squadron that would finally render sorties with the Bristol twin an unviable option. This was in relation to range that currently was adequate during the Battle of the Ruhr phase and even the subsequent Battle of Hamburg, Germany's second-largest industrial city located on the Elbe near its North Sea outflow (during July, long-range attacks were made on Turin in northern Italy and Montileard near the French–Swiss border, both well beyond the Serrate fighter's range; all the more ironic was the overall loss ratio of less than 4 per cent, but this acceptable statistic held no guarantee of being maintained as the campaign increased in intensity and distance. Having said that, return raids to Turin and Stuttgart in south-west Germany rendered similar low loss percentages).

Bad Night for NJG1

What was most certainly the peak of Serrate success enjoyed by No. 141 Squadron occurred on the night of 17–18 August 1943, when Bomber Command dispatched nearly 600 crews to attack the key rocket-research establishment at Peenemunde. The location was up on the Baltic coast and deep inside Germany with all that this presaged for a prolonged and bloody battle with the *Nachtjagd*. In the event, forty-one bombers were MIA, but a greater figure was denied the defences thanks to the successful efforts of No. 139 Squadron's Mosquitos, who drew off a sizeable proportion of the *Nachtjagd* strength by engaging in a spoof action over Berlin. This activity as the main assault to the north was nearing Peenemunde ensured a vital delay in the *Nachtjagd*'s involvement with the main force. The Berlin-directed aircrafts' belated transfer to and subsequent presence over the true target, although bearing fruit to the above stated degree, was arguably lower than would have been the case had they been on full hand over the target area prior to the attack's initiation.

Further to the west over central Holland, there had occurred a confrontation between No. 141 Squadron and NJG1 that had a small, if measurable, effect upon the overall battle. Leeuwarden was the current home for IV *Gruppe* of what was the longest-serving *Geschwader* operating within the Na*chtjagd*. Created back in 1940 by Wolfgang Falck, one of its current *Experten* was Heinz-Wolfgang Schnaufer who, by the end of the Second World War, would amass a frightening figure of 121 *Abschuss* and who was currently based at the Dutch airfield.

Radar reports of an RAF formation skirting the Frisian Island chain resulted in Schnaufer, along with four other pilots, being alerted and dispatched in pursuit. On the way north, the ground defence's hostile identification of Schnaufer's Bf 110G-4, if not the others, led to the flak gunners opening up and inflicting a degree of non-fatal damage that induced him to abort the sortie—good luck for him and his crew on this occasion as events were to confirm over the next hour or so. Instead of encountering the usual ever-vulnerable formation of RAF bombers, the surviving crews were heading straight into an aerial ambush, courtesy of No. 141 Squadron.

The small radar blip presented by the handful of Beaufighters on the German screens should have heralded a note of caution; after all, the main bomber stream was progressing somewhat to the north. On the other hand, it was not unknown for crews to stray off course, apart from which the existence of Serrate and its operators was not known. Braham had stationed himself in a patrol line near the island of Heligoland; he and his fellow pilot had throttled back to a speed similar to the bombers in order to heighten their 'straggler' image. The eight aircraft operated in two groups, one flying north of the Frisians as far as the approach to Heligoland, the other stationing itself between Emden and the northern fringe of the Zuiderzee. All was set for action as the twin lines of crews awaited the emergence of the *Nachtjagd* fighters on their northern-directed interception courses.

'Sticks' Gregory was on an operational 'rest period' that was mandatory in view of his exhausted state, and 'Jacko' Jacobs was standing in for him. The Serrate screens were casting up vague indications of the presence of bogeys, but only when an AI contact that had been initiated by a firm Serrate indication bore fruit was the chase commenced. The target was confirmed at 5,000 yards to port and above its assailant, and full throttle was applied. The bright moonlight condition should have made the Bf 110 outline clear when the visual distance was closed to only 400 yards; however, Braham's accumulating state of tiredness over the past few days was playing upon his vision and Jacobs' strained voice became more frustrated in tone at his pilot's inability to pick out the aircraft. Fortunately, his eyes finally focused properly for him to close in and open fire. The Bf 110 attempted to pull away in a dive as his pursuer fired again and this time set the fuselage on fire; the fighter now entered into a vertical dive and swooped towards the cold wastes of the North Sea.

Climbing back to their patrol altitude, the Braham–Jacobs team awaited further trade that turned up virtually as the Beaufighter was levelled off. This time, the combat was swift and arguably more brutal because of the almost too-swift rate of closure. In fact, fire was opened at less than 100 yards, and the resultant explosion of the Bf 110's airframe could easily have consumed the Beaufighter in its death throes. Amazingly, one crewmember was sighted under his deployed parachute; Braham's immediate reaction was to ensure its occupant never reached the ground alive, but he was dissuaded from this course of action by Jacobs. In any case, it is likely his descent into the sea would have consumed his life through drowning or exposure.

Despite Jacob's assertion that current fuel and ammunition reserves was more than enough to remain on station, his pilot decided to turn for home at this stage. This was probably a sensible decision given his physical state in general and particularly his impaired vision. His general state was also clearly due to carrying out sustained operations as well as carrying out his command duties. In truth, he was as ready for an operational rest as 'Sticks' Gregory, although this would only occur in early October.

Further NJG1 Travails

A second crew who were to realise a measure of success during the Peenemunde raid was Flt Lt Harry White and his RO, Fg Off. Mike Allen. Their appearance at Wittering heralded a permanent association with No. 141 up to January 1945, by which time they had notched up twelve confirmed kills. Following the damaging of a Bf 110 over Cologne on 3–4 July, the first of the confirmed victims was another Bf 110 that had been recorded on 15–16 July. Their joy at gaining the victory nearly proved costly since White's course took him over a searchlight belt whose support flak guns initiated an uncomfortable, if not near-lethal barrage. Now they were part of the squadron's twin screen for the Peenemunde-bound force.

In the course of their sortie, Mike picked up two contacts that were in tune with the Serrate equipment. However, the first interception should have proved fatal—for the Beaufighter crew, not the trio manning the Bf 110. For some reason, White's manoeuvring placed him ahead of his intended prey. At what was a range so minimal that Allan claimed to have heard the bark of the twin-MG151 and MK108 nose-mounted cannon above the Hercules engines, this should have sealed their fate.

Having miraculously survived the onslaught, whose tracer-directed course luckily cleared the top of the Beaufighter, White hauled his charge wildly around, but whether or not his first kill tonight subsequently involved this Bf 110 seems unclear (a well-researched book on RAF/Commonwealth aces credits the White–Allen team with a Bf 110 downed near Groningen and a Ju 88 at Lingen on this night; in addition, the former machine was probably the last of the three IV/NJG1 night fighters lost on 17–18 August).

A Change of Guard

As autumn 1943 faded into winter and Bomber Command reached ever-further into the Third Reich, with Berlin as its epicentre of overall assault, the need for Fighter Command to similarly extend its reach in support of the Lancaster, Halifax, and Stirling squadrons became paramount. The Beaufighter's stunted range capability tokened its withdrawal from this duty and the obvious candidate as a replacement was the Mosquito. This was sound in theory but was currently restricted in practical effect.

In No. 141 Squadron's case, the first assignments of the De Havilland fighter were arriving as early as September; however, these were examples of the original F Mk II that were just adequate for the task. In addition, they were still bearing the original AI Mk IV radar sets that were equally in the 'adequate' category in terms of general efficiency. For example, the set's range was equal to no more than the aircraft's altitude so with the bomber 'stream's' average altitude basically between 15,000 and 20,000 ft. the maximum AI range was 3–4 miles. The RAF Authorities were not yet prepared to commit the later Marks of AI to the battle for natural fear of exposure to the Germans with the almost inevitable loss of the Mosquitoes within which they were installed.

The revised *Nachtjagd* policy of feeding its night fighters into the bomber stream had been introduced in the wake of the Hamburg series of raids. On that occasion, the use of the radar-blinding strips of aluminium, known as Window, had thrown the defensive provisions into chaos. Now the dispatch of the Bf 110s and Ju 88s towards the incoming RAF force's ranks allowed the individual crews to close with any contact that was other than the Window dispensing aircraft at the stream's forefront. Worse still was the equally recent advent of the *Schräge Musik* upward-firing cannon that permitted closure from underneath the bombers who largely possessed no underside armament provision matching the USAAF's ball turret.

The internal fuel capacity of the Mosquito permitted the aircraft to range far into enemy territory. Adding to this was the carriage of supplementary wing-mounted tanks; these are seen here and range in capacity from 50 gallons (front), 100 gallons (centre), and 200 gallons (rear). This endurance was particularly advantageous when conducting Intruder operations with what appear to be FB Mk VIs seen in the left background.

As had been witnessed with the No. 141's experience, the crews had of necessity to carry out their duties at extended distance from the bombers in order to avoid any chance of those manning the gun turrets opening fire upon their own protectors. Now with the wholesale infiltration being carried out by the *Nachtjagd*, their RAF contemporaries were restricted to operating around the fringes of the stream with the hope of latching on to a target as the aircraft was either heading in towards or withdrawing from an engagement. The cards were, in effect, firmly stacked against the RAF fighters in their bid to bring a decent measure of punishment to bear against the bomber tormentors as they continued to inflict an increasingly serious degree of punishment. The revised form of attack approach that was basically indefensible was witnessing individual pilots notching anything up to six or seven kills during one sortie.

The known location of some *Nachtjagd* airfields provided a second line of opportunity for the RAF crews to interdict their adversary's ranks. However, there was a marked difference in how both nations flew nocturnal operations by this point in the Second World War. The RAF crews would take-off and return to their assigned airfield. In contrast, the *Luftwaffe* crews would be deployed across the greater length and breadth of the Third Reich; following their link-up and often prolonged action against the bombers, it often became necessary for them to divert into any available airfield since their diminished fuel reserves would not permit a return to their assigned airfield. Consequently, there was no guarantee of trade reappearing on the scene for a Mosquito or indeed any other nocturnal intruder assigned to or otherwise freelancing near a specific airfield.

No. 141 Squadron's Fighter Command status was destined to last only until November when it was transferred to the nascent No. 100 (Bomber Support) Group. This organisation would play a key role in placing increasing and finally unassailable electronic constraints upon the *Nachtjagd*'s hitherto largely unfettered access to Bomber Command's ranks with all this implied for its bomber crews' morale boost and a converse lowering in that of their opponents'.

Several other Mosquito squadrons were joining in bomber-support activities. No. 25 had commenced upgrading from the Mk II to the more multirole-suited FB Mk VI during August, but by September, when it was assigned to the aforementioned duty, only 'A' Flight had made the switch, although a full complement of aircraft was on hand over the intervening few weeks. Two further squadrons (Nos 157 and 410) were also assigned during August, albeit on a short-term basis for the latter, the crews' operational service in the role ending in October when they resumed home defence duties within No. 11 Group. No. 157 would serve out the Second World War in this manner, but under No. 100 (Bomber Support) Group's tutelage from May 1944 onwards.

No. 605 Squadron had also entered the fray during August while utilising an electronic variation to Serrate in the form of tail-warning radar. The ability to pick-up encroaching aircraft from this angle enabled the pilots to then describe a 360-degree circuit that would bring them in behind the target, which, if a night fighter, would be attacked with impunity since the German aircraft were not yet similarly outfitted. This activity, code-named 'Mahmoud' and indulged in by several squadrons, was sound in theory but posed a problem: the radar's inability to tell friend from foe, allied to the Bf 110's speed factor being not measurably greater than its RAF prey, probably led to false alarm situations as well as the possible risk of the Mosquito firing upon a bomber if the contact was acted upon too swiftly.

The squadron's initial sorties were flown directly above the bomber stream in an attempt to intercept the enemy aircraft releasing flares designed to illuminate the formations' presence, but no success attended their endeavours. This negative experience was to prove the virtual norm for Mahmoud and indeed for any of the other variations in attempting to seek out and attack the *Nachtjagd* crews during their direct interdiction of the main force attacks. Kills would be registered but in miniscule numbers spread between the RAF units concerned as the 1943–44 winter developed. It would take the steadily-mounting strength of No. 100 Group with its plethora of electronic devices to turn the tide in the RAF's favour and this desirable situation would not take effective hold until well into 1944.

In contrast to the entrance hatch directly under the cockpit on bomber and PR Mosquitos, the presence of cannon armament in the forward fuselage and bomb bay forced a switch to a side-access alternative on fighter airframes. The pilot is seen ascending the metal ladder with wide-spaced rungs. Note that the wheel cover intended to protect against oil seepage is still in place.

No. 157 Squadron converted on to the Mk II Mosquito in early 1942 and functioned initially in the night-fighter role. A year later, it was redirected onto Ranger patrols, as well as bomber support. This picture of one having the port wing fuel tanks replenished is taken at Hunsdon from where the aircraft flew until November; the squadron then transferred to Predannack to take part in Instep operations.

Intruder Operations

The Intruder aspect of RAF Fighter Command operations by the 1942–43 period of the Second World War was growing into a serious threat to the German forces located across Western Europe. Out of the often pinprick level of assault initiated by the Hurricane and Havoc squadrons over the preceding year or so was now emerging a much heavier weight of assault that, moreover, was ranging ever deeper into the Third Reich's hinterland as well as its ill-gotten empire as far as Austria and Czechoslovakia.

The geographic expansion was due to the entry of the Beaufighter and Mosquito into the battle. Although the Bristol-manufactured fighter was destined to share this specific activity, it would be the Mosquito that would make itself the leader in delivering the bulk of the punishment. The Beaufighter in turn would figure more prominently in the Ranger category of fighter function, although this parallel duty would be shared with the Mosquito though with fewer units assigned to the task.

AM Leigh-Mallory had decided in late 1942 that a Mosquito cadre drawn from five squadrons should be adapted to the Intruder–Ranger role. A necessary adaptation involved the removal of radar sets and their replacement by Gee navigation equipment, while cannon ammunition capacity was increased by

No. 456 (RAAF) Squadron's original cadre of night fighters were Mk I Defiants, but a switch to Beaufighters was followed in 1942 to the Mk II Mosquito with which the pilots pursued Ranger and Intruder operations, the French railway system being a prime target. RX:X/DD739 displays the gracefully-lethal outline of the de Havilland design during September 1943; by then, the camouflage pattern for RAF fighters was dark green bands over medium sea grey.

50 per cent. A specialist course was created at which a small number of crews assigned to the function could be trained-up, but the expansion of this type of specialist operations led to the opening of a proper OTU in May.

The Beau Leads the Way

No. 96 Squadron was operating on the Mk VIF and was unconsciously picking up the Intruder baton from No. 23 Squadron after the pioneer unit was posted to Malta the previous December to continue the same disruptive duty it had hitherto launched from Southern Britain. The rationale behind these operations required several conditions be met: first, any operation would involve a specific activity or target; second, the crews would be held at readiness; and third, radio links with the unit's airfield would be maintained throughout the sortie.

No. 141 Squadron was the second Beaufighter-equipped squadron to begin launching Intruder sorties in this case from Predannack on the western Channel coast around mid-March 1943, but it also participated in Instep patrols by providing escort for anti-shipping strikes by Coastal Command. The CO was newly-promoted Wg Cdr Bob Braham who would lead the squadron up to October (a preceding section in this chapter also deals with the squadrons' involvement in operating the Serrate equipment that was used to home-in upon the *Nachtjagd* fighters).

Ranger Operations

The disruptive intention behind Ranger compared to Intruder operations was differently pitched in several respects, as well as being more open-ended in execution. Whereas the Intruder crews were briefed for a specific location, the Ranger crews were not. On the other hand, their take-off times were predetermined compared to their Intruder contemporaries, who were held at a state of readiness. Once airborne, there was no mandatory radio link like that demanded for Intruder operations. In effect, the Ranger personnel had a roving brief that was probably intended to cause a degree of psychological as well as likely physical disturbance in the minds of the German military. Moonlit conditions were a prerequisite when flying these operations.

Ranger operations were commenced initially by day during February 1943 with No. 264 Squadron involved. However, an extension to night-launched operations by Nos 25 and 151 Squadrons, as well as No. 264, was quickly on hand. The overall scale of sorties was inevitably small when given the fighter strength on hand, but by April, two more squadrons were involved. In addition, an advance in striking power was on hand with the first FB Mk VI airframes that were allocated to No. 418 (Canadian) Squadron.

There was almost as much of a psychological as a material intention behind either form of intrusion, although any success in the latter category was very welcome. The depredations wrought upon the enemy by the RAF crews could be likened to that handed out by a bird of prey such as a sparrowhawk, with the avian example being replaced by a fighter. The German servicemen and civilian population were (unconsciously) placed in the same position as a flock of birds or mammals minding their own business, and therefore not anticipating any form of interference, lethal or otherwise.

Suddenly and often shockingly, out of the skies at any point of the twenty-four-hour cycle would emerge the RAF Sparrowhawk to catch a truck or train driver, a trainee pilot and instructor, a group of military personnel, or any other party forming a suitable target upon which a hail of gunfire and bombs would descend. Regardless of the damage or destruction inflicted by any attack, the result would likely be to create a state of permanent confusion and anxiety among the survivors. Who might be next for assault or summary treatment? Individual and corporate morale is an intangible but vital factor in sustaining a nation's will to continue prosecuting a conflict; any way in which to subvert that will had to be accommodated and the Intruder–Ranger tactic was a classic example of this basically debilitating tactic.

The nocturnal aspect of Ranger operations involved the more selective choice of target, since the visual constraints upon the pilots in circumstances other than full moonlight did not allow for the same time span in which to pick up and deliver their weaponry precisely. Airfields were an obvious choice for bombing and shooting-up, with the added prospect of catching any aircraft flying in the vicinity. Another target type was railway-borne—and to a lesser extent road—traffic. Added to the list were a range of permanent structures such as factories, railyards, and the like that ranged from France up into north-western Germany.

An anonymous FB Mk VI belonging to a Canadian Squadron is having its armament attended to. One mechanic is up on the aircraft while two other mechanics are working with the 20-mm belts, enclosing them within their drum frames. Note the tunic folded carefully and placed on the starboard gear framing—the owner is clearly confident no oil seepage through the cowling will occur.

The flame-scorched nose and feathered port propeller on this No. 410 Squadron's NF Mk II Mosquito provides stark evidence of its exposure to and potential destruction from burning fuel cast out by an exploding Do 217 encountered over Holland on 27 September 1943. Flt Lt M. Cybulski was fortunate enough to maintain control and land back safely at Coleby Grange; he is seen with Fg Off. H. Ladbrook (N) the following day.

A steady, if unspectacular haul of aircraft were damaged or shot down over the months, but the engagement of these victims could rebound on the assailant. A classic example involved No. 410 Squadron's Flt Lt M. Cybulski and Fg Off. H. Ladbrook on 26 September. Having patrolled the Dutch coast without result, the crew turned back, but almost immediately, the RO picked up a trace that evolved into a Do 217. Closure was made to 100 yards, and a burst of fire blew the bomber apart, but the resultant balloon of flame, smoke, and metal shards totally enveloped the Mosquito.

One engine was disabled, and the fighter assumed a diving attitude that cost over 4,000 feet before control was regained. Even then, the aircraft was yawing badly to port to the extent that Cybulski had to place both feet on the starboard rudder pedal. It was only after landing that both airmen realised their good fortune. The fuselage, fin, and a sizeable proportion of the upper and lower wing surfaces had lost its camouflage coating, while the rudder fabric was burnt off. Had the burning debris and fuel spray caught any degree of hold on the airframe, it is problematical whether the outcome would have been so positive.

Although the assault on most target types provided some measure of satisfaction, there was no greater satisfaction than the downing of an aircraft. The onset of Operation *Steinbeck* in January 1944 involved the greatest concentration of *Luftwaffe* bombers over Britain since the *Blitz*. The knock-on effect of this was to provide the regular chance of catching the crews on their return. On 18–19 February 1944, Flt Lts R. Kipp and P. Hulotsky were dispatched with infiltration of the retreating formation the intention. The squadron had set a fine standard in Ranger activities with their FB Mk VI Mosquitoes, and this night would further enhance matters.

No. 29 Squadron was yet another unit involved in nocturnal combat from 1940 on. By January 1945, when this NF Mk XIII from No. 29 Squadron was filmed at Hunsdon, the emphasis had switched from home defence to Intruder operations. The squadron finished the war operating on the NF Mk 30. Note the black undersides supplementing the standard dark green and medium sea grey on the remaining bulk of the airframe.

Laon–Athies was targeted, but when the first visual contact was made, the Ju 88 concerned was in fact heading west in the direction of Juvincourt; a flare shot up from Laon that Kipps regarded as being a warning of their bearing an exposed navigation light initiated no response as the machine flew on. Kipp's attack approach was too fast and he had recourse to lowering the wheels and throttling back in order to avoid overshooting before finally opening fire. His reflector sight was flickering, and the result was no strikes were landed on the bomber who by now had extinguished the navigation light that had originally betrayed its presence. The second burst delivered blind fortunately struck home, and the 'Me 410', as Kipps stated at debriefing, climbed briefly prior to reversing into a terminal dive.

The bomber's fiery grave was 2 miles north of Juvincourt's lit-up runway, towards which it was being directed. The Mosquito crew were still observing their diving victim when both caught sight of another aircraft west of the airfield that incredibly did not extinguish its navigation lights even after the explosive end of its companion machine that should have alerted the pilot. Kipps had quickly replaced the faulty gunsight bulb and apparently did not even retract the fighter's wheels as he closed-up upon a second 'Me 410' (his words) just as the pilot was lining-up with the south-east–north-west runway. The crew's thoughts of a meal and a night's sleep were viciously erased when the four-second burst of fire ignited both engines and cast the bomber into an equally explosive contact with French soil. Uffz. H. Framing was the pilot of this bomber from which two crewmembers managed to evacuate the aircraft but failed to survive thanks to parachute failure and drowning in a canal; Uffz. R. Backofen forfeited his life along with two of his three colleagues in the first crash. Both crews had been operating with 3/KG54.

The massive and speed-sapping aerial array on a Bf 110G-4 would be typical of the *Nachtjagd* crews' experience almost until the end of the Second World War. Not only did this affect the aircraft's performance, reception was adversely affected whenever wet conditions were encountered.

15
Towards D-Day

Structural Changes

Between 1936 and 1943, Fighter Command had retained direct control of all fighter-equipped squadrons based in the UK. However, the intention to invade Hitler's empire via a cross-Channel assault proved to be the catalyst for a separate entity, the 2nd Tactical Air Force (2TAF) that was brought into being during November. Also encompassing No. 2 (Medium Bomber) Group that had been declared independent from Bomber Command in late May, the new force would not only carry out tactical support operations from the UK, once the invasion troops and equipment were established ashore, the squadrons under 2TAF's charge would in time decamp to the continent with the intention of providing close air support as the Allied ground forces moved eastwards. Taking command was the veteran of North African operations, Air Marshal Sir Arthur Coningham, a New Zealander nicknamed 'Mary' (a corruption of the word 'Maori', the Native New Zealand element of the population).

The man selected to take charge of what was with the inclusion of the 9th USAAF, known as the Allied Expeditionary Air Forces (AEAF), was the current C-in-C of Fighter Command, the rather humourless Air Marshal Sir Trafford Leigh-Mallory, whose adoption of the Big Wing concept three years previous had caused so much disruption and ill-will during and after the Battle of Britain. The RAF element of the AEAF organisation in his hands comprised Nos 83, 84, and 85 Groups, as well as No. 2 Group. The first two sub-forces were allocated a string of Spitfire and Typhoon squadrons flying in a strike role, whose function was the respective support force for the British 2nd Army and Canadian 1st Army following the successful penetration of Hitler's Atlantic Wall around Normandy. No. 85 would operate in a more passive, albeit important role, namely providing direct air cover for the Army. Finally, No. 2 Group's Mosquitos, along with their Boston and Mitchell counterparts, would provide the vast bulk of the tactical bombing function.

Three Mk IID Hurricanes assigned to No. 164 Squadron are lined-up at Middle Wallop during June 1943. The 40-mm externally-mounted cannon was a potent weapon against a range of targets but pitting the now-venerable Hawker fighter against the *Jagdwaffe* was asking for trouble. In the event, this squadron surrendered the cannon for rocket rails, but operations were limited prior to conversion onto the more-robust Typhoon.

The creation of 2TAF was basically at the expense of Fighter Command from whose ranks the squadrons were to be drawn. The greatly depleted establishment of squadrons at the latter's command would continue to serve in defence of the UK as was made amply plain by its revised and almost banal title—Air Defence of Great Britain (ADGB). The name held none of the emotive ring of positive action about it compared to its predecessor and in fact a reversion to the original title would occur the following October 1944. Air Marshal Sir Roderick Hill was assigned as Leigh-Mallory's replacement during November and he would hold the post until the end of the Second World War.

Summer Fortunes in 1943

The command's emphasis on fighter escort for the daylight bombing forces was originally concentrated on the efforts of the RAF and USAAF mediums. In the latter case, the relative shortage of their own escort squadrons until the mid-point of the year had seen the duty of necessity falling primarily upon the Spitfire squadrons with Nos 11 and 12 Groups in the forefront. In June, the former possessed a total of five operating the Mk IX and five operating on the Mk VB; No. 12 Group's Spitfire cadre was based solely on the Mk VB, whose limitations against the Fw 190 in particular saw the variant serving in the close escort role whenever the squadrons were called upon.

A second apparent advantage held by No. 11 was the possession by two squadrons of the latest Spitfire variant in the form of the Mk XII that was also the first to switch over to the Rolls-Royce Griffon in its initial IIB format. Rated at 1,735 hp, the enhanced power coupled to a retractable tail wheel and broad-chord rudder were all features intended to provide an effective response to the 'tip and run' raids out of northern France. Their use on escort duties was accordingly rendered null and void, at least until the foregoing threat was erased or rather curtailed by the *Jagdwaffe* around mid-1943. A total of 100 airframes modified from Mk V, VIII, and IX stocks would be produced. However, waiting in the wings was the Mk XIV with a five-blade propeller compared to the standard four-blade unit; the Griffon 61, with a two-stage engine supercharger compared to the single-stage facility on the Griffon IIB; and two extra wing-installed fuel tanks. The Mk XIV's scale of production would prove to be ten-fold compared to the Mk XII.

The arrival of the four B-26 groups (322BG, 323BG, 386BG, and 387BG) to the VIII Bomber Command's 3rd Bomb Wing saw all units operational between May and July. With a good all-round performance added to by an armament provision close to that of its four-engined USAAF 'big brothers' and an equally sizeable bomb load, the design promised to add to the pressure already being placed upon the Germans. That it still required escort cover was demonstrated early on when the 323BG carried out a raid to IJmuiden in mid-May. One of the twelve aircraft aborted early on and the remainder ended up MIA—tacit proof if any were needed that the *Jagdwaffe* was very much still a potent force and likely to hold the advantage when challenging bombers alone.

That uncomfortable lesson was steadily being brought to bear upon the VIII Bomber Command hierarchy as the B-17 and B-24 groups began to push the geographic boundaries of their assault ever further into Western Europe. For the crews, the option of achieving their targets under enough as well as effective escort cover was not available as yet; the current paucity in P-47 fighters guaranteed this failing. As for Fighter Command, its dependence upon the Spitfire as its prime escort machine meant that the same limitation in range suffered by the P-47s on current hand would be corrected to some degree in the future whereas the same improvement would notably elude its RAF cousin.

Whenever the RAF was called to provide support to the USAAF heavies, the squadrons concerned would operate from forward airfields such as Manston in order to utilise their fuel reserves to the maximum degree. Even then, the pilots would be fortunate to reach as far as the eastern boundaries of Belgium or the Dutch coast, for example. Bradwell Bay was the choice for Wg Cdr 'Johnny' Johnson's Canadian Wing on 17 August, when they were briefed to pick up the B-17s returning from the disastrous initial strike on Schweinfurt. Rendezvous with the formations that were still under assault saw Johnson split his formation into sections that hunted down those fighters taking on straggling bombers. In Johnson's case, he gained credit for a quarter of a rocket-firing Bf 1110 that was decimated by all four Spitfires.

The opportunity for Fighter Command's pilots to engage in these operations did not provide very much in the way of positive contact with the *Jagdwaffe*

No. 401 (Canadian) Squadron alternated between the Mk VB and Mk IX Spitfire during the second half of 1942 and the autumn of 1943. An airman stands beside an example of the earlier mark as he watches a several section-strong formation parade over the airfield. A return to the Mk IX was only made when the squadron joined No. 126 Wing of the 2TAF during October.

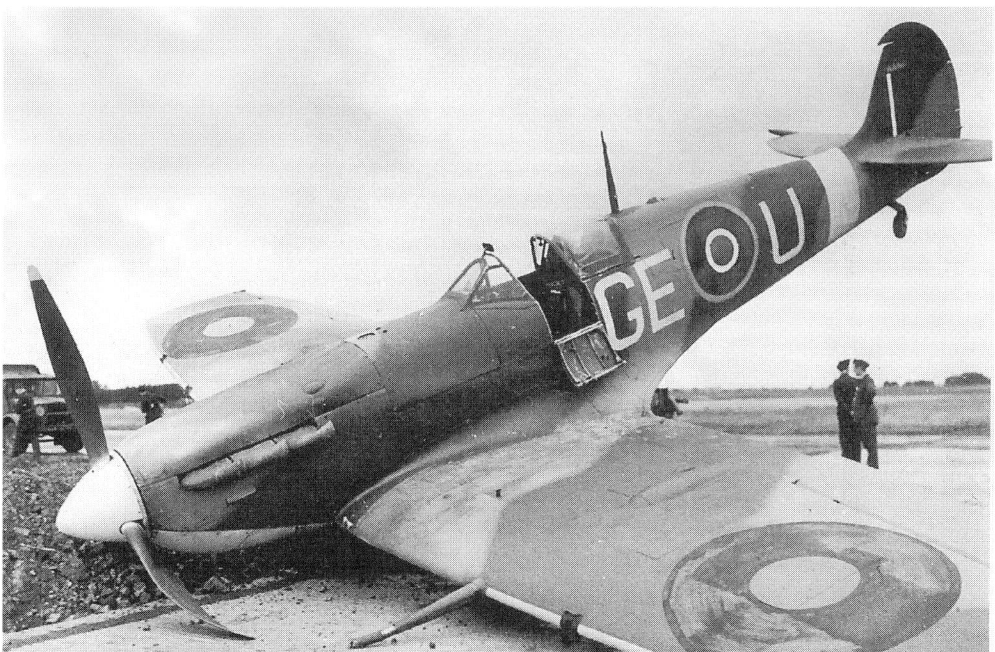

The second Belgian squadron (No. 349) was reformed in Britain in mid-1943 and assigned LF VBs for low-altitude operations. This example has suffered a collapsed port undercarriage with bent propeller blades on the Rotol propeller and the port cannon barrel. Aircraft serial AA944 is obliterated by the 'Sky S' fuselage band.

as 1943 entered its later stages. By then, the regular deep-penetration missions coupled with the still-minimal Allied long-range escort strength played into the *Jagdwaffe*'s hands. Far from initiating a challenge soon after the bombers had crossed into Europe, its pilots could 'stand-off' until their adversaries were well out of friendly fighter cover before launching their attacks. The cull of 148 B-17s MIA between 8 and 14 October was the worst shocking reverse to date accruing from the measure.

Tactical Disaster

Although the escort strength on hand for the medium-bomber sorties was largely sound to comprehensive, there were occasions when the planning went badly awry in practice. In addition, the seaport of Ijmuiden would be involved on two rebuffs, one RAF and one USAAF, during May. The first incident was on 3 May, when the seaport was a No. 2 Group target for the second time within twenty-four hours, but this time for No. 107 Squadron's Boston Mk 111A with No. 487 Squadron's fourteen Venturas striking a power station further east at Amsterdam. Both units would approach at minimum altitude, but whereas the entire 107 Squadron raid would be conducted at this height, No. 487 would climb to its 12,000-foot bombing altitude just before the coast. The selected installations at Ijmuiden were struck at the cost of one crew; as the second wave was withdrawing, a Ventura

The Lockheed Ventura was the poorest overall performer out of the four US medium bombers in RAF service, as No. 487 (New Zealand) Squadron's crews discovered on 3 May 1943; only one of the eleven aircraft attacking Amsterdam returned to Methwold, flying what was an adaptation of the Hudson patrol bomber. The aircraft being bombed-up was a clear exception in survival terms as it bears around twenty bomb symbols on its nose compartment.

was seen to hurtle into the sea, one of three 487 Squadron aircraft whose last resting place was thereunder.

The Bostons had approached and departed without traversing the Dutch landscape, but this was not the case for No. 487, whose westerly approach took the crews across 30 miles between the coastline and the target. A diversion by Spitfires over Flushing further south that went in too early was the suggested reason why the *Jagdwaffe* was alerted and ready for the Ventura crews with their trio of Spitfire escorts. The result was that one element of the enemy force successfully drew off the Spitfires while the second latched onto the totally exposed bombers, now down to thirteen thanks to one aircraft aborting.

The unequal battle witnessed the steady erosion of the formation until only five were on hand during the bomb run; fortune deserted all but Sqn Ldr L. Trent (CO), even before the target was reached, and his bid to escape the incessant fighter passes ended with a violent impact into a polder that left him and one of his three fellow crew surprisingly alive. Trent's determination to get his squadron through to the target later resulted in the award of the Victoria Cross, a fact that he would not be aware of until its post-war promulgation.

A surprising aspect of the fighter-to-fighter element of the air battle was the superiority in numbers of Spitfires (thirty-six) comprising the close escort compared to the twenty-plus quoted figure for the *Jagdwaffe* element engaging them. On the other hand, all of the former was of the Mk VB or VC variants, whose marked inferiority in all performance categories other than turning circle had long been demonstrated against the Fw 190 and less so the Bf 109F, although the current presence of the G 'Gustav' Model would have restored that disability. The sole Mk IX squadron on hand was No. 453, but their allocation to target support probably put its pilots out of the frame in making an immediate contribution to this air battle. The rear cover sub-force of thirty Mk Vs and eight Mustang Mk Is was clearly too far distant to similarly join in.

The overall technical inferiority of the Mk V does not appear to have resulted in more than one casualty on this occasion, but the individual pilot concerned proved to be a senior loss, namely the Coltishall Wing Leader Wg Cdr H. P. 'Cowboy' Blatchford. The Canadian had previously been a flight commander on Stanford-Tuck's No. 257 Squadron in 1940–41, assuming command after Tuck's departure. On this sortie, his Spitfire was badly damaged by a JG1 pilot; when still well short of friendly soil, he attempted to execute a ditching action that proved fatal.

By grim coincidence, a similar disaster would be inflicted upon the Marauders of the 322BG exactly two weeks later, with Ijmuiden the epicentre. The port had been bombed by the group on 14 May, but with no discernible success, so the perhaps ill-advised decision was made to send the bombers back three days later. One crew aborted from the low-level altitude being adopted, but the pilot's climb to a more suitable height was the probable catalyst for alerting the German radar system as to the formation's approach. At any rate, the waiting fighters along with the flak tore into the bombers that had unfortunately made landfall 30 miles

Ground crew for one of the squadrons operating on the Ventura are preparing to load several incendiary canisters. The bomb-bay doors are trapezoidal in design, a style also applied to the Marauder. Twin machine guns in the nose are supplemented by a third fitted into the upper fuselage and operated by the pilot. The design's Hudson lineage can be partially discerned from the Plexiglas panel layout.

south of Ijmuiden. Col. Stillman's (CO) B-26 was fatally crippled and crashed inverted into the coastal strip, but he miraculously survived. Numerous of his crew personnel were not so fortunate, while the survivors with two exceptions ended up as *Kriegsgefangenen* (POWs).

Tactical Success

A double Ramrod operation on 3 October provided a reasonable demonstration of how several targets could be effectively assaulted at minimal cost, allied to some degree of success against the *Jagdwaffe* defences. Five medium-bomber squadrons mustering over sixty aircraft between them enjoyed an escort umbrella of over 110 Spitfire Mk V, IX, and XIIs, as well as Typhoon Mk Is split between twelve squadrons. In addition, the targets were well spread between Paris, Orleans, and three others, extending as far as Guerlédan in central Brittany and therefore likely to attract the attention of both JG2 and JG26. By now, the dangerously inefficient Ventura, an adaptation of the Hudson, had ceased to operate within

No. 2 Group to be replaced by the Mosquito FB Mk VI in the case of all three squadrons concerned.

There were two phases to the overall operation that saw the Boston-equipped trio of squadrons launching the initial co-ordinated attacks. No. 88 Squadron was first off due to flying the greatest depth into France to bomb an electricity-production plant that was also the common target category for the day's activity. The Distre transformer station was struck almost simultaneously with No. 107 Squadron's lunge at a similar plant near Orleans; meanwhile, No. 342 Squadron was already homeward-bound from Chevilly-Larue, south of Paris, minus one from among its ranks. Additionally, two from No. 88's ranks ditched in the Channel.

The Mosquito contingent from Nos 464 and 487 Squadrons, being possessed of a much greater speed factor, had taken-off later to hammer their Brittany targets, after which they swept in a great clockwise circle out over the Bay of Biscay and back to their forward airfield of Predannack. Although more than capable of evading the *Jagdwaffe*'s presence, they, too, had enjoyed escort cover; on the other hand, the presence of the four assigned Spitfire and Typhoon squadrons was more likely deliberately directed at taking on the enemy fighters that did rise in challenge. In the event, two Fw 190s were credited to No. 183 Squadron.

No casualties were incurred by the Mosquito and escort squadrons, but on the eastern fringe of the operational zone, three Spitfires, all reportedly from No. 341 Squadron, had gone down to a combination of flak (one) and JG26 Fw 190s (two); in fact, no less than six claims were submitted, of which none were officially granted. In turn, only Ltn. H. Loerzer had been shot down in comparison to the RAF kill claims submitted.

A Mitchell raid on a power station at Rouen in the evening involved Nos 403 and 421 (Canadian) Squadrons staging a diversion that redressed the day's kill–loss ratio in the command's favour; no less than four Fw 190s were confirmed to pilots of the latter unit, although one Spitfire was shot down. JG26 records disclosed four counter claims, of which none were officially allowed, but which equally refuted any suggestion of the victims being from the *Geschwader*; presumably either JG2 or a training unit had been the source.

The operation was a typical and soundly-executed bid to bring disruption to what was one of several vital supply points. Their reduction or, better still, their deletion in function would adversely affect the overall German military structure by weakening its general ability to hold back any Allied attempt to gain access to the continent, let alone advance into its hinterland. Although the primary target categories were, for example, rail, road, and even canal communications, the denial of electrical power would adversely affect general production and repair facilities.

A secondary intention was to draw the *Jagdwaffe* into continuous combat with a view to similarly interdicting its aircraft and pilot strength to the point of helplessness. This highly desirable situation was, at this stage, still well away from being attained; the quality of both its fighters and pilots ensured this specific

The Boston III proved to be a fine all-round medium bomber for the RAF with a top speed of 304 mph and a 2,000-lb internal bombload. Low-level strikes were a regular feature as shown in this shot of No. 88 Squadron skimming the sea. Extreme pilot concentration was necessary in these circumstances since any error of judgement or mechanical lapse provided little leeway for recovery.

No. 197 Squadron was only formed in Nov. 1942 and had commenced patrols over Northeast England, with its Mk IB Typhoons. In March, it moved south to Tangmere, where the pilots assisted in countering 'tip-and-run' raids. By October, when this shot of Sqn Ldr Holmes's (CO) fighter was taken, the squadron was about to be switched to ground-assault operations with emphasis on bombing 'No-Ball' sites. Note how the serial number is extended onto the fuselage band. Holmes was KIA on 24 January 1944.

air campaign would only turn inexorably in the Allies favour around the ensuing March–April period. This would be primarily thanks to the depredations among both the *Jagdwaffe*'s material and particularly human resources wrought by the 8th Fighter Command.

Typhoon Depredations

The reputation the Typhoon was to earn as a rugged ground-attack fighter was being enhanced as the Allied air forces used every measure possible to apply effective pressure upon the enemy. The four-cannon layout provided the basic means of bringing a devastating degree of firepower to bear upon any target, aerial or ground-based, but added to this, during 1943 and into 1944, was the ability to carry a solid bomb load. As a result, the squadrons operating the design could and did deliver attacks against military locations that included assaults upon shipping.

One specific example against the latter category of target involved a merchant blockade runner, the *Münsterland*, but the normal sortie was directed against vessels sailing singly or in convoy. In such cases, the 'Bombphoons' would seek to deliver their bombs not by standard release, but rather by using the 'skip' technique similar to skimming a flat stone across the surface; the three-second fuse delay was sufficient for the fighter to clear its prey before the detonation, but timing was everything to ensuring the necessary margin in safe distance was achieved to avoid being embroiled in the explosion.

The dire shortage of key industrial products, such as precious metals, rubber, etc., impelled the Nazi regime to dispatch merchant vessels to countries where these commodities were available; the vessels faced a tough task in evading Royal Navy and RAF patrolling units, and so were known as blockade runners. In October 1943, one was the focus for Typhoon assault; named the *Münsterland*, it had progressed as far as Cherbourg, the major seaport in north-western France.

On 24 October, six No. 263 Squadron Whirlwinds and eight No. 183 Squadron Typhoons were sent out on separate sorties widely-spaced in time. The Whirlwind pilots were covered by Typhoons from No. 257 Squadron and delivered their bombs at the cost of two fighters. The afternoon sortie encountered the same fierce defensive reaction, and although damage was inflicted on the ship, it was at the cost of three aircraft, including that of the CO, Sqn Ldr A. Gowers.

Escort was reportedly provided by the Mk IXB Spitfires of No. 602 Squadron according to the French 'Ace' Pierre Clostermann, who recalled his fellow pilots had a task to maintain position thanks to the Typhoons' pace. Cherbourg forms the approximate base of an inverted geographic triangle with Newchurch in Kent (602 Squadron) and Predannack in Cornwall (183 Squadron) forming the other points; it seems odd that airfields several hundred miles distant as these were would have been involved in this manner unless No. 602 Squadron was detached to Predannack, an unlikely scenario considering the availability of similar-equipped squadrons much closer on hand.

EK176 one of 400 Typhoons built between February and July 1943 demonstrates little change in the Hawker fighter's original outline. The sole modification is the Plexiglas rear-cockpit frame in place of its solid predecessor. This aircraft was lost in a fatal crash-landing near Lydd on 14 August following engine failure, with Fg Off. L. Wood being the unfortunate pilot.

Rows of rockets with their fearsome 60-lb warheads are being loaded on to trailers for delivery to the Typhoons of No. 609 Squadron. A proportion of the warheads were inert as opposed to possessing explosive content; as it was, the sheer velocity of the weapon propelled at 800 feet per second would penetrate most solid structures.

The *Münsterland*'s condition was enough for it to be delayed in further completing the Channel run until January, although by then it had limped eastward to Boulogne close to the Dover–Calais bottleneck. It was reported to have sailed early on the 20th, and No. 198 Squadron duly set out to finish her off; the ship was picked up but by then the deed had been accomplished—not from the air but by the long-range heavy artillery batteries at Dover, whose shells had caused the vessel to founder, although the superstructure was still showing.

Rocket Debut

The day following the Cherbourg attack, there was an event that heralded use of the attack weapon with which the Tiffie has been primarily identified in post-war historic circles, namely the rocket. No. 181 Squadron had been selected to introduce the rocket operationally and had already aborted the initial briefed attack on shipping four days previous. This time around, the power-station target at Caen enjoyed no similar reprieve, although the result was bittersweet for the squadron that suffered a 50 per cent casualty rate from among the six pilots involved thanks to accurate flak.

The experience of No. 181's switch to rocket-based assault was not paralleled by any other contemporary until January, however. It was then that plans were put in force that had the intention of designating squadrons for the function; No. 174 Squadron was the first of twelve, all but one of which would be assigned to either Nos 83 or 84 Groups with a view to Army-support duties within 2TAF, and they attended one of four Armour Practice Camps (APC) in order to test the specialist equipment. An ironic twist to the programme lies in the fact that to date the Typhoon's armoury had followed the standard pattern of wing-mounted guns and bombs as a secondary although increasingly used item. There was an initial shortage of appropriately modified Typhoons with which to carry out unlimited practice flights, but a crash programme by Hawkers and RAF Maintenance Units soon corrected the situation.

The 60-lb solid heads to the rockets could and did provide a punch that, when delivered in a single eight-strong salvo, was credited with an effect equal to the firepower of a Royal Navy cruiser. True or not, the weapon would wreak a physical as well as a psychological effect among the *Wehrmacht*/*SS* forces, with emphasis upon those manning the *Panzer* units' vehicles. A noticeable gravity drop following discharge would deflect a good proportion away from landing a lethal strike as has been evidenced in post-war film clips. The die was nevertheless cast for serious and sustained punishment to be handed out by the remainder, a fact to which survivors of the 'Falaise Gap' massacre in August would surely testify.

Sqn Ldr J. Bryan (No. 198 Squadron CO) was leading an anti-shipping strike on 27 September 1943, when flak exploded the starboard outer gun bay's ammunition. Despite this, the wing structure held together sufficiently for Bryan to bring her home. On landing, the fighter veered sharply off the runway with the wing scraping the ground, but Bryan managed to keep control; he is seen examining the damage. Sadly, Bryan was listed KIA shortly after D-Day.

Human 'Prey'

The elimination of key figures within the German High Command was a desirable by-product accruing from the aerial offensive and *Generalfeldmarschall* Gerd von Rundstedt's movements by rail from southern France to Paris, as supplied by Allied intelligence during October 1943, provided the catalyst for an ambush that involved Sqn Ldr Pat Thornton-Browne's No. 609 Squadron. The cloud-strewn weather on the day in question provided the perceived condition for the operation to go ahead. 'Johnny' Johnson had been posted on rest to No. 11 Group where he served as a planner; his interest was personal since he had recommended No. 609 for the duty.

He recalled the event as he sat in the operations room where the squadron's progress from Lympne was being monitored. Surprise was later expressed to the controller when the plot on the operations table showed the squadron crossing-out appreciably earlier than scheduled. A subsequent telephone conversation with the CO elicited the fact that clearing weather during the inward leg had impelled Thornton-Browne to call off the attack. Despite this disappointment, the fact that five *Luftwaffe* aircraft were taken down in combat over Brétigny airfield with several ground targets successfully strafed took a degree of edge off the primary failure.

Typhoon Structural Improvements

The original Typhoon structure had undergone several improvements since its operational debut. The first involved the cockpit frame that had a 'solid' rear section leading to seriously-limited rearward vision. This was partially solved by replacing it with a Plexiglas equivalent that still did not provide unconditional clear sighting. Other improvements involved the replacement of the fixed radio mast with a whip aerial and complete fairing cover for the cannon barrels. However, a major change to the structure to date would basically solve what was currently a dangerously-cumbersome means of exit in an emergency.

The Typhoon's original cockpit was known as the 'car-door'; this was due to access being gained by a doorframe on the starboard side that was matched by one on the port side. Enclosure was completed by a Plexiglas frame above. This arrangement was similar to the P-38, although the Lockheed fighter possessed side panels that only extended down to the fuselage top line. Escape from either structure was more complicated compared to a standard sliding cockpit. The need to provide a far less risky means of exit provision was clearly of paramount importance.

This official line-up of No. 193 Squadron Typhoons was snapped at Harrowbeer during October 1943 when the occasion was a visit by the Brazilian ambassador. JP919 in foreground is modified with a whip aerial and plinth surround to the exhaust stubs. It survived the war while subsequently assigned to Nos. 257 and 168 Squadrons. Fully sheathed cannon barrels are visible on the first four aircraft.

MN454/HF: L bearing the CO's pennant is seen under inspection by King George VI at Northolt shortly before D-Day; a Mk IX Spitfire from No. 222 Squadron stands in the background. Delivered to No. 183 Squadron during March, the Typhoon failed to survive the launch of Overlord, being one of three shot down by Fw 190s.

In the Typhoon's case, the pilot had to cross both arms in order to operate the door release mechanisms before releasing the top panel. This was none too easy to accomplish swiftly, even in level flight, and was even more difficult to execute should the fighter be otherwise configured in attitude, something that probably led to numerous needless pilot losses. At last, in mid-1943, the 'door' framework was replaced by a simple, neatly-formed sliding canopy mounted on the former lower door space that was displaced by a solid panel containing the canopy runner slot. No. 486 Squadron were first to receive examples during September 1943, and the pilot's reaction to the enhanced prospect of a safe exit in an emergency must have bolstered their morale.

Apocalyptic Warning

The direct cover provided to the medium bomber squadrons that operated on Bostons, Marauders, and Mitchells along with a more diversionary support effort for the Mosquitos promised a better prospect of encountering fighter opposition as the year wore on. A sea change in medium bomber targeting occurred around November. Over the previous month or so, reconnaissance photos had shown the rapidly-growing number of sites primarily spread between the Pas-de-Calais and western Belgium heralding the advent during the following June of the V-1 offensive that encompassed the south-east region of Britain, with London the epicentre.

The robot weapon that was but a precursor of the immeasurably more volatile and indefensible V-2 ballistic rocket was as-yet an unknown quantity in terms of its function. Nevertheless, the Allied authorities were under little illusion that Germany's scientists were incapable of producing some form of reasonably-effective offensive weaponry. The consequence was that, commencing on 5 November, all available resources within No. 2 Group and the recently-formed 9USAAF and including whenever possible the RAF/VIIIBC strategic bombers would focus upon the region. However, the sprouting of what were dubbed 'Ski-sites' presented a particular difficulty in being targeted, this being due to their extremely compact size (12 × 30 feet) that impinged noticeably upon accurate bomb delivery.

The proximity of the main sites around the Pas-de-Calais and into Belgium and also to a lesser extent the Normandy region meant that the short distance between the medium bomber airfields in particular and the sites permitted a steady rate of attack. On the other hand, there was no guarantee that the minimum flight times would provide the basis for what was called a 'milk-run'—a sortie free from enemy interference. The supposition was to prove partially correct because fighter reaction was to largely prove conspicuous by its absence, this despite the presence of JG26 and elements of JG2 in the immediate vicinity.

The chances of surviving a ditching in a Typhoon were normally very slim, but Flt Lt Charles Brayshaw survived the experience after his fighter lost power as he was crossing-out over the coast and sank immediately on impact. He explains to two airmen how, although knocked out, he managed on recovering to release the canopy and get to the surface where he was hauled out by the crew of a fishing boat.

No. 2 Squadron was one of nine units originally with Army Co-operation Command that was ultimately absorbed into 2TAF when the former entity was dissolved in June 1943; the interim period up to November was spent in Fighter Command's charge. The squadron's regular airfield of Sawbridgeworth north of London was where this and the following picture were taken. Three Mustang Is are lined up and ready to taxi out.

A close-up of AG633 confirms the shapely outline of the North American aircraft as well as its dangerous similarity to the Bf 109. The Allison engine was efficient at altitudes up to around 10–12,000 feet, but fell away from then on, this being the likely reason the design was used in lower-level reconnaissance and ground-attack operations. By the summer of 1944, only Nos 2 and 269 Squadrons would still be using the Allison-Mustang within 2TAF.

What did prove an illusion was the expected minimal reaction from the ground in the form of flak guns. The *Flakartillerie* units on hand were quickly bolstered by the transfer of further weapons and manpower with which to create a fairly tight defensive barrier to the bomber incursions. To add to the No. 2 Group and 9USAAF crews' discomfort were the altitudes regularly adopted. The 88-mm that was the stock piece of equipment on hand could throw up a barrage that easily encompassed the 10,000 to 12,000-foot operational altitude at which the Allied mediums flew. Ploughing one's way through the gauntlet of explosive fire was to prove fatal for a good number of their crews as the campaign wended its several-month course.

Fighter opposition was probably reduced to marginal proportions but not through any reluctance on the *Jagdwaffe* pilots to tangle with their aerial adversaries. There seemed little advantage in entering what was primarily a gun zone and which could bring with it an increased risk of being crippled or shot down by one's own side. It was better that the *Geschwadern* resources be used to countering the parallel attacks being daily launched against other target categories. Another more critical matter was the burgeoning strength of the now retitled 8th Air Force as 1944 commenced. Every effort to minimise the effect of the USAAF strategic bombers strikes merited every diversion away from countering the regional assaults to punishing the American crews carrying out their brief to hammer the Reich's industrial base into oblivion. One way or another, the overall effect of Allied air operations was inexorably stretching the *Jagdwaffe*'s resources towards if not yet beyond unsustainable limits.

Tiffie Intervention

The sizeable bomb-carrying capacity and relatively better manoeuvrability of the Tiffie—as the Hawker fighter was dubbed by its personnel—*vis-à-vis* any standard bomber made it a logical candidate for joining in on the 'Ski' site assaults. The chances of landing more accurate strikes against the miniscule targets with the Typhoon compared to the saturation-pattern assault by the medium and heavy bombers seemed likely to yield better results. The one disability was provided by Mother Nature in the form of the ever-wayward winter weather that could and did effectively cloak the sites to make attacks inadvisable or impossible.

In the event, a second more intractable problem concerned the nature of the bombs being used. Although the 1,000-lb weapon could be borne, the decision was taken to mount the 500-lb bomb instead. In practice, it would be April before the former calibre of bomb would be first operationally deployed and its use more directed towards key transport structures, such as bridges, as the Transportation Plan was being implemented. The result was that even a direct strike would only affect the structure in a marginal and generally reparable manner. Therefore, the best that could be envisioned, with the regular involvement of the Hawker fighter, lay in disrupting the construction or refurbishment process being indulged in by the Organisation Todt labour force.

Adding to the problem was a total inability to aim using a bombsight since this item could not be installed without removing the gunsight, whose reverse absence would compromise any prospect of becoming positively involved should combat arise with the *Jagdwaffe*. Instead, the pilots had to have recourse to a crude time count of several seconds after pulling out of their dives before releasing their bombs—a process hardly guaranteed to achieve even an approximate strike on the selected target.

During the 1943–44 winter, the deployment of several Hurricane squadrons equipped with rocket rails against a range of targets that also included 'Ski' sites merited the use of the Typhoon in an escort role, adding to their operational flexibility (the 'Ski' term related to the lengthy storage buildings that were curved at their entrances to limit possible bomb-blast effect). On some sorties, the Hurricane rockets were added to with bombs dropped by the 'Bombphoon' element within the Typhoon support formation. The mounting value of the Typhoon as a multirole combat fighter was exemplified by the number of squadrons (twenty), all but three of which were operational at the year's end, with the other three working-up to operational standard.

As it was, by the year's end, enough damage had been inflicted upon many of the original site zones to impel a shift away from their more prominently visual presence to a clutch of revised sites primarily located between Calais and Rouen. These were more utilitarian in nature, with, for example, the actual launch ramps consisting of prefabricated sections that could be erected swiftly when required. The support buildings were, as before, concealed in wooded areas where possible, but they were smaller and more dispersed in nature and therefore harder to detect. This dispersal effort would not halt the proposed offensive but would delay its implementation. The fact would be vital in practice, being destined to militate against the Nazi plan to swamp London with the V-1 missile and thereby induce a morale lapse among the citizens, if not even among the British population that in turn would impel the government to consider peace or armistice negotiations.

Spitfire-Variant Supreme?

The operational advent of the second Griffon-powered Spitfire, the Mk XIV, during January 1944 held a real promise of domination over its current Bf 109G and Fw 190 contemporaries, especially when combined with its still-nascent Hawker twin, the Mk V Tempest, as well as the Mk III Mustang. ADFU tests drew the following conclusion:

> Fw 190A Series
>
> Maximum speed is 20 mph greater up to 5,000 feet and the 15,000–20,000-foot band. This advantage extends up to 60 mph at all other altitudes.
>
> Climb rate is noticeably superior at all heights.
>
> Dive rate varies, with the Fw 190 initially faster but only marginally so.
>
> Turning circle is better in either direction but less so when turning to starboard.

A No. 1 Squadron Typhoon fuselage is seen loaded on a French railroad wagon, ready for shipment to a German aircraft boneyard and possible smelting-down action. The fighter was force-landed by Fg Off. Wyatt (POW) on 22 December 1943, as the twisted propeller blade confirms. The solid bulk of the design provided a better basis for surviving the often hard and unpredictable impact with the ground.

No. 1 Squadron suffered a second loss on 22 December 1943, when Plt Off. J. Sutherland was also forced to belly-in JR237/JX: I. His Typhoon's fuselage is similarly stripped of its wings and appears to have been lowered by the crane onto a rail-borne turntable situated within what looks like a scrapyard. The action is watched by a mix of German military and civilians.

Roll rate is the one performance aspect where the Fw 190 has the advantage.

Conclusion: The RAF pilot should utilise his superior climb rate and turning circle when challenged. In attacking, he should watch for the faster roll rate and dive capability of his opponent; following the enemy would only result in a satisfactory rate of closure when the Fw 190 finally pulled up.

Bf 109G

Maximum speed is greater by 40 mph other than at 16,000 feet, when the margin falls sharply to 10 mph.

Climb rate is superior at all altitudes other than 16,000 feet, when it is identical for both fighters. Application of full throttle allows the Mk XIV to easily outclimb its adversary.

The Bf 109G eases slightly ahead when commencing a dive but when a speed of 380 mph is exceeded, the RAF fighter closes the gap.

The Mk XIV's turning circle is manifestly superior as is its roll rate.

Conclusion: The Mk XIV enjoys an overall superior performance to the Bf 109G.

The tests indicated that the Fw 190 presented the greater threat in any direct combat scenario compared to the Bf 109, whose inferiority in most of the

A side profile view of a Mk XIV Spitfire serving with No. 610 Squadron demonstrates the steady advance in refining the fighter's airframe. The tail-wheel retracts and the original radio mast is replaced by a neat whip aerial. Also notable is the increase in the area of both the fin and rudder, while the five-blade propeller and spinner cover also stand out.

performance aspects that had been examined was manifestly obvious. However, the unknown quantity in determining success or failure in an air battle was pilot skill that, in the latter case, could see the more experienced *Jagdwaffe* pilot coming out on top.

As regards the test runs involving the Tempest, there was a greater divergence in overall performance, with the Tempest leading the way in the dive, a zoom climb (but not after attaining normal climb speed), and, in general, when operating up to 20,000 feet. The Mk XIV held the edge in maximum speed above 22,000 feet, while its top ceiling was 40,000 feet compared to 30,000 feet for the Tempest. From these facts, the conclusion was drawn that squadrons converting from the Typhoon should take on the Tempest as opposed to the Mk XIV being utilised for the same function in respect of Spitfire-operating units.

The one inevitable weakness of the Mk XIV compared to the Mustang was range, or rather its lack. Maximum speed was almost identical, whereas the climb rate contest went to the Mk XIV as did the roll rate and turning circle. The sole Mustang advantage lay in the dive. The first recipient of the Mk XIV in January was No. 610 Squadron, but the pace of the variant's entry into service was destined to prove very slow and would involve just two more units by the summer; these were Nos 350 and 41 Squadrons, which took delivery in August and September. All would be heavily involved in the course of the V-1 offensive, however.

Specialist Assaults

No. 2 Group's C-in-C AVM Sir Basil Embry was to rightly earn a reputation for directing his Mosquito squadrons in particularly daring strikes against specialist targets during the Second World War. Attacks on locations such as *Gestapo* HQs would feature prominently, but the one strike that is arguably most associated with the performance and skills of the Mosquito and its airmen respectively would be the raid upon a French prison at Amiens, northern France, during February 1944. Reports filtered back to London regarding the imminent execution of several hundred resistance members incarcerated therein.

A plan was accordingly put in motion with a view to attacking the prison in a manner that would free as many as possible of the internees; this entailed no less than the blowing of holes in the perimeter walls and the main building structure that would permit their release—a seemingly doomed enterprise in terms of administering the destructive effect while still leaving the prisoners alive or even uninjured in order to attempt their break-out from the necessarily-fractured building in which they were currently housed.

The weather conditions were simply atrocious on 21 February when the Nos 21, 464, and 487 Squadron crews at Hunsdon were briefed for the sortie, appropriately named 'Jericho'. The attack would be delivered in three waves. The first would breach the north and west perimeter walls; the second would

No. 305 (Polish) Squadron converted from Mitchells to FB Mk VI Mosquitoes in December 1943. LR298 is pictured straining against the wheel-restraining chocks as full power is applied to the Merlins prior to taxiing out at Lasham. Operations within 2TAF later witnessed transfer to the Continent in October 1944.

do likewise with either end of the actual prison as well as destroying the Guards barracks; the third would stand by to be utilised if deemed necessary. The walls were 20 feet by 3 feet in height and thickness, so the bombing accuracy had to be spot on. Nineteen Mosquitos took off, but their strength was cut by nearly a quarter when two crews from both Nos 21 and 464 Squadrons became visually detached from the overall formation and failed to regain contact. The Mk IV camera aircraft had a particularly hard job in catching up after being delayed on take-off, but the crew did achieve their goal; the subsequent film brought back provided a superb record of the action.

The breaches in the perimeter walls and the main prison building were sufficient to permit the release of several hundred inmates of which nearly 300 managed to survive the gunfire from surviving guards to get clear; however, it was sadly certain that an added element of their number had not survived the actual strikes on the prison. The aerial cost was two Mosquitos including Grp Capt. Pickard the formation leader; in addition, one of the eight Typhoons out of the full escorting unit that had managed to make rendezvous also fell. It was fortunate that the nearby fighter airfield at Amiens–Glisy had only responded in time to intercept the tail-end of the operation with Pickard's aircraft one of the victims, otherwise the outcome could have been far more fraught for the attackers.

No. 486 (New Zealand) Squadron exchanged its Typhoons for Mk V Tempests around April 1944 and was assigned to No. 150 Wing, 2TAF operating out of Newchurch. The flat expanses of the Channel coast of Kent is demonstrated in the top picture as a pilot is directed by a ground crew member. The friendly fighter stripes would see a fuller application on D-Day, although the black element would feature broader bands. Lower picture presents a fine side view of a second squadron Tempest.

The Tempest Arrives

Production on Hawker's latest Storm offering in terms of fighters had commenced several months prior to the year's end, but it was the new year of 1944 before the first examples were received by No. 486 (New Zealand) Squadron during January only to be reassigned to No. 3 Squadron the following month. Both units along with No. 56 were due to form No. 150 Wing, whose primary task was perceived as pinning down the *Jagdwaffe* forces deployed between the river Seine and western Belgium.

The first two listed squadrons were declared non-operational in order to work-up their new charges to combat-efficiency level, but No. 56's similar conversion was delayed with its operational status only reached in late June. In the meantime, it joined the wing at Newchurch, still equipped with a Typhoon–Spitfire mix. The wing leader chosen to command was an officer extremely well versed in Hawker fighter experience, being none other than Wg Cdr 'Bee' Beamont. Ranger and Ramrod sorties became the letter of the day during the intervening weeks leading up to Overlord (although officially part of 2TAF's No. 85 Group, the wing would be retained at home as part of ADGB's strength until September).

1944 Instep Fortunes

The severe rebuffs now being handed out to the U-boat *Dienst* crews as they sought in growing vain to inflict any, let alone a destructive scale of punishment upon the Allied convoys did not mean that all available steps to interdict the Biscay routes into the Atlantic had been reduced by the Allied air forces. The Ju 88C-6s of the original V/KG40 that had been redesignated I/ZG1 the previous 13 October were still active in bringing counterstrikes to bear upon the Coastal Command crews trawling the Bay for their underwater prey as well as protecting the Gibraltar convoy route from the enemy's depredations. The presence of Fighter Command detachments based at Predannack over the past year in support of their coastal colleagues was continued into 1944.

No. 157 Squadron was destined to extend its late-1943 success rate as early as 7 January, although at an initial cost in Mosquitos. On this date, Fg Off. R. Perkins won out against Fw. J. Puetz in terms of personnel survival. Whatever damage was borne by the RAF fighter caused it to be ditched, but its two-man crew survived the experience unlike their three German counterparts. A single kill on 10 March by two aircraft was recorded, but the events of 11 April involved No. 151 Squadron.

On this day, the air battle was centred round *U-235* that was the target for two Tsetse Mosquitos bearing 57-mm fuselage-mounted guns and supported by five No. 248 Squadron Mosquitos and four from No. 151 flying top cover. The former unit's CO was downed fatally with one other Mosquito as the 'Tsetse' fighters attacked the U-boat and its flak ship while being engaged by a greater number of ZG1 Ju 88s (ten). The odds against survival for the remaining RAF crews seemed slim—that is, until No. 151 descended to bounce the enemy formation.

The tangle of manoeuvring aircraft saw the air battle conclude with two No. 151 aircraft failing to survive and one crash-landing on return, while the *Luftwaffe* survivors submitted claims for a total of ten kills, double the actual figure. Their enthusiasm must have been dampened by the absence of fully seven crews, although the counter claims among the RAF units only recorded three confirmed kills. The similar attrition rate suggested a combat draw, but the bald fact was that, in general, the technical, if not also human logistical advantage lay with the RAF who could replace both in far swifter time than its adversary.

The involvement of I/ZG1 over the Bay of Biscay would extend for a further two to three months, but the vast bulk of the 109 *Abschuss* granted the crews during the campaign's course had unknowingly been recorded. RAF records indicate a mere two aircraft MIA up to the end of May. The cost had been even greater, with 129 aircraft destroyed and 280 crewmembers MIA or killed in operational crashes. Moreover, the onset of Overlord witnessed the Ju 88s being redirected to provide air support for their ground-based colleagues attempting to block off the breaches in the Atlantic Wall created by the Anglo–American troops along with their massive sea and air support. The Biscay Battle was at a practical end as regards *Luftwaffe* fighter intervention, although only time would confirm the fact.

Instep Variation

The detachment of Fighter Command units to Predannack with a view to supporting Coastal Command operations over the Bay of Biscay was naturally centred upon the use of the longer-range Beaufighters and Mosquitos. Nevertheless, there was a place for their single-engined contemporaries as exemplified by No. 1 Squadron's experience, although it entailed just two months on either side of D-Day as far as this battle-hardened unit was concerned. In addition, the basic Instep brief as practiced by the twin-engined squadrons involved a greater degree of sorties devoted to other target categories as opposed to directly challenging the *Luftwaffe*'s interdiction of the Bay.

Having converted from the Typhoon, the Mk IXB Spitfires now on hand were fitted with Merlin 66 engines that could accommodate 150 Octane fuel. The greater boost output provided by the enhanced grade of fuel allowed for an increase in maximum speed and climb rate, albeit only for five minutes. Of more concern to the pilots was the equally increased consumption rate that gobbled up the fuel reserves—not a comfortable situation when bearing a maximum quantity of less than 200 gallons, even with drop tanks, as well as having to traverse the Channel at its widest point.

The radius of action the Mk IXBs could achieve encompassed the Brittany peninsula down to Lorient and Vannes, as well as Rennes further inland. The search for aircraft using the peninsula's airfields generally yielded little result, however. Escort cover for Beaufighters and Typhoons seeking out shipping targets was also indulged in, as was the occasional Rhubarb, although the latter type of sortie had already been scrapped by the RAF, overall success not being deemed to justify the cost in aircraft. This point was sharply brought home on 22 May, when rail targets were sought around Vannes. Although two trains were shot up, all four Spitfires involved were struck by flak and worse still was the loss of Sgt E. Jacobsen (killed) and Fg Off. A. Vale (POW).

The Instep aspect of operations from 6 June onwards tended to be subordinated to applying pressure upon the *Wehrmacht/SS* opposition to Overlord. On D-Day, two anti-shipping strikes, a convoy patrol, and a Ranger effort by two pilots who strafed goods-trains were launched. Over the ensuing sixteen-day period, intensive operations were flown with airfields and transport high on the target list; however, there was a compulsory four-day break up to the 12th thanks to adverse weather over the continent. The personnel were unaware of their impending departure from the region on the 22th, and before this was initiated, several bombing sorties were launched upon St Peter Port in the Channel Isles and two radar stations. The cursory forty-eight hours spent at Harrowbeer, near Plymouth, concluded with transfer back to Detling within No. 11 Group, from where the pilots would operate against the now-regular flow of V-1 flying bombs currently being directed against London.

Dive-Bombing Limitations

The concept of dive-bombing conferred a theoretically better opportunity of pinpoint accuracy than a level-flight approach; this was a seeming fact as proven by custom-built designs, with the Ju 87 and Ju 88 proving to be premier exponents of the art. The Allied experience by contrast was more piecemeal in that similar effort was not expended upon the same design technology, priority being largely given over to the standard bombing approach that although more dispersed in effect granted a greater individual tonnage to be borne.

A picture of ground crew working on a LF Mk VB Spitfire belonging to No. 322 Squadron and based at Hawkinge must be for the benefit of the press; a normal support team consisted of less than half this number. The squared-off wing-tip is a clear indicator of the fighter's LF (low-flying) capability. The squadron was manned primarily by men from Holland.

The regular deployment of both the Spitfire and Typhoon in the dive-bombing role from 1943 onward cast up the limitations of what were fighters converted to the function. The main disability was the absence of a bombsight in place of the normal gyro gunsight; the latter piece of equipment was needed anyway in the event of encountering *Jagdwaffe* aircraft or any other enemy aircraft that might be encountered. The other limitation related to the maximum bomb load capable of being carried, a factor that impinged more upon the Supermarine aircraft with its more delicate wing structure *vis-à-vis* the Tiffie.

'Johnny' Johnson had returned to combat with No. 144 (Canadian) Wing during March. The wing was part of No. 83 Group, and since all its squadrons would be involved in tactical operations and be deployed abroad after Operation Overlord, strafing and dive-bombing sorties would supplement their primary fighter function. The bomb loads of up to 1,000 lb—two 500-lb or three 250-lb bombs with the extra weapon carried on a centre-line rack—required the wings to be stressed. The bombing technique's perceived simplicity by aiming the aircraft and effecting release at the point of pull out was basically compromised, however.

The practical problem arose due to the bombs' trajectory not following the fighter's line of flight and falling short when employing the foregoing standard technique. Since the gunsight was of little use in assisting aiming in this context, the pilots had recourse to crude methods of (hopefully) striking the target. They

Several pilots from No. 485 (New Zealand) Squadron are gathered round a WAAF as she serves them with the universal British curative for all problems affecting the nervous system—tea. The squadron had just completed an escort sortie for 9USAAF B-26s. It had also recently completed an Armament Practice Camp (APC) course and was now ready to function in ground-assault operations. Picture was taken at Hornchurch on 30 March 1944.

could count up to three or four in some cases after pulling back on the control column and then release the bombs; some pilots, however, did aim through the gunsight, only releasing when the target had passed through a portion of the equipment's visual presentation. The overall degree of accuracy must have led to a 'scattered' bomb pattern at the very least.

The relatively lightweight structure of the Spitfire was another inhibiting issue affecting its capability in the role. The acceleration during a dive was accordingly much more moderate in scale compared to that achieved by the heavier frame of either the *Luftwaffe*'s Ju 87 and Ju 88 twins or the Typhoon. Johnson soon became well aware of this, as did his pilots when he led them into action. When asked his reaction to the Spitfire's deployment in this manner, one of the squadron COs, 'Wally' Macleod, caustically responded: 'Not much sir. If we could get two decent long-range tanks instead of these'—pointing to the bombs—'we could go to Berlin with the Yanks and get stuck into some real fighting!'

Unwelcome Contradiction

To a fighter pilot, the prime reason behind his training-up for operations was to engage enemy aircraft in the sky. The mass 1943–44 diversion away from this concept in favour of ground-attack in general and dive-bombing in particular was alien to his mindset, and accordingly almost universally unwelcome to anyone flying other than with the Typhoon and Hurricane units that were already assigned to the task. There were six Armament Practice Camps (APC) to which the squadrons were dispatched for around two weeks to learn the art, but the practical effect upon both the pilots, if not also the Germans, was to prove mixed to say the least as the foregoing paragraphs indicate.

There was a combination of practical and emotive reasons behind the RAF pilots' reluctance in assuming the supplementary duty. The involvement in aerial combat tended to (falsely in numerous instances) create the impression of a 'clean battle', with the target seen as just a machine rather than something with single or multiple men on board. Of course, the effects of gunfire upon the human frame were rarely witnessed, a factor that sustained the image of a sanitised contest. Shooting-up ground targets was a world away from the 'clean air war' image; the effect of a burst of fire against exposed personnel could be seen and elicit a sense of regret if not shame at actually inflicting death and injury upon a human being.

Contrast an air battle with launching an attack upon a ground target. Now the odds of an even contest tended to be stacked against the aircraft, especially when going against a well-defended target such as an airfield or radar site. The flak gunners generally had a clear view of the attackers and could track their passage all the way; the reverse ability to pick out the defenders against the surrounding geography especially in wooded regions and take them on was often denied to the pilots with the result that casualties in terms of loss or heavy damage became a constant.

Although Geoffrey Page (second from left) has taken charge of No. 132 Squadron in this 26 April 1944 picture, he still wears flight lieutenant bars on his jacket epaulettes; the Mk IXC Spitfire bears his CO's pennant below the windshield. Squadron was stationed at Ford and these pilots had just conducted a long-range 'sweep' that has extended beyond Aachen in Germany. Promotion to No. 125 wing leader within which Page's squadron served would follow in July.

Normal Service Resumed

Both Nos 83 and 84 Groups were subordinated to No. 11 Group's operational control and planning ahead of the invasion, and they continued to provide escort to the Allied medium bombers. The paucity in *Jagdwaffe* opposition to these incursions was undoubtedly frustrating to the Fighter Command pilots who obviously wanted to test their combat skills. Of course, by the late winter of 1943–1944, the enemy fighter *Geschwadern* were being forced to grant priority to the *Reichsverteidigung* against the 8th and 15th USAAF bombers, but sufficient numbers of fighters were still stationed along the Channel coast to potentially present some form of opposition.

In the case of No. 144 Wing, the decision was taken to send an element of the escort force well ahead of the escorted bombers, with the intention of catching aircraft near or over their airfields—a risky business given the often-formidable perimeter flak defences. Map reading a course designed to place any airfield out of the fighters' direct approach but near enough to sight any aircraft taking off or landing was difficult, and on one occasion proved potentially fatal. Johnson had

No. 313 Squadron was the third Czechoslovakian-staffed unit within 2TAF and was equipped with LF Mk IX Spitfires when this picture was taken at Appledram, home for No. 134 Wing in the spring of 1944. Also present were the other Czech Squadrons, Nos 310 and 312. The torpedo-shaped drop tank enabled the fighters to extend their range while carrying out bomber escort operations.

lost his bearings in the vicinity of Paris, and on cresting a wooded ridge, he and his fellow pilots found themselves approaching an airfield whose flak gunners were ready for them with much fire coming from hangar locations. The formation had no option but to hug the ground and apply full throttle; it was a minor miracle that the solid weight of the 20-mm barrage failed to claim a victim, but it was a thoroughly shaken, if also thankful group of airmen that later dismounted at Tangmere.

Johnson's wing enjoyed a greater degree of success on 5 May against JG26. The advanced 'sweep' tactic that had yielded a near-disaster near Paris was reversed when the entire wing trawled the Pas-de-Calais. Sighting the Fw 190 formation, Johnson ordered two flights to engage, and the resultant dogfight took out Fw. H. Schwentick (5/JG26) and Uffz. M. Talkenberg (8/JG26) at the cost of one No. 441 Squadron Spitfire. Adding to the *Geschwader*'s woes on the 7th was a No. 411 Squadron Flight's bounce of a 3/JG26 formation; the result was the deaths of Obfhr. E. Scheyda, a twenty-kill veteran with well over two years' service in JG26, and his *Katchmarek* (*Luftwaffe* term for a wingman) Ogfr. T. Schwertl. Encounters of this nature were inclined to be the exception rather than the rule as D-Day loomed, however.

Long-Range Resources—Courtesy the USA

The range-inhibition forced upon the Spitfire had witnessed its practical exclusion from the daylight bomber operations largely flown by the Americans until mid-1944. Fighter Command's natural desire to join in with besting the *Jagdwaffe* over the Third Reich received a potential boost with the arrival in the European theatre of operations (ETO) of the Packard-Merlin-powered Mustang commencing with the 354FG at the end of 1943. What is surprising as well as comprising a generous gesture by Britain's major Ally was the almost simultaneous equipping of No. 65 Squadron with the Mk III, the RAF's designation for the P-51B that also displaced the original Bf 109-style hinged canopy with the sliding Malcolm Hood. The surprise in the author's mind lies in the fact that the overall numbers of P-51 airframes at this point were minimal enough for the USAAF's need in terms of long-range escort provision, let alone any other air force sharing in the allocation.

The pace of conversion by what was the first of fifteen squadrons to operate on the Mustang during the Second World War was a steady one between December and mid-February, when a sufficient number of fighters were finally available to fly a sortie that involved a short-range sweep only. By that date, Nos 19 and 122 Squadrons were carrying out a similar conversion process and it seems likely that all three were operationally on hand when the first full-scale American thrust was made on Berlin (6 March). Mention was made of 'three RAF squadrons' being assigned to withdrawal support for the bombers. The rendezvous point was north-east of Hannover, a distance from Britain that would have rendered any Spitfire squadrons incapable of attaining.

No. 306 (Polish) Squadron converted to the Mustang III in April 1944 when 133 Wing was based at Coolham. The basic nature of this airfield, in common with numerous 2TAF locations, seems to be confirmed by the absence of a hard-surfaced dispersal point. The 75-Gall external tank permitted the fighter to extend its already sizeable range while flying a mix of escort and ground-assault operations.

By the end of April, a further expansion of Mustang-equipped units had added four more to the figure, all but one of which (No. 129) came from Polish Air Force ranks (Nos 306, 315, and 316 Squadrons). A mix of duties including escort for Beaufighter strike wings, Rangers, and Ramrods were indulged in during the period up to D-Day. As regards the Mustang's use as a long-range fighter, it seems the squadrons were not regularly used in this role. By the end of April, the 8th Fighter Command had basically asserted its ultimate domination over the *Jagdwaffe* so the RAF's involvement in the campaign seems to have been restricted at most to support cover over the continental approaches to central Europe rather than directly over Germany itself—a perceived waste of the design's capability if not also the aggressive spirit of the pilots, with particular emphasis upon the Polish contingent.

'Blinding' the Germans

In the four years since the Occupation of France and the Low Countries, the Germans had constructed a formidable array of radar stations totalling nearly 100 in the case of the French and Belgian coastal sectors. The massive electronic surveillance of the sea and air approaches to the continent so established now cast up a solid barrier against any prospect of an invasion-bound force from Britain being able to even approach the shoreline, let alone gain access to a secure landing zone while remaining undetected. It followed from this that a concerted effort had to be made against these locations in order to provide the means for the attacking forces to get ashore in sufficient numbers as well as in basically intact state in order to guarantee holding back any *Wehrmacht/SS* counter thrusts.

Once again, the Typhoon was called into action as early as mid-March. On the 16th, the *Wassermann* site at Ostend was struck by rockets borne by a third of the twelve-strong force, the remainder carrying out strafing attacks; later that day, a second similar strike was made, and although no visual sign of material damage was observed, the delicate mechanisms had been ruptured or affected to such a degree that nearly three months elapsed before the equipment was back in full service. The fact of this was naturally unknown so it was likely that further assaults were rendered during the course of the interim period.

The intensified attention being paid to the German's electronic 'screen' as May commenced naturally encountered the parallel intensified flak defences around these sites. The inevitable result was that the RAF pilots found themselves somewhat on the back foot in terms of survival. Their presence against the skyline even at low altitudes coupled with a need to maintain a steady course before releasing their bombs provided the gunners with the ability to better track their prey. This was especially the case with the lighter, rapid-fire 20-mm *Flak-Vierling* (four-gun) batteries and 37-mm guns, although the 88-mm guns did add their weight of equally-lethal fire to the overall barrage. An extra hazard was the presence of parachute-assisted cables (PAC) that were fired up in the

A group of Typhoon pilots are gathered around the nose of a No. 198 Squadron fighter awaiting the order to go into battle with their fully-armed charges. Complete D-Day stripes indicate photo taken shortly after D-Day as confirmed by the 15 June photo date when the squadron was stationed at Thorney Island; it was one of eleven units assigned to rocket-firing operations as opposed to the remaining seven Typhoon-equipped examples that were bomb-carrying in operational function.

Mk IX Spitfires from Nos 411 (DB), 332 (AH), and 56 (US) Squadrons are ranged behind airmen busy belting-up 20-mm rounds. Picture reportedly taken on 5 June, but sunny weather contradicts this, given the adverse conditions existing then. In addition, all three units were spread between the three groups in 2TAF, so picture was probably taken at some general location rather than at one of the squadrons' airfields.

hope of fatally ensnaring a fighter's structure. Attempts to divide the gunner's concentration of fire by making more than one attack angle at most only lessened the odds against survival.

Three specially-equipped electronic-signal monitoring fighters from No. 1320 Flight trawling the enemy coastline to detect whether a site was still functioning could not guarantee success since the Germans quickly learned to switch off as soon as the RAF aircraft 'traces' were detected on their screens. Consequently, the general inability to confirm that a specific site had been rendered permanently out of commission added to the Typhoon squadrons' task in that repeat assaults were then deemed necessary. The spread of the manifold gun-battery locations probably made any attempt at bringing about suppression of their fire by escorting fighters unlikely. Another potentially fatal disability related to the Sabre engines that, as with all in-line models, used glycol as a coolant. Any puncture of the fluid's container would result in engine seizure within a very short time, thereby causing the aircraft's loss even if getting clear of the target area.

Several squadron COs ended up among the casualty figures, hardly surprising since they usually were first into the attack. As an example, on 2 June, No. 198 Squadron headed out towards a radar site west of Dieppe and while the rest of the unit's pilots swooped down from a higher altitude Sqn Ldr J. Niblett approached at low level with his flight. When still well distant from the clifftop target, his Typhoon was squarely struck and immediately became totally enveloped in smoke and flame; it then slowly rolled over and plunged headlong into the cliff face. The other three pilots managed to discharge their rockets and emerge intact while madly 'jinking' their aircraft in evasion (survival prospects accruing from attacks of this nature were described by an anonymous pilot as akin to 'riding a thoroughbred racehorse through a snake-infested swamp'—a tragically apt analogy).

Painful as the losses in aircraft and pilots had been during the overall assault, the result during the final days leading up to Overlord's inception would prove to be a massive reduction in German surveillance. The combination of rockets strikes against the more sensitive elements of each site's structures coupled with the loss of power and telecommunications caused by the liberal cratering of the site's surrounds and approaches caused by bombing attacks were the twin reasons for this individual and corporate failure so vital for the approaching invasion forces. The electronic shield guarding the Channel was in effect gaping open.

The Transportation Plan Evolves

Following Anglo–American governmental discussions, Eisenhower's executive order for both Strategic Bomber Commands to grant priority to the Transportation Plan instead of focusing wholly upon their original brief of destroying German industrial output was applied. The duty entailed cutting all rail and road links to the proposed Overlord landings in Normandy. A secondary aspect of these

A 500-lb bomb from a trolley load is about to be attached to the port-side pylon on a Tiffie belonging to No. 181 Squadron. The WAAF holding a dog and observing the activity is operating a motorised unit that is hauling nothing more hostile than a roller with which to flatten out the airfield surface.

assaults involved a higher degree of concentration being deliberately paid to regular attacks upon the Pas-de-Calais region's facilities as opposed to those immediately leading into Normandy; this tactical ploy was intended to feed Hitler's obsession with the belief the Allies would attempt their invasion on the former-named coastline. Despite the apparent total switch away from strategic assaults demanded from the plan, both Bomber Commands would still devote a sizeable percentage of their sorties to the continued strategic hammering of the enemy's resources.

The RAF fighter-bombers' participation in these operations was now being paralleled by the fighter element of the 9th USAAF, with the P-47 and P-38 proving themselves to be worthy contemporaries in ground-attack operations. The enemy's ground movements by day were truly being circumscribed by the relentless weight of assault, and the Typhoon was a prominent partner in these operations. The other side of the coin was that the increased weight of *Flakartillerie* fire proved a mortal threat to any sortie, especially when being flown at low level; the result was the loss of a steady number of fighters not all of whose pilots survived the experience.

The new Ski sites, known now as 'No Balls', were well-provisioned in this manner as Plt Off. C. Tucker and FS D. Stack discovered during a fighter sweep conducted by No. 175 Squadron on 5 February that unconsciously skirted too

Typhoon JP853/ SA: K from No. 486 Squadron sweeps majestically alongside the photographer as its pilot describes a steep bank that shows off the black and white identity stripes. These would only give way to the more broad-based and fewer D-Day pattern the following June, but by then, the squadron would be one of five to convert to the Tempest, using these in Diver operations in the case of this squadron.

close to one location. Although this incident predated the plan's inception, it was nevertheless typical of the risks faced by Allied fighter pilots in particular in flying over France and the Low Countries during the lead up to D-Day and, indeed, for some time afterwards. The incessant pressure applied to the transport network structure within France and extending into Belgium was a vitally important factor in ensuring any reinforcement effort towards Normandy would be largely if not totally inhibited in its intention.

The involvement of Fighter Command in the offensive added to the punishment being handed out by 2TAF. Railways were a key target, with choke points being a favourite source of attack. An example of this arose on 23 May when Nos 193 and 257 Typhoons concentrated on a tunnel into which a train had supposed sped in safety—an illusion that was confirmed when bombs blocked off both entrances to leave the personnel therein with a lengthy wait before clearance was achieved as well as creating a through-traffic hindrance. Marshalling yards were an obvious source for disruption as No. 184 Squadron confirmed when it made several assaults upon one at Gamaches. These attacks were far from 'milk run' in character, however; in one instance, PAC units were on hand, and although no losses were sustained, one Typhoon returned trailing 25 yards of cable embedded deep into one wing.

A ground crewmember stands by and holds onto the ropes for the triangular wheel braces known as chocks that will be placed in front of the approaching Tempest once it has reached the dispersal point. Picture was taken prior to D-Day as the friendly fighter stripes denote. Squadron concerned may be one of the two attached to No. 150 Wing, Newchurch.

Overlord's Onset

As May headed towards June, the atmosphere in the Allied ranks reached a point of high tension. Operation Fortitude South, with its creation of a fictional 1st US Army Group (FUSAG) under the command of the brilliant but mercurial Gen. George Patton, had hopefully confirmed Hitler's phobia that the Pas-de-Calais was the true epicentre for the Allies invasion attempt and that anywhere else was just a deceptive ploy. From an Allied point of view, the one unknown factor was not human but natural in the form of conveniently-suitable weather and especially sea conditions in which to attempt this critical venture. As history has now confirmed, Mother Nature would blow hot and cold in this respect. All stood ready for Gen. Eisenhower's 'Great Crusade' to rid Europe of the scourge of the Swastika with all that this entailed for the 'light and life of the world to advance into broad and sunlit uplands', as stated by Churchill during the critical months of the 1940 summer.

16
D-Day and 'Diver'

D-Day Doubts

The final preparations for Overlord were well and truly in order as May transformed into June, with the 5th scheduled as its launch. The overall atmosphere of tension was raised to crisis point thanks to the weather conditions that had hitherto been relatively benign, but which then converted ominously into a persistent low pressure front, casting up solid wind and sea conditions; these in turn threatened any real prospect of a basic, let alone positive invasion effort for the projected 5 June date. The distinct possibility of a postponement in order to await the same tidal conditions as was now on hand with all it entailed for likely discovery by the enemy should the *Luftwaffe*'s hitherto absent aerial reconnaissance effort stumble upon the Allied concentrations comprised a real worry.

On the morning of the 5th, meteorological staff picked up a temporary break in the weather front of no more than one or two days that was reported to Gen. Eisenhower. At the briefing of his Allied staff, he was exhorted by Montgomery—himself a cautious individual—to proceed. After collating all his subordinates' views, he quietly said 'let's go', and the invasion was irreversibly launched. On a multitude of airfields across Southern Britain, the personnel had already applied the black and white fuselage and inner-wing bands that would signify a 'friendly' status upon the aircraft so marked. The procedure was extended as far as the Anglo–American paratrooper-dropping and glider-towing transports as well as the gliders; only the four-engined bombers of the strategic commands were not so designated due to the Germans having no mass-scale operational equivalent, the few He 177s notwithstanding.

Final Deception

As the RAF and USAAF transports bearing the three parachute divisions that would spearhead the invasion took off, a final electronic diversion was launched over the approaches to the Pas-de-Calais. It took the form of No. 617 Squadron's Lancaster and No. 218 Squadron's Stirling crews creating the electronic-based illusion of an invasion fleet. This was accomplished with the use of strips of Window dropped at precise intervals as the bombers flew a series of orbits advancing precisely towards the French coast. On the sea was a group of vessels bearing barrage balloons. Between the two sub-forces, they hoped to create the impression on the enemy radar screens of what was actually a phantom armada, and in so doing further delay any enemy attention upon the true invasion source. This intended misimpression was heightened by the release of 'dummies' armed with explosive devices over the Pas-de-Calais region that would indicate a parachute drop with all it seemed to entail in terms of an invasion effort.

Back at Uxbridge, London, home for No. 11 Group's HQ, one of the multitudes of staff present was Flt Lt 'Jimmy' Rawnsley, navigator to John Cunningham. Both were veterans of the nocturnal battles against the *Luftwaffe* in the dark days of 1940–41, and both of whom had known adversity in its worst and seemingly interminable form. Now fully three years on, with the conflict swinging inexorably in the opposite direction, Rawnsley was present as he sat and watched the advance of the Allied air forces as they progressed in stately form throughout the night and into the early morning hours. As he finally emerged into the morning gloom, he studied the faraway look on his colleagues' faces. In his words: 'They were like a matinee audience emerging from a theatre, not quite able to free their minds from the world of make-believe they had just left behind. But what they had seen was not make believe'.

Action Beckons

The constant nocturnal air traffic would have provided a reasonable indication to the fighter squadron personnel that they could expect to be called into action once daylight emerged. The dull weather conditions probably did not quash the general atmosphere of enthusiasm upon hearing the news. The natural expectation of a strong *Luftwaffe* reaction to the invasion surely imbued the pilots with the hope of encountering and punishing their adversaries severely; as events confirmed, such hopes would be disappointingly frustrated.

The Germans had thankfully been taken by surprise to the extent that Gen. Rommel, having regard to the apparently unrelenting weather conditions, had departed home for his wife's birthday the very day before Overlord's launch. Even more fortunate was the German hierarchy's reluctance to provide their Führer with the fact of the Normandy-based assault until he had awoken from his slumbers later in the day—a further indication of the luck as opposed to logic that is ever likely to attend military activity.

Opposition on the ground, although moderate to severe—with the American experience on Omaha beach by far the worst among the five assault sectors—was not anything like matched by the *Luftwaffe* whose overall absence was striking

Operation Overlord has now been launched and the Typhoons of No. 198 Squadron based at Thorney Island are taking to the air as part of the massive aerial-support assault. MN233 soars aloft as part of a formation that is being directed against any *Panzer* or support-vehicle transport echelons attempting to encroach upon the landing beaches. The aircraft letter is moved forward in place of its normal location that is now obliterated by the fuselage stripes.

by comparison. Whether this was due to being taken off guard or due to their planned assembling of a sufficiently-effective force with which to make an effective challenge is ever open to interpretation. Meantime, the Allied air forces progressed in almost unhindered fashion to support the Allied armies by striking at any and all suitable targets.

The onset of the early June daylight permitted the launch of the initial wave of fighter squadrons intended to repel any counter presence of the *Luftwaffe.* Little or nothing in aerial terms disturbed the progress of the Allied soldiers as they disembarked while their aerial cover wheeled over the beaches and further inland. The lowering cloud conditions probably assisted in hindering German air response, but this was of relief to the soldiers storming ashore if not also to the frustration of their colleagues hovering above and awaiting a reaction that was clearly not forthcoming.

Ground Support

The eighteen Typhoon squadrons assigned to Nos 83 and 84 Groups were utilised in exact 50 per cent portions. Nine were allocated to close support of the ground forces with the targets being strongpoints lining the three British–Canadian beaches to be bombed as the landings commenced. The other nine were briefed to attack either heavy-calibre gun sites in the background or, in one instance, a radar site acting in a gun-ranging capacity for guns challenging either the landings or the naval fleet. The afternoon's activities involved a widening of the target region to include armed reconnaissance sorties extending some distance inland. The groups between them flew over 400 sorties at a cost of eight Typhoons.

Several of the casualties demonstrated the danger inherent in flying low down and being bounced while concentrating fully upon the task at hand. A group of Bf 109s caught No. 183 Squadron out in the vicinity of the city of Caen and, in the course of the brief but bloody combat, shot down three fighters with none of their occupants emerging alive. One among the unfortunate trio was a Canadian, Fg Off. A. Taylor, who only nine days before had been victorious over two Bf 109G *Jabos*, having expended just forty cannon shells in the process.

The immediate absence on D-Day of suitable ground facilities for constructing advanced landing grounds (ALG) within the still constrained series of beachheads forced the RAF squadrons to operate from home territory, but within a mere four days, the first example (B-3 at Sainte-Croix-sur-Mer overlooking Juno beach) had been finished and ready to receive traffic, albeit only for emergency cases. A three-fold expansion out of the ultimate total of ten planned ALGs to be located between Caen and Bayeux was completed by the 13th. Now the fighters had the

This detailed picture of a No. 198 Typhoon is probably publicity-influenced, given the number of personnel involved. The eight-rocket battery is in the process of being loaded during the initial stage of Overlord to judge by the full and pristine condition of the D-Day stripes. The squadron letters 'TP' have been repositioned ahead of the cockpit, the D-Day fuselage bands having completely obliterated the letters' normal location.

The Typhoon's strong airframe enabled it to carry bombs weighing up to 1,000 lb under each wing. This example is being winched into position on a No. 440 (RCAF) Squadron fighter, using hand winches known as 'hockey sticks' from their shape. The bulged landing gear cover and non-tread tyre are other points of note.

opportunity to land, rearm, and refuel during operations but to head back to their airfields across the Channel at the day's end. The fact that the ALGs were squarely within range of the German guns and would remain so for over two months did not make for a comfortable existence but just had to be borne by both pilots and ground crews.

'Dust Devil' Menace

The delicate innards of any aircraft, especially its power source, are prone to failure thanks to weather conditions among other factors. The powder-like quality of dust constitutes a real threat to an engine that, if ingested to any degree, will lead to a faltering if not total failure in performance. The removal of the French topsoil as a necessary precondition to laying down the ALGs with their Sommerfield-Track metal surfaces soon revealed its malign consequences for any aircraft thanks to a fine residue cast up off the naked soil surface by the thrusting effect of the propellers. The massive radiator aperture on the Typhoon was extremely vulnerable to drawing-in the swirling dust cloud's particles with all that implied for engine efficiency—or rather inefficiency.

A remedy was urgently needed if the incidence of failure was not to hinder the pace of operations, if not also prevent needless loss of aircraft should engine performance be fatally compromised especially in the course of a sortie over enemy soil. The initial solution took the form of a metal 'dome' that fitted over the carburettor air-intake. The problem with this fitting was not from its own operation but rather thanks to a regular foible displayed by the Sabre—backfire on start-up. Should this occur, the result was the inadvertent and violent propulsion of the 'dome' into space; this was a potentially lethal issue for anyone who might be in the fitting's precipitate path. A more functional and secure alternative was the development of a 'Drum' pattern filter with a fine-mesh screen that possessed twin flexible panels in the centre. Just as on a cuckoo clock, these would open under the influence of a backfire action to permit dissipation of the air projected outwards.

There were two additional Typhoon-equipped units who were currently functioning outside the 2TAF umbrella. These were Nos 137 and 263 Squadrons, serving within ADGB, whose pilots were tasked with anti-shipping sorties while operating from their widely-spread Channel airfields at Manston and Bolt Head. The greater geographic spread at the western end with equally increased traffic as the *Kriegsmarine* sought to infiltrate its U-boats, in particular, into the Channel to challenge the Allied invasion fleet provided No. 263 with enhanced latitude in surface targets but conversely laid it open to more punishment. Flak ships were a constant hazard and probably were the primary cause for six losses, whereas No. 137 emerged unscathed from its less-pressurised experience. The squadrons' service within ADGB would end with transfer into 2TAF on 6 and 13 August respectively, by which stage the defence of Britain in terms of daylight operations was then in the hands of Spitfire, Tempest (one), and Mustang-equipped squadrons.

Sqn Ldr Pitt-Brown (Squadron CO) standing in the centre is one of seven No. 174 Squadron pilots talking to two members of the unit's servicing commando. Instead of each squadron retaining its own ground crew, personnel were assigned to a specific ALG in Normandy and serviced the aircraft stationed there. This was not a popular move since the ground crew naturally lost their identity with a specific squadron.

Overlord Air Activity

The complete Allied domination around the Normandy operation during the crucial first days was a foreboding issue not only for *Luftwaffe* hopes of a measurable counterstrike, but also for the chances of the *Wehrmacht/SS* units in being capable of similarly thwarting either the consolidation of the overall bridgehead or the burgeoning threat of an irresistible breakout into the French hinterland. The oft-quoted strafing pass by the JG26 *Kommodore* 'Pips' Priller and his wingman is held up as a key indicator of the *Luftwaffe*'s totally inadequate response on 6 June. In fact, even if sufficient forces had been promptly mustered and dispatched, the numbers involved would have constituted a fraction of the roughly 15,000 individual sorties flown by the Allied air forces. As regards the fighter element, RAF Fighter Command alone had ninety-five squadrons available in Southern England split between its tactical and pure fighter strength to add to the USAAF figure; between them, they displayed an estimated six-to-one numerical superiority.

The incidence of fighter *v.* fighter combat was to prove small in general, in addition to which it was the tactical squadrons within the Anglo–American ranks that bore the brunt of the casualties. The low- to medium-altitude nature of their operations not only rendered them particularly vulnerable to the enemy flak gunners, but if intercepted by a *Jagdwaffe* formation when still laden down with their external weaponry, the odds were in the enemy pilots' favour as to a successful outcome. The Bf 109G and Fw 190 were still redoubtable gun platforms when matched against virtually anything in the RAF or USAAF fighter inventory. It was the issue of numerically-inferior material and human resources almost as much as the Allies' technical superiority that was placing the *Luftwaffe* on the increasing back foot.

The ADGB units had been involved on 6 June, but the distance to be flown across the Channel did not permit too much time over the battle zone for the Spitfire squadrons, while the solid cloud formations along with a dearth in enemy aircraft numbers provided a disappointing scenario. The ten Mosquito and two Beaufighter squadrons on hand were available when called on to provide nocturnal surveillance of the overall landing zone and beyond as darkness closed upon the organized chaos and inevitable litter of battle below. Those on the ground under whose protective cover the nocturnal fliers were assembled could be certain that they were largely secure from counter assault from the air, a security that would not be materially impinged upon as the Normandy Campaign expanded.

Although some squadrons applied their D-Day stripes in precise fashion, other units such as No. 402 (RCAF) Squadron were more casual. The white paint has been roughly applied around parts of the fuselage roundel while the stripe edges are somewhat 'wavy' in general. The overall effect would be perfect when viewed from afar, however.

The fortunately-tardy deployment of the *Panzer* units close to the landings during D-Day was further hindered by the fighter-bomber assaults; this was a situation that would never materially improve over the weeks ahead, especially after the RAF contingent began to transfer across the Channel to permanent occupancy of the ALG sites. Within fifteen days, five squadrons had taken up residence, but the discovery by a *Luftwaffe* reconnaissance fighter allied to the airfields' close proximity to the frontline forced a return to British soil thanks to disruptive, if not generally effective artillery fire. It would be the month's end before the reduction in this countermeasure was such that a safe return could be deemed in order. The two rocket-equipped wings and one bomb-carrying wing assigned would pile on the punishment that would be further strengthened as the remaining wings followed suit and Fighter Command relinquished unfettered control to AM Conningham's 2TAF.

Mustang Fortunes over France

The seven out of a final figure of thirteen squadrons equipped with the Merlin-Mustang on hand at D-Day were with the exception of No. 316 currently formed into two wings: No. 122 assigned to 83 Group contained Nos 19, 65, and 122 Squadrons, with No. 133 serving in 84 Group absorbing Nos 129, 306 (Polish), and 315 (Polish) Squadrons. The single remaining unit was stationed at Coltishall in No. 12 Group. Although attached to 2TAF, only the first-mentioned wing would actually transfer to the continent and then only until around September before returning to Matlaske in Norfolk.

The vastly superior range capability of the Mustang compared to even the Typhoon made it an admirable choice for tactical reconnaissance sorties; the pilots could either cover a greater geographic spread or alternately monitor a specific sector over a longer time span. The aircraft's ability to carry bomb loads equal to the Typhoon provided it with a solid striking capacity against a range of targets from rail and road transport as well as river and canal traffic to the more vulnerable conduits such as bridges, locks, and viaducts. Added to this was the striking power of the design's .5-calibre machine guns.

The Immediate Reaction

The second volume on JG26's history provides a sound insight as regards the *Jagdwaffe*'s overall reaction to the invasion and its aftermath during June and up to September. The solo effort by Priller and his No. 2 as D-Day commenced was followed by the three available *Gruppen* transferring to airfields around Paris. It then seems that the two French-based *Geschwadern* provided all the opposition this day due to the non-arrival of other units; this was put down to the German High Command only treating Overlord as a diversionary tactic instead of a primary threat as the day wore on.

A Mustang III of No. 315 (Polish) Squadron is being rearmed for another post-Overlord operation while serving within No. 122 Wing, 2TAF. It is surprising that the original side-hinged cockpit frame has not been replaced by the more visually-efficient 'Malcolm' sliding alternative. The relatively crude application of the black-and-white stripes is evidence of the haste with which they were applied.

The single RAF squadron serving within No. 133 Wing was No. 129, two of whose Mustang IIIs are seen in the immediate aftermath of the Normandy invasion. The one in the foreground is under detailed maintenance with the fighter's tail jacked-up, engine cowling panels removed and armourers working on the port gun bay.

The arrival of seventeen further *Gruppen* over the next forty-eight hours promised a strong response to the invaders. In the event, the overall numbers of fighters on hand was barely one-quarter of the theoretical strength normally on hand within the units concerned. Worse still were the support logistics at the airfields where the newcomers were directed to. This was nowhere near even the minimum required to sustain operations; to the lack of supplies was added inadequate or non-existent buildings, communications systems, lighting, etc.

The generally inclement weather conditions that had nearly thrown the invasion effort off the rails now worked to a good degree in the Allies favour. Those aircraft already geared-up to carry bombs were stood ready to launch a concerted series of attacks on the 9th, but virtually all were cancelled. One of the few to be launched still could not gain visual access to the beachheads and the pilots reportedly contented themselves with shooting-up abandoned gliders, a totally meaningless gesture. A *Luftflotte* 3 order that all fighters be fitted with bomb racks and that priority must be unconditionally allotted to this activity would leave the skies clear of fighter interception for the Allied air forces. The *Jagdwaffe* in effect would be rendered wholly redundant in activating its normal primary role.

The order was rightly ignored by some units, but its issue and almost immediate cancellation was to prove symptomatic of the current and future chaotic state of the *Luftwaffe*'s defensive plan. By the end of the first full week of operations (the 13th), the *Jagdwaffe*'s attention was focused upon combating the Allied air forces' fighter-bombers and their companion fighters conducting sweeps. By this date, the Overlord bridgehead was continuous in length and extended well into the Normandy countryside, with the US 1st Army pushing relentlessly up into the Cherbourg Peninsula. Back in Britain, there was a sober mood of confidence that the final stages of the conflict could possibly be concluded before the year's end. The onset of a German counterassault as the 13th dawned would shake that positive mood. Hitler's manic desire to break his adversary's fighting spirit would be expressed over the same region of the country that had seen his dream of total European domination compromised for the first time four years before.

The Robot Age Beckons

The German genius in matters technical among a range of subjects had been expressed between the two major conflicts with manifold experiments in rocket science. The concept of an aerial means for delivering an explosive force had led to the construction of pilotless weapons, a measure that was economic in cost compared to manned aircraft as well as in terms of dispensing with aircrew. One of these featured a warhead on a simple cruciform-shaped airframe that was driven by a pulsejet. The project appeared to have Hitler's approval, but when in the later stage of completion, it was dropped; the events of April to June 1940 convinced the Führer that with the war all but won, the weapon was rendered redundant.

Although resurrected in the light of subsequent adverse military events, the delay was to prove somewhat fortuitous for Germany's opponents.

The *Vergeltungswaffen Nr. Eins* (revenge weapon No. 1) remained unknown to Allied intelligence even after mid-1943 photo reconnaissance sorties over the major research centre at Peenemunde revealed the existence of what was to be the follow-up V-2 ballistic rocket. However, the resultant discovery of the manifold launch sites in France allied to a Polish resistance group's confirmed details of the weapon's existence alerted the British Government as to the latent threat being posed. The code word Diver was instituted, and the wording of the 22 April supporting document issued to the Royal Observer Corps referred to the possibility of 'pilotless aircraft being launched from the Pas-de-Calais and Cherbourg regions. This was a statement that confirmed the authorities' clear knowledge of the admittedly still-uncertain nature of the weaponry. The stage was set for however imminent the assault might be as well as how it would evolve.

A specialist *Luftwaffe* unit had been created that would be central to the offensive's initiation and continuation. Ob. Wachtel was assigned to preside over *Flak-Regiment 155 (W)*'s handling of the V-1s, but the *Führerbefehl* for the campaign's initiation on 10 June found his subordinates not quite ready to oblige, although the seventy-two-hour delay would be of marginal comfort to the population in Southeast England. So it was that in the early hours of 13 June the first of four bombs to be successfully dispatched and attain their target shot off its ramp in a pall of smoke. The resultant strikes were well spread with one descending within inner London. Which one constituted the example picked up by a ROC team at Dymchurch who transmitted the Diver warning to their HQ is uncertain, but the die was cast for battle to commence. The team's location on top of a Martello Tower was unconsciously ironic; the defensive structure was one of a number erected in response to a possible invasion by an earlier dictator who, like Hitler, had once been a corporal—Napoleon Bonaparte.

Daylight quickly dispelled any doubt as to this remote form of attack as a succession of V-1s passed overhead in virtually unhindered fashion for at least several days. Casualties mounted steadily with the worst example a strike on the Guards Chapel (the 18th) that killed sixty-three serviceman and fifty-eight civilians. The immediate countermeasures involved the swift siting of numerous gun batteries that would later be supplied with proximity-fused shells; compared to a standard shell that had to strike directly home, the new missile only had to detonate in the V-1's vicinity for the resultant concussive effect to induce a sympathetic explosion of the warhead.

The original grouping of the batteries directly ahead of the barrage-balloon screen created on the southern approaches to London would also be subject to relocation in the light of operational circumstances. This technical and geographic combination was destined to claim a growing number of the Doodlebugs as the official version of the flying bomb was to be christened by the public. However, until these changes occurred, the guns' overall performance would not be equal to making a terminal dent in the rain of missiles. Less than 200 V-1s

The balding head of Wg Cdr Skalski is discernible within the cockpit of a Mustang III assigned to either 306 or 315 (Polish) Squadron following completion of a sortie. When this post D-Day picture was taken, he was leader for 133 Wing that conducted operations over France flying out of Ford in Southern England. The wing would soon be called upon to challenge the flood of V-1 missiles commencing in July.

No. 3 Squadron's Tempests were not called into action until late on D-Day, a fact that might account for the extremely precise application of D-Day stripes. The top picture shows JF: G under detailed maintenance; the lower picture depicts the Tempest flown by Wg Cdr Beamont, squadron CO and leader of No. 150 Wing based at Newchurch close to the Channel coast. The wing would soon be pitched into the fight against the V-1 Doodlebug.

would be claimed in this time compared to over 900 by the fighters along with a number snared by the balloons.

Tactical Conundrums: An Overview

Fighter Command's involvement in the counter campaign was mandatory, as well as crucial, but by no means easy to deploy in an unconditionally-efficient manner. For a start, the speed of the V-1 ranged from as low as 300 mph to nearly 400 mph; even the lower speed level was swallowed up in roughly fifteen to twenty minutes between three fighter patrol lines extending inwards from mid-Channel and the London area. This was one factor in a multi-fold test for the fighters on hand that included the Spitfire as the immediate prime weapon, although the Mosquito, Mustang, and Tempest would each add their individual weight. First of all, the interception had to be initiated with sufficient time to close upon the target and land effective fire. The miniscule shape of the V-1 posed the next problem in the ability to direct that fire accurately. Most critical was the ability or otherwise to avoid the weapon's detonation effect that would cast debris directly in the path of the attacker.

The initial positioning of the gun batteries well inland from the coast still left pilots with an uncomfortable time margin in which to accomplish their task before intruding over the barrage of shells, particularly in the case of interceptions initiated over the Channel 'neck' between Dover and Calais. Three patrol lines located between mid-Channel, the coast and adjacent to the gun belt represented the initial pattern of fighter cover between the campaign's inception and up to mid-July. During this period, there were regular occasions when a 'free for all' situation arose whereby the pursuing fighters became equally at risk of damage or destruction from the guns in common with their robotic prey as the pilots intruded upon the barrage of fire. This undesirable scenario seemed automatic in the case of the inner patrol line that clearly gave little or no latitude for the fighters so involved to engage and down their targets before they entered the gun belt.

The authorities were tardy in creating revised operational conditions that were intended to alleviate the problem. Only around 21 July were these put into force, being based upon the existing weather conditions. Should the visibility be clear then the airspace above the gun belt was turned exclusively over to RAF Fighter Command leaving its pilots uninterrupted pursuit of their targets. Otherwise, the gunners would be granted the same level of exclusivity. The code-names 'Flabby' and 'Spouse' were applied to the respective operational conditions.

The question was at least partially solved following an ADGB Memorandum issued on 15 July. Gen. Frederick Pile (C-in-C Anti-Aircraft Command) was requested to initiate the transfer of the array of what was a 400 heavy gun complement onto the coastline where they were backed by nearly 600 Bofors quick-firing 40-mm guns. That the act was accomplished within seventy-two hours speaks well of the general and his personnel. By the campaign's conclusion,

MK126, a Mk IX Spitfire, has the same number as the squadron that it was assigned to—No. 126. Picture is taken at Harrowbeer in mid-1944, following the unit's return from the Mediterranean theatre of operations. Operations from here involved cover for the Normandy bridgehead. Repetition of the aircraft letter on the fin is an unusual variation.

The Mk XII Spitfire was the first to be fitted with a Griffon engine, albeit one of lower power rating, as well as lacking the five-blade propeller applied to the Mk XIV variant. Its introduction in early 1943 to No. 41 Squadron was to counter *Jagdwaffe* tip-and-run raids on the Channel coast and the clipped wing tips were an addition to the low-altitude performance deemed necessary to properly engage the marauding Bf 109s and Fw 190s. The mark was retained until September 1944 and was used during the V-1 offensive.

no less than 2,300 individual guns would be involved in a proportion of one heavy to three Bofors. In addition, the original compact geographic arc of fire directly ahead of the balloon screen was now expanded to a roughly 60-mile length between a point east of Dover and Beachy Head. The defensive effort still covered the 'spread' of the launch sites between Dunkirk and Dieppe, but now the guns could engage their targets at a far greater distance from London.

The average height of no more than several thousand feet flown on an undeviating course by the Doodlebugs laid them particularly vulnerable to the hail of fire dispensed by the Bofors with their fast traversing motion compared to the static heavy guns, but the latter still added soundly to the overall weight of fire. There would be little doubt that the gun belt's transfer coupled with the availability of continuously-replenished stocks of proximity-fused shells would ultimately have a deleterious effect upon the proportion of the V-1s successfully running the gauntlet during the campaign, whose course would span around two and a half months.

The 3-mile firing zone straddling both sides of the coastline was primarily off limits to Allied aircraft under the memorandum's terms, but it still allowed for the latter to intercept out over the Channel; the time span granted the fighter pilots in which to engage a target over the water was inevitably minimal around the Dover–Calais zone, but extended up to around ten minutes as the Channel width expanded westwards—still a tight margin in which to accomplish the deed before

JN735 is photographed around March 1944 onward following assignment to No. 3 Squadron; her QO: A codes are still absent, although she does bear the friendly fighter underwing stripes. Her involvement in the V-1 campaign was swift in terms of success, since Plt Off. 'Buck' Feldman, an American pilot, downed a Doodlebug on 20 June.

intruding upon mutually hostile airspace for hunter and prey (the original 'mixed' involvement of fighters and guns was still to be allowed for, however. Code-named 'Fickle', this allowed for the heavy guns to fire up to 8,000 feet and the lighter-calibre guns to take on visual targets; meanwhile, the fighters could enter the zone if already in pursuit—a somewhat illogical reversal from the aforementioned strict limitations).

The barrage balloon screen, one that would be reinforced over three-fold by the end of July, presented a lesser hindrance, but the distance between the revised gun belt and the screen's southern boundary, although greater than the seaward approach to the former-named defensive network, still presented a fairly tight time span within which to down the weapon without intruding upon the cable-supported airbags that constituted a more passive, but still potentially lethal threat to any aircraft.

A more intractable problem facing the fighters when confronted with engaging their pilotless adversary over the south-eastern English landscape was the question of security of life and limb for the population therein. It was axiomatic to destroy the V-1s before they could break through to the capital and causing them to

The auxiliary nature of airfields such as Newchurch meant that the facilities were rather basic in terms of support structures; the use of tents was accordingly much more of a norm compared to a regular established airfield. Several mechanics are working over a No. 3 Squadron Tempest resplendent in its accurately-applied D-Day stripes and with the aircraft code letters intruding on the white stripes outlined in black.

disintegrate in mid-air was the naturally desired option. Sending one out of action by upsetting its stability in any manner possible was a second option, but success in doing so created a dilemma.

London's citizenry, along with the capital's military and commercial infrastructure, would obviously be spared thanks to the diversionary act—but what of those individuals below the now totally-errant flight attitude of the weapon when it inevitably detonated on the ground, there being no guarantee it would do so well away from inhabited areas. A sizeable number of casualties would be incurred in this tragic, but arguably necessary manner that constituted a crude case of 'The greater Good for the greater number' in terms of both lives and property.

The summer of 1944 was inordinately wayward in terms of sunny and dry conditions, and this was to be the case even when allowing for the ever-unpredictable weather patterns surrounding the British Isles. The jetting flames from the V-1's engine nacelle could remain concealed from sight in the case of solid cloud patterns at least in daylight; during the hours of darkness, there could be a better chance of picking up the reflection projected within the clouds, but it would be equally difficult if not impossible to close down the target and also gain the necessary visual contact in order to open fire unless the cloud barrier gave way to open space.

The Aerial Challenge

The relatively swift passage through the gun barrage for those V-1s surviving the experience left only the barrage balloon screen as the last resort to an unfettered access to their primary target. It was therefore crucial for the campaign's positive outcome that Fighter Command be fully engaged in culling the maximum number of Hitler's robotic weapons from their evil intent. Two essential requirements were a top speed that could be consistently maintained along with a heavy enough armament with which to land a lethal punch. The first of these needs was by now on regular hand thanks to the presence of the Mk XIV Spitfire and the Mustang III, as well as the current Mosquito fighter variants that would carry out a good proportion of the nocturnal interceptions.

What was to be the doyen of the single-engined range of fighter types on hand was the Mk V Tempest, which could more than hold its own with the onrushing Doodlebug in terms of constant pace. The Hawker machine would prove its value in this respect, and over the ensuing weeks, its pilots would cut particularly deep into the robots' ranks. It would moreover provide virtually half of the above force (five squadrons) compared to three—Nos 129, 306, and 315—flying the Mustang III and two—Nos 19 and 322 Squadron—the Mk XIV Spitfire during the campaign's course. Also on hand would be No. 41 Squadron's Spitfire Mk XIIs, whose low-level performance in terms of maximum speed was at least adequate in assuming this duty.

As regards firepower, the striking power of the Spitfire variants was reasonable but was somewhat limited in that only two cannon-calibre weapons were generally on hand along with four .303 machine guns; on the other hand, some Mk XIVs were fitted with two .5 weapons in place of the four .303s, and in such cases, the overall weight of firepower was enhanced. A similar limitation affected the Mustang III's complement of four .5 machine guns, although the US manufactured gun's ammunition possessed a solid 'punch' as well as being on hand in greater quantity compared to the more limited stowage capacity of its cannon contemporary. It was the Tempest that could deliver what was arguably the most concentrated weight of fire with its four 20-mm cannon.

'Bee' Beamont's Newchurch-based wing was perfectly positioned to answer the call for action, although only Nos 3 and 486 Squadrons were in possession of the Tempest; No. 56 was still several weeks away from converting from the Mk IX Spitfire, with which it had entered the fray. The number of Tempests on hand was still no more than adequate, this being due to delays in Maintenance Command completing the necessary range of modifications prior to squadron delivery. Operations commencing on 1 May involved regular sweeps, during which period several instances of mechanical failure that

No. 610 Squadron was first to convert onto the Mk XIV Spitfire that possessed a superior overall performance compared to the Mk XII. Its ability to virtually match the Tempest in speed witnessed a sizeable number of V-1s being downed by this and the several other squadrons so equipped and committed to the Diver campaign. The 2,050-hp Griffon 65 driving a five-blade propeller was a prime factor in this success.

including runaway propellers had rather dampened the pilots' confidence in their new mounts.

The wing's involvement on 6 June seemed illogically fragmented in that only No. 56 Squadron was dispatched for the first action of escort to Allied transport aircraft; the Tempest units were only called on until late in the day, with a brief to over-fly the landing beaches. The following week witnessed only one sortie where the *Luftwaffe* was encountered, but the resultant combat left the enemy force three Bf 109s short; the total included one credited to Beamont that brought him up to ace status as well as being his penultimate kill in the Second World War; he was fortunate to escape with no more than one hole in a wing after being himself bounced thanks to a momentary relaxation in attention. Today's wing score was added to the two Ju 88s strafed to destruction on 28 May. However, the wing's kill tally was unknowingly on the verge of being massively expanded, although the human cost to the *Luftwaffe* would be nil.

Although the first flurry of V-1s had been dispatched on the morning of the 13th, there was a total abstinence from further action until the late evening on the 15th when the full fury of Hitler's 'vengeance weapon' descended primarily upon London to inflict more than 700 fatalities and a further 2,600 injury cases within the first week. The destruction inflicted was inevitably random in nature, and with no signs of the offensive flagging in scale, the people's morale was undoubtedly becoming as it were 'frayed at the edges'. They could know little of the fact that the defensive chain was already rising to the challenge, however fitful in effect this might seem in the initial stage, but it was one already ensuring that the weight of assault was not destined to rise to an even higher degree of intensity.

'Let Battle Commence!'

Fighter Command's involvement was seemingly turgid in initial application to judge by the experience of the Tempest wing that was not called upon until the second full day of attack (the 16th). The designated patrol line on this occasion was over the Channel 'neck', but the first sight Wg Cdr Beamont gained of a V-1 was almost head-on and left him away behind by the time he had reversed course. The resultant tail chase was protracted, and he only closed to maximum firing range when over halfway between the coast and London. The miniscule outline was difficult to focus upon and he was nearly out of ammunition before the V-1 finally succumbed, not to his but rather Sgt Cole's (No. 2) gunfire.

The experience was a chastening one in terms of downing the weapons in minimal time despite another No. 3 Squadron pilot having shot down his target before it had even reached the English coast. The ability of the Tempest to accelerate quickly in a dive impelled Beamont among others to do so in cases where the V-1 was first picked up at a lower altitude, a situation that depended on luck. The wing leader's first solo kill owed much to this initial advantage coming his way and he duly opened fire after the range shortened to a minimal distance.

The application of D-Day stripes on most aircraft was a hasty and inevitably slap-dash affair. In sharp contrast, another No. 3 Squadron Tempest V demonstrates the markings very neat application. The squadron code letters are clearly defined, but the forward part of the serial number has been swallowed up.

What happened next provided a salutary if inevitable lesson in tacking a Doodlebug, namely its detonation. The latest of several bursts of fire induced a massive explosion that threw the fighter over into an incipient roll as it waded through the smoke pall within which were myriad pieces of the weapon. Beamont regained control of the Tempest that now displayed scorched paintwork and a blackened canopy. He would have one more such heart-stopping experience during his very next engagement that would leave his aircraft with damage to its tail plane, among other damage. His double dose of good fortune would not always be reflected in the experience of a number of other pilots who would succumb along with their target in similar circumstances.

Interception Problems (Day)

The experience of Wg Cdr Beamont's first 'solo' interception highlighted a key problem, namely its prompt achievement. The V-1's minimal outline made it difficult for it to be visually engaged; the flame output from the engine was only evident after the weapon was already ahead of the fighter. The fact that the chase had extended from mid-Channel to a point so far along the inland route did not bode well for a swift dispatch. The situation arguably became even more fraught when the hitherto unimpeded range factor from over the Channel was reduced to a point directly behind the realigned coastal gun belt, which accordingly reduced the overall distance in which a kill could be achieved.

Although every bit as expansive in size as the Typhoon, the Mk V Tempest possessed a more proportionally-streamlined appearance with the enlarged fin fairing compared to the more-upright and stubby Tiffie pattern adding to the impression. JN766 was an early-assigned aircraft to No. 486 (RNZAF) Squadron that went on to survive combat up to VE-Day.

However swiftly the Doodlebug was closed upon, the next problem was how to both accurately and quickly inflict a terminal burst of fire upon the speeding target. The normal harmonization of the guns provided a 'spread' pattern that was sufficient when aligned against an aircraft but wasted a good percentage of the ammunition unless the pilot closed to a short distance—at which point, the fighter was likely to be fatally involved should the V-1 explode. Beamont decided that his pilots should have their guns aligned in 'spot' fashion. The greatly-enhanced concentration of fire arising from this alteration was not permitted by the Fighter Command hierarchy, but it allowed a pilot to open-up at a distance that provided a better, albeit not guaranteed, prospect of not being enveloped in the explosive effect, should that occur.

The presence of sizeable numbers of fighters assigned to the campaign raised the problem of how to deploy them so that the available airspace was comprehensively 'policed' while simultaneously reducing the chances of pilots running across one another's path with all that entailed in near misses or collisions. Linked to this risk was the engaging of each V-1 by more than one or, at most, two fighters, which in turn critically limited the overall number being taken on hand as it were. The problem of gaining first sight of the incoming robots was ameliorated by the Observer Corps personnel firing flares whenever its personnel sighted one. However, the vagaries of Britain's weather patterns were a natural factor that both the aerial and ground-based defenders had no control over, but whose negative elements of cloud, in particular, was more likely to visually benefit the enemy assault.

Interception Problems (Night)

The task of nocturnal interception was initially lessened due to the visual trail left by the V-1 pulsejet exhaust, which accordingly permitted its more-prompt engagement. The perceived advantage compared to daylight operations was almost wholly compromised if the pilot attempted to close upon the weapon from the standard rear angle; this was due to his night vision almost certainly being degraded to a point where he had no visual focus. The practical alternative was found by the Tempest element of the defensive force at least. Instead of levelling out from a dive when in direct line, the pilot would descend marginally below the V-1's flightpath and hold this position until within firing range. He would then pull up into firing position. Having confirmed his correct alignment thanks to the motion created by the weapon's wake, he would open fire directly into the orb of the flame. The tactic certainly worked to some degree for the wing and was probably taken on board elsewhere.

Destabilisation Option: Pros and Cons

There is a plethora of film clips and still photos showing V-1s commencing or already being cast into an uncontrollable manoeuvre and striking the ground while still underway towards London. The cause of their welcome demise was due

A triumvirate of Second World War fighter successes are caught alongside one another. The FB Mk VI Mosquito is having its machine-gun compartment replenished with .303 ammunition as another mechanic works on the canopy. An impressive fifty-plus mission tally is recorded on the forward fuselage. All three aircraft bear D-Day stripes that appear to be reduced to indicate picture taken well after the invasion.

to the aerodynamic as opposed to explosive influence inflicted by the fighter or fighter pilots involved in their pursuit. The merit in what was to be an alternative method of dispatch was clear but brought with it a parallel degree of risk for those attackers who carried out the indulgence, usually after running out of ammunition.

One of those who did so was Beamont, but his first experience was unintentional in practice. During a night sortie, his attempt to act on a radar-directed plot almost ended in disaster when his track ran directly with that of the V-1 that he only avoided by opening-up power and shooting across in front. When he then looked for the Doodlebug, it had disappeared only to erupt into a ball of fire upon striking the ground; the malign influence of his slipstream upon its gyro-control had accomplished the act of destabilisation.

Several days later, he suffered gun malfunction and, having recalled the involuntary diversion of the aforementioned V-1, decided upon what was a deliberately-engineered variation. He closed slowly in upon the flying bomb until one wing tip was perched scant feet below his robotic adversary's wing tip. He held position but veered sharply away when the V-1 dipped towards the Tempest before resuming level and undeviating flight. The second attempt was initiated, and after an agonising, if short time span, the airflow's effect succeeded in tipping the weapon up and over into a terminal dive.

The Specialists

The V-1 campaign was to reveal a group of pilots demonstrating a penchant for tackling the weapons in a manner that saw them run up a high score. The Fighter Interception Unit had been examining how to best operate at night, and during June, it had been provided with a handful of Tempests for this purpose. Two of the pilots involved were accordingly seconded to the Newchurch Wing towards the month's end; they were Flt Lt Joe Berry and Sqn Ldr Daniel, nicknamed 'Tubby'. Berry's latent prowess in nocturnal operations was immediately confirmed during his first foray when he downed two V-1s. A similar tally was recorded by Daniel, who was already a night-fighter ace from his service in the Mediterranean, but his value was tragically cut short a week later when he was MIA following bale out from his blast-afflicted fighter.

The presence of FIU pilots within the wing was soon increased to flight strength, but the original number was whittled down by two more, including the FIU CO Wg Cdr Hartley, who was side-lined with a broken leg, the result of a mid-air collision that claimed the crew on the Mosquito involved. In the meantime, Flt Lt Berry's onslaught against the Doodlebugs went from strength to strength, so much so that by later July, his fifty-nine tally comprised the bulk of the fifty kills credited to the FIU Detachment. The peak of this success rate was attained on 23–24 June, when no less than seven were hauled from the sky. Five other wing pilots could claim a double-figure score, amounting to ninety-six overall, with Wg Cdr Beamont leading on twenty-three (one ahead of Flt Lt Van Lierde).

Sqn Ldr Joe Berry gained (sadly posthumous) fame arising from the V-1 campaign. As a member of the specialist Fighter Interception Unit (FIU) team assigned to these operations, he scored no less than fifty-nine kills scoring multiple victories of between four and seven on eight occasions. He then joined No. 501 Squadron as CO, but on 2 October, his Tempest was flak-stricken during a Ranger sortie and he died in the resultant crash.

Berry would advance to become the campaign's premier V-1 ace, with sixty and a half confirmed. The final eight were claimed after the FIU had been absorbed into No. 501 Squadron based at Manston, where he took over command during early August, having been promoted to squadron leader in the process. Sadly, having survived the battle against what were more unpredictable aerial adversaries than manned examples, during a subsequent Ranger sortie on 1 October, he failed to survive the gauntlet of flak guarding a German airfield that his flight was strafing.

Spitfire Fortunes

The need to maintain a constant speed at the top end of its range placed a heavy strain upon the engine of any fighter. The Mk IXB Spitfire was arguably the most-affected in terms of inordinate wear upon the Merlin 66's innards from among the three Supermarine variants on current hand; as it was, only Nos 1 and 165 Squadrons seem to have been called into the fight and then only for several weeks before being switched to bomber escort duties. The former unit had converted from the Typhoon during April with the availability of 150 Octane fuel that the Merlin 66s were adapted to accommodate. However, the maximum time period during which the enhanced +25-lb/square-inch boost pressure could be applied was five minutes. The result was that any engagement with a V-1 had to be even more promptly executed in comparison to any other fighter type so involved.

The combination of recurrent adverse weather conditions over the summer did not help in cutting down the odds against possible interception let alone success in gaining a kill. In spite of this frustrating limitation, the squadron did begin to make steady, if finally-modest inroads into the flow of V-1s. The first was shared between three pilots on 27 June and by 10 August, when the squadron was switched back to bomber escort duties it had amassed a total of forty-seven confirmed victories. The equivalent tally for No. 165 is unclear but was probably similar.

On the subject of the battle's tactical handling, it was ironic that complaints were raised about the Mk IX pilots sometimes being disturbed during interceptions by Tempests cutting them out—but the reverse complaint had been raised by Wg Cdr Beamont within days of the offensive's start. Whatever the truth, the withdrawal of the Mk IXs before the campaign's conclusion would seem to support his suggestion to Fighter Command regarding limiting the defensive complement to the higher-performance designs mentioned earlier in this chapter. If Beamont's view was taken up, then its application was only gradual. However, by early August, the situation had been improved in the Allies' favour to the extent

Sqn Ldr Eugeniusz Horbaczewski (believed to be second from left) was a legend with No. 315 (Polish) Squadron by August 1944. He had amassed around thirteen confirmed kills ranging back to late 1941 by 18 August, when he led a highly successful bounce on a *Jagdwaffe* formation. On return, the squadron was just one short—tragically, it was the man himself, who was posthumously awarded three of the sixteen confirmed victories.

No. 604 Squadron was the first dedicated night-fighter unit going back to the pioneer period of the *Blitz*. Four years later, the tide has fully turned as crews return from an operation with the *Luftwaffe* now firmly on the back foot. By now, the squadron was operating within No. 147 Wing, 2TAF, at Zeals and flying the NF Mk XIII Mosquito. The nose-mounted centimetric-wavelength radar sets reduced weaponry to the bomb bay's four 20-mm cannon, a scale of firepower still enough to hand out lethal strikes.

that the Mk IXs could be safely excluded without materially delaying the final positive outcome.

A similar operational pattern was enjoyed by the Mk XIIs flown by No. 41 Squadron, the sole RAF unit now using the variant. The original concept behind what was the first mark to switch from the Merlin to the Griffin as its power source was to provide a low-level challenge to the *Jagdwaffe*, with specific emphasis upon the enemy 'tip and run' raids. The 1,735-hp rating of the IIB and the four-blade propeller, although adequate to the task in Operation Diver, was overshadowed by the equivalent performance enjoyed by the Griffon 65/66 Series engine and five-blade propeller applied to the Mk XIV. And so, it was likely that the squadron's simultaneous switch to 'sweep' operations in mid-August was enacted on the same basis as for its Mk IX contemporaries.

The Mosquito's Share

The nocturnal cover for Operation Diver was largely placed in the hands of the Mosquito squadrons, with the initial cadre consisting of Nos 96, 219, 409, and 418; the greater endurance of the twin-engined fighter was a key reason for their deployment in this manner. As the battle progressed, additional squadrons, including two from No. 100 Group, would be allocated. The first kill was in fact gained by a No. 605 Squadron FB VI over the Channel and lasted a bare three minutes from interception to destruction. Whenever conditions allowed pilots would extend their patrols to the French coast in the hope of either witnessing the flash of an actual launching or picking up one already airborne. The likely engagement would then be granted a reasonable time span in which to take out the weapon before it reached the English coastline.

The resiting of the gun belt down onto the Channel coast imposed a limitation upon patrols over the Channel, in that the previously unhindered act of destruction now had to be achieved before the RAF crew encroached upon the barrage being thrown up, thereby losing contact by having to avoid becoming an unwitting target themselves. However, the primary difficulty experienced at night was that of accurate range with the V-1's flame exhaust, creating a second problem by degrading the crew's visual acuity, regardless of which stage the Doodlebug was first picked up.

The problem of range was solved through use of a stereoscopic gunsight. The device's optical system provided the pilot with two lights that gradually merged into one during the approach, at which point the exact range had been established. What could never be guaranteed was an immediate and effective burst of fire upon the V-1; in addition, the detonation effect of any successful impact laid the Mosquito particularly open to critical, if not lethal damage in two ways. To the puncturing of the Merlin's coolant tank was added the vulnerability of the wing-mounted radiator slots in sustaining a strike.

Summation

The overall effect of the V-1 offensive upon Southeast England was one that had created a degree of structural disruption as well as impinging upon an element of the population's morale. Had the Germans managed to complete the intended number of launch sites and operated these to their maximum capacity, the effect could have been immeasurably greater in scale, painful as the events of mid-June to late August had cast up. The total number of individual launchings has been assessed at anything up to 8.081 of which 5,400 gained access to the British landscape and 2,340 penetrated to London. In the initial weeks of the campaign, the figure of V-1s recorded rose steadily to a point where, by the end of June, a daily average of 100 weapons had been recorded; the intensity of assault rose to 800 during the first full week of July, unknowingly signalling the peak of attack over the entire spell (during one specific twenty-four-hour period, a total of 295 V-1s sped off their ramps but thankfully this was an exception in daily delivery).

The gun belt batteries were doing their best, but by mid-July, they had brought down barely a fraction of the Doodlebugs traversing their gauntlet of fire. This compared poorly to the RAF figures of 924, but even so, the combined figure, although healthy in statistical terms, was still well short of blunting the assault, let alone turning it permanently aside. A major change in operational procedure was mooted and applied from the middle of the month; the result was a transformation in the fortunes of the gunners. Between 17 July and 5 September, the now-coastal-located gunners ran up a staggering 400 per cent increase in confirmed kills, with the availability of the proximity-fused shells a major component in this operational improvement.

The nature of any mass-manufactured weapon lends itself to noticeable variations in operational performance and the V-1 was no exception to this. Although there was no evidence of regular failure at the point of launch, a percentage of those taking to the skies did not extend their progress further than between site and the English coast; the resultant premature descent into the Channel waters was likely due to mechanical or even structural failure. Whatever the cause, this added further to the dilution of the overall effect of the assault.

Fighter success was maintained albeit at a conversely reduced scale that by 5 September had still raked in a further 847 V-1s to provide a final figure of 1,902 against 1,584 credited to the gun batteries of AA Command and the Royal Navy, and a further 278 snared in the embrace of the barrage balloon screen. The swathe of capital destruction was most concentrated in the central and southern districts, with the surrounding Home Counties absorbing a varying degree of punishment that was inevitably mainly borne by those regions under the regular approach flight of the Doodlebugs.

The human and material cost meted out by Hitler's robot menace was sharp, albeit nowhere near the hoped-for result. The number of missiles striking the capital during the campaign was listed as 2,340; their malign influence led to over 5,000 individuals, mainly civilian in nature, forfeiting their lives. Nor was this the conclusion of V-1 directed assaults since between September and the following March, air- and ground-launched sorties, with the latter initiated from sites now roughly 200 miles distant, would garner further measures of death and destruction that were fortunately on a far lesser scale. Material damage to both commercial and housing properties was counted in the several hundreds of thousands.

Fortune Favours the Brave—and the Lucky!

The eighty-four-day-long Diver campaign that ended in success for the Allies was a serious enough threat to the hopes for the swift and comprehensive annihilation of Nazi influence throughout Europe. However, the situation could have been even worse for several reasons. The most critical one relates to the start of the offensive that only occurred on 13 June instead of several months earlier; the significance of this was to confer a positive influence upon the Allied conduct of the conflict compared to the following likely setbacks had the assault gone to time plan:

The availability of the Allies' first operational jet-propelled fighter, the Gloster Meteor, to take on the V-1 promised a degree of success that was never realised. The problem lay not with the airframe but rather the choice of engine. The Rolls-Royce Welland's output of 1,700-lb thrust was only capable of raising the fighter's maximum speed to around 410 mph and No. 616 Squadron's pilots achieved very little in the way of kills.

This Mustang IV assigned to No. 65 Squadron is under inspection by what appears to be a civilian technician judging by his headgear with two soldiers as an escort. The absence of D-Day stripes confirms the photo was taken during the final stage of the war; the downed aircraft's location is believed to be somewhere in Denmark, with the flat ground permitting a smooth forced-landing.

1. Had the bombing of the original spread of V-1 sites not been commenced in late 1943 the enforced switch to alternate site locations would not have proved necessary with all it entailed in slowing up the offensive's launch.
2. The consequent unobstructed availability of the original sites would have allowed the daily barrage of missiles to flow not only from the Pas-de-Calais region but also from the Cherbourg Peninsula. Subsequent counter bombing of the sites would have affected the scale of assault, but not necessarily blunted its overall effect in the short-term at least.
3. The absence of Allied forces ashore in France prior to 6 June would have meant that there would have been no realistic hopes for overrunning the launch sites in the immediate future. That was further assuming that the invasion attempt could even have been launched had the conditions listed at (4) arisen to cut deeply into the Allied preparations.
4. Had the Germans succeeded in discovering the main assembly areas for the planned Overlord invasion, the likely disruption to, if not chaos inflicted upon, the Allied facilities due to the V-1s launched from the latter region would surely have further blunted all prospects for a landing in France.
5. There was a visual benefit for Fighter Command in that the offensive's earlier initiation would have seen the pilots faced with a longer period of darkness compared to the shorter nocturnal time spans occurring during the mid-summer months that encompassed the actual campaign. This in turn would arguably have provided a sterner test in terms of gaining accurate range access to their targets among other issues.

17
'Final Pickings'

Escort Duties

By the time the curtain had finally been brought down upon the V-1 offensive, what was currently the Air Defence of Great Britain element of the nation's overall fighter strength (that would revert to the original Fighter Command nomenclature in October) was fully charged with Home Defence. The 2TAF squadrons were dominating the continental skies as they granted very effective support to the British Army units thrusting across France and into Belgium following the Allied breakout from the Normandy bridgehead. As it transpired, however, the single-engined home-based squadrons were by now more involved in active operations. *Luftwaffe* incursions over the British Isles had dwindled to miniscule proportions as Allied airpower continued to sweep all before it.

The former function related to supporting the burgeoning daylight aerial onslaught that had hitherto been delivered by the Allied four-engined and medium bombers upon the enemy forces initially entrenched within France and the Low Countries on either side of D-Day. That autocratic grip had been largely erased within the northern stretches of France by the end of August, but the pressure was accordingly transferred to military and industrial resources not only in Belgium and Holland, but also western Germany.

As regards RAF Bomber Command, up to the period ahead of and in the weeks beyond D-Day, the Lancasters and Halifaxes had of necessity flown their deep-penetration operations into the Third Reich by night. It had proven a fraught enough situation in nocturnally challenging the German air and flak defences, let alone attempting to do so bereft of escort cover by day. Now, with the advent of longer-range fighters, the Mustang III being the supreme example in providing this vital backup, the RAF crews could be dispatched in full visual sight of the enemy but with the same degree of security from regular and potentially unsustainable loss percentages as their USAAF contemporaries were enjoying.

This group of senior RAF officers include Air Marshal 'Mary' Conningham (2TAF CO) on the right with Air Vice-Marshal Harry Broadhurst (back to camera). On the left is Air Chief Marshal Arthur Tedder (Deputy Supreme Commander to Eisenhower) while Marshal of the Royal Air Force Peter Portal (Chief of the Air Staff) faces the camera.

Spitfire Operations

The Spitfire was not excluded from this duty, regardless of its range limitations that had seen it restricted to affording cover to the 2TAF and 9USAAF mediums. The experience of No. 1 Squadron that had witnessed its Mk IXs transferred from Diver to Ranger operations in company with Nos 165 and 310 during August was a clear indication of the added provision of support for the RAF heavies. The first-named pair were formed into a wing based at Detling in Kent, an airfield ironically still square in the path of the admittedly more staccato flow of V-1s when the operational switch occurred.

During September, the release of both Allied Bomber Commands from a primary commitment to supporting the campaign in Normandy—however loosely adhered to by their senior staff—allowed the RAF crews to operate regularly by day as well as night over Germany. The availability of the latest electronic bombing aid, coded G-H, saw No. 3 Group specifically tasked with putting the equipment to use. G-H was, in effect, the blind-bombing device Oboe in reverse; the aircraft's set interrogated two ground stations in order to confirm its positioning in relation to the briefed target. Bombers so outfitted bore two parallel yellow bars on the outer fin/rudder surfaces. These would act as the bombing leaders for two wingmen, all three releasing their bombs upon the relevant release point.

The need for the RAF bombers to be escorted during their daylight forays was of even more importance than the same provision enjoyed by the 8USAAF heavies. The firepower generated by the RAF's .303-calibre weaponry was measurably inferior to that of the greater mass of the .5 machine guns borne by the B-17s and B-24s that, until 1944, had hitherto availed their crews little in successfully prosecuting their offensive while penetrating well beyond fighter cover. A proportion of the Canadian-built Mk X Lancasters did bear .5 guns in their Martin mid-upper turrets, while the Rose-Rice Co. in Britain were turning out rear turrets similarly equipped for the RAF; however, this scale of armament was to remain minimal and could not guarantee freedom from high loss figures even if comprehensively adapted.

It was accordingly fortunate that the *Jagdwaffe*'s ranks were being thinned down by this point, not only in terms of numbers of pilots, but, more critically, their combat capability. Training standards had been drastically curtailed from the original almost two-year level to a matter of months, with fuel shortage playing its part in this downturn. There was still a cadre of experienced pilots on hand, although their numbers were likewise being pruned, but there were occasions when the bomber force was penetrated. As with the USAAF, so the RAF escort screen could not guarantee complete exclusion of their *Jagdwaffe* opponents from access to their targets.

The sortie to Witten in the Ruhr by No. 3 Group on 12 December was an example of this. For once, the aerial defenders had successfully engaged the escorts to the extent that an element among their ranks was free to close in upon the 140-strong bomber stream. One No. 218 Squadron crew recalled an Fw 190 swooping on a companion Lancaster, whose tail gunner baled out just before a fusillade of gunfire initiated a vast balloon of smoke and flame from one engine, with the bomber sagging into a curving dive; even had the individual stayed in post, the gunnery contest involving his .303s and the Fw 190's powerful battery would have been seriously if not fatally imbalanced. The final loss of eight bombers was statistically moderate in terms of casualties, albeit all too final for the fifty-six airmen involved; it was also a salutary remainder of the heavies' defensive frailty that, fortunately, was rarely again exploited on future daylight operations.

The availability of the 90-gallon external tank was key to the home-based Spitfire squadrons' ability to penetrate as far as the western edges of Germany when tasked with bomber-escort duties and a flight duration approaching three hours was regularly achieved. However, two forward Belgian airfields at Ursel and Maldegem were also utilised, so permitting even greater range penetration into the enemy heartland. The 150 Octane fuel was another boost to performance that ironically had its downside. This related to enhanced engine wear that, in conjunction with the longer flight times, was resulting in the grounding of aircraft with the knock-on effect on sufficient numbers of operationally-available machines.

Mustang Support

The arrival of the Mustang III into service with the RAF had witnessed a solid build-up in numbers by the autumn of 1944. Seven squadrons, all but one then assigned to 2TAF, were on hand by D-Day, and this figure would almost double to thirteen by the following April. The long-range capability of the North American fighter would seem to lend itself to the fighter being essentially directed towards escorting bombers into the continental hinterland rather than being deployed within 2TAF, where the emphasis tended to be on more range-restricted operations—a duty in which the 'shorter-legged', but basically efficient Spitfire in particular could serve.

As it was, prior to D-Day, the Mustang variant had been used for long-range escort duties; on the other hand, the growing strength of the 8USAAF in this field meant that the RAF's contribution was probably optional as opposed to mandatory. In addition, the RAF heavy bomber's involvement in daylight operations was nil in terms of deep-penetration runs until around the early autumn of 1944. Only then could renewed attention be paid to utilising the Mustang in its perceived primary role.

A further seeming contradiction regarding the Mustang III's existence within 2TAF is that only three of the squadrons on hand for Overlord's inception actually crossed the Channel and operated from airfields in France and, to a lesser degree, in Belgium. Their presence abroad only lasted until between September and October, when they were withdrawn to home soil with all being re-established at Matlaske in Norfolk.

Pilot comfort was a key matter of importance when flying sorties that, in the Mustang's case, could extend up to five hours or more. One negative issue with previous Mustang variants, including the initial P-51B/C production runs, was the

No. 122 Squadron was an early recipient of the Mustang, having converted from the Spitfire Mk VB in January 1944. The Mk III seen here bearing the 'K' aircraft letter is believed to be FB226; the D-day stripe restriction to the lower fuselage indicates a date during late 1944 or early 1945.

side-hinged cockpit frame that was also flat in its upper profile and accordingly left little headroom. In addition, the heavy framing badly, if not lethally, restricted side and rearward visibility—the last thing any pilot wanted when endeavouring to keep enemy fighters off his tail. A solution for the combined problem was on hand thanks to a British source.

The Martin-Baker Co. manufactured a 'bubble' canopy, designed by an RAF officer, Malcolm, after whom it was named, and this revised fitting was supplied and retrofitted to both the RAF and 8FC airframes. The immediate benefit for the pilots was in terms of both headroom and overall visibility. Now the physical constraint hitherto placed on the individual's upper torso was totally erased, with the ability to turn one's head and shoulders in relative comfort. Rearward visibility was similarly enhanced in quality, although the greater and unframed area of Plexiglas could exert an uncomfortable degree of heat and glare upon the body when flying in clear air. However, the fact that the new canopy was on runners meant that the discomfort could be countered by sliding it back if necessary. Moreover, exiting the fighter in an emergency had been greatly improved compared to attempting the evacuation with its side-hinged predecessor on hand.

V-1 Air-Mounted Threat

The main and intractable disability faced by the Germans in launching the V-1 offensive related to the static nature of the sites from which the missiles were dispatched. Although difficult to focus upon by Allied bombers, there was still a degree of punishment that could be handed out that, in turn, yielded a measure of dislocation to the scale of attack. The possibility of a mobile alternative had previously been considered by the Nazi military and was duly put into action as early as late June from north-eastern French airfields, although it was 7–8 July before the British defenders became aware of V-1s approaching from the direction of Belgium. As matters transpired, the benefit gained from this activity was much less severe, although it was spread in regular intensity over the period from July until November with more intermittent activity during the ensuing winter months (a total of just under 1,200 Doodlebugs were estimated to have been fired during the July–November spell for instance).

The chosen vehicle for this mobility was the *Luftwaffe*'s venerable design, the He 111 that in this instance involved the aircraft assigned to III/KG3 *Blitz*. The '*Dampfer*' or 'steamer', as the machine was affectionately dubbed by many of its crews, was a reliable and sturdy airframe that was more than capable of accommodating the carriage of the Doodlebug, the weapon being positioned below the starboard fuselage-wing junction to accommodate the height of the pulsejet. A modified ETC2000 rack was mounted as the V-1's attachment and steel plating was applied to the stabiliser to absorb the heat-effect of the engine. The offset position that was also to the rear of the He 111's centre of gravity

The Mk XIX Mosquito was the latest night-fighter variant that entered service just before D-Day. Radar equipment was a mix of the British Mk VIII and the USA's SCR720 that was housed in either a Thimble or Bull nose fairing, the latter being seen here. As regards these centimetric sets, the airflow drag created by external aerials was limited to the receivers aligned with the wing tips. No. 68 Squadron was the sole No. 11 Group unit out of the eight operating on the mark and participated in the anti-Diver campaign.

impelled pilots to be very careful on take-off, but progress to the release point likely proved an equally uncomfortable experience, given the air resistance arising from the V-1's bulk.

The appropriate course and flight-distance aspects of operation were of necessity factored in prior to take-off. The bomber's progress westward was made at minimum altitude until the firing point was attained. Then, the pilot pulled up to around 1,600 feet while also increasing speed to the minimum 250 mph required to match the weapon's launch speed—none too easy to achieve in a descent angle, let alone one at an ascending angle. As soon as the V-1 had been released, the bomber would regain its minimum altitude path for the return course—a necessary manoeuvre to confuse any night fighter trying to pick up its track and deliver a lethal 'punch'.

All was set for a successful foray, which proved fine in theory, but the aircraft's freedom of movement conferred a reverse problem for the crews not faced by their ground-bound colleagues in France. The exact distance to the London area was an established matter for the V-1 site operators as was the course. Contrast this with the He 111 crews who had to be precise in navigating to the exact point of release that moreover was bereft of any ground reference due to the bulk of operations occurring over the featureless North Sea. The nocturnal nature of operations also cast up a potentially lethal scenario. The firing-up of the V-1 naturally created a massive beacon that would attract the attention of any RAF night fighter orbiting the immediate area.

A head-on view of a Gloster Mk III Meteor displays little external difference from the original Mk I, apart from the sliding canopy replacing the side-hinged fitting. A major internal alteration is the substitution of the Rolls-Royce Welland producing 850-lb thrust for the company's Derwent; the new engine's output was more than double at 2,000-lb thrust. The Mk III entered service in January 1945 and more than 200 airframes were built.

On the Prowl

As with the main French-based assault, so a combination of air and anti-aircraft gun provision would be laid on to challenge the sorties made by III/KG3. The direction from which the assault emanated coupled with the presence of the Mosquito Mk XVII, with its superior-strength SCR720 radar sets as employed by Nos 25 and 125 Squadrons operating out of Coltishall, made these night fighter's deployment against the He 111s a primary choice; Manston and Castle Camps-based squadrons provided further cover, with No. 125 Squadron later operating against the attackers from the former location during 1944–45.

The apparent superiority in overall performance enjoyed by the Mosquito over the pedestrian-paced He 111 would seem to indicate a hard time ahead for the *Luftwaffe* airmen, but several factors were to militate against this. The first related to the method of target approach and withdrawal. First of all, the Mosquito crews patrolling at several thousand feet had to be relatively close to their prey in order to pick it up on radar, especially since the opportunity to do so usually only extended over the brief period surrounding the V-1's launch process when the He 111's signature registered on the tube.

Once electronically picked out, the race was on to catch the bomber as it was descending to minimum altitude, and most likely achieving this before the Mosquito crew was within range. If achieved by the bomber's pilot, flying at such a height over the flat expanses of the sea, especially in partial or heavy cloud cover, could easily lead to inadvertent and usually fatal contact with the surface, a circumstance that probably led to those RAF crews failing to return from a sortie when the reason for their loss was unconfirmed.

Making a successful interception would suggest only one end to the action, but here again there was a problem should the He 111 be other than at release altitude. The noticeably higher stalling speed of the RAF night fighter could work in the German pilot's favour should the engagement result in any protracted tail chase before the 20-mm cannon battery was brought to bear. A secondary problem in such cases was the disturbance created by the He 111's slipstream, inducing a swaying action on its assailant's airframe—a motion that could prove fatal when flying so low and attempting to match the He 111's more deliberate pace and stable flightpath.

In an attempt to narrow down the odds against being able to track down the bombers, the Royal Navy made available the frigate HMS *Caicos*, whose radar equipment was accordingly utilised, the service being supplemented by a Wellington similarly outfitted. In spite of this, the rate of interception was destined to be fairly low. On the other hand, a good number of the V-1s were picked up and destroyed thereby achieving the basic aim of disrupting the actual assault if not also causing the same degree of depredation among their flying 'launch pads'. As it was, around fifteen interceptions were to be granted as confirmed kills by Fighter Command, while post-war checks of *Luftwaffe* records indicate a loss rate from all causes of several times this figure.

The inaugural success for No. 125 Squadron went to a Fg Off. Beadle, who, on 25 September, made contact with a bomber as it was at launch altitude. The V-1 was released but the resultant descent was barely commenced before the Mosquito was within firing range. The desperate attempts by the bomber's gunner manning the H-22's *Drehlafette* (rotating turret) to ward off the assault totally failed, with the third 50-yard burst of cannon fire dispatching aircraft and crew into the remorseless depths of the North Sea. A second unit kill followed on the 30th, with Flt Lt Thompson the victor. The steady string of kills was to be shared among the several other units involved but an inevitable price was paid. For example, on 6 January, No. 68 Squadron's W/O Brooking called in a kill but soon after radioed that his Mosquito had developed problems, after which no more was heard or seen of the two-man team, whose fate was to join their adversaries in fatal communion beneath the sea.

Concentration of Effort

A secondary reported intention for the airborne weapons' use was to strike at Britain's industrial heartland, with the Black Country a primary source, and to do so without risking the *Luftwaffe*'s bomber force such as it might be. If this was the case, then the scale of involvement was to prove no more than adequate, as well as being very belated in terms of build-up in aircraft numbers. The original III/

KG3 force was only supplemented during the autumn by the withdrawal from the Eastern Front of II and III/KG53 Condor Legion that duly absorbed the original KG3 *Gruppe* within its ranks as I/KG53. By then, the original withdrawal from France to Gilze-Rijen and Venlo in southern Holland had been cancelled out thanks to the Allied advance, whereupon a group of nine German airfields ranging down along the borders with Holland accommodated each *Staffel*.

Whatever the intended plan was for attacking Britain's industrial base, its implantation by KG53 was to prove barely visible. On Christmas Eve, the one recorded mass assault was briefed and launched against Northwest England—at least that was the indication, as forty-five He 111s formed up and headed towards the coastline of Lincolnshire due west of Manchester. Two-thirds of the V-1s that had been launched roughly 40 miles out to sea landed in the city or came down around the general region. There were a few fatalities and injuries during what turned out to be the sole such variation during this aspect of V-1 operations. It seems surprising considering the number of bombers comprising the force that no aerial interceptions were reportedly made by Fighter Command.

V2 Menace: Big Ben's Wayward Strokes

The arrival of the ballistic missile era on 8 September 1944 via the V-2 rocket—even if ultimately proven to be limited in effect upon the conflict's conduct—at the time provided a sharp reminder to the Allies that the enemy's 'lights of perverted science' capability could not be taken for granted. Just as its predecessor had earned the code-name Diver, so the sobriquet Big Ben was to be hung upon what was officially titled the A4. In the course of the intervening seven months to 27 March, a total of 1,117 rockets were recorded around Southeast England, of which all but a handful that came down in the sea impacted on London or the immediate surrounding regions; a mini-concentration also descended upon the Norfolk and Suffolk coastal zone during the initial weeks of the assault.

The original intention for the V-2s to be launched from fixed sites in northern France, which moreover were deemed totally invulnerable to aerial assault due to their subterranean locations, was totally compromised following D-Day. This was thanks to the 12,000-lb Tallboy aerodynamic bombs delivered on to the several sites by No. 617 Squadron that collapsed the manifold passage ways connected to the central chamber and thereby rendered the overall facility *hors de combat*. The start of the campaign accordingly witnessed the distance to be traversed by the V-2 increase noticeably, but the regular flow of the weapons onto British, as well as Belgian soil, confirmed that alternate sites were in use. The subsequent search-and-strike operations by Fighter Command were to prove frustrating, if not fruitless, thanks to the Germans having dispensed with fixed locations.

The ironic feature of this switch in operational procedure lay in the fact that, whereas the V-1 had to have recourse to fixed-site launching, no such technical inhibition affected its 'big brother'—hence the waste of time and costly effort

No. 501 Squadron, in contrast to the other four Tempest-equipped squadrons, never deployed to the continent prior to disbandment in April 1945. The view of armourers laying out and with one airman feeding-in the ammunition belts for the 20-mm cannon is taken at Bradwell Bay in March. The slim wing layout compared to the Typhoon is only marginally spoilt by the feed drums that require streamlined blister bulges in the compartment panel's surface.

in constructing the redundant fixed sites now in Allied hands. Instead, giant custom-built trailers on to which the rockets were loaded were also to serve as the basic vertical support frame. These were towed to a location appropriately shielded within wooded areas. Also on hand and towing the actual launch platform was a halftrack, upon whose frame was mounted an armoured control post from which the operating staff would fire the rocket. The process of setting up the equipment, fuelling the V-2, and dispatching it extended over sixty to ninety minutes, during which time the weapon was vulnerable to attack, after which the dismantling and withdrawal of the launch platform and vertical support frames and their attendant gear cancelled out the threat.

The search for the V-2s' suspected sites became a regular feature of RAF operations, though with little or no success. A major suspected concentration believed to exist with the Dutch capital as the epicentre cast up a real dilemma, especially when giving consideration to bombing attacks. The Transportation Plan had inflicted many casualties upon the citizens living within the towns possessing rail facilities, but at least the Allied crews did have specific targets upon which to focus their bomb loads. By comparison, any similar attacks against unconfirmed rocket sites could see casualties being borne by the Dutch citizens living therein with no guarantee of any material dislocation being landed upon the enemy's resources.

Despite the presence of multiple fighter squadrons based on the continent and therefore close on hand to monitor the Dutch landscape, there was also a degree of home-based fighter involvement in the hunt for the sites. No. 1 Squadron was very early engaged in this activity, with sorties launched within several days of the first rocket striking home. However, the pilots were to fly double sorties involving Big Ben patrols and bomber escort whenever weather conditions allowed for the V-2 sites to be picked out. Nos 303 (Polish) and 312 (Czech) Squadrons were other home-based units launching these sorties.

There was at least one occasion when a Spitfire-equipped squadron unconsciously overflew a launch site in Holland, but whose pilots were unable to deliver a pre-emptive strike. The formation leader, who became a renowned post-war British television commentator, recalled his and his colleagues' amazement as the massive bulk of a V-2 blasted upward from a wooded area directly ahead. During the subsequent debriefing session, one pilot said he had reacted to the missile's presence by directing a burst of fire in its direction; it was perhaps fortunate this had no positive effect, otherwise the resultant detonation could easily have created multiple casualties among the squadron's ranks.

Nocturnal Intrusions

The need to provide fighter support to Bomber Command at night was inaugurated during 1943 with the introduction of the 'Flower' and 'Mahmoud' type of operations. By early 1944, the inception of No. 100 Group had included among its manifold specialist squadrons, several tasked with 'active' operations against the *Nachtjagd* force as opposed to the others that practiced a range of 'passive' measures designed to subvert the German electronic defensive mechanism.

By the autumn of 1944, No. 85 Squadron was to become a prominent leader in effectively delivering the Intruder sorties that took on the Bf 110G and Ju 88G night-fighter crews. However, the activity was not destined to be wholly allocated to No. 100 Group since Fighter Command was still being brought into the action with Nos 151 and 406—the latter Canada's first dedicated night-fighter unit—forming part of this additional force. The Flower operational pattern was twofold, with an initial wave attacking designated night-fighter airfields ahead of the bomber stream and the second wave heading out later with a view to snaring the enemy aircraft as they were returning back (the far greater mobility of the *Nachtjagd* crews did not guarantee an automatic return to their designated airfields and a consequent 'snaring'; on the other hand, it did not matter who was downed in terms of unit/airfield link-up—just as long as the deed was accomplished).

Regardless of the aforementioned potential limitation, there was to be a steady degree of interception made during the last months of the conflict as typified by the following account of a sortie made on 21 November by a Plt Off. Beynon (P) and Plt Off. Pearcy (N) whose departure was from the forward base of Hunsdon and their target an airfield at Sachsenheim. One of the five targeted locations for Bomber Command was Aschaffenberg, south-east of Frankfiurt, which lay roughly 40 miles north of the airfield that the Mosquito finally reached and orbited to the north of the conveniently-flashing identity beacon.

Pearcy made a radar contact on a bogey proceeding on a westerly course and which was closed upon as it headed towards and began to circle another lit-up airfield assumed to be at Speyer on the Rhine. The steady descent of what was finally identified as a 'Ju 188' and which had failed to respond to identity calls in English culminated in Beynon shortening the distance to 200 yards before raking his prey with a short burst of fire. The port wing was enveloped in flames that swiftly spread to the forward fuselage, whereupon the aircraft rolled sharply over and dived to its fiery destruction.

Intruder Variation

Nocturnal operations naturally rendered any viable form of direct escort to the bombers impossible; instead, fighters were dispatched with a view to flying well out on the flanks of the bomber stream with a view to encountering a *Nachtjagd* crew approaching or disengaging from an engagement. On 28 January, Fg Off. A. Sherrett and Flt Lt K. MacKenzie, serving with No. 406 Squadron, departed Manston flying their NF Mk 30 Mosquito. The Canadian crew's briefed zone was near Mannheim and north-west of the target at Stuttgart; interestingly, there was to be a twin assault on the city involving a total of over 300 main force bombers with No. 8 (PFF) Mosquitos that featured a three-hour lapse between the strikes.

The German night-fighter beacon Otto formed the epicentre for the patrol that was minutes into its duration before a contact was picked up 5 miles distant. The easterly heading was then transformed into a southerly direction as the bogey that was climbing took up the latter course. Then, a second contact was made approaching head-on and to starboard that Sherrett promptly diverted on to. Closure to minimum range was achieved and what was again identified as a 'Ju 188' failed to respond to the RAF crew's calls. Satisfied as to its hostile status, Sherrett delivered two bursts of fire that only produced a positive result the second time around, with an explosive, although not apparently lethal, result. The third firing approach was about to commence when the aircraft rolled on it back and fell the full 15,000-foot altitude to its doom (the recorded crash site was well over 60 miles due west of Mannheim, so the chase was seemingly protracted).

Operation Gisela's Pyrrhic Victory

The depredations that had been visited upon the *Nachtjagd* crews since 1943 and on their bomber contemporaries even further back in the Second World War had thankfully never been approached in scale, let alone balanced out by a similar campaign against Bomber Command. The involvement of I/NJG2 in roaming the night-shrouded British landscape in search of prey during 1940–41 had been curtailed by a *Führerbefehl* (ordinance) during the autumn, and from then until the final months of the Second World War, little in the way of Intruder sorties had been launched. The mass of bombers assembling for and returning from the average operation had long presented a vulnerable target whose regular exploitation would surely have had an inordinately disruptive effect in material and morale terms.

The events of 22 April 1944 had demonstrated the value of such attacks, in this case against the 2nd Bomb Division of the 8USAAF. The handful of Me 410s from II/KG51 had infiltrated the B-24 ranks as the daylight was almost spent, and either shot down or indirectly formed the catalyst for several airfield crashes as the bomber crews sought to either land or clear the area as quickly as possible. Here was a clear indication of the benefit accruing from repeat strikes, with RAF Bomber Command the source for assault. The foregoing action had only evolved due to the very late launching of the mission to Hamm compared to the normal USAAF experience of mission completion during daylight hours.

In fact, *Oberstgeneral* 'Beppo' Schmid, who had succeeded Kammhuber as *General der Nachtjagd* during 1943, had proposed the resumption of large-scale Intruder operations soon after taking over, but he had been solidly rebuffed by his superiors. Of course, the wholesale commitment of the night fighters to what was an increasingly effective challenge to Bomber Command's actual campaign during the winter of 1943–44 may well have played a part in the decision—why divert resources to such external operations when ACM Harris's force was being so severely shredded over the continent?

However, one of the rational counterpoints against sending night fighters on Intruder operations involved the deadly-efficient SN2 (*FuG* 220) radar set, whose existence was as-yet unknown to the Allies; should one of these fall into British hands and its secrets be unlocked, the likelihood of the system being exposed to dislocation by jamming could not be discounted (in fact, a set was to fall into British hands during July 1944 when a Ju 88G's pilot unwittingly flew a reciprocal course and landed at Woodbridge). Above all prevailed Hitler's comprehensive objection to such operations. As it was, by October 1944, with the *Nachtjagd* crews now being firmly placed on the back foot both numerically and technically, the second bid by Schmid for the plan's implementation was given the green light. Curiously, it was not acted upon until the beginning of the following March, when the die was irrevocably cast for Nazi Germany's comprehensive defeat.

On 3 March, 446 Bomber Command crews were briefed to attack two targets; having duly done so, the twin forces from Nos 4 and 5 Groups were approaching their airfields as midnight was on hand, wholly unaware of the impending chaos looming up. Ju 88Gs from seven *Gruppen* spread between four *Geschwadern* had taken-off earlier, and their ETA over eastern England was timed to coincide with their potential targets. The seeds were sown for a largely one-sided contest between the exhausted RAF crews with their fuel- and ammunition-depleted resources and the German crews possessing plenty of either resource.

In the course of little more than sixty minutes, fully thirty-four RAF aircraft were attacked, of which no less than twenty-one were shot down. To the fifteen Lancasters and Halifaxes directly involved in the raids was added six aircraft from No. 100 Group. The remaining thirteen crews involved landed or crash-landed their aircraft, with most individuals alive and unhurt. Although several Mosquito night-fighter squadrons were on hand, the marauders suffered no recorded losses from this operational source. This was not wholly surprising considering the maelstrom arising from the numbers of aircraft aloft and the resultant mass of radar 'signatures' that would have created problems in sorting out friend from foe for the navigators.

The notable degree of depredation wrought among the ranks of the command's and 100 Group's aircraft should have provided the *Nachtjagd* personnel with a clear sense of success, as well as a prospect of delivering further blows in the nights ahead. Instead, the losses borne by the attacking force was to render the operation as one meriting the pyrrhic title recorded here. To the three crews who came down on British soil was added a further ten declared MIA or crashing on the continent, two being the victim of *Flak* friendly-fire; five more were abandoned largely thanks to fuel shortage. The fact that none of the losses were directly attributed to the British defensive network should still not have created a permanent halt to the Intruder activity, but only once more was an assault made in any strength (sixteen Ju 88s on 20–21 March) before the conflict was concluded.

Strike Wing Support

The growing threat to the German merchant convoys deployed along the coastal fringes of Western Europe was reaching a sustained level of attack by 1944. This was a signal advance from the initial assaults between 1940 and 1942 by the Blenheims of No. 2 Group that had witnessed a high attrition rate among the crews in exchange for a poor return in vessels sunk or damaged. The several wings of Beaufighters and Mosquitos enfilading the shipping lanes were regularly hammering home the message with their heavy machine gun and cannon supplementing the batteries of rockets. However, the extended ranges from friendly shores when reaching up into Denmark and Norway, in particular, that left the attackers without fighter cover laid them accordingly open to lethal attention from the *Jagdwaffe* units based in these regions.

The availability of the Mustang from mid-year on promised a better prospect for survival, with the latest Mosquito and Beaufighter wings stationed respectively at Banff and Dallachy along Scotland's Moray Firth from around October destined to be a major beneficiary. Anti-shipping operations commenced around September, but it was only on 3 October that the first of four RAF squadrons to share the escort function arrived at Peterhead north of Aberdeen. It was joined by one of No. 309 (Polish) Squadron's flights, but both unit's presence was extremely

No. 309 Squadron was a fellow-Polish unit of No. 316 that was also stationed at Andrews Field at the same period of the war. By the beginning of 1945, camouflage was being excluded from RAF aircraft; in this picture of the squadron lining-up for take-off, the two nearside Mustang IIIs are in NMF finish. In addition, the Type 'B' wing roundels have given way to Type 'C'.

short, and it was only on 1 November that No. 315, another Polish squadron, took up a more permanent—or rather a less transitory—residence, where it was joined by No. 309.

The experience for the fighter pilots in this specific campaign would witness little action against the *Jagdwaffe*, but the few encounters would generally be sharp in nature. A more insidious adversary would intrude upon the scene, namely the need to make minimum altitude crossings of the North Sea in order not to alert the enemy defences of the attacking force. The several hundred miles to be flown demanded full concentration from the pilots; this was difficult enough for the twin-engined aircraft of the wing to maintain, but at least each pilot had a fellow airman with which to break the potentially-deadly monotony that could easily induce lapses in concentration. In addition, the loss of one engine still enabled the aircraft to remain aloft; as for ditching, the action could be survived if a sound sea surface and pilot skill were both on hand.

Contrast this with the Mustang pilots' lot. First, they were on their own in terms of concentration; second, their charges bore just one engine; and third, the risk inherent in ditching a Mustang was greatly heightened regardless of the sea conditions. The problem lay with the design's large air scoop beneath the fuselage centre that, like the equivalent nose-mounted facility on the Typhoon, could literally pull the airframe downwards almost immediately following contact with the water, so denying the pilot much prospect of surviving the incident.

The undoubted aggression and courage of the Poles could sometimes be carried to fatal lengths and an example of this occurred on an early No. 315 sortie when Sgt A. Ciundziewicki disengaged from the formation to initiate a pass

Above: A double view of FB357 (top) shows the Mustang III ready for an operation, all mechanical checks having been completed. The lower picture catches the fighter as it trundles along the Andrews Field perimeter track. Type 'C' upper wing roundels confirms picture taken after January 1945, when these displaced the Type 'B'. White triangle contains the unit motif, a cockerel.

Below: The tree line's defoliated state indicates this shot of two No. 315 Squadron Mustang IIIs was taken between January and April 1945 when the squadron had deployed from Peterhead to Andrews Field. The nearside fighter bears a fin strake that was only fitted to a proportion of this variant. Neither aircraft appears ever to have borne D-Day stripes despite being on hand with the squadron prior to the invasion.

upon a vessel that was close enough to the coast to earn support from flak units. Disregarding the leader's order to rejoin, he took on the gunners, but his fighter was struck squarely, set on fire, and soon after plunged into the sea. Several weeks later, a second pilot was lost on the return leg when his Merlin ground to a halt, and the resultant ditching attempt witnessed the sea seizing the aircraft and its occupant in a fatal embrace.

Elements of JG5, known as the *Eismeer-Geschwader* thanks to its near four-year service mainly in the Arctic regions of Norway and Finland, had deployed elements along Norway's coastline. On 7 December, the *Jagdwaffe* pilots rose to the challenge posed by a strike wing off Alesund, north of Bergen, and bounced the Mustang escorts to shoot down one Mustang. The remaining eleven Polish pilots rallied strongly, with the German victor dispatched almost immediately along with three further companions before the ever-feral combat was concluded. The squadron's spell at Peterhead extended to mid-January when it transferred south to Essex, where it linked up with No. 309 Squadron who had preceded it during December (the squadron appeared to have had no practical involvement in wing escort duties prior to transfer. Also, No. 315 Squadron's final sortie was for whatever reason launched from Wick, nearly 100 miles north of Peterhead).

No. 65 Squadron now took up the combat 'reins' at Peterhead, but within twelve days, the squadron moved to Banff where conversion onto the Mustang IV—the RAF's designation for the USAAF's P-51D—was effected. The cut-down rear fuselage and replacement of the Malcolm Hood with a full 'tear-drop' canopy provided the pilots with a greatly enhanced visual field with emphasis on rearward scanning—very important for survival from an attempted bounce. Operations began in earnest during early February, but the inaugural experience was rather negative. The strike wing's attack upon a naval force cost nine Beaufighters, a factor that undoubtedly dampened their escort's mood on return even given two Fw 190 kills at a cost of one Mustang. A week later, the formation was very fortunate to survive a bounce action that only damaged several aircraft; a series of dogfights then developed, by whose conclusion three of the marauding Bf 109Gs were later recorded as confirmed kills at debriefing.

Unknown to the pilots and arising from the former action was the latest in a long list of *Experten* lost to the *Jagdwaffe*. Ltn. Rudi Linz had served with JG5 for three years and had latterly assumed command of 12 *Staffel* the previous July. Now based at Herdla, he led his sub-force against the Beaufighters and quickly downed one, thus achieving his seventieth and final *Abschuss*. He never regained the airfield and was almost certainly one of the two victims claimed by No. 65 Squadron. As with many Second World War German aircrew, the award of the *Ritterkreuz* (Knight's Cross) would be posthumously bestowed. Joining him in death was Fw. Otto Liebfried.

A formation of No. 309 (Polish) Squadron Mustang IIIs are flying in a flat pattern as they head out on an operation. Although small in detail, the view of WC:X in the foreground demonstrates the pilot's head clearance with the Malcolm bubble canopy compared to the uncomfortable tight fit under the original flat-roofed frame on the Mk I. Drop tanks extended the fighter's already generous range provided by the internal fuel tanks.

Combat Pros and Cons

The Mustang III in current RAF service along with the more recent delivery of the Mk IV was the basic answer to taking on both the Bf 109G and the Fw 190 on an equal, if not superior manner. Its overall speed factor was ahead of both adversaries from medium to higher altitudes by between 30 and 50 mph. Turning circle *vis-à-vis* the Bf 109 was equally greater especially in a prolonged action and with the pilot properly utilising the flaps; however, there was little to choose in respect of the Fw 190's similar ability. The third advantage lay in the dive when this was indulged in a prolonged manoeuvre.

One limitation affected the ability to zoom climb, in which case the Bf 109G in particular held the distinct advantage, but this appeared to be the sole element of inferiority during a combat action. In turn, the Fw 190's roll rate was well ahead of the Mustang. Of course, any fighter's overall performance is still dependent upon one human factor—namely, pilot efficiency—in addition to which the *Jagdwaffe* still possessed an element of *Experten* among its ranks who could and did present a formidable challenge to their Anglo–American adversaries.

Final Actions

The last Peterhead-based unit to see prolonged action was No. 19 Squadron; it had been the first to be equipped with the Spitfire in 1938 and by now possessed a combat record second to none both at home and on the continent. The first sortie was flown on 3 March, and nine days later came the initial contact with Bf 109s. The resultant battle claimed the life of Sqn Ldr M. Hill who impacted with the sea during an evasive manoeuvre. In turn, Obltn. H. Schneider and Obfw. Theo Stebner (13/JG5) were declared *Vermisst* (MIA) in the *Geschwader* records; one had been downed by Sqn Ldr P. Hearne (CO) to be the first of three kills granted him.

Although escort sorties continued in a regular fashion, the incidence of fighter *v.* fighter actions continued albeit in a staccato manner, probably to the frustration of the RAF pilots, albeit not to their Beaufighter and Mosquito contemporaries. No. 65 was back in action on 5 April when an almost equal number of Mustangs and Bf 109Gs went head-to-head as the RAF Strike Wing was homeward-bound. The battle ended with a resounding defeat for 10/JG5; Uffzs. Erwin Angerer and Peter Wirz and Ogfr. Wilhelm Otage were three of the four casualties, all fatal.

No. 19 Squadron had entered and finished the war on Merlin-engine fighters, the difference being that the first example was British, the second American—Spitfire and Mustang IV respectively. These pilots are grouped around one of the latter types following the squadron's transfer around February 1945 to Peterhead in north-east Scotland to provide long-range escort for Coastal Command's Beaufighter and Mosquito strike wings.

An attempt by No. 19 Squadron to infiltrate the circuit of Lister airfield around which a group of Bf 109s were circling for landing came to naught when the Mustangs were picked out on final descent upon their prey. The series of dogfights ended in stalemate for both sides, but Sqn Ldr Hearne had one trick still up his sleeve. Minutes on the homeward route, he and his No. 2 reversed course for Lister where the duo swooped upon two Bf 109s with undercarriages deployed. The desperate attempts of the pilot fighter selected by Hearne to retrieve the situation, raising the wheels and taking evasive action by constant reversing course, culminated with the six-gun bursts from the Mustang dispatching his fighter into the sea. The same day (11 April), No. 65 Squadron suffered the reverse fate; having successfully warded off Bf 109G passes upon the Banff Wing force, both sub-forces were also on the return leg when the Bf 109s carried out a bounce that downed two Mosquitos and Flt Lt F. Bradford's Mustang IV.

One of if not the final contact with the *Jagdwaffe* again involved the No. 19 Squadron CO. Sqn Ldr Hearne repeated his action of the 11th by reversing course, but this time with the entire twelve-strong formation. Lister was again the focus towards which a single Bf 109G was picked up on initial landing approach. Its pilot, instead of continuing towards the airfield where the flak defences could have covered his landing, instead raised the undercarriage and began to manoeuvre his fighter. His superb flying ability coupled to some degree by the mass of Mustangs getting in one another's way gave him several minutes of immunity before the CO managed to inflict a telling blow. The Bf 109G slowly rolled over before the nose dropped inexorably towards a lethal impact with the sea.

A bright day, with the war drawing to its conclusion, catches the Mustang IIIs from No. 309 (Polish) Squadron. A collection of support vehicles surrounds the two nearest aircraft. The drop tanks in the foreground are of 108-Gall capacity compared to the teardrop examples under the wings that hold 75 Gallons. Andrews Field was the current home for several Mustang units.

The intervening several weeks up to VE-Day witnessed little or no contact with the *Jagdwaffe* as the Second World War in Europe drew to its close. The strike wings wended their paths along the Norwegian southern coastal approaches as well as venturing into the Skagerrak sea stretch separating Norway and Denmark. No. 234 Squadron arrived at Peterhead on 2 May and flew a minimal total of sorties; on 4 May, the flak gunners took down two Mustangs at low level, a situation that proved fatal for both pilots—a particularly cruel fate with peace just four days distant.

Bomber Command Provision

The escort provision for the heavies of Bomber Command was sustained during the four months of 1945 within which the Third Reich's very industrial heartland was put to the sword. No. 3 Group had basically led the way for daylight operations and their selection for this operational aspect within 'Butch' Harris's overall plan was logical. The various squadrons had been equipped with G-H, an electronic system that was similar to Oboe but which worked in reverse. Specific Lancasters were fitted out with a radar transmitter and receiver; a second ground-based receiver further extended the operational range.

The key difference with Oboe was that more than one bomber could utilise the equipment compared to the individual electronic limitation imposed upon the aircraft using the latter-named gear. The G-H-allocated bombers were intended to act as leaders for other aircraft. Their fins bore two horizontal yellow bars by way of identification and each lead bomber would in effect act as a visual indicator for the entire section to release its loads. The equipment ensured that when a target was visually obscured it would still feel the weight of assault, albeit in a more precise and therefore punishing manner than could be achieved by H2X for example.

No. 1 Squadron continued its involvement in this field with the Belgian airfields at Ursel and Maldegem in regular use for overnight or emergency use. By now, of course, the other groups within Bomber Command were adding their weight to the offensive, with oil production plants one of the key targets. The Ruhr's massive complex was generally hammered with up to 1,000 bombers dispatched. The largest-ever figure (1,108 Lancasters and Halifaxes) focusing on one target was achieved on 12 March when Dortmund was saturated with 4,851 tons—even greater than that handed out to Essen, home for the Krupp armament monster, forty-eight hours previous. Adding to the destruction of specific targets were Nos 9 and 617 Squadrons. Their aerodynamic bombs—the 12,000-lb Tallboy and 22,000-lb Grand Slam—took out pinpoint locations such as railway viaducts and U-boat pens.

The by-now general impotence of the *Jagdwaffe* was demonstrated by the virtually total immunity from loss by either RAF force. This was an obvious bonus for bomber crews but was probably frustrating for their fighter escorts who would have liked the occasional aerial reaction if only to break the monotony entailed

The Meteor's sleek outline is well demonstrated by EE457; even though this is a post-war picture of a Mk IV, the fighter's overall external layout remained the same up to the introduction of the final NF Mks 12 and 14. By now, cannon-calibre weapons were standard with the Gloster jet's foursome neatly slotted into the nose.

in flying cover. However, there was ever the thankfully few instances when the *Jagdwaffe* managed to strike with some force—in particular when the Me 262 units made contact. Several weeks prior to VE-Day, a raid against Hamburg witnessed the lumbering heavies being assailed by what was a minimal number of these frighteningly-functioning and heavily-armed machines. The available escorts were themselves well outperformed while the bombers were potentially sitting ducks in terms of manoeuvrability and defensive armament. The final single-figure losses said much more for the *Jagdwaffe* numbers on hand than the defensive response.

An Overview

By the conclusion of the Second World War, RAF Fighter Command was unrecognisable compared to its inauguration during 1936. The domination of the biplane as its primary weapon of deployment, which was still stubbornly holding sway at that time, was thankfully giving way to the steady introduction of monoplane designs with their perceived technological superiority as the conflict commenced. The fight against odds that dominated the period between September 1939 and the end of 1942 had witnessed both success and failure in challenging the *Luftwaffe*. This was a matter that affected the aircraft and the manner in which combat tactics were evolved in order to utilise their qualities as well as those of their pilots in order to match, if not ultimately exceed, that of the enemy.

The reverses suffered during the *Blitz* and to a lesser if not also debilitating degree following the introduction of the Fw 190 were being addressed in the former instance with the burgeoning introduction and expansion of airborne radar and its Bristol Beaufighter platform, while the advent of the Mk IX Spitfire redressed the balance in the latter specific instance. By 1943, the command was going evermore on the offensive. By day, the Spitfires and Typhoons were applying constant pressure; a parallel effort was building up in the nocturnal skies over Europe from 1941 onward, with early Intruder sorties by Hurricanes and Blenheims giving way to the even more lethal strikes conducted by Beaufighters and Mosquitos right into the Reich's heartland.

As the Third Reich's domination of the continent began to inexorably shrink and 1943 gave way to 1944, the combined strength of the command along with its newly-created 'partner' 2TAF laid the ground for the D-Day invasion along with its American 9USAAF contemporary. The very unwelcome advent of

No. 616 Squadron had been the sole unit to take the Mk I Meteor into action during the V-1 offensive but had transferred onto the Mk III in January 1945. A move to Gilze-Rijen in Holland culminated after VE-Day with a final move to Lübeck on Germany's Baltic coast in May, where this line-up of fighters is portrayed.

the V-I offensive did not distract from the task of consolidating the Normandy beachheads and indeed the robotic assaults were contained and finally thwarted thanks to the dedication of the fighter squadron pilots assigned to the duty in conjunction with the Army gunners and balloon operators. The final months of the Second World War involved the command in providing long-range bomber escort by day as well as similar cover to the strike wings of Coastal Command.

The image of 'The Greatest Flying Club in the World' with its naïve outlook on how fighter operations should be conducted had been firmly if belatedly 'put to bed' in the heat of combat. The cost of achieving a victorious conclusion in 1945 was inevitably high and relatively few of those who had been in the command's ranks in 1936 were around to attest to this mandatory advance, with a graveyard or the vast expanses of the ocean being their ever-tragic domain, to be shared with all who had fallen in battle during the Second World War. The legacy of their sacrifice remains in the fact that they and their fellow-servicemen in the Allied air forces, armies, and navies had granted future generations the priceless gift of freedom from oppression.

Appendix I

Order of Battle, 1 August 1940

No. 10 Group

Airfield	Squadron	Aircraft
Pembrey	No. 92	Spitfire Mk I
Exeter	No. 87	Hurricane Mk I
	No. 213	Hurricane Mk I
St Eval	No. 234	Spitfire Mk I
Risborough	No. 247 (one flight)	Gladiator Mk II
Middle Wallop	No. 238	Hurricane Mk I
	No. 604	Blenheim Mk IF
	No. 609	Spitfire Mk I
Warmwell	No. 152	Spitfire Mk I

No. 11 Group

Airfield	Squadron	Aircraft
Debden	No. 17	Hurricane Mk I
Martlesham Heath	No. 25	Blenheim Mk IF
	No. 85	Hurricane Mk I
Biggin Hill	No. 610	Spitfire Mk I
	No. 32	Hurricane Mk I
North Weald	No. 151	Hurricane Mk I
Rochford	No. 56	Hurricane Mk I
Hornchurch	No. 41	Spitfire Mk I
	No. 54	Spitfire Mk I
	No. 65	Spitfire Mk I
	No. 74	Spitfire Mk I
Tangmere	No. 43	Hurricane Mk I
	No. 601	Hurricane Mk I

Westhampnett	No. 145	Hurricane Mk I
Northolt	No. 1	Hurricane Mk I
	No. 257	Hurricane Mk I
Kenley	No. 64	Spitfire Mk I
	No. 615	Hurricane Mk I
Gravesend	No. 501	Hurricane Mk I
Croydon	No. 111	Hurricane Mk I
Manston	No. 600	Blenheim Mk IF

No. 12 Group

Airfield	Squadron	Aircraft
Church Fenton	No. 73	Hurricane Mk I
	No. 249	Hurricane Mk I
Leconfield	No. 616	Spitfire Mk I
Kirton-in-Lindsay	No. 222	Spitfire Mk I
	No. 264 ('B' Flight)	Defiant Mk I
Ringway	No. 264 ('A' Flight)	Defiant Mk I
Digby	No. 29	Blenheim Mk IF
	No. 46	Hurricane Mk I
	No. 611	Spitfire Mk I
Coltishall	No. 66	Spitfire Mk I
	No. 242	Hurricane Mk I
Wittering	No. 229	Hurricane Mk I
	No. 266	Spitfire Mk I
Collyweston	No. 23	Blenheim Mk IF
Duxford	No. 19	Spitfire Mk I

No. 13 Group

Airfield	Squadron	Aircraft
Acklington	No. 72	Spitfire Mk I
	No. 79	Hurricane Mk I
Usworth	No. 607	Hurricane Mk I
Drem	No. 605	Hurricane Mk I
Turnhouse	No. 232	Hurricane Mk I
	No. 253	Hurricane Mk I
Prestwick	No. 141	Defiant Mk I
Catterick	No. 219	Blenheim Mk IF
Aldergrove	No. 245	Hurricane Mk I
Wick	No. 3	Hurricane Mk I
Castletown	No. 504	Hurricane Mk I
Sumburgh	No. 232 (one flight)	Hurricane Mk I
Dyce	No. 603 ('A' Flight)	Spitfire Mk I
Montrose	No. 603 ('B' Flight)	Spitfire Mk I

Appendix II

Order of Battle, 6 June 1944

2nd Tactical Air Force

No. 83 Group

Airfield	Squadrons	Wing	Type
Odiham	Nos 168, 414, 430	39 (Recce)	Mustang I
	No. 400		Spitfire Mk XI
Holmsley South	Nos 174, 175, 245	No. 121	Typhoon Mk IB
Funtinton	Nos 19, 65, 122	No. 122	Mustang III
Hurn	Nos 181, 182, 247	No. 124	Typhoon Mk IB
	Nos 438, 439, 440	No. 143	Typhoon Mk IB
Ford	Nos 132, 453, 602	No. 125	Spitfire Mk IX
	Nos 441, 442, 443	No. 144	Spitfire Mk IX
Tangmere	Nos 401, 411, 412	No. 126	Spitfire Mk IX
	Nos 403, 416, 421	No. 122	Spitfire Mk IX
Westhampnett	No. 184	No. 129	Typhoon Mk IB

No. 84 Group

Airfield	Squadrons	Wing	Type
Gatwick	Nos 2, 268	35 (Recce)	Mustang I
	No. 4		Spitfire Mk XI
Thorney Island	Nos 198, 609	No. 123	Typhoon Mk IB
Chailey	Nos 302, 308, 317	No. 131	Spitfire Mk IX
Bognor	Nos 66, 331, 332	No. 132	Spitfire Mk IX
Coolham	Nos 129, 306, 315	No. 133	Mustang III

Appeldram	Nos 310, 312, 313	No. 134	Spitfire Mk IX
Selsey	Nos 222, 349, 485	No. 135	Spitfire Mk IX
Thorney Island	Nos 164, 183,	No. 136	Typhoon Mk IB
Merston	Nos 329, 340, 341	No. 145	Spitfire Mk IX
Needs Oar Point	Nos 193, 197, 257,266	No. 146	Typhoon Mk IB

No. 85 Group

Airfield	Squadrons	Wing	Type
Newchurch	No. 56		Spitfire Mk IX
	Nos 3, 486		Tempest Mk V
West Malling	Nos 29, 409		Mosquito NF Mk XIII
	No. 91		Spitfire Mk XIV
Bradwell Bay	No. 124		Spitfire Mk VII
Hartford Bridge Flats	No. 322		Spitfire Mk IX
	No. 264		Mosquito Mk XIII
Hunsdon	No. 410		Mosquito NF Mk XIII
Zeals	No. 488		Mosquito NF Mk XIII
Hern	No. 604		Mosquito NF MK XIII

Air Defence of Great Britain

No. 10 Group

Airfield	Squadrons	Wing	Type
Predannack	Nos 1, 165		Spitfire Mk IX
	No. 151		Mosquito NF Mk XIII
Bolt Head	No. 41		Spitfire Mk XII
Culmhead	No. 126		Spitfire Mk IX
	Nos 131, 616		Spitfire Mk VII
Harrowbeer	No. 610		Spitfire Mk XIV
	No. 263		Typhoon Mk IB
Fairwood Common	No. 68		Beaufighter Mk VIF
Winkleigh	No. 406		Beaufighter Mk VIF

No. 11 Group

Airfield	Squadrons	Wing	Type
Lympne	Nos 33, 74, 127		Spitfire Mk IX
Deanland	Nos 64, 234, 611		Spitfire Mk VB

Detling	Nos 80, 229, 274		Spitfire Mk IX
Shoreham	No. 345		Spitfire Mk VB
Friston	No. 350		Spitfire Mk VB
	No. 501		Spitfire Mk IX
Manston	No. 137		Typhoon Mk IB
	No. 605		Mosquito FB Mk VI
West Malling	No. 96		Mosquito NF Mk XIII
Hurn	No. 125		Mosquito NF Mk XVII
Bradwell Bay	No. 219		Mosquito NF Mk XVII
Ford	No. 456		Mosquito NF Mk XVII
Holmesley South	No. 418		Mosquito FB Mk VI
Horne	Nos 130, 303, 402		Spitfire Mk VB

No. 12 Group

Airfield	Squadrons	Wing	Type
Coltishall	No. 25		Mosquito NF Mk XVII
	No. 316		Mustang III
Church Fenton	No. 307		Mosquito NF Mk XII
Castletown	No. 504		Spitfire Mk VB
Digby	No. 504 (detachment)		Spitfire Mk VB
Acklington	No. 504 (detachment)		Spitfire Mk VB

No. 13 Group

Airfield	Squadrons	Wing	Type
Skeabrae	No. 118	Spitfire Mk VB	
Sumburgh	No. 118		Spitfire Mk VB
Peterhead	No. 309		Hurricane Mk IIC

Bibliography

Bowyer, M., *No. 2 Group 1936–1945* (Faber and Faber, 1974)

Brookes, A. J., *Fighter Squadron At War* (Ian Allen, 1980)

Caldwell, D., *The JG26 War Diary (Vol. 1, 1939–1942)* (Grub Street, 1996); *The JG26 War Diary (Vol. 2, 1943–1945)* Grub Street, 1998)

Cull, B., Lander, B., and Weiss, H., *Twelve Days in May* (Grub Street, 1999)

Filley, B., *Junkers Ju88 in Action (Part Two)* (Squadron/Signal Inc., 1991)

Goss, C., *Bloody Biscay* (Crecy Publishing Ltd, 1997)

Hinchliffe, P., *The Other Battle* (Airlife Publishing Ltd, 1996)

Holland, J. *The Battle of Britain* (Bantam Press, 1020)

Mackay, R., and Parry, S. W., *The Last Blitz* (Red Kite, 2011)

Mackay, R., *DH.98 Mosquito In Action* (Squadron/Signal Inc., 2017); *Heinkel He111* (Crowood Press, 2000); *Junkers Ju88* (Crowood Press, 2001); *Messerschmitt Bf110* (Crowood Press, 2000)

Mason, F. K., *The Hawker Hurricane* (Aston Publications Ltd, 1987); *The Hawker Typhoon and Tempest* (Aston Publications, 1988)

Morgan, E. B., and Shacklady, E., *Spitfire: The History* (Key Publishing Ltd, 1987)

Parry, S. W., *Intruders over Britain (1940–1945)* (Air Research Publications, 1987)

Price, Dr A., *The Hardest Day* (Arms and Armour Press, 1988)

Ramsey, W. G., *The Blitz, Then and Now*, Vol. 2 (Battle of Britain Prints International Ltd, 1988); *The Blitz, Then and Now*, Vol. 3 (Battle of Britain Prints International Ltd, 1990)

Rawlings, J. D. R., *Fighter Squadrons of the R.A.F. and Their Aircraft* (MacDonald and Co. (Publishers), 1969)

Shores, C., and Williams, C., *Aces High* (Grub Street, 1994)

Thetford, O., *Aircraft of the RAF since 1918* (Putnam, 1988)